CISSP Cert Guide

Troy McMillan
Robin M. Abernathy

800 East 96th Street,
Indianapolis, Indiana 46240 USA

CISSP Cert Guide

Troy McMillan
Robin M. Abernathy

Copyright © 2014 by Pearson Certification

All rights reserved. No part of this book shall be reproduced, stored in a retrieval system, or transmitted by any means, electronic, mechanical, photocopying, recording, or otherwise, without written permission from the publisher. No patent liability is assumed with respect to the use of the information contained herein. Although every precaution has been taken in the preparation of this book, the publisher and authors assume no responsibility for errors or omissions. Nor is any liability assumed for damages resulting from the use of the information contained herein.

ISBN-13: 978-0-7897-5151-5

ISBN-10: 0-7897-5151-8

Library of Congress Control Number: 2013949991

Printed in the United States on America

First Printing: October 2013

Trademarks

All terms mentioned in this book that are known to be trademarks or service marks have been appropriately capitalized. Pearson cannot attest to the accuracy of this information. Use of a term in this book should not be regarded as affecting the validity of any trademark or service mark.

Windows is a registered trademark of Microsoft Corporation.

Warning and Disclaimer

Every effort has been made to make this book as complete and as accurate as possible, but no warranty or fitness is implied. The information provided is on an "as is" basis. The authors and the publisher shall have neither liability nor responsibility to any person or entity with respect to any loss or damages arising from the information contained in this book or from the use of the CD or programs accompanying it.

Bulk Sales

Pearson offers excellent discounts on this book when ordered in quantity for bulk purchases or special sales. For more information, please contact

    U.S. Corporate and Government Sales
    1-800-382-3419
    corpsales@pearsontechgroup.com

For sales outside of the U.S., please contact

    International Sales
    international@pearsoned.com

Associate Publisher
Dave Dusthimer

Acquisitions Editor
Betsy Brown

Development Editor
Allison Beaumont Johnson

Managing Editor
Sandra Schroeder

Project Editor
Seth Kerney

Copy Editor
Paula Lowell

Indexer
Erika Millen

Proofreader
Anne Goebel

Technical Editors
Chris Crayton
Brock Pearson

Publishing Coordinator
Vanessa Evans

Multimedia Developer
Eric Miller

Book Designer
Chuti Prasertsith

Composition
Jake McFarland

Contents at a Glance

	Introduction
CHAPTER 1	The CISSP Certification 3
CHAPTER 2	Access Control 13
CHAPTER 3	Telecommunications and Network Security 65
CHAPTER 4	Information Security Governance and Risk Management 159
CHAPTER 5	Software Development Security 203
CHAPTER 6	Cryptography 243
CHAPTER 7	Security Architecture and Design 297
CHAPTER 8	Operations Security 343
CHAPTER 9	Business Continuity and Disaster Recovery 369
CHAPTER 10	Legal, Regulations, Investigations, and Compliance 405
CHAPTER 11	Physical (Environmental) Security 445
	Glossary 481
	Index 538
APPENDIX A	Memory Tables On CD
APPENDIX B	Memory Tables Answer Key On CD

Table of Contents

Chapter 1 The CISSP Certification 3

The Goals of the CISSP Certification 3
  Sponsoring Bodies 3
  Stated Goals 4
The Value of the CISSP Certification 4
  To the Security Professional 5
  To the Enterprise 5
The Common Body of Knowledge 5
  Access Control 5
  Telecommunications and Network Security 6
  Information Security Governance and Risk Management 6
  Software Development Security 7
  Cryptography 7
  Security Architecture and Design 8
  Operations Security 8
  Business Continuity and Disaster Recovery Planning 8
  Legal, Regulations, Investigations, and Compliance 9
  Physical and Environmental Security 9
Steps to Becoming a CISSP 10
  Qualifying for the Exam 10
  Signing Up for the Exam 10
  About the CISSP Exam 10

Chapter 2 Access Control 13

Foundation Topics 13
Access Control Concepts 13
  CIA 13
  Default Stance 14
  Defense In Depth 14
  Access Control Process 15
    Identify Resources 15
    Identify Users 15
    Identify Relationships between Resources and Users 16

Identification and Authentication Concepts   16
    Three Factors for Authentication   17
    Knowledge Factors   17
    Identity and Account Management   *18*
    Password Types and Management   *19*
    Ownership Factors   22
    Synchronous and Asynchronous Token   *22*
    Memory Cards   *22*
    Smart Cards   *23*
    Characteristic Factors   23
    Physiological Characteristics   *24*
    Behavioral Characteristics   *25*
    Biometric Considerations   *26*
Authorization Concepts   28
    Access Control Policies   28
    Separation of Duties   29
    Least Privilege/Need-to-Know   29
    Default to No Access   30
    Directory Services   30
    Single Sign-on   31
    Kerberos   *32*
    SESAME   *34*
    Federated Identity Management   *35*
    Security Domains   35
Accountability   35
    Auditing and Reporting   36
    Vulnerability Assessment   37
    Penetration Testing   38
Access Control Categories   39
    Compensative   40
    Corrective   40
    Detective   40
    Deterrent   40
    Directive   40

Preventive   41
Recovery   41
Access Control Types   41
  Administrative (Management) Controls   41
  Logical (Technical) Controls   43
  Physical Controls   43
Access Control Models   46
  Discretionary Access Control   46
  Mandatory Access Control   47
  Role-based Access Control   47
  Rule-based Access Control   48
  Content-dependent Versus Context-dependent   48
  Access Control Matrix   48
  Capabilities Table   48
  Access Control List (ACL)   49
Access Control Administration   49
  Centralized   49
  Decentralized   49
  Provisioning Life Cycle   50
Access Control Monitoring   50
  IDS   50
  IPS   52
Access Control Threats   52
  Password Threats   53
  Dictionary Attack   53
  Brute-Force Attack   53
  Social Engineering Threats   53
  Phishing/Pharming   54
  Shoulder Surfing   54
  Identity Theft   54
  Dumpster Diving   55
  DoS/DDoS   55
  Buffer Overflow   55
  Mobile Code   56

                    Malicious Software   56

                    Spoofing   56

                    Sniffing and Eavesdropping   57

                    Emanating   57

                    Backdoor/Trapdoor   57

            Exam Preparation Tasks   57

            Review All Key Topics   57

            Complete the Tables and Lists from Memory   58

            Define Key Terms   59

            Review Questions   59

            Answers and Explanations   61

Chapter 3   **Telecommunications and Network Security   65**

            Foundation Topics   66

            OSI Model   66

                    Application Layer   67

                    Presentation Layer   67

                    Session Layer   67

                    Transport Layer   68

                    Network Layer   68

                    Data Link Layer   68

                    Physical Layer   69

            Multi-Layer Protocols   70

            TCP/IP Model   71

                    Application Layer   72

                    Transport Layer   72

                    Internet Layer   74

                    Link Layer   76

                    Encapsulation   76

            Common TCP/UDP Ports   77

            Logical and Physical Addressing   78

                IPv4   78

                IP Classes   80

                Public Versus Private IP Addresses   81

                NAT   81

IPv4 Versus IPv6   82
MAC Addressing   82
Network Transmission   83
    Analog Versus Digital   83
    Asynchronous Versus Synchronous   84
    Broadband Versus Baseband   84
    Unicast, Multicast, and Broadcast   85
    Wired Versus Wireless   86
Cabling   87
    Coaxial   87
    Twisted Pair   88
    Fiberoptic   90
Network Topologies   91
    Ring   91
    Bus   92
    Star   92
    Mesh   93
    Hybrid   94
Network Technologies   94
    Ethernet 802.3   94
    Token Ring 802.5   96
    FDDI   97
    Contention Methods   97
    CSMA/CD Versus CSMA/CA   98
    Collision Domains   98
    CSMA/CD   99
    CSMA/CA   100
    Token Passing   101
    Polling   101
Network Protocols/Services   101
    ARP   101
    DHCP   102
    DNS   103
    FTP, FTPS, SFTP   103

      HTTP, HTTPS, SHTTP   104
      ICMP   104
      IMAP   105
      NAT   105
      PAT   105
      POP   105
      SMTP   105
      SNMP   105
Network Routing   106
      Distance Vector, Link State, or Hybrid Routing   106
      RIP   107
      OSPF   107
      IGRP   108
      EIGRP   108
      VRRP   108
      IS-IS   108
      BGP   108
Network Devices   109
      Patch Panel   109
      Multiplexer   109
      Hub   109
      Switch   110
      VLANs   111
      Layer 3 Versus Layer 4   111
      Router   111
      Gateway   112
      Firewall   112
      Types   113
      Architecture   114
      Virtualization   116
      Proxy Server   116
      PBX   116
      Honeypot   117

Cloud Computing   117
Endpoint Security   119
Network Types   119
    LAN   119
    Intranet   119
    Extranet   120
    MAN   120
    WAN   120
WAN Technologies   121
    T Lines   121
    E Lines   121
    OC Lines (SONET)   122
    CSU/DSU   122
    Circuit-Switching Versus Packet-Switching   123
    Frame Relay   123
    ATM   123
    X.25   124
    Switched Multimegabit Data Service   124
    Point-to-Point Protocol   124
    High-Speed Serial Interface   124
    PSTN (POTS, PBX)   125
    VoIP   125
Remote Connection Technologies   126
    Dial-up   126
    ISDN   127
    DSL   127
    Cable   128
    VPN   129
    RADIUS and TACACS   132
    Remote Authentication Protocols   133
    Telnet   134
    TLS/SSL   134
    Multimedia Collaboration   134

Wireless Networks   135
    FHSS, DSSS, OFDM, FDMA, TDMA, CDMA, OFDMA, and GSM   135
    802.11 Techniques   *136*
    Cellular or Mobile Wireless Techniques   *136*
    WLAN Structure   137
    Access Point   *137*
    SSID   *137*
    Infrastructure Mode Versus Ad Hoc Mode   *137*
    WLAN Standards   137
    802.11a   *138*
    802.11b   *138*
    802.11f   *138*
    802.11g   *138*
    802.11n   *138*
    Bluetooth   *139*
    Infrared   *139*
    WLAN Security   139
    WEP   *139*
    WPA   *140*
    WPA2   *140*
    Personal Versus Enterprise   *140*
    SSID Broadcast   *141*
    MAC Filter   *141*
    Satellites   141
Network Threats   142
    Cabling   142
    Noise   *142*
    Attenuation   *142*
    Crosstalk   *143*
    Eavesdropping   *143*
    ICMP Attacks   143
    Ping of Death   *143*

     Smurf 144
     Fraggle 144
     ICMP Redirect 144
     Ping Scanning 145
     DNS Attacks 145
     DNS Cache Poisoning 145
     DoS 146
     DDoS 146
     DNSSEC 146
     URL Hiding 146
     Domain Grabbing 147
     Cybersquatting 147
     Email Attacks 147
     Email Spoofing 147
     Spear Phishing 148
     Whaling 148
     Spam 148
     Wireless Attacks 148
     Wardriving 149
     Warchalking 149
     Remote Attacks 149
     Other Attacks 149
     SYN ACK Attacks 149
     Session Hijacking 150
     Port Scanning 150
     Teardrop 150
     IP Address Spoofing 150
Exam Preparation Tasks 151
Review All Key Topics 151
    Define Key Terms 151
    Review Questions 153
    Answers and Explanations 155

Chapter 4   Information Security Governance and Risk Management   159

    Foundation Topics   159

    Security Principles and Terms   159

        CIA   160

        Vulnerability   160

        Threat   161

        Threat Agent   161

        Risk   161

        Exposure   161

        Countermeasure   161

        Due Care and Due Diligence   162

        Job Rotation   163

        Separation of Duties   163

    Security Frameworks and Methodologies   163

        ISO/IEC 27000 Series   164

        Zachman Framework   166

        The Open Group Architecture Framework (TOGAF)   168

        Department of Defense Architecture Framework (DoDAF)   168

        British Ministry of Defence Architecture Framework (MODAF)   168

        Sherwood Applied Business Security Architecture (SABSA)   168

        Control Objectives for Information and Related Technology (CobiT)   170

        National Institute of Standards and Technology (NIST) Special Publication (SP)   170

        Committee of Sponsoring Organizations (COSO) of the Treadway Commission Framework   171

        Information Technology Infrastructure Library (ITIL)   172

        Six Sigma   173

        Capability Maturity Model Integration (CMMI)   174

        Top-Down Versus Bottom-Up Approach   174

        Security Program Life Cycle   174

    Risk Assessment   175

        Information and Asset (Tangible/Intangible) Value and Costs   177

        Vulnerabilities and Threats Identification   177

        Quantitative Risk Analysis   178

Qualitative Risk Analysis 179
Safeguard Selection 179
Total Risk Versus Residual Risk 180
Handling Risk 180
Risk Management Principles 181
Risk Management Policy 181
Risk Management Team 181
Risk Analysis Team 182
Information Security Governance Components 182
Policies 183
Organizational Security Policy 184
System-Specific Security Policy 185
Issue-Specific Security Policy 185
Policy Categories 185
Standards 185
Baselines 185
Guidelines 186
Procedures 186
Information Classification and Life Cycle 186
Commercial Business Classifications 186
Military and Government Classifications 187
Information Life Cycle 188
Security Governance Responsibilities and Roles 188
Board of Directors 188
Management 189
Audit Committee 189
Data Owner 190
Data Custodian 190
System Owner 190
System Administrator 190
Security Administrator 190
Security Analyst 191
Application Owner 191
Supervisor 191

　　　　User   191
　　　　Auditor   191
　　　　Third-Party Governance   191
　　　　Onsite Assessment   192
　　　　Document Exchange/Review   192
　　　　Process/Policy Review   192
　　　　Personnel Security (Screening, Hiring, and Termination)   192
　　Security Awareness Training   193
　　Security Budget, Metrics, and Effectiveness   194
　　Exam Preparation Tasks   195
　　Review All Key Topics   195
　　　　Complete the Tables and Lists from Memory   195
　　　　Define Key Terms   196
　　　　Review Questions   196
　　　　Answers and Explanations   198

Chapter 5   Software Development Security   203
　　Foundation Topics   203
　　System Development Life Cycle   203
　　　　Initiate   204
　　　　Acquire/Develop   204
　　　　Implement   205
　　　　Operate/Maintain   205
　　　　Dispose   205
　　Software Development Life Cycle   206
　　　　Gather Requirements   206
　　　　Design   207
　　　　Develop   207
　　　　Test/Validate   208
　　　　Release/Maintain   209
　　　　Change Management and Configuration Management   209
　　Software Development Security Best Practices   209
　　　　WASC   210
　　　　OWASP   210
　　　　BSI   210

ISO/IEC 27000   210
Software Development Methods   211
    Build and Fix   211
    Waterfall   212
    V-Shaped   213
    Prototyping   214
    Incremental   214
    Spiral   215
    Rapid Application Development (RAD)   216
    Agile   216
    JAD   218
    Cleanroom   218
    CMMI   218
Programming Concepts   219
    Machine Languages   219
    Assembly Languages and Assemblers   219
    High-level Languages, Compilers, and Interpreters   219
    Object-Oriented Programming   220
    Polymorphism   221
    Cohesion   221
    Coupling   221
    Data Structures   221
    Distributed Object-Oriented Systems   222
    CORBA   222
    COM and DCOM   222
    OLE   223
    Java   223
    SOA   223
    Mobile Code   223
    Java Applets   223
    ActiveX   224
Database Concepts and Security   224
    DBMS Architecture and Models   224
    Database Interface Languages   226

      ODBC 226
      JDBC 227
      XML 227
      OLE DB 227
      Data Warehouses and Data Mining 227
      Database Threats 228
      Database Views 228
      Database Locks 228
      Polyinstantiation 228
      OLTP ACID Test 229
Knowledge-Based Systems 229
Software Threats 230
      Malware 230
      Virus 230
      Worm 231
      Trojan Horse 231
      Logic Bomb 232
      Spyware/Adware 232
      Botnet 232
      Rootkit 233
      Source Code Issues 233
      Buffer Overflow 233
      Escalation of Privileges 235
      Backdoor 235
      Malware Protection 235
      Antivirus Software 235
      Antimalware Software 236
      Security Policies 236
Software Security Effectiveness 236
      Certification and Accreditation 236
      Auditing 237
Exam Preparation Tasks 237

Review All Key Topics   237
    Define Key Terms   238
    Complete the Tables and Lists from Memory   238
    Review Questions   238
    Answers and Explanations   240

Chapter 6   Cryptography   243

Foundation Topics   244
Cryptography Concepts   244
    Cryptographic Life Cycle   246
Cryptography History   246
    Julius Caesar and the Caesar Cipher   247
    Vigenere Cipher   248
    Kerckhoff's Principle   249
    World War II Enigma   249
    Lucifer by IBM   250
Cryptosystem Features   250
    Authentication   250
    Confidentiality   250
    Integrity   251
    Authorization   251
    Non-repudiation   251
Encryption Systems   251
    Running Key and Concealment Ciphers   251
    Substitution Ciphers   252
    Transposition Ciphers   253
    Symmetric Algorithms   253
    Stream-based Ciphers   254
    Block Ciphers   255
    Initialization Vectors (IVs)   255
    Asymmetric Algorithms   255
    Hybrid Ciphers   256
Substitution Ciphers   257
    One-Time Pads   257
    Steganography   258

Symmetric Algorithms 258
    Digital Encryption Standard (DES) and Triple DES (3DES) 259
    DES Modes 259
    Triple DES (3DES) and Modes 262
    Advanced Encryption Standard (AES) 263
    IDEA 263
    Skipjack 264
    Blowfish 264
    Twofish 264
    RC4/RC5/RC6 264
    CAST 265
Asymmetric Algorithms 265
    Diffie-Hellman 266
    RSA 267
    El Gamal 267
    ECC 267
    Knapsack 268
    Zero Knowledge Proof 268
Message Integrity 268
    Hash Functions 269
    One-Way Hash 269
    MD2/MD4/MD5/MD6 271
    SHA/SHA-2/SHA-3 271
    HAVAL 272
    RIPEMD-160 272
    Tiger 272
    Message Authentication Code 273
    HMAC 273
    CBC-MAC 274
    CMAC 274
Digital Signatures 274
Public Key Infrastructure 275
    Certification Authority (CA) and Registration Authority (RA) 275
    OCSP 276

        Certificates   276
        Certificate Revocation List (CRL)   277
        PKI Steps   277
        Cross-Certification   278
    Key Management   278
    Trusted Platform Module (TPM)   279
    Encryption Communication Levels   280
        Link Encryption   280
        End-to-End Encryption   281
    E-mail Security   281
        PGP   281
        MIME and S/MIME   282
        Quantum Cryptography   282
    Internet Security   282
        Remote Access   283
        SSL/TLS   283
        HTTP, HTTPS, and SHTTP   284
        SET   284
        Cookies   284
        SSH   285
        IPsec   285
    Cryptography Attacks   286
        Ciphertext-Only Attack   287
        Known Plaintext Attack   287
        Chosen Plaintext Attack   287
        Chosen Ciphertext Attack   287
        Social Engineering   287
        Brute Force   288
        Differential Cryptanalysis   288
        Linear Cryptanalysis   288
        Algebraic Attack   288
        Frequency Analysis   288
        Birthday Attack   289
        Dictionary Attack   289

Replay Attack 289
Analytic Attack 289
Statistical Attack 289
Factoring Attack 289
Reverse Engineering 289
Meet-in-the-Middle Attack 290
Exam Preparation Tasks 290
Review All Key Topics 290
Complete the Tables and Lists from Memory 290
Define Key Terms 291
Review Questions 291
Answers and Explanations 293

Chapter 7 Security Architecture and Design 297

Foundation Topics 297
Security Model Concepts 297
Confidentiality 297
Integrity 297
Availability 298
Defense in Depth 298
System Architecture 298
System Architecture Steps 299
ISO/IEC 42010:2011 299
Computing Platforms 300
Mainframe/Thin Clients 300
Distributed Systems 300
Middleware 301
Embedded Systems 301
Mobile Computing 301
Virtual Computing 301
Security Services 302
Boundary Control Services 302
Access Control Services 302
Integrity Services 303

Cryptography Services 303
Auditing and Monitoring Services 303
System Components 303
CPU and Multiprocessing 303
Memory and Storage 304
Input/Output Devices 307
Operating Systems 307
Multitasking 308
Memory Management 309
System Security Architecture 310
Security Policy 310
Security Requirements 310
Security Zones 311
Security Architecture Frameworks 312
Zachman Framework 312
SABSA 312
TOGAF 312
ITIL 313
Security Architecture Documentation 314
ISO/IEC 27000 Series 314
CobiT 314
Security Model Types and Security Models 314
Security Model Types 315
State Machine Models 315
Multilevel Lattice Models 315
Matrix-Based Models 315
Noninference Models 316
Information Flow Models 316
Security Models 317
Bell-LaPadula Model 317
Biba Model 318
Clark-Wilson Integrity Model 319
Lipner Model 320
Brewer-Nash (Chinese Wall) Model 320

Graham-Denning Model 320
Harrison-Ruzzo-Ullman Model 321
Security Modes 321
Dedicated Security Mode 321
System High Security Mode 321
Compartmented Security Mode 321
Multilevel Security Mode 321
Assurance 322
System Evaluation 322
- TCSEC 322
- *Rainbow Series* 323
- *Orange Book* 323
- *Red Book* 326
- ITSEC 326
- Common Criteria 328

Certification and Accreditation 329
Security Architecture Maintenance 330
- Security Architecture Threats 330
- *Maintenance Hooks* 331
- *Time-of-Check/Time-of-Use Attacks* 331
- *Web-Based Attacks* 332
- *XML* 332
- *SAML* 332
- *OWASP* 333
- *Server-Based Attacks* 333
- *Data Flow Control* 333
- Database Security 333
- *Inference* 333
- *Aggregation* 334
- *Contamination* 334
- *Data Mining Warehouse* 334
- *Distributed Systems Security* 334
- *Cloud Computing* 335

    Grid Computing 335

    Peer-to-Peer Computing 335

  Exam Preparation Tasks 336

  Review All Key Topics 336

    Complete the Tables and Lists from Memory 336

    Define Key Terms 336

    Review Questions 337

    Answers and Explanations 339

Chapter 8 **Operations Security 343**

  Foundation Topics 343

  Operations Security Concepts 343

    Need-to-Know/Least Privilege 343

    Separation of Duties 344

    Job Rotation 344

    Sensitive Information Procedures 344

    Record Retention 345

    Monitor Special Privileges 345

  Resource Protection 345

    Protecting Tangible and Intangible Assets 346

    Facilities 346

    Hardware 346

    Software 347

    Information Assets 347

    Asset Management 348

    Redundancy and Fault Tolerance 348

    Backup and Recovery Systems 348

    Identity and Access Management 349

    Media Management 349

    SAN 353

    NAS 353

    HSM 353

    Media History 354

    Media Labeling and Storage 354

Sanitizing and Disposing of Media 355
Network and Resource Management 355
Operations Processes 356
  Incident Response Management 356
  Change Management 357
  Configuration Management 358
  Patch Management 359
  Audit and Review 360
Operations Security Threats and Preventative Measures 361
  Clipping Levels 361
  Deviations from Standards 361
  Unusual or Unexplained Events 361
  Unscheduled Reboots 362
  Trusted Recovery 362
  Trusted Paths 362
  Input/Output Controls 362
  System Hardening 362
  Vulnerability Management Systems 363
  IDS/IPS 363
  Monitoring and Reporting 363
  Antimalware/Antivirus 364
Exam Preparation Tasks 364
Review All Key Topics 364
  Complete the Tables and Lists from Memory 364
  Define Key Terms 364
  Review Questions 365
  Answers and Explanations 367

Chapter 9 Business Continuity and Disaster Recovery 369
Foundation Topics 369
Business Continuity and Disaster Recovery Concepts 369
  Disruptions 370
  Disasters 370
    Technological Disasters 371
    Man-made Disasters 371

Natural Disasters 371
Disaster Recovery and the Disaster Recovery Plan (DRP) 371
Continuity Planning and the Business Continuity Plan (BCP) 372
Business Impact Analysis (BIA) 372
Contingency Plan 372
Availability 373
Reliability 373
Business Impact Analysis (BIA) Development 373
Identify Critical Processes and Resources 374
Identify Outage Impacts, and Estimate Downtime 374
Identify Resource Requirements 375
Identify Recovery Priorities 376
Recoverability 376
Fault Tolerance 376
Business Continuity Scope and Plan 376
Personnel Components 377
Project Scope 377
Business Continuity Steps 377
Preventive Controls 378
Redundant Systems, Facilities, and Power 379
Fault-Tolerant Technologies 379
Insurance 379
Data Backup 380
Fire Detection and Suppression 380
Create Recovery Strategies 380
Categorize Asset Recovery Priorities 381
Business Process Recovery 382
Facility Recovery 382
Hot Site 383
Cold Site 383
Warm Site 384
Tertiary Site 384
Reciprocal Agreements 384
Redundant Sites 385

Contents   xxvii

        Supply and Technology Recovery   385
        Hardware Backup   386
        Software Backup   386
        Human Resources   387
        Supplies   387
        Documentation   388
        User Environment Recovery   388
        Data Recovery   388
        Data Backup Types and Schemes   389
        Electronic Backup   392
        High Availability   392
        Training Personnel   393
    Critical Teams and Duties   393
        Damage Assessment Team   394
        Legal Team   394
        Media Relations Team   394
        Recovery Team   395
        Relocation Team   395
        Restoration Team   395
        Salvage Team   395
        Security Team   395
    BCP Testing   396
        Checklist Test   396
        Table-top Exercise   396
        Structured Walk-Through Test   397
        Simulation Test   397
        Parallel Test   397
        Full-Interruption Test   397
        Functional Drill   397
        Evacuation Drill   397
    BCP Maintenance   398
    Exam Preparation Tasks   398
    Review All Key Topics   398
    Complete the Tables and Lists from Memory   399
    Exam Preparation Tasks   398

Define Key Terms 399
Review Questions 399
Answers and Explanations 401

Chapter 10 Legal, Regulations, Investigations, and Compliance 405

Foundation Topics 406

Computer Crime Concepts 406

    Computer-Assisted Crime 406

    Computer-Targeted Crime 406

    Incidental Computer Crime 406

    Computer Prevalence Crime 407

    Hackers Versus Crackers 407

Major Legal Systems 407

    Civil Code Law 408

    Common Law 408

    Criminal Law 408

    Civil/Tort Law 408

    Administrative/Regulatory Law 409

    Customary Law 409

    Religious Law 409

    Mixed Law 409

Intellectual Property Law 409

    Patent 410

    Trade Secret 410

    Trademark 411

    Copyright 411

    Software Piracy and Licensing Issues 412

    Internal Protection 413

Privacy 413

    Personally Identifiable Information (PII) 414

    Laws and Regulations 414

    Sarbanes-Oxley (SOX) Act 415

    Health Insurance Portability and Accountability Act (HIPAA) 415

    Gramm-Leach-Bliley Act (GLBA) of 1999 415

    Computer Fraud and Abuse Act (CFAA) 416

  Federal Privacy Act of 1974 416
  Federal Intelligence Surveillance Act (FISA) of 1978 416
  Electronic Communications Privacy Act (ECPA) of 1986 416
  Computer Security Act of 1987 417
  United States Federal Sentencing Guidelines of 1991 417
  Communications Assistance for Law Enforcement Act (CALEA) of 1994 417
  Personal Information Protection and Electronic Documents Act (PIPEDA) 417
  Basel II 417
  Payment Card Industry Data Security Standard (PCI DSS) 418
  Federal Information Security Management Act (FISMA) of 2002 418
  Economic Espionage Act of 1996 418
  USA PATRIOT Act 418
  Health Care and Education Reconciliation Act of 2010 418
  Employee Privacy Issues and Expectation of Privacy 419
  European Union 419
  Export/Import Issues 420
  Compliance 420
Liability 420
  Due Diligence Versus Due Care 421
  Negligence 421
  Liability Issues 422
Incident Response 423
  Event Versus Incident 423
  Incident Response Team and Incident Investigations 424
  Rules of Engagement, Authorization, and Scope 424
  Incident Response Procedures 424
Forensic and Digital Investigations 425
  Identify Evidence 427
  Preserve and Collect Evidence 427
  Examine and Analyze Evidence 428
  Present Findings 428
  Decide 428
  IOCE/SWGDE 429

Crime Scene   429
MOM   429
Chain of Custody   430
Interviewing   430
Evidence   430
Five Rules of Evidence   431
Types of Evidence   431
Best Evidence   432
Secondary Evidence   432
Direct Evidence   432
Conclusive Evidence   432
Circumstantial Evidence   432
Corroborative Evidence   433
Opinion Evidence   433
Hearsay Evidence   433
Surveillance, Search, and Seizure   433
Media Analysis   434
Software Analysis   434
Network Analysis   435
Hardware/Embedded Device Analysis   435
Security Professional Ethics   435
(ISC)² Code of Ethics   436
Computer Ethics Institute   436
Internet Architecture Board   437
Organizational Ethics   437
Exam Preparation Tasks   437
Review All Key Topics   437
Define Key Terms   438
Review Questions   439
Answers and Explanations   441

Chapter 11   Physical (Environmental) Security   445
Foundation Topics   445
Geographical Threats   445
Internal Versus External Threats   445
Natural Threats   446

  Hurricane/Tropical Storm 446
  Tornadoes 446
  Earthquakes 446
  Floods 447
  System Threats 447
  Electrical 447
  Communications 447
  Utilities 448
  Man-Made Threats 449
  Explosions 449
  Fire 449
  Vandalism 450
  Fraud 450
  Theft 450
  Collusion 451
  Politically Motivated Threats 451
  Strikes 451
  Riots 451
  Civil Disobedience 452
  Terrorist Acts 452
  Bombing 452
Site and Facility Design 453
  Layered Defense Model 453
  CPTED 453
  Natural Access Control 453
  Natural Surveillance 454
  Natural Territorials Reinforcement 454
  Physical Security Plan 454
  Deter Criminal Activity 454
  Delay Intruders 454
  Detect Intruders 455
  Assess Situation 455
  Respond to Intrusions and Disruptions 455

Facility Selection Issues   455
Visibility   455
Surrounding Area and External Entities   456
Accessibility   456
Construction   456
Internal Compartments   457
Computer and Equipment Rooms   457
Perimeter Security   458
Gates and Fences   458
Barriers (Bollards)   458
Fences   459
Gates   459
Walls   460
Perimeter Intrusion Detection   460
Infrared Sensors   460
Electromechanical Systems   460
Photoelectric Systems   460
Acoustical Detection Systems   461
Wave Motion Detector   461
Capacitance Detector   461
CCTV   461
Lighting   461
Types of Systems   461
Types of Lighting   462
Patrol Force   462
Access Control   462
Building and Internal Security   463
Doors   463
Door Lock Types   463
Turnstiles and Mantraps   464
Locks   464
Biometrics   466
Glass Entries   466
Visitor Control   466

Contents   xxxiii

　　　　Equipment Rooms   467
　　　　Work Areas   467
　　　　Secure Data Center   467
　　　　Restricted Work Area   468
　　Environmental Security   468
　　　　Fire Protection   468
　　　　Fire Detection   468
　　　　Fire Suppression   468
　　　　Power Supply   470
　　　　Types of Outages   470
　　　　Preventative Measures   470
　　　　HVAC   471
　　　　Water Leakage and Flooding   471
　　　　Environmental Alarms   472
　　Equipment Security   472
　　　　Corporate Procedures   472
　　　　Tamper Protection   472
　　　　Encryption   472
　　　　Inventory   473
　　　　Physical Protection of Security Devices   473
　　　　Tracking Devices   473
　　　　Portable Media Procedures   473
　　　　Safes, Vaults, and Locking   473
　　Personnel Privacy and Safety   474
　　Exam Preparation Tasks   475
　　Review All Key Topics   475
　　　　Define Key Terms   475
　　　　Review Questions   476
　　　　Answers and Explanations   478
　Glossary   481
　Index   538
Appendix A   Memory Tables   On CD
Appendix B   Memory Tables Answer Key   On CD

About the Authors

Troy McMillan is a Product Developer and Technical Editor for Kaplan Cert Prep as well as a full time trainer and writer. He became a professional trainer 12 years ago teaching Cisco, Microsoft, CompTIA, and Wireless classes.

Troy's book *CCNA Essentials* by Sybex Publishing was released in November 2011. It has been chosen as the textbook for both online and instructor-led classes at several colleges in the United States.

Troy also is a courseware developer. Among the work he has done in this area is wireless training materials for Motorola in 2011 and instructor materials for a series of books by Sybex on Windows Server 2008 R2 in 2011.

Troy also teaches Cisco, Microsoft, CompTIA, and Security classes for several large corporate training companies. Among these are Global Knowledge and New Horizons.

He now creates certification practice tests and study guides for the Transcender and Self-Test brands. Troy lives in Atlanta, Georgia.

Troy's professional accomplishments include B.B.A., MCSE (NT/2000/ 2003, 2008), CCNA, CCNP, MCP+I, CNA, A+, Net+, MCT, Server+, I-Net+, MCSA, CIW p, CIWa, CIW security analyst, CWNA, CWSP, CWNT, CWNE, MCTS: Vista Configuration, MCITP: Enterprise Support Technician, MCITP: Server Administrator, MCITP: Consumer Support Technician, MCTS: Forefront Client and Server Configuration, MCTS: Business Desktop Deployment with BDD, MCTS: Office Project Server 2007, MCTS: Windows Active Directory: Configuration, MCTS: Applications Infrastructure: Configuration, MCTS: Network Infrastructure: Configuration, CCSI, and VCP.

Robin M. Abernathy has been working in the IT certification preparation industry at Kaplan IT Certification Preparation, the owners of the Transcender and Self Test brands, for more than a decade. Robin has written and edited certification preparation materials for many (ISC)^2, Microsoft, CompTIA, PMI, Cisco, and ITIL certifications and holds multiple IT certifications from these vendors.

Robin provides training on computer hardware and software, networking, security, and project management. Over the past couple years, she has ventured into the traditional publishing industry by technically editing several publications. More recently, she has presented at technical conferences and hosted webinars on IT certification topics.

Dedications

This is dedicated to my soulmate and wife, Heike. —Troy

For my husband Michael and my son Jonas. —Robin

Acknowledgments

From Troy: Special thanks to all that helped with this book, but especially to Dave Dusthimer for suggesting me for this book, to Betsy Brown for guiding us through the process, to Andrew Cupp and Allison Johnson for keeping us on schedule, and most of all to my co-author, Robin Abernathy.

From Robin: I would be remiss if I did not first of all mention my gratitude to God for blessing me throughout my life. I do nothing on my own. It is only through Him that I have the strength and wisdom to accomplish my goals.

When my father and his business partner asked me to take over a retail computer store in the mid-1990s, I had no idea that a BIG journey was just starting. So thanks, Wayne McDaniel (a.k.a. Dad) and Roy Green for seeing something in me that I didn't even see in myself and for taking a chance on a very green techie. Also, thanks to my mom, Lucille McDaniel, for supporting my career changes over the years, even if you didn't understand them. Thanks to Mike White for sharing your knowledge and giving me a basis on which to build my expertise over the coming years. Thanks to Zackie Bosarge, a great mentor who gave me my first "real" job in the IT field at Alabama Institute for the Deaf and Blind.

Thanks also to my little family, my husband Michael and my son Jonas. Thanks for being willing to have Friday night fun nights without me while I spent my extra time knee-deep in CISSP topics. Thanks to Michael for always making sure that I knew that everything was easier on a Mac. Thanks to Jonas for keeping mom humble by making sure she understood that you couldn't see why someone was paying mom to write a book where Percy Jackson or Harry Potter was NOT the main character. I love you both immensely!

Pearson has put together an outstanding team to help me on my journey. Thanks to Betsy Brown, Andrew Cupp, Allison Johnson, and Seth Kerney for making this first foray into authorship so easy for me. Also, thanks to Chris Crayton and Brock Pearson for providing such a great technical review and giving us suggestions on improvement.

Finally, a thank you to Troy McMillan for contacting me when this book idea was first introduced to you. It has been a great journey! We make a great team, and I look forward to working with you on future projects.

It is my wish that you, the reader, succeed in your IT certification and career goals. I wish you the very best.

About the Technical Editors

Chris Crayton is an author, technical consultant, trainer, and SkillsUSA technology competition judge. Formerly, he worked as a computer technology and networking instructor at Keiser University; as network administrator for Protocol, a global electronic customer relationship management (eCRM) company; and at Eastman Kodak as a computer and network specialist. Chris has authored several print and online books on PC repair, CompTIA A+, CompTIA Security+, and Microsoft Windows. He has also served as technical editor and content contributor on numerous technical titles for several of the leading publishing companies. He holds MCSE, A+, and Network+ certifications.

Brock Pearson has more than 20 years of experience in the Information Technology/Information Security industry specializing in cybersecurity and cyberoperations. As a manager in a large security practice, Brock has assisted fortune 100 companies and government agencies, in the United States and abroad, in their efforts to defend themselves against hackers, cybertheft, and cyberterrorism. Brock Pearson has developed and delivered customized, technical security training; enhanced security policies, processes, and procedures; and integrated multiple information technologies to facilitate a holistic and proactive security posture for his clients.

We Want to Hear from You!

As the reader of this book, *you* are our most important critic and commentator. We value your opinion and want to know what we're doing right, what we could do better, what areas you'd like to see us publish in, and any other words of wisdom you're willing to pass our way.

We welcome your comments. You can email or write us directly to let us know what you did or didn't like about this book—as well as what we can do to make our books better.

Please note that we cannot help you with technical problems related to the topic of this book.

When you write, please be sure to include this book's title and authors as well as your name, email address, and phone number. We will carefully review your comments and share them with the authors and editors who worked on the book.

Email: feedback@pearsonitcertification.com

Mail: Pearson IT Certification
ATTN: Reader Feedback
800 East 96th Street
Indianapolis, IN 46240 USA

Reader Services

Visit our website and register this book at www.pearsonitcertification.com/register for convenient access to any updates, downloads, or errata that might be available for this book.

Introduction

(ISC)² Certified Information Systems Security Professional (CISSP) Certification is widely respected in the IT world as a premier security certification.

(ISC)² CISSP Certification is designed to be a vendor-neutral exam that measures your knowledge of industry-standard security practices.

Goals and Methods

The number one goal of this book is a simple one: to help you pass the current version of the (ISC)² CISSP Certification exam. The CISSP Certification stresses a Common Body of Knowledge (CBK) that defines the architecture, design, management, risk, and controls necessary to secure a business environment. The Candidate Information Bulletin (CIB) from (ISC)² provides an exam blueprint, reference list, format description, and registration policies.

To aid you in mastering and understanding the CISSP objectives, this book uses the following methods:

- The beginning of each chapter defines the topics to be covered in the chapter.

- The body of the chapter explains the topics from a hands-on and a theory-based standpoint. This includes in-depth descriptions, tables, and figures geared to build your knowledge so that you can pass the exam. The chapters are broken down into several topics each.

- The key topics indicate important figures, tables, and lists of information that you should know for the exam. They are interspersed throughout each chapter and are listed in table format at the end of each chapter.

- You can find memory tables and lists on the disc as Appendix A, "Memory Tables," and Appendix B, "Memory Tables Answer Key." Use them to help memorize important information.

- Key terms without definitions are listed at the end of each chapter. Write down the definition of each term, and check your work against the complete key terms in the Glossary.

- Each chapter includes review questions meant to gauge your knowledge of the subjects. If an answer to a question doesn't come readily to you, be sure to review that portion of the chapter. The answers with detailed explanations are at the end of each chapter.

- The disc accompanying this book includes two practice exams that test you on all the CISSP exam topics.

Who Should Read This Book?

The (ISC)² CISSP exam measures the necessary competencies for a full-time security professional with a minimum of five years in two or more of the 10 domains in the CISSP CBK or a minimum of four years in two or more domains with a four-year college degree. This book is written for people who have that amount of experience working with information systems security.

Readers will range from people who are attempting to attain a position in the IT security field to people who want to keep their skills sharp or perhaps retain their job due to a company policy that mandates that they take the new exams. However, readers with no knowledge of IT security should be cautioned against attempting the CISSP certification as their first IT certification. Beginners would be best served to pursue a more basic IT certification, such as CompTIA's A+, Network+, or Security+ certification.

This book is also aimed at the reader who wants to acquire additional certifications beyond the CISSP certification. The book is designed in such a way to offer easy transition to future certification studies.

Strategies for Exam Preparation

Strategies for exam preparation will vary depending on your existing knowledge. We recommend that you have access to as many devices and hardware as possible so as to be able to examine the different security methods mentioned in this book. A hands-on approach will really help to reinforce the ideas and concepts expressed in the book. However, not everyone has access to this equipment, so the next best step you can take is to read through the chapters in this book, jotting down notes with key concepts or configurations on a separate notepad. Each chapter contains a quiz that you can use to test your knowledge of the chapter's topics. It's located near the end of the chapter.

After you have read through the book, look at the current exam blueprint for the (ISC)² CISSP Certification Exam from https://www.isc2.org/exam-outline/Default.aspx. If there are any areas shown in the blueprint that you would still like to study, find those sections in the book and review them.

When you feel confident in your skills, attempt the practice exams included on the disc with this book. As you work through the practice exams, note the areas where you lack confidence and review those concepts in the book. After you review the areas, work through the practice exam a second time and rate your skills. Keep in mind that the more you work through the practice exam, the more familiar the questions will become.

(ISC)² CISSP Exam Objectives

Table I-1 lists the objectives for the CISSP exam. Each domain has been given its own chapter in this book.

Table I-1 (ISC)² CISSP Exam Objectives

Objective
1.0 Access Control
1.1 Control access by applying the following concepts/methodologies/techniques: - Policies - Types of controls (preventive, detective, corrective, etc.) - Techniques (that is, non-discretionary, discretionary, and mandatory) - Identification and authentication - Decentralized/distributed access control techniques - Authorization mechanisms - Logging and monitoring
1.2 Understand access control attacks: - Threat modeling - Asset valuation - Vulnerability analysis - Access aggregation
1.3 Assess effectiveness of access controls: - User entitlement - Access review and audit
1.4 Identity and access provisioning life cycle (e.g., provisioning, review, revocation)
2.0 Telecommunications and Network Security
2.1 Understand secure network architecture and design (e.g., IP and non-IP protocols, segmentation): - OSI and TCP/IP models - IP networking - Implications of multilayer protocols
2.2 Securing network components: - Hardware (e.g., modems, switches, routers, wireless access points) - Transmission media (e.g., wired, wireless, fiber) - Network access control devices (e.g., firewalls, proxies) - End-point security

2.3 Establish secure communication channels (e.g., VPN, TLS/SSL, VLAN):
- Voice (e.g., POTS, PBX, VoIP)
- Multimedia collaboration (e.g., remote meeting technology, instant messaging)
- Remote access (e.g., screen scraper, virtual application/desktop, telecommuting)
- Data communications

2.4 Understand network attacks (e.g., DDOS, spoofing)

3.0 Information Security Governance and Risk Management

3.1 Understand and align security function to goals, mission, and objectives of the organization

3.2 Understand and apply security governance:
- Organizational processes (e.g., acquisitions, divestitures, governance committees)
- Security roles and responsibilities
- Legislative and regulatory compliance
- Privacy requirements compliance
- Control frameworks
- Due care
- Due diligence

3.3 Understand and apply concepts of confidentiality, integrity, and availability

3.4 Develop and implement security policy:
- Security policies
- Standards/baselines
- Procedures
- Guidelines
- Documentation

3.5 Manage the information life cycle (e.g., classification, categorization, ownership)

3.6 Manage third-party governance (e.g., onsite assessment, document exchange and review, process/policy review)

3.7 Understand and apply risk management concepts:
- Identify threats and vulnerabilities
- Risk assessment/analysis (qualitative, quantitative, hybrid)
- Risk assignment/acceptance
- Countermeasure selection
- Tangible and intangible asset valuation

3.8 Manage personnel security:
- Employment candidate screening (e.g., reference checks, education verification)
- Employment agreements and policies
- Employee termination processes
- Vendor, consultant, and contractor controls

3.9 Develop and manage security education, training, and awareness

3.10 Manage the security function:
- Budget
- Metrics
- Resources
- Develop and implement security strategies
- Assess the completeness and effectiveness of the security program

4.0 Software Development Security

4.1 Understand and apply security in the software development life cycle:
- Development life cycle
- Maturity models
- Operation and maintenance
- Change management

4.2 Understand the environment and security controls:
- Security of the software environment
- Security issues of programming languages
- Security issues in source code (e.g., buffer overflow, escalation of privilege, backdoor)
- Configuration management

4.3 Assess the effectiveness of software security

5.0 Cryptography

5.1 Understand the application and use of cryptography:
- Data at rest (that is, hard drive)
- Data in transit (that is, "on the wire")

5.2 Understand the cryptographic life cycle (e.g., cryptographic limitations, algorithm/protocol governance)

5.3 Understand encryption concepts:
- Foundational concepts
- Symmetric cryptography
- Asymmetric cryptography
- Hybrid cryptography
- Message digests
- Hashing

5.4 Understand key management processes:
- Creation/distribution
- Storage/destruction
- Recovery
- Key escrow

5.5 Understand digital signatures

5.6 Understand non-repudiation

5.7 Understand methods of cryptanalytic attacks:
- Chosen plaintext
- Social engineering for key discovery
- Brute force (i.e., rainbow tables, specialized/scalable architecture)
- Cipher-text only
- Known plaintext
- Frequency analysis
- Chosen ciphertext
- Implementation attacks

5.8 Use cryptography to maintain network security

5.9 Use cryptography to maintain application security

5.10 Understand Public Key Infrastructure (PKI)

5.11 Understand certificate-related issues

5.12 Understand information hiding alternatives (e.g., steganography, watermarking)

6.0 Security Architecture and Design

6.1 Understand the fundamental concepts of security models (e.g., Confidentiality, Integrity, and Multilevel models)

6.2 Understand the components of information systems security evaluation models:
- Product evaluation models (e.g., common criteria)
- Industry and international security implementation guidelines (e.g., PCI-DSS, ISO)

6.3 Understand security capabilities of information systems (e.g., memory protection, virtualization, trusted platform module)

6.4 Understand the vulnerabilities of security architectures:
- System (e.g., covert channels, state attacks, emanations)
- Technology and process integration (e.g., single point of failure, service-oriented architecture)

6.5 Understand software and system vulnerabilities and threats:
- Web-based (e.g., XML, SAML, OWASP)
- Client-based (e.g., applets)
- Server-based (e.g., data flow control)
- Database security (e.g., inference, aggregation, data mining, warehousing)
- Distributed systems (e.g., cloud computing, grid computing, peer to peer)

6.6 Understand countermeasure principles (e.g., defense in depth)

7.0 Security Operations

7.1 Understand security operations concepts:
- Need-to-know/least privilege
- Separation of duties and responsibilities
- Monitor special privileges (e.g., operators, administrators)
- Job rotation
- Marking, handling, storing, and destroying of sensitive information
- Record retention

7.2 Employ resource protection:
- Media management
- Asset management (e.g., equipment life cycle, software licensing)

7.3 Manage incident response:
- Detection
- Response
- Reporting
- Recovery
- Remediation and review (e.g., root cause analysis)

7.4 Implement preventive measures against attacks (e.g., malicious code, zero-day exploit, denial of service)

7.5 Implement and support patch and vulnerability management

7.6 Understand change and configuration management (e.g., versioning, baselining)

7.7 Understand system resilience and fault tolerance requirements

8.0 Business Continuity and Disaster Recovery Planning

8.1 Understand business continuity requirements:
- Develop and document project scope and plan

8.2 Conduct business impact analysis:
- Identify and prioritize critical business functions
- Determine maximum tolerable downtime and other criteria
- Assess exposure to outages (e.g., local, regional, global)
- Define recovery objectives

8.3 Develop a recovery strategy:
- Implement a backup storage strategy (e.g., offsite storage, electronic vaulting, tape rotation)
- Recovery site strategies

8.4 Understand disaster recovery process:
- Response
- Personnel
- Communications
- Assessment
- Restoration
- Provide training

8.5 Exercise, assess, and maintain the plan (e.g., version control, distribution)

9.0 Legal, Regulations, Investigations, and Compliance

9.1 Understand legal issues that pertain to information security internationally:
- Computer crime
- Licensing and intellectual property (e.g., copyright, trademark)
- Import/export
- Trans-border data flow
- Privacy

9.2 Understand professional ethics:
- (ISC)² Code of Professional Ethics
- Support organization's code of ethics

9.3 Understand and support investigations:
- Policy, roles, and responsibilities (e.g., rules of engagement, authorization, scope)
- Incident handling and response
- Evidence collection and handling (e.g., chain of custody, interviewing)
- Reporting and documenting

9.4 Understand forensic procedures:
- Media analysis
- Network analysis
- Software analysis
- Hardware/embedded device analysis

9.5 Understand compliance requirements and procedures:
- Regulatory environment
- Audits
- Reporting

9.6 Ensure security in contractual agreements and procurement processes (e.g., cloud computing, outsourcing, vendor governance)

10.0 Physical (Environmental) Security
10.1 Understand site and facility design considerations
10.2 Support the implementation and operation of perimeter security (e.g., physical access control and monitoring, audit trails/access logs)
10.3 Support the implementation and operation of internal security (e.g., escort requirements/visitor control, keys and locks)
10.4 Support the implementation and operation of facilities security (e.g. technology convergence): ■ Communications and server rooms ■ Restricted and work area security ■ Data center security ■ Utilities and Heating, Ventilation, and Air Conditioning (HVAC) considerations ■ Water issues (e.g., leakage, flooding) ■ Fire prevention, detection, and suppression
10.5 Support the protection and securing of equipment
10.6 Understand personnel privacy and safety (e.g., duress, travel, monitoring)

Pearson IT Certification Practice Test Engine and Questions on the Disc

The disc in the back of the book includes the Pearson IT Certification Practice Test engine—software that displays and grades a set of exam-realistic multiple-choice questions. Using the Pearson IT Certification Practice Test engine, you can either study by going through the questions in Study Mode or take a simulated exam that mimics real exam conditions.

The installation process requires two major steps: installing the software and then activating the exam. The disc in the back of this book has a recent copy of the Pearson IT Certification Practice Test engine. The practice exam—the database of exam questions—is not on the disc.

NOTE The cardboard disc case in the back of this book includes the disc and a piece of paper. The paper lists the activation code for the practice exam associated with this book. Do not lose the activation code. On the opposite side of the paper from the activation code is a unique, one-time use coupon code for the purchase of the Premium Edition eBook and Practice Test.

Install the Software from the Disc

The Pearson IT Certification Practice Test is a Windows-only desktop application. You can run it on a Mac using a Windows Virtual Machine, but it was built specifically for the PC platform.

The software installation process is pretty routine compared with other software installation processes. If you have already installed the Pearson IT Certification Practice Test software from another Pearson product, there is no need for you to reinstall the software. Simply launch the software on your desktop and proceed to activate the practice exam from this book by using the activation code included in the disc sleeve.

The following steps outline the installation process:

1. Insert the disc into your PC.
2. The software that automatically runs is the Pearson software to access and use all disc-based features, including the exam engine and the disc-only appendixes. From the main menu, click the option to Install the Exam Engine.
3. Respond to Windows prompts as with any typical software installation process.

The installation process gives you the option to activate your exam with the activation code supplied on the paper in the disc sleeve. This process requires that you establish a Pearson website login. You need this login to activate the exam, so please do register when prompted. If you already have a Pearson website login, there is no need to register again. Just use your existing login.

Activate and Download the Practice Exam

After the exam engine is installed, you should then activate the exam associated with this book (if you did not do so during the installation process) as follows:

1. Start the Pearson IT Certification Practice Test software from the Windows Start menu or from your desktop shortcut icon.
2. To activate and download the exam associated with this book, from the My Products or Tools tab, select the Activate button.
3. At the next screen, enter the Activation Key from the paper inside the cardboard disc holder in the back of the book. When it's entered, click the Activate button.
4. The activation process downloads the practice exam. Click Next and then click Finish.

After the activation process finishes, the My Products tab should list your new exam. If you do not see the exam, make sure you have selected the My Products tab on the menu. At this point, the software and practice exam are ready to use. Simply select the exam, and click the Open Exam button.

To update a particular exam you have already activated and downloaded, simply select the Tools tab, and select the Update Products button. Updating your exams will ensure you have the latest changes and updates to the exam data.

If you want to check for updates to the Pearson Cert Practice Test exam engine software, simply select the Tools tab, and select the Update Application button. This will ensure you are running the latest version of the software engine.

Activating Other Exams

The exam software installation process, and the registration process, must happen only once. Then, for each new exam, only a few steps are required. For instance, if you buy another new Pearson IT Certification Cert Guide or Cisco Press Official Cert Guide, extract the activation code from the disc sleeve in the back of that book—you don't even need the disc at this point. From there, all you need to do is start the exam engine (if not still up and running), and perform steps 2–4 from the previous list.

Premium Edition

In addition to the two free practice exams provided on the disc, you can purchase two additional exams with expanded functionality directly from Pearson IT Certification. The Premium Edition eBook and Practice Test for this title contains two additional full practice exams as well as an eBook (in both PDF and ePub format). In addition, the Premium Edition title also has remediation for each question to the specific part of the eBook that relates to that question.

If you have purchased the print version of this title, you can purchase the Premium Edition at a deep discount. There is a coupon code in the disc sleeve that contains a one-time use code as well as instructions for where you can purchase the Premium Edition.

This chapter covers the following topics:

- **The goals of the CISSP certification:** A description of its sponsoring bodies and the stated goals of the certification
- **The value of the CISSP certification:** An examination of the career and business drivers that comprise the value of the certification
- **The Common Body of Knowledge:** The ten domains of information that make up the topics covered in the certification
- **Steps to becoming a CISSP:** The process involved in achieving the CISSP certification

CHAPTER 1

The CISSP Certification

The Certified Information Systems Security Professional (CISSP) is one of the most respected and sought after security certifications available today. It is a globally recognized credential that demonstrates that the holder has knowledge and skills across a broad range of security topics.

As the number of security threats to organizations grows and the nature of these threats broaden, companies large and small have realized that security can no longer be an afterthought. It must be built into the DNA of the enterprise to be successful. This requires trained professionals who are versed not only in technology security but in all aspects of security. It also requires a holistic approach to protecting the enterprise.

In today's world, security is no longer a one-size-fits-all proposition. The CISSP credential is a way security professionals can demonstrate the ability to design, implement, and maintain the correct security posture for an organization based on the complex environments in which today's organizations exist.

The Goals of the CISSP Certification

The CISSP certification is created and managed by one of the most prestigious security organizations in the world and has a number of stated goals. Although not critical for passing the exam, having knowledge of the organization and of these goals is helpful in understanding the motivation behind the creation of the exam.

Sponsoring Bodies

The CISSP is created and maintained by the International Information Systems Security Certification Consortium (ISC)^2. The (ISC)^2 is a global not-for-profit organization that provides both a vendor-neutral certification process and supporting educational materials.

The CISSP is one of a number of security-related certifications offered by (ISC)². Other certifications offered by this organization include the following:

- Systems Security Certified Practitioner (SSCP)
- Certified Authorization Professional (CAP)
- Certified Secure Software Lifecycle Professional (CSSLP)

Several additional versions of the CISSP are offered that focus in particular areas. These include:

- CISSP-Information Systems Security Architecture Professional (CISSP-IS-SAP)
- CISSP-Information Systems Security Engineering Professional (CISSP-ISSEP)
- CISSP-Information Systems Security Management Professional (CISSP-ISSMP)

(ISC)² derives some of its prestige from the fact that it was the first security certification body to meet the requirements set forth by the ANSI/ISO/IEC Standard 17024, a global benchmark for personnel certification. This ensures certifications offered by this organization are both highly respected and sought after.

Stated Goals

The goal of (ISC)², operating through its administration of the CISSP certification, is to provide a reliable instrument to measure an individual's knowledge of security. This knowledge is not limited to technology issues alone, but to all aspects of security that face an organization.

In that regard, the topics are technically more shallow than those tested by some other security certifications while covering a much wider range of issues than those same certifications. Later in this section, the topics that comprise the 10 domains of knowledge are covered in detail, but it is a wide range of topics. This vast breadth of knowledge and the experience needed to pass the exam are what set the CISSP certification apart.

The Value of the CISSP Certification

The CISSP certification holds value for both the exam candidate and the enterprise. This certification is routinely in the top 10 of yearly lists that rank the relative demand for various IT certifications.

To the Security Professional

Numerous reasons exist for why the security professional would spend the time and effort required to achieve this credential:

- To meet growing demand for security professionals
- To become more marketable in an increasingly competitive job market
- To enhance skills in a current job
- To qualify for or compete more successfully for a promotion
- To increase one's salary

In short, this certification demonstrates that the holder not only has the knowledge and skills tested in the exam, but also that the candidate has the wherewithal to plan and implement a study plan that addresses an unusually broad range of security topics.

To the Enterprise

For the organization, the CISSP certification offers a reliable benchmark to which job candidates can be measured by validating knowledge and experience. Candidates who successfully pass the rigorous exam are required to submit documentation verifying experience in the security field. Individuals holding this certification will stand out from the rest, not only making the hiring process easier but also adding a level of confidence in the final hire.

The Common Body of Knowledge

The material contained in the CISSP is divided into 10 domains, which comprise what is known as the *Common Body of Knowledge*. This book devotes a chapter to each of these domains. Inevitable overlap occurs between the domains, leading to some overlap between topics covered in the chapters; the topics covered in each chapter are described next.

Access Control

The access control domain covers aspects of controlling access to information, including the identification of security principles. Topics include

- Access control concepts
- Access control types and techniques

- Access control models
- Access control administration and monitoring
- Access control attacks
- Access control review and auditing
- Access control life cycle

Telecommunications and Network Security

The telecommunications and network security domain focuses on protecting data in transit and securing the underlying networks over which the data travels. Topics include:

- OSI and TCP/IP model
- Network topologies and technologies
- Network protocols and services
- Network routing
- WAN and remote connection technologies
- Wireless networks
- Secure network design
- Network device security
- Protecting communication channels
- Network attack methods

Information Security Governance and Risk Management

The information security governance and risk management domain addresses the processes involved in developing security polices and their constituent procedures, standards, and guidelines. Topics include:

- Security governance and risk management concepts
- Security frameworks and methods
- Risk assessment and management
- Alignment of security goals to business processes
- Compliance with industry regulations and legal obligations

- Management of the information life cycle
- Integration of third-party governance
- Personnel security
- Security training and awareness
- Security budgeting and assessment

Software Development Security

The software development security domain explores the software development life cycle and development best practices. The topics include:

- System and software development life cycle
- Change management
- Software development methods
- Security control in the software environment
- Assessment of software security
- Software threats

Cryptography

The cryptography domain discusses maintaining the confidentiality of data, both in transit and at rest. Topics include:

- Cryptography concepts
- The role of cryptography in information security
- The cryptographic life cycle
- Cryptography methods
- Encryption system types
- The role of a public key infrastructure (PKI)
- Key management processes
- The relationship between digital signatures and non-repudiation
- E-mail and Internet security
- Methods of crypto-analytic attacks

Security Architecture and Design

The security architecture and design domain covers design models and the proper alignment of these models to support an organization's strategic objectives. The topics include:

- Security models and their respective fundamental concepts
- Security modes
- Security evaluation models
- Current capabilities of information systems
- Vulnerabilities of security architectures
- Software-based attacks
- Countermeasures

Operations Security

The operations security domain surveys the execution of security measures and maintenance of proper security posture. Topics include:

- Principle of secure operations control
- Resource protection
- Operations processes, including incident response, patch management, and change control
- Attack prevention and mitigation
- Maintaining availability

Business Continuity and Disaster Recovery Planning

The business continuity and disaster recovery planning domain describes the processes involved in maintaining business livelihood during incidents both large and small. Topics include:

- Identification of requirements for business continuity
- Development and execution of a business impact analysis
- Recovery strategies
- Critical teams and duties
- Disaster preparedness and recovery

Legal, Regulations, Investigations, and Compliance

The legal, regulations, investigations, and compliance domain focuses on aligning security policies to an increasing amount of regulations and legal requirements facing organizations today. Topics include:

- Computer crime concepts
- Major legal systems
- Intellectual property law
- Legal issues pertaining to integration law and the transfer of data
- Professional ethics prescribed by the (ISC)^2
- Procedures and roles that support successful investigations
- Forensic procedures
- Evidence
- Proper auditing and reporting
- Security issues involved in contracts and the procurement process

Physical and Environmental Security

The physical and environmental security domain addresses processes designed to physically protect all assets, including people, devices, facilities, and support systems. Topics include:

- Threats to physical and environmental security
- Site and facility design issues impacting security
- Network perimeter security
- Internal physical security
- Environmental security
- Equipment security
- Facility security
- Secure device placement
- Personnel privacy and safety

Steps to Becoming a CISSP

To become a CISSP, certain prerequisites must be met and procedures followed. This final section covers those topics.

Qualifying for the Exam

Candidates must have a minimum of five years of direct full-time professional security work experience in two or more of the ten domains in the Common Body of Knowledge. You may receive a one-year experience waiver with a four-year college degree or additional credential from the approved list, available at the $(ISC)^2$ website, thus requiring four years of direct full-time professional security work experience in two or more of the ten domains of the CISSP.

If you lack this experience, you can become an Associate of $(ISC)^2$ by successfully passing the CISSP exam. You'll then have six years to earn your experience to become a CISSP.

Signing Up for the Exam

The steps required to sign up for the CISSP are as follows:

- Complete the exam registration form that is found at the site www.isc2.org. Send this form in to $(ISC)^2$.
- Supply work history as well as documents for the necessary educational requirements (see the previous section "Qualifying for the Exam").
- Sign the Code of Ethics form indicating you will abide by the code.
- Provide payment and indicate the exam site and date. The locations and dates can be found at www.isc2.org.

About the CISSP Exam

The CISSP exam is a paper-based test that the candidate can spend up to 4 hours completing. There are no formal breaks but you are allowed to bring a snack and eat it at the back of the test room, but any time used for that will count toward the 4 hours. You must bring a government-issued identification card. No other forms of ID will be accepted.

The test consists of 250 items with 4 choices per item. Some of the items will not be scored and are for research, which will not be identified to the candidate. The passing grade is 700 out of a possible 1,000. Results will be released via e-mail within four to six weeks.

This chapter covers the following topics:

- **Access control concepts:** Concepts discussed include the confidentiality, integrity, and availability (CIA) triad, default stance, defense in depth, and the access control process.

- **Identification and authentication concepts:** Concepts discussed include the identification concepts and the three factors for authentication.

- **Authorization concepts:** Concepts discussed include access control policies, separation of duties, least privilege, need to know, default to no access, Kerberos and Directory Services, single sign-on, and security domains.

- **Accountability:** Concepts discussed include auditing and reporting, vulnerability assessment, penetration testing, and threat modeling.

- **Access control categories:** Categories include compensative, corrective, detective, deterrent, directive, preventive, and recovery.

- **Access control types:** Types include administrative (management) controls, logical (technical) controls, and physical controls.

- **Access control models:** Models include discretionary access control, mandatory access control, role-based access control, rule-based access control, content-dependent versus context-dependent access control, and access control matrix.

- **Access control administration:** Administration topics include centralized administration, decentralized administration, and provisioning life cycle.

- **Access control monitoring:** Monitoring topics include intrusion detection system (IDS) and intrusion prevention system (IPS).

- **Access control threats:** Threats include password threats, social engineering threats, DoS/DDoS, buffer overflow, mobile code, malicious software, spoofing, sniffing and eavesdropping, emanating, and backdoor/trapdoor.

CHAPTER 2

Access Control

Access occurs when information flows between a subject and an object. A subject is an entity that requests access to an object, and an object is an entity that contains information. A user is an example of a subject, and a file on a computer is an example of an object.

Access control is the means by which a subject's ability to communicate with an object is allowed or denied based on an organization's security requirements. It is the mechanism by which managers and administrators can control access to the objects. Access control mechanisms include a broad range of controls that protect information, computers, networks, and even buildings.

The most important factor when implementing access control is to determine the value of the information being protected. If the cost of the access control mechanism is higher than the value of the information being protected, the access control mechanism is not a good value.

Foundation Topics

Access Control Concepts

When implementing access control, you should always keep several security principles in mind. Confidentiality, integrity, and availability are the three components of the CIA triad and the three main security principles that security professionals should understand when designing access controls. Other security principles that organizations and security professionals should understand are the organization's default security stance and defense in depth.

CIA

The three main security principles of the CIA triad must be considered throughout any security design. Although the CIA triad is being introduced here, each principle of the triad should be considered in every aspect of security design. The CIA triad could easily be discussed in any domain of the CISSP exam.

To ensure *confidentiality*, you must prevent the disclosure of data or information to unauthorized entities. As part of confidentiality, the sensitivity level of data must be determined before putting any access controls in place. Data with a higher sensitivity level will have more access controls in place than data at a lower sensitivity level. The opposite of confidentiality is disclosure.

Integrity, the second part of the CIA triad, ensures that data is protected from unauthorized modification or data corruption. The goal of integrity is to preserve the consistency of data. The opposite of integrity is corruption.

Finally, *availability* means ensuring that data is accessible when and where it is needed. Only individuals who need access to data should be allowed access to that data. Availability is the opposite of destruction or isolation.

Every security control that is put into place by an organization fulfills at least one of the security principles of the CIA triad. Understanding how to circumvent these security principles is just as important as understanding how to provide them.

Default Stance

An organization's approach to information security directly affects its access control strategy. For a default stance, organizations must choose between an allow-by-default or deny-by-default stance. As implied by its name, an allow-by-default stance permits access to any data unless a need exists to restrict access. The deny-by-default stance is much stricter because it denies any access that is not explicitly permitted. Government and military institutions and many commercial organizations use a deny-by-default stance.

Today few organizations implement either of these stances to its fullest. In most organizations, you see some mixture of the two. Although the core stance should guide the organization, organizations often find that this mixture is necessary to ensure that data is still protected while providing access to a variety of users. For example, a public Web site might grant an allow-by-default stance, whereas a SQL database might have a deny-by-default stance.

Defense In Depth

A defense-in-depth strategy refers to the practice of using multiple layers of security between data and the resources on which it resides and possible attackers. The first layer of a good defense-in-depth strategy is appropriate access control strategies. Access controls exist in all areas of an Information Systems (IS) infrastructure (more commonly referred to as an IT infrastructure), but a defense-in-depth strategy goes beyond access control. It also considers software development security, cryptography, and all other domains of the CISSP realm.

Figure 2-1 shows an example of the defense-in-depth concept.

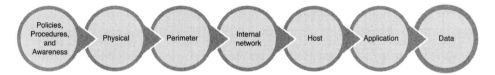

Figure 2-1 Defense-In-Depth Example

Access Control Process

Although many approaches to implementing access controls have been designed, all the approaches generally involve the following steps:

1. Identify resources.
2. Identify users.
3. Identify the relationships between the resources and users.

Identify Resources

This first step in the access control process involves defining all resources in the IT infrastructure by deciding which entities need to be protected. When defining these resources, you must also consider how the resources will be accessed. The following questions can be used as a starting point during resource identification:

- Will this information be accessed by members of the general public?
- Should access to this information be restricted to employees only?
- Should access to this information be restricted to a smaller subset of employees?

Keep in mind that data, applications, services, servers, and network devices are all considered resources. Resources are any organizational asset that users can access. In access control, resources are often referred to as objects.

Identify Users

After identifying the resources, an organization should identify the users who need access to the resources. A typical security professional must manage multiple levels of users who require access to organizational resources. During this step, only identifying the users is important. The level of access these users will be given will be analyzed further in the next step.

As part of this step, you must analyze and understand the users' needs and then measure the validity of those needs against organizational needs, policies, legal issues, data sensitivity, and risk.

Remember that any access control strategy and the system deployed to enforce it should avoid complexity. The more complex an access control system is, the harder that system is to manage. In addition, anticipating security issues that could occur in more complex systems is much harder. As security professionals, we must balance the organization's security needs and policies with the needs of the users. If a security mechanism that we implement causes too much difficulty for the user, the user might engage in practices that subvert the mechanisms that we implement. For example, if you implement a password policy that requires a very long, complex password, users might find remembering their passwords to be difficult. Users might then write their passwords on sticky notes that are attached to their monitor or keyboard.

Identify Relationships between Resources and Users

The final step in the access control process is to define the access control levels that need to be in place for each resource and the relationships between the resources and users. For example, if an organization has defined a Web server as a resource, general employees might need a less restrictive level of access to the resource than the public and a more restrictive level of access to the resource than the Web development staff. Access controls should be designed to support the business functionality of the resources that are being protected. Controlling the actions that can be performed for a specific resource based on a user's role is vital.

Identification and Authentication Concepts

To be able to access a resource, a user must profess his identity, provide the necessary credentials, and have the appropriate rights to perform the tasks he is completing. The first step in this process is called *identification*, which is the act of a user professing an identity to an access control system.

Authentication, the second part of the process, is the act of validating a user with a unique identifier by providing the appropriate credentials. When trying to differentiate between the two, security professionals should know that identification identifies the user and authentication verifies that the identity provided by the user is valid. Authentication is usually implemented through a user password provided at logon. When a user logs into a system, the login process should validate the login after the user supplies all the input data.

The most popular forms of user identification include user IDs or user accounts, account numbers, and personal identification numbers (PINs).

Three Factors for Authentication

After establishing the user identification method, an organization must decide which authentication method to use.

Authentication methods are divided into three broad categories:

- **Knowledge factor authentication:** Something a person knows
- **Ownership factor authentication:** Something a person has or possesses
- **Characteristic factor authentication:** Something a person is

Authentication usually ensures that a user provide at least one factor from these categories, which is referred to as single-factor authentication. An example of this would be providing a user name and password at login. Two-factor authentication ensures that the user provides two of the three factors. An example of two-factor authentication would be providing a user name, password, and smart card at login. Three-factor authentication ensures that a user provides three factors. An example of three-factor authentication would be providing a user name, password, smart card, and fingerprint at login. For authentication to be considered strong authentication, a user must provide factors from at least two different categories. (Note that the user name is the identification factor, not an authentication factor.)

You should understand that providing multiple authentication factors from the same category is still considered single-factor authentication. For example, if a user provides a user name, password, and the user's mother's maiden name, single-factor authentication is being used. In this example, the user is still only providing factors that are something a person knows.

Knowledge Factors

As briefly described in the preceding section, *knowledge factor authentication* is authentication that is provided based on something that a person knows. This type of authentication is referred to as a Type I authentication factor. Although the most popular form of authentication used by this category is password authentication, other knowledge factors can be used, including date of birth, mother's maiden name, key combination, or PIN.

Identity and Account Management

Identity and account management is vital to any authentication process. As a security professional, you must ensure that your organization has a formal procedure to control the creation and allocation of access credentials or identities. If invalid accounts are allowed to be created and are not disabled, security breaches will occur. Most organizations implement a method to review the identification and authentication process to ensure that user accounts are current. Questions that are likely to help in the process include:

- Is a current list of authorized users and their access maintained and approved?
- Are passwords changed at least every 90 days or earlier if needed?
- Are inactive user accounts disabled after a specified period of time?

Any identity management procedure must include processes for creating (provisioning), changing and monitoring (reviewing), and removing users from the access control system (revoking). This is referred to as the access control provisioning life cycle. When initially establishing a user account, new users should be required to provide valid photo identification and should sign a statement regarding password confidentiality. User accounts must be unique. Policies should be in place that standardize the structure of user accounts. For example, all user accounts should be firstname.lastname or some other structure. This ensures that users within an organization will be able to determine a new user's identification, mainly for communication purposes.

After creation, user accounts should be monitored to ensure that they remain active. Inactive accounts should be automatically disabled after a certain period of inactivity based on business requirements. In addition, any termination policy should include formal procedures to ensure that all user accounts are disabled or deleted. Elements of proper account management include the following:

- Establish a formal process for establishing, issuing, and closing user accounts.
- Periodically review user accounts.
- Implement a process for tracking access authorization.
- Periodically rescreen personnel in sensitive positions.
- Periodically verify the legitimacy of user accounts.

User account reviews are a vital part of account management. User accounts should be reviewed for conformity with the principle of least privilege. (The principle of least privilege is explained later in this chapter.) User account reviews can be performed on an enterprise-wide, system-wide, or application-by-application basis. The size of the organization will greatly affect which of these methods to use. As part of user account reviews, organizations should determine whether all user accounts are active.

Password Types and Management

As mentioned earlier, password authentication is the most popular authentication method implemented today. However, password types can vary from system to system. Understanding all the types of passwords that can be used is vital.

The types of passwords that you should be familiar with include:

- **Standard word or simple passwords:** As the name implies, these passwords consist of single words that often include a mixture of upper- and lowercase letters. The advantage of this password type is that it is easy to remember. A disadvantage of this password type is that it is easy for attackers to crack or break, resulting in a compromised account.

- **Combination passwords:** This password type uses a mix of dictionary words, usually two unrelated words. These are also referred to as composition passwords. Like standard word passwords, they can include upper- and lowercase letters and numbers. An advantage of this password is that it is harder to break than simple passwords. A disadvantage is that it can be hard to remember.

- **Static passwords:** This password type is the same for each login. It provides a minimum level of security because the password never changes. It is most often seen in peer-to-peer networks.

- **Complex passwords:** This password type forces a user to include a mixture of upper- and lowercase letters, numbers, and special characters. For many organizations today, this type of password is enforced as part of the organization's password policy. An advantage of this password type is that it is very hard to crack. A disadvantage is that it is harder to remember and can often be much harder to enter correctly than standard or combination passwords.

- **Passphrase passwords:** This password type requires that a long phrase be used. Because of the password's length, it is easier to remember but much harder to attack, both of which are definite advantages. Incorporating upper- and lowercase letters, numbers, and special characters in this type of password can significantly increase authentication security.

- **Cognitive passwords:** This password type is a piece of information that can be used to verify an individual's identity. This information is provided to the system by answering a series of questions based on the user's life, such as favorite color, pet's name, mother's maiden name, and so on. An advantage to this type is that users can usually easily remember this information. The disadvantage is that someone who has intimate knowledge of the person's life (spouse, child, sibling, and so on) might be able to provide this information as well.

- **One-time passwords:** Also called a dynamic password, this type of password is only used once to log in to the access control system. This password type provides the highest level of security because passwords are discarded when they are used.

- **Graphical passwords:** Also called CAPTCHA passwords, this type of password uses graphics as part of the authentication mechanism. One popular implementation requires a user to enter a series of characters in the graphic displayed. This implementation ensures that a human is entering the password, not a robot. Another popular implementation requires the user to select the appropriate graphic for his account from a list of graphics given.

- **Numeric passwords:** This type of password includes only numbers. Keep in mind that the choices of a password are limited by the number of digits allowed. For example, if all passwords are 4 digits, then the maximum number of password possibilities is 10,000, from 0000 through 9999. After an attacker realized that only numbers are used, cracking user passwords would be much easier because the possibilities would be known.

Passwords are considered weaker than passphrases, one-time passwords, token devices, and login phrases. After an organization has decided which type of password to use, the organization must establish its password management policies.

Password management considerations include, but might not be limited to

- **Password life:** How long the password will be valid. For most organizations, passwords are valid for 60 to 90 days.

- **Password history:** How long before a password can be reused. Password policies usually remember a certain number of previously used passwords.

- **Authentication period:** How long a user can remain logged in. If a user remains logged in for the period without activity, the user will be automatically logged out.

- **Password complexity:** How the password will be structured. Most organizations require upper- and lowercase letters, numbers, and special characters.

- **Password length:** How long the password must be. Most organizations require 8–12 characters.

As part of password management, organizations should establish a procedure for changing passwords. Most organizations implement a service that allows users to automatically reset their password before the password expires. In addition, most organizations should consider establishing a password reset policy in cases where users have forgotten their password or passwords have been compromised. A self-service password reset approach allows users to reset their own passwords without the assistance of help desk employees. An assisted password reset approach requires that users contact help desk personnel for help in changing their passwords.

Password reset policies can also be affected by other organizational policies, such as account lockout policies. Account lockout policies are security policies that organizations implement to protect against attacks that are carried out against passwords. Organizations often configure account lockout policies so that user accounts are locked after a certain number of unsuccessful login attempts. If an account is locked out, the system administrator might need to unlock or re-enable the user account. Security professionals should also consider encouraging organizations to require users to reset their password if their account has been locked or after a password has been used for a certain amount of time (90 days for most organizations). For most organizations, all the password policies, including account lockout policies, are implemented at the enterprise level on the servers that manage the network.

NOTE An older term that you might need to be familiar with is *clipping level*. A clipping level is a configured baseline threshold above which violations will be recorded. For example, an organization might want to start recording any unsuccessful login attempts after the first one, with account lockout occurring after five failed attempts.

Depending on which servers are used to manage the enterprise, security professionals must be aware of the security issues that affect user account and password management. Two popular server operating systems are Linux and Windows.

For Linux, passwords are stored in the */etc/passwd* and */etc/shadow* file. Because the */etc/passwd* file is a text file that can be easily accessed, you should ensure that any Linux servers use the */etc/shadow* file where the passwords in the file can be protected using a hash. The *root* user in Linux is a default account that is given administrative-level access to the entire server. If the *root* account is compromised, all passwords should be changed. Access to the *root* account should be limited only to systems administrators, and root login should only be allowed via a local system console, not remotely.

For Windows computers that are in workgroups, the Security Accounts Manager (SAM) stores user passwords in a hashed format. However, known security issues exist with a SAM, including the ability to dump the password hashes directly from the registry. You should take all Microsoft-recommended security measures to protect this file. If you manage a Windows network, you should change the name of the default Administrator account or disable it. If this account is retained, make sure that you assign it a password. The default Administrator account might have full access to a Windows server.

Ownership Factors

Ownership factor authentication is authentication that is provided based on something that a person has. This type of authentication is referred to as a Type II authentication factor. Ownership factors can include token devices, memory cards, and smart cards.

Synchronous and Asynchronous Token

The token device (often referred to as a password generator) is a handheld device that presents the authentication server with the one-time password. If the authentication method requires a token device, the user must be in physical possession of the device to authenticate. So although the token device provides a password to the authentication server, the token device is considered a Type II authentication factor because its use requires ownership of the device.

Two basic token device authentication methods are used: synchronous or asynchronous. A synchronous token generates a unique password at fixed time intervals with the authentication server. An asynchronous token generates the password based on a challenge/response technique with the authentication server, with the token device providing the correct answer to the authentication server's challenge.

A token device is usually only implemented in very secure environments because of the cost of deploying the token device. In addition, token-based solutions can experience problems because of the battery lifespan of the token device.

Memory Cards

A memory card is a swipe card that is issued to valid users. The card contains user authentication information. When the card is swiped through a card reader, the information stored on the card is compared to the information that the user enters. If the information matches, the authentication server approves the login. If it does not match, authentication is denied.

Because the card must be read by a card reader, each computer or access device must have its own card reader. In addition, the cards must be created and programmed. Both of these steps add complexity and cost to the authentication process. However, it is often worth the extra complexity and cost for the added security it provides, which is a definite benefit of this system. However, the data on the memory cards is not protected, a weakness that organizations should consider before implementing this type of system. Memory-only cards are very easy to counterfeit.

Smart Cards

Similar to a memory card, a smart card accepts, stores, and sends data but can hold more data than a memory card. Smart cards, often known as integrated circuit cards (ICCs), contain memory like a memory card but also contain an embedded chip like bank or credit cards. Smart cards use card readers. However, the data on the smart card is used by the authentication server without user input. To protect against lost or stolen smart cards, most implementations require the user to input a secret PIN, meaning the user is actually providing both a Type I (PIN) and Type II (smart card) authentication factor.

Two basic types of smart cards are used: contact cards and contactless cards. Contact cards require physical contact with the card reader, usually by swiping. Contactless cards, also referred to as proximity cards, simply need to be in close proximity to the reader. Hybrid cards are available that allow a card to be used in both contact and contactless systems.

For comparative purposes, security professionals should remember that smart cards have processing power due to the embedded chips. Memory cards do not have processing power. Smart card systems are much more reliable than memory card systems or callback systems (which are discussed in Chapter 3, "Telecommunications and Network Security").

Smart cards are even more expensive to implement than memory cards. Many organizations prefer smart cards over memory cards because they are harder to counterfeit and the data on them can be protected using encryption.

Characteristic Factors

Characteristic factor authentication is authentication that is provided based on something that a person is. This type of authentication is referred to as a Type III authentication factor. Biometric technology is the technology that allows users to be authenticated based on physiological or behavioral characteristics. Physiological characteristics include any unique physical attribute of the user, including iris, retina, and fingerprints. Behavioral characteristics measure a person's actions in a situation, including voice patterns and data entry characteristics.

Physiological Characteristics

Physiological systems use a biometric scanning device to measure certain information about a physiological characteristic. You should understand the following physiological biometric systems:

- Fingerprint
- Finger scan
- Hand geometry
- Hand topography
- Palm or hand scans
- Facial scans
- Retina scans
- Iris scans
- Vascular scans

A fingerprint scan usually scans the ridges of a finger for matching. A special type of fingerprint scan called minutiae matching is more microscopic in that it records the bifurcations and other detailed characteristics. Minutiae matching requires more authentication server space and more processing time than ridge fingerprint scans. Fingerprint scanning systems have a lower user acceptance rate than many systems because users are concerned with how the fingerprint information will be used and shared.

A finger scan extracts only certain features from a fingerprint. Because a limited amount of the fingerprint information is needed, finger scans require less server space or processing time than any type of fingerprint scan.

A hand geometry scan usually obtains size, shape, or other layout attributes of a user's hand but can also measure bone length or finger length. Two categories of hand geometry systems are mechanical and image-edge detective systems. Regardless of which category is used, hand geometry scanners require less server space and processing time than fingerprint or finger scans.

A hand topography scan records the peaks and valleys of the hand and its shape. This system is usually implemented in conjunction with hand geometry scans because hand topography scans are not unique enough if used alone.

A palm or hand scan combines fingerprint and hand geometry technologies. It records fingerprint information from every finger as well as hand geometry information.

A facial scan records facial characteristics, including bone structure, eye width, and forehead size. This biometric method uses eigenfeatures or eigenfaces. Neither of these methods actually captures a picture of a face. With eigenfeatures, the distance between facial features are measured and recorded. With eigenfaces, measurements of facial components are gathered and compared to a set of standard eigenfaces. For example, a person's face might be composed of the average face plus 21% from eigenface 1, 83% from eigenface 2, and -18% from eigenface 3. Many facial scan biometric devices will use a combination of eigenfeatures and eigenfaces.

A retina scan scans the retina's blood vessel pattern. A retina scan is considered more intrusive than an iris scan.

An iris scan scans the colored portion of the eye, including all rifts, coronas, and furrows. Iris scans have a higher accuracy than any other biometric scan.

A vascular scan scans the pattern of veins in the user's hand or face. Although this method can be a good choice because it is not very intrusive, physical injuries to the hand or face, depending on which the system uses, could cause false rejections.

Behavioral Characteristics

Behavioral systems use a biometric scanning device to measure a person's actions. You should understand the following behavioral biometric systems:

- Signature dynamics
- Keystroke dynamics
- Voice pattern or print

Signature dynamics measure stroke speed, pen pressure, and acceleration and deceleration while the user writes his signature. Dynamic Signature Verification (DSV) analyzes signature features and specific features of the signing process.

Keystroke dynamics measure the typing pattern that a user uses when inputting a password or other predetermined phrase. In this case, even if the correct password or phrase is entered but the entry pattern on the keyboard is different, the user will be denied access. Flight time, a term associated with keystroke dynamics, is the amount of time it takes to switch between keys. Dwell time is the amount of time you hold down a key.

Voice pattern or print measures the sound pattern of a user stating a certain word. When the user attempts to authenticate, he will be asked to repeat those words in different orders. If the pattern matches, authentication is allowed.

Biometric Considerations

When considering biometric technologies, security professionals should understand the following terms:

- **Enrollment time:** The process of obtaining the sample that is used by the biometric system. This process requires actions that must be repeated several times.

- **Feature extraction:** The approach to obtaining biometric information from a collected sample of a user's physiological or behavioral characteristics.

- **Accuracy:** The most important characteristic of biometric systems. It is how correct the overall readings will be.

- **Throughput rate:** The rate at which the biometric system will be able to scan characteristics and complete the analysis to permit or deny access. The acceptable rate is 6–10 subjects per minute. A single user should be able to complete the process in 5–10 seconds.

- **Acceptability:** Describes the likelihood that users will accept and follow the system.

- **False rejection rate (FRR):** A measurement of valid users that will be falsely rejected by the system. This is called a Type I error.

- **False acceptance rate (FAR):** A measurement of the percentage of invalid users that will be falsely accepted by the system. This is called a Type II error. Type II errors are more dangerous than Type I errors.

- **Crossover error rate (CER):** The point at which FRR equals FAR. Expressed as a percentage, this is the most important metric.

When analyzing biometric systems, security professionals often refer to a Zephyr chart that illustrates the comparative strengths and weaknesses of biometric system. However, you should also consider how effective each biometric system is and its level of user acceptance. The following is a list of the more popular biometric methods ranked by effectiveness, with the most effective being first:

1. Iris scan
2. Retina scan
3. Fingerprint
4. Hand print
5. Hand geometry
6. Voice pattern
7. Keystroke pattern
8. Signature dynamics

The following is a list of the more popular biometric methods ranked by user acceptance, with the methods that are ranked more popular by users being first:

1. Voice pattern
2. Keystroke pattern
3. Signature dynamics
4. Hand geometry
5. Hand print
6. Fingerprint
7. Iris scan
8. Retina scan

When considering FAR, FRR, and CER, smaller values are better. FAR errors are more dangerous than FRR errors. Security professionals can use the CER rate for comparative analysis when helping their organization decide which system to implement. For example, voice print systems usually have higher CERs than iris scans, hand geometry, or fingerprints.

Figure 2-2 shows the biometric enrollment and authentication process.

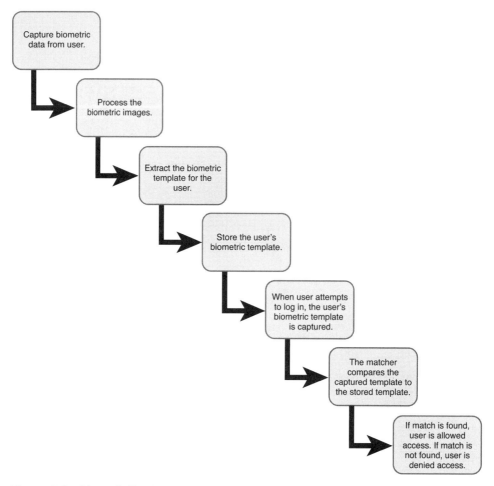

Figure 2-2 Biometric Enrollment and Authentication Process

Authorization Concepts

After a user is authenticated, the user must be granted the rights and permissions to resources. The process is referred to as authorization. Identification and authentication are necessary steps to providing authorization. The next sections cover important components in authorization: access control policies, separation of duties, least privilege/need to know, default to no access, Kerberos and directory services, single sign-on, and security domains.

Access Control Policies

An access control policy defines the method for identifying and authenticating users and the level of access that is granted to users. Organizations should put access control policies in place to ensure that access control decisions for users are based on formal guidelines. If an access control policy is not adopted, organizations will have trouble assigning, managing, and administering access management.

Separation of Duties

Separation of duties is an important concept to keep in mind when designing an organization's authentication and authorization policies. Separation of duties prevents fraud by distributing tasks and their associated rights and privileges between more than one user. This helps to deter fraud and collusion because it requires collusion for any fraudulent act to occur. A good example of separation duties is authorizing one person to manage backup procedures and another to manage restore procedures.

Separation of duties is associated with dual controls and split knowledge. With dual controls, two or more users are authorized and required to perform certain functions. For example, a retail establishment might require two managers to open the safe. Split knowledge ensures that no single user has all the information to perform a particular task. An example of a split control is the military's requiring two individuals to each enter a unique combination to authorize missile firing.

Least Privilege/Need-to-Know

The principle of least privilege requires that a user or process is given only the minimum access privilege needed to perform a particular task. Its main purpose is to ensure that users only have access to the resources they need and are authorized to perform only the tasks they need to perform. To properly implement the least privilege principle, organizations must identify all users' jobs and restrict users only to the identified privileges.

The need-to-know principle is closely associated with the concept of least privilege. Although least privilege seeks to reduce access to a minimum, the need-to-know principle actually defines what the minimums for each job or business function are. Excessive privileges become a problem when a user has more rights, privileges, and permissions than he needs to do his job. Excessive privileges are hard to control in large environments.

A common implementation of the least privilege and need-to-know principles is when a systems administrator is issued both an administrative-level account and a normal user account. In most day-to-day functions, the administrator should use his normal user account. When the systems administrator needs to perform administrative-level tasks, he should use the administrative-level account. If the administrator uses his administrative-level account while performing routine tasks, he risks compromising the security of the system and user accountability.

Organizational rules that support the principle of least privilege include the following:

- Keep the number of administrative accounts to a minimum.
- Administrators should use normal user accounts when performing routine operations.
- Permissions on tools that are likely to be used by attackers should be as restrictive as possible.

To more easily support the least privilege and need-to-know principles, users should be divided into groups to facilitate the confinement of information to a single group or area. This process is referred to as compartmentalization.

Default to No Access

During the authorization process, you should configure an organization's access control mechanisms so that the default level of security is to default to *no access*. This means that if nothing has been specifically allowed for a user or group, then the user or group will not be able to access the resource. The best security approach is to start with no access and add rights based on a user's need to know and least privilege needed to accomplish their daily tasks.

Directory Services

A directory service is a database designed to centralize data management regarding network subjects and objects. A typical directory contains a hierarchy that includes users, groups, systems, servers, client workstations, and so on. Because the directory service contains data about users and other network entities, it can be used by many applications that require access to that information.

The three most common directory service standards are

- X.500
- Lightweight Directory Access Protocol (LDAP)
- X.400

X.500 uses the directory access protocol (DAP). In X.500, the distinguished name (DN) provides the full path in the X.500 database where the entry is found. The relative distinguished name (RDN) in X.500 is an entry's name without the full path.

Based on X.500's DAP, LDAP is simpler than X.500. LDAP supports DN and RDN, but includes more attributes such as the common name (CN), domain component (DC), and organizational unit (OU) attributes. Using a client/server architecture, LDAP uses TCP port 389 to communicate. If advanced security is needed, LDAP over SSL communicates via TCP port 636.

Microsoft's implementation of LDAP is Active Directory, which organizes directories into forests and trees.

X.400 is mainly for message transfer and storage. It uses elements to create a series of name/value pairs separated by semicolons. X.400 has gradually been replaced by Simple Mail Transfer Protocol (SMTP) implementations.

Single Sign-on

In a single sign-on (SSO) environment, a user enters his login credentials once and can access all resources in the network. The Open Group Security Forum has defined many objectives for an SSO. Some of the objectives for the user sign-on interface and user account management include the following:

- The interface should be independent of the type of authentication information handled.
- The creation, deletion, and modification of user accounts should be supported.
- Support should be provided for a user to establish a default user profile.
- They should be independent of any platform or operating system.

NOTE To obtain more information about the Open Group's Single Sign-On Standard, you should access the Web site at www.opengroup.org/security/sso_scope.htm.

SSO provides many advantages and disadvantages when it is implemented.

Advantages of an SSO system include:

- Users are able to use stronger passwords.
- User and password administration is simplified.
- Resource access is much faster.
- User login is more efficient.
- Users only need to remember the login credentials for a single system.

Disadvantages of an SSO system include:

- After a user obtains system access through the initial SSO login, the user is able to access all resources to which he is granted access. Although this is also an advantage for the user (only one login needed), it is also considered a disadvantage because only one signin can compromise all the systems that participate in the SSO network.

- If a user's credentials are compromised, attackers will have access to all resources to which the user has access.

Although the discussion on SSO so far has been mainly on how it is used for networks and domains, SSO can also be implemented in Web-based systems. Enterprise Access Management (EAM) provides access control management for Web-based enterprise systems. Its functions include accommodation of a variety of authentication methods and role-based access control.

SSO can be implemented in Kerberos and Secure European System for Applications in a Multi-vendor Environment (SESAME) environments.

Kerberos

Kerberos is an authentication protocol that uses a client/server model developed by MIT's Project Athena. It is the default authentication model in the recent editions of Windows Server and is also used in Apple, Sun, and Linux operating systems. Kerberos is an SSO system that uses symmetric key cryptography. Kerberos provides confidentiality and integrity.

Kerberos assumes that messaging, cabling, and client computers are not secure and are easily accessible. In a Kerberos exchange involving a message with an authenticator, the authenticator contains the client ID and a timestamp. Because a Kerberos ticket is valid for a certain time, the timestamp ensures the validity of the request.

In a Kerberos environment, the Key Distribution Center (KDC) is the repository for all user and service secret keys. The client sends a request to the authentication server (AS), which might or might not be the KDC. The AS forwards the client credentials to the KDC. The KDC authenticates clients to other entities on a network and facilitates communication using session keys. The KDC provides security to clients or principals, which are users, network services, and software. Each principal must have an account on the KDC. The KDC issues a ticket-granting ticket (TGT) to the principal. The principal will send the TGT to the ticket-granting service (TGS) when the principal needs to connect to another entity. The TGS then transmits a ticket and sessions keys to the principal. The set of principles for which a single KDC is responsible is referred to as a realm.

Some advantages of implementing Kerberos include the following:

- User passwords do NOT need to be sent over the network.
- Both the client and server authenticate each other.
- The tickets passed between the server and client are timestamped and include lifetime information.
- The Kerberos protocol uses open Internet standards and is not limited to proprietary codes or authentication mechanisms.

Some disadvantages of implementing Kerberos include:

- KDC redundancy is required if providing fault tolerance is a requirement. The KDC is a single point of failure.
- The KDC must be scalable to ensure that performance of the system does not degrade.
- Session keys on the client machines can be compromised.
- Kerberos traffic needs to be encrypted to protect the information over the network.
- All systems participating in Kerberos process must have synchronized clocks.
- Kerberos systems are susceptible to password-guessing attacks.

Figure 2-3 shows the ticket-issuing process for Kerberos.

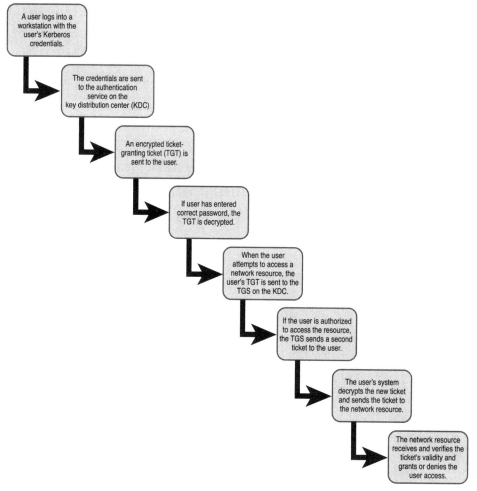

Figure 2-3 Kerberos Ticket-Issuing Process

SESAME

The Secure European System for Applications in a Multi-vendor Environment (SESAME) project extended Kerberos' functionality to fix Kerberos' weaknesses. SESAME uses both symmetric and asymmetric cryptography to protect interchanged data. SESAME uses a trusted authentication server at each host.

SESAME uses Privileged Attribute Certificates (PACs) instead of tickets. It incorporates two certificates: one for authentication and one for defining access privileges. The trusted authentication server is referred to as the Privileged Attribute Server (PAS), which performs roles similar to the KDC in Kerberos. SESAME can be integrated into a Kerberos system.

Federated Identity Management

A federated identity is a portable identity that can be used across businesses and domains. In federated identity management, each organization that joins the federation agrees to enforce a common set of policies and standards. These policies and standards define how to provision and manage user identification, authentication, and authorization. Federated identity management uses two basic models for linking organizations within the federation: cross certification and trusted third-party or bridge model.

In the cross-certification model, each organization certifies that every other organization is trusted. This trust is established when the organizations review each other's standards. Each organization must verify and certify through due diligence that the other organizations meet or exceed standards. One disadvantage of cross certification is that the number of trust relationships that must be managed can become a problem.

In the trusted third-party or bridge model, each organization subscribes to the standards of a third party. The third party manages verification, certification, and due diligence for all organizations. This is usually the best model if an organization needs to establish federated identity management relationships with a large number of organizations.

Security Domains

A domain is a set of resources that are available to a subject over a network. Subjects that access a domain include users, processes, and applications. A security domain is a set of resources that follow the same security policies and are available to a subject. The domains are usually arranged in a hierarchical structure of parent and child domains.

> **NOTE** Do not confuse the term *security domain* with protection domain. Although a security domain usually encompasses a network, a protection domain resides within a single resource. A *protection domain* is a group of processes that share access to the same resource.

Accountability

Accountability is an organization's ability to hold users responsible for the actions they perform. To ensure that users are accountable for their actions, organizations must implement an auditing mechanism. In addition, the organization should periodically carry out vulnerability assessments, penetration testing, and threat modeling.

Although organizations should internally complete these accountability mechanisms, they should also periodically have a third party perform these audits and tests. This is important because the outside third party can provide objectivity that internal personnel often cannot provide.

Auditing and Reporting

Auditing and reporting ensure that users are held accountable for their actions, but an auditing mechanism can only report on events that it is configured to monitor. You should monitor network events, system events, application events, user events, and keystroke activity. Keep in mind that any auditing activity will impact the performance of the system being monitored. Organizations must find a balance between auditing important events and activities and ensuring that device performance is maintained at an acceptable level. Also, organizations must ensure that any monitoring that occurs is in compliance with all applicable laws.

When designing an auditing mechanism, security professionals should remember the following guidelines:

- Develop an audit log management plan that includes mechanisms to control the log size, backup processes, and periodic review plans.

- Ensure that the ability to delete an audit log is a two-man control that requires the cooperation of at least two administrators. This ensures that a single administrator is not able to delete logs that might hold incriminating evidence.

- Monitor all high-privilege accounts (including all root users and administrative-level accounts).

- Ensure that the audit trail includes who processed the transaction, when the transaction occurred (date and time), where the transaction occurred (which system), and whether the transaction was successful or not.

- Ensure that deleting the log and deleting data within the logs cannot occur unless the user has the appropriate administrative-level permissions.

> **NOTE** *Scrubbing* is the act of deleting incriminating data within an audit log.

Audit trails detect computer penetrations and reveal actions that identify misuse. As a security professional, you should use the audit trails to review patterns of access to individual objects. To identify abnormal patterns of behavior, you should first identify normal patterns of behavior. Also, you should establish the clipping level, which is a baseline of user errors above which violations will be recorded. For example, your organization might choose to ignore the first invalid login attempt, knowing that initial failed login attempts are often due to user error. Any invalid login after the first would be recorded because it could be a sign of an attack. A common clipping level that is used is three failed login attempts. Any failed login attempt above the limit of three would be considered malicious. In most cases, a lockout policy would lock out a user's account after this clipping level is reached.

Audit trails deter attacker attempts to bypass the protection mechanisms that are configured on a system or device. As a security professional, you should specifically configure the audit trails to track system/device rights or privileges being granted to a user and data additions, deletions, or modifications.

Finally, audit trails must be monitored, and automatic notifications should be configured. If no one monitors the audit trail, then the data recorded in the audit trail is useless. Certain actions should be configured to trigger automatic notifications. For example, you might want to configure an e-mail alert to occur after a certain number of invalid login attempts because invalid login attempts might be a sign that a brute-force password attack is occurring.

Vulnerability Assessment

A vulnerability assessment helps to identify the areas of weakness in a network. It can also help to determine asset prioritization within an organization. A comprehensive vulnerability assessment is part of the risk management process. But for access control, security professionals should use vulnerability assessments that specifically target the access control mechanisms.

Vulnerability assessments usually fall into one of three categories:

- **Personnel testing:** Reviews standard practices and procedures that users follow.
- **Physical testing:** Reviews facility and perimeter protections.
- **System and network testing:** Reviews systems, devices, and network topology.

The security analyst who will be performing the vulnerability assessment must understand the systems and devices that are on the network and the job they perform. Having this information ensures that the analyst can assess the vulnerabilities of the systems and devices based on the known and potential threats to the systems and devices.

After gaining knowledge regarding the systems and devices, the security analyst should examine existing controls in place and identify any threats against these controls. The security analyst can then use all the information gathered to determine which automated tools to use to analyze for vulnerabilities. After the vulnerability analysis is complete, the security analyst should verify the results to ensure that they are accurate and then report the findings to management with suggestions for remedial action. With this information in hand, the analyst should carry out threat modeling to identify the threats that could negatively affect systems and devices and the attack methods that could be used.

Penetration Testing

The goal of penetration testing, also known as ethical hacking, is to simulate an attack to identify any threats that can stem from internal or external resources that plan to exploit the vulnerabilities of a system or device.

The steps in performing a penetration test are as follows:

1. Document information about the target system or device.

2. Gather information about attack methods against the target system or device. This includes performing port scans.

3. Identify the known vulnerabilities of the target system or device.

4. Execute attacks against the target system or device to gain user and privileged access.

5. Document the results of the penetration test, and report the findings to management with suggestions for remedial action.

Both internal and external tests should be performed. Internal tests occur from within the network, whereas external tests originate outside the network by targeting the servers and devices that are publicly visible.

Strategies for penetration testing are based on the testing objectives as defined by the organization. The strategies that you should be familiar with include the following:

- **Blind test:** The testing team is provided with limited knowledge of the network systems and devices using publicly available information. The organization's security team knows that an attack is coming. This test requires more effort by the testing team, and the testing team must simulate an actual attack.

- **Double-blind test:** This test is like a blind test except the organization's security team does NOT know that an attack is coming. Only a few individuals at the organization know about the attack, and they do not share this information with the security team. This test usually requires equal effort for both the testing team and the organization's security team.

- **Target test:** Both the testing team and the organization's security team are given maximum information about the network and the type of test that will occur. This is the easiest test to complete but will not provide a full picture of the organization's security.

Penetration testing is also divided into categories based on the amount of information to be provided. The main categories that you should be familiar with include the following:

- **Zero-knowledge test:** The testing team is provided with no knowledge regarding the organization's network. Testing team can use any means at their disposal to obtain information about the organization's network. This is also referred to as closed or black box testing.

- **Partial-knowledge test:** The testing team is provided with public knowledge regarding the organization's network. Boundaries might be set for this type of test.

- **Full-knowledge test:** The testing team is provided with all available knowledge regarding the organization's network. This test is focused more on what attacks can be carried out.

Access Control Categories

You implement access controls as a countermeasure to identified vulnerabilities. Access control mechanisms that you can use are divided into seven main categories:

- Compensative
- Corrective
- Detective
- Deterrent
- Directive
- Preventive
- Recovery

Any access control that you implement will fit into one or more access control category.

> **NOTE** Access controls are also defined by the type of protection they provide. Access control types are discussed in the next section.

Compensative

Compensative controls are in place to substitute for a primary access control and mainly act as a mitigation to risks. Using compensative controls, you can reduce the risk to a more manageable level. Examples of compensative controls include requiring two authorized signatures to release sensitive or confidential information and requiring two keys owned by different personnel to open a safety deposit box.

Corrective

Corrective controls are in place to reduce the effect of an attack or other undesirable event. Using corrective controls fixes or restores the entity that is attacked. Examples of corrective controls include installing fire extinguishers, isolating or terminating a connection, implementing new firewall rules, and using server images to restore to a previous state.

Detective

Detective controls are in place to detect an attack while it is occurring to alert appropriate personnel. Examples of detective controls include motion detectors, intrusion detection systems (IDSs), logs, guards, investigations, and job rotation.

Deterrent

Deterrent controls deter or discourage an attacker. Via deterrent controls, attacks can be discovered early in the process. Deterrent controls often trigger preventive and corrective controls. Examples of deterrent controls include user identification and authentication, fences, lighting, and organizational security policies, such as a non-disclosure agreement (NDA).

Directive

Directive controls specify acceptable practice within an organization. They are in place to formalize an organization's security directive mainly to its employees. The most popular directive control is an acceptable use policy (AUP) that lists proper (and often examples of improper) procedures and behaviors that personnel must follow. Any organizational security policies or procedures usually fall into this access control category. You should keep in mind that directive controls are only efficient if there is a stated consequence for not following the organization's directions.

Preventive

Preventive controls prevent an attack from occurring. Examples of preventive controls include locks, badges, biometric systems, encryption, intrusion prevention systems (IPSs), antivirus software, personnel security, security guards, passwords, and security awareness training.

Recovery

Recovery controls recover a system or device after an attack has occurred. The primary goal of recovery controls is restoring resources. Examples of recovery controls include disaster recovery plans, data backups, and offsite facilities.

Access Control Types

Whereas the access control categories classify the access controls based on where they fit in time, access control types divide access controls on their method of implementation. The three types of access controls are

- Administrative (management) controls
- Logical (technical) controls
- Physical controls

In any organization where defense in depth is a priority, access control requires the use of all three types of access controls. Even if you implement the strictest physical and administrative controls, you cannot fully protect the environment without logical controls.

Administrative (Management) Controls

Administrative or management controls are implemented to administer the organization's assets and personnel and include security policies, procedures, standards, baselines, and guidelines that are established by management. These controls are commonly referred to as soft controls. Specific examples are personnel controls, data classification, data labeling, security awareness training, and supervision.

Security awareness training is a very important administrative control. Its purpose is to improve the organization's attitude about safeguarding data. The benefits of security awareness training include reduction in the number and severity of errors and omissions, better understanding of information value, and better administrator recognition of unauthorized intrusion attempts. A cost-effective way to ensure that employees take security awareness seriously is to create an award or recognition program.

Table 2-1 lists many administrative controls and includes in which access control categories the controls fit.

Table 2-1 Administrative (Management) Controls

Administrative (Management) Controls	Compensative	Corrective	Detective	Deterrent	Directive	Preventive	Recovery
Personnel procedures						x	
Security policies				x	x		
Monitoring			x				
Separation of duties						x	
Job rotation	x		x				
Information classification						x	
Security awareness training						x	
Investigations			x				
Disaster recovery plan						x	x
Security reviews			x				
Background checks			x				
Termination		x					
Supervision	x						

Logical (Technical) Controls

Logical or technical controls are software or hardware components used to restrict access. Specific examples of logical controls include firewalls, IDSs, IPSs, encryption, authentication systems, protocols, auditing and monitoring, biometrics, smart cards, and passwords.

Although auditing and monitoring are logical controls and are often listed together, they are actually two different controls. Auditing is a one-time or periodic event to evaluate security. Monitoring is an ongoing activity that examines either the system or users.

Table 2-2 lists many logical controls and includes in which access control categories the controls fit.

Physical Controls

Physical controls are implemented to protect an organization's facilities and personnel. Personnel concerns should take priority over all other concerns. Specific examples of physical controls include perimeter security, badges, swipe cards, guards, dogs, man traps, biometrics, and cabling.

Table 2-3 lists many physical controls and includes in which access control categories the controls fit.

Table 2-2 Logical (Technical) Controls

Logical (Technical) Controls	Compensative	Corrective	Detective	Deterrent	Directive	Preventive	Recovery
Password						x	
Biometrics						x	
Smart cards						x	
Encryption						x	
Protocols						x	
Firewalls						x	
IDS			x				
IPS						x	
Access control lists						x	
Routers						x	
Auditing			x				
Monitoring			x				
Data backups							x
Antivirus software						x	
Configuration standards					x		
Warning banner				x			
Connection isolation and termination		x					

Table 2-3 Physical Controls

Physical Controls	Compensative	Corrective	Detective	Deterrent	Directive	Preventive	Recovery
Fencing				x		x	
Locks						x	
Guards			x			x	
Fire extinguisher		x					
Badges						x	
Swipe cards						x	
Dogs			x				
Man traps						x	
Biometrics						x	
Lighting				x			
Motion detectors			x				
CCTV	x		x				
Data backups							x
Antivirus software						x	
Configuration standards					x		
Warning banner				x			
Hot, warm, and cold sites							x

Access Control Models

An access control model is a formal description of an organization's security policy. Access control models are implemented to simplify access control administration by grouping objects and subjects. Subjects are entities that request access to an object or data within an object. Users, programs, and processes are subjects. Objects are entities that contain information or functionality. Computers, databases, files, programs, directories, and fields are objects. A secure access control model must ensure that secure objects cannot flow to a less secure subject.

The access control models and concepts that you need to understand include the following:

- Discretionary access control
- Mandatory access control
- Role-based access control
- Rule-based access control
- Content-dependent versus context-dependent access control
- Access control matrix
- Capabilities table
- Access control list

Discretionary Access Control

In discretionary access control (DAC), the owner of the object specifies which subjects can access the resource. DAC is typically used in local, dynamic situations. The access is based on the subject's identity, profile, or role. DAC is considered to be a need-to-know control.

DAC can be an administrative burden because the data custodian or owner grants access privileges to the users. Under DAC, a subject's rights must be terminated when the subject leaves the organization. Identity-based access control is a subset of DAC and is based on user identity or group membership.

Non-discretionary access control is the opposite of DAC. In non-discretionary access control, access controls are configured by a security administrator or other authority. The central authority decides which subjects have access to objects based on the organization's policy. In non-discretionary access control, the system compares the subject's identity with the objects' access control list.

Mandatory Access Control

In mandatory access control (MAC), subject authorization is based on security labels. MAC is often described as prohibitive because it is based on a security label system. Under MAC, all that is not expressly permitted is forbidden. Only administrators can change the category of a resource.

MAC is more secure than DAC. DAC is more flexible and scalable than MAC. Because of the importance of security in MAC, labeling is required. Data classification reflects the data's sensitivity. In a MAC system, a clearance is a subject's privilege. Each subject and object is given a security or sensitivity label. The security labels are hierarchical. For commercial organizations, the levels of security labels could be confidential, proprietary, corporate, sensitive, and public. For government or military institutions, the levels of security labels could be top secret, secret, confidential, and unclassified.

In MAC, the system makes access decisions when it compares the subject's clearance level with the object's security label.

Role-based Access Control

In role-based access control (RBAC), each subject is assigned to one or more roles. Roles are hierarchical. Access control is defined based on the roles. RBAC can be used to easily enforce minimum privileges for subjects. An example of RBAC is implementing one access control policy for bank tellers and another policy for loan officers.

RBAC is not as secure as the previously mentioned access control models because security is based on roles. RBAC usually has a much lower cost to implement than the other models and is popular in commercial applications. It is an excellent choice for organizations with high employee turnover. RBAC can effectively replace DAC and MAC because it allows you to specify and enforce enterprise security policies in a way that maps to the organization's structure.

RBAC is managed in four ways. In non-RBAC, no roles are used. In limited RBAC, users are mapped to single application roles, but some applications do not use RBAC and require identity-based access. In hybrid RBAC, each user is mapped to a single role, which gives them access to multiple systems, but each user can be mapped to other roles that have access to single systems. In full RBAC, users are mapped to a single role as defined by the organization's security policy, and access to the systems is managed through the organizational roles.

Rule-based Access Control

Rule-based access control facilitates frequent changes to data permissions and is defined in RFC 2828. Using this method, a security policy is based on global rules imposed for all users. Profiles are used to control access. Many routers and firewalls use this type of access control and define which packet types are allowed on a network. Rules can be written allowing or denying access based on packet type, port number used, MAC address, and other parameters.

Content-dependent Versus Context-dependent

Content-dependent access control makes access decisions based on the data contained within the object. With this access control, the data that a user sees might change based on the policy and access rules that are applied.

Context-dependent access control is based on subject or object attributes or environmental characteristics. These characteristics can include location or time of day. An example of this is if administrators implement a security policy that ensures that a user only logs in from a particular workstation during certain hours of the day.

Security experts consider a constrained user interface as another method of access control. An example of a constrained user interface is a shell, which is a software interface to an operating system that implements access control by limiting the system commands that are available. Another example is database views that are filtered based on user or system criteria. Constrained user interfaces can be content- or context-dependent based on how the administrator constrains the interface.

Access Control Matrix

An access control matrix is a table that consists of a list of subjects, a list of objects, and a list of the actions that a subject can take upon each object. The rows in the matrix are the subjects, and the columns in the matrix are the objects. Common implementations of an access control matrix include a capabilities table and an access control list (ACL).

Capabilities Table

A capability corresponds to a subject's row from an access control matrix. A capability table lists the access rights that a particular subject has to objects. A capability table is about the subject.

Access Control List (ACL)

An ACL corresponds to an object's column from an access control matrix. An ACL lists all the access rights that subjects have to a particular object. An ACL is about the object.

Figure 2-4 shows an access control matrix and how a capability and ACL are part of it.

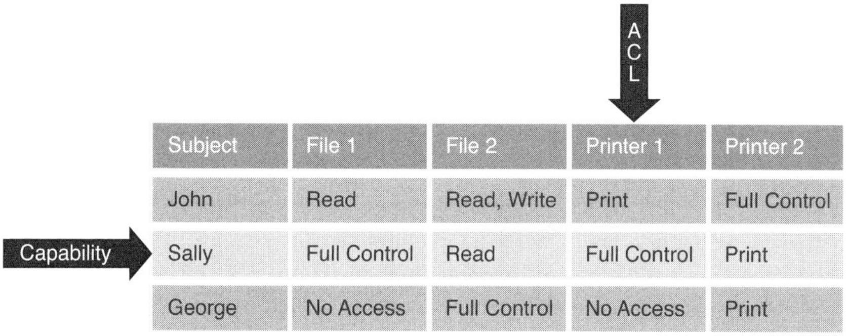

Subject	File 1	File 2	Printer 1	Printer 2
John	Read	Read, Write	Print	Full Control
Sally	Full Control	Read	Full Control	Print
George	No Access	Full Control	No Access	Print

Figure 2-4 Access Control Matrix

Access Control Administration

After deciding on which access control model to use, an organization must decide how the system will be administered. Access control administration occurs in two basic manners: centralized and decentralized.

Centralized

In centralized access control, a central department or personnel oversee the access for all organizational resources. This administration method ensures that user access is controlled in a consistent manner across the entire enterprise. However, this method can be slow because all access requests are processed by the central entity.

Decentralized

In decentralized access control, personnel closest to the resources, such as department managers and data owners, oversee the access control for individual resources. This administration method ensures that those who know the data control the access rights to it. However, this method can be hard to manage because not just one entity is responsible for configuring access rights, thereby losing the uniformity and fairness of security.

Provisioning Life Cycle

Organizations should create a formal process for creating, changing, and removing users, which is the provisioning life cycle. This process includes user approval, user creation, user creation standards, and authorization. Users should sign a written statement that explains the access conditions, including user responsibilities. Finally, access modification and removal procedures should be documented.

User provision policies should be integrated as part of human resource management. Human resource policies should include procedures whereby the human resource department formally requests the creation or deletion of a user account when new personnel are hired or terminated.

Access Control Monitoring

Access control monitoring is the process of tracking resource access attempts. The primary goals of access control monitoring are accountability and response. The "Accountability" section earlier in this chapter covers auditing and reporting, vulnerability assessments, penetration testing, and threat modeling. This section covers two additional methods of monitoring: intrusion detection systems (IDSs) and intrusion prevention systems (IPSs).

IDS

An IDS is a system responsible for detecting unauthorized access or attacks against systems and networks. It can verify, itemize, and characterize threats from outside and inside the network. Most IDSs are programmed to react certain ways in specific situations. Event notification and alerts are crucial to an IDS. They inform administrators and security professionals when and where attacks are detected.

The most common way to classify an IDS is based on its information source: network-based or host-based.

A network-based IDS is the most common IDS and monitors network traffic on a local network segment. To monitor traffic on the network segment, the network interface card (NIC) must be operating in promiscuous mode. A network-based IDS (NIDS) can only monitor the network traffic. It cannot monitor any internal activity that occurs within a system, such as an attack against a system that is carried out by logging on to the system's local terminal. An NIDS is affected by a switched network because generally an NIDS only monitors a single network segment.

NOTE Network hardware, such as hubs and switches, is covered in detail in Chapter 3.

A host-based IDS monitors traffic on a single system. Its primary responsibility is to protect the system on which it is installed. A host-based IDS (HIDS) uses information from the operating system audit trails and system logs. The detection capabilities of an HIDS are limited by how complete the audit logs and system logs are.

IDS implementations are furthered divided into the following categories:

- **Signature-based:** This type of IDS analyzes traffic and compares it to attack or state patterns, called signatures that reside within the IDS database. It is also referred to as a misuse-detection system. Although this type of IDS is very popular, it can only recognize attacks as compared with its database and is only as effective as the signatures provided. Frequent updates are necessary. The two main types of signature-based IDSs are

    - **Pattern-matching:** The IDS compares traffic to a database of attack patterns. The IDS carries out specific steps when it detects traffic that matches an attack pattern.

    - **Stateful-matching:** The IDS records the initial operating system state. Any changes to the system state that specifically violate the defined rules result in an alert or notification being sent.

- **Anomaly-based:** This type of IDS analyzes traffic and compares it to normal traffic to determine whether said traffic is a threat. It is also referred to as a behavior-based or profile-based system. The problem with this type of system is that any traffic outside of expected norms is reported, resulting in more false positives than signature-based systems. The three main types of anomaly-based IDSs are

    —**Statistical anomaly-based:** The IDS samples the live environment to record activities. The longer the IDS is in operation, the more accurate a profile that will be built. However, developing a profile that will not have a large number of false positives can be difficult and time consuming. Thresholds for activity deviations are important in this IDS. Too low a threshold results in false positives, whereas too high a threshold results in false negatives.

    —**Protocol anomaly-based:** The IDS has knowledge of the protocols that it will monitor. A profile of normal usage is built and compared to activity.

    —**Traffic anomaly-based:** The IDS tracks traffic pattern changes. All future traffic patterns are compared to the sample. Changing the threshold will reduce the number of false positives or negatives. This type of filter is excellent for detecting unknown attacks, but user activity might not be static enough to effectively implement this system.

- **Rule- or heuristic-based:** This type of IDS is an expert system that uses a knowledge base, inference engine, and rule-based programming. The knowledge is configured as rules. The data and traffic is analyzed, and the rules are applied to the analyzed traffic. The inference engine uses its intelligent software to "learn." If characteristics of an attack are met, alerts or notifications trigger. This is often referred to as an IF/THEN or expert system.

An application-based IDS is a specialized IDS that analyzes transaction log files for a single application. This type of IDS is usually provided as part of the application or can be purchased as an add-on.

Tools that can complement an IDS include vulnerability analysis systems, honeypots, and padded cells. Honeypots are systems that are configured with reduced security to entice attackers so that administrators can learn about attack techniques. Padded cells are special hosts to which an attacker is transferred during an attack.

IPS

An IPS is a system responsible for preventing attacks. When an attack begins, an IPS takes actions to prevent and contain the attack. An IPS can be network- or host-based, like an IDS. Although an IPS can be signature- or anomaly-based, it can also use a rate-based metric that analyzes the volume of traffic as well as the type of traffic.

In most cases, implementing an IPS is more costly than an IDS because of the added security of preventing attacks versus simply detecting attacks. In addition, running an IPS is more of an overall performance load than running an IDS.

Access Control Threats

Access control threats directly impact the confidentiality, integrity, and availability of organizational assets. The purpose of most access control threats is to cause harm to an organization. Because harming an organization is easier to do from within its network, outsiders usually first attempt to attack any access controls that are in place.

Access control threats that you should understand include:

- Password threats
- Social engineering threats
- DoS/DDoS
- Buffer overflow

- Mobile code
- Malicious software
- Spoofing
- Sniffing and eavesdropping
- Emanating
- Backdoor/trapdoor

Password Threats

A password threat is any attack that attempts to discover user passwords. The two most popular password threats are dictionary attacks and brute-force attacks.

The best countermeasures against password threats are to implement complex password policies, require users to change passwords on a regular basis, employ account lockout policies, encrypt password files, and use password-cracking tools to discover weak passwords.

Dictionary Attack

A dictionary attack occurs when attackers use a dictionary of common words to discover passwords. An automated program uses the hash of the dictionary word and compares this hash value to entries in the system password file. Although the program comes with a dictionary, attackers also use extra dictionaries that are found on the Internet.

You should implement a security rule that says that a password must NOT be a word found in the dictionary to protect against these attacks.

Brute-Force Attack

Brute-force attacks are more difficult to carry out because they work through all possible combinations of numbers and characters. A brute-force attack is also referred to as an exhaustive attack. It carries out password searches until a correct password is found. These attacks are also very time consuming.

Social Engineering Threats

Social engineering attacks occur when attackers use believable language and user gullibility to obtain user credentials or some other confidential information. Social engineering threats that you should understand include phishing/pharming, shoulder surfing, identity theft, and dumpster diving.

The best countermeasure against social engineering threats is to provide user security awareness training. This training should be required and must occur on a regular basis because social engineering techniques evolve constantly.

Phishing/Pharming

Phishing is a social engineering attack in which attackers try to learn personal information, including credit card information and financial data. This type of attack is usually carried out by implementing a fake Web site that very closely resembles a legitimate Web site. Users enter data, including credentials on the fake Web site, allowing the attackers to capture any information entered. Spear phishing is a phishing attack carried out against a specific target by learning about the target's habits and likes. Spear phishing attacks take longer to carry out than phishing attacks because of the information that must be gathered.

Pharming is similar to phishing, but pharming actually pollutes the contents of a computer's DNS cache so that requests to a legitimate site are actually routed to an alternate site.

Caution users against using any links embedded in e-mail messages, even if the message appears to have come from a legitimate entity. Users should also review the address bar any time they access a site where their personal information is required to ensure that the site is correct and that SSL is being used, which is indicated by an HTTPS designation at the beginning of the URL address.

Shoulder Surfing

Shoulder surfing occurs when an attacker watches when a user enters login or other confidential data. Encourage users to always be aware of who is observing their actions. Implementing privacy screens helps to ensure that data entry cannot be recorded.

Identity Theft

Identity theft occurs when someone obtains personal information, including driver's license number, bank account number, and Social Security number, and uses that information to assume an identity of the individual whose information was stolen. After the identity is assumed, the attack can go in any direction. In most cases, attackers open financial accounts in the user's name. Attackers also can gain access to the user's valid accounts.

Dumpster Diving

Dumpster diving occurs when attackers examine garbage contents to obtain confidential information. This includes personnel information, account login information, network diagrams, and organizational financial data.

Organizations should implement policies for shredding documents that contain this information.

DoS/DDoS

A denial-of-service (DoS) attack occurs when attackers flood a device with enough requests to degrade the performance of the targeted device. Some popular DoS attacks include SYN floods and teardrop attacks.

A distributed DoS (DDoS) attack is a DoS attack that is carried out from multiple attack locations. Vulnerable devices are infected with software agents, called zombies. This turns the vulnerable devices into botnets, which then carry out the attack. Because of the distributed nature of the attack, identifying all the attacking botnets is virtually impossible. The botnets also help to hide the original source of the attack.

NOTE More information about this type of attack is in Chapter 3.

Buffer Overflow

Buffers are portions of system memory that are used to store information. A buffer overflow occurs when the amount of data that is submitted to the application is larger than the buffer can handle. Typically, this type of attack is possible because of poorly written application or operating system code. This can result in an injection of malicious code.

To protect against this issue, organizations should ensure that all operating systems and applications are updated with the latest service packs and patches. In addition, programmers should properly test all applications to check for overflow conditions. Finally, programmers should use input validation to ensure that the data submitted is not too large for the buffer.

Mobile Code

Mobile code is any software that is transmitted across a network to be executed on a local system. Examples of mobile code include Java applets, Java script code, and ActiveX controls. Mobile code includes security controls, Java implements sandboxes, and ActiveX uses digital code signatures. Malicious mobile code can be used to bypass access controls.

Organizations should ensure that users understand the security concerns of malicious mobile code. Users should only download mobile code from legitimate sites and vendors.

Malicious Software

Malicious software, also called malware, is any software that is designed to perform malicious acts.

The following are the four classes of malware you should understand:

- **Virus:** Any malware that attaches itself to another application to replicate or distribute itself.
- **Worm:** Any malware that replicates itself, meaning that it does not need another application or human interaction to propagate.
- **Trojan horse:** Any malware that disguises itself as a needed application while carrying out malicious actions.
- **Spyware:** Any malware that collects private user data, including browsing history or keyboard input.

The best defense against malicious software is to implement anti-virus and anti-malware software. Today most vendors package these two types of software in the same package. Keeping anti-virus and anti-malware software up to date is vital. This includes ensuring that the latest virus and malware definitions are installed.

Spoofing

Spoofing, also referred to as masquerading, occurs when communication from an attacker appears to come from trusted sources. Spoofing examples include IP spoofing and hyperlink spoofing. The goal of this type of attack is to obtain access to credentials or other personal information.

A man-in-the-middle attack uses spoofing as part of the attack. Some security professionals consider phishing attacks as a type of spoofing attack.

Sniffing and Eavesdropping

Sniffing, also referred to as eavesdropping, occurs when an attacker inserts a device or software into the communication medium that collects all the information transmitted over the medium. Network sniffers are used by both legitimate security professionals and attackers.

Organizations should monitor and limit the use of sniffers. To protect against their use, you should encrypt all traffic on the network.

Emanating

Emanations are electromagnetic signals that are emitted by an electronic device. Attackers can target certain devices or transmission mediums to eavesdrop on communication without having physical access to the device or medium.

The TEMPEST program, initiated by the U.S. and UK, researches ways to limit emanations and standardizes the technologies used. Any equipment that meets TEMPEST standards suppresses signal emanations using shielding material. Devices that meet TEMPEST standards usually implement an outer barrier or coating, called a Faraday cage or Faraday Shield. TEMPEST devices are most often used in government, military, or law enforcement.

Backdoor/Trapdoor

A backdoor or trapdoor is a mechanism implemented in many devices or applications that gives the user who uses the backdoor unlimited access to the device or application. Privileged backdoor accounts are the most common method of backdoor that you will see today.

Most established vendors no longer release devices or applications with this security issue. You should be aware of any known backdoors in the devices or applications you manage.

Exam Preparation Tasks

Review All Key Topics

Review the most important topics in this chapter, noted with the Key Topics icon in the outer margin of the page. Table 2-4 lists a reference of these key topics and the page numbers on which each is found.

Table 2-4 Key Topics for Chapter 2

Key Topic Element	Description	Page Number
Paragraph	Access control process	15
Paragraph	Three factors for authentication	17
List	Password Types	19
Paragraph	Physiological Systems	24
Paragraph	Behavioral Systems	25
List	Biometric terms	26
Paragraph	Directory service standards	30
List	SSO advantages	31
List	SSO disadvantages	32
List	Kerberos disadvantages	33
List	Auditing guidelines	36
Paragraph	Vulnerability assessment categories	37
List	Penetration testing steps	38
List	Penetration testing strategies	38
List	Penetration testing categories	39
Paragraph	Access control categories	39
Paragraph	Access control types	41
Table 2-1	Administrative controls	42
Table 2-2	Logical controls	44
Table 2-3	Physical controls	45
Paragraph	Access control models and concepts	46
Paragraph	Access control threats	52
List	Malicious software types	56

Complete the Tables and Lists from Memory

Print a copy of the CD Appendix A, "Memory Tables," or at least the section for this chapter, and complete the tables and lists from memory. The CD Appendix B,

"Memory Tables Answer Key," includes completed tables and lists to check your work.

Define Key Terms

Define the following key terms from this chapter and check your answers in the glossary:

access control, confidentiality, integrity, availability, default stance, identification, authentication, knowledge factors, ownership factors, synchronous token, asynchronous token, memory card, smart card, characteristic factors, physiological characteristics, fingerprint scan, finger scan, hand geometry, hand topography, palm or hand scan, facial scan, retinal scan, iris scan, vascular scan, behavioral characteristics, signature dynamics, keystroke dynamics, voice pattern or print, biometric enrollment time, biometric feature extraction, biometric accuracy, biometric throughput rate, biometric acceptability, false rejection rate, false acceptance rate, crossover error rate, authorization, access control policy, separation of duties, least privilege, need to know, single sign-on, Kerberos, SESAME, federated identity, cross-certification federated identity model, trusted third-party federated identity model, bridge federated identity model, security domain, accountability, vulnerability assessment, penetration testing, compensative controls, corrective controls, detective controls, deterrent controls, directive controls, preventive controls, recovery controls, administrative controls, logical controls, physical controls, discretionary access control, mandatory access control, role-based access control, rule-based access control, content-dependent, context-dependent, access control matric, capabilities table, access control list, centralized access control, decentralized access control, IDS, network-based IDS, host-based IDS, phishing, spear phishing, pharming, shoulder surfing, dumpster diving, backdoor, and trapdoor.

Review Questions

1. Which security principle is the opposite of disclosure?

    a. integrity

    b. availability

    c. confidentiality

    d. authorization

2. Which of the following is NOT an example of a knowledge authentication factor?

   a. password

   b. mother's maiden name

   c. city of birth

   d. smart card

3. Which of the following statements about memory cards and smart cards is false?

   a. A memory card is a swipe card that contains user authentication information.

   b. Memory cards are also known as integrated circuit cards (ICCs).

   c. Smart cards contain memory and an embedded chip.

   d. Smart card systems are more reliable than memory card systems.

4. Which biometric method is MOST effective?

   a. Iris scan

   b. Retina scan

   c. Fingerprint

   d. Hand print

5. What is a Type I error in a biometric system?

   a. crossover error rate (CER)

   b. false rejection rate (FRR)

   c. false acceptance rate (FAR)

   d. throughput rate

6. Which penetration test provides the testing team with limited knowledge of the network systems and devices using publicly available information and the organization's security team knows an attack is coming?

   a. target test

   b. physical test

   c. blind test

   d. double-blind test

7. Which access control type reduces the effect of an attack or other undesirable event?

    a. compensative control

    b. preventive control

    c. detective control

    d. corrective control

8. Which of the following controls is an administrative control?

    a. security policy

    b. CCTV

    c. data backups

    d. locks

9. Which access control model is most often used by routers and firewalls to control access to networks?

    a. discretionary access control

    b. mandatory access control

    c. role-based access control

    d. rule-based access control

10. Which threat is NOT considered a social engineering threat?

    a. phishing

    b. pharming

    c. DoS attack

    d. dumpster diving

Answers and Explanations

1. **c.** The opposite of disclosure is confidentiality. The opposite of corruption is integrity. The opposite of destruction is availability. The opposite of disapproval is authorization.

2. **d.** Knowledge factors are something a person knows, including passwords, mother's maiden name, city of birth, and date of birth. Ownership factors are something a person has, including a smart card.

3. **b.** Memory cards are NOT also known as integrated circuit cards (ICCs). Smart cards are also known as ICCs.

4. **a.** Iris scans are considered more effective than retina scans, fingerprints, and hand prints.

5. **b.** A Type I error in a biometric system is false rejection rate (FRR). A Type II error in a biometric system is false acceptance rate (FAR). Crossover error rate (CER) is the point at which FRR equals FAR. Throughput rate is the rate at which users are authenticated.

6. **c.** A blind test provides the testing team with limited knowledge of the network systems and devices using publicly available information and the organization's security team knows an attack is coming.

    A target test occurs when the testing team and the organization's security team are given maximum information about the network and the type of test that will occur.

    A physical test is not a type of penetration test. It is a type of vulnerability assessment.

    A double-blind test is like a blind test except the organization's security team does not know that an attack is coming.

7. **d.** A corrective control reduces the effect of an attack or other undesirable event.

    A compensative control substitutes for a primary access control and mainly acts as mitigation to risks. A preventive control prevents an attack from occurring. A detective control detects an attack while it is occurring to alert appropriate personnel.

8. **a.** A security policy is an administrative control. CCTV and locks are physical controls. Data backups are a technical control.

9. **d.** Rule-based access control is most often used by routers and firewalls to control access to networks. The other three types of access control models are not usually implemented by routers and firewalls.

10. **c.** A Denial of Service (DoS) is not considered a social engineering threat. The other three options are considered to be social engineering threats.

This chapter covers the following topics:

- **OSI model:** An explanation of the functions of the seven layers of the OSI model

- **TCP/IP model:** A discussion of the TCP/IP model and its relationship to the OSI model

- **Common TCP/UDP ports:** A description of the function of port numbers and common standard ports

- **IP addressing:** A look at both logical and physical addressing systems and their interrelationship in routing and switching

- **Network transmission:** An examination of the processes used to transfer data across various media types

- **Cabling:** Types of bounded media, their characteristics, and proper use

- **Network topologies:** A survey of both logical and physical network topologies

- **Network technologies:** A discussion of the various technologies used to accomplish networking

- **Network protocols/services:** The functions of the major network protocols and services that provide network functionality

- **Network routing:** An explanation of how static and dynamic routing works and a discussion of the major interior and exterior routing protocols

- **Network devices:** Covers the function and placement of major network devices

CHAPTER 3

Telecommunications and Network Security

- **Network types:** An explanation of local area network types including MAN, WAN, LAN, extranet, and intranet
- **WAN technologies:** A discussion of the various methods of connecting local area networks (LANs) with wide area networks (WANs)
- **Remote connection technologies:** A description of the methods of connecting remote users and networks to the LAN and the Internet
- **Wireless networks:** Covers the types of wireless networks and the processes required to secure them
- **Network threats:** An introduction to the various security threats facing networks

Sensitive data must be protected from unauthorized access when the data is at rest (on a hard drive) and in transit (moving through a network). Moreover, sensitive communications of other types such as emails, instant messages, and phone conversations must also be protected from prying eyes and ears. Many communication processes send information in a form that can be read and understood if captured with a protocol analyzer or sniffer.

In today's communication world, assume that your communications are being captured regardless of how unlikely you think that might be. You should also take steps to protect or encrypt the transmissions so they will be useless to anyone capturing them. This chapter covers the protection of wired and wireless transmissions and of the network devices that perform the transmissions, as well as some networking fundamentals required to understand transmission security.

Foundation Topics

OSI Model

A complete understanding of networking requires an understanding of the Open Systems Interconnect (OSI) model. Created in the 1980s by the International Standards Organization (ISO) as a part of its mission to create a protocol set to be used as a standard for all vendors, it breaks the communication process into layers. Although the ensuing protocol set did not catch on as a standard Transmission Control Protocol/Internet Protocol [TCP/IP] was adopted), the model has guided the development of technology since its creation. It also has helped generations of students understand the network communication process between two systems.

The OSI model breaks up the process into seven layers or modules. The benefits of doing this are

- It breaks up the communication process into layers with standardized interfaces between the layers, allowing for changes and improvements on one layer without necessitating changes on other layers.

- It provides a common framework for hardware and software developers, fostering interoperability.

The goal of this open systems architecture is that no vendor owns it and it acts as a blueprint or model for developers to work with. Various protocols operate at different layers of this model. A protocol is a set of communication rules two systems must both use and understand to communicate. Some protocols depend on other protocols for services, and as such, these protocols work as a team to get transmissions done, much like the team at the post office that gets your letters delivered. Some people sort, others deliver, and still others track lost shipments.

The OSI model and the TCP/IP model, explained in the next section, are often both used to describe the process called *packet creation* or *encapsulation*. Until a packet is created to hold the data, it cannot be sent on the transmission medium.

With a modular approach, it becomes possible for a change in a protocol or the addition of a new protocol to be accomplished without having to rewrite the entire protocol *stack* (a term for all the protocols that work together at all layers). The model has seven layers. This section discusses each layer's function and its relationship to the layer above and below it in the model. The layers are often referred to by their number with the numbering starting at the bottom of the model at layer 1, the Physical layer.

The process of creating a packet or encapsulation begins at layer 7, the Application layer rather than layer 1, so we discuss the process starting at layer 7 and work down the model to layer 1, the Physical layer, where the packet is sent out on the transmission medium.

Application Layer

The Application layer (layer 7) is where the encapsulation process begins. This layer receives the raw data from the application in use and provides services, such as file transfer and message exchange to the application (and thus the user). An example of a protocol that operates at this layer is Hypertext Transfer Protocol (HTTP), which is used to transfer web pages across the network. Other examples of protocols that operate at this layer are DNS queries, FTP transfers, and SMTP email transfers.

The user application interfaces with these application protocols through a standard interface called an Application Programming Interface (API). The Application layer protocol receives the raw data and places it in a container called a protocol data unit (PDU). When the process gets down to layer 4, these PDUs have standard names, but at layers 5–7 we simply refer to the PDU as "data."

Presentation Layer

The information that is developed at layer 7 is then handed to layer 6, the Presentation layer. Each layer makes no changes to the data received from the layer above it. It simply adds information to the developing packet. In the case of the Presentation layer, information is added that standardizes the formatting of the information if required.

Layer 6 is responsible for the manner in which the data from the Application layer is represented (or presented) to the Application layer on the destination device (explained more fully in the section "Encapsulation"). If any translation between formats is required, it will take care of it. It also communicates the type of data within the packet and the application that might be required to read it on the destination device.

Session Layer

The Session layer or layer 5 is responsible for adding information to the packet that makes a communication session between a service or application on the source device possible with the same service or application on the destination device. Do not confuse this process with the one that establishes a session between the two physical devices. That occurs not at this layer but at layers 3 and 4. This session is built and closed after the physical session between the computers has taken place.

The application or service in use is communicated between the two systems with an identifier called a port number. This information is passed on to the Transport layer, which also makes use of these port numbers.

Transport Layer

The protocols that operate at the Transport layer (layer 4) work to establish a session between the two physical systems. The service provided can be either connection-oriented or connectionless, depending on the transport protocol in use. The "TCP/IP Model" section (TCP/IP being the most common standard networking protocol in use) discusses the specific transport protocols used by TCP/IP in detail.

The Transport layer receives all the information from layers 7, 6, and 5 and adds information that identifies the transport protocol in use and the specific port number that identifies the required layer 7 protocol. At this layer, the PDU is called a segment because this layer takes a large transmission and segments it into smaller pieces for more efficient transmission on the medium.

Network Layer

At layer 3 or the Network layer, information required to route the packet is added. This is in the form of a source and destination logical address (meaning one that is assigned to a device in some manner and can be changed). In TCP/IP, this is in terms of a source and destination IP address. An IP address is a number that uniquely differentiates a host from all other devices on the network. It is based on a numbering system that makes it possible for computers (and routers) to identify whether the destination device is on the local network or on a remote network. Any time a packet needs to be sent to a different network or subnet (IP addressing is covered later in the chapter), it must be routed and the information required to do that is added here. At this layer, the PDU is called a packet.

Data Link Layer

The Data Link layer is responsible for determining the destination physical address. Network devices have logical addresses (IP addresses) and the network interfaces they possess have a physical address (Media Access Control [MAC] address), which is permanent in nature. When the transmission is handed off from routing device to routing device, at each stop this source and destination address pair changes, whereas the source and destination logical addresses (in most cases IP addresses) do not. This layer is responsible for determining what those MAC addresses should be at each hop (router interface) and adding them to this part of the packet. The later section "TCP/IP Model" covers how this resolution is performed in TCP/IP. After this is done, we call the PDU a frame.

Something else happens at this layer that is unique to this layer. Not only is a layer 2 header placed on the packet but also a trailer at the "end" of the frame. Information contained in the trailer is used to verify that none of the data contained has been altered or damaged en route.

Physical Layer

Finally, the packet (or frame as it is called at layer 2) is received by the Physical layer (layer 1). Layer 1 is responsible for turning the information into bits (ones and zeros) and sending it out on the medium. The way in which this is accomplished can vary according to the media in use. For example, in a wired network, the ones and zeros are represented as electrical charges. In wireless, they are represented by altering the radio waves. In an optical network, they are represented with light.

The ability of the same packet to be routed through various media types is a good example of the independence of the layers. As a PDU travels through different media types, the physical layer will change but all the information in layers 2–7 will not. Similarly, when a frame crosses routers or hops, the MAC addresses change but none of the information in layers 3–7 changes. The upper layers depend on the lower layers for various services but the lower layers leave the upper layer information unchanged.

Figure 3-1 shows common protocols mapped to the OSI model.

The next section covers another model that perhaps more accurately depicts what happens in a TCP/IP network. Because TCP/IP is the standard now for transmission, comparing these two models is useful. Although they have a different number of layers and some of the layer names are different, they describe the same process of packet creation or encapsulation.

OSI model

7. Application layer
NNTP · SIP · SSI · DNS · FTP · Gopher · HTTP · NFS · NTP · SMPP · SMTP * SNMP · Telnet · DHCP · Netconf · (more)

6. Presentation layer
MIME · XDR

5. Session layer
Named pipe · NetBIOS · SAP · PPTP · RTP · SOCKS · SPDY · TLS/SSL

4. Transport layer
TCP · UDP · SCTP · DCCP · SPX

3. Network layer
IP · (IPv4 · IPV6) · ARP · ICMP · IPsec · IGMP · IPX · Apple Talk

2. Data link layer
ATM · SDLC · HDLC · CSLIP · SLIP · GFP · PLIP · IEEE 802.2 · LLC · L2TP · IEEE 802.3 · Frame Relay · ITU-T G.hn DLL · PPP · X.25

1. Physical layer
EIA/TIA-232 · EIA/TIA-449 · ITU-T V-Series · 1.430 · 1.431 · PDH · SONET/SDH · PON · OTN · DSL · IEEE 802.3 - IEEE 802.11 · IEEE 802.15 · IEEE 802.16 · IEEE 1394 · ITU-T G.hn PHY · USB · Bluetooth · RS-232 · RS-449

Figure 3-1 Protocol Mappings

Multi-Layer Protocols

Many protocols, such as FTP and DNS, operate on a single layer of the OSI model. However, many protocols operate at multiple layers of the OSI model. The best example is TCP/IP, the networking protocol used on the Internet and on the vast majority of local area networks (LANs). In fact, this protocol has its own model that describes the layers on which it operates and the parts of the protocol that operate on each layer. The next section covers this model and the protocol it was designed to describe.

TCP/IP Model

The protocols developed when the OSI model was developed (sometimes referred to as OSI protocols) did not become the standard for the Internet. The Internet as we know it today has its roots in a wide area network (WAN) developed by the Department of Defense (DoD) with TCP/IP being the protocol developed for that network. The Internet is a global network of public networks and Internet Service Providers (ISPs) throughout the world.

Although the OSI model is still often referenced, of the protocols themselves only X.400, X.500, and IS-IS have had much lasting impact. For that reason, a second model exists based on TCP/IP. In a discussion of this model, the protocols that are part of what is called the TCP/IP suite can be mapped to the layer on which they perform their function.

This model bears many similarities to the OSI model, which is not unexpected because they both describe the process of packet creation or encapsulation. The difference is that the OSI model breaks the process into seven layers, whereas the TCP/IP model breaks it into four. If you examine them side by side, however, it becomes apparent that many of the same functions occur at the same layers, while the TCP/IP model combines the top three layers of the OSI model into one and the bottom two layers of the OSI model into one. Figure 3-2 show the two models next to one another.

Figure 3-2 TCP/IP and OSI Models

The TCP/IP model has only four layers and is useful to study because it focuses its attention on TCP/IP. This section explores those four layers and their functions and relationships to one another and to layers in the OSI model.

Application Layer

Although the Application layer in the TCP/IP model has the same name as the top layer in the OSI model, the Application layer in the TCP/IP model encompasses all the functions performed in layers 5–7 in the OSI model. Not all functions map perfectly because both are simply conceptual models. Within the Application layer, applications create user data and communicate this data to other processes or applications on another host. For this reason, it is sometimes also referred to as the process-to-process layer.

Examples of protocols that operate at this layer are SMTP, FTP, SSH, and HTTP. These protocols are discussed in the section "Network Protocols/Services" later in this chapter. In general, however, these are usually referred to as higher layer protocols that perform some specific function, whereas protocols in the TCP/IP suite that operate at the Transport and Internet layers perform location and delivery service on behalf of these higher layer protocols.

A port number identifies to the receiving device these upper layer protocols and the programs on whose behalf they function. The number identifies the protocol or service. Many port numbers have been standardized. For example, Domain Name System (DNS) is identified with the standard port number of 53. The "Common TCP/UDP Ports" section covers these port numbers in more detail.

Transport Layer

The Transport layers of the OSI model and the TCP/IP model perform the same function, which is to open and maintain a connection between hosts. This must occur before the session between the processes can occur as described in the Application layer section and can be done in TCP/IP in two ways: connectionless and connection-oriented. A connection-oriented transmission means that a connection will be established before any data is transferred, whereas in a connectionless transmission this is not done. One of two different transport layer protocols is used for each process. If a connection-oriented transport protocol is required, Transmission Control Protocol (TCP) will be used. If the process will be connectionless, User Datagram Protocol (UDP) is used.

Application developers can choose to use either TCP or UDP as the Transport layer protocol used with the application. Regardless of which transport protocol is used, the application or service will be identified to the receiving device by its port number and the transport protocol (UDP or TCP). Port numbers are discussed in more detail in the section "Common TCP/UDP Ports" later in this chapter.

Although TCP provides more functionality and reliability, the overhead required by this protocol is substantial when compared to UDP. This means that a much higher percentage of the packet consists of the header when using TCP than when using UDP. This is necessary to provide the fields required to hold the information needed to provide the additional services. Figure 3-3 shows a comparison of the size of the two respective headers.

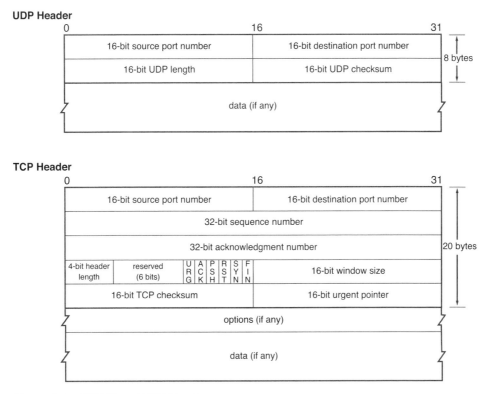

Figure 3-3 TCP/IP and UDP Headers

When an application is written to use TCP, a state of connection is established between the two hosts before any data is transferred. This occurs using a process known as the TCP three-way handshake. This process is followed exactly, and no data is transferred until it is complete. Figure 3-4 shows the steps in this process. The steps are as follows:

1. The initiating computer sends a packet with the SYN flag set (one of the fields in the TCP header), which indicates a desire to create a connection.

2. The receiving host acknowledges receiving this packet and indicates a willingness to create a state of connection by sending back a packet with both the SYN and ACK flags set.

3. The first host acknowledges completion of the connection process by sending a final packet back with only the ACK flag set.

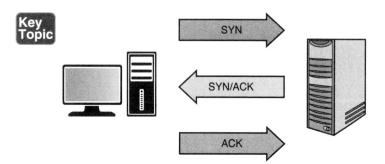

Figure 3-4 TCP Three-Way Handshake

So what exactly is gained by using the extra overhead to use TCP? The following are examples of the functionality provided with TCP:

- **Guaranteed delivery:** If the receiving host does not specifically acknowledge receipt of each packet, the sending system will resend the packet.

- **Sequencing:** In today's routed networks, the packets might take many different routes to arrive and might not arrive in the order in which they were sent. A sequence number added to each packet allows the receiving host to reassemble the entire transmission using these numbers.

- **Flow control:** The receiving host has the capability of sending the acknowledgement packets back to signal the sender to slow the transmission if it cannot process the packets as fast as they are arriving.

Many applications do not require the services provided by TCP or cannot tolerate the overhead required by TCP. In these cases the process will use UDP, which sends on a "best effort" basis with no guarantee of delivery. In many cases some of these functions are provided by the Application layer protocol itself rather than relying on the Transport layer protocol.

Internet Layer

The Transport layer can neither create a state of connection nor send using UDP until the location and route to the destination are determined, which occurs on the Internet layer. The four protocols in the TCP/IP suite that operate at this layer are

- **Internet Protocol (IP):** Responsible for putting the source and destination IP addresses in the packet and for routing the packet to its destination.

- **Internet Control Message Protocol (ICMP):** Used by the network devices to send messages regarding the success or failure of communications and used by humans for troubleshooting. When you use the PING or TRACEROUTE commands, you are using ICMP.

- **Internet Group Management Protocol (IGMP):** Used when multicasting, which is a form of communication whereby one host sends to a group of destination hosts rather than a single host (called a unicast transmission) or to all hosts (called a broadcast transmission).
- **Address Resolution Protocol (ARP):** Resolves the IP address placed in the packet to a physical or layer 2 address (called a MAC address in Ethernet).

The relationship between IP and ARP is worthy of more discussion. IP places the source and destination IP addresses in the header of the packet. As we saw earlier, when a packet is being routed across a network, the source and destination IP addresses never change but the layer 2 or MAC address pairs change at every router hop. ARP uses a process called the ARP broadcast to learn the MAC address of the interface that matches the IP address of the next hop. After it has done this, a new layer 2 header is created. Again, nothing else in the upper layer changes in this process, just layer 2.

That brings up a good point concerning the mapping of ARP to the TCP/IP model. Although we generally place ARP on the Internet layer, the information it derives from this process is placed in the Link layer or layer 2, the next layer in our discussion.

Just as the Transport layer added a header to the packet, so does the Internet layer. One of the improvements made by IPv6 is the streamlining of the IP header. Although the same information is contained in the header and the header is larger, it has a much simpler structure. Figure 3-5 shows a comparison of the two.

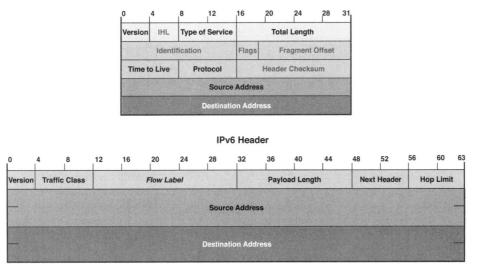

Figure 3-5 IPv6 and IPv4 Headers

Link Layer

The Link layer of the TCP/IP model provides the services provided by both the Data Link and the Physical layers in the OSI model. The source and destination MAC addresses are placed in this layer's header. A trailer is also placed on the packet at this layer with information in the trailer that can be used to verify the integrity of the data.

This layer is also concerned with placing the bits on the medium, as discussed in the section on the OSI model earlier in this chapter. Again, the exact method of implementation varies with the physical transmission medium. It might be in terms of electrical impulses, light waves, or radio waves.

Encapsulation

In either model as the packet is created, information is added to the header at each layer and then a trailer is placed on the packet before transmission. This process is called *encapsulation*. Intermediate devices, such as routers and switches, only read the layers of concern to that device (for a switch, layer 2 and for a router, layer 3). The ultimate receiver strips off the entire header with each layer, making use of the information placed in the header by the corresponding layer on the sending device. This process is called *de-encapsulation*. Figure 3-6 shows a visual representation of encapsulation.

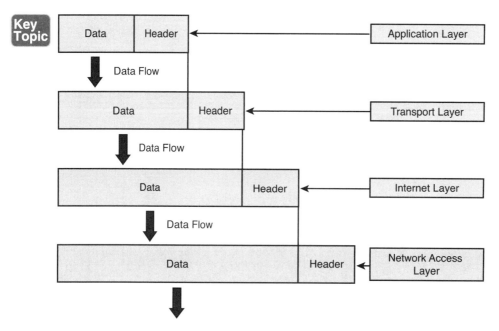

Figure 3-6 Encapsulation and De-encapsulation

Common TCP/UDP Ports

When the Transport layer learns the required port number for the service or application required on the destination device from the Application layer, it is recorded in the header as either a TCP or UDP port number. Both UDP and TCP use 16 bits in the header to identify these ports. These port numbers are software based or logical, and there are 65,535 possible numbers. Port numbers are assigned in various ways, based on three ranges:

- System or well-known ports (0–1023)
- User Ports (1024–49151)
- Dynamic and/or Private Ports (49152–65535)

System Ports are assigned by the Internet Engineering Task Force (IETF) for standards-track protocols, as per [RFC6335]. User ports can be registered with the Internet Assigned Numbers Authority (IANA) and assigned to the service or application using the "Expert Review" process, as per [RFC6335]. Dynamic ports are used by source devices as source ports when accessing a service or application on another machine. For example, if computer A is sending an FTP packet, the destination port will be the well-known port for FTP and the source will be selected by the computer randomly from the dynamic range.

The combination of the destination IP address and the destination port number is called a *socket*. The relationship between these two values can be understood if viewed through the analogy of an office address. The office has a street address but the address also must contain a suite number as there could be thousands (in this case 65,535) suites in the building. Both are required to get the information where it should go.

As a security professional, you should be aware of well-known port numbers of common services. In many instances, firewall rules and access control lists (ACLs) are written or configured in terms of the port number of what is being allowed or denied rather than the name of the service or application. Table 3-1 lists some of the more important port numbers. Some use more than one port.

Table 3-1 Common TCP/UDP Port Numbers

Application Protocol	Transport Protocol	Port Number
Telnet	TCP and UDP	23
SMTP	UDP	25
HTTP	TCP	80
SNMP	TCP and UDP	161 and 162

Application Protocol	Transport Protocol	Port Number
FTP	TCP and UDP	21 and 20
POP3	TCP and UDP	110
DNS	TCP and UDP	53
DHCP	UDP	67 and 68
SSH	TCP	22
LDAP	TCP and UDP	389

Logical and Physical Addressing

During the process of encapsulation at layer 3 of the OSI model, IP places source and destination IP addresses in the packet. Then at layer 2, the matching source and destination MAC addresses that have been determined by ARP are placed in the packet. IP addresses are examples of logical addressing, and MAC addresses are examples of physical addressing. IP addresses are considered logical because these addresses are administered by humans and can be changed at any time. MAC addresses on the other hand are assigned permanently to the interface cards of the devices when the interfaces are manufactured. It is important to note, however, that although these addresses are permanent, they can be spoofed. When this is done, however, the hacker is not actually changing the physical address, but rather telling the interface to place a different MAC address in the layer 2 headers.

This section discusses both address types with a particular focus on how IP addresses are used to create separate networks or subnets in the larger network. It also discusses how IP addresses and MAC addresses are related and used during a network transmission.

IPv4

IPv4 addresses are 32 bits in length and can be represented in either binary or in dotted-decimal format. The number of possible IP addresses using 32 bits can be calculated by raising the number 2 (the number of possible values in the binary number system) to the 32nd power. The result is 4,294,967,296, which on the surface appears to be enough IP addresses. But with the explosion of the Internet and the increasing number of devices that require an IP address, this number has proven to be insufficient.

Due to the eventual exhaustion of the IPv4 address space, several methods of preserving public IP addresses (more on that in a bit, but for now these are addresses that are legal to use on the Internet) have been implemented, including the use of private addresses and Network Address Translation (NAT), both discussed in the following sections. The ultimate solution lies in the adoption of IPv6, a new system that uses 128 bits and allows for enough IP addresses for each man, woman, and child on the planet to have as many IP addresses as the entire IPv4 numbering space. IPv6 is discussed later in this section.

IP addresses that are written in dotted-decimal format, the format in which humans usually work with them, have four fields called octets separated by dots or periods. Each field is called an octet because when we look at the addresses in binary format, we devote 8 bits in binary to represent each decimal number that appears in the octet when viewed in dotted-decimal format. Therefore, if we look at the address 216.5.41.3, four decimal numbers are separated by dots, where each would be represented by 8 bits if viewed in binary. The following is the binary version of this same address:

11011000.00000101.00101001.00000011

There are 32 bits in the address, 8 in each octet.

The structure of IPv4 addressing lends itself to dividing the network into subdivisions called subnets. Each IP address also has a required companion value called a subnet mask. The subnet mask is used to specify which part of the address, is the *network* part and which part is the *host*. The network part, on the left side of the address, determines on which network the device resides whereas the host portion on the right identifies the device on that network. Figure 3-7 shows the network and host portion of the three default classes of IP address.

Class A Subnet Mask	Network	Host	Host	Host
	255	0	0	0

Class B Subnet Mask	Network	Network	Host	Host
	255	255	0	0

Class C Subnet Mask	Network	Network	Network	Host
	255	255	255	0

www.smartPCtricks.com

Figure 3-7 Network and Host Bits

When the IPv4 system was first created, there were only three default subnet masks. This yielded only three sizes of networks, which later proved to be inconvenient and wasteful of public IP addresses. Eventually a system called Classless Interdomain Routing (CIDR) was adopted that uses subnet masks that allow you to make subnets or subdivisions out of the major classful networks possible before CIDR. CIDR is beyond the scope of the exam but it is worth knowing about. You can find more information about how CIDR works at http://searchnetworking.techtarget.com/definition/CIDR.

IP Classes

Classful subnetting (pre-CIDR) created five classes of networks. Each class represented a range of IP addresses. Table 3-2 shows the five classes. Only the first three (A, B, and C) are used for individual network devices. The other ranges are for special use.

Table 3-2 Classful Addressing

Class	Range	Mask	Initial Bit Pattern of First Octet	Network/Host Division
Class A	0.0.0.0 – 127.255.255.255	255.0.0.0	01	net.host.host.host
Class B	128.0.0.0 – 191.255.255.255	255.255.0.0	10	net.net.host.host
Class C	192.0.0.0 –223.255.255.255	255.255.255.0	11	net.net.net.host
Class D	224.0.0.0 – 239.255.255.255	Used for multicasting		
Class E	240.0.0.0 – 255.255.255.255	Reserved for research		

As you can see, the key value that changes as you move from one class to another is the value of the first octet (the one on the far left). What might not be immediately obvious is that as you move from one class to another, the dividing line between the host portion and network portion also changes. This is where the subnet mask value comes in. When the mask is overlaid with the IP addresses (thus we call it a mask), every octet in the subnet mask where there is a 255 is a network portion and every octet where there is a 0 is a host portion. Another item to mention is that each class has a distinctive pattern in the first two bits of the first octet. For example, ANY IP address that begins with 01 in the first bit positions MUST be in Class A, also indicated in Table 3-2.

The significance of the network portion is that two devices must share the same values in the network portion to be in the same network. If they do not, they will not be able to communicate.

Public Versus Private IP Addresses

The initial solution used (and still in use) to address the exhaustion of the IPv4 space involved the use of private addresses and NAT. Three ranges of IP addresses were set aside to be used ONLY within private networks and are NOT routable on the Internet. RFC 1918 set aside the IP address ranges in Table 3-3 to be used for this purpose. Because these addresses are not routable on the public network, they must be translated to public addresses before being sent to the Internet. This process, called NAT is discussed in the next section.

Table 3-3 Address Classes

Class	Range
Class A	10.0.0.0 – 10.255.255.255
Class B	172.16.0.0 – 172.31.255.255
Class C	192.168.0.0 – 192.168.255.255

NAT

Network Address Translation (NAT) is a service that can be supplied by a router or by a server. The device that provides the service stands between the LAN and the Internet. When packets need to go to the Internet, the packets go through the NAT service first. The NAT service changes the private IP address to a public address that is routable on the Internet. When the response is returned from the Web, the NAT service receives it, translates the address back to the original private IP address, and sends it back to the originator.

This translation can be done on a one-to-one basis (one private address to one public address), but to save IP addresses, usually the NAT service will represent the entire private network with a single public IP address. This process is called Port Address Translation (PAT). This name comes from the fact that the NAT service keeps the private clients separate from one another by recording their private address and the source port number (usually a unique number) selected when the packets were built.

Allowing NAT to represent an entire network (perhaps thousands of computers) with a single public address has been quite effective in saving public IP addresses.

However, many applications do not function properly through NAT, and thus it has never been seen as a permanent solution to resolving the lack of IP addresses. That solution is IPv6.

IPv4 Versus IPv6

IPv6 was developed to more cleanly address the issue of the exhaustion of the IPv4 space. Although private addressing and the use of NAT have helped to delay the inevitable, the use of NAT introduces its own set of problems. The IPv6 system uses 128 bits so it creates such a large number of possible addresses that it is expected to suffice for many, many years.

The details of IPv6 are beyond the scope of the exam but these addresses look different than IPv4 addresses because they use a different format and use the hexadecimal number system, so there are letters and numbers in them such as you would see in a MAC address (discussed in the next section). There are eight fields separated by colons, not dots. Here is an example address:

2001:00000:4137:9e76:30ab:3035:b541:9693

Many of the security features that were add-ons to IPv4 (such as IPsec) have been built into IPv6, increasing its security. Moreover, while Dynamic Host Configuration Protocol (DHCP) can be used with IPv6, IPv6 provides a host the ability to locate its local router, configure itself, and discover the IP addresses of its neighbors. Finally, broadcast traffic is completely eliminated in IPv6 and replaced by multicast communications.

MAC Addressing

All the discussion about addressing thus far has been addressing that is applied at layer 3, which is IP addressing. At layer 2, physical addresses reside. In Ethernet, these are called Media Access Control (MAC) addresses. They are called physical addresses because these 48-bit addresses expressed in hexadecimal are permanently assigned to the network interfaces of devices. Here is an example of a MAC address:

01:23:45:67:89:ab

As a packet is transferred across a network, at every router hop and then again when it arrives at the destination network, the source and destination MAC addresses change. ARP resolves the next hop address to a MAC address using a process called the ARP broadcast. MAC addresses are unique. This comes from the fact that each manufacturer has a different set of values assigned to it at the beginning of the address called the Organizationally Unique Identifier (OUI). Each manufacturer ensures that it assigns no duplicate within its OUI. The OUI is the first three bytes of the MAC address.

Network Transmission

Data can be communicated across a variety of media types, using several possible processes. These communications can also have a number of characteristics that need to be understood. This section discusses some of the most common methods and their characteristics.

Analog Versus Digital

Data can be represented in various ways on a medium. On a wired medium, the data can be transmitted in either analog or digital format. Analog represents the data as sound and is used in analog telephony. Analog signals differ from digital in that there are an infinite possible number of values. If we look at an analog signal on a graph, it looks like a wave going up and down. Figure 3-8 shows an analog waveform compared to a digital one.

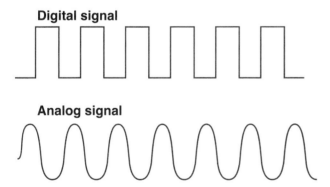

Figure 3-8 Digital and Analog Signals

Digital signaling on the other hand, which is the type used in most computer transmissions, does not have an infinite number of possible values, but only two: on and off. A digital signal shown on a graph exhibits a sawtooth pattern as shown in Figure 3-8. Digital signals are usually preferable to analog because they are more reliable and less susceptible to noise on the line. Transporting more information on the same line at a higher quality over a longer distance than with analog is also possible.

Asynchronous Versus Synchronous

When two systems are communicating, they not only need to represent the data in the same format (analog/digital) but they must also use the same synchronization technique. This process tells the receiver when a specific communication begins and ends so two-way conversations can happen without talking over one another. The two types of techniques are asynchronous transmission and synchronous transmission.

With asynchronous transmissions, the systems use *start* and *stop* bits to communicate when each byte is starting and stopping. This method also uses *parity bits* for the purpose of ensuring that each byte has not changed or been corrupted en route. This introduces additional overhead to the transmission.

Synchronous transmission uses a clocking mechanism to synch up the sender and receiver. Data is transferred in a stream of bits with no start, stop, or parity bits. This clocking mechanism is embedded into the layer 2 protocol. It uses a different form of error checking (cyclical redundancy check or CRC) and is preferable for high-speed, high-volume transmissions. Figure 3-9 shows a visual comparison of the two techniques.

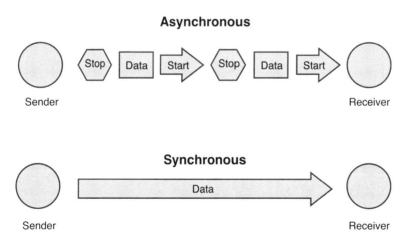

Figure 3-9 Asynchronous Versus Synchronous

Broadband Versus Baseband

All data transfers use a communication channel. Multiple transmissions might need to use the same channel. Sharing this medium can be done in two different ways: broadband or baseband. The difference is in how the medium is shared.

In baseband, the entire medium is used for a single transmission, and then multiple transmission types are assigned time slots to use this single circuit. This is called Time Division Multiplexing (TDM). Multiplexing is the process of using the same medium for multiple transmissions. The transmissions take turns rather than sending at the same time.

Broadband, on the other hand, divides the medium in different frequencies, a process called Frequency Division Multiplexing (FDM). This has the benefit of allowing true simultaneous use of the medium.

An example of broadband transmission is Digital Subscribers Line (DSL), where the phone signals are sent at one frequency and the computer data at another. This is why you can talk on the phone and use the Web at the same time. Figure 3-10 illustrates these two processes.

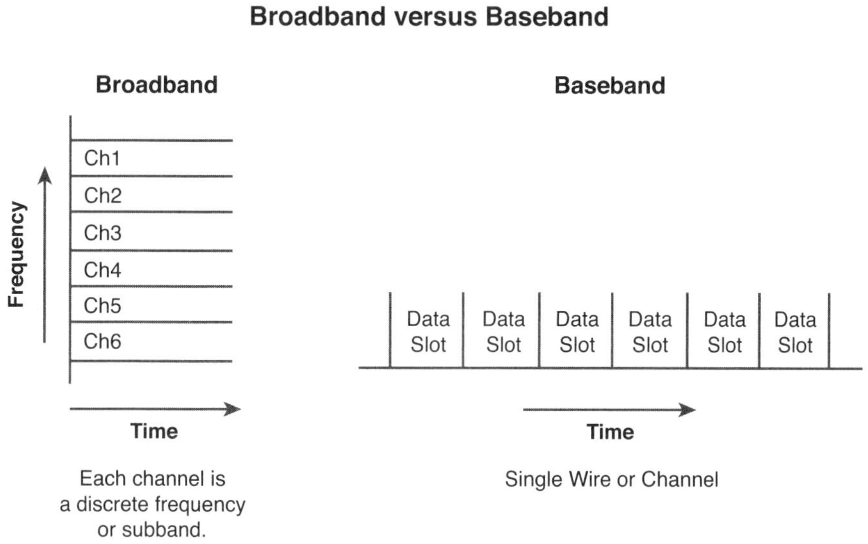

Figure 3-10 Broadband Versus Baseband

Unicast, Multicast, and Broadcast

When systems are communicating in a network, they might send out three types of transmissions. These methods differ in the scope of their reception as follow:

- **Unicast:** Transmission from a single system to another single system. It is considered one-to-one.

- **Multicast:** A signal is received by all others in a group called a multicast group. It is considered one-to-many.

- **Broadcast:** A transmission sent by a single system to all systems in the network. It is considered one-to-all.

Figure 3-11 illustrates the three methods.

Figure 3-11 Unicast, Multicast, and Broadcast

Wired Versus Wireless

As you probably know by now, not all transmissions occur over a wired connection. Even within the category of wired connections, the way in which the ones and zeros are represented can be done in different ways. In a copper wire, the ones and zeros are represented with changes in the voltage of the signal, whereas in a fiberoptic cable, they are represented with manipulation of a light source (lasers or light-emitting diodes [LEDs]).

In wireless transmission, radios waves or light waves are manipulated to represent the ones and zeros. When infrared technology is used, this is done with infrared light. With wireless LANs (WLANs), radio waves are manipulated to represent the ones and zeros. These differences in how the bits are represented occur at the physical and data link layers of the OSI model. When a packet goes from a wireless section of the network to a wired section, these two layers are the only layers that change.

When a different physical medium is used, typically a different layer 2 protocol is called for. For example, while the data is traveling over the wired Ethernet network, the 802.3 standard is used. However, when the data gets to a wireless section of the network, it needs a different layer 2 protocol. Depending on the technology in use, it could be either 802.11 (WLAN) or 802.16 (WiMAX).

The ability of the packet to traverse various media types is just another indication of the independence of the OSI layers because the information in layers 3–7 remains unchanged regardless of how many layer 2 transitions must be made to get the data to its final destination.

Cabling

Cabling resides at the physical layer of the OSI model and simply provides a medium on which data can be transferred. The vast majority of data is transferred across cables of various types, including coaxial, fiberoptic, and twisted pair. Some of these cables represent the data in terms of electrical voltages whereas fiber cables manipulate light to represent the data. This section discusses each type.

You can compare cables to one another using several criteria. One of the criteria that is important with networking is the cable's susceptibility to *attenuation*. Attenuation occurs when the signal meets resistance as it travels through the cable. This weakens the signal, and at some point (different in each cable type), the signal is no longer strong enough to be read properly at the destination. For this reason, all cables have a maximum length. This is true regardless of whether the cable is fiberoptic or electrical.

Another important point of comparison between cable types is their data rate, which describes how much data can be sent through the cable per second. This area has seen great improvement over the years, going from rates of 10 Mbps in a LAN to 1000 Mbps in today's networks (and even higher rates in data centers).

Another consideration when selecting a cable type is the ease of installation. Some cable types are easier than others to install, and fiberoptic cabling requires a special skill set to install, raising its price of installation.

Finally (and most importantly for our discussion) is the security of the cable. Cables can leak or radiate information. Cables can also be tapped into by hackers if they have physical access to them. Just as the cable types can vary in allowable length and capacity, they can also vary in their susceptibility to these types of data losses.

Coaxial

One of the earliest cable types to be used for networking was coaxial, the same basic type of cable that brought cable TV to millions of homes. Although coaxial cabling is still used, due to its low capacity and the adoption of other cable types, its use is almost obsolete now in LANs.

Coaxial cabling comes in two types or thicknesses. The thicker type, called Thicknet, has an official name of 10Base5. This naming system, used for other cable types as well, imparts several facts about the cable. In the case of 10Bbase5, it means that it is capable of transferring 10 Mbps and can go roughly 500 meters. Thicknet uses two types of connectors: a vampire tap (named thusly because it has a spike that pierces the cable) and N-connectors.

Thinnet or 10Base2 also operates at 10 Mbps. Although when it was named it was anticipated to be capable of running 200 feet, this was later reduced to 185 feet. Both types are used in a bus topology (more on topologies in the section "Network Topologies" later in this chapter). Thinnet uses two types of connectors: BNC connectors and T-connectors.

Coaxial has an outer cylindrical covering that surrounds either a solid core wire (Thicknet) or a braided core (Thinnet). This type of cabling has been replaced over time with more capable twisted-pair and fiberoptic cabling. Coaxial cabling can be tapped, so physical access to this cabling should be restricted or prevented if possible. It should be out of sight if it is used. Figure 3-12 shows the structure of a coaxial cable.

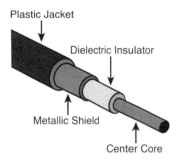

Figure 3-12 Coaxial Cabling

Another security problem with coax in a bus topology is that it is broadcast-based, which means a sniffer attached anywhere in the network can capture all traffic. In switched networks (more on that topic later in this chapter in the section "Network Devices"), this is not a consideration.

Twisted Pair

The most common type of network cabling found today is called twisted-pair cabling. It is called this because inside the cable are four pairs of smaller wires that are braided or twisted. This twisting is designed to eliminate a phenomenon called crosstalk, which occurs when wires that are inside a cable interfere with one another. The number of wire pairs that are used depends on the implementation. In some implementations, only two pairs are used, and in others all four wire pairs are used. Figure 3-13 shows the structure of a twisted-pair cable.

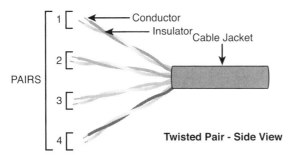

Figure 3-13 Twisted-Pair Cabling

Twisted-pair cabling comes in shielded (STP) and unshielded (UTP) versions. Nothing is gained from the shielding except protection from Radio Frequency Interference (RFI) and Electromagnetic Interference (EMI). RFI is interference from radio sources in the area, whereas EMI is interference from power lines. A common type of EMI is called common mode noise, which is interference that appears on both signal leads (signal and circuit return) or the terminals of a measuring circuit, and ground. If neither EMI nor RFI are a problem, nothing is gained by using STP, and it costs more.

The same naming system used with coaxial and fiber is used with twisted pair. The following are the major types of twisted pair you will encounter:

- **10BaseT:** Operates at 10 Mbps
- **100BaseT:** Also called Fast Ethernet; operates at 100 Mbps
- **1000BaseT:** Also called Gigabit Ethernet; operates at 1000 Mbps
- **10GBaseT:** Operates at 10 Gbps

Twisted-pair cabling comes in various capabilities and is rated in categories. Table 3-4 lists the major types and their characteristics. Regardless of the category, twisted-pair cabling can be run about 100 meters before attenuation degrades the signal.

Table 3-4 Twisted-Pair Categories

Name	Maximum Transmission Speed
Cat3	10 Mbps
Cat4	16 Mbps
Cat5	100 Mbps
Cat5e	100 Mbps

Name	Maximum Transmission Speed
Cat6	1 Gbps
Cat6a	10 Gbps

Fiberoptic

Fiberoptic cabling uses a source of light that shoots down an inner glass or plastic core of the cable. This core is covered by cladding that causes light to be confined to the core of the fiber. Figure 3-14 shows the structure of a fiberoptic cable.

Figure 3-14 Fiberoptic Cabling

Fiberoptic cabling manipulates light such that it can be interpreted as ones and zeros. Because it is not electrically based, it is totally impervious to EMI, RFI, and crosstalk. Moreover, although not impossible, tapping or eavesdropping on a fiber cable is much more difficult. In most cases, attempting to tap into it results in a failure of the cable, which then becomes quite apparent to all.

Fiber comes in a single and multi-mode format. The single mode uses a single beam of light provided by a laser, goes the further of the two, and is the most expensive. Multi-mode uses several beams of light at the same time, uses LEDs, will not go as far, and is less expensive. Either type goes much further than electrical cabling in a single run and also typically provides more capacity. Fiber cabling has its drawbacks, however. It is the most expensive to purchase and the most expensive to install. Table 3-5 shows some selected fiber specifications and their theoretical maximum distances.

Table 3-5 Selected Fiber Specifications

Standard	Distance
100Base-FX	Maximum length is 400 meters for half-duplex connections (to ensure collisions are detected) or 2 kilometers for full-duplex.
1000Base-SX	550 meters

Standard	Distance
1000Base-LX	Multi-mode fiber (up to 550 m) or single-mode fiber (up to 2 km; can be optimized for longer distances, up to 10 km).
10GBase-LR	10 km
10GBase-ER	40 km

Network Topologies

Networks can be described by their logical topology (the data path used) and by their physical topology (the way in which devices are connected to one another. In most cases the logical topology and the physical topology will be the same but not in all. This section discusses both logical and physical network topologies.

Ring

A physical ring topology is one in which the devices are daisy-chained one to another in a circle or ring. If the network is also a logical ring, the data circles the ring from one device to another. Two technologies use this topology, Fiber Distributed Data Interface (FDDI) and Token Ring. Both these technologies are discussed in detail in the section, "Network Technologies." Figure 3-15 shows a typical ring topology.

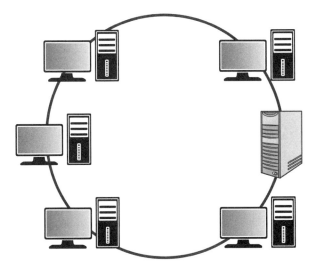

Figure 3-15   Ring Topology

One of the drawbacks of the ring topology is that if a break occurs in the line, all systems will be affected as the ring will be broken. As you will see in the section "Network Technologies," a FDDI network addresses this issue with a double ring for fault tolerance.

Bus

The bus topology was the earliest Ethernet topology used. In this topology, all devices are connected to a single line that has two definitive endpoints. The network does NOT loop back and form a ring. This topology is broadcast-based, which can be a security issue in that a sniffer or protocol analyzer connected at any point in the network will be capable of capturing all traffic. From a fault tolerance standpoint, the bus topology suffers the same danger as a ring. If a break occurs anywhere in the line, all devices are affected. Moreover, a requirement specific to this topology is that each end of the bus must be terminated. This prevents signals from "bouncing" back on the line causing collisions. (More on collisions later, but collisions require the collided packets to be sent again, lowering overall throughput.) If this termination is not done properly, the network will not function correctly. Figure 3-16 shows a bus topology.

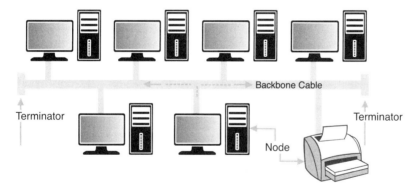

Figure 3-16 Bus Topology

Star

The star topology is the most common in use today. In this topology, all devices are connected to a central device (either a hub or a switch). One of the advantages of this topology is that if a connection to any single device breaks, ONLY that device is affected and no others. The downside of this topology is that a single point of failure (the hub or switch) exists. If the hub or switch fails, all devices are affected. Figure 3-17 shows a star topology.

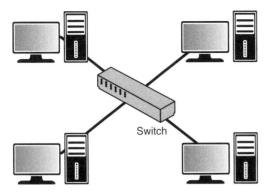

Figure 3-17 Star Topology

Mesh

Although the mesh topology is the most fault tolerant of any discussed thus far, it is also the most expensive to deploy. In this topology, all devices are connected to all other devices. This provides complete fault tolerance but also requires multiple interfaces and cables on each device. For that reason, it is deployed only in rare circumstances where such an expense is warranted. Figure 3-18 shows a mesh topology.

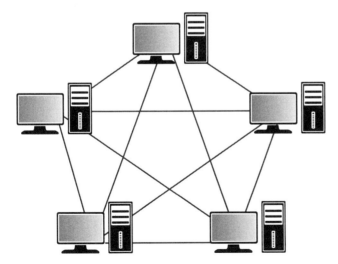

Figure 3-18 Mesh Topology

Hybrid

In many cases an organization's network is a combination of these network topologies, or a hybrid network. For example, one section might be a star that connects to a bus network or a ring network. Figure 3-19 shows an example of a hybrid network.

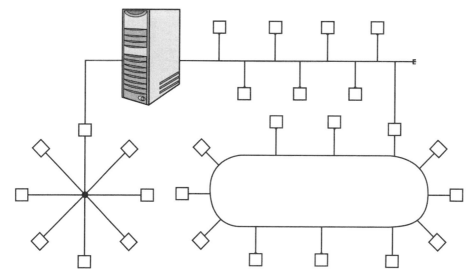

Figure 3-19 Hybrid Topology

Network Technologies

Just as a network can be connected in various topologies, different technologies have been implemented over the years that run over those topologies. These technologies operate at layer 2 of the OSI model, and their details of operation are specified in various standards by the Institute of Electrical and Electronics Engineers (IEEE). Some of these technologies are designed for Local Area Network (LAN) applications whereas others are meant to be used in a Wide Area Network (WAN). In this section, we look at the main LAN technologies and some of the processes that these technologies use to arbitrate access to the network.

Ethernet 802.3

The IEEE specified the details of Ethernet in the 802.3 standard. Prior to this standardization, Ethernet existed in several earlier forms, the most common of which was called Ethernet ll or DIX Ethernet (DIX stands for the three companies that collaborated on its creation, DEC, Intel, and Xerox).

In the section on the OSI model, you learned that the PDU created at layer 2 is called a frame. Because Ethernet is a layer 2 protocol, we refer to the individual Ethernet packets as *frames*. There are small differences in the frame structures of Ethernet ll and 802.3, although they are compatible in the same network. Figure 3-20 shows a comparison of the two frames. The significant difference is that during the IEEE standardization process, the EtherType field was changed to a (data) length field in the new 802.3 standard. For purposes of identifying the data type, another field called the 802.2 header was inserted to contain that information.

Ethernet

Preamble	Destination Address	Source Address	Type	DATA	FCS
8	6	6	2	46-1500	4

IEEE 802.3

Preamble	SOF	Destination Address	Source Address	Length	802.2 Header	DATA	FCS
7	1	6	6	2		46-1500	4

Field lengths are in bytes

Figure 3-20 Ethernet ll and 802.3

Ethernet has been implemented on coaxial, fiber, and twisted-pair wiring. Table 3-6 lists some of the more common Ethernet implementations.

Table 3-6 Ethernet Implementations

Ethernet Type	Cable Type	Speed
10Base2	Coaxial	10 Mbps
10Base5	Coaxial	10 Mbps
10BaseT	Twisted pair	10 Mbps
100BaseTX	Twisted pair	100 Mbps
1000BaseT	Twisted pair	1000 Mbps
1000BaseX	Fiber	1000 Mbps
10GBaseT	Twisted pair	10 Gbps

NOTE Despite the fact that 1000BaseT and 1000BaseX are faster, 100BaseTX is called *Fast Ethernet*! Also both 1000BaseT and 1000BaseX are usually referred to as Gigabit Ethernet.

Ethernet calls for devices to share the medium on a frame-by-frame basis. It arbitrates access to the media using a process called Carrier Sense Multiple Access with Collision Detection (CSMA/CD). This process is discussed in detail in the section "CSMA/CD Versus CSMA/CA" where the process is contrasted with the method used in 802.11 wireless networks.

Token Ring 802.5

Ethernet is the most common layer 2 protocol, but it has not always been that way. An example of a proprietary layer 2 protocol that enjoyed some small success is IBM Token Ring. This protocol operates using specific IBM connective devices and cables, and the nodes must have Token Ring network cards installed. It can operate at 16 Mbps, which at the time of its release was impressive, but the proprietary nature of the equipment and the soon-to-be faster Ethernet caused Token Ring to fall from favor.

As mentioned earlier, in most cases the physical network topology is the same as the logical topology. Token Ring is the exception to that general rule. It is logically a ring and physically a star. It is a star in that all devices are connected to a central device called a Media Access Unit (MAU), but the ring is formed in the MAU and when you investigate the flow of the data, it goes from one device to another in a ring design by entering and exiting each port of the MAU, as shown in Figure 3-21.

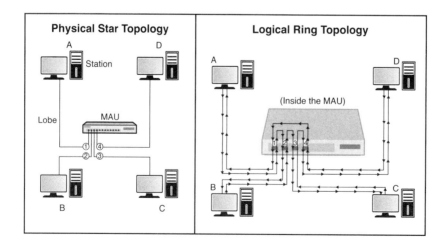

Figure 3-21 Token Ring

FDDI

Another layer 2 protocol that uses a ring topology is Fiber Distributed Data Interface (FDDI). Unlike Token Ring, it is both a physical and a logical ring. It is actually a double ring, each going in a different direction to provide fault tolerance. It also is implemented with fiber cabling. In many cases it is used for a network backbone and is then connected to other network types, such as Ethernet, forming a hybrid network. It is also used in Metropolitan Area Networks (MANs) because it can be deployed up to 100 kilometers.

Figure 3-22 shows an example of an FFDI ring.

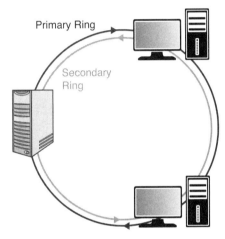

Figure 3-22 FDDI

Contention Methods

Regardless of the layer 2 protocol in use, there must be some method used to arbitrate the use of the shared media. Four basic processes have been employed to act as the traffic cop, so to speak:

- CSMA/CD
- CSMA/CA
- Token passing
- Polling

This section compares and contrasts each and provides examples of technologies that use each.

CSMA/CD Versus CSMA/CA

To appreciate CSMA/CD and CSMA/CA, you must understand the concept of collisions and collision domains in a shared network medium. Collisions occur when two devices send a frame at the same time causing the frames and their underlying electrical signals to collide on the wire. When this occurs, both signals and the frames they represent are destroyed or at the very least corrupted such that they are discarded when they reach the destination. Frame corruption or disposal causes both devices to resend the frames, resulting in a drop in overall throughput.

Collision Domains

A collision domain is any segment of the network where the possibility exists for two or more devices' signals to collide. In a bus topology, that would constitute the entire network because the entire bus is a shared medium. In a star topology, the scope of the collision domain or domains depends on the central connecting device. Central connecting devices include hubs and switches. Hubs and switches are discussed more fully in the section "Network Devices" but their differences with respect to collision domains need to be discussed here.

A hub is an unintelligent junction box into which all devices plug. All the ports in the hub are in the same collision domain because when a hub receives a frame, the hub broadcasts the frame out all ports. So logically, the network is still a bus.

A star topology with a switch in the center does not operate this way. A switch has the intelligence to record the MAC address of each device on every port. After all the devices' MAC addresses are recorded, the switch sends a frame ONLY to the port on which the destination device resides. Because each device's traffic is then segregated from any other device's traffic, each device is considered to be in its own collision domain.

This segregation provided by switches has both performance and security benefits. From a performance perspective, it greatly reduces the number of collisions, thereby significantly increasing overall throughput in the network. From a security standpoint, it means that a sniffer connected to a port in the switch will ONLY capture traffic destined for that port, not all traffic. Compare this security to a hub-centric network. When a hub is in the center of a star network, a sniffer will capture all traffic regardless of the port to which it is connected because all ports are in the same collision domain.

In Figure 3-23, a switch has several devices and a hub connected to it with each collision domain marked to show how the two devices create collision domains. Note that each port on the switch is a collision domain whereas the entire hub is a single collision domain.

Chapter 3: Telecommunications and Network Security

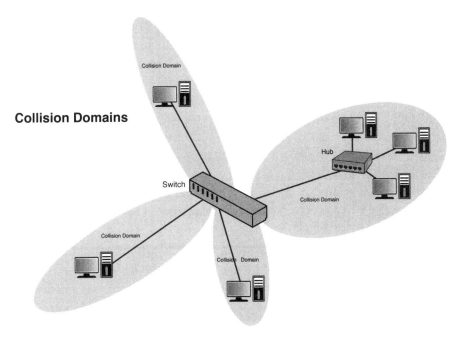

Collision Domains

Figure 3-23 Collision Domains

CSMA/CD

In 802.3 networks, a mechanism called Carrier Sense Multiple Access Collision Detection (CSMA/CD) is used when a shared medium is in use to recover from inevitable collisions. This process is a step-by-step mechanism that each station follows every time it needs to send a single frame. The steps to the process are as follow:

1. When a device needs to transmit, it checks the wire for existing traffic. This process is called carrier sense.

2. If the wire is clear, the device transmits and continues to perform carrier sense.

3. If a collision is detected, both devices issue a jam signal to all the other devices, which indicates to them to NOT transmit. Then both devices increment a retransmission counter. This is a cumulative total of the number of times this frame has been transmitted and a collision occurred. There is a maximum number at which it aborts the transmission of the frame.

4. Both devices calculate a random amount of time (called a random back off) and wait that amount of time before transmitting again.

5. In most cases because both devices choose random amounts of time to wait, another collision will not occur. If it does, the procedure repeats.

CSMA/CA

In 802.11 wireless networks, CSMA/CD cannot be used as an arbitration method because unlike when using bounded media, the devices cannot detect a collision. The method used is called Carrier Sense Multiple Access Collision Avoidance (CSMA/CA). It is a much more laborious process because each station must acknowledge each frame that is transmitted.

The "Wireless Networks" section covers 802.11 network operations in more detail, but for the purposes of understanding CSMA/CA we must at least lay some groundwork. The typical wireless network contains an access point (AP) and at least one or more wireless stations. In this type of network (called Infrastructure Mode wireless network), traffic never traverses directly between stations but is always relayed through the AP. The steps in CSMA/CA are as follows:

1. Station A has a frame to send to Station B. It checks for traffic in two ways. First, it performs carrier sense, which means it listens to see whether any radio waves are being received on its transmitter. Secondly, after the transmission is sent, it will continue to monitor the network for possible collisions.

2. If traffic is being transmitted, Station A decrements an internal countdown mechanism called the random back-off algorithm. This counter will have started counting down after the last time this station was allowed to transmit. All stations will be counting down their own individual timers. When a station's timer expires, it is allowed to send.

3. If Station A performs carrier sense, there is no traffic and its timer hits zero, it sends the frame.

4. The frame goes to the AP.

5. The AP sends an acknowledgment back to Station A. Until that acknowledgment is received by Station A, all other stations must remain silent. For each frame that AP needs to relay, it must wait its turn to send using the same mechanism as the stations.

6. When its turn comes up in the cache queue, the frame from Station A is relayed to Station B.

7. Station B sends an acknowledgment back to the AP. Until that acknowledgment is received by the AP, all other stations must remain silent.

As you can see, these processes create a lot of overhead but are required to prevent collisions in a wireless network.

Token Passing

Both FDDI and Token Ring networks use a process called token passing. In this process, a special packet called a token is passed around the network. A station cannot send until the token comes around and is empty. Using this process, NO collisions occur because two devices are never allowed to send at the same time. The problem with this process is that the possibility exists for a single device to gain control of the token and monopolize the network.

Polling

The final contention method to discuss is polling. In this system, a primary device polls each other device to see whether it needs to transmit. In this way, each device gets a transmit opportunity. This method is common in the mainframe environment.

Network Protocols/Services

Many protocols and services have been developed over the years to add functionality to networks. In many cases these protocols reside at the Application layer of the OSI model. These Application layer protocols usually perform a specific function and rely on the lower layer protocols in the TCP/IP suite and protocols at layer 2 (like Ethernet) to perform routing and delivery services.

This section covers some of the most important of these protocols and services, including some that do NOT operate at the Application layer, focusing on the function and port number of each. Port numbers are important to be aware of from a security standpoint because in many cases port numbers are referenced when configuring firewall rules. In cases where a port or protocol number is relevant, they will be given as well.

ARP

Address Resolution Protocol (ARP), one of the protocols in the TCP/IP suite, operates at layer 3 of the OSI model. The information it derives is utilized at layer 2, however. ARP's job is to resolve the destination IP address placed in the header by IP to a layer 2 or MAC address. Remember, when frames are transmitted on a local segment the transfer is done in terms of MAC addresses not IP addresses, so this information must be known.

Whenever a packet is sent across the network, at every router hop and again at the destination subnet, the source and destination MAC address pairs change but the source and destination IP addresses not. The process that ARP uses to perform this resolution is called an ARP broadcast.

First an area of memory called the ARP cache is consulted. If the MAC address has been recently resolved, the mapping will be in the cache and a broadcast is not required. If the record has aged out of the cache, ARP sends a broadcast frame to the local network that all devices will receive. The device that possesses the IP address responds with its MAC address. Then ARP places the MAC address in the frame and sends the frame. Figure 3-24 illustrates this process.

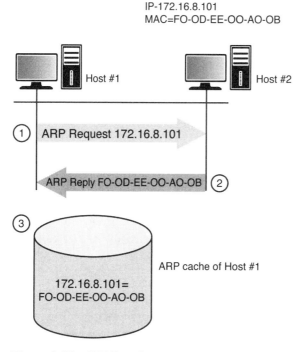

Figure 3-24 ARP Broadcast

DHCP

Dynamic Host Configuration Protocol (DHCP) is a service that can be used to automate the process of assigning an IP configuration to the devices in the network. Manual configuration of an IP address, subnet mask, default gateway, and DNS server is not only time consuming but fraught with opportunity for human error. Using DHCP can not only automate this, but can also eliminate network problems from this human error.

DHCP is a client/server program. All modern operating systems contain a DHCP client, and the server component can be implemented either on a server or on a router. When a computer that is configured to be a DHCP client starts, it performs a precise four-step process to obtain its configuration. Conceptually, the client broadcasts for the IP address of the DHCP server. All devices receive this broadcast, but only DHCP servers respond. The device accepts the configuration offered by the first DHCP server from which it hears. The process uses four packets with distinctive names (see Figure 3-25). DHCP uses UDP ports 67 and 68. Port 67 sends data to the server, and port 68 sends data to the client.

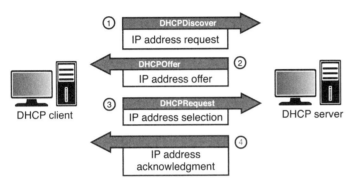

Figure 3-25 DHCP

DNS

Just as DHCP relieves us from having to manually configure the IP configuration of each system, Domain Name System (DNS) relieves all humans from having to know the IP address of every computer with which they want to communicate. Ultimately, an IP address must be known to connect to another computer. DNS resolves a computer name (or in the case of the Web, a domain name) to an IP address.

DNS is another client/server program with the client included in all modern operating systems. The server part resides on a series of DNS servers located both in the local network and on the Internet. When a DNS client needs to know the IP address that goes with a particular computer name or domain name, it queries the local DNS server. If the local DNS server does not have the resolution, it contacts other DNS servers on the client's behalf, learns the IP address, and relays that information to the DNS client. DNS uses UDP port 53 and TCP port 53. The DNS servers use TCP port 53 to exchange information, and the DNS clients use UDP port 53 for queries.

FTP, FTPS, SFTP

File Transfer Protocol (FTP), and its more secure versions FTPS and SFTP, transfers files from one system to another. FTP is insecure in that the username and password is transmitted in clear text. The original clear text version uses TCP port 20 for data and TCP port 21 as the control channel. Using FTP when security is a consideration is not recommended.

FTPS is FTP that adds support for the Transport Layer Security (TLS) and the Secure Sockets Layer (SSL) cryptographic protocols. FTPS uses TCP ports 989 and 990.

FTPS is not the same as and should not be confused with another secure version of FTP, SSH File Transfer Protocol (SFTP). This is an extension of the Secure Shell Protocol (SSH). There have been a number of different versions with version 6 being the latest. Because it uses SSH for the file transfer, it uses TCP port 22.

HTTP, HTTPS, SHTTP

One of the most frequently used protocols today is Hypertext Transfer Protocol (HTTP) and its secure versions, HTTPS and SHTTP. This protocol is used to view and transfer web pages or web content. The original version (HTTP) has no encryption so when security is a concern, one of the two secure versions should be used. HTTP uses TCP port 80.

Hypertext Transfer Protocol Secure (HTTPS) layers the HTTP on top of the SSL/TLS protocol, thus adding the security capabilities of SSL/TLS to standard HTTP communications. It is often used for secure websites because it requires no software or configuration changes on the web client to function securely. When HTTPS is used, port 80 is not used. Rather, it uses port 443.

Unlike HTTPS, which encrypts the entire communication, SHTTP encrypts only the served page data and submitted data such as POST fields, leaving the initiation of the protocol unchanged. Secure-HTTP and HTTP processing can operate on the same TCP port, port 80. This version is rarely used.

ICMP

Internet Control Message Protocol (ICMP) operates at layer 3 of the OSI model and is used by devices to transmit error messages regarding problems with transmissions. It also is the protocol used when the ping and traceroute commands are used to troubleshoot network connectivity problems. Because IP is part of the TCP/IP suite, it doesn't use a port number but is identified in the packet by its protocol number. Its protocol number is 1.

ICMP is a protocol that can be leveraged to mount several network attacks based on its operation, and for this reason many networks choose to block ICMP. These attacks are discussed in the section "Network Threats."

IMAP

Internet Message Access Protocol (IMAP) is an Application layer protocol for email retrieval. Its latest version is IMAP4. It is a client email protocol used to access email from a server. Unlike POP3, another email client that can only download messages from the server, IMAP4 allows one to download a copy and leave a copy on the server. IMAP 4 uses port 143. A secure version also exists, IMAPS (IMAP over SSL), that uses port 993.

NAT

Network Address Translation (NAT) is a service that maps private IP addresses to public IP addresses. It is discussed in the section "Logical and Physical Addressing" earlier in this chapter.

PAT

Port Address Translation (PAT) is a specific version of NAT that uses a single public IP address to represent multiple private IP addresses. Its operation is discussed in the section "Logical and Physical Addressing" earlier in this chapter.

POP

Post Office Protocol (POP) is an Application layer email retrieval protocol. POP3 is the latest version. It allows for downloading messages only and does not allow the additional functionality provided by IMAP4. POP3 uses port 110. A version that runs over SSL is also available that uses port 995.

SMTP

POP and IMAP are client email protocols used for retrieving email, but when email servers are talking to each other they use a protocol called Simple Mail Transfer Protocol (SMTP), a standard Application layer protocol. This is also the protocol used by clients to send email. SMTP uses port 25, and when it is runs over SSL, it uses port 465.

SNMP

Simple Network Management Protocol (SNMP) is an Application layer protocol that is used to retrieve information from network devices and to send configuration changes to those devices. SNMP uses TCP port 162 and UDP ports 161 and 162.

SNMP devices are organized into communities and the community name must be known to either access information from or send a change to a device. It also can be used with a password. SNMP versions 1 and 2 are susceptible to packet sniffing, and all versions are susceptible to brute-force attacks on the community strings and password used. The defaults of community string names, which are widely known, are often left in place. The latest version, SNMPv3, is the most secure.

Network Routing

Routing occurs at layer 3 of the OSI model, which is also the layer at which IP operates and where the source and destination IP addresses are placed in the packet. Routers are devices that transfer traffic between systems in different IP networks. When computers are in different IP networks, they cannot communicate unless a router is available to route the packets to the other networks.

Routers keep information about the paths to other networks in a routing table. These tables can be populated several ways. Administrators manually enter these routes, or dynamic routing protocols allow the routers running the same protocol to exchange routing tables and routing information. Manual configuration, also called static routing, has the advantage of avoiding the additional traffic created by dynamic routing protocols and allows for precise control of routing behavior, but requires manual intervention when link failures occur. Dynamic routing protocols create traffic but are able to react to link outages and reroute traffic without manual intervention.

From a security standpoint, routing protocols introduce the possibility that routing update traffic might be captured, allowing a hacker to gain valuable information about the layout of the network. Moreover, Cisco devices (perhaps the most widely used) also use a proprietary layer 2 protocol by default called Cisco Discovery Protocol (CDP) that they use to inform each other about their capabilities. If the CDP packets are captured, additional information can be obtained that can be helpful to mapping the network in advance of an attack.

This section compares and contrasts routing protocols.

Distance Vector, Link State, or Hybrid Routing

Routing protocols have different capabilities and operational characteristics that impact when and where they are utilized. Routing protocols come in two basic types: interior and exterior. Interior routing protocols are used within an autonomous system, which is a network managed by one set of administrators, typically a single enterprise. Exterior routing protocols route traffic between systems or company networks. An example of this type of routing is what occurs on the Internet.

Routing protocols also can fall into three categories that describe their operations more than their scope: distance vector, link state, and hybrid (or advanced distance vector). The difference in these mostly revolves around the amount of traffic created and the method used to determine the best path out of possible paths to a network. The value used to make this decision is called a metric, and each has a different way of calculating the metric and thus determining the best path.

Distance vector protocols share their entire routing table with their neighboring routers on a schedule, thereby creating the most traffic of the three categories. They also use a metric called *hop count*. Hop count is simply the number of routers traversed to get to a network.

Link state protocols only share network changes (link outages and recoveries) with neighbors, thereby greatly reducing the amount of traffic generated. They also use a much more sophisticated metric that is based on many factors, such as the bandwidth of each link on the path and the congestion on each link. So when using one of these protocols, a path might be chosen as best even though it has more hops because the path chosen has better bandwidth, meaning less congestion.

Hybrid or advanced distance vector protocols exhibit characteristics of both types. EIGRP, discussed later in this section, is the only example of this type. In the past, EIGRP has been referred to as a hybrid protocol but in the last several years, Cisco (which created IGRP and EIGRP) has been calling this an advanced distance vector protocol so you might see both terms used. In the following sections, several of the most common routing protocols are discussed briefly.

RIP

Routing Information Protocol (RIP) is a standards-based distance vector protocol that has two versions: RIPv1 and RIPv2. Both use hop count as a metric and share their entire routing tables every 30 seconds. Although RIP is the simplest to configure, it has a maximum hop count of 15, so it is only useful in very small networks. The biggest difference between the two versions is that RIPv1 can only perform classful routing whereas RIPv2 can route in a network where CIDR has been implemented.

OSPF

Open Shortest Path First (OSPF) is a standards-based link state protocol. It uses a metric called cost that is calculated based on many considerations. Thus it makes much more sophisticated routing decisions than a distance vector routing protocol such as RIP. It also only updates other routers with changes, greatly reducing the amount of traffic generated. To take full of advantage of OSPF, a much deeper knowledge of routing and OSPF itself is required. It can scale successfully to very large networks because it has no minimum hop count.

IGRP

Interior Gateway Routing Protocol (IGRP) is an obsolete classful Cisco-proprietary routing protocol that you will not likely see in the real world because of its inability to operate in an environment where CIDR has been implemented. It has been replaced with the classless version Enhanced IGRP (EIGRP) discussed next.

EIGRP

Enhanced IGRP (EIGRP) is a classless Cisco-proprietary routing protocol that is considered a hybrid or advanced distance vector protocol. It exhibits some characteristics of both link state and distance vector operations. It also has no limitations on hop count and is much simpler to implement than OSPF. It does, however, require that all routers be Cisco.

VRRP

When a router goes down, all hosts that use that router for routing will be unable to send traffic to other networks. Virtual Router Redundancy Protocol (VRRP) is not really a routing protocol but rather is used to provide multiple gateways to clients for fault tolerance in the case of a router going down. All hosts in a network are set with the IP address of the *virtual router* as their default gateway. Multiple physical routers are mapped to this address so there will be an available router even if one goes down.

IS-IS

Intermediate System to Intermediate System (IS-IS) is a complex interior routing protocol that is based on OSI protocols rather than IP. It is a link state protocol. The TCP/IP implementation is called Integrated IS-IS. OSPF has more functionality, but IS-IS creates less traffic than OSPF and is much less widely implemented than OSPF.

BGP

Border Gateway Protocol (BGP) is an exterior routing protocol considered to be a path vector protocol. It routes between autonomous systems (ASs) and is used on the Internet. It has a rich set of attributes that can be manipulated by administrators to control path selection and to control the exact way in which traffic enters and exits the AS. However, it is one of the most complex to understand and configure.

Network Devices

Network devices operate at all layers of the OSI model. The layer at which they operate reveals quite a bit about their level of intelligence and about the types of information used by each device. This section covers common devices and their respective roles in the overall picture.

Patch Panel

Patch panels operate at the Physical layer (layer 1) of the OSI model and simply function as a central termination point for all the cables running through the walls from wall outlets, which in turn are connected to computers with cables. The cables running through the walls to the patch panel are permanently connected to the panel. Short cables called patch cables are then used to connect each panel port to a switch or hub.

Multiplexer

A multiplexer is a Physical layer (layer 1) device that combines several input information signals into one output signal, which carries several communication channels, by means of some multiplex technique. Conversely, a demultiplexer takes a single input signal that carries many channels and separates those over multiple output signals. Sharing the same physical medium can be done in a number of different ways: on the basis of frequencies used (frequency division multiplexing or FDM) or by using time slots (time division multiplexing or TDM).

Hub

A hub is a Physical layer (layer 1) device that functions as a junction point for devices in a star topology. It is considered a Physical layer device because it has no intelligence. When a hub receives traffic, it broadcasts that traffic out of every port because it does not have the intelligence to make any decisions about where the destination is located.

Although this results in more collisions and poor performance, from a security standpoint the problem is that it broadcasts all traffic to all ports. A sniffer connected to any port will be able to sniff all traffic. The operation of a hub is shown in Figure 3-26. When a switch is used, that is not the case (more on those next).

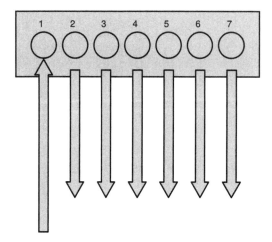

Figure 3-26 Hub

Switch

Switches are intelligent and operate at layer 2 of the OSI model. We say they map to this layer because they make switching decisions based on MAC addresses, which reside at layer 2. This process is called *transparent bridging*. Figure 3-27 shows this process.

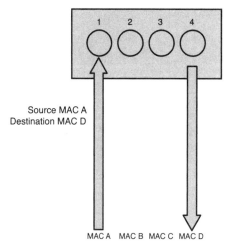

Figure 3-27 Transparent Bridging

Switches improve performance over hubs because they eliminate collisions. Each switch port is in its own collision domain, whereas all ports of a hub are in the same collision domain. From a security standpoint, switches are more secure in that a sniffer connected to any single port will only be able to capture traffic destined for or originating from that port.

Some switches, however, are both routers and switches, and in that case we call them layer 3 switches because they route and switch.

VLANs

Enterprise-level switches are also capable of another functionality called virtual local area networks (VLANs). These are logical subdivisions of a switch that segregate ports from one another as if they were in different LANs. These VLANs can also span multiple switches, meaning that devices connected to switches in different parts of a network can be placed in the same VLAN regardless of physical location.

VLANs offer another way to add a layer of separation between sensitive devices and the rest of the network. For example, if only two devices should be able to connect to the HR server, the two devices and the HR server could be placed in a VLAN separate from the other VLANs. Traffic between VLANs can only occur through a router. Routers can be used to implement ACLs that control the traffic allowed between VLANs.

Layer 3 Versus Layer 4

Typically we map the switching process to layer 2 of the OSI model because layer 2 addresses are used to make frame-forwarding decisions. That doesn't mean that a single physical device cannot be capable of both functions. A layer 3 switch is such a device. It is a switch with the routing function also built in. It can both route and switch and can combine the two functions in an integrated way such that a single data stream can be routed when the first packet arrives and then the rest of the packets in the stream can be fast switched, resulting in better performance.

Layer 4 switches take this a step further by providing additional routing above layer 3 by using the port numbers found in the Transport layer header to make routing decisions. The largest benefit of layer 4 switching is the ability to prioritize data traffic by application, which means a quality of service (QoS) can be defined for each user.

Router

Routers operate at layer 3 (Network layer) when we are discussing the routing function in isolation. As previously discussed, certain devices can combine routing functionality with switching and layer 4 filtering. However, because routing uses layer 3 information (IP addresses) to make decisions, it is a layer 3 function.

Routers use a routing table that tells the router in which direction to send traffic destined for a particular network. Although routers can be configured with routes to individual computers, typically they route toward networks, not individual computers. When the packet arrives at the router that is directly connected to the destination network, that particular router performs an ARP broadcast to learn the MAC address of the computer and send the packets as frames at layer 2.

Routers perform an important security function because on them ACLs are typically configured. These are ordered sets of rules that control the traffic that is permitted or denied the use of a path through the router. These rules can operate at layer 3 making these decisions on the basis of IP addresses or at layer 4 when only certain types of traffic are allowed. When this is done, the ACL typically references a port number of the service or application that is allowed or denied.

Gateway

The term *gateway* doesn't refer to a particular device but rather to any device that performs some sort of translation or acts as a control point to entry and exit. For example, if a router has one interface that uses TCP/IP and another interface that uses IPX/SPX (a now obsolete LAN protocol), we would say it performs as a gateway between the two protocols.

Another example of a device performing as a gateway would be an email server. It receives email from all types of email servers (Exchange, IBM Notes, Novell GroupWise) and performs any translation of formats that is necessary between these different implementations.

Finally, but certainly not the last example would be a Network Access Server (NAS) that controls access to a network. This would be considered a gateway in that all traffic might need to be authenticated before entry is allowed. This type of server might even examine the computers themselves for the latest security patches and updates before entry is allowed.

Firewall

The network device that perhaps is most connected with the idea of security is the firewall. Firewalls can be software programs that are installed over server operating systems or they can be appliances that have their own operating system. In either case their job is to inspect and control the type of traffic allowed.

Firewalls can be discussed on the basis of their type and their architecture. They can also be physical devices or exist in a virtualized environment. This section looks at them from all angles.

Types

When we discuss *types* of firewalls, we are focusing on the differences in the way they operate. Some firewalls make a more thorough inspection of traffic than others. Usually there is tradeoff in the performance of the firewall and the type of inspection that it performs. A deep inspection of the contents of each packet results in the firewall having a detrimental effect on throughput whereas a more cursory look at each packet has somewhat less of an impact on performance. It is for this reason we make our selections of what traffic to inspect wisely, keeping this tradeoff in mind.

Packet filtering firewalls are the least detrimental to throughput because they only inspect the header of the packet for allowed IP addresses or port numbers. Although even performing this function will slow traffic, it involves only looking at the beginning of the packet and making a quick allow or disallow decision.

Although packet filtering firewalls serve an important function, they cannot prevent many attack types. They cannot prevent IP spoofing, attacks that are specific to an application, attacks that depend on packet fragmentation, or attacks that take advantage of the TCP handshake. More advanced inspection firewall types are required to stop these attacks.

Stateful firewalls are those that are aware of the proper functioning of the TCP handshake, keep track of the state of all connections with respect to this process, and can recognize when packets are trying to enter the network that don't make sense in the context of the TCP handshake. You might recall the discussion of how the TCP handshake occurs from the section "Transport Layer" earlier in this chapter.

To review that process, a packet should never arrive at a firewall for delivery that has both the SYN flag and the ACK flag set unless it is part of an existing handshake process and it should be in response to a packet sent from inside the network with the SYN flag set. This is the type of packet that the stateful firewall would disallow. It also has the ability to recognize other attack types that attempt to misuse this process. It does this by maintaining a state table about all current connections and the status of each connection process. This allows it to recognize any traffic that doesn't make sense with the current state of the connection. Of course, maintaining this table and referencing the table causes this firewall type to have more effect on performance than a packet filtering firewall.

Proxy firewalls actually stand between each connection from the outside to the inside and make the connection on behalf of the endpoints. Therefore there is no direct connection. The proxy firewall acts as a relay between the two endpoints. Proxy firewalls can operate at two different layers of the OSI model. Both are discussed shortly.

Circuit-level proxies operate at the Session layer (layer 5) of the OSI model. They make decisions based on the protocol header and Session layer information. Because they do not do deep packet inspection (at layer 7 or the Application layer), they are considered application-independent and can be used for wide ranges of layer 7 protocol types.

A SOCKS firewall is an example of a circuit-level firewall. This requires a SOCKS client on the computers. Many vendors have integrated their software with SOCKS to make using this type of firewall easier.

Application-level proxies perform deep packet inspection. This type of firewall understands the details of the communication process at layer 7 for the application of interest. An application-level firewall maintains a different proxy function for each protocol. For example, for HTTP the proxy will be able to read and filter traffic based on specific HTTP commands. Operating at this layer requires each packet to be completely opened and closed, making this firewall the most impactful on performance.

Dynamic packet filtering rather than describing a different type of firewall describes functionality that a firewall might or might not possess, When internal computers attempt to establish a session with a remote computer, it places both a source and destination port number in the packet. For example, if the computer is making a request of a web server, because HTTP uses port 80, the destination will be port 80.

The source computer selects the source port at random from the numbers available above the well-known port numbers, or above 1023. Because predicting what that random number will be is impossible, creating a firewall rule that anticipates and allows traffic back through the firewall on that random port is impossible. A dynamic packet filtering firewall will keep track of that source port and dynamically add a rule to the list to allow return traffic to that port.

A kernel proxy firewall is an example of a *fifth-generation firewall*. It inspects the packet at every layer of the OSI model but does not introduce the performance hit that an Application layer firewall will because it does this at the kernel layer. It also follows the proxy model in that it stands between the two systems and creates connections on their behalf.

Architecture

Although the type of firewall speaks to the internal operation of the firewall, the architecture refers to the way in which the firewall or firewalls are deployed in the network to form a system of protection. This section looks at the various ways firewalls can be deployed and what the names of these various configurations are.

A bastion host might or might not be a firewall. The term actually refers to the position of any device. If it is exposed directly to the Internet or to any untrusted network, we would say it is a bastion host. Whether it is a firewall, a DNS server, or a web server, this means all standard hardening procedures become even more important for these exposed devices. Any unnecessary services should be stopped, all unneeded ports should be closed, and all security patches must be up to date. These procedures are referred to as *reducing the attack surface*.

A dual-homed firewall is one that has two network interfaces, one pointing to the internal network and another connected to the untrusted network. In many cases routing between these interfaces is turned off. The firewall software allows or denies traffic between the two interfaces based on the firewall rules configured by the administrator. The danger of relying on a single dual-homed firewall is that there is a single point of failure. If this device is compromised, the network is also. If it suffers a denial of service (DoS) attack, no traffic will pass. Neither is a good situation.

In some cases the firewall may be multihomed. One popular type is the three-legged firewall. In this configuration are three interfaces: one connected to the untrusted network, one to the internal network, and the last to a part of the network called a Demilitarized Zone (DMZ). A DMZ is a portion of the network where systems are placed that will be accessed regularly from the untrusted network. These might be web servers or an email server, for example. The firewall can then be configured to control the traffic that flows between the three networks, being somewhat careful with traffic destined for the DMZ and then treating traffic to the internal network with much more suspicion.

Although the firewalls discussed thus far typically connect directly to the untrusted network (at least one interface does), a screened host is a firewall that is between the final router and the internal network. When traffic comes into the router and is forwarded to the firewall, it will be inspected before going into the internal network.

Taking this concept a step further is a screened subnet. In this case, two firewalls are used, and traffic must be inspected at both firewalls to enter the internal network. It is called a screen subnet because there will be a subnet between the two firewalls that can act as a DMZ for resources from the outside world.

In the real world, these various approaches are mixed and matched to meet requirements, so you might find elements of all these architectural concepts being applied to a specific situation.

Virtualization

Today physical servers are increasingly being consolidated as virtual servers on the same physical box. Virtual networks using virtual switches even exist in the physical devices that host these virtual servers. These virtual network systems and their traffic can be segregated in all the same ways as in a physical network using subnets, VLANs, and of course, virtual firewalls. Virtual firewalls are software that has been specifically written to operate in the virtual environment. Increasingly, virtualization vendors such as VMware are making part of their code available to security vendors to create firewalls (and antivirus products) that integrate closely with the product.

Keep in mind that in any virtual environment each virtual server that is hosted on the physical server must be configured with its own security mechanisms. These mechanisms include antivirus and antimalware software and all the latest service packs and security updates for ALL the software hosted on the virtual machine. Also, remember that all the virtual servers share the resources of the physical device.

Proxy Server

Proxy servers can be appliances or they can be software that is installed on a server operating system. These servers act like a proxy firewall in that they create the web connection between systems on their behalf, but they can typically allow and disallow traffic on a more granular basis. For example, a proxy server might allow the Sales group to go to certain websites while not allowing the Data Entry group access to these same sites. The functionality extends beyond HTTP to other traffic types, such as FTP and others.

Proxy servers can provide an additional beneficial function called *web caching*. When a proxy server is configured to provide web caching, it saves a copy of all web pages that have been delivered to internal computers in a web cache. If any user requests the same page later, the proxy server has a local copy and need not spend the time and effort to retrieve it from the Internet. This greatly improves web performance for frequently requested pages.

PBX

A private branch exchange (PBX) is a private telephone switch that resides on the customer premises. It has a direct connection to the telecommunication provider's switch. It performs call routing within the internal phone system. This is how a company can have two "outside" lines but 50 internal phones. The call comes in on one of the two outside lines, and the PBX routes it to the proper extension. Sometimes the system converts analog to digital but not always.

The security considerations with these devices revolve around their default configurations. They typically are configured with default administrator passwords that should be changed, and they often contain backdoor connections that can be used by vendor support personnel to connect in and help with problems. These back doors are usually well known and should be disabled until they are needed.

Honeypot

Honeypots are systems that are configured to be attractive to hackers and lure them into spending time attacking them while information is gathered about the attack. In some cases entire networks called honeynets are attractively configured for this purpose. These types of approaches should only be undertaken by companies with the skill to properly deploy and monitor them.

Care should be taken that the honeypots and honeynets do not provide direct connections to any important systems. This prevents providing a jumping-off point to other areas of the network. The ultimate purpose of these systems is to divert attention from more valuable resources and to gather as much information about an attack as possible. A *tarpit* is a type of honeypot designed to provide a very slow connection to the hacker so that the attack can be analyzed.

Cloud Computing

Cloud computing is all the rage these days, and it comes in many forms. The basic idea of cloud computing is to make resources available in a web-based data center so the resources can be accessed from anywhere. When a company pays another company to host and manage this environment, we call it a public cloud solution. When companies host this environment themselves, we call it a private cloud solution.

There is trade-off when a decision must be made between the two architectures. The private solution provides the most control over the safety of your data but also requires the staff and the knowledge to deploy, manage, and secure the solution. A public cloud puts your data's safety in the hands of a third party, but that party is often more capable and knowledgeable about protecting data in this environment and managing the cloud environment.

When a public solution is selected, various levels of service can be purchased. Some of these levels include

- **Infrastructure as a service (IaaS)** involves the vendor providing the hardware platform or data center and the company installing and managing its own operating systems and application systems. The vendor simply provides access to the data center and maintains that access.

- **Platform as a service (PaaS)** involves the vendor providing the hardware platform or data center and the software running on the platform. This includes the operating systems and infrastructure software. The company is still involved in managing the system.
- **Software as a service (SaaS)** involves the vendor providing the entire solution. This includes the operating system, infrastructure software, and the application. It might provide you with an email system, for example, whereby the vendor hosts and manages everything for you.

Figure 3-28 shows the relationship of these services to one another.

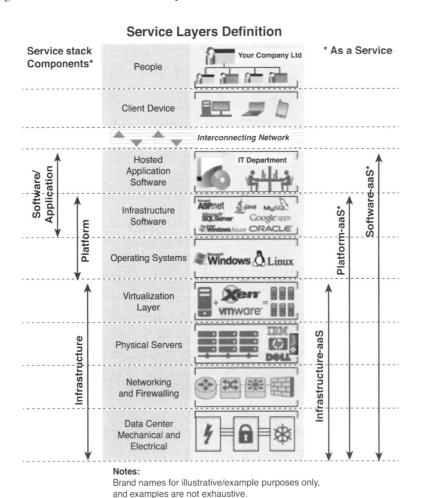

Figure 3-28 Cloud Computing

Endpoint Security

Endpoint security is a field of security that attempts to protect individual systems in a network by staying in constant contact with these individual systems from a central location. It typically works on a client server model in that each system will have software that communicates with the software on the central server. The functionality provided can vary.

In its simplest form, this incudes monitoring and automatic updating and configuration of security patches and personal firewall settings. In more advanced systems, it might include an examination of the system each time it connects to the network. This examination would ensure that all security patches are up to date and in even more advanced scenarios it could automatically provide remediation to the computer. In either case the computer would not be allowed to connect to the network until the problem is resolved, either manually or automatically.

Network Types

So far we have discussed network topologies and technologies, so now let's look at a third way to describe networks: *network type*. Network type refers to the scope of the network. Is it a LAN or a WAN? Is it a part of the internal network, or is it an extranet? This section discusses and differentiates all these network types.

LAN

First let's talk about what makes a local area network (LAN) local. Although classically we think of a LAN as a network located in one location, such as a single office, referring to a LAN as a group of systems that are connected with a *fast* connection is more correct. For purposes of this discussion, that is any connection over 10 Mbps.

That might not seem very fast to you, but it is when compared to a wide area connection (WAN). Even a T1 connection is only 1.544 Mbps. Using this as our yardstick, if a single campus network has a WAN connection between two buildings, then the two networks are considered two LANs rather than a single LAN. In most cases, however, networks in a single campus are typically NOT connected with a WAN connection, which is why usually you hear a LAN defined as a network in a single location.

Intranet

Within the boundaries of a single LAN, there can be subdivisions for security purposes. The LAN might be divided into an intranet and an extranet. The intranet is the internal network of the enterprise. It would be considered a trusted network and typically houses any sensitive information and systems and should receive maximum protection with firewalls and strong authentication mechanisms.

Extranet

An extranet is a network logically separate from the intranet where resources that will be accessed from the outside world are made available. Access might be granted to customers, business partners, and the public in general. All traffic between this network and the intranet should be closely monitored and securely controlled. Nothing of a sensitive nature should be placed in the extranet.

MAN

A Metropolitan Area Network (MAN) is a type of LAN that encompasses a large area such as the downtown of a city. In many cases it is a backbone that is provided for LANs to hook into. Three technologies are usually used in a MAN:

- Fiber Distributed Data Interface (FDDI)
- Synchronous Optical Networks (SONET)
- Metro Ethernet

FDDI and SONET rings, which both rely on fiber cabling, can span large areas, and businesses can connect to the rings using T1, fractional T1, or T3 connections. As you saw earlier, FDDI rings are a double ring with fault tolerance built in. SONET is also *self-healing*, meaning it has a double ring with a backup line if a line goes bad.

Metro Ethernet is the use of Ethernet technology over a wide area. It can be pure Ethernet or a combination of Ethernet and other technologies such as the ones mentioned in this section. Traditional Ethernet (the type used on a LAN) is less scalable. It is often combined with Multiple Protocol Label Switching (MPLS) technology, which is capable of carrying packets of various types, including Ethernet.

Less capable MANs often feed into MANs of higher capacity. Conceptually, you can divide the MAN architecture into three sections: customer, aggregation, and core layer. The customer section is the local loop that connects from the customer to the aggregation network, which then feeds into the high-speed core. The high-speed core connects the aggregation networks to one another.

WAN

Finally, WANs are used to connect LANs and MANs together. Many technologies can be used for these connections. They vary in capacity and cost, and access to these networks is purchased from a telecommunications company. The ultimate WAN is the Internet, the global backbone to which all MANs and LANs are connected. However, not all WANs connect to the Internet because some are private, dedicated links to which only the company paying for them has access. WAN technologies are discussed more fully in the next section.

WAN Technologies

Many different technologies have evolved for delivering WAN access to a LAN. They differ in capacity, availability, and, of course, cost. This section compares the various technologies.

T Lines

T carriers are dedicated lines to which the subscriber has private access and does not share with another customer. Customers can purchase an entire T1, or they can purchase a part of a T1 called a fractional T1. T1 lines consist of 24 channels, each capable of 64 Kbps. This means a T1 has a total capacity of 1.544 Mbps. The T1 is split into channels through a process called time division multiplexing (TDM).

The drawback of a T1 is that the customer is buying the full capacity of the number of channels purchased, and any capacity left unused is wasted. This inflexibility and the high cost have made this option less appealing that it was at one time. The cost is a function of not only the number of channels but the distance of the line as well.

T carriers also come in larger increments as well. Table 3-7 shows a summary of T carriers and their capacity.

Table 3-7 T Carriers

Carrier	# of T1s	# of Channels	Speed (Mbps)
Fractional	1/24	1	.064
T1	1	24	1.544
T3	28	672	44.736

E Lines

In Europe, a similar technology to T-carrier lines exists called E carriers. With this technology, 30 channels are bundled rather than 24. These technologies are not compatible, and the available sizes are a bit different. Table 3-8 shows some selected increments of E carriers.

Table 3-8 E Carriers

Signal	Rate
E0	64 Kbps
E1	2.048 Mbps
E3	8.448 Mbps

OC Lines (SONET)

Synchronous Optical Networks (SONET) use fiber-based links that operate over lines measured in optical carrier (OC) transmission rates. These lines are defined by an integer value of the basic unit of rate. The basic OC-1 rate is 55.84 Mbps, and all other rates are multiples of that. For example, an OC3 yields 155.52 Mbps. Table 3-9 shows some of these rates. Smaller increments such as OC-2 or OC-9 might be used by a company, whereas the larger pipes such as OC-3072 would be used by a service provider.

Table 3-9 Carrier Rates

Optical Carrier	Speed
OC-9	466.56 Mbps
OC-19	933.12 Mbps
OC-48	2.488 Gbps
OC-3072	160 Gbps

CSU/DSU

A discussion of WAN connections would not be complete without discussing a device that many customers connect to for their WAN connection. A Channel Service Unit/Data Service Unit (CSU/DSU) connects a LAN to a WAN. This device performs a translation of the information from a format that is acceptable on the LAN to one that can be transmitted over the WAN connection.

The CSU/DSU is considered a Data Communications Equipment (DCE) device, and it provides an interface for the router, which is considered a Data Terminal Equipment (DTE) device. The CSU/DSU will most likely be owned by the Telco, but not always, and in some cases this functionality might be built into the interface of the router, making a separate device unnecessary.

Circuit-Switching Versus Packet-Switching

On the topic of WAN connections, discussing the types of networks that these connections might pass through is also helpful. Some are circuit-switched, whereas others are packet-switched. Circuit-switching networks (such as the telephone) establish a set path to the destination and only use that path for the entire communication. It results in a predictable operation with fixed delays. These networks usually carry voice-oriented traffic.

Packet-switching networks (such as the Internet or a LAN) establish an optimal *path-per-packet*. This means each packet might go a different route to get to the destination. The traffic on these networks experiences performance bursts and the amount of delay can vary widely. These types of networks usually carry data-oriented traffic.

Frame Relay

Frame relay is a layer 2 protocol used for WAN connections. Therefore, when Ethernet traffic must traverse a frame relay link, the layer 2 header of the packet will be completely recreated to conform to frame relay. When the frame relay frame arrives at the destination, a new Ethernet layer 2 header will be placed on the packet for that portion of the network.

When frame relay connections are provisioned, the customer pays for a minimum amount of bandwidth called the Committed Information Rate (CIR). That will be the floor of performance. However, because frame relay is a packet-switched network using frame relay switches, the actual performance will vary based on conditions. Customers are sharing the network rather than having a dedicated line, such as a T1 or Integrated Services Digital Network (ISDN) line. So in many cases the actual performance will exceed the CIR.

ATM

Asynchronous Transfer Mode (ATM) is a cell-switching technology. It transfers fixed size cells of 53 bytes rather than packets, and after a path is established, it uses the same path for the entire communication. The use of a fixed path makes performance more predictable, making it a good option for voice and video, which need such predictability. Where IP networks depend on the source and destination devices to ensure data is properly transmitted, this responsibility falls on the shoulders of the devices between the two in the ATM world.

ATM is used mostly by carriers and service providers for their backbones, but some companies have implemented their own ATM backbones and ATM switches. This allows them to make an ATM connection to the carrier, which can save money over connection with a T link because the ATM connection cost will be based on usage, unlike the fixed cost of the T1.

X.25

X.25 is somewhat like frame relay in that traffic moves through a packet-switching network. It charges by bandwidth used. The data is divided into 128-byte High-Level Data Link Control (HDLC) frames. It is, however, an older technology created in a time when noisy transmission lines were a big concern. Therefore, it has many error-checking mechanisms built in that make it very inefficient.

Switched Multimegabit Data Service

Switched Multimegabit Data Service (SMDS) is a connectionless, packet-switched technology that communicates across an established public network. It has been largely repacked with other WAN technologies. It can provide LAN-like performance to a WAN. It's generally delivered over a SONET ring with a maximum effective service radius of around 30 miles.

Point-to-Point Protocol

Point-to-Point-Protocol (PPP) is a layer 2 protocol that performs framing and encapsulation of data across point-to-point connections. These are connections to the ISP where only the customer device and the ISP device reside on either end. It can encapsulate a number of different LAN protocols such as TCP/IP, IPX/SPX, and so on. It does this by using a Network Core Protocol (NCP) for each of the LAN protocols in use.

Along with the use of multiple NCPs, it uses a single Link Control Protocol (LCP) to establish the connection. PPP provides the ability to authenticate the connection between the devices using either Password Authentication Protocol (PAP) or Challenge Handshake Authentication Protocol (CHAP). Whereas PAP transmits the credentials in clear text, CHAP does NOT send the credentials across the line and is much safer.

High-Speed Serial Interface

High-Speed Serial Interface (HSSI) is one of the many physical implementations of a serial interface. Because these interfaces exist on devices, they are considered to operate at layer 1 of the OSI model. The Physical layer is the layer that is concerned with the signaling of the message and the interface between the sender or receiver and the medium. Examples of other serial interface are

- X.25
- V.35
- X.21

The HSSI interface is found on both routers and multiplexers and provides a connection to services such as frame relay and ATM. It operates at speeds up to 52 Mbps.

PSTN (POTS, PBX)

Probably the least attractive WAN connection available, at least from a performance standpoint, is the Public Switched Telephone Network (PSTN). Also referred to as the Plain Old Telephone Service (POTS), this is the circuit-switched network that has been used for analog phone service for years and is now mostly a digital operation.

This network can be utilized using modems for an analog line or with ISDN for digital phone lines. Both these options are discussed in more detail in the section "Remote Connection Technologies" because that is their main use. In some cases these connections might be used between offices but due to the poor performance, typically only as a backup solution in case a more capable option fails. These connections must be established each time they are used as opposed to "always on" solutions, such as cable or DSL.

PBX devices were discussed in the earlier section "Network Devices."

VoIP

Although voice over the PSTN is circuit-switched, voice can also be encapsulated in packets and sent across packet-switching networks. When this is done over an IP network, it is called Voice over IP (VoIP). Where circuit-switching networks use the Signaling System 7 (SS7) protocol to set up, control, and disconnect a call, VoIP uses Session Initiation Protocol (SIP) to break up the call sessions. In VoIP implementations, QoS is implemented to ensure that certain traffic (especially voice) is given preferential treatment over the network.

SIP is an application layer protocol that can operate over either TCP or UDP. Addressing is in terms of IP addresses, and the voice traffic uses the same network used for regular data. Because latency is always possible on these networks, protocols have been implemented to reduce the impact as this type of traffic is much more affected by delay. Applications such as voice and video need to have protocols and devices that can provide an isochronous network. Isochronous networks guarantee continuous bandwidth without interruption. It doesn't use an internal clock source or start and stop bits. All bits are of equal importance and are anticipated to occur at regular intervals.

VoIP can be secured by taking the following measures:

- Create a separate VLAN or subnet for the IP phones and prevent access to this VLAN by PCs.
- Deploy a VoIP-aware firewall at the perimeter.
- Ensure that all passwords related to VoIP are strong.
- Secure the network layer with IPsec.

Remote Connection Technologies

In many cases connections must be made to the main network from outside the network. The reasons for these connections are varied. In some cases it is for the purpose of allowing telecommuters to work on the network as if sitting in the office with all network resources available to them. In another instance, it is for the purposes of managing network devices, whereas in others it could be to provide connections between small offices and the main office.

In this section, some of these connection types are discussed along with some of the security measures that go hand in hand with them. These measures include both encryption mechanisms and authentication schemes.

Dial-up

A dial-up connection is one that uses the PSTN. If it is initiated over an analog phone line, it requires a modem that converts the digital data to analog on the sending end with a modem on the receiving end converting it back to digital. These lines operate up to 56 Kbps.

Dial-up connections can use either Serial Line Internet Protocol (SLIP) or PPP at layer 2. SLIP is an older protocol that has been made obsolete by PPP. PPP provides authentication and multilink capability. The caller is authenticated by the remote access server. This authentication process can be centralized by using either a TACACS+ or RADIUS server. These servers are discussed more fully later in this section.

Some basic security measures that should be in place when using dial-up are

- Have the remote access server call back the initiating caller at a preset number. Do NOT allow call forwarding because it can be used to thwart this security measure.
- Modems should be set to answer after a set number of rings to thwart war dialers (more on them later).

- Consolidate the modems in one place for physical security, and disable modems not in use.
- Use the strongest possible authentication mechanisms.

If the connection is done over a digital line, it can use ISDN. It also must be dialed up to make the connection but offers much more capability and the entire process is all digital. ISDN is discussed next.

ISDN

Integrated Services Digital Network (ISDN) is sometimes referred to as digital dial-up. The really big difference between ISDN and analog dial-up is the performance. ISDN can be provisioned in two ways:

- **Basic rate (BRI):** Provides three channels—two B channels that provide 64 Kbps each and a D channel that is 16 Kbps for a total of 144 Kbps.
- **Primary Rate (PRI):** Can provide up to 23 B channels and a D channel for a total of 1.544 Mbps.

Although ISDN is typically now only used as a backup connection solution and many consider ISDN to be a dedicated connection and thus safe, attacks can be mounted against ISDN connections, including

- **Physical attacks:** These are attacks by persons who are able to physically get to network equipment. With regard to ISDN, shared telecom closets can provide an AP. Physical security measures to follow are described in Chapter 11, "Physical (Environmental) Security."
- **Router attacks:** If a router can be convinced to accept an ISDN call from a rogue router, it might allow an attacker access to the network. Routers should be configured to authenticate with one another before accepting call requests.

DSL

Digital Subscribers Line (DSL) is a very popular option that provides a high-speed connection from a home or small office to the ISP. Although it uses the existing phone lines, it is an always-on connection. By using different frequencies than the voice transmissions over the same copper lines, talking on the phone and using the data network (Internet) at the same time is possible.

It also is many times faster than ISDN or dial-up. It comes in several variants, some of which offer the same speed uploading and downloading (which is called symmetric service) while most offer better download performance than upload performance (called asymmetric service). Some possible versions are:

- **Symmetric DSL (SDSL)** usually provides from 192 Kbps to 1.1 Gbps in both directions. It is usually used by businesses.
- **Asymmetric DSL (ADSL)** usually provides uploads from 128 Kbps–384 Kbps and downloads up to 768 Kbps. It is usually used in homes.
- **High Bit-Rate DSL (HDSL)** provides T1 speeds.
- **Very High Bit-Rate DSL (VDSL)** is capable of supporting High Definition TV (HDTV) and VoIP.

Unlike cable connections, DSL connections are dedicated links, but there are still security issues to consider. The PCs that are used to access the DSL line should be set with the following options in Internet Options:

- Check for publisher's certificate revocation.
- Enable memory protection to help mitigate online attacks.
- Enable SmartScreen Filter.
- Use SSL 3.0.
- Use TLS 1.0.
- Warn about certificate address mismatch.
- Warn if POST submittal is redirected to a zone that does not permit posts.

Another issue with DSL is the fact it is always connected. This means that the PC typically keeps the same IP address. A static IP address provides a fixed target for the attacker. Therefore, taking measures such as NAT helps to hide the true IP address of the PC to the outside world.

Cable

Getting connections to the ISP using the same cabling system used to deliver cable TV is also possible. Cable modems can provide up to 50 Mbps over the coaxial cabling used for cable TV. Cable modems conform to the Data-Over-Cable Service Interface Specification (DOCSIS) standard.

A security and performance concern with cable modems is that each customer is on a shared line with neighbors. This means performance varies with the time of day and congestion and the data is traveling over a shared medium. For this reason, many cable companies now encrypt these transmissions.

VPN

Virtual Private Network (VPN) connections are those that use an untrusted carrier network but provide protection of the information through strong authentication protocols and encryption mechanisms. Although we typically use the most untrusted network, the Internet as the classic example, and most VPNs do travel through the Internet, they can be used with interior networks as well whenever traffic needs to be protected from prying eyes.

When discussing VPN connections, many new to the subject become confused by the number and type of protocols involved. Let's break down what protocols are required, which are optional, and how they all play together. Recall how the process of encapsulation works. Earlier we discussed this concept when we talked of packet creation, and in that context we applied it to how one layer of the OSI model "wraps around" or encapsulates the other data already created at the other layers.

In VPN operations, entire protocols wrap around other protocols (a process called encapsulation). They include

- A LAN protocol (required)
- A remote access or line protocol (required)
- An authentication protocol (optional)
- An encryption protocol (optional)

Let's start with the original packet before it is sent across the VPN. This is a LAN packet, probably a TCP/IP packet. The change that will be made to this packet is it will be wrapped in a line or remote access protocol. This protocol's only job is to carry the TCP/IP packet still fully intact across the line and then, just like a ferry boat drops a car at the other side of a river, it de-encapsulates the original packet and delivers it to the destination LAN unchanged.

Several of these remote access or line protocols are available. Among them are

- Point-to-Point-Tunneling Protocol (PPTP)
- Layer 2 Tunneling Protocol (L2TP)

PPTP is a Microsoft protocol based on PPP. It uses built-in Microsoft Point-to-Point Encryption (MPPE) and can use a number of authentication methods, including CHAP, MS-CHAP, and EAP-TLS. One shortcoming of PPTP is that it only works on IP-based networks. If a WAN connection is in use that is not IP-based, L2TP must be used.

MS-CHAP comes in two versions. Both versions can be susceptible to password attacks. Version 1 is inherently insecure and should be avoided. Version 2 is much safer but can still suffer brute-force attacks on the password, although such attacks usually take up to 23 hours to crack the password. Moreover, the MPPE used with MS-CHAP can suffer attacks on the RC4 algorithm on which it is based. Although PPTP is a better solution, it also has been shown to have known vulnerabilities related to the PPP authentication protocols used and is no longer recommended by Microsoft.

Although EAP-TLS is superior to both MS-CHAP and PPTP, its deployment requires a public key infrastructure (PKI), which is often not within the technical capabilities of the network team or the resources to maintain it are not available.

L2TP is a newer protocol that operates at layer 2 of the OSI model. It can use various authentication mechanisms such as PPTP can but does not provide any encryption. It is typically used with IPsec, a very strong encryption mechanism.

With PPTP, the encryption is included, and the only remaining choice to be made is the authentication protocol. These authentication protocols are discussed later in the section "Remote Authentication Protocols."

With L2TP, both encryption and authentication protocols, if desired, must be added. IPsec can provide encryption, data integrity, and system-based authentication, which makes it a flexible and capable option. By implementing certain parts of the IPsec suite, these features can be used or not.

IPsec is actually a suite of protocols in the same way that TCP/IP is. It includes the following components:

- **Authentication Header (AH):** Provides data integrity, data origin authentication, and protection from replay attacks.

- **Encapsulating Security Payload (ESP):** Provides all that AH does as well as data confidentiality.

- **Internet Security Association and Key Management Protocol (ISAKMP):** Handles the creation of a security association for the session and the exchange of keys.

- **Internet Key Exchange (IKE), also sometimes referred to as IPsec Key Exchange:** Provides the authentication material used to create the keys exchanged by ISAKMP during peer authentication. This was proposed to be performed by a protocol called Oakley that relied on the Diffie-Hellman algorithm, but Oakley has been superseded by IKE.

You can find more information on IPsec in Chapter 6, "Cryptography."

IPsec is a framework, which means it does not specify many of the components used with it. These components must be identified in the configuration, and they must match for the two ends to successfully create the required security association that must be in place before any data is transferred. The selections that must be made are:

- The encryption algorithm (encrypts the data)
- The hashing algorithm (ensures the data has not been altered and verifies its origin)
- The mode (tunnel or transport)
- The protocol (AH, ESP, or both)

All these settings must match on both ends of the connection. It is not possible for the systems to select these on the fly. They must be preconfigured correctly to match.

When the tunnel is configured in tunnel mode, the tunnel exists only between the two gateways but all traffic that passes through the tunnel is protected. This is normally used to protect all traffic between two offices. The security association (SA) is between the gateways between the offices. This is the type of connection that would be called a site-to-site VPN.

The SA between the two endpoints is made up of the security parameter index (SPI) and the AH/ESP combination. The SPI, a value contained in each IPsec header, help the devices maintain the relationship between each SA (of which there could be several happening at once) and the security parameters (also called the transform set) used for each SA.

Each session has a unique session value which help to prevent:

- Reverse engineering
- Content modification
- Factoring attacks (the attacker tries all the combinations of numbers that can be used with the algorithm to decrypt ciphertext)

With respect to authenticating the connection, the keys can be pre-shared or derived from a PKI. A PKI creates a public/private key pair that is associated with individual users and computers that use a certificate. These key pairs are used in the place of pre-shared keys in that case. Certificates can also be used that are not derived from a PKI.

In transport mode, the SA is either between two end stations or an end station and a gateway or remote access server. In this mode, the tunnel extends from computer to computer or from computer to gateway. This is the type of connection that would be for a remote access VPN. This is but one application of IPsec. It is also used in other applications such as a General Packet Radio Service (GPRS), a VPN solution for devices using a 2G cell phone network.

When the communication is from gateway to gateway or host to gateway, either transport or tunnel mode can be used. If the communication is computer to computer, the tunnel must be in transport mode. If the tunnel is configured in transport mode from gateway to host, the gateway must operate as a host.

The most effective attack against IPsec VPN is a man-in-the-middle attack. In this attack, the attacker proceeds through the security negotiation phase until the key negotiation when the victim reveals its identity. In a well-implemented system, the attacker will fail when the attacker cannot likewise prove his identity.

RADIUS and TACACS

When users are making connections to the network through a variety of mechanisms, they should be authenticated first. These users could be accessing the network through

- Dial-up remote access servers
- VPN access servers
- Wireless Access Points
- Security-enabled switches

At one time each of these access devices would perform the authentication process locally on the device. The administrators would need to ensure that all remote access policies and settings were consistent across them all. When a password required changing, it had to be done on all devices.

Remote Authentication Dial In User Service (RADIUS) and Terminal Access Controller Access-Control System Plus (TACACS+) are networking protocols that provide centralized authentication and authorization. These services can be run at a central location, and all the access devices (AP, remote access, VPN, and so on) can be made clients of the server. Whenever authentication occurs, the TACACS+ or RADIUS server performs the authentication and authorization. This provides one location to manage the remote access policies and passwords for the network. Another advantage of using these systems is that the audit and access information (logs) are not kept on the access server.

TACACS and TACACS+ are Cisco proprietary services that operate in Cisco devices, whereas RADIUS is a standard defined in RFC 2138. Cisco has implemented several versions of TACACS over time. It went from TACACS to XTACACS to the latest version, TACACS+. The latest version provides authentication, accounting, and authorization, which is why it is sometimes referred to as an AAA service. TACACS+ employs tokens for two-factor, dynamic password authentication. It also allows users to change their passwords.

RADIUS is designed to provide a framework that includes three components. The *supplicant* is the device seeking authentication. The authenticator is the device to which they are attempting to connect (AP, switch, remote access server), and the RADIUS server is the authentication server. With regard to RADIUS, the device seeking entry is *not* the RADIUS client. The authenticating server is the RADIUS server, and the authenticator (AP, switch, remote access server) is the RADIUS client.

In some cases a RADIUS server can be the client of another RADIUS server. In that case the RADIUS server acts as a proxy client for its RADIUS clients.

Diameter is another authentication protocol based on RADIUS and is *not* compatible with RADIUS. Diameter has a much larger set of attribute-value pairs (AVPs) than RADIUS, allowing more functionality and services to communicate, but has not been widely adopted.

Remote Authentication Protocols

Earlier we said that one of the protocol choices that must be made when provisioning a remote access solution is the authentication protocol. This section discusses some of the most important of those protocols:

- **Password Authentication Protocol (PAP)** provides authentication but the credentials are sent in clear text and can be read with a sniffer.

- **Challenge Handshake Authentication Protocol (CHAP)** solves the cleartext problem by operating without sending the credentials across the link. The server sends the client a set of random texts called a challenge. The client encrypts the text with the password and sends it back. The server then decrypts it with the same password and compares the result with what was sent originally. If the results match, then the server can be assured that the user or system possesses the correct password without ever needing to send it across the untrusted network.

- **Extensible Authentication Protocol (EAP)** is not a single protocol but a framework for port-based access control that uses the same three components that are used in RADIUS. A wide variety of these implementations can use all sorts of authentication mechanisms, including certificates, a PKI, or even simple passwords.

Telnet

Telnet is a remote access protocol used to connect to a device for the purpose of executing commands on the device. It can be used to access servers, routers, switches, and many other devices for the purpose of managing them. Telnet is not considered a secure remote management protocol because like another protocol used with UNIX-based systems, rlogin, it transmits all information including the authentication process in clear text. Alternatives such as SSH have been adopted to perform the same function while providing encryption. Telnet and rlogin connections are connection-oriented so they use TCP as the transport protocol.

TLS/SSL

Transport Layer Security/Secure Sockets Layer (TLS/SSL) is another option for creating secure connections to servers. It works at the Application layer of the OSI model. It is used mainly to protect HTTP traffic or web servers. Its functionality is embedded in most browsers, and its use typically requires no action on the part of the user. It is widely used to secure Internet transactions. It can be implemented in two ways:

- **SSL portal VPN**, in which a user has a single SSL connection used to access multiple services on the web server. After being authenticated, the user is provided a page that acts as a portal to other services.

- **SSL tunnel VPN** uses an SSL tunnel to access services on a server that is not a web server. It uses custom programming to provide access to non-web services through a web browser.

TLS and SSL are very similar but not the same. TLS 1.0 is based on the SSL 3.0 specification but they are not operationally compatible. Both implement confidentiality, authentication, and integrity above the Transport layer. The server is always authenticated and optionally the client also can be. SSL v2 must be used for client-side authentication. When configuring SSL, a session key length must be designated. The two options are 40 bit and 128 bit. It prevents man-in-the middle attacks by using self-signed certificates to authenticate the server public key.

Multimedia Collaboration

In today's modern enterprises, the sharing of multimedia during both web presentations or meetings and instant messaging programs has exploded. Note that not all collaboration tools and products are created equally in regard to the security. Many were built with an emphasis on ease of use rather than security. This is a key issue to consider when choosing a product. For both the presenter and the recipient, the following security requirements should be met:

- Data confidentiality
- Origin authentication
- Identity confidentiality
- Data integrity
- Non-repudiation of receipt
- Repudiation of transmission
- Non-repudiation of transmission
- Availability to present
- Availability to receive

Wireless Networks

Perhaps the area of the network that keeps more administrators awake at night is the wireless portion of the network. In the early days of 802.11 WLAN deployments, many chose to simply not implement wireless for fear of the security holes it creates. However, it became apparent that not only did users demand this, but in some cases users were bringing home APs to work and hooking them up and suddenly there was a wireless network!

Today WLAN security has evolved to the point that security is no longer a valid reason to avoid wireless. This section offers a look at the protocols used in wireless, the methods used to convert the data into radio waves, the various topologies in which WLANs can be deployed, and security measures that should be taken.

FHSS, DSSS, OFDM, FDMA, TDMA, CDMA, OFDMA, and GSM

When data leaves an Ethernet network interface controller (NIC) and is sent out on the network, the ones and zeros that constitute the data are represented with different electric voltages. In wireless, this information must be represented in radio waves. A number of different methods exist for performing this operation, which is called modulation. You should also understand some additional terms to talk intelligently about wireless. This section defines a number of terms to provide a background for the discussion found in the balance of this section. The first section covers techniques used in WLAN and the second covers techniques used in cellular networking.

802.11 Techniques

- **Frequency Hopping Spread Spectrum (FHSS)** is one of two technologies (along with DSSS) that were a part of the original 802.11 standard. It is unique in that it changes frequencies or channels every few seconds in a set pattern that both transmitter and receiver know. This is not a security measure because the patterns are well known, although it does make capturing the traffic difficult. It helps avoid inference by only occasionally using a frequency where the inference is present. Later amendments to the 802.11 standard did not include this technology. It can attain up to 2 Mbps.

- **Direct Sequence Spread Spectrum (DSSS)** is one of two technologies (along with FHSS) that were a part of the original 802.11 standard. This is the modulation technique used in 802.11b. The modulation technique used in wireless has a huge impact on throughput. In the case of DSSS, it spreads the transmission across the spectrum at the same time as opposed to hopping from one to another as in FHSS. This allows it to attain up to 11 Mbps.

- **Orthogonal Frequency Division Multiplexing (OFDM)** is a more advanced technique of modulation where a large number of closely spaced orthogonal sub-carrier signals are used to carry the data on several parallel data streams. It is used in 802.11a and 802.11g. It makes speed up to 54 Mbps possible.

Cellular or Mobile Wireless Techniques

- **Frequency Division Multiple Access (FDMA)** is one of the modulation techniques used in cellular wireless networks. It divides the frequency range into bands and assigns a band to each subscriber. This was used in 1G cellular networks.

- **Time Division Multiple Access (TDMA)** increases the speed over FDMA by dividing the channels into time slots and assigning slots to calls. This also helps to prevent eavesdropping in calls.

- **Code Division Multiple Access (CDMA)** assigns a unique code to each call or transmission and spreads the data across the spectrum, allowing a call to make use of all frequencies.

- **Orthogonal Frequency Division Multiple Access (OFDMA)** takes FDMA a step further by subdividing the frequencies into subchannels. This is the technique required by 4G devices.

- **Global System Mobile (GSM)** is a type of cellphone that contains a Subscriber Identity Module (SIM) chip. These chips contain all the information about the subscriber and must be present in the phone for it to function. One of the dangers with these phones is cell *phone cloning*, a process where copies of the SIM chip are made, allowing another user to make calls as the original user. Secret key cryptography is used (using a common secret key) when authentication is performed between the phone and the network.

WLAN Structure

Before we can discuss 802.11 wireless, which has come to be known as WLAN, we need to discuss the components and the structure of a WLAN. This section covers basic terms and concepts.

Access Point

An access point (AP) is a wireless transmitter and receiver that hooks into the wired portion of the network and provides an access point to this network for wireless devices. In some cases they are simply wireless switches, and in other cases they are also routers. Early APs were devices with all the functionality built into each device, but increasingly these "fat" or intelligent APs are being replaced with "thin" APs that are really only antennas that hook back into a central system called a controller.

SSID

The service set identifier (SSID) is a name or value assigned to identify the WLAN from other WLANs. The SSID can either be broadcast by the AP as is done in a free hot spot or it can be hidden. When it is hidden, a wireless station will have to be configured with a profile that includes the SSID to connect. Although some view hiding the SSID as a security measure, it is not an effective measure because hiding the SSID only removes one type of frame, the beacon frame, while it still exists in other frame types and can be easily learned by sniffing the wireless network.

Infrastructure Mode Versus Ad Hoc Mode

In most cases a WLAN includes at least one AP. When an AP is present, the WLAN is operating in *Infrastructure* mode. In this mode, all transmissions between stations go through the AP, and no direct communication between stations occurs. In *Ad Hoc* mode, there is no AP, and the stations communicate directly with one another.

WLAN Standards

The original 802.11 wireless standard has been amended a number of times to add features and functionality. This section discusses these amendments, which are sometimes referred to as standards although they really are amendments to the original standard. The original 802.11 standard specified the use of either FHSS or DSSS and supported operations in the 2.4 GHz frequency range at speeds of 1 Mbps and 2 Mbps.

802.11a

The first amendment to the standard was 802.11a. This standard called for the use of OFDM. Because that would require hardware upgrades to existing equipment, this standard saw limited adoption for some time. It operates in a different frequency than 802.11 (5 GHz) and by using OFDM supports speeds up to 54 Mbps.

802.11b

The 802.11b amendment dropped support for FHSS and enabled an increase of speed to 11 Mbps. It was widely adopted because it both operates in the same frequency as 802.11 and is backward compatible with it and can coexist in the same WLAN.

802.11f

The 802.11f amendment addressed problems introduced when wireless clients roam from one AP to another. This causes the station to need to reauthenticate with the new AP, which in some cases introduced a delay that would break the application connection. This amendment improves the sharing of authentication information between APs.

802.11g

The 802.11g amendment added support for OFDM, which made it capable of 54 Mbps. This also operates in the 2.4 GHz frequency so it is backward compatible with both 802.11 and 802.11b. While just as fast as 802.11a, one reason many switched to 802.11a is that the 5 GHz band is much less crowded than the 2.4 GHz band.

802.11n

The 802.11n standard uses several newer concepts to achieve up to 650 Mbps. It does these using channels that are 40 MHz wide, using multiple antennas that allow for up to four spatial streams at a time (a feature called Multiple Input Multiple Output or MIMO). It can be used in both the 2.4 GHz and 5.0 GHz bands but performs best in a pure 5.0 GHz network because in that case it does not need to implement mechanisms that allow it to coexist with 802.11b and 802.11g devices. These mechanisms slow the performance.

Bluetooth

Bluetooth is a wireless technology that is used to create Personal Area Networks (PANs). These are simply short-range connections that are between devices and peripherals, such as headphones. It operates in the 2.4 GHz frequency at speeds of 1 Mbps to 3 Mbps at a distance of up to 10 meters.

Several attacks can take advantage of Bluetooth technology. Bluejacking is when an unsolicited message is sent to a Bluetooth-enabled device often for the purpose of adding a business card to the victim's contact list. This can be prevented by placing the device in non-discoverable mode.

Bluesnarfing is the unauthorized access to a device using the Bluetooth connection. In this case the attacker is trying to access information on the device rather than send messages to the device.

Infrared

Finally, infrared is a short-distance wireless process that uses light rather than radio waves, in this case infrared light. It is used for short connections between devices that both have an infrared port. It operates up to 5 meters at speeds up to 4 Mbps and requires a direct line of sight between the devices. There is one infrared mode or protocol that can introduce security issues. The IrTran-P (image transfer) protocol is used in digital cameras and other digital image capture devices. All incoming files sent over IrTran-P are automatically accepted. Because incoming files might contain harmful programs, users should ensure that the files originate from a trustworthy source.

WLAN Security

To safely implement 802.11 wireless technologies, you must understand all the methods used to secure a WLAN. In this section, the most important measures are discussed including some measures that, although they are often referred to as security measures, provide no real security whatsoever.

WEP

Wired Equivalent Privacy (WEP) was the first security measure used with 802.11. It was specified as the algorithm in the original specification. It can be used to both authenticate a device and encrypt the information between the AP and the device. The problem with WEP is that it implements the RC4 encryption algorithm in a way that allows a hacker to crack the encryption. It also was found that the mechanism designed to guarantee the integrity of data (that the data has not changed) was inadequate and that it was possible for the data to be changed and for this fact to go undetected.

WEP is implemented with a secret key or password that is configured on the AP, and any station will need that password to connect. Above and beyond the problem with the implementation of the RC4 algorithm, it is never good security for all devices to share the same password in this way.

WPA

To address the widespread concern with the inadequacy of WEP, the Wi-Fi Alliance, a group of manufacturers that promotes interoperability, created an alternative mechanism called Wi-Fi Protected Access (WPA) that is designed to improve on WEP. There are four types of WPA but first let's talk about how the original version improves over WEP.

First, WPA uses the Temporal Key Integrity Protocol (TKIP) for encryption, which generates a new key for each packet. Second, the integrity check used with WEP is able to detect any changes to the data. WPA uses a message integrity check algorithm called Michael to verify the integrity of the packets. There are two versions of WPA (covered in the section "Personal Versus Enterprise").

Some legacy devices might only support WPA. You should always check with a device's manufacturer to find out whether a security patch has been released that allows for WPA2 support.

WPA2

WPA2 is an improvement over WPA. WPA2 uses Counter Cipher Mode with Block Chaining Message Authentication Code Protocol (CCMP) based on Advanced Encryption Standard (AES), rather than TKIP. AES is a much stronger method and is required for Federal Information Processing Standards (FIPS)-compliant transmissions. There are also two versions of WPA2 (covered in the next section).

Personal Versus Enterprise

Both WPA and WPA2 come in Enterprise and Personal versions. The Enterprise versions require the use of an authentication server, typically a RADIUS server. The Personal versions do not and use passwords configured on the AP and the stations. Table 3-10 provides a quick overview of WPA and WPA2.

Table 3-10 WPA and WPA2

Variant	Access Control	Encryption	Integrity
WPA Personal	Preshared key	TKIP	Michael
WPA Enterprise	802.1X (RADIUS)	TKIP	Michael
WPA2 Personal	Preshared key	CCMP, AES	CCMP
WPA2 Enterprise	802.1X (RADIUS)	CCMP, AES	CCMP

SSID Broadcast

Issues surrounding the SSID broadcast were covered in the section "WLAN Structure" earlier in this chapter.

MAC Filter

Another commonly discussed security measure that can be taken is to create a list of allowed MAC addresses on the AP. When this is done, only the devices with MAC addresses on the list can make a connection to the AP. Although on the surface, this might seem like a good security measure, in fact a hacker can easily use a sniffer to learn the MAC addresses of devices that have successfully authenticated. Then by changing the MAC address on his device to one that is on the list he can gain entry.

MAC filters can also be configured to deny access to certain devices. The limiting factor in this method is that only the devices with the denied MAC addresses are specifically denied access. All other connections will be allowed.

Satellites

Satellites can be used to provide TV service and have for some time but now they can also be used to deliver Internet access to homes and businesses. The connection is two-way rather than one-way as is done with TV service. This is typically done using microwave technology. In most cases, the downloads come from the satellite signals, whereas the uploads occur through a ground line. Microwave technology can also be used for *terrestrial transmission*, which means ground station to ground station rather than satellite to ground. Satellite connections are very slow but are useful in remote locations where no other solution is available.

Network Threats

Before you can address network security threats, you must be aware of them, understand how they work, and know the measures to take to prevent the attacks from succeeding. This section covers a wide variety of attack types along with measures that should be taken to prevent them from occurring.

Cabling

Although it's true that a cabled network is easier to secure from eavesdropping than a wireless network, you must still be aware of some security issues. You should also understand some general behaviors of cabling that affect performance and ultimately can affect availability. As you might recall, maintaining availability to the network is also one of the goals of CIA, which is explained in Chapter 2, "Access Control." Therefore, performance characteristics of cabling that can impact availability are also discussed.

Noise

Noise is a term used to cover several types of interference than can be introduced to the cable that causes problems. This can be from large electrical motors, other computers, lighting, and other sources. This noise combines with the data signals (packets) on the line and distorts the signal. When even a single bit in a transmission is misread (read as a 1 when it should be a 0 or vice versa), nonsense data is received and retransmissions must occur. Retransmissions lead to lower throughput and in some cases no throughput whatsoever.

In any case where this becomes a problem, the simplest way to mitigate the problem is use shielded cabling. In cases where the noise is still present, locating the specific source and taking measures to remove it (or least the interference it is generating) from the environment might be necessary.

Attenuation

Attenuation is the weakening of the signal as it travels down the cable and meets resistance. In the discussion on cabling earlier in this chapter, you learned that all cables have a recommended maximum length. When you use a cable that is longer than its recommended length, attenuation weakens the signal to the point it cannot be read correctly, resulting in the same problem that is the end result of noise. The data must be sent again lowering throughput.

The solution to this problem is in design. Follow the length recommendations listed in the section on cables earlier in this chapter with any type of cabling. This includes coaxial, twisted pair, and fiberoptic. All types have maximum lengths that should not be exceeded without risking attenuation.

Crosstalk

Crosstalk is a behavior that can occur whenever individual wires within a cable are run parallel to one another. Crosstalk occurs when the signals from the two wires (or more) interfere with one another and distort the transmission. Cables such as twisted-pair cables would suffer from this were the cables not twisted as they are. The twisting prevents the crosstalk from occurring.

Eavesdropping

Although cabling is a bounded media and much easier to secure than wireless, eavesdropping can still occur. All cabling that depends on electrical voltages, such as coaxial and twisted pair, can be tapped or monitored with the right equipment. The least susceptible to eavesdropping (although not completely immune) is fiberoptic cabling because it doesn't use electrical voltages, but rather light waves. In any situation where eavesdropping is a concern, using fiberoptic cabling can be a measure that will at least drastically raise the difficulty of eavesdropping. The real solution is ensuring physical security of the cabling. The cable runs should not be out in the open and available.

ICMP Attacks

Earlier in this chapter you learned about Internet Control Message Protocol (ICMP), one of the protocols in the TCP/IP suite. This protocol is used by devices to send error messages to sending devices when transmission problems occur and is also used when either the ping command or the traceroute command is used for troubleshooting. Like many tools and utilities that were created for good purposes, this protocol can also be used by attackers who take advantage of its functionality.

This section covers ICMP-based attacks. One of the ways to prevent ICMP-based attacks is disallow its use by blocking the protocol number for ICMP, which is 1. Many firewall products also have the ability to only block certain types of ICMP messages as opposed to prohibiting its use entirely. Some of these problematic ICMP message types are discussed in this section as well.

Ping of Death

The Ping of Death is an attack that takes advantage of the normal behavior of devices that receive oversized ICMP packets. ICMP packets are normally a predictable 65,536 bytes in length. Hackers have learned how to insert additional data into

ICMP packets. The Ping of Death attack sends several of these oversized packets, which can cause the victim system to be unstable at the least and possibly freeze up. That results in a denial-of-service attack because it makes the target system less able or even unable to perform its normal function in the network.

Smurf

The Smurf attack is also a denial-of-service attack that uses a type of ping packet called an ICMP ECHO REQUEST. This is an example of a Distributed Denial of Service (DDoS) attack in that the perpetuator enlists the aid of other machines in the network.

When a system receives an ICMP ECHO REQUEST packet, it attempts to answer this request with an ICMP ECHO REPLY packet (usually four times by default). Normally this reply is sent to a single sending system. In this attack, the ECHO REQUEST has its destination address set to the network broadcast address of the network in which the target system resides and the source address is set to the target system. When every system in the network replies to the request, it overwhelms the target device causing it to freeze or crash.

Fraggle

Although not really an ICMP attack because it uses UDP, the Fraggle attack is a DDoS attack with the same goal and method as the Smurf attack. In this attack, an attacker sends a large amount of UDP echo traffic to an IP broadcast address, all of it having a fake source address, which will, of course, be the target system. When all systems in the network reply, the target is overwhelmed.

ICMP Redirect

One of the many types of error messages that ICMP uses is called an ICMP redirect or an ICMP Packet type 5. ICMP redirects are used by routers to specify better routing paths out of one network. When it does this, it changes the path that the packet will take.

By crafting ICMP redirect packets, the attacker alters the route table of the host that receives the redirect message. This changes the way packets are routed in the network to his advantage. After its routing table is altered, the host will continue to use the path for 10 minutes. For this reason, ICMP redirect packets might be one of the types you might want to disallow on the firewall.

Ping Scanning

ICMP can be used to scan the network for live or active IP addresses. This attack basically pings every IP address and keeps track of which IP addresses respond to the ping. This attack is usually accompanied or followed by a port scan, covered later in this chapter.

DNS Attacks

As you might recall in the discussion of DNS earlier in this chapter, DNS resolves computer and domain names to IP addresses. It is a vital service to the network and for that reason multiple DNS servers are always recommended for fault tolerance. DNS servers are a favorite target of DoS and DDoS attacks because of the mayhem taking them down causes.

DNS servers also can be used to divert traffic to the attacker by altering DNS records. In this section, all types of DNS attacks are covered along with practices that can eliminate or mitigate the effect of these attacks.

DNS Cache Poisoning

DNS clients send requests for name-to-IP address resolution (called queries) to a DNS server. The search for the IP address that goes with a computer or domain name usually starts with a local DNS server that is not authoritative for the DNS domain in which the requested computer or website resides. When this occurs, the local DNS server makes a request of the DNS server that does hold the record in question. After the local DNS server receives the answer, it returns it to the local DNS client. After this, the local DNS server maintains that record in its DNS cache for a period called the Time to Live (TTL), which is usually an hour but can vary.

In a DNS cache poisoning attack, the attacker attempts to refresh or update that record when it expires with a different address than the correct address. If he can convince the DNS server to accept this refresh, the local DNS server will then be responding to client requests for that computer with the address inserted by the attacker. Typically the address they now receive is for a fake website that appears to look in every way like the site the client is requesting. The hacker can then harvest all the name and password combinations entered on his fake site.

To prevent this type of attack, the DNS servers should be limited in the updates they accept. In most DNS software, you can restrict the DNS servers from which a server will accept updates. This can help prevent the server from accepting these false updates.

DoS

DNS servers are a favorite target of Denial of Service (DoS) attacks. This is because the loss of DNS service in the network typically brings the network to a halt as many network services depend on its functioning. Any of the assorted type of DoS attacks discussed in this book can be targeted to DNS servers. For example, the Ping of Death might be the attack of choice.

DDoS

Any of the assorted DoS attacks can be amplified by the attacker by recruiting other devices to assist in the attack. Some examples of these attacks are the Smurf and Fraggle attacks (covered earlier).

In some cases the attacker might have used malware to install software on thousands of computers (called zombies) to which he sends commands at a given time, instructing all the devices to launch the attack. Not only does this amplify the attack but it also helps to hide the source of the attack because it appears to come from many places at once.

DNSSEC

One of the newer approaches to preventing DNS attacks is a stronger authentication mechanism called Domain Name System Security Extensions (DNSSEC). Many current implementations of DNS software contain this functionality. It uses digital signatures to validate the source of all messages to ensure they are not spoofed.

The problem with DNSSEC illustrates the classic tradeoff between security and simplicity. To deploy DNSSEC, a PKI must be built and maintained to issue, validate, and renew the public/private key pairs and certificates that must be issued to all the DNS servers. (PKI is covered more fully in Chapter 6.) Moreover, for complete security of DNS, all the DNS servers on the Internet would also need to participate, which complicates the situation further. The work on this continues today.

URL Hiding

An alternate and in some ways simpler way for an attacker to divert traffic to a fake website is a method called URL hiding. This attack takes advantage of the ability to embed URLs in web pages and email. The attacker might refer to the correct name of the website in the text of the webpage or email, but when he inserts the URL that goes with the link he inserts the URL for the fake site. The best protection against this issue is to ask users to not click links on unknown or untrusted websites.

Domain Grabbing

Domain grabbing occurs when individuals register a domain name of a well-known company before the company has the chance to do so. Then later the individuals hold the name hostage until the company becomes willing to pay to get the domain name. In some cases these same individuals monitor the renewal times for well-known websites and register the name before the company has a chance to perform the renewal. Some practices that can help to prevent this are to register domain names for longer periods of time and to register all permutations of the chosen domain name (misspellings and so on).

Cybersquatting

When domain names are registered with no intent to use them but with intent to hold them hostage (as described in the preceding), it is called cybersquatting. The same practices to prevent domain grabbing are called for to prevent the company from becoming a victim of cybersquatting.

Email Attacks

One of the most popular avenues for attacks is a tool we all must use every day, email. In this section, several attacks that use email as the vehicle are covered. In most cases the best way to prevent these attacks is user training and awareness because many of these attacks are based upon poor security practices on the part of the user.

Email Spoofing

Email spoofing is the process of sending an email that appears to come from one source when it really comes from another. It is made possible by altering the fields of email headers such as From, Return Path, and Reply-to. Its purpose is to convince the receiver to trust the message and reply to it with some sensitive information that the receiver would not have shared unless it was a trusted message.

Often this is one step in an attack designed to harvest usernames and passwords for banking or financial sites. This attack can be mitigated in several ways. One is SMTP authentication, which when enabled, disallows the sending of an email by a user that cannot authenticate with the sending server.

Another possible mitigation technique is to implement a Sender Policy Framework (SPF). An SPF is an email validation system that works by using DNS to determine whether an email sent by someone has been sent by a host sanctioned by that domain's administrator. If it can't be validated, it is not delivered to the recipient's box.

Spear Phishing

Phishing is a social engineering attack where a recipient is convinced to click on a link in an email that appears to go to a trusted site but in fact goes to the hacker's site. This is used to harvest usernames and passwords.

Spear phishing is the process of foisting this attack on a specific person rather than a random set of people. The attack might be made more convincing by learning details about the person through social media that the email might reference to boost its appearance of legitimacy.

Whaling

Just as spear phishing is a subset of phishing, whaling is a subset of spear phishing. It targets a single person and in the case of whaling, that person is someone of significance or importance. It might be a CEO, COO, or CTO, for example. The attack is based on the assumption that these people have more sensitive information to divulge.

Spam

No one enjoys the way our email boxes fill every day with unsolicited emails, usually trying to sell us something. In many cases we cause ourselves to receive this email by not paying close attention to all the details when we buy something or visit a site. When email is sent out on a mass basis that is not requested, it is called spam.

Spam is more than an annoyance because it can clog email boxes and cause email servers to spend resources delivering it. Sending spam is illegal so many spammers try to hide the source of the spam by relaying through other corporations' email servers. Not only does this practice hide the email's true source, but it can cause the relaying company to get in trouble.

Today's email servers have the ability to deny relaying to any email servers that you do not specify. This can prevent your email system from being used as a spamming mechanism. This type of relaying should be disallowed on your email servers.

Wireless Attacks

Wireless attacks are some of the hardest to prevent because of the nature of the medium. If you want to make the radio transmissions available to the users then you must make them available to anyone else in the area as well. Moreover, there is no way to determine when someone is capturing your radio waves! You might be able to prevent someone from connecting to or becoming a wireless client on the network, but you can't stop them from using a wireless sniffer to capture the packets.

In this section, some of the more common attacks are covered and some mitigation techniques are discussed as well.

Wardriving

Wardriving is the process of riding around with a wireless device connected to a high-power antenna searching for WLANs. It could be for the purpose of obtaining free Internet access, or it could be to identify any open networks vulnerable to an attack.

Warchalking

Warchalking is a practice that typically accompanies wardriving. When a wardriver locates a WLAN, he indicates in chalk on the sidewalk the SSID and the types of security used on the network. This activity has gone mostly online now as many sites are dedicated to compiling lists of found WLANs and their locations.

Remote Attacks

Although in a sense all attacks such as DoS attacks, DNS poisoning, port scanning, and ICMP attacks are remote in the sense they can be launched from outside the network, remote attacks can also be focused on remote access systems such as VPN servers or dial-up servers. As security practices have evolved, these types of attacks have somewhat diminished.

Wardialing is not the threat that it once was simply because we don't use modems and modem banks as much as we used to. In this attack, software programs attempt to dial large lists of phone numbers for the purpose of identifying numbers attached to modems. When a person or fax machine answers, it records that fact, and when a modem answers, it attempts to make a connection. If this connection is successful, the hacker now has an entryway into the network.

Other Attacks

In this final section of this chapter, some other attacks are covered that might not fall into any of the other categories discussed thus far.

SYN ACK Attacks

The SYN ACK attack takes advantage of the TCP three-way handshake, covered in the section "Transport Layer" earlier in this chapter.

In this attack, the hacker sends a large number of packets with the SYN flag set, which causes the receiving computer to set aside memory for each ACK packet it expects to receive in return. These packets never come and at some point the resources of the receiving computer are exhausted, making this a form of DoS attack.

Session Hijacking

In a session highjacking attack, the hacker attempts to place himself in the middle of an active conversation between two computers for the purpose of taking over the session of one of the two computers, thus receiving all data sent to that computer. A couple of tools can be used for this attack. Juggernaut and the Hunt Project allow the attacker to spy on the TCP session between the computers. Then he uses some sort of DoS attack to remove one of the two computers from the network while spoofing the IP address of that computer and replacing that computer in the conversation. This results in the hacker receiving all traffic that was originally intended for the computer that suffered the DoS attack.

Port Scanning

ICMP can also be used to scan the network for open ports. Open ports indicate services that might be running and listening on a device that might be susceptible to being used for an attack. This attack basically pings every address and port number combination and keeps track of which ports are open on each device as the pings are answered by open ports with listening services and not answered by closed ports.

Teardrop

A teardrop attack is a type of fragmentation attack. The Maximum Transmission Unit (MTU) of a section of the network might cause a packet to be broken up or fragmented, which requires the fragments to be reassembled when received. The hacker sends malformed fragments of packets that when reassembled by the receiver cause the receiver to crash or become unstable.

IP Address Spoofing

IP address spoofing is one of the techniques used by hackers to hide their trail or to masquerade as another computer. The hacker alters the IP address as it appears in the packet. This can sometimes allow the packet to get through an ACL that is based on IP addresses. It also can be used to make a connection to a system that only trusts certain IP addresses or ranges of IP addresses.

Exam Preparation Tasks

Review All Key Topics

Review the most important topics in this chapter, noted with the Key Topics icon in the outer margin of the page. Table 3-11 lists a reference of these key topics and the page numbers on which each is found.

Table 3-11 Key Topics

Key Topic Element	Description	Page Number
Figure 3-1	Protocol Mappings	70
Figure 3-2	TCP/IP and OSI models	71
Figure 3-4	TCP three-way handshake	74
Figure 3-6	Encapsulation and de-encapsulation	76
Table 3-1	Common UDP and TCP ports	77
Table 3-2	Classful IP addressing	80
Table 3-3	Private IP address ranges	81
Table 3-4	Twisted-pair categories	89
Table 3-6	Ethernet implementations	95
Ordered steps	CSMA/CD	99
Ordered steps	CSMA/CA	100
Section	Cloud computing services	117
Table 3-7	T carriers	121
Table 3-8	E-carriers	122
Table 3-9	Optical carriers	122
Section	WLAN Standards	138
Table 3-10	WPA and WPA2	141

Define Key Terms

Define the following key terms from this chapter and check your answers in the glossary:

Open Systems Interconnect (OSI) model, Application layer, Presentation layer, Session layer, Transport layer (layer 4), Network layer (layer 3), Data Link layer

(layer 2), Physical layer (layer 1), TCP/IP model, TCP three-way handshake, Internet Protocol (IP), Internet Message Control Protocol (ICMP), Internet Group Messaging Protocol (IGMP), Address Resolution Protocol (ARP), Encapsulation, Private IP addresses, Media Access Control (MAC) addresses, Digital, Asynchronous transmission, Synchronous transmission, Baseband, Time Division Multiplexing (TDM), Broadband, Frequency Division Multiplexing (FDM), Unicast, Multicast, Broadcast, Attenuation, Coaxial, Thicknet, Thinnet, Twisted Pair, Radio Frequency Interference (RFI), EMI, Fiberoptic, Single mode, Multimode, Ring, Bus, Star, Mesh, Hybrid, Ethernet, Token Ring, Fiber Distributed Data Interface (FDDI), Carrier Sense Multiple Access Collision Detection (CSMA/CD), Carrier Sense Multiple Access Collision Avoidance (CSMA/CA), token passing, polling, Dynamic Host Configuration Protocol (DHCP), DNS, File Transfer Protocol (FTP), FTPS, Secure File Transfer Protocol (SFTP), HTTP, Hypertext Transfer Protocol Secure (HTTPS), SHTTP, Internet Message Access Protocol (IMAP), Network Address Translation (NAT), Port Address Translation (PAT), Post Office Protocol (POP), Simple Mail Transfer Protocol (SMTP), Simple Network Management Protocol (SNMP), distance vector, link state, hybrid, Routing Internet Protocol (RIP), Open Shortest Path First (OSPF), Interior Gateway Protocol, Enhanced IGRP (EIGRP), Virtual Router Redundancy Protocol (VRRP), Intermediate System to Intermediate System (IS-IS), Border Gateway Protocol (BGP), patch panels, multiplexer, demultiplexer, hub, switches, VLANs, layer 3 switch, layer 4 switches, routers, gateway, Network Access Server (NAS), firewall, packet filtering firewalls, stateful firewalls, proxy firewalls, circuit level proxies, SOCKS firewall, application-level proxies, dynamic packet filtering firewall, kernel proxy firewall, bastion host, dual-homed firewall, three legged firewall, DMZ, screened host, screened subnet, virtual firewalls, proxy firewall, private branch exchange (PBX), honeypots, honeynets, cloud computing, Infrastructure as a Service (IaaS), Platform as a Service (PaaS), Software as a Service (SaaS), LAN, intranet, extranet, Metropolitan Area Network (MAN), Metro Ethernet, wide area networks (WANs), T carriers, fractional T1, E carriers, Synchronous Optical Networks (SONET), Channel Service Unit/Data Service Unit (CSU/DSU), circuit-switching networks, packet-switching networks, Asynchronous Transfer Mode (ATM), X.25, Switched Multimegabit Data Service (SMDS), Point-to-Point Protocol (PPP), HSSI, PSTN, VOIP, Signaling System 7 (SS7), Session Initiation Protocol (SIP), dial-up, SLIP, Integrated Services Digital Network (ISDN), Basic Rate (BRI), Primary Rate (PRI), Digital Subscribers Line (DSL), Asymmetric DSL (ADSL), High Bit Data Rate DSL (HDSL), Very High Bit Data Rate DSL (VDSL), cable modems, Data-Over-Cable Service Interface Specifications (DOCSIS), Virtual Private Network (VPN), PPTP, L2TP, IPsec, Authentication Header (AH), Encapsulating Security Payload (ESP), Internet Security Association and Key Management Protocol (ISAKMP), Internet Key Exchange

(IKE), TACACS+, RADIUS, supplicant, authenticator, authenticating server, Password Authentication Protocol (PAP), Challenge Handshake Authentication Protocol (CHAP), Extensible Authentication Protocol (EAP), Telnet, Transport Layer Security/Secure Sockets Layer (TLS/SSL), Frequency Hopping Spread Spectrum (FHSS), Direct Sequence Spread Spectrum (DSSS), Orthogonal Frequency Division Multiplexing (OFDM), Frequency Division Multiple Access (FDMA), Code Division Multiple Access (CDMA), Global System Mobile (GSM), phone cloning, access point, Service Set Identifier (SSID), Infrastructure mode, Ad Hoc mode, 802.11a, 802.11b, 802.11f, 802.11g, 802.11n, Multiple Input Multiple Output, Bluetooth, bluejacking, bluesnarfing, infrared, Wired Equivalent Privacy (WEP), Wi-Fi Protected Access (WPA), WPA2, noise, attenuation, crosstalk, Ping of Death, Distributed Denial of Service (DDOS), Smurf attack, ping scanning, DNS cache poisoning attack, DNSSEC (DNS security), URL hiding, domain grabbing, cybersquatting, email spoofing, phishing, spear phishing, whaling, spam, wardriving, warchalking, SYN ACK attack, session highjacking attack, port scan, teardrop, IP address spoofing

Review Questions

1. At which layer of the OSI model does the encapsulation process begin?

    a. Transport

    b. Application

    c. Physical

    d. Session

2. Which two layers of the OSI model are represented by the Link layer of the TCP/IP model? (Choose two.)

    a. Data Link

    b. Physical

    c. Session

    d. Application

    e. Presentation

3. Which of the following represents the range of port numbers that are referred to as "well-known" port numbers?

    a. 49152–65535

    b. 0–1023

    c. 1024–49151

    d. all above 500

4. What is the port number for HTTP?
   a. 23
   b. 443
   c. 80
   d. 110

5. What protocol in the TCP/IP suite resolves IP addresses to MAC addresses?
   a. ARP
   b. TCP
   c. IP
   d. ICMP

6. How many bits are contained in an IPv4 IP address?
   a. 128
   b. 48
   c. 32
   d. 64

7. Which of the following is a Class C address?
   a. 172.16.5.6
   b. 192.168.5.54
   c. 10.6.5.8
   d. 224.6.6.6

8. Which of the following is a private IP address?
   a. 10.2.6.6
   b. 172.15.6.6
   c. 191.6.6.6
   d. 223.54.5.5

9. Which service converts private IP addresses to public IP addresses?
   a. DHCP
   b. DNS
   c. NAT
   d. WEP

10. Which type of transmission uses stop and start bits?

    a. Asynchronous

    b. Unicast

    c. Multicast

    d. Synchronous

Answers and Explanations

1. **b.** The Application Layer (layer 7) is where the encapsulation process begins. This layer receives the raw data from the application in use and provides services such as file transfer and message exchange to the application (and thus the user).

2. **a, b.** The Link layer of the TCP/IP model provides the services provided by both the Data Link and the Physical layers in the OSI model.

3. **b.** System Ports, also called well-known ports, are assigned by the IETF for standards-track protocols, as per [RFC6335].

4. **c.** The listed ports numbers are as follows:

    23–Telnet

    443–HTTPS

    80–HTTP

    110–POP3

5. **a.** Address Resolution Protocol (ARP) resolves IP addresses to MAC addresses.

6. **c.** IPv4 addresses are 32 bits in length and can be represented in either binary or in dotted decimal format.

7. **b.** The calls C range of addresses is from 192.0.0.0 -223.255.255.255.

8. **a.**

    Here are the private IP address ranges:

Class	Range
Class A	10.0.0.0 – 10.255.255.255
Class B	172.16.0.0 – 172.31.255.255
Class C	192.168.0.0 – 192.168.255.255

9. **c.** Network Address Translation (NAT) is a service that can be supplied by a router or by a server. The device that provides the service stands between the local LAN and the Internet. When packets need to go to the Internet, the packets go through the NAT service first. The NAT service changes the private IP address to a public address that is routable on the Internet. When the response is returned from the Web, the NAT service receives it and translates the address back to the original private IP address and sends it back to the originator.

10. **a.** With asynchronous transmission, the systems use what are called start and stop bits to communicate when each byte is starting and stopping. This method also uses what are called parity bits to be used for the purpose of ensuring that each byte has not changed or been corrupted en route. This introduces additional overhead to the transmission.

This chapter covers the following topics:

- **Security principles and terms:** Principles and terms discussed include CIA, vulnerability, threat, threat agent, risk, exposure, countermeasure, due care, due diligence, job rotation, and separation of duties.

- **Security frameworks and methodologies:** Frameworks and methodologies discussed include ISO/IEC 27000 series, CobiT, NIST 800-53, COSO, ITIL, Six Sigma, and CMMI.

- **Risk assessment:** Assessment topics discussed include information and asset (tangible/intangible) value and cost, quantitative risk analysis, qualitative risk analysis, steps in risk assessment, total risk versus residual risk, and handling risk.

- **Risk management principles:** Principles discussed include risk management policy, risk management team, and risk analysis team.

- **Information security governance components:** Components include policies, procedures, standards, guidelines, baselines, and information classification and life cycle.

- **Security governance roles and responsibilities:** Roles and responsibilities discussed include board of directors, high-level management, CEO/CFO/CIO/CPO/CSO, audit committee, data owner, data custodian, system owner, system administrator, security administrator, security analyst, application owner, supervisor, user, auditor, third-party governance, and personnel security.

- **Security awareness and training:** Topics include the why, when, how, and who of security awareness and training.

- **Security budget, metrics, and effectiveness:** Topics include understanding a security budget, understanding security metrics, and measuring security effectiveness.

CHAPTER 4

Information Security Governance and Risk Management

Information security governance involves the principles, frameworks, and methods that establish criteria for protecting information assets, including security awareness. Risk management allows organizations to identify, measure, and control organizational risks. These two facets ensure that security controls that are implemented are in balance with the operations of the organization. Each organization must develop a well-rounded, customized security program that addresses the needs of the organization while ensuring that the organization exercises due care and due diligence in its security plan.

Security professionals must take a lead role in their organization's security program and act as risk advisors to management. In addition, security professionals must ensure that they understand current security issues and risks, governmental and industry regulations, and security controls that can be implemented. Security is an ever-evolving, continuous process, and security professionals must be watchful.

In this chapter, you will learn how to use the information security governance and risk management components to assess risks, implement controls for identified risks, monitor control effectiveness, and perform future risk assessments.

Foundation Topics

Security Principles and Terms

When assessing and implementing information security governance and risk management, you should always understand the following concepts:

- CIA triad
- Vulnerability
- Threat

- Threat agents
- Risk
- Exposure
- Countermeasure
- Due care
- Due diligence
- Job rotation
- Separation of duties

CIA

The three fundamentals of security are confidentiality, integrity, and availability (CIA). Most security issues result in a violation of at least one facet of the CIA triad. Understanding these three security principles will help security professionals ensure that the security controls and mechanisms implemented protect at least one of these principles.

Confidentiality ensures that data is protected from unauthorized disclosure. Integrity ensures that data is accurate and reliable. Availability ensures that data is accessible when and where it is needed. A balanced security approach should be implemented to ensure that all three facets are considered when security controls are implemented. When implementing any control, you should identify the facet that the control addresses. For example, RAID addresses data availability, file hashes address data integrity, and encryption addresses data confidentiality. A balanced approach ensures that no facet of the CIA triad is ignored.

NOTE Refer to Chapter 2, "Access Control" for more in-depth information regarding the CIA triad.

Vulnerability

A vulnerability is an absence or weakness of a countermeasure that is in place. Vulnerabilities can occur in software, hardware, or personnel. An example of a vulnerability is unrestricted access to a folder on a computer. Most organizations implement a vulnerability assessment to identify vulnerabilities.

> **NOTE** Refer to Chapter 2 for more in-depth information regarding vulnerability assessments.

Threat

A threat is the next logical progression in risk management. A threat occurs when vulnerability is identified or exploited. A threat would occur when an attacker identified the folder on the computer that has an inappropriate or absent access control list (ACL).

Threat Agent

A threat is carried out by a threat agent. Continuing with the example, the attacker who takes advantage of the inappropriate or absent ACL is the threat agent. Keep in mind, though, that threat agents can discover and/or exploit vulnerabilities. Not all threat agents will actually exploit an identified vulnerability.

Risk

A risk is the probability that a threat agent will exploit a vulnerability and the impact if the threat is carried out. The risk in the vulnerability example would be fairly high if the data residing in the folder is confidential. However, if the folder only contains public data, then the risk would be low. Identifying the potential impact of a risk often requires security professionals to enlist the help of subject matter experts.

Exposure

An exposure occurs when an organizational asset is exposed to losses. If the folder with the inappropriate or absent ACL is compromised by a threat agent, the organization is exposed to the possibility of data exposure and loss.

Countermeasure

A countermeasure reduces the potential risk. Countermeasures are also referred to as safeguards or controls. Three things must be considered when implementing a countermeasure: vulnerability, threat, and risk. For our example, a good countermeasure would be to implement the appropriate ACL and to encrypt the data. The ACL protects the integrity of the data, and the encryption protects the confidentiality of the data.

Countermeasures or controls come in many categories and types. The categories and types of controls are discussed in depth in Chapter 2.

All the aforementioned security concepts work together in a relationship that is demonstrated in Figure 4-1.

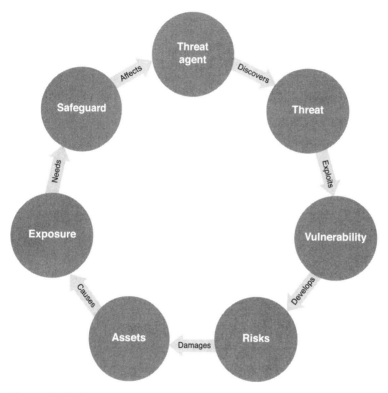

Figure 4-1 Security Concept Cycle

Due Care and Due Diligence

Due care and *due dilligence* are legal terms. Due care means that an organization took all reasonable measures to prevent security breaches and also took steps to mitigate damages caused by successful breaches. This includes making sure that the correct policies, procedures, and standards are in place and being followed. Due diligence means that an organization investigated all vulnerabilities. This includes performing the appropriate audits and assessments to ensure that the organization is protected. Both of these legal terms have bearing on the security governance and risk management process.

Job Rotation

Job rotation ensures that more than one person fulfills the job tasks of a single position within an organization. This job rotation ensures that more than one person is capable of performing those tasks, providing redundancy. It is also an important tool in helping an organization to recognize when fraudulent activities have occurred.

Separation of Duties

Separation of duties ensures that one person is not capable of compromising organizational security. Any activities that are identified as high risk should be divided into individual tasks, which can then be allocated to different personnel or departments. When an organization implements adequate separation of duties, collusion between two or more personnel would be required to carry out fraud against the organization. Split knowledge, a variation of separation of duties, ensures that no single employee knows all the details to perform a task. An example would be two individuals knowing parts of a safe combination. Another variation is dual control, which requires that two employees must be available to complete a specific task to complete the job. An example is two managers being required to turn keys simultaneously in separate locations to launch a missile.

Security Frameworks and Methodologies

Many organizations have developed security management frameworks and methodologies to help guide security professionals. These frameworks and methodologies include security program development standards, enterprise and security architect development frameworks, security controls development methods, corporate governance methods, and process management methods. This section discusses the following frameworks and methodologies and explains where they are used:

- ISO/IEC 27000 Series
- Zachman Framework
- TOGAF
- DoDAF
- MODAF
- SABSA
- CobiT
- NIST

- COSO
- ITIL
- Six Sigma
- CMMI
- Top-down versus bottom-up approach
- Security program life cycle

ISO/IEC 27000 Series

International Organization for Standardization (ISO), often incorrectly referred to as the International Standards Organization, joined with the International Electrotechnical Commission (IEC) to standardize the British Standard 7799 (BS7799) to a new global standard that is now referred to as ISO/IEC 27000 Series. ISO 27000 is a security program development standard on how to develop and maintain an information security management system (ISMS).

The 27000 Series includes a list of standards, each of which addresses a particular aspect of ISMS. These standards are either published or in development. The following standards are included as part of the ISO/IEC 27000 Series at the time of this writing:

- 27000: Published overview of ISMS and vocabulary
- 27001: Published ISMS requirements
- 27002: Published code of practice for information security management
- 27003: Published ISMS implementation guidelines
- 27004: Published ISMS measurement guidelines
- 27005: Published information security risk management guidelines
- 27006: Published requirements for bodies providing audit and certification of ISMS
- 27007: Published ISMS auditing guidelines
- 27008: Published auditor of ISMS guidelines
- 27010: Published information security management for inter-sector and inter-organizational communications guidelines
- 27011: Published telecommunications organizations information security management guidelines

- 27013: Published integrated implementation of ISO/IEC 27001 and ISO/IEC 20000-1 guidance
- 27014: In-development information security governance guidelines
- 27015: Published financial services information security management guidelines
- 27016: In-development ISMS organizational economics guidelines
- 27017: In-development cloud computing services information security control guidelines based on ISO/IEC 27002
- 27018: In-development code of practice for public cloud computing services data protection controls
- 27019: In-development energy industry process control system ISMS guidelines based on ISO/IEC 27002
- 27031: Published information and communication technology readiness for business continuity guidelines
- 27032: Published cybersecurity guidelines
- 27033-1: Published network security overview and concepts
- 27033-2: Published network security design and implementation guidelines
- 27033-3: Published network security threats, design techniques, and control issues guidelines
- 27034-1: Published application security overview and concepts
- 27034-2: In-development application security organization normative framework guidelines
- 27034-3: In-development application security management process guidelines
- 27034-4: In-development application security validation guidelines
- 27034-5: In-development application security protocols and controls data structure guidelines
- 27034-6: In-development security guidance for specific applications
- 27035: Published information security incident management guidelines
- 27035-1: In-development information security incident management principles
- 27035-2: In-development information security incident response readiness guidelines
- 27035-3: In-development computer security incident response team (CSIRT) operations guidelines

- 27036-1: In-development information security for supplier relationships overview and concepts
- 27036-2: In-development information security for supplier relationships common requirements guidelines
- 27036-3: In-development information and communication technology (ICT) supply chain security guidelines
- 27036-4: In-development information security for supplier relationships outsourcing security guidelines
- 27037: Published digital evidence identification, collection, acquisition, and preservation guidelines
- 27038: In-development information security digital redaction specification
- 27039: In-development intrusion detection systems (IDS) selection, deployment, and operations guidelines
- 27040: In-development storage security guidelines
- 27042: In-development digital evidence analysis and interpretation guidelines
- 27044: In-development security information and event management (SIEM) guidelines
- 27799: Published information security in health organizations guidelines

These standards are developed by the ISO/IEC bodies, but certification or conformity assessment is provided by third parties.

NOTE You can find more information regarding ISO standards at www.iso.org.

Zachman Framework

The Zachman framework, an enterprise architecture framework, is a two-dimensional classification system based on six communication questions (What, Where, When, Why, Who, and How) that intersect with different views (Planner, Owner, Designer, Builder, Subcontractor, and Actual System). This system allows analysis of an organization to be presented to different groups in the organization in ways that relate to the groups' responsibilities. Although this framework is not security oriented, using this framework helps you to relay information for personnel in a language and format that is most useful to them (see Table 4-1).

Table 4-1 Zachman Framework Matrix with Examples

Order	Viewpoints	Layer	What (Data)	How (Function)	Where (Network)	Who (People)	When (Time)	Why (Motivation)
1	Planner	Scope context	List things important to the business	List processes the business performs	List locations where business operates	List organizations important to business	List events significant to business	List business goals/strategies
2	Owner	Conceptual enterprise model	For example, semantic model	For example, business process model	For example, business logistics system	For example, workflow model	For example, master schedule	For example, business plan
3	Designer	Logical system model	For example, logical data model	For example, application architecture	For example, distributed system architecture	For example, human interface architecture	For example, process structure	For example, business rule mode
4	Builder	Physical technology model	For example, physical data model	For example, system design	For example, technology architecture	For example, presentation architecture	For example, control structure	For example, rule design
5	Implementer	Component configuration	For example, data definition	For example, program	For example, network architecture	For example, security architecture	For example, timing definition	For example, rule specification
6	Worker	Functioning system	For example, data	For example, function	For example, network	For example, organization	For example, schedule	For example, strategy

The Open Group Architecture Framework (TOGAF)

TOGAF, another enterprise architecture framework, helps organizations design, plan, implement, and govern an enterprise information architecture. TOGAF is based on four inter-related domains: technology, applications, data, and business.

Department of Defense Architecture Framework (DoDAF)

DoDAF is an architecture framework that organizes a set of products under four views: operational view (OV), system view (SV), technical standards view (TV), and all view (AV). It is used to ensure that new DoD technologies integrate properly with the current infrastructures.

British Ministry of Defence Architecture Framework (MODAF)

MODAF is an architecture framework that divides information into seven viewpoints: strategic viewpoint (StV), operational viewpoint (OV), service-oriented viewpoint (SOV), systems viewpoint (SV), acquisition viewpoint (AcV), technical viewpoint (TV), and all viewpoint (AV).

> **NOTE** Organizations should select the enterprise architecture framework that represents the organization in the most useful manner based on the needs of the stakeholders.

Sherwood Applied Business Security Architecture (SABSA)

SABSA is an enterprise security architecture framework that is similar to the Zachman framework. It uses the six communication questions (What, Where, When, Why, Who, and How) that intersect with six layers (operational, component, physical, logical, conceptual, and contextual). It is a risk-driven architecture. See Table 4-2.

Table 4-2 SABSA Framework Matrix

Viewpoints	Layer	Assets (What)	Motivation (Why)	Process (How)	People (Who)	Location (Where)	Time (When)
Business	Contextual	Business	Risk model	Process model	Organizations and relationships	Geography	Time dependencies
Architect	Conceptual	Business attributes profile	Control objectives	Security strategies and architectural layering	Security entity model and trust framework	Security domain model	Security-related lifetimes and deadlines
Designer	Logical	Business information model	Security policies	Security services	Entity schema and privilege profiles	Security domain definitions and associations	Security processing cycle
Builder	Physical	Business data model	Security rules, practices, and procedures	Security mechanism	Users, applications, and interfaces	Platform and network infrastructure	Control structure execution
Tradesman	Component	Detailed data structures	Security standards	Security tools and products	Identities, functions, actions, and ACLs	Processes, nodes, addresses, and protocols	Security step timing and sequencing
Facilities Manager	Operational	Operational continuity assurance	Operation risk management	Security service management and support	Application and user management and support	Site, network, and platform security	Security operations schedule

Control Objectives for Information and Related Technology (CobiT)

CobiT is a security controls development framework that uses a process model to subdivide IT into four domains: Plan and Organize (PO), Acquire and Implement (AI), Deliver and Support (DS), and Monitor and Evaluate (ME). These four domains are further broken down into 34 processes. CobiT aligns with the ITIL, PMI, ISO, and TOGAF frameworks and is mainly used in the private sector. See Figure 4-2.

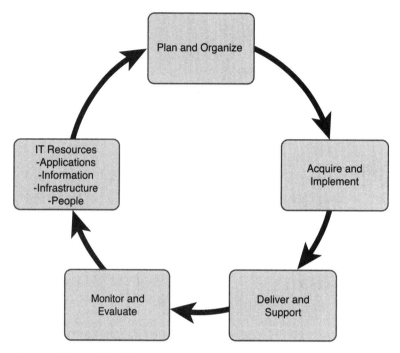

Figure 4-2 CobiT 4.0 Framework

National Institute of Standards and Technology (NIST) Special Publication (SP)

NIST SP 800-53 is a security controls development framework developed by the NIST body of the U.S. Department of Commerce. SP 800-53 divides the controls into three classes: technical, operational, and management. Each class contains control families or categories.

Table 4-3 lists the NIST SP 800-53 control families.

Table 4-3 NIST SP 800-53 Control Families

Family	Class
Access Control (AC)	Technical
Awareness and Training (AT)	Operational
Audit and Accountability (AU)	Technical
Security Assessment and Authorization (SAA)	Management
Configuration Management (CM)	Operational
Contingency Planning (CP)	Operational
Identification and Authentication (IA)	Technical
Incident Response (IR)	Operational
Maintenance (MA)	Operational
Media Protection (MP)	Operational
Physical and Environmental Protection (PE)	Operational
Planning (PL)	Management
Program Management (PM)	Management
Personnel Security (PS)	Operational
Risk Assessment (RA)	Management
System and Services Acquisition (SA)	Management
System and Communications Protection (SC)	Technical
System and Information Integrity (SI)	Operational

NIST 800-55 is an information security metrics framework that provides guidance on developing performance measuring procedures with a U.S. government viewpoint.

Committee of Sponsoring Organizations (COSO) of the Treadway Commission Framework

COSO is a corporate governance framework that consists of five interrelated components: control environment, risk assessment, control activities, information and communication, and monitoring. CobiT was derived from the COSO framework. COSO is for corporate governance; CobiT is for IT governance.

Information Technology Infrastructure Library (ITIL)

ITIL is a process management development standard developed by the Office of Management and Budget in OMB Circular A-130. ITIL has five core publications: ITIL Service Strategy, ITIL Service Design, ITIL Service Transition, ITIL Service Operation, and ITIL Continual Service Improvement. These five core publications contain 26 processes. Although ITIL has a security component, it is primarily concerned with managing the service-level agreements (SLAs) between an IT department or organization and its customers. As part of the OMB Circular A-130, an independent review of security controls should be performed every three years.

Table 4-4 lists the five ITIL version 3 core publications and the 26 processes within them.

Table 4-4 *ITIL v3 Core Publications and Processes*

ITIL Service Strategy	ITIL Service Design	ITIL Service Transition	ITIL Service Operation	ITIL Continual Service Improvement
Strategy Management	Design Coordination	Transition Planning and Support	Event Management	Continual Service Improvement
Service Portfolio Management	Service Catalogue	Change Management	Incident Management	
Financial Management for IT Services	Service Level Management	Service Asset and Configuration Management	Request Fulfillment	
Demand Management	Availability Management	Release and Deployment Management	Problem Management	
Business Relationship Management	Capacity Management	Service Validation and Testing	Access Management	
	IT Service Continuity Management	Change Evaluation		
	Information Security Management System	Knowledge Management		
	Supplier Management			

Six Sigma

Six Sigma is a process improvement standard that includes two project methodologies that were inspired by Deming's Plan/Do/Check/Act cycle. The DMAIC methodology includes Define, Measure, Analyze, Improve, and Control. The DMADV methodology includes Define, Measure, Analyze, Design, and Verify. Six Sigma was designed to identify and remove defects in the manufacturing process, but can be applied to many business functions, including security.

Figures 4-3 and 4-4 show both of the Six Sigma methodologies.

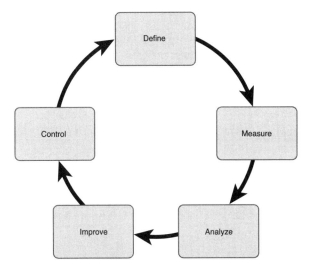

Figure 4-3   Six Sigma DMAIC

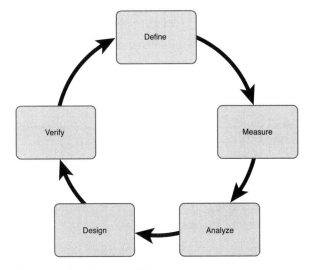

Figure 4-4   Six Sigma DMADV

Capability Maturity Model Integration (CMMI)

Capability Maturity Model Integration (CMMI) is a process improvement approach that addresses three areas of interest: product and service development (CMMI for development), service establishment and management (CMMI for services), and product service and acquisition (CMMI for acquisitions). CMMI has five levels of maturity for processes: Level 1 Initial, Level 2 Managed, Level 3 Defined, Level 4 Quantitatively Managed, and Level 5 Optimizing. All processes within each level of interest are assigned one of the five levels of maturity.

> **NOTE** No organization will implement all the aforementioned frameworks or methodologies. Security professionals should help their organization pick the framework that best fits the needs of the organization.

Top-Down Versus Bottom-Up Approach

In a top-down approach, management initiates, supports, and directs the security program. In a bottom-up approach, staff members develop a security program prior to receiving direction and support from management. A top-down approach is much more efficient than a bottom-up approach because management's support is one of the most important components of a security program.

Security Program Life Cycle

Any security program has a continuous life cycle and should be assessed and improved constantly. The security program life cycle includes the following steps:

1. **Plan and Organize:** Includes performing risk assessment, establishing management and steering committee, evaluating business drivers, and obtaining management approval.
2. **Implement:** Includes identifying and managing assets, managing risk, managing identity and access control, training on security and awareness, implementing solutions, assigning roles, and establishing goals.
3. **Operate and Maintain:** Includes performing audits, carrying out tasks, and managing SLAs.
4. **Monitor and Evaluate:** Include reviewing auditing and logs, evaluating security goals, and developing improvement plans for integration into the Plan and Organize step (step 1).

Figure 4-5 shows a diagram of the security program life cycle.

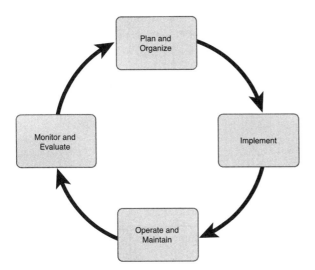

Figure 4-5 Security Program Life Cycle

Risk Assessment

A risk assessment is a tool used in risk management to identify vulnerabilities and threats, assess the impact of those vulnerabilities and threats, and determine which controls to implement. Risk assessment or analysis has four main goals:

- Identify assets and asset value.
- Identify vulnerabilities and threats.
- Calculate threat probability and business impact.
- Balance threat impact with countermeasure cost.

Prior to starting the risk assessment, management and the risk assessment team must determine which assets and threats to consider. This process determines the size of the project. The risk assessment team must then provide a report to management on the value of the assets considered. Management can then review and finalize the asset list, adding and removing assets as it sees fit, and then determine the budget of the risk assessment project.

If a risk assessment is not supported and directed by senior management, it will not be successful. Management must define the risk assessment's purpose and scope and allocate the personnel, time, and monetary resources for the project.

According to NIST SP 800-30, common information-gathering techniques used in risk analysis include automated risk assessment tools, questionnaires, interviews, and policy document reviews. Keep in mind that multiple sources should be used to determine the risks to a single asset. The NIST SP 800-30 identifies the following steps in the risk assessment process:

1. Identify the assets and their value.
2. Identify threats.
3. Identify vulnerabilities.
4. Determine likelihood.
5. Identify impact.
6. Determine risk as a combination of likelihood and impact.

Figure 4-6 shows the risk assessment process according to NIST SP 800-30.

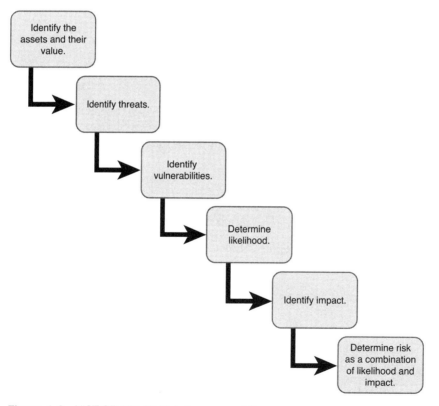

Figure 4-6 NIST SP 800-30 Risk Assessment Process

Information and Asset (Tangible/Intangible) Value and Costs

As stated earlier, the first step of any risk assessment is to identify the assets and determine the asset value. Assets are both tangible and intangible. Tangible assets include computers, facilities, supplies, and personnel. Intangible assets include intellectual property, data, and organizational reputation. The value of an asset should be considered in respect to the asset owner's view. The six following considerations can be used to determine the asset's value:

- Value to owner
- Work required to develop or obtain the asset
- Costs to maintain the asset
- Damage that would result if the asset were lost
- Cost that competitors would pay for asset
- Penalties that would result if asset was lost

After determining the value of the assets, you should determine the vulnerabilities and threats to each asset.

Vulnerabilities and Threats Identification

When determining vulnerabilities and threats to an asset, considering the threat agents first is often easiest. Threat agents can be grouped into the following six categories:

- **Human:** Includes both malicious and non-malicious insiders and outsiders, terrorists, spies, and terminated personnel.
- **Natural:** Includes floods, fires, tornadoes, hurricanes, earthquakes, or other natural disaster or weather event.
- **Technical:** Includes hardware and software failure, malicious code, and new technologies.
- **Physical:** Includes CCTV issues, perimeter measures failure, and biometric failure.
- **Environmental:** Includes power and other utility failure, traffic issues, biological warfare, and hazardous material issues (such as spillage).
- **Operational:** Includes any process or procedure that can affect CIA.

When the vulnerabilities and threats have been identified, the loss potential for each must be determined. This loss potential is determined by using the likelihood of the event combined with the impact that such an event would cause. An event with a high likelihood and a high impact would be given more importance than an event with a low likelihood and a low impact. Different types of risk analysis, including quantitative risk analysis and qualitative risk analysis, should be used to ensure that the data that is obtained is maximized.

Quantitative Risk Analysis

A quantitative risk analysis assigns monetary and numeric values to all facets of the risk analysis process, including asset value, threat frequency, vulnerability severity, impact, safeguard costs, and so on. Equations are used to determine total and residual risks. The most common equations are for single loss expectancy (SLE) and annual loss expectancy (ALE).

The SLE is the monetary impact of each threat occurrence. To determine the SLE, you must know the asset value (AV) and the exposure factor (EF). The EF is the percent value or functionality of an asset that will be lost when a threat event occurs. The calculation for obtaining the SLE is as follows:

$SLE = AV \times EF$

For example, an organization has a Web server farm with an AV of $20,000. If the risk assessment has determined that a power failure is a threat agent for the Web server farm and the exposure factor for a power failure is 25%, the SLE for this event equals $5,000.

The ALE is the expected risk factor of an annual threat event. To determine the ALE, you must know the SLE and the annualized rate of occurrence (ARO). The ARO is the estimate of how often a given threat might occur annually. The calculation for obtaining the ALE is as follows:

$ALE = SLE \times ARO$

Using the previously mentioned example, if the risk assessment has determined that the ARO for the power failure of the Web server farm is 50%, the ALE for this event equals $2,500.

Using the ALE, the organization can decide whether to implement controls or not. If the annual cost of the control to protect the Web server farm is more than the ALE, the organization could easily choose to accept the risk by not implementing the control. If the annual cost of the control to protect the Web server farm is less than the ALE, the organization should consider implementing the control.

Keep in mind that even though quantitative risk analysis uses numeric value, a purely quantitative analysis cannot be achieved because some level of subjectivity is always part of the data. In our example, how does the organization know that damage from the power failure will be 25% of the asset? This type of estimate should be based on historical data, industry experience, and expert opinion.

An advantage of quantitative over qualitative risk analysis is that quantitative uses less guesswork than qualitative. Disadvantages of quantitative risk analysis include the difficulty of the equations, the time and effort needed to complete the analysis, and the level of data that must be gathered for the analysis.

Qualitative Risk Analysis

Qualitative risk analysis does *not* assign monetary and numeric values to all facets of the risk analysis process. Qualitative risk analysis techniques include intuition, experience, and best practice techniques, such as brainstorming, focus groups, surveys, questionnaires, meetings, interviews, and Delphi. Although all of these techniques can be used, most organizations will determine the best technique(s) based on the threats to be assessed. Experience and education on the threats are needed.

Each member of the group who has been chosen to participate in the qualitative risk analysis uses his experience to rank the likelihood of each threat and the damage that might result. After each group member ranks the threat possibility, loss potential, and safeguard advantage, data is combined in a report to present to management.

Advantages of qualitative over quantitative risk analysis include qualitative prioritizes the risks and identifies areas for immediate improvement in addressing the threats. Disadvantages of qualitative risk analysis include all results are subjective and a dollar value is not provided for cost-benefit analysis or for budget help.

NOTE When performing a risk analysis, all organizations will experience issues with any estimate they obtain. This lack of confidence in an estimate is referred to as uncertainty and is expressed as a percentage. Any reports regarding a risk assessment should include the uncertainty level.

Most risk analysis includes some hybrid use of both quantitative and qualitative risk analyses. Most organizations favor using quantitative risk analysis for tangible assets and qualitative risk analysis for intangible assets.

Safeguard Selection

The most common criteria for choosing a safeguard is the cost effectiveness of the safeguard or control. Planning, designing, implementing, and maintenance costs need to be included in determining the total cost of a safeguard. To calculate a cost-benefit analysis, use the following equation:

(ALE before safeguard) − (ALE after safeguard) − (annual cost of safeguard) = safeguard value

To complete this equation, you have to know the revised ALE after the safeguard is implemented. Implementing a safeguard can improve the ARO but will not completely do away with it. In the example mentioned earlier in the "Quantitative Risk Analysis" section, the ALE for the event is $2,500. Let's assume that implementing the safeguard reduces the ARO to 10%, so the ALE after the safeguard is calculated as: $5,000 × 10% or $500. You could then calculate the safeguard value for a control that costs $1,000 as follows:

$2,500 − $500 − $1,000 = $1,000

Knowing the corrected ARO after the safeguard is implemented is necessary for determining the safeguard value. A legal liability exists if the cost of the safeguard is less than the estimated loss that would occur if the threat is exploited.

Maintenance costs of safeguards are not often fully considered during this process. Organizations should fully research the costs of maintaining safeguards. New staff or extensive staff training often must occur to properly maintain a new safeguard. In addition, the cost of the labor involved must be determined. So the cost of a safeguard must include the actual cost to implement plus any training costs, testing costs, labor costs, and so on. Some of these costs might be hard to identify but a thorough risk analysis will account for these costs.

Total Risk Versus Residual Risk

Total risk is the risk that an organization could encounter if it decides not to implement any safeguards. As you already know, any environment is never fully secure so you must always deal with residual risk. Residual risk is risk that is left over after safeguards have been implemented. Residual risk is represented using the following equation:

Residual risk = total risk − countermeasures

This equation is considered to be more conceptual than for actual calculation.

Handling Risk

Risk reduction is the process of altering elements of the organization is response to risk analysis. After an organization understands its total and residual risk, it must determine how to handle the risk. The following four basic methods are used to handle risk:

- **Risk avoidance:** Terminating the activity that causes a risk or choosing an alternative that is not as risky.

- **Risk transfer:** Passing the risk on to a third party, including insurance companies.

- **Risk mitigation:** Defining the acceptable risk level the organization can tolerate and reducing the risk to that level.

- **Risk acceptance:** Understanding and accepting the level of risk as well as the cost of damages that can occur.

Risk Management Principles

After the risk assessment is complete, the organization must manage the risk. This step involves implementing and maintaining the safeguards. In addition, the organization must decide on any future risk analysis that occurs because risk analysis should be carried out on a regular basis. Risk management involves developing and maintaining a risk management policy and maintaining a risk management and risk analysis team.

Risk Management Policy

Senior management must commit to the risk management process. The risk management policy is a formal statement of senior management's commitment to risk management. The policy also provides risk management direction.

A risk management policy must include the overall risk management plan and list the risk management team and must specifically list the risk management team's objectives, responsibilities and roles, acceptable level of risk, risk identification process, risk and safeguards mapping, safeguard effectiveness, monitoring process and targets, and future risk analysis plans and tasks.

Risk Management Team

Depending on the size of the organization, the risk management team might be an actual team of employees or might consist only of a single team member. For any organization, the team's goal is to protect the organization and its assets from risk in the most cost-effective way. Because in most cases the risk management team members are not dedicated solely to risk management, senior management must specifically put a resource allocation measure in place to ensure the success of the risk management process.

Management must also ensure that the members of the risk management team, particularly the team leader, be given the necessary training and tools for risk management. In larger organizations, the team leader should be able to dedicate the majority of his time to the risk management process.

Risk Analysis Team

To perform the most comprehensive risk analysis, the risk analysis team must consist of a representative from as many departments and as many employment levels as possible. Having a diverse risk analysis team ensures that risks from all areas of the organization can be determined.

If the risk analysis team cannot contain members from all departments, the members must interview each department to understand all the threats encountered by that department. During the risk analysis process, the risk analysis team should determine the threat events that could occur, the potential impact of the threats, the frequency of the threats, and the level of confidence in the information gathered.

Information Security Governance Components

Within an organization, information security governance consists of several components that are used to provide comprehensive security management. Data and other assets should be protected mainly based on their value and sensitivity. Strategic plans guide the long-term security activities (3–5 years or more). Tactical plans achieve the goals of the strategic plan and are shorter in length (6–18 months).

Because management is the most critical link in the computer security chain, management approval must be obtained as part of the first step in forming and adopting an information security policy. Senior management must complete the following steps prior to the development of any organizational security policy:

- Define the scope of the security program.
- Identify all the assets that need protection.
- Determine the level of protection that each asset needs.
- Determine personnel responsibilities.
- Develop consequences for noncompliance with the security policy.

By fully endorsing an organizational security policy, senior management accepts the ownership of an organization's security. High-level polices are statements that indicate senior management's intention to support security.

After senior management approval has been obtained, the first step in establishing an information security program is to adopt an organizational information security statement. The organization's security policy comes from this organizational information security statement. The security planning process must define how security will be managed, who will be responsible for setting up and monitoring compliance, how security measures will be tested for effectiveness, who is involved in establishing the security policy, and where the security policy is defined.

Security professionals must understand how information security components work together to form a comprehensive security plan. Information security governance components include:

- Policies
- Standards
- Baselines
- Guidelines
- Procedures
- Information classification and life cycle

Policies

A security policy dictates the role of security as provided by senior management and is strategic in nature, meaning it provides the end result of security. Policies are defined in two ways: the level in the organization at which they are enforced and the category to which they are applied. Policies must be general in nature, meaning they are independent of a specific technology or security solution. Policies outline goals but do not give any specific ways to accomplish the stated goals. All policies must contain an exception area to ensure that management will be able to deal with situations that might require exceptions.

Policies are broad and provide the foundation for development of standards, baselines, guidelines, and procedures, all of which provide the security structure. Administrative, technical, and physical access controls fill in the security and structure complete the security program.

The policy levels used in information security are organizational security policies, system-specific security policies, and issue-specific security policies. The policy categories used in information security are regulatory security policies, advisory security policies, and informative security policies. The policies are divided as shown in Figure 4-7.

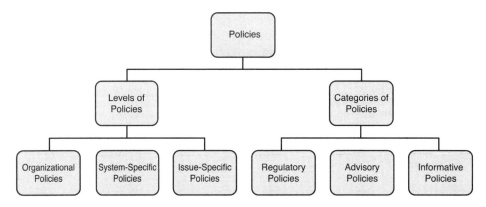

Figure 4-7 Levels and Categories of Security Policies

Organizational Security Policy

An organizational security policy is the highest level security policy adopted by an organization. Business goals steer the organizational security policy. An organizational security policy contains general directions and should have the following components:

- Define overall goals of security policy.
- Define overall steps and importance of security.
- Define security framework to meet business goals.
- State management approval of policy, including support of security goals and principles.
- Define all relevant terms.
- Define security roles and responsibilities.
- Address all relevant laws and regulations.
- Identify major functional areas.
- Define compliance requirements and noncompliance consequences.

An organizational security policy must be supported by all stakeholders and should have high visibility for all personnel and be discussed regularly. In addition, it should be reviewed on a regular basis and revised based on the findings of the regular review. Each version of the policy should be maintained and documented with each new release.

System-Specific Security Policy

A system-specific security policy addresses security for a specific computer, network, technology, or application. This policy type is much more technically focused than an issue-specific security policy. It outlines how to protect the system or technology.

Issue-Specific Security Policy

An issue-specific security policy addresses specific security issues. Issue-specific policies include e-mail privacy policies, virus checking policies, employee termination policies, no expectation of privacy policies, and so on. Issue-specific policies support the organizational security policy.

Policy Categories

Regulatory security policies address specific industry regulations, including mandatory standards. Examples of industries that must consider regulatory security policies include healthcare facilities, public utilities, and financial institutions.

Advisory security policies provide instruction on acceptable and unacceptable activities. In most cases, this policy is considered to be strongly suggested, not compulsory. This type of policy usually gives examples of possible consequences if users engage in unacceptable activities.

Informative security policies provide information on certain topics and act as an educational tool.

Standards

Standards describe how policies will be implemented within an organization. They are mandatory actions or rules that are tactical in nature, meaning they provide the steps necessary to achieve security. Just like policies, standards should be regularly reviewed and revised.

Baselines

A baseline is a reference point that is defined and captured to be used as a future reference. Although capturing baselines is important, using those baselines to assess the security state is just as important. Even the most comprehensive baselines are useless if they are never used.

Capturing a baseline at the appropriate point in time is also important. Baselines should be captured when a system is properly configured and fully updated. When updates occur, new baselines should be captured and compared to the previous baselines. At that time, adopting new baselines based on the most recent data might be necessary.

Guidelines

Guidelines are recommended actions that are much more flexible than standards, thereby providing allowance for circumstances that can occur. Guidelines provide guidance when standards do not apply.

Procedures

Procedures embody all the detailed actions that personnel are required to follow and are the closest to the computers and other devices. Procedures often include step-by-step lists on how policies, standards, and guidelines are implemented.

Information Classification and Life Cycle

Data should be classified based on its value to the organization and its sensitivity to disclosure. Assigning a value to data allows an organization to determine the resources that should be used to protect the data. Resources that are used to protect data include personnel resources, monetary resources, access control resources, and so on. Classifying data allows you to apply different protective measures. Data classification is critical to all systems to protect the confidentiality, integrity, and availability (CIA) of data.

After data is classified, the data can be segmented based on its level of protection needed. The classification levels ensure that data is handled and protected in the most cost-effective manner possible. An organization should determine the classification levels it uses based on the needs of the organization. A number of commercial business and military and government information classifications are commonly used.

The information life cycle should also be based on the classification of the data. Organizations are required to retain certain information, particularly financial data, based on local, state, or government laws and regulations.

Commercial Business Classifications

Commercial businesses usually classify data using four main classification levels, listed from highest sensitivity level to lowest:

1. Confidential
2. Private

3. Sensitive
4. Public

Data that is confidential includes trade secrets, intellectual data, application programming code, and other data that could seriously affect the organization if unauthorized disclosure occurred. Data at this level would only be available to personnel in the organization whose work relates to the data's subject. Access to confidential data usually requires authorization for each access. Confidential data is exempt from disclosure under the Freedom of Information Act. In most cases, the only way for external entities to have authorized access to confidential data is as follows:

- After signing a confidentiality agreement
- When complying with a court order
- As part of a government project or contract procurement agreement

Data that is private includes any information related to personnel, including human resources records, medical records, and salary information, that is only used within the organization. Data that is sensitive includes organizational financial information and requires extra measures to ensure its CIA and accuracy. Public data is data that would not cause a negative impact on the organization.

Military and Government Classifications

Military and governmental entities usually classify data using five main classification levels, listed from highest sensitivity level to lowest:

1. Top Secret
2. Secret
3. Confidential
4. Sensitive but unclassified
5. Unclassified

Data that is top secret includes weapon blueprints, technology specifications, spy satellite information, and other military information that could gravely damage national security if disclosed. Data that is secret includes deployment plans, missile placement, and other information that could seriously damage national security if disclosed. Data that is confidential includes patents, trade secrets, and other information that could seriously affect the government if unauthorized disclosure occurred. Data that is sensitive but unclassified includes medical or other personal data that might not cause serious damage to national security but could cause citizens to question the reputation of the government. Military and government information that does not fall into any of the other four categories is considered unclassified and usually has to be granted to the public based on the Freedom of Information Act.

Information Life Cycle

All organizations need procedures in place for the retention and destruction of data. Data retention and destruction must follow all local, state, and government regulations and laws. Documenting proper procedures ensures that information is maintained for the required time to prevent financial fines and possible incarceration of high-level organizational officers. These procedures must include both retention period and destruction process.

Security Governance Responsibilities and Roles

Although all organizations have layers of responsibility within the organization, computer security is generally considered the responsibility of everyone in the organization. This section covers the responsibilities of the different roles within an organization.

Board of Directors

An organization's board of directors includes individuals who are elected by shareholders to ensure that the organization is run properly. The loyalty of the board of directors should be to the shareholders, not high-level management. Members of the board of directors should maintain their independence from all organizational personnel, especially if the Sarbanes-Oxley (SOX) Act or Gramm-Leach-Bliley Act (GLBA) applies to the organization.

> **NOTE** All laws that are pertinent to the CISSP exam are discussed in Chapter 10, "Legal, Regulations, Investigations, and Compliance." Keep in mind that for testing purposes, security professionals only need to understand the types of organizations and data that these laws affect.

Senior officials, including the board of directors and senior management, must perform their duties with the care that ordinary, prudent people would exercise in similar circumstances. This is known as the prudent-man rule. Due care and due diligence, discussed earlier in this chapter, also affect members of the board of directors and high-level management.

Management

High-level management has the ultimate responsibility for preserving and protecting organizational data. High-level management includes the CEO, CFO, CIO, CPO, and CSO. Other management levels, including business unit managers and business operations managers, have security responsibilities as well.

The chief executive officer (CEO) is the highest managing officer in any organization and reports directly to the shareholders. The CEO must ensure that an organization grows and prospers.

The chief financial officer (CFO) is the officer responsible for all financial aspects of an organization. Although structurally the CFO might report directly to the CEO, the CFO must also provide financial data for the shareholders and government entities.

The chief information officer (CIO) is the officer responsible for all information systems and technology used in the organization and reports directly to the CEO or CFO. The CIO usually drives the effort to protect company assets, including any organizational security program.

The chief privacy officer (CPO) is the officer responsible for private information and usually reports directly to the CIO. As a newer position, this role is still considered optional but is becoming increasingly popular, especially in organizations that handle lots of private information, including medical institutions, insurance companies, and financial institutions.

The chief security officer (CSO) is the officer that leads any security effort and reports directly to the CEO. Although this role is considered optional, this role must solely be focused on security matters. Its independence from all other roles must be maintained to ensure that the organization's security is always the focus of the CSO.

Business unit managers provide departmental information to ensure that appropriate controls are in place for departmental data. Often business unit managers are classified as the data owner for all departmental data. Some business unit managers have security duties. For example, the business operations department manager would be best suited to oversee the security policy development.

Audit Committee

An audit committee evaluates an organization's financial reporting mechanism to ensure that financial data is accurate. This committee performs an internal audit and engages independent auditors as needed. Members of this committee must obtain appropriate education on a regular basis to ensure that they can oversee financial reporting and enforce accountability in the financial processes.

Data Owner

The main responsibility of the data or information owner is to determine the classification level of the information he owns and to protect the data for which he is responsible. This role approves or denies access rights to the data. However, the data owner usually does not handle the implementation of the data access controls.

The data owner role is usually filled by an individual who understands the data best through membership in a particular business unit. Each business unit should have a data owner. For example, a human resources department employee better understands the human resources data than an accounting department employee.

Data Custodian

The data custodian implements the information classification and controls after they are determined by the data owner. Although the data owner is usually an individual who understands the data, the data custodian does not need any knowledge of the data beyond its classification levels. Although a human resources manager should be the data owner for the human resources data, an IT department member could act as the data custodian for the data.

System Owner

A system owner owns one or more systems and must ensure that the appropriate controls are in place on those systems. Although a system has a single system owner, multiple data owners can be responsible for the information on the system. Therefore, system owners must be able to manage the needs of multiple data owners and implement the appropriate procedures to ensure that the data is secured.

System Administrator

A system administrator performs the day-to-day administration of one or more systems. These day-to-day duties include adding and removing system users and installing system software.

Security Administrator

A security administrator maintains security devices and software, including firewalls, antivirus software, and so on. The main focus of the security administrator is security, whereas the main focus of a system administrator is the system availability and the main focus of the network administrator is network availability. The security administrator reviews all security audit data.

Security Analyst

A security analyst analyzes the security needs of the organization and develops the internal information security governance documents, including policies, standards, and guidelines. The role focuses on the design of security, not its implementation.

Application Owner

An application owner determines the personnel who can access an application. Because most applications are owned by a single department, business department managers usually fill this role. However, the application owner does not necessarily perform the day-to-day administration of the application. This responsibility can be delegated to a member of the IT staff because of the technical skills needed.

Supervisor

A supervisor manages a group of users and any assets owned by this group. Supervisors must immediately communicate any personnel role changes that affect security to the security administrator.

User

A user is any person who accesses data to perform their job duties. Users should understand any security procedures and policies for the data to which they have access. Supervisors are responsible for ensuring that users have the appropriate access rights.

Auditor

An auditor monitors user activities to ensure that the appropriate controls are in place. Auditors need access to all audit and event logs to verify compliance with security policies. Both internal and external auditors can be used.

Third-Party Governance

For many organizations, a third party ensures that an organization complies with industry or governmental standards and regulations. This third party performs analysis of organizational operations and any other area dictated by the certifying or regulating organization. The third party reports all results of its findings to the certifying or regulating organization. The contract with the third party should stipulate that any findings or results should only be communicated with the organization that is being analyzed and with the regulating organization.

A member of high-level management usually manages this process so that the third party is given access as needed. As part of this analysis, the third party might need to perform an onsite assessment, a document exchange, or a process/policy review.

Onsite Assessment

An onsite assessment involves a team from the third party. This team needs access to all aspects of the organization under regulation. This assessment might include observing employees performing their day-to-day duties, reviewing records, reviewing documentation, and other tasks. Management should delegate a member of management to which the team can make formal requests.

Document Exchange/Review

A document exchange/review involves transmitting a set of documents to the third party. The process used for the document exchange must be secure on both ends of the exchange.

Process/Policy Review

A process/policy review focuses on a single process or policy within the organization and ensures that the process or policy follows regulations.

Personnel Security (Screening, Hiring, and Termination)

Personnel are responsible for the vast majority of security issues within an organization. For this reason, it is vital that an organization implement the appropriate personnel security policies. Organizations should have personnel security policies in place that include screening, hiring, and termination policies.

Personnel screening should occur prior to the offer of employment and might include a criminal background check, work history, background investigations, credit history, driving records, substance-abuse testing, and education and licensing verification. Each organization should determine the screening needs based on the organization's needs and the perspective personnel's employment level.

Personnel hiring procedures should include signing all the appropriate documents, including government-required documentation, no expectation of privacy statements, and non-disclosure agreements (NDAs). Organizations usually have a personnel handbook and other hiring information that must be communicated to the employee. The hiring process should include a formal verification that the employee has completed all the training. Employee IDs and passwords are issued at this time.

Personnel termination must be handled differently based on whether the termination is friendly or unfriendly. Procedures defined by the human resources department can ensure that the organizational property is returned, user access is removed at the appropriate time, and exit interviews are completed. With unfriendly terminations, organizational procedures must be proactive to prevent damage to organizational assets. Therefore, unfriendly termination procedures should include system and facility access termination prior to employee termination notification as well as security escort from the premises.

Management must also ensure that appropriate security policies are in place during employment. Separation of duties and job rotation were covered earlier in this chapter. Another management control is mandatory vacations, which requires that employees take their vacations and that another employee performs their job duties during that vacation time. Some positions might require employment agreements to protect the organization and its assets even after the employee is no longer with the organization. These agreements can include NDAs, non-compete clauses, and code of conduct and ethics agreements.

> **NOTE** Code of conduct and ethics are discussed in more depth in Chapter 10.

Security Awareness Training

Security awareness training, security training, and security education are three terms that are often used interchangeably but they are actually three different things. Awareness training reinforces the fact that valuable resources must be protected by implementing security measures. Security training teaches personnel the skills to enable them to perform their jobs in a secure manner. Awareness training and security training are usually combined as security awareness training, which improves user awareness of security and ensures that users can be held accountable for their actions. Security education is more independent and is targeted at security professionals who require security expertise to act as in-house experts for managing the security programs. Awareness training is the what, security training is the how, and security education is the why.

Security awareness training should be developed based on the audience. In addition, trainers must understand the corporate culture and how it will affect security. The audiences you need to consider when designing training include high-level management, middle management, technical personnel, and regular staff.

For high-level management, the security awareness training must provide a clear understanding of potential risks and threats, effects of security issues on organizational reputation and financial standing, and any applicable laws and regulations that pertain to the organization's security program. Middle management training should discuss policies, standards, baselines, guidelines, and procedures, particularly how these components map to the individual departments. Also, middle management must understand their responsibilities regarding security. Technical staff should receive technical training on configuring and maintaining security controls, including how to recognize an attack when it occurs. In addition, technical staff should be encouraged to pursue industry certifications and higher education degrees. Regular staff need to understand their responsibilities regarding security so that they perform their day-to-day tasks in a secure manner. With regular staff, providing real-world examples to emphasize proper security procedures is effective.

Personnel should sign a document that indicates they have completed the training and understand all the topics. Although the initial training should occur when personnel is hired, security awareness training should be considered a continuous process, with future training sessions occurring annually at a minimum.

Security Budget, Metrics, and Effectiveness

The CSO or other designated high-level manager prepares the organization's security budget, determines the security metrics, and reports on the effectiveness of the security program. This officer must work with other subject matter experts (SMEs) to ensure that all security costs are accounted for, including development, testing, implementation, maintenance, personnel, and equipment. The budgeting process requires an examination of all risks and ensures that security projects with this best cost-benefit ratio are implemented. Projects that take longer than 12–18 months are long-term and strategic and require more resources and funding to complete.

Security metrics provide information on both short- and long-term trends. By collecting these metrics and comparing them on a day-to-day basis, a security professional can determine the daily workload. When the metrics are compared over a longer period of time, the trends that occur can help to shape future security projects and budgets. Procedures should state who will collect the metrics, which metrics will be collected, when the metrics will be collected, and what the thresholds are that will trigger corrective actions. Security professionals should consult with the information security governance frameworks listed earlier in this chapter, particularly ISO/IEC 27004 and NIST 800-55, for help in establishing metrics guidelines and procedures.

Although the security team should analyze metrics on a daily basis, periodic analysis of the metrics by a third party can ensure the integrity and effectiveness of the security metrics by verifying the results of the internal team. Data from the third party should be used to improve the security program and security metrics process.

Exam Preparation Tasks

Review All Key Topics

Review the most important topics in this chapter, noted with the Key Topics icon in the outer margin of the page. Table 4-5 lists a reference of these key topics and the page numbers on which each is found.

Table 4-5 Key Topics for Chapter 4

Key Topic Element	Description	Page Number
Paragraph	Security principles and terms	159
Paragraph	Security frameworks and methodologies	163
List	ISO/IEC 27000 standards	164
List	NIST SP 800-53 control families	171
List	NIST SP 800-30 steps	176
List	Threat agent categories	177
Paragraph	SLE calculation	178
Paragraph	ALE calculation	178
Paragraph	Cost-benefit analysis	179
Paragraph	Handling risk	180
Paragraph	Information security governance components	183
List	Commercial business data classifications	186
List	Military and government data classifications	187

Complete the Tables and Lists from Memory

Print a copy of CD Appendix A, "Memory Tables," or at least the sections for this chapter, and complete the tables and lists from memory. Appendix B, "Memory Tables Answer Key," includes completed tables and lists to check your work.

Define Key Terms

Define the following key terms from this chapter and check your answers in the glossary:

risk management, confidentiality, integrity, availability, vulnerability, threat, threat agent, risk, exposure, countermeasure, safeguard, due care, due diligence, job rotation, separation of duties, split knowledge, dual control, tangible assets, intangible assets, quantitative risk analysis, qualitative risk analysis, SLE, AV, EF, ALE, ARO, total risk, residual risk, risk avoidance, risk transfer, risk mitigation, risk acceptance, strategic plans, tactical plans, policy, organizational security policy, system-specific security policy, issue-specific security policy, regulatory security policy, advisory security policy, informative security policy, standard, baseline, guideline, procedure.

Review Questions

1. What is a vulnerability?

    a. the entity that carries out a threat

    b. when an organizational asset is exposed to losses

    c. an absence or weakness of a countermeasure that is in place

    d. a control that reduces risk

2. Which ISO/IEC standard gives an overview and vocabulary of information security management?

    a. ISO/IEC 27000

    b. ISO/IEC 27001

    c. ISO/IEC 27002

    d. ISO/IEC 27003

3. Which framework uses the six communication questions (What, Where, When, Why, Who, and How) that intersect with six layers (operational, component, physical, logical, conceptual, and contextual)?

    a. Six Sigma

    b. SABSA

    c. ITIL

    d. ISO/IEC 27000 series

4. What is the first stage of the security program life cycle?

    a. Plan and Organize

    b. Implement

    c. Operate and Maintain

    d. Monitor and Evaluate

5. Which group of threat agents includes hardware and software failure, malicious code, and new technologies?

    a. human

    b. natural

    c. environmental

    d. technical

6. Which term indicates the monetary impact of each threat occurrence?

    a. ARO

    b. ALE

    c. EF

    d. SLE

7. What is risk avoidance?

    a. risk that is left over after safeguards have been implemented

    b. terminating the activity that causes a risk or choosing an alternative that is not as risky

    c. passing the risk on to a third party

    d. defining the acceptable risk level the organization can tolerate and reducing the risk to that level

8. Which security policies provide instruction on acceptable and unacceptable activities?

    a. informative security policies

    b. regulatory security policies

    c. system-specific security policies

    d. advisory security policies

9. What is the highest military security level?

    a. Confidential

    b. Top Secret

    c. Private

    d. Sensitive

10. Which organization role determines the classification level of the information to protect the data for which he is responsible?

    a. data owner

    b. data custodian

    c. security administrator

    d. security analyst

Answers and Explanations

1. **c.** A vulnerability is an absence or weakness of a countermeasure that is in place. A threat occurs when a vulnerability is identified or exploited. A threat agent is the entity that carries out a threat. Exposure occurs when an organizational asset is exposed to losses. A countermeasure or safeguard is a control that reduces risk.

2. **a.** The ISO/IEC 27000 standard gives an overview and vocabulary of information security management. The ISO/IEC 27001 standard lists information security requirements. The ISO/IEC 27002 standard gives the code of practice for information security management. The ISO/IEC 27003 standard gives implementation guidelines for information security management.

3. **b.** SABSA uses the six communication questions (What, Where, When, Why, Who, and How) that intersect with six layers (operational, component, physical, logical, conceptual, and contextual). Six Sigma is a process improvement standard that includes two project methodologies that were inspired by Deming's Plan/Do/Check/Act cycle. ITIL is a process management development standard that has five core publications: ITIL Service Strategy, ITIL Service Design, ITIL Service Transition, ITIL Service Operation, and ITIL Continual Service Improvement. ISO/IEC 27000 series includes a list of standards, each of which addresses a particular aspect of information security management.

4. **a**. The four stages of the security program life cycle, in order, are as follows:

    1. Plan and Organization
    2. Implement
    3. Operate and Maintain
    4. Monitor and Evaluate

5. **d**. Technical threat agents include hardware and software failure, malicious code, and new technologies. Human threat agents include both malicious and non-malicious insiders and outsiders, terrorists, spies, and terminated personnel. Natural threat agents include floods, fires, tornadoes, hurricanes, earthquakes, or other natural disaster or weather event. Environmental threat agents include power and other utility failure, traffic issues, biological warfare, and hazardous material issues (such as spillage).

6. **d**. SLE indicates the monetary impact of each threat occurrence. ARO is the estimate of how often a given threat might occur annually. ALE is the expected risk factor of an annual threat event. EF is the percent value or functionality of an asset that will be lost when a threat event occurs.

7. **b**. Risk avoidance is terminating the activity that causes a risk or choosing an alternative that is not as risky. Residual risk is risk that is left over after safeguards have been implemented. Risk transfer is passing the risk on to a third party. Risk mitigation is defining the acceptable risk level the organization can tolerate and reducing the risk to that level.

8. **d**. Advisory security policies provide instruction on acceptable and unacceptable activities. Informative security policies provide information on certain topics and act as an educational tool. Regulatory security policies address specific industry regulations, including mandatory standards. System-specific security policies address security for a specific computer, network, technology, or application.

9. **b**. Military and governmental entities classify data using five main classification levels, listed from highest sensitivity level to lowest:

Top Secret

Secret

Confidential

Sensitive but unclassified

Unclassified

Commercial businesses classify data using four main classification levels, listed from highest sensitivity level to lowest:

Confidential

Private

Sensitive

Public

10. **a.** The data owner determines the classification level of the information to protect the data for which he is responsible. The data custodian implements the information classification and controls after they are determined. The security administrator maintains security devices and software. The security analyst analyzes the security needs of the organizations and develops the internal information security governance documents.

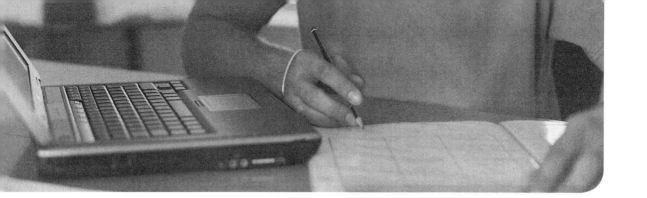

This chapter covers the following topics:

- **System development life cycle:** Covers development steps, including Initiate, Acquire/Develop, Implement, Operate/Maintain, and Dispose

- **Software development life cycle:** Describes the steps in the software development life cycle, including Gather Requirements, Design, Develop, Test/Validate, Release/Maintain, and Change Management/Configuration Management

- **Software development security best practices:** Includes a survey of industry approaches to ensuring best practices in securing software development

- **Software development methods:** Explains common software development methods and terms important to understanding their application

- **Programming concepts:** Discusses software architectures and languages used to implement them

- **Database concepts and security:** Surveys database concepts and security

- **Knowledge-based systems:** Covers artificial intelligence (AI) and its use in knowledge-based or expert systems

- **Software threats:** Describes common security issues presented by insecure code and malware

- **Software security effectiveness:** Describes methods of validating and certifying software security

CHAPTER 5

Software Development Security

Software is at the heart of all functionality in computer systems. Various types of software, including operating systems, applications, and utilities, work together to deliver instructions from the human to his hardware. All of these instructions are created with the intent of making some operation possible.

When software is written and developed the focus can be placed on its functionality and ease of use or on its security. In many cases the two goals might work at cross purposes. Giving inadequate attention to the security of a piece of software results in software that can introduce security issues to both the application and the systems on which it is run.

Moreover, some types of software are intentionally developed to create security openings in a network or system. This chapter discusses software development methodology, best practices for secure development, and types of malware and methods of mitigating the effects of malware.

Foundation Topics

System Development Life Cycle

When an organization defines new functionality that must be provided either to its customers or internally, it must create systems to deliver that functionality. Many decisions have to be made, and a logical process should be followed in making those decisions. This process is called the System Development Life Cycle. Rather than being a haphazard approach, a System Development Life Cycle provides clear and logical steps to follow to ensure that the system that emerges at the end of the development process provides the intended functionality with an acceptable level of security.

System Development Life Cycle:

1. Initiate
2. Acquire/Develop
3. Implement

4. Operate/Maintain

5. Dispose

This section explains the five steps in the System Development Life Cycle.

Initiate

In the Initiate phase, the realization is made that a new feature or functionality is desired or required in an existing piece of software. This new feature might constitute an upgrade to an existing product or the development of a whole new piece of software. In either case the Initiate phase includes making a decision on whether to purchase or develop the product internally.

In this stage an organization must also give thought to the security requirements of the solution. Creating a *preliminary risk assessment* can be used to detail the confidentiality, integrity, and availability (CIA) requirement and concerns. Identifying these issues at the outset is important so these considerations can guide the purchase or development of the solution. The earlier in the System Development Life Cycle that the security requirements are identified, the more likely that the issues will be successfully addressed in the final product.

NOTE Chapter 4, "Information Security Governance and Risk Management," covers risk assessment in depth.

Acquire/Develop

In the Acquire/Develop stage of the System Development Life Cycle, a series of activities take place that provide input to facilitate making a decision about acquiring or developing the solution; the organization then makes a decision on the solution. The activities are designed to get answers to the following questions:

- What functions does the system need to perform?
- What are the potential risks to CIA exposed by the solution?
- What protection levels must be provided to satisfy legal and regulatory requirements?
- What tests are required to ensure that security concerns have been mitigated?

- How do various third-party solutions address these concerns?
- How do the security controls required by the solution affect other parts of the company security policy?
- What metrics will be used to evaluate the success of the security controls?

The answers to these questions should guide the acquisition/develop decision as well as the steps that follow this stage of the System Development Life Cycle.

Implement

In the Implement stage, the solution is introduced to the live environment but not without its completing both certification and accreditation. Certification is the process of technically verifying the solution's effectiveness and security. The Accreditation process involves a formal authorization to introduce the solution into the production environment by management.

Operate/Maintain

After the system is operating in the environment, the process does not end. Doing a performance baseline is important so that continuous monitoring can take place. The baseline ensures that performance issues can be quickly determined. Any changes over time (addition of new features, patches to the solution, and so on) should be closely monitored with respect to the effects on the baseline.

Instituting a formal change management process ensures that all changes are both approved and documented. Because any changes can affect both security and performance, special attention should be given to monitoring the solution after any changes.

Finally, vulnerability assessments and penetration testing after the solution is implemented can help discover any security or performance problems that might either be introduced by a change or arise as a result of a new threat.

Dispose

The Dispose stage consists of removing the solution from the environment when it reaches the end of its usefulness. When this occurs, an organization must consider certain issues. They include:

1. Does removal or replacement of the solution introduce any security holes in the network?

2. How can the system be terminated in an orderly fashion so as not to disrupt business continuity?

3. How should any residual data left on any systems be removed?

4. How should any physical systems that were a part of the solution be disposed of safely?

5. Are there any legal or regulatory issues that would guide the destruction of data?

Software Development Life Cycle

The Software Development Life Cycle can be seen as a subset of the System Development Life Cycle in that any system under development could (but not necessarily) include the development of software to support the solution. The goal of the Software Development Life Cycle is to provide a predictable framework of procedures designed to identify all requirements with regard to functionality, cost, reliability, and delivery schedule and ensure that each are met in the final solution. This section breaks down the steps in the Software Development Life Cycle and describes how each step contributes to this ultimate goal. Keep in mind that steps in the SDLC can vary based on the provider and this is but one popular example. The following sections flesh out the Software Development Life Cycle steps in detail:

1. Gather requirements

2. Design

3. Develop

4. Release/Maintain

5. Change Management and Configuration Management

Gather Requirements

In the Gather Requirements phase of the Software Development Life Cycle, both the functionality and the security requirements of the solution are identified. These requirements could be derived from a variety of sources such as evaluating competitor products for a commercial product to surveying the needs of users for an internal solution. In some cases these requirements could come from a direct request from a current customer.

From a security perspective, an organization must identify potential vulnerabilities and threats. When this assessment is performed, the intended purpose of the software and the expected environment must be considered. Moreover, the data that will be generated or handled by the solution must be assessed for its sensitivity. Assigning a privacy impact rating to the data to help guide measures intended to protect the data from exposure might be useful.

Design

In the Design phase of the Software Development Life Cycle, an organization develops a detailed description of how the software will satisfy all functional and security goals. It attempts to map the internal behavior and operations of the software to specific requirements to identify any requirements that have not been met prior to implementation and testing.

During this process the state of the application is determined in every phase of its activities. The state of the application refers to its functional and security posture during each operation it performs. Therefore all possible operations must be identified. This is done to ensure that at no time does the software enter an insecure state or act in an unpredictable way.

Identifying the attack surface is also a part of this analysis. The attack surface describes what is available to be leveraged by an attacker. The amount of attack surface might change at various states of the application but at no time should the attack surface provided violate the security needs identified in the Gather Requirements stage.

Develop

The Develop phase is where the code or instructions that make the software work is written. The emphasis of this phase is strict adherence to secure coding practices. Some models that can help promote secure coding are covered later in this chapter in the section "Software Development Security Best Practices."

Many security issues with software are created through insecure coding practices such as lack of input validation or data type checks. Identifying these issues in a code review that attempts to assume all possible attack scenarios and their impact on the code is needed. Not identifying these issues can lead to attacks such as buffer overflows and injection and to other error conditions, which are covered later in this chapter in the section "Source Code Issues."

Test/Validate

In the Test/Validate phase, several types of testing should occur, including ways to identify both functional errors and security issues. The auditing method that assesses the extent of the system testing and identifies specific program logic that has not been tested is called the *test data method*. This method tests not only expected or valid input but also invalid and unexpected values to assess the behavior of the software in both instances. An active attempt should be made to attack the software, including attempts at buffer overflows and denial of service (DoS) attacks. Some goals of testing performed at this time are

- **Verification testing:** Determines whether the original design specifications have been met
- **Validation testing:** Takes a higher level view and determines whether the original purpose of the software has been achieved

NOTE Chapter 2, "Access Control," covers buffer overflows and DoS attacks.

Software is typically developed in pieces or modules of code that are later assembled to yield the final product. Each module should be tested separately in a procedure called *unit testing*. Having development staff carry out this testing is critical, but using a different group of engineers than the ones who wrote the code can ensure an impartial process occurs. This is a good example of the concept of separation of duties.

NOTE Separation of duties is discussed in more depth in Chapter 2 and Chapter 4.

The following should be characteristics of the unit testing:

- The test data is part of the specifications.
- Testing should check for out-of-range values and out-of bounds conditions.
- Correct test output results should be developed and known beforehand.

Live or actual field data is *not* recommended for use in the unit testing procedures.

Additional testing that is recommended includes:

- **Integration testing:** Assesses the way in which the modules work together and determines whether functional and security specifications have been met
- **Acceptance testing:** Ensures that the customer (either internal or external) is satisfied with the functionality of the software
- **Regression testing:** Takes places after changes are made to the code to ensure the changes have neither reduced functionality or security

Release/Maintain

Also called the release/maintenance phase in some documentation, this phase includes the implementation of the software into the live environment and the continued monitoring of its operation. Finding additional functional and security problems at this point as the software begins to interface with other elements of the network is not unusual.

In many cases vulnerabilities are discovered in the live environments for which no current fix or patch exists. In that case, it is referred to as *zero-day vulnerability*. Having the supporting development staff discover these rather than those looking to exploit the vulnerability is best.

Change Management and Configuration Management

After the solution is deployed in the live environment, there will inevitably be additional changes that must be made to the software due to security issues. In some cases the software might be altered to enhance or increase its functionality. In either case changes must be handled through a formal change and configuration management process.

The purpose of this process is to ensure that all changes to the configuration of and to the source code itself are approved by the proper personnel and are implemented in a safe and logical manner. This process should always ensure continued functionality in the live environment and changes should be documented fully, including all changes to hardware and software.

Software Development Security Best Practices

To support the goal of ensuring that software is soundly developed with regard to both functionality and security, a number of organizations have attempted to assemble a set of software development best practices. In this section, we'll look at some of those organizations and in the section that follows list a number of their most important recommendations.

WASC

The Web Application Security Consortium (WASC) is an organization that provides best practices for web-based applications along with a variety of resources, tools, and information that organizations can make use of in developing web applications.

One of the functions undertaken by WASC is continual monitoring of attacks leading to the development of a list of top attack methods in use. This list can aid in ensuring that organizations are not only aware of the latest attack methods and how widespread these attacks are but also can assist them in making the proper changes to their web applications to mitigate these attack types.

OWASP

The Open Web Application Security Project (OWASP) is another group that monitors attacks, specifically web attacks. OWASP maintains a list of top 10 attacks on an ongoing basis. This group also holds regular meetings at chapters throughout the world, providing resources and tools including testing procedures, code review steps, and development guidelines.

BSI

The Department of Homeland Security (DHS) also has become involved in promoting software security best practices. The Build Security In (BSI) initiative promotes a process-agnostic approach that makes security recommendations with regard to architectures, testing methods, code reviews, and management processes. The DHS Software Assurance program addresses ways to reduce vulnerabilities, mitigate exploitations, and improve the routine development and delivery of software solutions.

ISO/IEC 27000

The International Organization for Standardization (ISO) and the International Electrotechnical Commission (IEC) created the 27034 standard, which is part of a larger body of standards called the ISO/IEC 27000 series. These standards provide guidance to organizations in integrating security into the development and maintenance of software applications. These suggestions are relevant not only to the development of in-house applications but also to the safe deployment and management of third-party solutions in the enterprise.

> **NOTE** All the standards that are part of ISO/IEC 27000 are discussed in more depth in Chapter 4.

Software Development Methods

In the course of creating software over the last 30 years, developers have learned many things about the development process. As development projects have grown from a single developer to small teams to now large development teams working on massive projects with many modules that must securely interact, development models have been created to increase the efficiency and success of these projects. Lessons learned have been incorporated into these models and methods. This section covers some of the more common models along with concepts and practices that must be understood to implement them.

This section discusses the following software development methods:

- Build and Fix
- Waterfall
- V-shaped
- Prototyping
- Incremental
- Spiral
- Rapid Application Development
- Agile
- JAD
- Cleanroom
- CMMI

Build and Fix

Although it's not a formal model, the Build and Fix approach describes a method that while certainly used in the past has been largely discredited and is now used as a template for how *not* to manage a development project. Simply put, in this method, the software is developed as quickly as possible and released.

No formal control mechanisms are used to provide feedback during the process. The product is rushed to market, and problems are fixed on an as-discovered basis with patches and service packs. Although this approach gets the product to market faster and cheaper, in the long run, the costs involved in addressing problems and the collateral damage to the product in the marketplace outweigh any initial cost savings.

Despite the fact that this model still seems to be in use today, most successful developers have learned to implement one of the other models discussed in this section so that the initial product, though not necessarily perfect, comes much closer to meeting all the functional and security requirements of the design. Moreover, using these models helps to identify and eliminate as many bugs as possible without using the customer as "quality control."

In this simplistic model of the software development process, certain unrealistic assumptions are made, including:

- Each step can be completed and finalized without any effect from the later stages that might require rework.
- Iteration (reworking and repeating) among the steps in the process that is typically called for in other models is not stressed in this model.
- Phases are not seen as individual milestones as in some other models discussed here.

Waterfall

The original Waterfall model breaks the process into distinct phases. Although this model is somewhat of a rigid approach, the basic process is as a sequential series of steps that are followed without going back to earlier steps. This approach is called *incremental development*. Figure 5-1 is a representation of the Waterfall process.

In the *modified* Waterfall model, each phase in the development process is considered its own milestone in the project management process. Unlimited backward iteration (returning to earlier stages to address problems) is not allowed in this model. However, product verification and validation are performed in this model. Problems that are discovered during the project do *not* initiate a return to earlier stages, but rather are dealt with after the project is complete.

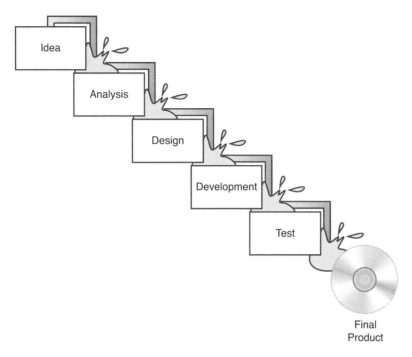

Figure 5-1 Waterfall Method

V-Shaped

The V-shaped model is also somewhat rigid but differs primarily from the Waterfall method in that verification and validation are performed at each step. Although this model can work when all requirements are well understood upfront (frequently not the case) and potential scope changes are small, it does not provide for handling events concurrently because it is also a sequential process like the Waterfall. It does build in a higher likelihood of success because it performs testing at every stage. Figure 5-2 is a representation of this process.

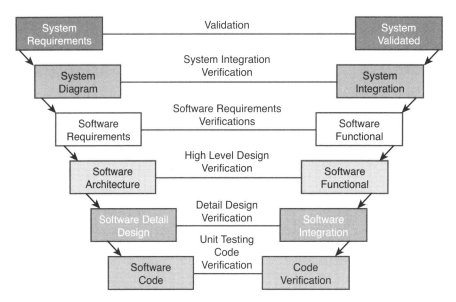

Figure 5-2 V-shaped Model

Prototyping

Although it's not a formal model unto itself, prototyping is the use of a sample of code to explore a specific approach to solving a problem before extensive time and cost have been invested in the approach. This allows the team to both identify the utility of the sample code as well as identify design problems with the approach. Prototype systems can provide significant time and cost savings because you don't have to make the whole final product to begin testing it.

Incremental

A refinement to the basic Waterfall model that states that software should be developed in increments of functional capability is called the Incremental model. In this model, a working version or iteration of the solution is produced, tested, and redone until the final product is completed. You could think of it as a series of waterfalls. After each iteration or version of the software is completed, testing occurs to identify gaps in functionality and security from the original design. Then the gaps are addressed by proceeding through the same analysis, design, code, and test stages again. When the product is deemed to be acceptable with respect to the original design, it is released. Figure 5-3 is a representation of this process.

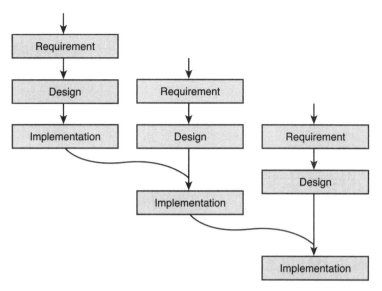

Figure 5-3 Incremental Model

Spiral

The Spiral model is actually a meta-model that incorporates a number of the software development models. It is also an iterative approach but places more emphasis on risk analysis at each stage. Prototypes are produced at each stage, and the process can be seen as a loop that keeps circling back to take a critical look at risks that have been addressed while still allowing visibility into new risks that might been created in the last iteration.

This model assumes that knowledge will be gained at each iteration and should be incorporated into the design as it evolves. Some cases even involve the customer making comments and observations at each iteration as well. Figure 5-4 is a representation of this process. The radial dimension of the diagram represents cumulative cost, and the angular dimension represents progress made in completing each cycle.

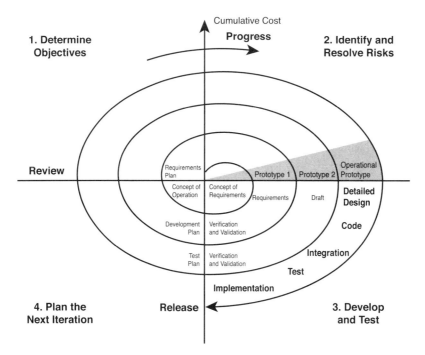

Figure 5-4 Spiral Model

Rapid Application Development (RAD)

In the Rapid Application Development (RAD) model, less time is spent upfront on design while emphasis is placed on rapidly producing prototypes with the assumption that crucial knowledge can only be gained through trial and error. This model is especially helpful when requirements are not well understood at the outset and are developed as issues and challenges arise during the building of prototypes. Figure 5-5 is a comparison of the RAD model to traditional models where the project is completed fully and then verified and validated.

Agile

Many of the processes discussed thus far rely on a rigid adherence to process-oriented models. In many cases the focus is more on following procedural steps than on reacting to changes quickly and increasing efficiency. The Agile model puts more emphasis on continuous feedback and cross-functional teamwork.

It attempts to be nimble enough to react to situations that arise during development. Less time is spent on the upfront analysis and more emphasis is placed on learning from the process and incorporating lessons learned in real time. There is also more interaction with the customer throughout the process. Figure 5-6 is a comparison of the Agile model with the Waterfall model.

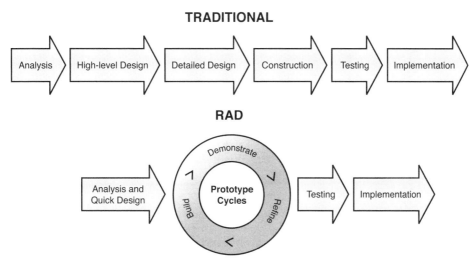

Figure 5-5 Traditional and RAD Models

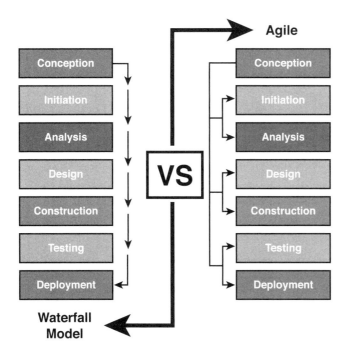

Figure 5-6 Agile and Waterfall Comparison Model

JAD

The Joint Analyses Development or Joint Application Development (JAD) model is one that uses a team approach. It uses workshops to both agree on requirements and to resolve differences. The theory is that by bringing all parties together at all stages, a more satisfying product will emerge at the end of the process.

Cleanroom

In contrast to the JAD model, the Cleanroom model strictly adheres to formal steps and a more structured method. It attempts to prevent errors and mistakes through extensive testing. This method works well in situations where high quality is a must, the application is mission critical, or the solution must undergo a strict certification process.

CMMI

The Capability Maturity Model Integration (CMMI) is a comprehensive set of guidelines that addresses all phases of the software development life cycle. It describes a series of stages or maturity levels that a development process can advance through as it goes from the ad hoc (Build and Fix) model to one that incorporates a budgeted plan for continuous improvement. Figure 5-7 shows its five maturity levels along with an explanation of each.

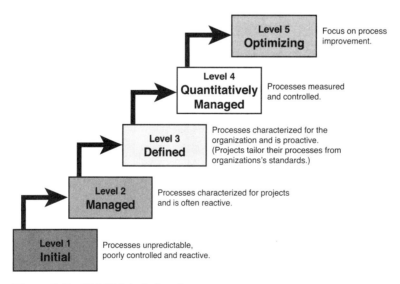

Figure 5-7 CMMI Maturity Levels

Programming Concepts

Software comprises the written instructions that allow humans to communicate with the computer hardware. These instructions are written in various *programming languages*. As programming has evolved over the years, each successive language has delivered more functionality to programmers. Programming languages can be classified in categories based on the type of instructions they create and to which part of the system they speak. This section covers the main categories.

Machine Languages

Machine languages are those that deliver instructions directly to the processor. This was the only type of programming done in the 1950s and uses basic binary instructions without a compiler or interpreter (programs that convert higher language types to a form that can be executed by the processor). This type of programming is both time consuming and prone to errors. Most of these programs were very rudimentary due to the need to keep a tight rein on their length.

Assembly Languages and Assemblers

Considered to be "one step above" machine languages, *assembly languages* use symbols or mnemonics to represent sections of complicated binary code. Consequently, these languages use an assembler to convert the code to machine level. Although this greatly simplifies and shortens the code, it still requires extensive knowledge of the computer's architecture. It also means that any code written in these languages will be hardware specific. Although assembly language is simpler to write than machine language, it is not as easy to create as the high-level languages discussed next.

High-level Languages, Compilers, and Interpreters

In the 1960s, a third level of language emerged called *high-level languages*. These instructions use abstract statements (for example, IF-THEN-ELSE) and are processor independent. They are easier to work with, and their syntax is more similar to human language. This code uses either assemblers or compilers to convert the instructions into machine code. The end result is a decrease in the total amount of code writers required for a particular project.

A fourth generation of languages called *very-high-level languages* focus on abstract algorithms that hide some of the complexity from the programmer. This frees the programmer to focus on the real world problems they are trying to solve rather than the details that go on behind the scenes.

Finally, in the 1990s, a fifth generation of languages began to emerge called *natural languages*. The goal is to use these languages to create software that can solve problems on its own rather than require a programmer to create code to deal with the problem. Although this goal is not fully realized, using knowledge-based processing and artificial intelligence is worth pursuing.

A significant distinction exists with respect to security between compiled code and interpreted code. Because compiled code has already been translated to binary language, detecting malicious code inside an application is very difficult. Interpreted code, on the other hand, uses a language interpreter that is a piece of software that allows the end user to write a program in some human-readable language and have this program executed directly by the interpreter. In this case spotting malicious code is somewhat easier because the code is a bit more readable by humans.

Object-Oriented Programming

In classic software development, data is input into a program, the program manages the data from beginning to end, and a result is returned. Object-Oriented Programming (OOP) supplies the same functionality but it is more efficiently introduced through different techniques. In OOP, *objects* are organized in a hierarchy of *classes* with characteristics called *attributes* attached to each. OOP emphasizes the employment of objects and methods rather than types or transformations as in other software approaches.

The programmer creates the classes of objects but not all the objects themselves. Software in the program allows for objects to be created on demand when needed through requests. When a request comes in, usually from an existing object for a new object to carry out some function, it is built (instantiated) with necessary code. It does not matter if objects are written in a different programming language as long as the objects have the ability to communicate with one another, a process usually made possible through an application programming interface (API).

Moreover, because objects are organized in hierarchical classes, object *methods* (functionalities or procedures) can be passed from a class to a subclass through a process called *inheritance*. The objects contain or *encapsulate* attribute *values*. Objects communicate with messages sent to another object's API. Different objects might react differently to the same message, which is called the object's *behavior*. The code that defines how an object will behave with respect to a message is called its *method*.

Some parts of an object might be private, which means its internal data and operation is not visible by other objects. This privacy is provided through the encapsulation process and is sometimes called *data hiding*. *Abstraction* is the ability to suppress these unnecessary internal details. Other objects, subjects, and applications can make use of objects' functionality through standardized interfaces without worrying about the details of the functionality.

Examples of OOP languages are C++, Simula 67, and Smalltalk. The many advantages to this approach include:

- Modularity in design through autonomous objects
- Definition of internal components without impacting other parts of the system
- Reusability of components
- More readily maps to business needs

Polymorphism

In an object-oriented system, polymorphism denotes objects of many different classes that are related by some common superclass; thus, any object denoted by this name can respond to some common set of operations in a different way. Polymorphism is the ability of different objects with a common name to react to the same message or input with different output. For example, three objects might receive the input "Dodge Dart." One object's output might be "subcompact," another's might be "uses unleaded fuel," and another's might be "costs 35,000." In some cases these differences derive from the fact that the objects have inherited different characteristics from their parent classes.

Cohesion

Cohesion is a term used to describe how many different tasks a module can carry out. If it is limited to a small number or a single function, it is said to have *high cohesion*. High cohesion is good in that changes can be made to the model without affecting other modules. It also makes reusing the module easier. The highest cohesion is provided by limiting the scope of a module's operation.

Coupling

Coupling describes how much interaction one module requires from another module to do its job. Low or loose coupling indicates a module does not need much help from other modules, whereas high coupling indicates the opposite. If Module A needs to wait on results from messages it sent to three other modules before it can proceed, it is said to have high coupling. To sum up these last two sections, the best programming provides high cohesion and low coupling.

Data Structures

Data structure refers to the logical relationship between elements of data. It describes the extent to which elements, methods of access, and processing alternatives are associated and the organization of data elements. These relationships can be simple or complex. From a security standpoint, these relationships or the way in which various software components communicate and the data formats that they use must be well understood to understand the vulnerabilities that might be exposed by these data structures.

Distributed Object-Oriented Systems

When an application operates in a client/server framework as many do, the solution is performing *distributed computing*. This means that components on different systems must be able to both locate each other and communicate on a network. Typically, the bulk of the solution is on the server, and a smaller piece is located on the client. This requires some architecture to support this process-to-process communication. There are several that can be used as discussed shortly.

CORBA

Common Object Request Broker Architecture (CORBA) is an open object-oriented standard developed by the Object Management Group (OMG). This standard uses a component called the Object Request Broker (ORB) to implement exchanges among objects in a heterogeneous, distributed environment.

The ORB manages all communication between components. It accepts requests for service from the client application, directs the request to the server, and then relays the response back to the client application. The ORB makes communication possible locally or remotely. This is even possible between components that are written in different languages because they use a standard interface to communicate with the ORB.

COM and DCOM

Component Object Model (COM) is a model for communication between processes on the same computer, whereas as its name implies, the Distributed Component Object Model (DCOM) is a model for communication between processes in different parts of the network. DCOM works as the middleware between these remote processes (called interprocess communication or IPC).

DCOM provides the same services as those provided by the ORB in the CORBA framework; that is, data connectivity, message service, and distributed transaction service. All of these functions are integrated into one technology that uses the same interface as COM.

OLE

Object Linking and Embedding (OLE) is a method for sharing objects on a local computer that uses COM as its foundation. In fact, OLE is sometimes described as the predecessor of COM. It allows objects to be embedded in documents (spreadsheets, graphics, and so on). The term *linking* refers to the relationship between one program and another, and the term *embedding* refers to the placement of data into a foreign program or document.

Java

Java Platform, Enterprise Edition (Java EE) is another distributed component model that relies on the Java programming language. It is a framework used to develop software that provides APIs for networking services and uses an interprocess communication process that is based on CORBA. Its goal is to provide a standardized method of providing back-end code that carries out business logic for enterprise applications.

SOA

A newer approach to providing a distributed computing model is the Service-Oriented Architecture (SOA). It operates on the theory of providing web-based communication functionality without each application requiring redundant code to be written per application. It uses standardized interfaces and components called service brokers to facilitate communication among web-based applications.

Mobile Code

Mobile code is a type that can be transferred across a network and then executed on a remote system or device. The security concerns with mobile code revolve around the prevention of the execution of malicious code without the knowledge of the user. This section covers the two main types of mobile code, Java applets and ActiveX applets, and the way they operate.

Java Applets

A *Java applet* is a small component created using Java that runs in a web browser. It is platform independent and creates intermediate code called byte code that is not processor-specific. When the applet downloads to the computer, the Java virtual machine (JVM), which must be present on the destination computer, converts the byte code to machine code.

The JVM executes the applet in a protected environment called a *sandbox*. This critical security feature, called the Java Security Model (JSM), helps to mitigate the extent of damage that could be caused by malicious code. However, it does not eliminate the problem with hostile applets (also called active content modules) so Java applets should still be regarded with suspicion because they might launch an intentional attack after being downloaded from the Internet.

ActiveX

ActiveX is a Microsoft technology that uses OOP and is based on the COM and DCOM. These self-sufficient programs, called *controls*, become a part of the operating system after they're downloaded. The problem is that these controls execute under the security context of the current user, which in many cases has administrator rights. This means that a malicious ActiveX control could do some serious damage.

ActiveX uses Authenticode technology to digitally sign the controls. This system has been shown to have significant flaws, and ActiveX controls are generally regarded with more suspicion than Java applets.

Database Concepts and Security

Databases have become the technology of choice for storing, organizing, and analyzing large sets of data. Users generally access a database though a client interface. As the need arises to provide access to entities outside the enterprise, the opportunities for misuse increase. In this section, concepts necessary to discuss database security are covered as well as the security concerns surrounding database management.

DBMS Architecture and Models

Databases contain data and the main difference in database models is how that information is stored and organized. The model describes the relationships among the data elements, how the data is accessed, how integrity is ensured, and acceptable operations. The five models or architectures we discuss are:

- Relational
- Hierarchical
- Network
- Object-oriented
- Object-relational

The **relational** model uses *attributes* (columns) and *tuples* (rows) to organize the data in two-dimensional tables. Each cell in the table, representing the intersection of an attribute and a tuple, represents a record.

When working with relational database management systems, you should understand the following terms:

- **Relation:** Fundamental entity in a relational database in the form of a table.
- **Tuple:** A row in a table.
- **Attribute:** A column in a table.
- **Schema:** Description of a relational database.
- **Record:** Collection of related data items.
- **Base relation:** In SQL, a relation that is actually existent in the database.
- **View:** The set of data available to a given user. Security is enforced through the use of these.
- **Degree:** The number of columns in a table.
- **Cardinality:** The number of rows in a relation.
- **Domain:** The set of allowable values that an attribute can take.
- **Primary key:** Columns that make each row unique.
- **Foreign key:** An attribute in one relation that has values matching the primary key in another relation. Matches between the foreign key to the primary key are important because they represent references from one relation to another and establish the connection among these relations.
- **Candidate key:** An attribute in one relation that has values matching the primary key in another relation.
- **Referential integrity:** Requires that for any foreign key attribute, the referenced relation must have a tuple with the same value for its primary key.

An important element of database design that ensures that the attributes in a table depend only on the primary key is a process called *normalization*. Normalization includes

- Eliminating repeating groups by putting them into separate tables
- Eliminating redundant data (occurring in more than one table)
- Eliminating attributes in a table that are not dependent on the primary key of that table

In the **hierarchical** model, data is organized into a hierarchy. An object can have one child (an object that is a subset of the parent object), multiple children, or no children. To navigate this hierarchy, you must know the branch in which the object is located. An example of the use of this system is the Windows registry and a Lightweight Directory Access Protocol (LDAP) directory.

In the **network** model, like in the hierarchical model, data is organized into a hierarchy but unlike the hierarchical model, objects can have multiple parents. Because of this, knowing which branch to find a data element in is not necessary because there will typically be multiple paths to it.

The **object-oriented** model has the ability to handle a variety of data types and is more dynamic than a relational database. Object-Oriented Database (OODB) systems are useful in storing and manipulating complex data, such as images and graphics. Consequently, complex applications involving multimedia, computer-aided design (CAD), video, graphics, and expert systems are more suited to it. It also has the characteristics of ease of reusing code and analysis and reduced maintenance.

Objects can be created as needed, and the data and the procedure (or methods) go with the object when it is requested. A *method* is the code defining the actions that the object performs in response to a message. This model uses some of the same concepts of a relational model. In the object-oriented model, a relation, column, and tuple (relational terms) are referred to as class, attribute, and instance objects.

The **object-relational** model is the marriage of object-oriented and relational technologies, combining the attributes of both. This is a relational database with a software interface that is written in an OOP language. The logic and procedures are derived from the front-end software rather than the database. This means each front-end application can have its own specific procedures.

Database Interface Languages

Access to information in a database is facilitated by an application that allows you to obtain and interact with data. These interfaces can be written in several different languages. This section discusses some of the more important data programming languages.

ODBC

Open Database Connectivity (ODBC) is an API that allows communication with databases either locally or remotely. An API on the client sends requests to the ODBC API. The ODBC API locates the database and a specific driver converts the request into a database command that the specific database will understand.

JDBC

As one might expect from the title, Java Database Connectivity (JDBC) makes it possible for Java applications to communicate with a database. A Java API is what allows Java programs to execute SQL statements. It is database agnostic and allows communication with various types of databases. It provides the same functionality as the ODBC.

XML

Data can now be created in XML format, but the XML:DB API allows XML applications to interact with more traditional databases, such as relational databases. It requires that the database have a database-specific driver that encapsulates all the database access logic.

OLE DB

Object Linking and Embedding Database (OLE DB) is a replacement for ODBC, extending its functionality to non-relational databases. Although it is COM-based and limited to Microsoft Windows-based tools, it provides applications with uniform access to a variety of data sources, including service through ActiveX objects.

Data Warehouses and Data Mining

Data warehousing is the process of combining data from multiple databases or data sources in a central location called a warehouse. The warehouse is used to carry out analysis. The data is not simply combined but is processed and presented in a more useful and understandable way. Data warehouses require stringent security because the data is not dispersed but located in a central location.

Data mining is the process of using special tools to organize the data into a format that makes it easier to make business decisions based on the content. It analyzes large data sets in a data warehouse to find non-obvious patterns. These tools locate associations between data and correlate these associations into metadata. It allows for more sophisticated inferences (sometimes called business intelligence [BI]) to be made about the data. Three measures should be taken when using data warehousing applications:

- Control metadata from being used interactively.
- Monitor the data purging plan.
- Reconcile data moved between the operations environment and data warehouse.

Database Threats

Security threats to databases usually revolve around unwanted access to data. Two security threats that exist in managing databases involve the processes of *aggregation* and *inference*. Aggregation is the act of combining information from various sources. The way this can become a security issue with databases is when a user does not have access to a given set of date objects, but does have access to them individually or least some of them and is able to piece together the information to which he should *not* have access. The process of piecing the information together is called inference. Two types of access measures can be put in place to help prevent access to inferable information:

- **Content-dependent access control** bases access on the sensitivity of the data. For example, a department manager might have access to the salaries of the employees in his/her department but not to the salaries of employees in other departments. The cost of this measure is an increased processing overhead.

- **Context-dependent access control** bases the access to data on multiple factors to help prevent inference. Access control can be a function of factors such as location, time of day, and previous access history.

Database Views

Access to the information in a database is usually controlled through the use of database views. A view refers to the given set of data that a user or group of users can see when they access the database. Before a user is able to use a view, she must have both permission on the view and all dependent objects. Views enforce the concept of least privilege.

Database Locks

Database locks are used when one user is accessing a record that prevents another user from accessing the record at the same time to prevent edits until the first user is finished. Locking not only provides exclusivity to writes but also controls reading of unfinished modifications or uncommitted data.

Polyinstantiation

Polyinstantiation is a process used to prevent data inference violations like the ones discussed in the section "Database Threats." It does this by enabling a relation to contain multiple tuples with the same primary keys with each instance distinguished by a security level. It prevents low-level database users from inferring the existence of higher level data.

OLTP ACID Test

An Online Transaction Processing (OLTP) system is used to monitor for problems such as processes that stop functioning. Its main goal is to prevent transactions that don't happen properly or are not complete from taking effect. An ACID test ensures that each transaction has the following properties before it is committed:

- **Atomicity:** Either all operations are complete, or the database changes are rolled back.

- **Consistency:** The transaction follows an integrity process that ensures that data is consistent in all places where it exists.

- **Isolation:** A transaction does not interact with other transactions until completion.

- **Durability:** After it's verified, the transaction is committed and cannot be rolled back.

Knowledge-Based Systems

Knowledge-based systems, also called expert systems, use artificial intelligence to emulate human logic when solving problems. They use rules-based programming to determine how to react through if-then statements and an inference engine to match patterns and facts to determine whether an operation should be allowed.

In an expert system, the process of beginning with a possible solution and using the knowledge in the knowledge base to justify the solution based on the raw input data is called backward chaining. This mode allows determining whether a given hypothesis is valid. Developing these systems requires the input of both a knowledge engineer and a domain expert.

An off-the-shelf software package that implements an inference engine, a mechanism for entering knowledge, a user interface, and a system to provide explanations of the reasoning used to generate a solution is called an *expert system shell*, which provides the fundamental building blocks of an expert system and supports the entering of domain knowledge.

A *fuzzy expert system* is an expert system that uses fuzzy membership functions and rules, instead of Boolean logic, to reason about data. Thus, fuzzy variables can have an approximate range of values instead of the binary True or False used in conventional expert systems.

Software Threats

Software threats can also be created in the way software is coded or developed. Following development best practices can help prevent this inadvertent creation of security issues when creating software. Software threats also can be introduced through malware. In this section, malware and software coding issues are discussed as well as options to mitigate the threat.

Malware

Malicious software (or malware) is a term that describes any software that harms a computer, deletes data, or takes actions the user did not authorize. It includes a wide array of malware types, including ones you have probably heard of such as viruses, and many you might not have heard of, but of which you should be aware.

The malware that you need to understand includes the following:

- Virus
    - Boot sector virus
    - Parasitic virus
    - Stealth virus
    - Polymorphic virus
    - Macro virus
    - Multipartite virus
- Worm
- Trojan horse
- Logic bomb
- Spyware/adware
- Botnet
- rootkit

Virus

A virus is a self-replicating program that infects software. It uses a host application to reproduce and deliver its payload and typically attaches itself to a file. It differs from a worm in that it usually requires some action on the part of the user to help it spread to other computers.

The following list shows virus types along with a brief description of each.

- **Boot sector:** These infect the boot sector of a computer and either overwrite files or install code into the sector so the virus initiates at startup.
- **Parasitic:** This virus attaches itself to a file, usually an executable file, and then delivers the payload when the program is used.
- **Stealth:** This virus hides the modifications that it is making to the system to help avoid detection.
- **Polymorphic:** This virus makes copies of itself, and then makes changes to those copies. It does this in hopes of avoiding detection from antivirus software.
- **Macro:** These infect programs written in Word, Basic, Visual Basic, or VB-Script that are used to automate functions. These viruses infect Microsoft Office files. They are easy to create because the underlying language is simple and intuitive to apply. They are especially dangerous in that they infect the operating system itself. They also can be transported between different operating systems because the languages are platform independent.
- **Multipartite:** These viruses can infect both program files and boot sectors.

Worm

A worm is a type of malware that can spread without the assistance of the user. They are small programs that, like viruses, are used to deliver a payload. One way to help mitigate the effects of worms is to place limits on sharing, writing, and executing programs.

Trojan Horse

A Trojan horse is a program or rogue application that appears to or is purported to do one thing but it does another when executed. For example, it might appear to be a screensaver program when it is really a Trojan horse. When the user unwittingly uses the program, it executes its payload, which could be to delete files or create backdoors. Backdoors are alternative ways to access the computer undetected in the future.

One type of Trojan targets and attempts to access and make use of smart cards. A countermeasure to prevent this attack is to use "single-access device driver" architecture. Using this approach, the operating system allows only one application to have access to the serial device (and thus the smart card) at any given time. Another way to prevent the attack is by using a smart card that enforces a "one private key usage per PIN entry" policy model. In this model, the user must enter her PIN every single time the private key is used, and therefore the Trojan horse would not have access to the key.

Logic Bomb

A logic bomb is a type of malware that executes when a particular event takes place. For example, that event could be a time of day or a specific date or it could be the first time you open notepad.exe. Some logic bombs execute when forensics are being undertaken, and in that case the bomb might delete all digital evidence.

Spyware/Adware

Adware doesn't actually steal anything, but tracks your Internet usage in an attempt to tailor ads and junk email to your interests. Spyware also tracks your activities and can also gather personal information that could lead to identity theft. In some cases, spyware can even direct the computer to install software and change settings.

Botnet

A bot is a type of malware that installs itself on large numbers of computers through infected emails, downloads from websites, Trojan horses, and shared media. After it's installed, the bot has the ability to connect back to the hacker's computer. After that, his server controls all the bots located on these machines. At a set time, the hacker might direct the bots to take some action, such as direct all the machines to send out spam messages, mount a DoS attack, or perform phishing or any number of malicious acts. The collection of computers that act together is called a *botnet*, and the individual computers are called *zombies*. Figure 5-8 shows this relationship.

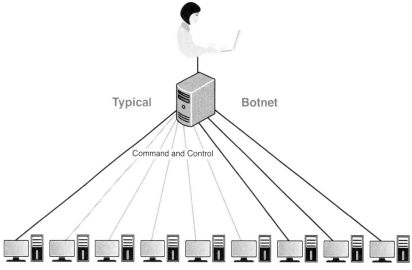

Figure 5-8 Botnet

Rootkit

A rootkit is a set of tools that a hacker can use on a computer after he has managed to gain access and elevate his privileges to administrator. It gets its name from the root account, the most powerful account in UNIX-based operating systems. The rootkit tools might include a backdoor for the hacker to access. This is one of the hardest types of malware to remove, and in many cases only a reformat of the hard drive will completely remove it.

Some of the actions a rootkit can take are

- Installation of a backdoor
- Removal of all entries from the security log (log scrubbing)
- Replacement of default tools with compromised version (Trojaned programs)
- Malicious kernel changes

Source Code Issues

Many security issues with software find their basis in poor development practices. A number of threats can be minimized by following certain coding principles. In this section, source code issues are discussed along with some guidelines for secure development processes.

Buffer Overflow

A buffer is an area of memory where commands and data are placed until they can be processed by the CPU. A buffer overflow occurs when too much data is accepted as input to a specific process. Hackers can take advantage of this phenomenon by submitting too much data, which can cause an error or in some cases execute commands on the machine if he can locate an area where commands can be executed. Not all attacks are designed to execute commands. Some just lock up the computer and are used as a DoS attack.

A packet containing a long string of *no-operation instructions* (NOPs) followed by a command is usually indicative of a type of buffer overflow attack called an NOP slide. The purpose is to get the CPU to locate where a command can be executed. The following is an example of a packet as seen from a sniffer where you can see a long string of 90s in the middle of the packet that pads the packet and causes it to overrun the buffer:

```
TCP Connection Request
---- 14/03/2004 15:40:57.910
68.144.193.124 : 4560 TCP Connected ID = 1
```

```
---- 14/03/2004 15:40:57.910
Status Code: 0 OK
68.144.193.124 : 4560 TCP Data In Length 697 bytes
MD5 = 19323C2EA6F5FCEE2382690100455C17
---- 14/03/2004 15:40:57.920
0000 90 90 90 90 90 90 90 90 90 90 90 90 90 90 90 90  ................
0010 90 90 90 90 90 90 90 90 90 90 90 90 90 90 90 90  ................
0020 90 90 90 90 90 90 90 90 90 90 90 90 90 90 90 90  ................
0030 90 90 90 90 90 90 90 90 90 90 90 90 90 90 90 90  ................
0040 90 90 90 90 90 90 90 90 90 90 90 90 90 90 90 90  ................
0050 90 90 90 90 90 90 90 90 90 90 90 90 90 90 90 90  ................
0060 90 90 90 90 90 90 90 90 90 90 90 90 90 90 90 90  ................
0070 90 90 90 90 90 90 90 90 90 90 90 90 90 90 90 90  ................
0080 90 90 90 90 90 90 90 90 90 90 90 90 90 90 90 90  ................
0090 90 90 90 90 90 90 90 90 90 90 90 90 90 90 90 90  ................
00A0 90 90 90 90 90 90 90 90 90 90 90 90 90 90 90 90  ................
00B0 90 90 90 90 90 90 90 90 90 90 90 90 90 90 90 90  ................
00C0 90 90 90 90 90 90 90 90 90 90 90 90 90 90 90 90  ................
00D0 90 90 90 90 90 90 90 90 90 90 90 90 90 90 90 90  ................
00E0 90 90 90 90 90 90 90 90 90 90 90 90 90 90 90 90  ................
00F0 90 90 90 90 90 90 90 90 90 90 90 90 90 90 90 90  ................
0100 90 90 90 90 90 90 90 90 90 90 90 90 4D 3F E3 77  ............M?.w
0110 90 90 90 90 FF 63 64 90 90 90 90 90 90 90 90 90  .....cd.........
0120 90 90 90 90 90 90 90 90 90 90 90 90 90 90 90 90  ................
0130 90 90 90 90 90 90 90 90 EB 10 5A 4A 33 C9 66 B9  ..........ZJ3.f.
0140 66 01 80 34 0A 99 E2 FA EB 05 E8 EB FF FF FF 70  f..4...........p
0150 99 98 99 99 C3 21 95 69 64 E6 12 99 12 E9 85 34  .....!.id......4
0160 12 D9 91 12 41 12 EA A5 9A 6A 12 EF E1 9A 6A 12  ....A....j....j.
0170 E7 B9 9A 62 12 D7 8D AA 74 CF CE C8 12 A6 9A 62  ...b....t......b
0180 12 6B F3 97 C0 6A 3F ED 91 C0 C6 1A 5E 9D DC 7B  .k...j?.....^..{
0190 70 C0 C6 C7 12 54 12 DF BD 9A 5A 48 78 9A 58 AA  p....T....ZHx.X.
01A0 50 FF 12 91 12 DF 85 9A 5A 58 78 9B 9A 58 12 99  P.......ZXx..X..
01B0 9A 5A 12 63 12 6E 1A 5F 97 12 49 F3 9A C0 71 E5  .Z.c.n._..I...q.
01C0 99 99 99 1A 5F 94 CB CF 66 CE 65 C3 12 41 F3 9D  ...._...f.e..A..
01D0 C0 71 F0 99 99 99 C9 C9 C9 C9 F3 98 F3 9B 66 CE  .q............f.
01E0 69 12 41 5E 9E 9B 99 9E 24 AA 59 10 DE 9D F3 89  i.A^....$.Y.....
01F0 CE CA 66 CE 6D F3 98 CA 66 CE 61 C9 C9 CA 66 CE  ..f.m...f.a...f.
0200 65 1A 75 DD 12 6D AA 42 F3 89 C0 10 85 17 7B 62  e.u..m.B......{b
0210 10 DF A1 10 DF A5 10 DF D9 5E DF B5 98 98 99 99  .........^......
0220 14 DE 89 C9 CF CA CA CA F3 98 CA CA 5E DE A5 FA  ............^...
0230 F4 FD 99 14 DE A5 C9 CA 66 CE 7D C9 66 CE 71 AA  ........f.}.f.q.
0240 59 35 1C 59 EC 60 C8 CB CF CA 66 4B C3 C0 32 7B  Y5.Y.`....fK..2{
```

```
0250 77 AA 59 5A 71 62 67 66 66 DE FC ED C9 EB F6 FA  w.YZqbgff.......
0260 D8 FD FD EB FC EA EA 99 DA EB FC F8 ED FC C9 EB  ................
0270 F6 FA FC EA EA D8 99 DC E1 F0 ED C9 EB F6 FA FC  ................
0280 EA EA 99 D5 F6 F8 FD D5 F0 FB EB F8 EB E0 D8 99  ................
0290 EE EA AB C6 AA AB 99 CE CA D8 CA F6 FA F2 FC ED  ................
02A0 D8 99 FB F0 F7 FD 99 F5 F0 EA ED FC F7 99 F8 FA  ................
```

The key to preventing many buffer overflow attacks is *input validation*. This method requires that any input be checked for format and length before it is used. Buffer overflows and boundary errors (when input exceeds the boundaries allotted for the input) are considered to be a family of error conditions called input validation errors.

Escalation of Privileges

Privilege escalation is the process of exploiting a bug or weakness in an operating system to allow a user to receive privileges to which they are not entitled. These privileges can be used to delete files, view private information, or install unwanted programs such as viruses.

Backdoor

Backdoors have been mentioned in passing several times here already. A backdoor is a piece of software installed by a hacker using one of the delivery mechanisms previously discussed that allows her to return later and connect to the computer without going through the normal authentication process. Some commercial applications inadvertently include backdoors because programmers forget to remove them before release to market. In many cases the program is listening on a specific port number and when the attacker attempts to connect to that port she is allowed to connect without authentication. An example is Back Orifice 2000 (BO2K), an application-level Trojan horse used to give an attacker backdoor network access.

Malware Protection

We are not totally helpless in the fight against malware. Programs and practices can help to mitigate the damage malware can cause. This section discusses some of the ways to protect a network from malware.

Antivirus Software

The first line of defense is antivirus software. This software is designed to identify viruses, Trojans, and worms and delete them or at least quarantine them until they can be removed. This identification process requires that you frequently update the software's *definition files*, the files that make it possible for the software to identify the latest viruses. If a new virus is created that has not yet been identified in the list, you will not be protected until the virus definition is added and the new definition file is downloaded.

Antimalware Software

Closely related to and in some cases part of the same software package, antimalware software focuses on other types of malware, such as adware and spyware. A way to help prevent malware infection is training the user on appropriate behavior when using the Internet. For that reason, user education in safe practices is a necessary part of preventing malware. This should be a part of security policies, covered in the next section.

Security Policies

Security policies are covered in detail in Chapter 4, but it is important to mention here that encouraging or requiring safe browsing and data handling practices should be formalized into the security policy of the organization. Some of the items to stress in this policy and perhaps include in training for users are the importance of the following:

- Antivirus and antimalware updates
- Reporting any error message concerning an update failure on the user machine
- Reporting any strange computer behavior that might indicate a virus infection

Software Security Effectiveness

Regardless of whether a software program is purchased from a third party or developed in-house, being able to verify and prove how secure the application is can be useful. The two ways to approach this are auditing the program's actions and determining whether it performs any insecure actions, or assessing it through a formal process. This section covers the two formal approaches.

Certification and Accreditation

In Chapter 7, "Security Architecture and Design," you will learn about rating systems for both operating systems and applications. Although third-party ratings are an input to the process, the terms *certification* and *accreditation* do not simply refer to the use of these ratings.

- **Certification** is the process of evaluating the software for its security effectiveness with regard to the customer's needs. Ratings can certainly be an input to this but are not the only consideration.
- **Accreditation** is the formal acceptance of the adequacy of a system's overall security by the management.

Auditing

Another approach and a practice that should continue after the software has been introduced to the environment is continual auditing of its actions and regular reviewing of the audit data. By monitoring the audit logs, security weaknesses that might not have been apparent in the beginning or that might have gone unreported until now can be identified. Auditing is discussed in more depth in Chapter 2.

Exam Preparation Tasks

Review All Key Topics

Review the most important topics in this chapter, noted with the Key Topics icon in the outer margin of the page. Table 5-1 lists a reference of these key topics and the page numbers on which each is found.

Table 5-1 Key Topics

Key Topic Element	Description	Page number
Section	System Development Life Cycle	203
Section	Software Development Life Cycle	206
List	Software Development Methods	211
Section	DBMS Architecture and Models	224
List	Malware	230

Define Key Terms

Define the following key terms from this chapter and check your answers in the glossary:

System Development Life Cycle, Software Development Life Cycle, Web Application Security Consortium (WASC), Open Web Application Security Project (OWASP), Build Security In (BSI), ISO/IEC 27000, build and fix, waterfall, V-shaped, prototyping, incremental, spiral, Rapid Application Development (RAD), agile, Joint Analyses Development Model, cleanroom, Capability Maturity Model Integration (CMMI), machine languages, assembly languages, high-level languages, very-high-level languages, natural languages, object-oriented programming, polymorphism, cohesion, coupling, data structure, distributed object-oriented systems, Common Object Request Broker Architecture (CORBA), Component Object Model (COM), Distributed Component Object Model (DCOM), Object Linking and Embedding (OLE), Java Platform, Enterprise Edition (J2EE), Service-Oriented Architecture (SOA), mobile code, Java applet, ActiveX, relational database, relation, row or tuple, column or attribute, schema, record, base relation, view, degree, cardinality, domain, primary key, foreign key, candidate key, referential integrity, hierarchical database, network database, object-oriented database, object-relational database, Open Database Connectivity (ODBC), Java Database Connectivity (JDBC), XML:DB API, Object Linking and Embedding Database (OLE DB), content-dependent access control, context-dependent access control, database views, database locks, polyinstantiation, OLTP ACID test, atomicity, consistency, isolation, durability, knowledge-based systems, data warehousing, data mining, malware, virus, boot sector virus, parasitic virus, stealth virus, polymorphic virus, macro virus, multipartite virus, worm, Trojan horse, logic bomb, adware, spyware, botnet, rootkit, buffer overflow, privilege, backdoor, certification, accreditation

Complete the Tables and Lists from Memory

Print a copy of the CD Appendix A, "Memory Tables," or at least the sections for this chapter, and complete the tables and lists from memory. The CD Appendix B, "Memory Tables Answer Key," includes completed tables and lists to check your work.

Review Questions

1. Which of the following is the last step in the System Development Life Cycle?

    a. Operate/Maintain

    b. Dispose

c. Acquire/Develop

d. Initiate

2. In which of the following stages of the Software Development Life Cycle is the software actually coded?

   a. Gather Requirements
   b. Design
   c. Develop
   d. Test/Validate

3. Which of the following initiatives was developed by the Department of Homeland Security?

   a. WASC
   b. BSI
   c. OWASP
   d. ISO

4. Which of the following development models provides no formal control mechanisms to provide feedback?

   a. Waterfall
   b. V-Shaped
   c. Build and Fix
   d. Spiral

5. Which language type delivers instructions directly to the processor?

   a. Assembly languages
   b. High-level languages
   c. Machine languages
   d. Natural languages

6. Which term describes how many different tasks a module can carry out?

   a. Polymorphism
   b. Cohesion
   c. Coupling
   d. Data structures

7. Which term describes a standard for communication between processes on the same computer?

    a. CORBA

    b. DCOM

    c. COM

    d. SOA

8. Which of the following is a Microsoft technology?

    a. ActiveX

    b. Java

    c. SOA

    d. CORBA

9. Which of the following is the number or rows in a relation?

    a. Tuple

    b. Schema

    c. Cardinality

    d. Degree

10. In which database model can an object have multiple parents?

    a. Hierarchical

    b. Object-oriented

    c. Network

    d. Object-relational

Answers and Explanations

1. b. The five steps, in order, are as follows:

    1. Initiate

    2. Acquire/Develop

    3. Implement

    4. Operate/Maintain

    5. Dispose

2. **c**. In the Develop stage, the code or instructions that make the software work is written. The emphasis of this phase is strict adherence to secure coding practice.

3. **b**. The Department of Homeland Security (DHS) also has become involved in promoting software security best practices. The Build Security In (BSI) initiative promotes a process-agnostic approach that makes security recommendations with regard to architectures, testing methods, code reviews, and management processes.

4. **c**. Though it's not a formal model, the Build and Fix approach describes a method that while certainly used in the past has been largely discredited and is now used as a template for how *not* to manage a development project. Simply put, using this method, the software is developed as quickly as possible and released.

5. **c**. Machine languages are those that deliver instructions directly to the processor. This was the only type of programming done in the 1950s and uses basic binary instructions using no complier or interpreter. (These are programs that convert higher language types to a form that can be executed by the processor.)

6. **b**. *Cohesion* is a term used to describe how many different tasks a module can carry out. If it is limited to a small number or a single function, it is said to have *high cohesion*. Coupling describes how much interaction one module requires from another module to do its job. Low or loose coupling indicates a module does not need much help from other modules whereas high coupling indicates the opposite.

7. **c**. Component Object Model (COM) is a model for communication between processes on the same computer, while as the name implies, the Distributed Component Object Model (DCOM) is a model for communication between processes in different parts of the network.

8. **a**. ActiveX is a Microsoft technology that uses Object-Oriented Programming (OOP) and is based on the COM and DCOM.

9. **c**. The number of rows in a relation describes its cardinality.

10. **c**. Like the hierarchical model, data is organized into a hierarchy but unlike the hierarchical model, objects can have multiple parents.

This chapter covers the following topics:

- **Cryptographic concepts:** Concepts discussed include encryption, decryption, keys, synchronous, asynchronous, symmetric, asymmetric, digital signatures, hash, digital certificates, plaintext, cleartext, ciphertext, cryptosystem, cryptanalysis, key clustering, key space, collision, algorithm, cryptology, encoding, decoding, transposition, substitution, confusion, diffusion, avalanche effect, work factor, trapdoor, and cryptographic life cycle.

- **Cryptography history:** The following components in cryptography history are discussed: Julius Caesar and the Caesar cipher, Vigenere cipher, Kerckhoff's Principle, World War II Enigma, and Lucifer by IBM.

- **Cryptosystem features:** Cryptosystem features discussed include authentication, confidentiality, integrity, authorization, and non-repudiation.

- **Encryption systems:** Encryption systems explained include running key and concealment ciphers, substitution ciphers, transposition ciphers, symmetric algorithms, asymmetric algorithms, and hybrid ciphers.

- **Substitution ciphers:** Substitution ciphers discussed include monoalphabetic ciphers, polyalphabetic ciphers, key ciphers, one-time pads, steganography, and watermarking.

- **Symmetric algorithms:** Symmetric algorithms discussed include DES, 3DES, AES, IDEA, Blowfish, Twofish, RC4, RC5, RC6, Countermode with CBC-MAC, and CAST.

- **Asymmetric algorithms:** Asymmetric algorithms discussed include Diffie-Hellman, RSA, El Gamal, ECC, Knapsack, and Zero Knowledge Proof.

- **Message integrity:** Message integrity topics explained include hash functions and message authentication code.

- **Digital signatures:** Digital signatures are explained, including DSS.

CHAPTER 6

Cryptography

- **PKI:** PKI topics explained include CAs and RAs, OCSP, certificates, CRLs, PKI steps, and cross-certification.
- **Key management:** Key management topics discussed include key management principles.
- **TPM:** The TPM chip is discussed.
- **Encryption communication levels:** Levels discussed include link encryption and end-to-end encryption.
- **E-mail security:** E-mail security topics discussed include PGP, MIME, S/MIME, and Quantum Cryptography.
- **Internet security:** Internet security topics discussed include remote access, SSL/TLS, HTTP, HTTPS, S-HTTP, SET, cookies, SSH, and IPsec.
- **Cryptography attacks:** Cryptography attacks discussed include ciphertext-only, known plaintext, chosen plaintext, chosen ciphertext, social engineering, brute force, differential cryptanalysis, linear cryptanalysis, algebraic, frequency analysis, birthday, dictionary, replay, analytic, statistical, factoring, reverse engineering, and meet-in-the-middle.

Cryptography is one of the most complicated domains of the CISSP knowledge base. Cryptography is a crucial factor to protecting data in rest and in transmission. It is a science that either hides data or makes data unreadable by transforming it. In addition, cryptography provides message author assurance, source authentication, and delivery proof.

Cryptography concerns itself with integrity, confidentiality, and authentication, but not with availability. It helps prevent or detect the fraudulent insertion, deletion, and modification of data.

In this chapter, you learn about cryptography concepts, cryptography history, cryptosystem features, cryptography methods, encryption systems (including substitution, symmetric, asymmetric, and hybrid ciphers), message integrity, public key infrastructure, key management, encryption communication levels, e-mail security, Internet security, and cryptography attacks.

Foundation Topics

Cryptography Concepts

As a security professional, you should understand many terms and concepts related to cryptography. These terms are often used when discussing cryptography:

- **Encryption:** The process of converting data from plaintext to ciphertext. Also referred to as enciphering.

- **Decryption:** The process of converting data from ciphertext to plaintext. Also referred to as deciphering.

- **Key:** A parameter that controls the transformation of plaintext into ciphertext or vice versa. Determining the original plaintext data without the key is impossible. Keys can be both public and private. Also referred to as a cryptovariable.

- **Synchronous:** When encryption or decryption occurs immediately.

- **Asynchronous:** When encryption or decryption requests are processed from a queue. This method utilizes hardware and multiple processors in the process.

- **Symmetric:** An encryption method whereby a single private key both encrypts and decrypts the data. Also referred to as private or secret key encryption.

- **Asymmetric:** An encryption method whereby a key pair, one private key and one public key, performs encryption and decryption. One key performs the encryption, whereas the other key performs the decryption. Also referred to as public key encryption.

- **Digital signature:** A method of providing sender authentication and message integrity. The message acts as an input to a hash function, and the sender's private key encrypts the hash value. The receiver can perform a hash computation on the received message to determine the validity of the message.

- **Hash:** A one-way function that reduces a message to a hash value. A comparison of the sender's hash value to the receiver's hash value determines message integrity. If the resultant hash values are different, then the message has been altered in some way, provided that both the sender and receiver used the same hash function.

- **Digital certificate:** An electronic document that identifies the certificate holder.

- **Plaintext:** A message in its original format. Also referred to as cleartext.

- **Ciphertext:** An altered form of a message that is unreadable without knowing the key and the encryption system used. Also referred to as a cryptogram.

- **Cryptosystem:** The entire cryptographic process, including the algorithm, key, and key management functions. The security of a cryptosystem is measured by the size of the keyspace and available computational power.
- **Cryptanalysis:** The science of decrypting ciphertext without prior knowledge of the key or cryptosystem used. The purpose of cryptanalysis is to forge coded signals or messages that will be accepted as authentic signals or messages.
- **Key clustering:** Occurs when different encryption keys generate the same ciphertext from the same plaintext message.
- **Keyspace:** All the possible key values when using a particular algorithm or other security measure. A 40-bit key would have 2^{40} possible values, whereas a 128-bit key would have 2^{128} possible values.
- **Collision:** An event that occurs when a hash function produces the same hash value on different messages.
- **Algorithm:** A mathematical function that encrypts and decrypts data. Also referred to as a cipher.
- **Cryptology:** The science that studies encrypted communication and data.
- **Encoding:** The process of changing data into another form using code.
- **Decoding:** The process of changing an encoded message back into its original format.
- **Transposition:** The process of shuffling or reordering the plaintext to hide the original message. Also referred to as permutation. For example, AEEGMSS is a transposed version of MESSAGE.
- **Substitution:** The process of exchanging one byte in a message for another. For example, ABCCDEB is a substituted version of MESSAGE.
- **Confusion:** The process of changing a key value during each round of encryption. Confusion is often carried out by substitution. Confusion conceals a statistical connection between the plaintext and ciphertext. Claude Shannon first discussed confusion.
- **Diffusion:** The process of changing the location of the plaintext within the ciphertext. Diffusion is often carried out using transposition. Claude Shannon first introduced diffusion.
- **Avalanche effect:** The condition where any change in the key or plaintext, no matter how minor, will significantly change the ciphertext. Horst Feistel first introduced avalanche effect.

- **Work factor:** The amount of time and resources that would be needed to break the encryption.

- **Trapdoor:** A secret mechanism that allows the implementation of the reverse function in a one-way function.

- **One-way function:** A mathematical function that can be more easily performed in one direction than in the other.

Cryptographic Life Cycle

When considering implementing cryptography or encryption techniques in an organization, security professionals must fully analyze the needs of the organization. Each technique has strengths and weaknesses. In addition, they each have specific purposes. Analyzing the needs of the organization will ensure that you identify the best algorithm to implement.

Professional organizations manage algorithms to ensure that they provide the protection needed. It is essential that security professionals research the algorithms they implement and understand any announcements from the governing organization regarding updates, retirements, or replacements to the implemented algorithms. The life cycle of any cryptographic algorithm involves implementation, maintenance, and retirement or replacement. Any security professional who fails to obtain up-to-date information regarding the algorithms implemented might find the organization's reputation and his or her own personal reputation damaged as the result of his or her negligence.

Cryptography History

Cryptography finds its roots in ancient civilizations. Although the early cryptography solutions were simplistic in nature, they were able to provide leaders with a means of hiding messages from enemies.

In their earliest forms, most cryptographic methods implemented some sort of substitution cipher, where each character in the alphabet was replaced with another. A mono-alphabetic substitution cipher uses only one alphabet, and a polyalphabetic substitution cipher uses multiple alphabets. As with all other cryptography methods, the early substitution ciphers had to be replaced by more complex methods.

The Spartans created the scytale cipher, which used a sheet of papyrus wrapped around a wooden rod. The encrypted message had to be wrapped around a rod of the correct size to be deciphered, as shown in Figure 6-1.

Figure 6-1 Scytale Cipher

Other notable advances in cryptography history include the following:

- Caesar cipher
- Vigenere cipher
- Kerchoff's Principle
- World War II Enigma
- Lucifer by IBM

Julius Caesar and the Caesar Cipher

Julius Caesar developed a mono-alphabetic cipher that shifts the letters of the alphabet three places. Although this technique is very simplistic, variations of it were very easy to develop because the key (the number of locations that the alphabet shifted) can be changed. Because it was so simple, it is easy to reverse engineer and led to the development of polyalphabetic ciphers.

An example of a Caesar cipher-encrypted message is shown in Figure 6-2. In this example, the letters of the alphabet are applied to a three-letter substitution shift, meaning the letters were shifted three letters. As you can see, the standard English alphabet is listed first. Underneath it, the substitution letters are listed.

Standard Alphabet
ABCDEFGHIJKLMNOPQRSTUVWXYZ
DEFGHIJKLMNOPQRSTUVWXYZABC
Caesar Cipher

Plaintext – PEARSON EDUCATION
Ciphertext – SHDUVRQ HGXFDWLRQ

Figure 6-2 Caesar Cipher

Vigenere Cipher

In the sixteenth century, Blaise de Vigenere of France developed one of the first polyalphabetic substitution ciphers that is referred to as the Vigenere cipher. Although it is based on the Caesar cipher, it is considerably more complicated because it uses 27 shift alphabets with letters being shifted up one place. To encrypt a message, you must know the security key. The security key is then used in conjunction with the plaintext message to determine the ciphertext.

Figure 6-3 shows the Vigenere table.

	A	B	C	D	E	F	G	H	I	J	K	L	M	N	O	P	Q	R	S	T	U	V	W	X	Y	Z
A	A	B	C	D	E	F	G	H	I	J	K	L	M	N	O	P	Q	S	S	T	U	V	W	X	Y	Z
B	B	C	D	E	F	G	H	I	J	K	L	M	N	O	P	Q	R	S	T	U	V	W	X	Y	Z	A
C	C	D	E	F	G	H	I	J	K	L	M	N	O	P	Q	R	S	T	U	V	W	X	Y	Z	A	B
D	D	E	F	G	H	I	J	K	L	M	N	O	P	Q	R	S	T	U	V	W	X	Y	Z	A	B	C
E	E	F	G	H	I	J	K	L	M	N	O	P	Q	R	S	T	U	V	W	X	Y	Z	A	B	C	D
F	F	G	H	I	J	K	L	M	N	O	P	Q	R	S	T	U	V	W	X	Y	Z	A	B	C	D	E
G	G	H	I	J	K	L	M	N	O	P	Q	R	S	T	U	V	W	X	Y	Z	A	B	C	D	E	F
H	H	I	J	K	L	M	N	O	P	Q	R	S	T	U	V	W	X	Y	Z	A	B	C	D	E	F	G
I	I	J	K	L	M	N	O	P	Q	R	S	T	U	V	W	X	Y	Z	A	B	C	D	E	F	G	H
J	J	K	L	M	N	O	P	Q	R	S	T	U	V	W	X	Y	Z	A	B	C	D	E	F	G	H	I
K	K	L	M	N	O	P	Q	R	S	T	U	V	W	X	Y	Z	A	B	C	D	E	F	G	H	I	J
L	L	M	N	O	P	Q	R	S	T	U	V	W	X	Y	Z	A	B	C	D	E	F	G	H	I	J	K
M	M	N	O	P	Q	R	S	T	U	V	W	X	Y	Z	A	B	C	D	E	F	G	H	I	J	K	L
N	N	O	P	Q	R	S	T	U	V	W	X	Y	Z	A	B	C	D	E	F	G	H	I	J	K	L	M
O	O	P	Q	R	S	T	U	V	W	X	Y	Z	A	B	C	D	E	F	G	H	I	J	K	L	M	N
P	P	Q	R	S	T	U	V	W	X	Y	Z	A	B	C	D	E	F	G	H	I	J	K	L	M	N	O
Q	Q	R	S	T	U	V	W	X	Y	Z	A	B	C	D	E	F	G	H	I	J	K	L	M	N	O	P
R	R	S	T	U	V	W	X	Y	Z	A	B	C	D	E	F	G	H	I	J	K	L	M	N	O	P	Q
S	S	T	U	V	W	X	Y	Z	A	B	C	D	E	F	G	H	I	J	K	L	M	N	O	P	Q	R
T	T	U	V	W	X	Y	Z	A	B	C	D	E	F	G	H	I	J	K	L	M	N	O	P	Q	R	S
U	U	V	W	X	Y	Z	A	B	C	D	E	F	G	H	I	J	K	L	M	N	O	P	Q	R	S	T
V	V	W	X	Y	Z	A	B	C	D	E	F	G	H	I	J	K	L	M	N	O	P	Q	R	S	T	U
W	W	X	Y	Z	A	B	C	D	E	F	G	H	I	J	K	L	M	N	O	P	Q	R	S	T	U	V
X	X	Y	Z	A	B	C	D	E	F	G	H	I	J	K	L	M	N	O	P	Q	R	S	T	U	V	W
Y	Y	Z	A	B	C	D	E	F	G	H	I	J	K	L	M	N	O	P	Q	R	S	T	U	V	W	X
Z	Z	A	B	C	D	E	F	G	H	I	J	K	L	M	N	O	P	Q	R	S	T	U	V	W	X	Y

Figure 6-3 Vigenere Table

As an example of a message on which the Vigenere cipher is applied, let's use the security key PEARSON and the plaintext message of MEETING IN CONFERENCE ROOM. The first letter in the plaintext message is M, and the first letter in the key is P. We should locate the letter M across the headings for the columns. We follow that column down until it intersects with the row that starts with the letter P, resulting in the letter B. The second letter of the plaintext message is E, and the second letter in the key is E. Using the same method, we obtain the letter I. We continue in this same manner until we run out of key letters, then we start over with the key, which would result in the second letter I in the plaintext message working with the letter P of the key.

So applying this technique to the entire message, the MEETING IN CONFERENCE ROOM plaintext message converts to BIEKABT XR CFFTRGINTW FBDQ ciphertext message.

Kerckhoff's Principle

In the nineteenth century, Auguste Kerckhoff developed six design principles for the military use of ciphers. The six principles are as follows:

1. The system must be practically, if not mathematically, indecipherable.
2. It must not be required to be secret, and it must be able to fall into the hands of the enemy without inconvenience.
3. Its key must be communicable and retainable without the help of written notes, and changeable or modifiable at the will of the correspondents.
4. It must be applicable to telegraphic correspondence.
5. It must be portable, and its usage and function must not require the concourse of several people.
6. Finally, given the circumstances that command its application, the system needs to be easy to use, requiring neither mental strain nor the knowledge of a long series of rules to observe.

In Kerckhoff's Principle, remember that the key is secret and the algorithm is known.

World War II Enigma

During World War II, most of the major military powers developed encryption machines. The most famous of the machines used during the war was the Enigma machine developed by Germany. The Enigma machine consisted of rotors and a plug board.

To convert a plaintext message to ciphertext, the machine operator would first configure its initial settings. Then the operator would type each letter of the original plaintext message into the machine one at a time. The machine would display a different letter for each letter entered. After the operator wrote down the ciphertext letter, the operator would advance the rotors to the new setting. So with each letter entered, the operator had to change the machine setting. The key of this process was the initial machine setting and the series of increments used to advance the rotor, both of which had to be known by the receiver to properly convert the ciphertext back to plaintext.

As complicated as the system was, a group of Polish cryptographers were able to break the code, thereby being credited with shortening World War II by two years.

Lucifer by IBM

The Lucifer project, developed by IBM, developed complex mathematical equations. These equations later were used by the U.S. National Security Agency in the development of the U.S. Data Encryption Standard (DES), which is still used today in some form. Lucifer used a Feistel cipher, an iterated block cipher that encrypts the plaintext by breaking the block into two halves. The cipher then applies a round of transformation to one of the halves using a subkey. The output of this transformation is XORed with the other block half. Finally, the two halves are swapped to complete the round.

Cryptosystem Features

A cryptosystem consists of software, protocols, algorithms, and keys. The strength of any cryptosystem comes from the algorithm and the length and secrecy of the key. For example, one method of making a cryptographic key more resistant to exhaustive attacks is to increase the key length. If the cryptosystem uses a weak key, it facilitates attacks against the algorithm.

While a cryptosystem supports the three core principles of the confidentiality, integrity, and availability (CIA) triad, cryptosystems directly provide authentication, confidentiality, integrity, authorization, and non-repudiation. The availability tenet of the CIA triad is supported by cryptosystems, meaning that implementing cryptography will help to ensure that an organization's data remains available. However, cryptography does not directly ensure data availability although it can be used to protect the data.

Authentication

Cryptosystems provide authentication by being able to determine the sender's identity and validity. Digital signatures verify the sender's identity. Protecting the key ensures that only valid users can properly encrypt and decrypt the message.

Confidentiality

Cryptosystems provide confidentiality by altering the original data in such a way as to ensure that the data cannot be read except by the valid recipient. Without the proper key, unauthorized users are unable to read the message.

Integrity

Cryptosystems provide integrity by allowing valid recipients to verify that data has not been altered. Hash functions do not prevent data alteration but provide a means to determine whether data alteration has occurred.

Authorization

Cryptosystems provide authorization by providing the key to a valid user after that user proves his identity through authentication. The key given to the user will allow the user to access a resource.

Non-repudiation

Non-repudiation in cryptosystems provides proof of the origin of data, thereby preventing the sender from denying that he sent the message and supporting data integrity. Public key cryptography and digital signatures provide non-repudiation.

Encryption Systems

Algorithms that are used in computer systems implement complex mathematical formulas when converting plaintext to ciphertext. The two main components to any encryption system are the key and the algorithm. In some encryption systems, the two communicating parties use the same key. In other encryption systems, the two communicating parties use different keys in the process, but the keys are related.

In this section, we discuss the following:

- Running key and concealment ciphers
- Substitution ciphers
- Transposition ciphers
- Symmetric algorithms
- Asymmetric algorithms
- Hybrid ciphers

Running Key and Concealment Ciphers

Running key ciphers and concealment ciphers are considered classical methods of producing ciphertext. The running key cipher uses a physical component, usually a book, to provide the polyalphabetic characters. An indicator block must be included somewhere within the text so that the receiver knows where in the book the originator started. Therefore, the two parties must agree upon which book to use and where the indicator block will be included in the cipher message. Running ciphers are also referred to as key ciphers and running key ciphers.

A concealment cipher, also referred to as a null cipher, occurs when plaintext is interspersed somewhere within other written material. The two parties must agree on the key value, which defines which letters are part of the actual message. For example, every third letter or the first letter of each word is part of the real message. A concealment cipher belongs in the steganography realm.

> **NOTE** Steganography is discussed later in this chapter.

Substitution Ciphers

A substitution cipher uses a key to substitute characters or character blocks with different characters or character blocks. The Caesar cipher and Vigenere cipher are two of the earliest forms of substitution ciphers.

Another example of a substitution cipher is a modulo 26 substitution cipher. With this cipher, the 26 letters of the alphabet are numbered in order starting at zero. The sender takes the original message and determines the number of each letter in the original message. Then the letter values for the keys are added to the original letter values. The value result is then converted back to text.

Figure 6-4 shows an example of a modulo 26 substitution cipher encryption. With this example, the original message is PEARSON, and the key is KEY. The ciphertext message is ZIYBSMX.

Orginal Message	Orginal Value	Key	Key Value	Result	Mod 26	Cipher Message
P	15	K	10	25	25	Z
E	4	E	4	8	8	I
A	0	Y	24	24	24	Y
R	17	K	10	27	1	B
S	18	E	0	18	18	S
O	14	Y	24	38	12	M
N	13	K	10	23	23	X

Modulo 26 Letter Chart

a	0		h	7		o	14		v	21
b	1		i	8		p	15		w	22
c	2		j	9		q	16		x	23
d	3		k	10		r	17		y	24
e	4		l	11		s	18		z	25
f	5		m	12		t	19			
g	6		n	13		u	20			

Figure 6-4 Modulo 26 Substitution Cipher Example

Transposition Ciphers

A transposition cipher scrambles the letters of the original message in a different order. The key determines the positions to which the letters are moved.

Figure 6-5 shows an example of a simple transposition cipher. With this example, the original message is PEARSON EDUCATION, and the key is 4231 2314. The ciphertext message is REAP ONSE AUCD IOTN. So you take the first four letters of the plaintext message (PEAR) and use the first four numbers (4231) as the key for transposition. In the new ciphertext, the letters would be REAP. Then you take the next four letters of the plaintext message (SONE) and use the next four numbers (2314) as the key for transposition. In the new ciphertext, the letters would be ONSE. Then you take the next four letters of the original message and apply the first four numbers of the key because you do not have any more numbers in the key. Continue this pattern until complete.

Original message:	PEARSON EDUCATION
Broken into groups:	PEAR SONE DUCA TION
Key:	4231 2314 4231 2314
Ciphertext message:	REAP ONSE AUCD IOTN

Figure 6-5 Transposition Example

Symmetric Algorithms

Symmetric algorithms use a private or secret key that must remain secret between the two parties. Each party pair requires a separate private key. Therefore, a single user would need a unique secret key for every user with whom she communicates.

Consider an example where there are 10 unique users. Each user needs a separate private key to communicate with the other users. To calculate the number of keys that would be needed in this example, you would use the following formula:

# of users * (# of users – 1) / 2

Using our example, you would calculate 10 * (10–1) / 2 or 45 needed keys.

With symmetric algorithms, the encryption key must remain secure. To obtain the secret key, the users must find a secure out-of-band method for communicating the secret key, including courier or direct physical contact between the users.

A special type of symmetric key called a session key encrypts messages between two users during one communication session.

Symmetric algorithms can be referred to as single-key, secret-key, private-key, or shared-key cryptography.

Symmetric systems provide confidentiality but not authentication or non-repudiation. If both users use the same key, determining where the message originated is impossible.

Symmetric algorithms include DES, AES, IDEA, Skipjack, Blowfish, Twofish, RC4/RC5/RC6, and CAST. All these algorithms will be discussed later in this chapter.

Table 6-1 lists the strengths and weaknesses of symmetric algorithms.

Table 6-1 Symmetric Algorithm Strengths and Weaknesses

Strengths	Weaknesses
1,000 to 10,000 times faster than asymmetric algorithms	Number of unique keys needed can cause key management issues
Hard to break	Secure key distribution critical
Cheaper to implement than asymmetric	Key compromise occurs if one party compromised, thereby allowing impersonation

The two broad types of symmetric algorithms are stream-based ciphers and block ciphers. Initialization vectors (IVs) are an important part of block ciphers. These three components will be discussed in the next sections.

Stream-based Ciphers

Stream-based ciphers perform encryption on a bit-by-bit basis and use keystream generators. The keystream generators create a bit stream that is XORed with the plaintext bits. The result of this XOR operation is the ciphertext.

A synchronous stream-based cipher depends only on the key, and an asynchronous stream cipher depends on the key and plaintext. The key ensures that the bit stream that is XORed to the plaintext is random.

An example of a stream-based cipher is RC4, which is discussed later in this chapter.

Advantages of stream-based ciphers include the following:

- Generally have lower error propagation because encryption occurs on each bit.
- Generally used more in hardware implementation.
- Use the same key for encryption and decryption.
- Generally cheaper to implement than block ciphers.
- Employ only confusion.

> **NOTE** Confusion is defined in the "Cryptography Concepts" section earlier in this chapter. Remember to refer to that list anytime you encounter terms in this chapter with which you are unfamiliar.

Block Ciphers

Blocks ciphers perform encryption by breaking the message into fixed-length units. A message of 1,024 bits could be divided into 16 blocks of 64 bits each. Each of those 16 blocks is processed by the algorithm formulas, resulting in a single block of ciphertext.

Examples of block ciphers include IDEA, Blowfish, RC5, and RC6, which are discussed later in this chapter.

Advantages of block ciphers include the following:

- Implementation is easier than stream-based cipher implementation.
- Generally less susceptible to security issues.
- Generally used more in software implementations.

Block ciphers employ both confusion and diffusion. Block ciphers often use different modes: ECB, CBC, CFB, and CTR. These modes are discussed in detail later in this chapter.

Initialization Vectors (IVs)

The modes mentioned earlier use IVs to ensure that patterns are not produced during encryption. These IVs provide this service by using random values with the algorithms. Without using IVs, a repeated phrase within a plaintext message could result in the same ciphertext. Attackers can possibly use these patterns to break the encryption.

Asymmetric Algorithms

Asymmetric algorithms use both a public key and a private or secret key. The public key is known by all parties, and the private key is known only by its owner. One of these keys encrypts the message, and the other decrypts the message.

In asymmetric cryptography, determining a user's private key is virtually impossible even if the public key is known, although both keys are mathematically related. However, if a user's private key is discovered, the system can be compromised.

Asymmetric algorithms can be referred to as dual-key or public-key cryptography.

Asymmetric systems provide confidentiality, integrity, authentication, and non-repudiation. Because both users have one unique key that is part of the process, determining where the message originated is possible.

If confidentiality is the primary concern for an organization, a message should be encrypted with the receiver's public key, which is referred to as secure message format. If authentication is the primary concern for an organization, a message should be encrypted with the sender's private key, which is referred to as open message format. When using open message format, the message can be decrypted by anyone with the public key.

Asymmetric algorithms include Diffie-Hellman, RSA, El Gamal, ECC, Knapsack, DSA, and Zero Knowledge Proof. All of these algorithms will be discussed later in this chapter.

Table 6-2 lists the strengths and weaknesses of asymmetric algorithms.

Table 6-2 Asymmetric Algorithm Strengths and Weaknesses

Strengths	Weaknesses
Key distribution is easier and more manageable than symmetric algorithms	More expensive to implement than symmetric algorithms
Key management is easier because the same public key is used by all parties	1,000 to 10,000 times slower than symmetric algorithms

Hybrid Ciphers

Because both symmetric and asymmetric algorithms have weaknesses, solutions have been developed that use both types of algorithms in a hybrid cipher. By using both algorithm types, the cipher provides confidentiality, authentication, and non-repudiation.

The process for hybrid encryption is as follows:

1. The symmetric algorithm provides the keys used for encryption.
2. The symmetric keys are then passed to the asymmetric algorithm, which encrypts the symmetric keys and automatically distributes them.
3. The message is then encrypted with the symmetric key.
4. Both the message and the key are sent to the receiver.

5. The receiver decrypts the symmetric key and uses the symmetric key to decrypt the message.

An organization should use hybrid encryption if the parties do not have a shared secret key and large quantities of sensitive data must be transmitted.

Substitution Ciphers

As mentioned earlier, a substitution cipher uses a key to substitute characters or character blocks with different characters or character blocks. Mono-alphabetic and polyalphabetic ciphers, including the Caesar cipher and Vigenere cipher, and running key ciphers have been explained earlier in this chapter.

Substitution ciphers explained in this section include the following:

- One-time pads
- Steganography

One-Time Pads

A one-time pad, invented by Gilbert Vernam, is the most secure encryption scheme that can be used. If it's used properly, an attacker cannot break a one-time pad. A one-time pad works likes a running cipher in that the key value is added to the value of the letters. However, a one-time pad uses a key that is the same length as the plaintext message, whereas the running cipher uses a smaller key that is repeatedly applied to the plaintext message.

Figure 6-6 shows an example of a one-time pad encryption. With this example, the original message is PEARSON, and the key is JOHNSON. The ciphertext message is YSHEKCA.

Orginal Message	Orginal Value	Key	Key Value	Result	Mod 26	Cipher Message
P	15	J	9	24	24	Y
E	4	O	14	18	18	S
A	0	H	7	7	7	H
R	17	N	13	30	4	E
S	18	S	18	36	10	K
O	14	O	14	28	2	C
N	13	N	13	26	0	A

Modulo 26 Letter Chart

a	0	h	7	o	14	v	21
b	1	i	8	p	15	w	22
c	2	j	9	q	16	x	23
d	3	k	10	r	17	y	24
e	4	l	11	s	18	z	25
f	5	m	12	t	19		
g	6	n	13	u	20		

Figure 6-6 One-time Pad Example

To ensure that the one-time pad is secure, the following conditions must exist:

- Must be used only one time.
- Must be as long (or longer) than the message.
- Must consist of random values.
- Must be securely distributed.
- Must be protected at its source and destination.

Although the earlier example uses a one-time pad in a Mod 26 scheme, one-time pads can also be used at the bit level. When the bit level is used, the message is converted into binary, and an XOR operation occurs two bits at a time. The bits from the original message are combined with the key values to obtain the encrypted message. When you combine the values, the result is 0 if both values are the same and 1 if both values are different. An example of an XOR operation is as follows:

Original message	0 1 1 0 1 1 0 0
Key	1 1 0 1 1 1 0 0
Cipher message	1 0 1 1 0 0 0 0

Steganography

Steganography occurs when a message is hidden inside another object, such as a picture or document. In steganography, it is crucial that only those who are expecting the message know that the message exists.

A concealment cipher, discussed earlier, is one method of steganography. Another method of steganography is digital watermarking. Digital watermarking is a logo or trademark that is embedded in documents, pictures, or other objects. The watermarks deter people from using the materials in an unauthorized manner.

Symmetric Algorithms

Symmetric algorithms were explained earlier in this chapter. In this section, we discuss some of the most popular symmetric algorithms. Some of these might no longer be commonly used because there are more secure alternatives.

Security professionals should be familiar with the following symmetric algorithms:

- DES/3DES
- AES

- IDEA
- Skipjack
- Blowfish
- Twofish
- RC4/RC5/RC6
- CAST

Digital Encryption Standard (DES) and Triple DES (3DES)

Digital Encryption Standard (DES) is a symmetric encryption system created by the National Security Agency (NSA) but based on the 128-bit Lucifer algorithm by IBM. Originally, the algorithm was named Data Encryption Algorithm (DEA), and the DES acronym was used to refer to the standard. But in today's world, DES is the more common term for both.

> **NOTE** Test candidates might see both acronyms used on the CISSP exam.

DES uses a 64-bit key, 8 bits of which are used for parity. Therefore, the effective key length for DES is 56 bits. DES divides the message into 64-bit blocks. Sixteen rounds of transposition and substitution are performed on each block, resulting in a 64-bit block of ciphertext.

DES has mostly been replaced by 3DES and AES, both of which are discussed later in this chapter.

DES-X is a variant of DES that uses multiple 64-bit keys in addition to the 56-bit DES key. The first 64-bit key is XORed to the plaintext, which is then encrypted with DES. The second 64-bit key is XORed to the resulting cipher.

Double-DES, a DES version that used a 112-bit key length, is no longer used. After it was released, a security attack occurred that reduced Double-DES security to the same level as DES.

DES Modes

DES comes in the following five modes:

- Electronic Code Book (ECB)
- Cipher Block Chaining (CBC)

- Cipher Feedback (CFB)
- Output Feedback (OFB)
- Counter Mode (CTR)

In ECB, 64-bit blocks of data are processed by the algorithm using the key. The ciphertext produced can be padded to ensure that the result is a 64-bit block. If an encryption error occurs, only one block of the message is affected. ECB operations run in parallel, making it a fast method.

Although ECB is the easiest and fastest mode to use, it has security issues because every 64-bit block is encrypted with the same key. If an attacker discovers the key, all the blocks of data can be read. If an attacker discovers both versions of the 64-bit block (plaintext and ciphertext), the key can be determined. For these reasons, the mode should not be used when encrypting a large amount of data because patterns would emerge.

ECB is a good choice if an organization needs encryption for its databases because ECB works well with the encryption of short messages. Figure 6-7 shows the ECB encryption process.

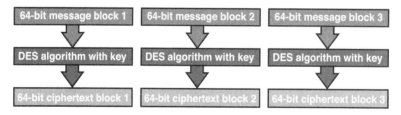

Figure 6-7 ECB Mode of DES

In CBC, each 64-bit block is chained together because each resultant 64-bit ciphertext block is applied to the next block. So plaintext message block 1 is processed by the algorithm using an IV (discussed earlier in this chapter). The resultant ciphertext message block 1 is XORed with plaintext message block 2, resulting in ciphertext message 2. This process continues until the message is complete.

Unlike ECB, CBC encrypts large files without having any patterns within the resulting ciphertext. If a unique IV is used with each message encryption, the resultant ciphertext will be different every time even in cases where the same plaintext message is used. Figure 6-8 shows the CBC encryption process.

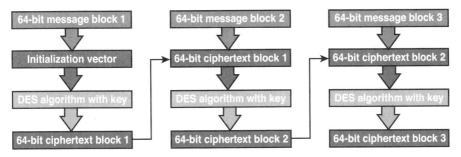

Figure 6-8 CBC Mode of DES

Whereas CBC and ECB require 64-bit blocks, CFB works with 8-bit (or smaller) blocks and uses a combination of stream ciphering and block ciphering. Like CBC, the first 8-bit block of the plaintext message is XORed by the algorithm using a keystream, which is the result of an IV and the key. The resultant ciphertext message is applied to the next plaintext message block. Figure 6-9 shows the CFB encryption process.

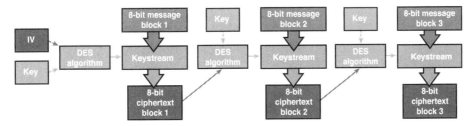

Figure 6-9 CFB Mode of DES

The size of the ciphertext block must be the same size as the plaintext block. The method that CFB uses can have issues if any ciphertext result has errors because those errors will affect any future block encryption. For this reason, CFB should not be used to encrypt data that can be affected by this problem, particularly video or voice signals. This problem led to the need for DES OFB mode.

Similar to CFB, OFB works with 8-bit (or smaller) blocks and uses a combination of stream ciphering and block ciphering. However, OFB uses the previous keystream with the key to create the next keystream. Figure 6-10 shows the OFB encryption process.

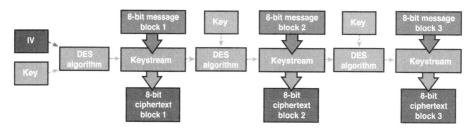

Figure 6-10 OFB Mode of DES

With OFB, the size of the keystream value must be the same size as the plaintext block. Because of the way in which OFB is implemented, OFB is less susceptible to the error type that CFB has.

CTR mode is similar to OFB mode. The main difference is that CTR mode uses an incrementing IV counter to ensure that each block is encrypted with a unique keystream. Also, the ciphertext is not chaining into the encryption process. Because this chaining does not occur, CTR performance is much better than the other modes. Figure 6-11 shows the CTR encryption process.

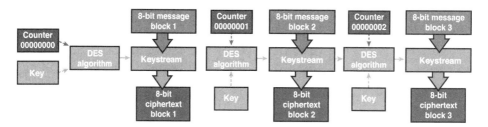

Figure 6-11 CTR Mode of DES

Triple DES (3DES) and Modes

Because of the need to quickly replace DES, Triple DES (3DES), a version of DES that increases security by using three 56-bit keys, was developed. Although 3DES is resistant to attacks, it is up to three times slower than DES. 3DES did serve as a temporary replacement to DES. However, the National Institute of Standards and Technology (NIST) has actually designated the Advanced Encryption Standard (AES) as the replacement for DES, even though 3DES is still in use today.

3DES comes in the following four modes:

- **3DES-EEE3:** Each block of data is encrypted three times, each time with a different key.

- **3DES-EDE3:** Each block of data is encrypted with the first key, decrypted with the second key, and encrypted with the third key.

- **3DES-EEE2:** Each block of data is encrypted with the first key, encrypted with the second key, and finally encrypted again with the first key.

- **3DES-EDE2:** Each block of data is encrypted with the first key, decrypted with the second key, and finally encrypted again with the first key.

Advanced Encryption Standard (AES)

AES is the replacement algorithm for DES. When the NIST decided a new standard was needed because DES had been cracked, the NIST was presented with five industry options:

- IBM's MARS
- RSA Laboratories' RC6
- Anderson, Biham, and Knudsen's Serpent
- Counterpane Systems' Twofish
- Daemen and Rijmen's Rijndael

Of these choices, the NIST selected Rijndael. So although AES is considered the standard, the algorithm that is used in the AES standard is the Rijndael algorithm. The AES and Rijndael terms are often used interchangeably.

The three block sizes that are used in the Rijndael algorithm are 128, 192, and 256 bits. A 128-bit key with a 128-bit block size undergoes 10 transformation rounds. A 192-bit key with a 192-bit block size undergoes 12 transformation rounds. Finally, a 256-bit key with a 256-bit block size undergoes 14 transformation rounds.

Rijndael employs transformations comprised of three layers: the non-linear layer, key addition layer, and linear-maxing layer. The Rijndael design is very simple, and its code is compact, which allows it to be used on a variety of platforms. It is the required algorithm for sensitive but unclassified U.S. government data.

IDEA

International Data Encryption Algorithm (IDEA) is a block cipher that uses 64-bit blocks. Each 64-bit block is divided into 16 smaller blocks. IDEA uses a 128-bit key and performs eight rounds of transformations on each of the 16 smaller blocks.

IDEA is faster and harder to break than DES. However, IDEA is not as widely used as DES or AES because it was patented and licensing fees had to be paid to IDEA's owner, a Swiss company named Ascom. However, the patent expired in 2012. IDEA is used in PGP, which is discussed later in this chapter.

Skipjack

Skipjack is a block-cipher, symmetric algorithm developed by the U.S. NSA. It uses an 80-bit key to encrypt 64-bit blocks. This is the algorithm that is used in the Clipper chip. Algorithm details are classified.

Blowfish

Blowfish is a block cipher that uses 64-bit data blocks using anywhere from 32- to 448-bit encryption keys. Blowfish performs 16 rounds of transformation. Initially developed with the intention of serving as a replacement to DES, Blowfish is one of the few algorithms that are not patented.

Twofish

Twofish is a version of Blowfish that uses 128-bit data blocks using 128-, 192-, and 256-bit keys. It uses 16 rounds of transformation. Like Blowfish, Twofish is not patented.

RC4/RC5/RC6

A total of six RC algorithms have been developed by Ron Rivest. RC1 was never published, RC2 was a 64-bit block cipher, and RC3 was broken before release. So the main RC implementations that a security professional needs to understand are RC4, RC5, and RC6.

RC4, also called ARC4, is one of the most popular stream ciphers. It is used in SSL (discussed later this chapter) and WEP (discussed in Chapter 2, "Telecommunications and Network Security"). RC4 uses a variable key size of 40 to 2,048 bits and up to 256 rounds of transformation.

RC5 is a block cipher that uses a key size of up to 2,048 bits and up to 255 rounds of transformation. Block sizes supported are 32, 64, or 128 bits. Because of all the possible variables in RC5, the industry often uses an RC5=*w*/*r*/*b* designation, where *w* is the block size, *r* is the number of rounds, and *b* is the number of 8-bit bytes in the key. For example, RC5-64/16/16 denotes a 64-bit word (or 128-bit data blocks), 16 rounds of transformation, and a 16-byte (128-bit) key.

RC6 is a block cipher based on RC5, and it uses the same key size, rounds, and block size. RC6 was originally developed as an AES solution, but lost the contest to Rijndael. RC6 is faster than RC5.

CAST

CAST, invented by Carlisle Adams and Stafford Tavares, has two versions: CAST-128 and CAST-256. CAST-128 is a block cipher that uses a 40- to 128-bit key that will perform 12 or 16 rounds of transformation on 64-bit blocks. CAST-256 is a block cipher that uses a 128-, 160-, 192-, 224-, or 256-bit key that will perform 48 rounds of transformation on 128-bit blocks.

Table 6-3 lists the key facts about each symmetric algorithm.

Table 6-3 Symmetric Algorithms Key Facts

Algorithm Name	Block or Stream Cipher?	Key Size	Number of Rounds	Block Size
DES	Block	64 bits (effective length 56 bits)	16	64 bits
3DES	Block	56, 112, or 168 bits	48	64 bits
AES	Block	128, 192, or 256 bits	10, 12, or 14 (depending on block/key size)	128, 192, or 256 bits
IDEA	Block	128 bits	8	64 bits
Skipjack	Block	80 bits	32	64 bits
Blowfish	Block	32 – 448 bits	16	64 bits
Twofish	Block	128, 192, or 256 bits	16	128 bits
RC4	Stream	40 – 2,048 bits	Up to 256	N/A
RC5	Block	Up to 2,048	Up to 255	32, 64, or 128 bits
RC6	Block	Up to 2,048	Up to 255	32, 64, or 128 bits

Asymmetric Algorithms

Asymmetric algorithms were explained earlier in this chapter. In this section, we discuss some of the most popular asymmetric algorithms. Some of these might no longer be commonly used because there are more secure alternatives.

Security professionals should be familiar with the following symmetric algorithms:

- Diffie-Hellman
- RSA
- El Gamal
- ECC
- Knapsack
- Zero Knowledge Proof

Diffie-Hellman

Diffie-Hellman is an asymmetric key agreement algorithm created by Whitfield Diffie and Martin Hellman. Diffie-Hellman is responsible for the key agreement process. The key agreement process includes the following steps:

1. John and Sally need to communicate over an encrypted channel and decide to use Diffie-Hellman.
2. John generates a private and public key, and Sally generates a private and a public key.
3. John and Sally share their public keys with each other.
4. An application on John's computer takes John's private key and Sally's public key and applies the Diffie-Hellman algorithm, and an application on Sally's computer takes Sally's private key and John's public key and applies the Diffie-Hellman algorithm.
5. Through this application, the same shared value is created for John and Sally, which in turn creates the same symmetric key on each system using the asymmetric key agreement algorithm.

Through this process, Diffie-Hellman provides secure key distribution, but not confidentiality, authentication, or non-repudiation. The key to this algorithm is dealing with discrete logarithms. Diffie-Hellman is susceptible to man-in-the-middle attacks unless an organization implements digital signatures or digital certificates for authentication at the beginning of the Diffie-Hellman process.

NOTE Man-in-the-middle attacks are discussed later in this chapter.

RSA

RSA is the most popular asymmetric algorithm and was invented by Ron Rivest, Adi Shamir, and Leonard Adleman. RSA can provide key exchange, encryption, and digital signatures. The strength of the RSA algorithm is the difficulty of finding the prime factors of very large numbers. RSA uses a 1,024- to 4,096-bit key and performs one round of transformation.

RSA-768 and RSA-704 have been factored. If factorization of the prime numbers used by an RSA implementation occurs, then the implementation is considered breakable and should not be used. RSA-2048 is the largest RSA number and carries a cash prize of $200,000 US if successful factorization occurs.

As a key exchange protocol, RSA encrypts a DES or AES symmetric key for secure distribution. RSA uses a one-way function to provide encryption/decryption and digital signature verification/generation. The public key works with the one-way function to perform encryption and digital signature verification. The private key works with the one-way function to perform decryption and signature generation.

In RSA, the one-way function is a trapdoor. The private key knows the one-way function. The private key is capable of determining the original prime numbers. Finally, the private key knows how to use the one-way function to decrypt the encrypted message.

Attackers can use Number Field Sieve (NFS), a factoring algorithm, to attack RSA.

El Gamal

El Gamal is an asymmetric key algorithm based on the Diffie-Hellman algorithm. Like Diffie-Hellman, El Gamal deals with discrete logarithms. However, whereas Diffie-Hellman can only be used for key agreement, El Gamal can provide key exchange, encryption, and digital signatures.

With El Gamal, any key size can be used. However, a larger key size negatively affects performance. Because El Gamal is the slowest asymmetric algorithm, using a key size of 1,024 bit or less would be wise.

ECC

Elliptic Curve Cryptosystem (ECC) provides secure key distribution, encryption, and digital signatures. The elliptic curve's size defines the difficulty of the problem.

Although ECC can use a key of any size, it can use a much smaller key than RSA or any other asymmetric algorithm and still provide comparable security. Therefore, the primary benefit promised by ECC is a smaller key size, reducing storage and transmission requirements. ECC is more efficient and provides better security than RSA keys of the same size.

Figure 6-12 shows an elliptic curve example with the elliptic curve equation.

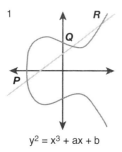

$y^2 = x^3 + ax + b$

Figure 6-12 Elliptic Curve Example with Equation

Knapsack

Knapsack is a series of asymmetric algorithms that provide encryption and digital signatures. This algorithm family is no longer used due to security issues.

Zero Knowledge Proof

A Zero Knowledge Proof is a technique used to ensure that only the minimum need information is disclosed without giving all the details. An example of this technique occurs when one user encrypts data with his private key and the receiver decrypts with the originator's public key. The originator has not given his private key to the receiver. But the originator is proving that he has his private key simply because the receiver can read the message.

Message Integrity

Integrity is one of the three basic tenets of security. Message integrity ensures that a message has not been altered by using parity bits, cyclic redundancy checks (CRCs), or checksums.

The parity bit method adds an extra bit to the data. This parity bit simply indicates if the number of 1 bits is odd or even. The parity bit is 1 if the number of 1 bits is odd, and the parity bit is 0 if the number of 1 bits is even. The parity bit is set before the data is transmitted. When the data arrives, the parity bit is checked against the other data. If the parity bit doesn't match the data sent, then an error is sent to the originator.

The CRC method uses polynomial division to determine the CRC value for a file. The CRC value is usually 16- or 32-bits long. Because CRC is very accurate, the CRC value will not match up if a single bit is incorrect.

The checksum method adds up the bytes of data being sent and then transmits that number to be checked later using the same method. The source adds up the values of the bytes and sends the data and its checksum. The receiving end receives the information, adds up the bytes in the same way the source did, and gets the checksum. The receiver then compares his checksum with the source's checksum. If the values match, message integrity is intact. If the values do not match, the data should be resent or replaced. Checksums are also referred to as hash sums because they typically use hash functions for the computation.

Message integrity is provided by hash functions and message authentication code.

Hash Functions

Hash functions were explained earlier in this chapter. In this section, we discuss some of the most popular hash functions. Some of these might no longer be commonly used because more secure alternatives are available.

Security professionals should be familiar with the following hash functions:

- One-way hash
- MD2/MD4/MD5/MD6
- SHA/SHA-2/SHA-3
- HAVAL
- RIPEMD-160
- Tiger

One-Way Hash

A hash function takes a message of variable length and produces a fixed-length hash value. Hash values, also referred to as message digests, are calculated using the original message. If the receiver calculates a hash value that is the same, then the original message is intact. If the receiver calculates a hash value that is different, then the original message has been altered.

Using a given function H, the following equation must be true to ensure that the original message, M1, has not been altered or replaced with a new message, M2:

H(M1) < > H(M2)

For a one-way hash to be effective, creating two different messages with the same hash value must be mathematically impossible. Given a hash value, discovering the original message from which the hash value was obtained must be mathematically impossible. A one-way hash algorithm is collision free if it provides protection against creating the same hash value from different messages.

Unlike symmetric and asymmetric algorithms, the hashing algorithm is publicly known. Hash functions are always performed in one direction. Using it in reverse is unnecessary.

However, one-way hash functions do have limitations. If an attacker intercepts a message that contains a hash value, the attacker can alter the original message to create a second invalid message with a new hash value. If the attacker then sends the second invalid message to the intended recipient, the intended recipient will have no way of knowing that he received an incorrect message. When the receiver performs a hash value calculation, the invalid message will look valid because the invalid message was appended with the attacker's new hash value, not the original message's hash value. To prevent this from occurring, the sender should use message authentication code (MAC).

Encrypting the hash function with a symmetric key algorithm generates a keyed MAC. The symmetric key does not encrypt the original message. It is used only to protect the hash value.

NOTES The basic types of MAC are discussed later in this chapter.

The basic steps of a hash function are shown in Figure 6-13.

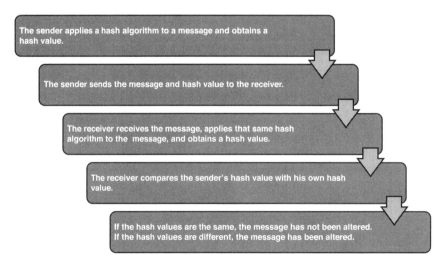

Figure 6-13 Hash Function Process

MD2/MD4/MD5/MD6

The MD2 message digest algorithm produces a 128-bit hash value. It performs 18 rounds of computations. Although MD2 is still in use today, it is much slower than MD4, MD5, and MD6.

The MD4 algorithm also produces a 128-bit hash value. However, it performs only three rounds of computations. Although MD4 is faster than MD2, its use has significantly declined because attacks against it have been so successful.

Like the other MD algorithms, the MD5 algorithm produces a 128-bit hash value. It performs four rounds of computations. It was originally created because of the issues with MD4, and it is more complex than MD4. However, MD5 is not collision free. For this reason, it should not be used for SSL certificates or digital signatures. The U.S. government requires the usage of SHA-2 instead of MD5. However, in commercial usage, many software vendors publish the MD5 hash value when they release software patches so customers can verify the software's integrity after download.

The MD6 algorithm produces a variable hash value, performing a variable number of computations. Although it was originally introduced as a candidate for SHA-3, it was withdrawn because of early issues the algorithm had with differential attacks. MD6 has since been re-released with this issue fixed. However, that release was too late to be accepted as the NIST SHA-3 standard.

SHA/SHA-2/SHA-3

Secure Hash Algorithm (SHA) is a family of four algorithms published by the U.S. NIST. SHA-0, originally referred to as simply SHA because there were no other "family members," produces a 160-bit hash value after performing 80 rounds of computations on 512-bit blocks. SHA-0 was never very popular because collisions were discovered.

Like SHA-0, SHA-1 produces a 160-bit hash value after performing 80 rounds of computations on 512-bit blocks. SHA-1 corrected the flaw in SHA-0 that made it susceptible to attacks.

SHA-2 is actually a family of hash functions, each of which provides different functional limits. The SHA-2 family is as follows:

- **SHA-224:** Produces a 224-bit hash value after performing 64 rounds of computations on 512-bit blocks.

- **SHA-256:** Produces a 256-bit hash value after performing 64 rounds of computations on 512-bit blocks.

- **SHA-384:** Produces a 384-bit hash value after performing 80 rounds of computations on 1,024-bit blocks.

- **SHA-512:** Produces a 512-bit hash value after performing 80 rounds of computations on 1,024-bit blocks.

- **SHA-512/224:** Produces a 224-bit hash value after performing 80 rounds of computations on 1,024-bit blocks. The 512 designation here indicates the internal state size.

- **SHA-512/256:** Produces a 256-bit hash value after performing 80 rounds of computations on 1,024-bit blocks. Once again, the 512 designation indicates the internal state size.

SHA-3, like SHA-2, will be a family of hash functions. However, this standard has not been formally adopted as of March 2013. The hash value sizes will range from 224 to 512 bits. Although the block sizes are unknown, SHA-3 will perform 120 rounds of computations, by default.

Keep in mind that SHA-1 and SHA-2 are still widely used today. SHA-3 was not developed because of some security flaw with the two previous standards but was instead proposed as an alternative hash function to the others.

HAVAL

HAVAL is a one-way function that produces variable-length hash values, including 128 bits, 160 bits, 192 bits, 224 bits, and 256 bits, and uses 1,024-bit blocks. The number of rounds of computations can be 3, 4, or 5. Collision issues have been discovered if producing a 128-bit hash value with three rounds of computations. All other variations do not have any discovered issues as of this printing.

RIPEMD-160

Although several variations of the RIPEMD hash function exist, security professionals should only worry about RIPEMD-160 for exam purposes. RIPEMD-160 produces a 160-bit hash value after performing 160 rounds of computations on 512-bit blocks.

Tiger

Tiger is a hash function that produces 128-, 160-, or 192-bit hash values after performing 24 rounds of computations on 512-bit blocks, with the most popular version being the one that produces 192-bit hash values. Unlike MD5, RIPEMD, SHA-0, and SHA-1, Tiger is *not* built on the MD4 architecture.

Message Authentication Code

MAC was explained earlier in this chapter. In this section, we discuss the three types of MACs with which security professionals should be familiar:

- HMAC
- CBC-MAC
- CMAC

HMAC

A hash MAC (HMAC) is a keyed-hash MAC that involves a hash function with symmetric key. HMAC provides data integrity and authentication. Any of the previously listed hash functions can be used with HMAC, with the HMAC name being appended with the hash function name, as in HMAC-SHA-1. The strength of HMAC is dependent upon the strength of the hash function, including the hash value size, and the key size.

HMAC's hash value output size will be the same as the underlying hash function. HMAC can help to reduce the collision rate of the hash function.

Figure 6-14 shows the basic steps of an HMAC process.

1. The sender and receiver agree on which symmetric key to use.
2. The sender joins the symmetric key to the message.
3. The sender applies a hash algorithm to the message and obtains a hash value.
4. The sender adds a hash value to the original message, and the sender sends the new message to the receiver.
5. The receiver receives the message and joins the symmetric key to the message.
6. The receiver applies the hash algorithm to the message and obtains a hash value.
7. If the hash values are the same, the message has not been altered. If the hash values are different, the message has been altered.

Figure 6-14 HMAC Process

CBC-MAC

Cipher block chaining MAC (CBC-MAC) is a block-cipher MAC that operates in CBC mode. CBC-MAC provides data integrity and authentication.

Figure 6-15 shows the basic steps of a CBC-MAC process.

1. The sender and receiver agree on which symmetric block cipher to use.
2. The sender encrypts the message with the symmetric block cipher in CBC mode. The last block is the MAC.
3. The sender adds the MAC to the original message, and the sender sends the new message to the receiver.
4. The receiver receives the message and encrypts the message with the symmetric block cipher in CBC mode.
5. The receiver obtains the MAC and compares it to the sender's MAC.
6. If the values are the same, the message has not been altered. If the values are different, the message has been altered.

Figure 6-15 CBC-MAC Process

CMAC

Cipher-based MAC (CMAC) operates in the same manner as CBC-MAC but with much better mathematical functions. CMAC addresses some security issues with CBC-MAC and is approved to work with AES and 3DES.

Digital Signatures

A digital signature is a hash value encrypted with the sender's private key. A digital signature provides authentication, non-repudiation, and integrity. A blind signature is a form of digital signature where the contents of the message are masked before it is signed.

Public key cryptography, which is discussed in the next section, is used to create digital signatures. Users register their public keys with a certification authority (CA), which distributes a certificate containing the user's public key and the CA's digital signature. The digital signature is computed by the user's public key and validity period being combined with the certificate issuer and digital signature algorithm identifier.

The Digital Signature Standard (DSS) is a federal digital security standard that governs the Digital Security Algorithm (DSA). DSA generates a message digest of 160 bits. The U.S. federal government requires the use of DSA, RSA (discussed earlier in this chapter), or Elliptic Curve DSA (ECDSA) and SHA for digital signatures. DSA is slower than RSA and only provides digital signatures. RSA provides digital signatures, encryption, and secure symmetric key distribution.

When considering cryptography, keep the following facts in mind:

- Encryption provides confidentiality.
- Hashing provides integrity.
- Digital signatures provide authentication, non-repudiation, and integrity.

Public Key Infrastructure

A public key infrastructure (PKI) includes systems, software, and communication protocols that distribute, manage, and control public key cryptography. A PKI publishes digital certificates. Because a PKI establishes trust within an environment, a PKI can certify that a public key is tied to an entity and verify that a public key is valid. Public keys are published through digital certificates.

The X.509 standard is a framework that enables authentication between networks and over the Internet. A PKI includes timestamping and certificate revocation to ensure that certificates are managed properly. A PKI provides confidentiality, message integrity, authentication, and non-repudiation.

The structure of a PKI includes CAs, certificates, registration authorities, certificate revocation lists, cross-certification, and the Online Certificate Status Protocol (OCSP). In this section, we discuss these PKI components as well as a few other PKI concepts.

Certification Authority (CA) and Registration Authority (RA)

Any participant that requests a certificate must first go through the registration authority (RA), which verifies the requestor's identity and registers the requestor. After the identity is verified, the RA passes the request to the CA.

A certification authority (CA) is the entity that creates and signs digital certificates, maintains the certificates, and revokes them when necessary. Every entity that wants to participate in the PKI must contact the CA and request a digital certificate. It is the ultimate authority for the authenticity for every participant in the PKI by signing each digital certificate. The certificate binds the identity of the participant to the public key.

There are different types of CAs. Organizations exist who provide a PKI as a payable service to companies who need them. An example is VeriSign. Some organizations implement their own private CAs so that the organization can control all aspects of the PKI process. If an organization is large enough, it might need to provide a structure of CAs with the root CA being the highest in the hierarchy.

Because more than one entity is often involved in the PKI certification process, certification path validation allows the participants to check the legitimacy of the certificates in the certification path.

OCSP

The Online Certificate Status Protocol (OCSP) is an Internet protocol that obtains the revocation status of an X.509 digital certificate. OCSP is an alternative to the standard certificate revocation list (CRL) that is used by many PKIs. OCSP automatically validates the certificates and reports back the status of the digital certificate by accessing the CRL on the CA.

Certificates

A digital certificate provides an entity, usually a user, with the credentials to prove its identity and associates that identity with a public key. At minimum, a digital certification must provide the serial number, the issuer, the subject (owner), and the public key.

An X.509 certificate complies with the X.509 standard. An X.509 certificate contains the following fields:

- Version
- Serial Number
- Algorithm ID
- Issuer
- Validity
- Subject
- Subject Public Key Info
    - Public Key Algorithm
    - Subject Public Key
- Issuer Unique Identifier (optional)

- Subject Unique Identifier (optional)
- Extensions (optional)

VeriSign first introduced the following digital certificate classes:

- **Class 1:** For individuals intended for e-mail. These certificates get saved by Web browsers.
- **Class 2:** For organizations that must provide proof of identity.
- **Class 3:** For servers and software signing in which independent verification and identity and authority checking is done by the issuing CA.

Certificate Revocation List (CRL)

A CRL is a list of digital certificates that a CA has revoked. To find out whether a digital certificate has been revoked, the browser must either check the CRL or the CA must push out the CRL values to clients. This can become quite daunting when you consider that the CRL contains every certificate that has ever been revoked.

One concept to keep in mind is the revocation request grace period. This period is the maximum amount of time between when the revocation request is received by the CA and when the revocation actually occurs. A shorter revocation period provides better security but often results in a higher implementation cost.

PKI Steps

The steps involved in requesting a digital certificate are as follow:

1. A user requests a digital certificate, and the RA receives the request.
2. The RA requests identifying information from the requestor.
3. After the required information is received, the RA forwards the certificate request to the CA.
4. The CA creates a digital certificate for the requestor. The requestor's public key and identity information are included as part of the certificate.
5. The user receives the certificate.

After the user has a certificate, he is ready to communicate with other trusted entities. The process for communication between entities is as follows:

1. User 1 requests User 2's public key from the certificate repository.
2. The repository sends User 2's digital certificate to User 1.

3. User 1 verifies the certificate and extracts User 2's public key.

4. User 1 encrypts the session key with User 2's public key and sends the encrypted session key and User 1's certificate to User 2.

5. User 2 receives User 1's certificate and verifies the certificate with a trusted CA.

After this certificate exchange and verification process occurs, the two entities are able to communicate using encryption.

Cross-Certification

Cross-certification establishes trust relationships between CAs so that the participating CAs can rely on the other participants' digital certificates and public keys. It enables users to validate each other's certificates when they are actually certified under different certification hierarchies. A CA for one organization can validate digital certificates from another organization's CA when a cross-certification trust relationship exists.

Key Management

Key management in cryptography is essential to ensure that the cryptography provides confidentiality, integrity, and authentication. If a key is compromised, it can have serious consequences throughout an organization.

Key management involves the entire process of ensuring that keys are protected during creation, distribution, transmission, and storage. As part of this process, keys must also be destroyed properly. When you consider the vast number of networks over which the key is transmitted and the different types of system on which a key is stored, the enormity of this issue really comes to light.

As the most demanding and critical aspect of cryptography, it is important that security professionals understand key management principles.

Keys should always be stored in ciphertext when stored on a non-cryptographic device. Key distribution, storage, and maintenance should be automatic by integrating the processes into the application.

Because keys can be lost, backup copies should be made and stored in a secure location. A designated individual should have control of the backup copies with other individuals designated serving as emergency backups. The key recovery process should also require more than one operator to ensure that only valid key recovery requests are completed. In some cases, keys are even broken into parts and deposited with trusted agents, who provide their part of the key to a central authority when authorized to do so. Although other methods of distributing parts of a key are used, all the solutions involve the use of trustee agents entrusted with part of the key and a central authority tasked with assembling the key from its parts. Also, key recovery personnel should span across the entire organization and not just be members of the IT department.

Organizations should also limit the number of keys that are used. The more keys that you have, the more keys you must worry about and ensure are protected. Although a valid reason for issuing a key should never be ignored, limiting the number of keys issued and used reduces the potential damage.

When designing the key management process, you should consider how to do the following:

- Securely store and transmit the keys.
- Use random keys.
- Issue keys of sufficient length to ensure protection.
- Properly destroy keys when no longer needed.
- Back up the keys to ensure that they can be recovered.

Trusted Platform Module (TPM)

Trusted Platform Module (TPM) is a security chip installed on computer motherboards that is responsible for managing symmetric and asymmetric keys, hashes, and digital certificates. This chip provides service to protect passwords, encrypt drives, and manage digital rights, making it much harder for attackers to gain access to the computers that have a TPM-chip enabled.

Two particularly popular uses of TPM are binding and sealing. Binding actually "binds" the hard drive through encryption to a particular computer. Because the decryption key is stored in the TPM chip, the hard drive's contents are available only when connected to the original computer. But keep in mind that all the contents are at risk if the TPM chip fails and a backup of the key does not exist.

Sealing, on the other hand, "seals" the system state to a particular hardware and software configuration. This prevents attacks from making any changes to the system. However, it can also make installing a new piece of hardware or a new operating system much harder. The system can only boot after the TPM verifies system integrity by comparing the original computed hash value of the system's configuration to the hash value of its configuration at boot time.

The TPM consists of both static memory and dynamic memory that is used to retain the important information when the computer is turned off. The memory used in a TPM chip is as follows:

- **Endorsement Key (EK):** Persistent memory installed by the manufacturer that contains a public/private key pair.
- **Storage Root Key (SRK):** Persistent memory that secures the keys stored in the TPM.
- **Attestation Identity Key (AIK):** Dynamic memory that ensures the integrity of the EK.
- **Platform Configuration Register (PCR) Hashes:** Dynamic memory that stores data hashes for the sealing function.
- **Storage keys:** Dynamic memory that contains the keys used to encrypt the computer's storage, including hard drives, USB flash drives, and so on.

Encryption Communication Levels

Encryption can provide different protection based on which level of communication is being used. The two types of encryption communication levels are link encryption and end-to-end encryption.

Link Encryption

Link encryption encrypts all the data that is transmitted over a link. In this type of communication, the only portion of the packet that is not encrypted is the data-link control information, which is needed to ensure that devices transmit the data properly. All the information is encrypted, with each router or other device decrypting its header information so that routing can occur and then re-encrypting before sending the information to the next device.

If the sending party needs to ensure that data security and privacy is maintained over a public communication link, then link encryption should be used. This is often the method used to protect e-mail communication or when banks or other institutions that have confidential data must send that data over the Internet.

Link encryption protects against packet sniffers and other forms of eavesdropping and occurs at the data link and physical layers of the OSI model. Advantages of link encryption include: All the data is encrypted, and no user interaction is needed for it to be used. Disadvantages of link encryption include: Each device that the data must be transmitted through must receive the key, key changes must be transmitted to each device on the route, and packets are decrypted at each device.

End-to-End Encryption

End-to-end encryption encrypts less of the packet information than link encryption. In end-to-end encryption, packet routing information, as well as packet headers and addresses, are not encrypted. This allows potential hackers to obtain more information if a packet is acquired through packet sniffing or eavesdropping.

End-to-end encryption has several advantages. A user usually initiates end-to-end encryption, which allows the user to select exactly what gets encrypted and how. It affects the performance of each device along the route less than link encryption because every device does not have to perform encryption/decryption to determine how to route the packet.

E-mail Security

E-mail has become an integral part of almost everyone's life, particularly as it relates to their business communication. But many e-mail implementations provide very little security natively without the incorporation of encryption, digital signatures, or keys. For example, e-mail authenticity and confidentiality are provided by signing the message using the sender's private key and encrypting the message with the receiver's public key.

In the following sections, we briefly discuss the PGP, MIME, and S/MIME e-mail standards that are popular in today's world and also give a brief description of quantum cryptography.

PGP

Pretty Good Privacy (PGP) provides e-mail encryption over the Internet and uses different encryption technologies based on the needs of the organization. PGP can provide confidentiality, integrity, and authenticity based on which encryption methods are used.

PGP provides key management using RSA. PGP uses a web of trust to manage the keys. By sharing public keys, users create this web of trust, instead of relying on a CA. The public keys of all the users are stored on each user's computer in a key ring file. Within that file, each user is assigned a level of trust. The users within the web vouch for each other. So if user 1 and user 2 have a trust relationship and user 1 and user 3 have a trust relationship, user 1 can recommend the other two users to each other. Users can choose the level of trust initially assigned to a user but can change that level later if circumstances warrant a change. But compromise of a user's public key in the PGP system means that the user must contact everyone with whom he has shared his key to ensure that this key is removed from the key ring file.

PGP provides data encryption for confidentiality using IDEA. However, other encryption algorithms can be used. Implementing PGP with MD5 provides data integrity. Public certificates with PGP provide authentication.

MIME and S/MIME

Multipurpose Internet Mail Extension (MIME) is an Internet standard that allows e-mail to include non-text attachments, non-ASCII character sets, multiple-part message bodies, and non-ASCII header information. In today's world, SMTP in MIME format transmits a majority of e-mail.

MIME allows the e-mail client to send an attachment with a header describing the file type. The receiving system uses this header and the file extension listed in it to identify the attachment type and open the associated application. This allows the computer to automatically launch the appropriate application when the user double-clicks the attachment. If no application is associated with that file type, the user is able to choose the application using the Open With option or a website might offer the necessary application.

Secure MIME (S/MIME) allows MIME to encrypt and digitally sign e-mail messages and encrypt attachments. It adheres to the Public Key Cryptography Standards (PKCS), which is a set of public-key cryptography standards designed by the owners of the RSA algorithm.

S/MIME uses encryption to provide confidentiality, hashing to provide integrity, public key certificates to provide authentication, and message digests to provide non-repudiation.

Quantum Cryptography

Quantum cryptography is a method of encryption that combines quantum physics and cryptography and offers the possibility of factoring the products of large prime numbers. Quantum cryptography provides strong encryption and eavesdropping detection.

This would be an excellent choice for any organizations that transmit Top Secret data, including the U.S. government.

Internet Security

The World Wide Web is a collection of HTTP servers that manage websites and their services. The Internet is a network that includes all the physical devices and protocols over which web traffic is transmitted. The web browser that is used allows users to read web pages via HTTP. Browsers can natively read many protocols. Any protocols not natively supported by the web browser can only be read by installing a plug-in or application viewer, thereby expanding the browser's role.

In our discussion of Internet security, we cover the following topics:

- Remote access
- SSL/TLS
- HTTP, HTTPS, and SHTTP
- SET
- Cookies
- SSH
- IPsec

NOTE All the topics in this "Internet Security" section are also discussed in Chapter 3, "Telecommunications and Network Security."

Remote Access

Remote access applications allow users to access an organization's resources from a remote connection. These remote connections can be direct dial-in connections but are increasingly using the Internet as the network over which the data is transmitted. If an organization allows remote access to internal resources, the organization must ensure that the data is protected using encryption when the data is being transmitted between the remote access client and remote access server. Remote access servers can require encrypted connections with remote access clients, which means that any connection attempt that does not use encryption will be denied.

SSL/TLS

Secure Sockets Layer (SSL) is a transport-layer protocol that provides encryption, server and client authentication, and message integrity. SSL was developed by Netscape to transmit private documents over the Internet. While SSL implements either 40-bit (SSL 2.0) or 128-bit encryption (SSL 3.0), the 40-bit version is susceptible to attacks because of its limited key size. SSL allows an application to have encrypted, authenticated communication across a network.

Transport Layer Security (TLS) is an open-community standard that provides many of the same services as SSL. TLS 1.0 is based upon SSL 3.0 but is more extensible.

The main goal of TLS is privacy and data integrity between two communicating applications.

SSL and TLS are most commonly used when data needs to be encrypted while it is being transmitted (in transit) over a medium from one system to another.

HTTP, HTTPS, and SHTTP

Hypertext Transfer Protocol (HTTP) is the protocol used on the Web to transmit website data between a web server and a web client. With each new address that is entered into the web browser, whether from initial user entry or by clicking a link on the page displayed, a new connection is established because HTTP is a stateless protocol.

HTTP Secure (HTTPS) is the implementation of HTTP running over the SSL/TLS protocol, which establishes a secure session using the server's digital certificate. SSL/TLS keeps the session open using a secure channel. HTTPS websites will *always* include the https:// designation at the beginning.

Although it sounds very similar, Secure HTTP (S-HTTP) protects HTTP communication in a different manner. S-HTTP only encrypts a single communication message, not an entire session (or conversation). S-HTTP is not as common as HTTPS.

SET

Secure Electronic Transaction (SET), proposed by Visa and MasterCard, secures credit card transaction information over the Internet. It was based on X.509 certificates and asymmetric keys. It used an electronic wallet on a user's computer to send encrypted credit card information. But to be fully implemented, SET would have required the full cooperation of financial institutions, credit card users, wholesale and retail establishments, and payment gateways. It was never fully adopted.

Visa now promotes the 3-D Secure protocol, which is not covered on the CISSP exam as of this writing.

Cookies

Cookies are text files that are stored on a user's hard drive or memory. These files store information on the user's Internet habits, including browsing and spending information. Because a website's servers actually determine how cookies are used, malicious sites can use cookies to discover a large amount of information about a user.

Although the information retained in cookies on the hard drive usually does not include any confidential information, it can still be used by attackers to obtain information about a user that can help an attacker develop a better targeted attack. For example, if the cookies reveal to an attack that a user accesses a particular bank's public website on a daily basis, that action can indicate that a user has an account at that bank, resulting in the attacker's attempting a phishing attack using an e-mail that looks to come from the user's legitimate bank.

Many anti-virus or anti-malware applications include functionality that allows you to limit the type of cookies downloaded and to hide personally identifiable information (PII), such as e-mail addresses. Often these types of safeguards end up proving to be more trouble than they are worth because they often affect legitimate Internet communication.

SSH

Secure Shell (SSH) is an application and protocol that is used to remotely log in to another computer using a secure tunnel. After the secure channel is established after a session key is exchanged, all communication between the two computers is encrypted over the secure channel.

IPsec

Internet Protocol Security (IPsec) is a suite of protocols that establishes a secure channel between two devices. IPsec is commonly implemented over VPNs. IPsec provides traffic analysis protection by determining the algorithms to use and implementing any cryptographic keys required for IPsec.

IPsec includes Authentication Header (AH), Encapsulating Security Payload (ESP), and security associations. AH provides authentication and integrity, whereas ESP provides authentication, integrity, and encryption (confidentiality). A security association (SA) is a record of a device's configuration that needs to participate in IPsec communication. A security parameter index (SPI) is a type of table that tracks the different SAs used and ensures that a device uses the appropriate SA to communicate with another device. Each device has its own SPI.

IPsec runs in one of two modes: transport mode or tunnel mode. Transport mode only protects the message payload, whereas tunnel mode protects the payload, routing, and header information. Both of these modes can be used for gateway-to-gateway or host-to-gateway IPsec communication.

IPsec does not determine which hashing or encryption algorithm is used. Internet Key Exchange (IKE), which is a combination of OAKLEY and Internet Security Association and Key Management Protocol (ISAKMP), is the key exchange method that is most commonly used by IPsec. OAKLEY is a key establishment protocol based on Diffie-Hellman that was superseded by IKE. ISAKMP was established to set up and manage SAs. IKE with IPsec provides authentication and key exchange.

The authentication method used by IKE with IPsec includes pre-shared keys, certificates, and public key authentication. The most secure implementations of pre-shared keys require a PKI. But a PKI is not necessary if a pre-shared key is based on simple passwords.

Cryptography Attacks

Cryptography attacks are categorized as either passive or active attacks. A passive attack is usually implemented just to discover information and is much harder to detect because it is usually carried out by eavesdropping or packet sniffing. Active attacks involve an attacker actually carrying out steps, like message alteration or file modification. Cryptography is usually attacked via the key, algorithm, execution, data, or people. But most of these attacks are attempting to discover the key used.

Cryptography attacks that are discussed include the following:

- Ciphertext-only attack
- Known plaintext attack
- Chosen plaintext attack
- Chosen ciphertext attack
- Social engineering
- Brute force
- Differential cryptanalysis
- Linear cryptanalysis
- Algebraic attack
- Frequency analysis
- Birthday attack
- Dictionary attack
- Replay attack
- Analytic attack
- Statistical attack

- Factoring attack
- Reverse engineering
- Meet-in-the-middle attack

Ciphertext-Only Attack

In a ciphertext-only attack, an attacker uses several encrypted messages (ciphertext) to figure out the key used in the encryption process. Although it is a very common type of attack, it is usually not successful because so little is known about the encryption used.

Known Plaintext Attack

In a known plaintext attack, an attacker uses the plaintext and ciphertext versions of a message to discover the key used. This type of attack implements reverse engineering, frequency analysis, or brute force to determine the key so that all messages can be deciphered.

Chosen Plaintext Attack

In a chosen plaintext attack, an attacker chooses the plaintext to get encrypted to obtain the ciphertext. The attacker sends a message hoping that the user will forward that message as ciphertext to another user. The attacker captures the ciphertext version of the message and tries to determine the key by comparing the plaintext version he originated with the captured ciphertext version. Once again, key discovery is the goal of this attack.

Chosen Ciphertext Attack

A chosen ciphertext attack is the opposite of a chosen plaintext attack. In a chosen ciphertext attack, an attacker chooses the ciphertext to be decrypted to obtain the plaintext. This attack is more difficult because control of the system that implements the algorithm is needed.

Social Engineering

Social engineering attacks against cryptographic algorithms do not differ greatly from social engineering attacks against any other security area. Attackers attempt to trick users into giving the attacker the cryptographic key used. Common social engineering methods include intimidation, enticement, or inducement.

Brute Force

As with a brute-force attack against passwords, a brute-force attack executed against a cryptographic algorithm uses all possible keys until a key is discovered that successfully decrypts the ciphertext. This attack requires considerable time and processing power and is very difficult to complete.

Differential Cryptanalysis

Differential cryptanalysis, also referred to as a side-channel attack, measures the execution times and power required by the cryptographic device. The measurements help the key and algorithm used.

Linear Cryptanalysis

Linear cryptanalysis is a known plaintext attack that uses linear approximation, which describes the behavior of the block cipher. An attacker is more successful with this type of attack when more plaintext and matching ciphertext messages are obtained.

Algebraic Attack

Algebraic attacks rely on the algebra used by cryptographic algorithms. If an attacker exploits known vulnerabilities of the algebra used, looking for those vulnerabilities can help the attacker to determine the key and algorithm used.

Frequency Analysis

Frequency analysis is an attack that relies on the fact that substitution and transposition ciphers will result in repeated patterns in ciphertext. Recognizing the patterns of eight bits and counting them can allow an attacker to use reverse substitution to obtain the plaintext message.

Frequency analysis usually involves the creation of a chart that lists all the letters of the alphabet alongside the number of times that letter occurs. So if the letter Q in the frequency lists has the highest value, a good possibility exists that this letter is actually E in the plaintext message because E is the most used letter in the English language. The ciphertext letter is then replaced in the ciphertext with the plaintext letter.

Today's algorithms are considered too complex to be susceptible to this type of attack.

Birthday Attack

A birthday attack uses the premise that finding two messages that result in the same hash value is easier than matching a message and its hash value. Most hash algorithms can resist simple birthday attacks.

Dictionary Attack

Similar to a brute-force attack, a dictionary attack uses all the words in a dictionary until a key is discovered that successfully decrypts the ciphertext. This attack requires considerable time and processing power and is very difficult to complete. It also requires a comprehensive dictionary of words.

Replay Attack

In a replay attack, an attacker sends the same data repeatedly in an attempt to trick the receiving device. This data is most commonly authentication information. The best countermeasures against this type of attack are timestamps and sequence numbers.

Analytic Attack

In analytic attacks, attackers use known structural weaknesses or flaws to determine the algorithm used. If a particular weakness or flaw can be exploited, then the possibility of a particular algorithm being used is more likely.

Statistical Attack

Whereas analytic attacks look for structural weaknesses or flaws, statistical attacks use known statistical weaknesses of an algorithm to aid in the attack.

Factoring Attack

A factoring attack is carried out against the RSA algorithm by using the solutions of factoring large numbers.

Reverse Engineering

One of the most popular cryptographic attacks, reverse engineering occurs when an attacker purchases a particular cryptographic product to attempt to reverse engineer the product to discover confidential information about the cryptographic algorithm used.

Meet-in-the-Middle Attack

In a meet-in-the middle attack, an attacker tries to break the algorithm by encrypting from one end and decrypting from the other to determine the mathematical problem used.

Exam Preparation Tasks

Review All Key Topics

Review the most important topics in this chapter, noted with the Key Topics icon in the outer margin of the page. Table 6-4 lists a reference of these key topics and the page numbers on which each is found.

Table 6-4 Key Topics for Chapter 6

Key Topic Element	Description	Page Number
List	Cryptography concepts	244
List	Cryptography history	247
List	Encryption systems	251
List	Substitution ciphers	257
List	Symmetric algorithms	258
List	DES modes	259
List	3DES modes	262
List	Symmetric algorithms key facts	265
List	Asymmetric algorithms	266
List	Hash functions	269
List	MAC types	273
List	Internet security topics	283
List	Cryptographic attacks	286

Complete the Tables and Lists from Memory

Print a copy of CD Appendix A, "Memory Tables," or at least the section for this chapter, and complete the tables and lists from memory. CD Appendix B, "Memory Tables Answer Key," includes completed tables and lists to check your work.

Define Key Terms

Define the following key terms from this chapter and check your answers in the glossary:

cryptography, encryption, decryption, key, cryptovariable, synchronous encryption, asynchronous encryption, symmetric encryption, private key encryption, secret key encryption, asymmetric encryption, public key encryption, digital signature, hash, digital certificate, plaintext, cleartext, ciphertext, cryptogram, cryptosystem, cryptanalysis, key clustering, keyspace, collision, algorithm, cipher, cryptology, encoding, decoding, transposition, permutation, substitution, confusion, diffusion, avalanche effect, work factor, trapdoor, one-way function, mono-alphabetic substitution cipher, polyalphabetic substitution cipher, authentication, confidentiality, integrity, authorization, non-repudiation, running key cipher, concealment cipher, null cipher, substitution cipher, transposition cipher, stream-based cipher, block cipher, one-time pad, steganography, Digital Encryption Standard, DES, DES-X, Double-DES, Electronic Code Book (ECB), Cipher Block Chaining (CBC), Cipher Feedback (CFB), Output Feedback (OFB), Counter Mode (CTR), Triple DES, 3DES, Rijndael algorithm, International Data Encryption Algorithm (IDEA), Skipjack, Blowfish, Twofish, RC4, RC5, RC6, CAST-128, CAST-256, MD2, MD4, MD5, MD6, HAVAL, RIPEMD-160, Tiger, Hash MAC (HMAC), cipher block chaining MAC (CBC-MAC), Digital Signature Standard (DSS), certification authority (CA), registration authority (RA), online certificate status protocol (OCSP), certificate revocation list (CRL), trusted platform module (TPM), Secure Sockets Layer (SSL), HTTP Secure (HTTPS), Secure Electronic Transaction (SET), Secure Shell (SSH), ciphertext-only attack, known plaintext attack, chosen plaintext attack, chosen ciphertext attack.

Review Questions

1. Which process converts plaintext into ciphertext?
    a. hashing
    b. decryption
    c. encryption
    d. digital signature

2. What occurs when different encryption keys generate the same ciphertext from the same plaintext message?
    a. key clustering
    b. cryptanalysis

c. keyspace

d. confusion

3. Which type of cipher is the Caesar cipher?

   a. polyalphabetic substitution

   b. mono-alphabetic substitution

   c. polyalphabetic transposition

   d. mono-alphabetic transposition

4. Which encryption system uses a private or secret key that must remain secret between the two parties?

   a. running key cipher

   b. concealment cipher

   c. asymmetric algorithm

   d. symmetric algorithm

5. What is the most secure encryption scheme?

   a. concealment cipher

   b. symmetric algorithm

   c. one-time pad

   d. asymmetric algorithm

6. Which 3DES implementation encrypts each block of data three times, each time with a different key?

   a. 3DES-EDE3

   b. 3DES-EEE3

   c. 3DES-EDE2

   d. 3DES-EEE2

7. Which of the following is an asymmetric algorithm?

   a. IDEA

   b. Twofish

   c. RC6

   d. RSA

8. Which of the following is NOT a hash function?

    a. ECC

    b. MD6

    c. SHA-2

    d. RIPEMD-160

9. Which PKI component contains a list of all the certificates that have been revoked?

    a. CA

    b. RA

    c. CRL

    d. OCSP

10. Which attack executed against a cryptographic algorithm uses all possible keys until a key is discovered that successfully decrypts the ciphertext?

    a. frequency analysis

    b. reverse engineering

    c. ciphertext-only attack

    d. brute force

Answers and Explanations

1. **c.** Encryption converts plaintext into ciphertext.

    Hashing reduces a message to a hash value. Decryption converts ciphertext into plaintext. A digital signature is an object that provides sender authentication and message integrity by including a digital signature with the original message.

2. **a.** Key clustering occurs when different encryption keys generate the same ciphertext from the same plaintext message.

    Cryptanalysis is the science of decrypting ciphertext without prior knowledge of the key or cryptosystem used. A keyspace is all the possible key values when using a particular algorithm or other security measure. Confusion is the process of changing a key value during each round of encryption.

3. **b.** The Caesar cipher is a mono-alphabetic substitution cipher.

    The Vigenere substitution is a polyalphabetic substitution.

4. **d**. A symmetric algorithm uses a private or secret key that must remain secret between the two parties.

   A running key cipher uses a physical component, usually a book, to provide the polyalphabetic characters. A concealment cipher occurs when plaintext is interspersed somewhere within other written material. An asymmetric algorithm uses both a public key and a private or secret key.

5. **c**. A one-time pad is the most secure encryption scheme because it is used only once.

6. **b**. The 3DES-EEE3 implementation encrypts each block of data three times, each time with a different key.

   The 3DES-EDE3 implementation encrypts each block of data with the first key, decrypts each block with the second key, and encrypts each block with the third key. The 3DES-EEE2 implementation encrypts each block of data with the first key, encrypts each block with the second key, and then encrypts each block with the third key. The 3DES-EDE2 implementation encrypts each block of data with the first key, decrypts each block with the second key, and then encrypts each block with the first key.

7. **d**. RSA is an asymmetric algorithm. All the other algorithms are symmetric algorithms.

8. **a**. ECC is NOT a hash function. It is an asymmetric algorithm. All the other options are hash functions.

9. **c**. A CRL contains a list of all the certificates that have been revoked.

   A CA is the entity that creates and signs digital certificates, maintains the certificates, and revokes them when necessary. An RA verifies the requestor's identity, registers the requestor, and passes the request to the CA. The OCSP is an Internet protocol that obtains the revocation status of an X.509 digital certificate.

10. **d**. A brute-force attack executed against a cryptographic algorithm uses all possible keys until a key is discovered that successfully decrypts the ciphertext.

    A frequency analysis attack relies on the fact that substitution and transposition ciphers will result in repeated patterns in ciphertext. A reverse engineering attack occurs when an attacker purchases a particular cryptographic product to attempt to reverse engineer the product to discover confidential information about the cryptographic algorithm used. A ciphertext-only attack uses several encrypted messages (ciphertext) to figure out the key used in the encryption process.

This chapter covers the following topics:

- **Security model concepts:** Discusses the four main goals of security
- **System architecture:** Describes a process for designing a system architecture
- **System security architecture:** Focuses on the security aspects of the system architecture
- **Security architecture frameworks:** Explores frameworks that have been developed to aid in secure architecture design
- **Security architecture documentation:** Covers the documentation process and describes best practices and guidelines by the ISO
- **Security model types and security models:** Surveys some of the most common security models
- **Security modes:** Examines various modes in which an operating system can function and the security effects of each
- **System evaluation:** Discusses formal evaluation systems used to assess the security of a system
- **Certification and accreditation:** Compares and contrasts these two processes
- **Security architecture maintenance:** Covers tasks required to maintain system security on an ongoing basis
- **Security architecture threats:** Examines common threats a security architecture must address

CHAPTER 7

Security Architecture and Design

Although much progress has been made in protecting the edge or perimeter of networks, the software we create and purchase *inside the network* still can contain vulnerabilities that can be exploited. In a rush to satisfy the increasing demands placed on software, developers sometimes sacrifice security goals to meet other goals. In this chapter we take a closer look at some of the security issues that can be created during development, some guidelines for secure practices, and some of the common attacks on software that need to be mitigated.

Foundation Topics

Security Model Concepts

Security measures must have a defined goal if we want to ensure that the measure is successful. All measures are designed to provide one of a core set of protections. In this section, the three fundamental principles of security are discussed. Also an approach to delivering these goals is covered.

Confidentiality

Confidentiality is provided if the data cannot be read either through access controls and encryption for data as it exists on a hard drive or through encryption as the data is in transit. With respect to information security, confidentiality is the opposite of disclosure. The essential security principles of confidentiality, integrity, and availability are referred to as the CIA triad.

Integrity

Integrity is provided if you can be assured that the data has not changed in any way. This is typically provided with a hashing algorithm or a checksum of some kind. Both methods create a number that is sent along with the data. When the data gets to the destination, this number can be used to determine whether even a single bit has changed in the data by calculating the hash value from the data that was received. This helps to protect data against undetected corruption.

Some additional integrity goals are to

- Prevent unauthorized users from making modifications
- Maintain internal and external consistency
- Prevent authorized users from making improper modifications

Availability

Availability describes what percentage of the time the resource or the data is available. This is usually measured as a percentage of "up" time with 99.9 % of up time representing more availability than 99% up time. Making sure that the data is accessible when and where it is needed is a prime goal of security.

Defense in Depth

Communications security management and techniques are designed to prevent, detect, and correct errors so that the CIA of transactions over networks might be maintained. Most computer attacks result in a violation of one of the security properties confidentiality, integrity, or availability. A defense-in-depth approach refers to deploying layers of protection. For example, even when deploying firewalls, access control lists should still be applied to resources to help prevent access to sensitive data in case the firewall is breached.

System Architecture

Developing a system architecture refers to the process of describing and representing the components that make up the planned system and the interrelationships between the components. It also attempts to answer questions such as:

- What is the purpose of the system?
- Who will use it?
- What environment will it operate in?

Developing the architecture of a planned system should go through logical steps to ensure that all considerations have been made. This section discusses these basic steps and covers the design principles, definitions, and guidelines offered by the ISO/IEC 42010:2011 standard.

System Architecture Steps

Various models and frameworks discussed in this chapter might differ in the exact steps toward developing a system architecture but do follow a basic pattern. The main steps include:

1. **System design phase:** In this phase system requirements are gathered and the manner in which the requirements will be met are mapped out using modeling techniques that usually graphically depict the components that satisfy each requirement and the interrelationships of these components. At this phase many of the frameworks and security models discussed later in this chapter are used to help meet the architectural goals.

2. **Development phase:** In this phase hardware and software components are assigned to individual teams for development. At this phase the work done in the first phase can help to ensure these independent teams are working toward components that will fit together to satisfy requirements.

3. **Maintenance phase:** In this phase the system and security architecture are evaluated to ensure that the system operates properly and that security of the systems are maintained. The system and security should be periodically reviewed and tested.

ISO/IEC 42010:2011

The International Organization for Standardization (ISO) and the International Electrotechnical Commission (IEC) 42010:2011 uses specific terminology when discussing architectural frameworks. The following is a review of some of the more important terms:

- **Architecture**: Describes the organization of the system, including its components and their interrelationships along with the principles that guide its design and evolution.

- **Architectural description (AD)**: Comprises the set of documents that convey the architecture in a formal manner.

- **Stakeholder**: Individuals, teams, and departments, including groups outside the organization with interests or concerns to consider.

- **View**: The representation of the system from the perspective of a stakeholder or a set of stakeholders.

- **Viewpoint:** A template used to develop individual views that establish the audience, techniques, and assumptions made.

Computing Platforms

A computing platform comprises the hardware and software components that allow software to run. This typically incudes the physical components, the operating systems, and the programming languages used. From a physical and logical perspective, a number of possible frameworks or platforms are in use. This section discusses some of the most common.

Mainframe/Thin Clients

When a mainframe/thin client platform is used, a client/server architecture exists. The server holds the application and performs all the processing. The client software runs on the user machines and simply sends requests for operations and displays the results. When a true thin client is used, very little exists on the user machine other than the software that connects to the server and renders the result.

Distributed Systems

The distributed platform also uses a client/server architecture, but the division of labor between the server portion and the client portion of the solution might not be quite as one-sided as you would find in a mainframe/thin client scenario. In many cases multiple locations or systems in the network might be part of the solution. Also, sensitive data is more likely to be located on the user's machine, and therefore the users play a bigger role in protecting it with best practices.

Another characteristic of a distributed environment is multiple processing locations that can provide alternatives for computing in the event a site becomes unavailable.

Data is stored at multiple, geographically separate locations. Users can access the data stored at any location with the users' distance from those resources transparent to the user.

Distributed systems can introduce security weaknesses into the network that must be considered. Among these are

- Desktop systems can contain sensitive information that might be at risk of being exposed.
- Users might generally lack security awareness.
- Modems present a vulnerability to dial-in attacks.
- Lack of proper backup might exist.

Middleware

In a distributed environment, middleware is software that ties the client and server software together. It is neither a part of the operating system nor a part of the server software. It is the code that lies between the operating system and applications on each side of a distributed computing system in a network. It might be generic enough to operate between several types of client-server systems of a particular type.

Embedded Systems

An embedded system is a piece of software built into a larger piece of software that is in charge of performing some specific function on behalf of the larger system. The embedded part of the solution might address specific hardware communications and might require drivers to talk between the larger system and some specific hardware.

Mobile Computing

Mobile code is instructions passed across the network and executed on a remote system. An example of mobile code is Java and ActiveX code downloaded into a web browser from the World Wide Web. Any introduction of code from one system to another is a security concern but is required in some situations. An active content module that attempts to monopolize and exploits system resources is called a hostile applet. The main objective of the Java Security Model (JSM) is to protect the user from hostile, network mobile code. As you might recall from Chapter 5, "Software Development Security," it does this by placing the code in a sandbox, which restricts its operations.

Virtual Computing

Virtual environments are increasingly being used as the computing platform for solutions. In Chapter 3, "Telecommunications and Network Security," you learned that most of the same security issues that must be mitigated in the physical environment must also be addressed in the virtual network.

In a virtual environment, instances of an operating system are called virtual machines (VMs). A host system can contain many VMs. Software called a hypervisor manages the distribution of resources (CPU, memory, and disk) to the VMs. Figure 7-1 shows the relationship between the host machine, its physical resources, the resident VMs, and the virtual resources assigned to them.

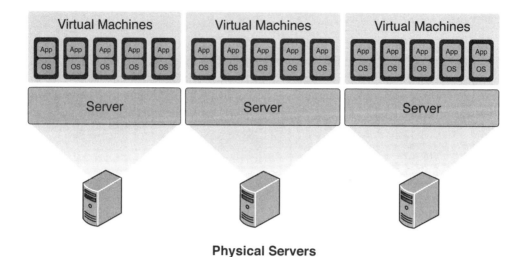

Figure 7-1 Virtualization

Security Services

The process of creating system architecture also includes design of the security that will be provided. These services can be classified into several categories depending on the protections they are designed to provide. This section briefly examines and compares types of security services.

Boundary Control Services

These services are responsible for placing various components in security zones and maintaining boundary control among them. Generally, this is accomplished by indicating components and services as trusted or not trusted. As an example, memory space insulated from other running processes in a multiprocessing system is part of a protection *boundary*.

Access Control Services

In Chapter 2, "Access Control," you learned about various methods of access control and how they can be deployed. An appropriate method should be deployed to control access to sensitive material and to give users the access they need to do their jobs.

Integrity Services

As you might recall, *integrity* implies that data has not been changed. When integrity services are present, they ensure that data moving through the operating system or application can be verified to not have been damaged or corrupted in the transfer.

Cryptography Services

If the system is capable of scrambling or encrypting information in transit, it is said to provide cryptography services. In some cases this service is not natively provided by a system and if desired must be provided in some other fashion, but if the capability is present it is valuable, especially in instances where systems are distributed and talk across the network.

Auditing and Monitoring Services

If the system has a method of tracking the activities of the users and of the operations of the system processes, it is said to provide auditing and monitoring services. Although our focus here is on security, the value of this service goes beyond security because it also allows for monitoring what the system itself is actually doing.

System Components

When discussing the way security is provided in an architecture, having a basic grasp of the components in computing equipment is helpful. This section discusses those components and some of the functions they provide.

CPU and Multiprocessing

The central processing unit (CPU) is the hardware in the system that executes all the instructions in the code. It has its own set of instructions for its internal operation, and those instructions define its architecture. The software that runs on the system must be compatible with this architecture, which really means the CPU and the software can communicate.

When more than one processor is present and available the system becomes capable of multiprocessing. This allows the computer to execute multiple instructions in parallel. It can be done with separate physical processors or with a single processor with multiple cores. Each core operates as a separate CPU.

CPUs have their own memory, and the CPU is able to access this memory faster than any other memory location. It also typically has cache memory where the most recently executed instructions are kept in case they are needed again. When a CPU gets an instructions from memory the process is called *fetching*.

An arithmetic logic unit (ALU) in the CPU performs the actual execution of the instructions. The control unit acts as the system manager while instructions from applications and operating systems are executed. CPU registers contain the instruction set information and data to be executed and include general registers, special registers, and a program counter register.

CPUs can work in user mode or privileged mode, which is also referred to as kernel or supervisor mode. When applications are communicating with the CPU, it is in user mode. If an instruction that is sent to the CPU is marked to be performed in privileged mode, it must be a trusted operating system process and is given functionality not available in user mode.

The CPU is connected to an address bus. Memory and I/O devices recognize this address bus. These devices can then communicate with the CPU, read requested data, and send it to the data bus.

When microcomputers were first developed, the instruction fetch time was much longer than the instruction execution time because of the relatively slow speed of memory access. This situation led to the design of the Complex Instruction Set Computer (CISC) CPU. In this arrangement, the set of instructions were reduced (while made more complex) to help mitigate the relatively slow memory access.

After memory access was improved to the point where not much difference existed in memory access times and processor execution times, the Reduced Instruction Set Computer (RISC) architecture was introduced. The objective of the RISC architecture was to reduce the number of cycles required to execute an instruction, which was accomplished by making the instructions less complex.

Memory and Storage

A computing system needs somewhere to store information, both on a long-term and short-term basis. There are two types of storage locations: memory, for temporary storage needs, and long-term storage media. Information can be accessed much faster from memory than from long-term storage, which is why the most recently used instructions or information is typically kept in cache memory for a short period of time, which ensures the second and subsequent accesses will be faster than returning to long-term memory.

Computers can have both Random Access Memory (RAM) and Read Only Memory (ROM). RAM is volatile, meaning the information must continually be refreshed and will be lost if the system shuts down. Table 7-1 contains some types of RAM used in laptops and desktops.

Table 7-1 Memory Types

Desktop Memory	Description
SDRAM—Synchronous Dynamic Random Access Memory	Synchronizes itself with the CPU's bus
DDR SDRAM—Double Data Rate Synchronous Dynamic Random Access Memory	Supports data transfers on both edges of each clock cycle (the rising and falling edges), effectively doubling the memory chip's data throughput
DDR2 SDRAM—Double Data Rate Two (2) Synchronous Dynamic Random Access Memory	Transfers 64 bits of data twice every clock cycle and is not compatible with current DDR SDRAM memory slots
DDR3-SDRAM—Double Data Rate Three (3) Synchronous Dynamic Random Access Memory	Offers reduced power consumption, a doubled pre-fetch buffer, and more bandwidth because of its increased clock rate.
Laptop Memory	**Description**
SODIMM (Small Outline DIMM)	Differs from desktop RAM in its physical size and its pin configuration. A full-size DIMM has 100, 168, 184, or 240 pins and is usually 4.5 to 5 inches in length. In contrast, a SODIMM has 72, 100, 144, or 200 pins and is smaller—2.5 to 3 inches.

ROM, on the other hand, is not volatile and also cannot be overwritten without executing a series of operations that depend on the type of ROM. It usually contains low-level instructions of some sort that make the device on which it is installed operational. Some examples of ROM are

- **Flash memory:** A type of electrically programmable ROM
- **Programmable Logic Device (PLD):** An integrated circuit with connections or internal logic gates that can be changed through a programming process
- **Field Programmable Gate Array (FPGA):** A type of PLD that is programmed by blowing fuse connections on the chip or using an antifuse that makes a connection when a high voltage is applied to the junction
- **Firmware:** A type of ROM where a program or low-level instructions are installed

Memory directly addressable by the CPU, which is for the storage of instructions and data that are associated with the program being executed, is called *primary* memory. Regardless of which type of memory in which the information is located, in most cases the CPU must get involved in fetching the information on behalf of other components. If a component has the ability to access memory directly without the help of the CPU, it is called *Direct Memory Access* (DMA).

Some additional terms you should be familiar with in regards to memory include the following:

- **Associative memory:** Searches for a specific data value in memory rather than using a specific memory address
- **Implied addressing:** Refers to registers usually contained inside the CPU
- **Absolute addressing:** Addresses the entire primary memory space. The CPU uses the physical memory addresses that are called absolute addresses.
- **Cache:** A relatively small amount (when compared to primary memory) of very high speed RAM that holds the instructions and data from primary memory and that has a high probability of being accessed during the currently executing portion of a program
- **Indirect addressing:** The type of memory addressing where the address location that is specified in the program instruction contains the address of the final desired location.
- **Logical address:** The address at which a memory cell or storage element appears to reside from the perspective of an executing application program
- **Relative address:** Specifies its location by indicating its distance from another address
- **Virtual memory:** A location on the hard drive used temporarily for storage when memory space is low
- **Memory leak:** Occurs when a computer program incorrectly manages memory allocations, which can exhaust available system memory as an application runs

Input/Output Devices

Input/output (I/O) devices are used to send and receive information to the system. Examples are the keyboard, mouse (input), and printers. The operating system controls the interaction between the I/O devices and the system. In cases where the I/O device requires the CPU to perform some action, it signals the CPU with a message called an *interrupt*.

Operating Systems

The operating system is the software that enables a human to interact with the hardware that comprises the computer. Without the operating system, the computer would be useless. Operating systems perform a number of noteworthy and interesting functions as part of the interfacing between the human and the hardware. In this section, we look some of these activities.

A *thread* is an individual piece of work done for a specific process. A *process* is a set of threads that are part of the same larger piece of work done for a specific application. An application's instructions are not considered processes until they have been loaded into memory where all instructions must first be copied to be processed by the CPU. A process can be in a running state, ready state, or blocked state. When a process is blocked, it is simply waiting for data to be transmitted to it, usually through user data entry. A group of processes that share access to the same resources is called a protection domain.

CPUs can be categorized according to the way in which they handle processes. A *superscalar* computer architecture is characterized by a processor that enables concurrent execution of multiple instructions in the same pipeline stage. A processor in which a single instruction specifies more than one CONCURRENT operation is called a *Very Long Instruction Word processor*. A *pipelined processor* overlaps the steps of different instructions whereas a *scalar processor* executes one instruction at a time, consequently increasing *pipelining*.

From a security perspective, processes are placed in a ring structure according to the concept of least privilege, meaning they are only allowed to access resources and components required to perform the task. A common visualization of this structure is shown in Figure 7-2.

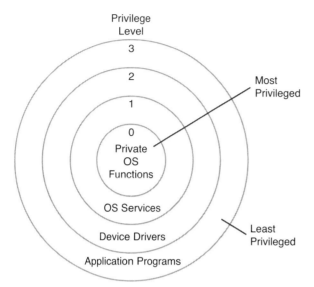

Figure 7-2 Ring Structure

When a computer system processes I/O instructions, it is operating in *Supervisor mode*. The termination of selected, non-critical processing when a hardware or software failure occurs and is detected is referred to as a *fail soft*. It is in a *fail safe* state if the system automatically leaves system processes and components in a secure state when a failure occurs or is detected in the system.

Multitasking

Multitasking is the process of carrying out more than one task at a time. Multitasking can be done in two different ways. When the computer has a single processor, it is not really doing multiple tasks at once. It is dividing its CPU cycles between tasks at such a high rate of speed that it appears to be doing multiple tasks at once. However, when a computer has more than one processor or has a processor with multiple cores, then it is capable of actually performing two tasks at the same time. It can do this in two different ways:

- **Symmetric mode:** In this mode the processors or cores are handed work on a round-robin basis, thread by thread.

- **Asymmetric mode:** In this mode a processor is dedicated to a specific process or application—when work needs done for that process it always is done by the same processor. Figure 7-3 shows the relationship between these two modes.

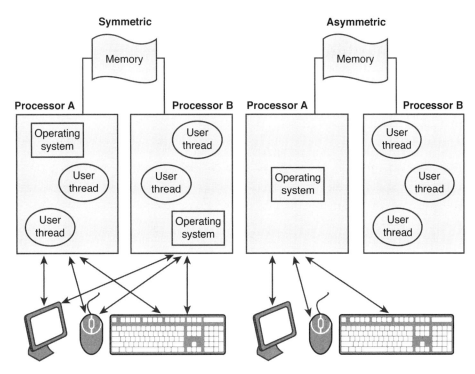

Figure 7-3 Types of Multiprocessing

Preemptive multitasking means that task switches can be initiated directly out of interrupt handlers. With *cooperative* (non-preemptive) multitasking, a task switch is only performed when a task calls the kernel and allows the kernel a chance to perform a task switch.

Memory Management

Because all information goes to memory before it can be processed, secure management of memory is critical. Memory space insulated from other running processes in a multiprocessing system is part of a *protection domain*.

System Security Architecture

Beyond their functional roles, the components that comprise the system can also be viewed from a security perspective, which describes its *system security architecture*. In this section, concepts used to maintain security within the system are discussed.

Security Policy

The security requirements of a system should be derived from the security policy of the organization. Although this policy makes statements regarding the general security posture and goals of the organization, a system-specific policy that speaks to the level of security required on the device, operating system, or application level must be much more detailed. This section covers some terms and concepts required to discuss security at this level.

NOTE Security policies are covered in detail in Chapter 4, "Information Security Governance and Risk Management."

Security Requirements

In 1972, the Computer Security Technology Planning Study was commissioned by the U.S. government to outline the basic and foundational security requirements of systems purchased by the government. This eventually led to a Trusted Computer System Evaluation Criteria or *Orange Book* (discussed later in this chapter). This section defines some of the core tenets as follows:

- **Trusted Computer Base (TCB):** The TCB comprises the components (hardware, firmware, and/or software) that are trusted to enforce the security policy of the system and that if compromised jeopardize the security properties of the entire system. The reference monitor is a primary component of the TCB. This term is derived from the *Orange Book*. All changes to the TCB should be audited and controlled, which is an example of a Configuration Management control.

NOTE Configuration Management is discussed in Chapter 8, "Operations Security."

- **Security Perimeter:** This is the dividing line between the trusted parts of the system and those that are untrusted. According to security design best practices, components that lie within this boundary (which means they lie within the TCB) should never permit untrusted components to access critical resources in an insecure manner.

- **Reference Monitor:** A reference monitor is a system component that enforces access controls on an object. It is an access control concept that refers to an abstract machine that mediates all accesses to objects by subjects. It was introduced for circumventing difficulties in classic approaches to computer security by limiting damages produced by malicious programs. The security risk created by a *covert channel* is that it bypasses the reference monitor functions. The reference monitor function should exhibit isolation, completeness, and verifiability. Isolation is required because of the following:
    - It can't be of public access. The less access the better.
    - It must have a sense of completeness to provide the whole information and process cycles.
    - It must be verifiable, to provide security, audit, and accounting functions.

- **Security Kernel:** A security kernel is the hardware, firmware, and software elements of a TCB that implements the reference monitor concept. It is an access control concept, not an actual physical component. The security kernel should be as small as possible to make it easier to formally verify it. The security kernel implements the authorized access relationship between subjects and objects of a system as established by the reference monitor. While performing this role, all accesses must be mediated, protected from modification, and verifiable. In the ring protection system discussed earlier in the CPU discussion (see Figure 7-2), the security kernel is usually located in the lowest ring number or ring 0.

Security Zones

In the context of this discussion, a security zone or security perimeter is the dividing line between the trusted parts of the system and the untrusted parts. An example of this is the ring structure for CPUs discussed earlier (see Figure 7-2). The most trusted components are allowed in ring 0 whereas less trusted components might be located in outer rings. Communication between components in different rings is tightly controlled to prevent a less trusted component from compromising one that has more trust and thus more access to the system.

Security Architecture Frameworks

Security architecture frameworks are used to help define the security goals during development of a system and to ensure those goals are achieved in the final product. This section covers some of the more widely known security architecture frameworks.

Zachman Framework

The Zachman Framework is a two-dimensional model that intersects communication interrogatives (what, why, where, and so on) with various viewpoints (planner, owner, designer, and so on). It is designed to help optimize communication between the various viewpoints during the creation of the security architecture. This framework is detailed in Chapter 4 in Table 4-1.

SABSA

A similar model to Zachman for guiding the creation and design of a security architecture is the Sherwood Applied Business Security Architecture (SABSA). It also attempts to enhance the communication process between stakeholders. It is a framework in addition to a methodology in that it prescribes the processes to follow to build and maintain the architecture. This framework is detailed in Chapter 4 in Table 4-2.

TOGAF

The Open Group Architecture Framework (TOGAF) was based on the Technical Architecture Framework for Information Management (TAFIM), developed since the late 1980s by the U.S. Department of Defense (DoD). It calls for an Architectural Development Method (ADM) that employs an iterative process that calls for individual requirements to be continuously monitored and updated as needed. It also enables the technology architect to understand the enterprise from four different views, allowing for the team to ensure that the proper environment and components are present to meet business and security requirements. Figure 7-4 shows the TOGAF 8.1.1 version of the ADM.

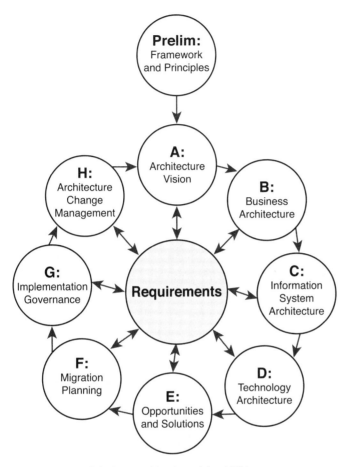

Figure 7-4 TOGAF 8.1.1 Version of the ADM

ITIL

A discussion of architectural frameworks would not be complete without mentioning the Information Technology Infrastructure Library (ITIL). In Chapter 4, you learned about this set of best practices, which have become the de facto standard for IT service management, of which creating the framework is a subset. If you review the ITIL discussion in Chapter 4, you will see that service design is a major portion of the process.

NOTE All these security frameworks and several others are discussed in greater detail in Chapter 4 in the "Security Frameworks and Methodologies" section.

Security Architecture Documentation

Documentation is important in the design of any system and with regards to the security architecture it is even more so. Documentation of the architecture provides valuable insight into how the architecture is supposed to operate and what the designers intended for various components to contribute to the security of a system. For example, any test plans and results should be retained as part of the system's permanent documentation.

This section discusses two influential documents providing guidance for best practices for security architecture documentation.

ISO/IEC 27000 Series

The ISO/IEC 27000 series establishes information security standards published jointly by the International Organization for Standardization (ISO) and the International Electrotechnical Commission (IEC). Although each individual standard in the series addresses a different issue, all standards in the series provide guidelines for documentation. The ISO/IEC 27000 series including both 27001 and 27002 are covered in more detail in the section "Security Frameworks and Methodologies" in Chapter 4.

CobiT

The Information Systems Audit and Control Association (ISACA) and the IT Governance Institute (ITGI), two important organizations with regard to offering guidance in operating and maintaining secure systems, created a set of control objectives used as a framework for IT governance called the Control Objectives for Information and Related Technology. It was derived from the COSO framework created by the Committee of Sponsoring Organizations of the Treadway Commission. Whereas the COSO framework deals with corporate governance, the CobiT deals with IT governance. It is covered in more detail in Chapter 4.

Security Model Types and Security Models

A security model describes the theory of security that is designed into a system from the outset. Formal models have been developed to approach the design of the security operations of a system. In the real world, the use of formal models is often skipped because it delays the design process somewhat (although the cost might be a lesser system). This section discusses some basic model *types* along with some *formal models* derived from the various approaches available.

Security Model Types

A security model maps the desires of the security policy makers to the rules that a computer system must follow. Different model *types* exhibit various approaches to achieving this goal. The specific models that are contained in the section "Security Models" incorporate various combinations of these model *types*.

State Machine Models

The state of a system is its posture at any specific point in time. Activities that occur in the processing of the system operating alter the state of the system. By examining every possible state the system could be in and ensuring that the system maintains the proper security relationship between objects and subjects in each state, the system is said to be secure. The Bell-LaPadula model discussed in the later section "Security Models" is an example of a state machine model.

Multilevel Lattice Models

The lattice-based access control model was developed mainly to deal with confidentiality issues and focuses itself mainly on information flow. Each security subject is assigned a security label that defines the upper and lower bounds of the subject's access to the system. Controls are then applied to all objects by organizing them into levels or lattices. Objects are containers of information in some format. These pairs of elements (object and subject) are assigned a least upper bound of values and a greatest lower bound of values that define what can be done by that subject with that object.

A subject's label (remember a subject can be a person but it can also be a process) defines what level one can access and what actions can be performed at that level. With the lattice-based access control model, a security label is also called a security *class*. This model associates every resource and every user of a resource with one of an ordered set of classes. The lattice-based model aims at protecting against illegal information flow among the entities.

Matrix-Based Models

A matrix-based model organizes tables of subjects and objects indicating what actions individual subjects can take upon individual objects. This concept is found in other model types as well such as the lattice model discussed in the previous section. Access control to objects is often implemented as a control *matrix*. It is a straightforward approach that defines access rights to subjects for objects. The two most common implementations of this concept are access control lists and capabilities. In its table structure, a row would indicate the access one subject has to an array of objects. Therefore, a row could be seen as a capability list for a specific subject. It consists of the following parts:

- A list of objects
- A list of subjects
- A function that returns an object's type
- The matrix itself, with the objects making the columns and the subjects making the rows

Noninference Models

In multilevel security models, the concept of non-interface prescribes those actions that take place at a higher security level but do not affect or influence those that occur at a lower security level. Because this model is less concerned with the flow of information and more concerned with a subject's knowledge of the state of the system at a point in time, it concentrates on preventing the actions that take place at one level from altering the state presented to another level.

One of the attack types that this conceptual model is meant to prevent is *inference*. This occurs when someone has access to information at one level that allows them to infer, information about another level.

Information Flow Models

Any of the models discussed in the next section that attempt to prevent the flow of information from one entity to another that violates or negates the security policy is called an information flow model. In the information flow model, what relates two versions of the same object is called the *flow*. A flow is a type of dependency that relates two versions of the same object, and thus the transformation of one state of that object into another, at successive points in time. In a multilevel security system (MLS), a one-way information flow device called a *pump* prevents the flow of information from a lower level of security classification or sensitivity to a higher level.

For example, the Bell-LaPadula model (discussed in the section "Security Models") concerns itself with the flow of information in the following three cases:

- When a subject alters an object.
- When a subject accesses an object.
- When a subject observes an object.

The prevention of illegal information flow among the entities is the aim of an information flow model.

Security Models

A number of formal models incorporating the concepts discussed in the previous section have been developed and used to guide the security design of systems. This section discusses some of the more widely used or important security models including the following:

- Bell-LaPadula model
- Biba model
- Clark-Wilson integrity model
- Lipner model
- Brewer-Nash model
- Graham-Denning model
- Harrison-Ruzzo-Ullman model

Bell-LaPadula Model

The Bell-LaPadula model was the first mathematical model of a multilevel system that used both the concepts of a state machine and those of controlling information flow. It formalizes the U.S. DoD multilevel security policy. It is a state machine model capturing confidentiality aspects of access control. Any movement of information from a higher level to a lower level in the system must be performed by a *trusted subject*.

It incorporates three basic rules with respect to the flow of information in a system:

- **The simple security rule:** A subject cannot read data located at a higher security level than that possessed by the subject (also called no read up).
- **The *- property rule:** A subject cannot write to a lower level than that possessed by the subject (also called *no write down* or the *confinement* rule).
- **The strong star property rule:** A subject can perform both read and write functions only at the same level possessed by the subject.

The *-property rule is depicted in Figure 7-5.

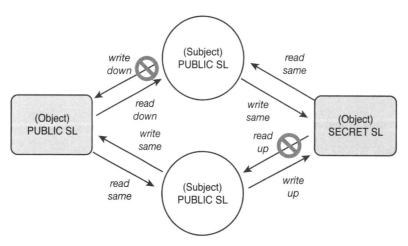

Figure 7-5 The *- Property Rule

The main concern of the Bell-LaPadula security model and its use of these rules is confidentiality. Although its basic model is a Mandatory Access Control (MAC) system, another property rule called the Discretionary Security Property (ds-property) makes a mixture of mandatory and discretionary controls possible. This property allows a subject to pass along permissions at its own discretion. In the discretionary portion of the model, access permissions are defined through an Access Control matrix using a process called *authorization*, and security policies prevent information flowing downward from a high security level to a low security level.

The Bell-LaPadula security model does have limitations. Among those are

- It contains no provision or policy for changing data access control. Therefore, it works well only with access systems that are static in nature.

- It does not address what are called *covert channels*. A low-level subject can sometimes detect the existence of a high-level object when it is denied access. Sometimes it is not enough to hide the content of an object; also their existence might have to be hidden.

- Its main contribution at the expense of other concepts is confidentiality.

This security policy model was the basis for the *Orange Book* (discussed in the later section TCSEC.

Biba Model

The Biba model came after the Bell-LaPadula model and shares many characteristics with that model. These two models are the most well-known of the models discussed in this section. It is also a state machine model that uses a series of lattices or security levels, but the Biba model concerns itself more with the integrity of information rather than the confidentiality of that information. It does this by relying on a data classification system to prevent unauthorized modification of data. Subjects are assigned classes according to their trustworthiness; objects are assigned integrity labels according to the harm that would be done if the data were modified improperly.

Like the Bell-LaPadula model, it applies a series of properties or axioms to guide the protection of integrity. Its effect is that data must not flow from a receptacle of given integrity to a receptacle of higher integrity:

- *** integrity axiom:** A subject cannot write to a higher integrity level than that to which he has access (no write up).
- **Simple integrity axiom:** A subject cannot read to a lower integrity level than that to which he has access (no read down).
- **Invocation property:** A subject cannot invoke (request service) of higher integrity.

Clark-Wilson Integrity Model

Developed after the Biba model, this model also concerns itself with data integrity. The model describes a series of elements that are used to control the integrity of data as listed here:

- **User:** An active agent
- **Transformation procedure (TP):** An abstract operation, such as read, write, and modify, implemented through programming
- **Constrained data item (CDI):** An item that can only be manipulated through a TP
- **Unconstrained data item (UDI):** An item that can be manipulated by a user via read and write operations
- **Integrity verification procedure (IVP):** A check of the consistency of data with the real world

This model enforces these elements by only allowing data to be altered through programs and not directly by users. Rather than employing a lattice structure, it uses a three-part relationship of subject/program/object known as a triple. It also sets as its goal the concepts of separation of duties and well-formed transactions:

- **Separation of duties:** This concept ensures that certain operations require additional verification.

- **Well-formed transaction:** This concept ensures that all values are checked before and after the transaction by carrying out particular operations to complete the change of data from one state to another.

To ensure that integrity is attained and preserved, the Clark-Wilson model asserts, integrity-monitoring and integrity-preserving rules are needed. Integrity-monitoring rules are called certification rules, and integrity-preserving rules are called enforcement rules.

Lipner Model

The Lipner model is an implementation that combines elements of the Bell-LaPadula model and the Biba model. The first way of implementing integrity with the Lipner model uses Bell-LaPadula and assigns subjects to one of two sensitivity levels—system manager and anyone else—and to one of four job categories. Objects are assigned specific levels and categories. Categories become the most significant integrity (such as access control) mechanism. The second implementation uses both Bell-LaPadula and Biba. This method prevents unauthorized users from modifying data and prevents authorized users from making improper data modifications. The implementations also share characteristics with the Clark-Wilson model in that it separates objects into data and programs.

Brewer-Nash (Chinese Wall) Model

This model introduced the concept of allowing access controls to change dynamically based on a user's previous actions. One of its goals is to do this while protecting against *conflicts of interest*. This model is also based on an information flow model. Implementation involves grouping data sets into discrete classes, each class representing a different conflict of interest. Isolating data set within a class provides the capability to keep one department's data separate from another in an integrated database.

Graham-Denning Model

The Graham-Denning model attempts to address an issue ignored by the Bell-LaPadula (with the exception of the ds-property) and Biba models. It deals with the delegate and transfer rights. It focuses on issues such as:

- Securely creating and deleting objects and subjects
- Securely providing or transferring access right

Harrison-Ruzzo-Ullman Model

This model deals with access rights as well. It restricts the set of operations that can be performed on an object to a finite set to ensure integrity. It is used by software engineers to prevent unforeseen vulnerabilities from being introduced by overly complex operations.

Security Modes

In MAC access systems, the system operates in different security modes at various times based on variables, such as sensitivity of data, the clearance level of the user, and the actions they are authorized to take. This section provides a description of these modes.

Dedicated Security Mode

A system is operating in dedicated security mode if it employs a single classification level. In this system, all users can access all data, but they must sign a non-disclosure agreement (NDA) and be formally approved for access on a need-to-know basis.

System High Security Mode

In a system operating in system high security mode, all users have the same security clearance (as in the dedicated security model) but they do not all possess a need-to-know clearance for all the information in the system. Consequently, although a user might have clearance to access an object, he still might be restricted if he does not have need-to-know clearance pertaining to the object.

Compartmented Security Mode

In the compartmented security mode system, all users must possess the highest security clearance (as in both dedicated and system high security), but they must also have valid need-to-know clearance, a signed NDA, and formal approval for all information to which they have access. The objective is to ensure that the minimum number of people possible have access to information at each level or compartment.

Multilevel Security Mode

When a system allows two or more classification levels of information to be processed at the same time, it is said to be operating in multilevel security mode. They must have a signed NDA for all the information in the system and will have access to subsets based on their clearance level, and need-to-know and formal access approval. These systems involve the highest risk because information is processed at more than one level of security even when all system users do not have appropriate clearances or a need-to-know for all information processed by the system. This is also sometimes called controlled security mode. Table 7-2 shows a comparison of the four security modes and their requirements.

Table 7-2 Security Model Summary

	Signed NDA	Proper Clearance	Formal Approval	Valid Need-to-Know
Dedicated	ALL information	ALL information	ALL information	ALL information
System High	ALL information	ALL information	ALL information	Some information
Compartmented	ALL information	ALL information	Some information	Some information
Multilevel	ALL information	Some information	Some information	Some information

Assurance

Whereas a trust level describes the protections that can be expected from a system, the assurance level refers to the level of confidence that the protections will operate as planned. Typically, higher levels of assurance are achieved by dedicating more scrutiny to security in the design process. The next section discusses various methods of rating systems for trust levels and assurance.

System Evaluation

In an attempt to bring order to the security chaos that surrounds both in-house and commercial software products (operating system, applications, and so on), several evaluation methods have been created to assess and rate the security of these products. An *assurance level* examination attempts to examine the security-related components of a system and assign a level of confidence that the system can provide a particular level of security. In the following sections, organizations that have created such evaluation systems are discussed.

TCSEC

The Trusted Computer System Evaluation Criteria (TCSEC) was developed by the National Computer Security Center (NCSC) for the U.S. DoD to evaluate products. They have issued a series of books focusing on both computer systems and the networks in which they operate. They address confidentiality, but not integrity. In 2005, TCSEC was replaced by the Common Criteria, discussed later in the chapter. However, security professionals still need to understand TCSEC because of its effect on security practices today and because some of its terminology is still in use.

With TCSEC, functionality and assurance are evaluated separately and form a basis for assessing the effectiveness of security controls built into automatic data-processing system products. For example, the concept of least privilege is derived from TSEC. In this section, those books and the ratings they derive are discussed.

Rainbow Series

The original publication created by the TCSEC was the *Orange Book* (discussed in the next section), but as time went by, other books were also created that focused on additional aspects of the security of computer systems. Collectively, this set of more than 20 books is now referred to as the Rainbow Series, alluding to the fact that each book is a different color. For example, the *Green Book* focuses solely on password management. The balance of this section covers the most important books, the *Red Book* and the *Orange Book*.

Orange Book

The *Orange Book* is a collection of criteria based on the Bell-LaPadula model that is used to grade or rate the security offered by a computer system product. Covert channel analysis, trusted facility management, and trusted recoveries are concepts discussed in this book. As an example of specific guidelines, it recommends that diskettes be formatted seven times to prevent any possibility of data remaining.

The goals of this system can be divided into two categories, operational assurance requirements and life cycle assurance requirements, the details of which are defined next.

The operational assurance requirements specified in the *Orange Book* are as follows:

- System architecture
- System integrity
- Covert channel analysis
- Trusted facility management
- Trusted recovery

The life cycle assurance requirements specified in the *Orange Book* are as follows:

- Security testing
- Design specification and testing
- Configuration management
- Trusted distribution

TCSEC uses a classification system that assigns a letter and number to describe systems' security effectiveness. The letter refers to a security assurance level or *division*, of which there are four, and the number refers to gradients within that security assurance level or *class*. Each division and class incorporate all the required elements of the ones below it. In order of least secure to most secure, the four classes and their constituent divisions and requirements are as follows:

D — Minimal Protection

Reserved for those systems that have been evaluated but that fail to meet the requirements for a higher division.

C — Discretionary Protection

C1 — Discretionary Security Protection

- Requires identification and authentication.
- Requires separation of users and data.
- Uses Discretionary Access Control (DAC) capable of enforcing access limitations on an individual or group basis.
- Requires system documentation and user manuals.

C2 — Controlled Access Protection

- Uses a more finely grained DAC.
- Provides individual accountability through login procedures.
- Requires protected audit trails.
- Invokes object reuse theory.
- Requires resource isolation.

B — Mandatory Protection

B1 — Labeled Security Protection

- Uses an informal statement of the security policy.
- Requires data sensitivity or classification labels.

- Uses MAC over selected subjects and objects.
- Capable of label exportation.
- Requires removal or mitigation of discovered flaws.
- Uses design specifications and verification.

B2 — Structured Protection

- Requires a clearly defined and formally documented security policy.
- Uses DAC and MAC enforcement extended to all subjects and objects.
- Analyzes and prevents covert storage channels for occurrence and bandwidth.
- Structures elements into protection-critical and non–protection-critical categories.
- Enables more comprehensive testing and review through design and implementation.
- Strengthens authentication mechanisms.
- Provides trusted facility management with administrator and operator segregation.
- Imposes strict configuration management controls.

B3 — Security Domains

- Satisfies reference monitor requirements.
- Excludes code not essential to security policy enforcement.
- Minimizes complexity through significant system engineering.
- Defines the security administrator role.
- Requires an audit of security-relevant events.
- Automatically detects and responds to imminent intrusion detection, including personnel notification.
- Requires trusted system recovery procedures.
- Analyzes and prevents covert timing channels for occurrence and bandwidth.
- An example of such a system is the XTS-300, a precursor to the XTS-400.

A — Verified Protection

A1 — Verified Design

- Provides higher assurance than B3, but is functionally identical to B3.
- Uses formal design and verification techniques, including a formal top-level specification.
- Requires that formal techniques are used to prove the equivalence between the TCB specifications and the security policy model.
- Provides formal management and distribution procedures.
- An example of such a system is Honeywell's Secure Communications Processor (SCOMP), a precursor to the XTS-400.

Red Book

The Trusted Network Interpretation (TNI) extends the evaluation classes of the TCSEC (DOD 5200.28-STD) to trusted network systems and components in the *Red Book*. So where the *Orange Book* focuses on security for a single system, the *Red Book* addresses network security.

ITSEC

TCSEC addresses confidentiality only and bundles functionality and assurance. In contrast to TCSEC, the Information Technology Security Evaluation Criteria (ITSEC) addresses integrity and availability as well as confidentiality. Another difference is that the ITSEC was mainly a set of guidelines used in Europe, whereas the TCSEC was relied on more in the United States.

ITSEC has a rating system in many ways similar to that of TCSEC. ITSEC has 10 classes, F1 to F10, to evaluate the functional requirements and 7 TCSEC classes, E0 to E6, to evaluate the assurance requirements.

Security functional requirements include the following:

- **F00:** Identification and authentication
- **F01:** Audit
- **F02:** Resource utilization
- **F03:** Trusted paths/channels
- **F04:** User data protection
- **F05:** Security management
- **F06:** Product access
- **F07:** Communications

- **F08:** Privacy
- **F09:** Protection of the product's security functions
- **F10:** Cryptographic support

Security assurance requirements include the following:
- **E00:** Guidance documents and manuals
- **E01:** Configuration management
- **E02:** Vulnerability assessment
- **E03:** Delivery and operation
- **E04:** Life-cycle support
- **E05:** Assurance maintenance
- **E06:** Development
- Testing

The two systems can be mapped to one another, but the ITSEC provides a number of ratings that have no corresponding concept in the TCSEC ratings. Table 7-3 shows a mapping of the two systems.

Table 7-3 Mapping of ITSEC and TCSEC

ITSEC	TCSEC
E0	D
F1+E1	C1
F2+E2	C2
F3+E3	B1
F4+E4	B2
F5+E5	B3
F6+E6	A1
F6	Systems that provide high integrity
F7	Systems that provide high availability
F8	Systems that provide high data integrity during communication
F9	Systems that provide high confidentiality (using cryptography)
F10	Networks with high demands on confidentiality and integrity

The ITSEC has been largely replaced by Common Criteria, discussed in the next section.

Common Criteria

In 1990 the ISO identified the need for a standardized rating system that could be used globally. The Common Criteria (CC) was the result of a cooperative effort to establish this system. This system uses Evaluation Assurance levels (EALs) to rate systems with each representing a successively higher level of security testing and design in a system. The resulting rating represents the potential the system has to provide security. It assumes that the customer will properly configure all available security solutions so it is required that the vendor always provide proper documentation to allow the customer to fully achieve the rating. ISO/IEC 15408-1:2009 is the International Standards version of CC.

CC represents requirements for IT security of a product or system in two categories: functionality and assurance. This means that the rating should describe what the system does (functionality), and the degree of certainty the raters have that the functionality can be provided (assurance).

CC has seven assurance levels, which range from EAL1 (lowest), where functionality testing takes place, through EAL7 (highest), where thorough testing is performed and the system design is verified. The assurance designators used in the CC are as follows:

- **EAL1:** Functionally tested
- **EAL2:** Structurally tested
- **EAL3:** Methodically tested and checked
- **EAL4:** Methodically designed, tested, and reviewed
- **EAL5:** Semi-formally designed and tested
- **EAL6:** Semi-formally verified design and tested
- **EAL7:** Formally verified design and tested

CC uses a concept called a *protection profile* during the evaluation process. The protection profile describes a set of security requirements or goals along with functional assumptions about the environment. Therefore, if someone identified a security need not currently addressed by any products, he could write a protection profile that describes the need and the solution and all issues that could go wrong during the development of the system. This would be used to guide the development of a new product. A protection profile contains the following elements:

- **Descriptive elements:** The name of the profile and a description of the security problem that is to be solved.

- **Rationale:** Justification of the profile and a more detailed description of the real-world problem to be solved. The environment, usage assumptions, and threats are given along with security policy guidance that can be supported by products and systems that conform to this profile.

- **Functional requirements:** Establishment of a protection boundary, meaning the threats or compromises that are within this boundary to be countered. The product or system must enforce the boundary.

- **Development assurance requirements:** Identification of the specific requirements that the product or system must meet during the development phases, from design to implementation.

- **Evaluation assurance requirements:** Establishment of the type and intensity of the evaluation.

The result of following this process will be a *security target.* This is the vendor's explanation of what the product brings to the table from a security standpoint. Intermediate groupings of security requirement developed along the way to a security target are called *packages*.

Certification and Accreditation

Although the terms are used as synonyms in casual conversation, *accreditation* and *certification* are two different concepts in the context of assurance levels and ratings, although they are closely related. Certification evaluates the technical system components, whereas accreditation occurs when the adequacy of a system's overall security is accepted by management.

The National Information Assurance Certification and Accreditation Process (NIACAP) provides a standard set of activities, general tasks, and a management structure to certify and accredit systems that will maintain the information assurance and security posture of a system or site. The accreditation process developed by NIACAP has four phases:

- **Phase 1:** Definition
- **Phase 2:** Verification
- **Phase 3:** Validation
- **Phase 4:** Post Accreditation

NIACAP defines the following three types of accreditation:

- *Type accreditation* evaluates an application or system that is distributed to a number of different locations.
- *System accreditation* evaluates an application or support system.
- *Site accreditation* evaluates the application or system at a specific self-contained location.

Security Architecture Maintenance

Unfortunately, after a product has been evaluated, certified, and accredited, the story is not over. The product typically evolves over time as updates and patches are developed to either address new security issues that arise or to add functionality or fix bugs. When these changes occur, as ongoing maintenance, the security architecture must be maintained.

Ideally, solutions should undergo additional evaluations, certification, and accreditation as these changes occur, but in many cases the pressures of the real world prevent this time-consuming step. This is unfortunate because as developers fix and patch things, they often drift further and further from the original security design as they attempt to put out time-sensitive fires.

This is where maturity modeling becomes important. Most maturity models are based on the Software Engineer Institute's CMMI, which is discussed in Chapter 5. It has five levels: initial, managed, defined, quantitatively managed, and optimized.

ITGI developed the Information Security Governance Maturity Model to rank organizations against industry best practices and international guidelines. It includes six rating levels, numbered from zero to five: nonexistent, initial, repeatable, defined, managed, and optimized. The nonexistent level does not correspond to any CMMI level, but all the other levels do.

Security Architecture Threats

Despite all efforts to design a secure architecture, attacks to the security system still occur and still succeed. In this section, we examine some of the more common types of attacks. Some of these have already been mentioned in passing or in the process of explaining the need for a particular protection mechanism.

Maintenance Hooks

From the perspective of software development, a *maintenance hook* is a set of instructions built into the code that allows someone who knows about the so-called "back door" to use the instructions to connect to view and edit the code without using the normal access controls. In many cases they are placed there to make it easier for the vendor to provide support to the customer. In other cases they are placed there to assist in testing and tracking the activities of the product and never removed later.

> **NOTE** A maintenance account is often confused with a maintenance hook. A maintenance account is a backdoor account created by programmers to give someone full permissions in a particular application or operating system. A maintenance account can usually be deleted or disabled easily, but a true maintenance hook is often a hidden part of the programming and much easier to disable. Both of these can cause security issues because many attackers try the documented maintenance hooks and maintenance accounts first. You would be surprised at the number of computers attacked on a daily basis because these two security issues are left unaddressed.

Regardless of how the maintenance hooks got into the code, they can present a major security issue if they become known to hackers who can use them to access the system. Countermeasures on the part of the customer to mitigate the danger are

- Use a host IDS to record any attempt to access the system using one of these hooks.
- Encrypt all sensitive information contained in the system.
- Implement auditing to supplement the IDS.

The best solution is for the vendor to remove all maintenance hooks before the product goes into production. Coded reviews should be performed to identify and remove these hooks.

Time-of-Check/Time-of-Use Attacks

Time-of-check/time-of-use attacks attempt to take advantage of the sequence of events that occur as the system completes common tasks. It relies on knowledge of the dependencies present when a specific series of events occur in multiprocessing systems. By attempting to insert himself between events and introduce changes, the hacker can gain control of the result.

A term often used as a synonym for a time-of-check/time-of-use attack, is a *race condition*, which is actually a different attack. In this attack, the hacker inserts himself between instructions, introduces changes, and alters the order of execution of the instructions, thereby altering the outcome.

Countermeasures to these attacks are to make critical sets of instructions atomic. This means that they either execute in order and in entirety or the changes they make are rolled back or prevented. It is also best for the system to lock access to certain items it will use or touch when carrying out these sets of instructions.

Web-Based Attacks

Attacks upon information security infrastructures have continued to evolve steadily over time, and the latest attacks use largely more sophisticated web application-based attacks. These attacks have proven more difficult to defend with traditional approaches using perimeter firewalls. All web application attacks operate by making at least one normal request or a modified request aimed at taking advantage of inadequate input validation and parameters or instruction spoofing. In this section, two web markup languages are compared on their security merits, followed by a look at an organization that supports the informed use of security technology.

XML

Extensible Markup Language (XML) is the most widely used web language now and has come under some criticism. The method currently used to sign data to verify its authenticity has been described as inadequate by some, and the other criticisms have been directed at the architecture of XML security in general. In the next section, an extension of this language that attempts to address some of these concerns is discussed.

SAML

Security Assertion Markup Language (SAML) is an XML-based open standard data format for exchanging authentication and authorization data between parties, in particular, between an identity provider and a service provider. The major issue on which it focuses is called the web browser single sign-on (SSO) problem.

As you might recall, SSO, which is discussed in Chapter 2, is the ability to authenticate once to access multiple sets of data. SSO at the Internet level is usually accomplished with cookies but extending the concept beyond the Internet has resulted in many propriety approaches that are not interoperable. SAML's goal is to create a standard for this process.

OWASP

The Open Web Application Security Project (OWASP) is an open-source application security project. This group creates guidelines, testing procedures, and tools to assist with web security. They are also known for maintaining a top-ten list of web application security risks.

Server-Based Attacks

In many cases an attack focuses on the operations of the server operating system itself rather than the web applications running on top of it. Later in this section, we look at the way in which these attacks are implemented focusing mainly on the issue of data flow manipulation.

Data Flow Control

Software attacks often subvert the intended dataflow of a vulnerable program. For example, attackers exploit buffer overflows (discussed in Chapter 2 and Chapter 5) and format string vulnerabilities to write data to unintended locations. The ultimate aim is either to read data from prohibited locations or write data to memory locations for the purpose of executing commands, crashing the system, or making malicious changes to the system. As you have already learned, the proper mitigation for these types of attacks is proper input validation and data flow controls that are built into the system.

With respect to databases in particular, a dataflow architecture is one that delivers the instruction tokens to the execution units and returns the data tokens to the content addressable memory (CAM). (CAM is hardware memory, not the same as RAM.) In contrast to the conventional architecture, data tokens are not permanently stored in memory; rather they are transient messages that only exist when in transit to the instruction storage. This makes them less likely to be compromised.

Database Security

In many ways, the database is the Holy Grail for the attacker. It is typically where the sensitive information resides. Some specific database attacks are reviewed briefly in this section.

Inference

Inference occurs when someone has access to information at one level that allows them to infer information about another level. The main mitigation technique for inference is *polyinstantiation*, which is the development of a detailed version of an object from another object using different values in the new object. It prevents low-level database users from inferring the existence of higher level data.

Aggregation

Aggregation is defined as assembling or compiling units of information at one sensitivity level and having the resultant totality of data being of a higher sensitivity level than the individual components. So you might think of aggregation as a different way of achieving the same goal as inference, which is to learn information about data on a level to which one does not have access.

Contamination

Contamination is the intermingling or mixing of data of one sensitivity or need-to-know level with that of another. Proper implementation of security levels is the best defense against these problems.

Data Mining Warehouse

A data warehouse is a repository of information from heterogeneous databases. It allows for multiple sources of data to not only be stored in one place but to be organized in such a way that redundancy of data is reduced (called data normalizing) and more sophisticated data mining tools are used to manipulate the data to discover relationships that may not have been apparent before. Along with the benefits they provide, they also offer more security challenges.

The following are control steps that should be performed in data warehousing applications:

- Monitor summary tables for regular use.
- Monitor the data purging plan.
- Reconcile data moved between the operations environment and data warehouse.

Distributed Systems Security

Some specific security issues need discussion when operating in certain distributed environments. This section covers three special cases in which additional security concerns might be warranted.

Cloud Computing

Cloud computing is the centralization of data in a web environment that can be accessed from anywhere anytime. An organization can create a cloud environment (private cloud) or it can pay a vendor to provide this service (public cloud). While this arrangement offers many benefits, using a public cloud introduces all sorts of security concerns. How do you know your data is kept separate from other customers? How do you know your data is safe? It makes many uncomfortable to outsource the security of their data.

Grid Computing

Grid computing is the process of harnessing the CPU power of multiple physical machines to perform a job. In some cases individual systems might be allowed to leave and rejoin the grid. Although the advantage of additional processing power is great, there has to be concern for the security of data that could be present on machines that are entering and leaving the grid. Therefore, grid computing is not a safe implementation when secrecy of the data is a key issue.

Peer-to-Peer Computing

Any client-server solution in which any platform may act as a client or server or both is called *peer-to-peer computing*. A widely used example of this is instant messaging (IM). These implementations present security issues that do not present themselves in a standard client-server arrangement. In many cases these systems operate outside the normal control of the network administrators.

Problems this can present are

- Viruses, worms, and Trojan horses can be sent through this entry point to the network.
- In many cases, lack of strong authentication allows for account spoofing.
- Buffer overflow attacks and attacks using malformed packets can sometimes be successful.

If these systems must be tolerated in the environment, the following guidelines should be followed:

- Security policies should address the proper use of these applications.
- All systems should have a firewall and antivirus products installed.
- Configure firewalls to block unwanted IM traffic.
- If possible, only allow products that provide encryption.

Exam Preparation Tasks

Review All Key Topics

Review the most important topics in this chapter, noted with the Key Topics icon in the outer margin of the page. Table 7-4 lists a reference of these key topics and the page numbers on which each is found.

Table 7-4 Key Topics

Key Topic Element	Description	Page number
Section	Security services	302
Bullet list	Memory terms	306
Section	*Orange Book* terms and concepts	310
Bullet list	Security models	317
Bullet list	Bell-LaPadula rules	317
Table 7-2	Security model summary	322
List	TCSEC classification system	324

Complete the Tables and Lists from Memory

Print a copy of the CD Appendix A, "Memory Tables," or at least the sections for this chapter, and complete the tables and lists from memory. The CD Appendix B, "Memory Tables Answer Key," includes completed tables and lists to check your work.

Define Key Terms

Define the following key terms from this chapter and check your answers in the glossary:

confidentiality, integrity, availability, defense in depth, architecture, architectural description (AD), stakeholder, view, viewpoint, middleware, embedded system, mobile code, fetching, flash memory, FPGA, firmware, associative memory, implied addressing, absolute addressing, cache, indirect addressing, interrupt, thread, process, superscalar, Very Long Instruction Word processor, pipelined processor, supervisor mode, fail soft fail safe state, multitasking, symmetric mode, asymmetric mode, Trusted Computer Base (TCB), security perimeter, reference monitor, security kernel, Zachman framework, TOGAF, Sherwood Applied Business Security Architecture (SABSA), ISO/IEC 27000,

CobiT, state machine models, multilevel lattice models, matrix-based model, noninference models, information flow model, Bell-LaPadula model, Biba model, Clark-Wilson Integrity model, Lipner model, Brewer-Nash (Chinese Wall) model, Graham–Denning model, Harrison-Ruzzo-Ullman model, Trusted Computer System Evaluation Criteria (TCSEC), *Orange Book*, *Red Book*, Information Technology Security Evaluation Criteria (ITSEC), Common Criteria, certification, accreditation, maintenance hook, time-of-check/time-of-use attacks, Extensible Markup Language (XML), Security Assertion Markup Language (SAML), Open Web Application Security Project (OWASP), inference, polyinstantiation, aggregation, contamination, data warehouse, cloud computing, grid computing, peer-to-peer computing

Review Questions

1. Which of the following is provided if the data cannot be read?

    a. integrity

    b. confidentiality

    c. availability

    d. defense in depth

2. Which of the following ISO/IEC 42010:2011 terms is the set of documents that convey the architecture in a formal manner?

    a. architecture

    b. stakeholder

    c. architectural description (AD)

    d. view

3. In a distributed environment, which of the following is software that ties the client and server software together?

    a. embedded systems

    b. mobile code

    c. virtual computing

    d. middleware

4. Which of the following is a relatively small amount of very high speed RAM, which holds the instructions and data from primary memory?

    a. cache

    b. firmware

c. flash memory

d. FPGA

5. In which CPU mode are the processors or cores handed work on a round-robin basis, thread by thread?

   a. Cache mode

   b. Symmetric mode

   c. Asymmetric mode

   d. Overlap mode

6. Which of the following comprises the components (hardware, firmware, and/or software) that are trusted to enforce the security policy of the system?

   a. security perimeter

   b. reference monitor

   c. trusted computer base (TCB)

   d. security kernel

7. Which of the following is the dividing line between the trusted parts of the system and those that are untrusted?

   a. security perimeter

   b. reference monitor

   c. trusted computer base (TCB)

   d. security kernel

8. Which of the following is a system component that enforces access controls on an object?

   a. security perimeter

   b. reference monitor

   c. trusted computer base (TCB)

   d. security kernel

9. Which of the following is the hardware, firmware, and software elements of a TCB that implements the reference monitor concept?

   a. security perimeter

   b. reference monitor

c. trusted computer base (TCB)

   d. security kernel

10. Which of the following frameworks is a two-dimensional model that intersects communication interrogatives (what, why, where, and so on) with various viewpoints (planner owner, designer, and so on)?

    a. SABSA

    b. Zachman framework

    c. TOGAF

    d. ITIL

Answers and Explanations

1. **b**. Confidentiality is provided if the data cannot be read. This can be provided either through access controls and encryption for data as it exists on a hard drive or through encryption as the data is in transit.

2. **c**. The ISO/IEC 42010:2011 uses specific terminology when discussing architectural frameworks. Architectural description (AD) comprises the set of documents that convey the architecture in a formal manner.

3. **d**. In a distributed environment, middleware is software that ties the client and server software together. It is neither a part of the operating system nor a part of the server software. It is the code that lies between the operating system and applications on each side of a distributed computing system in a network.

4. **a**. Cache is a relatively small amount (when compared to primary memory) of very high speed RAM, which holds the instructions and data from primary memory, that has a high probability of being accessed during the currently executing portion of a program.

5. **b**. In this CPU mode, the processors or cores are handed work on a round-robin basis, thread by thread.

6. **c**. The TCB comprises the components (hardware, firmware, and/or software) that are trusted to enforce the security policy of the system and that if compromised jeopardize the security properties of the entire system.

7. **a**. This is the dividing line between the trusted parts of the system and those that are untrusted. According to security design best practices, components that lie within this boundary (which means they lie within the TCB) should never permit untrusted components to access critical resources in an insecure manner.

8. **b**. A reference monitor is a system component that enforces access controls on an object. It is an access control concept that refers to an abstract machine that mediates all accesses to objects by subjects.

9. **d**. A security kernel is the hardware, firmware, and software elements of a TCB that implements the reference monitor concept. It is an access control concept, not an actual physical component.

10. **b**. The Zachman framework is a two-dimensional model that intersects communication interrogatives (what, why, where, and so on) with various viewpoints (planner owner, designer and so on). It is designed to help optimize communication between the various viewpoints during the creation of the security architecture.

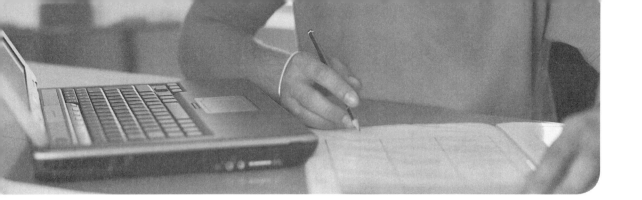

This chapter covers the following topics:

- **Operations security concepts:** Discusses concepts concerning maintaining security operations such as need-to-know/least privilege, separation of duties, job rotation, sensitive information procedures, record retention, and monitoring special privileges.

- **Resource protection:** Describes procedures used to protect tangible and intangible assets. Topics include redundancy and fault tolerance, backup and recovery systems, identity and access management, media management, and network and resource management.

- **Operations processes:** Focuses on managing ongoing security measures. Topics include incident response management, change management, configuration management, patch management, and audit and review.

- **Operations security threats and preventative measures:** Covers preventative measures to security threats. Topics include clipping levels, deviations from standards, unusual or unexplained events, unscheduled reboots, trusted recovery, trusted paths, input/output controls, system hardening, vulnerability management systems, IDS/IPS, monitoring and reporting, and antimalware/antivirus.

CHAPTER 8

Operations Security

After an enterprise has implemented a secure network, the job is not complete. Numerous policies, procedures, and processes must be developed and followed faithfully to maintain a secure posture. Operations security comprises the activities that support continual maintenance of the security of the system on a daily basis. This chapter covers those concepts and their application to an ever-changing environment.

Foundation Topics

Operations Security Concepts

Throughout this book, you've seen references made to policies and principals that can guide all security operations. In this section, we review some concepts more completely that have already been touched on and introduce some new issues concerned with maintaining security operations.

Need-to-Know/Least Privilege

In regard to allowing access to resources and assigning rights to perform operations, always apply the concept of least privilege (also called need-to-know). In the context of resource access, that means that the default level of access should be *no access*. Give users access only to resources required to do their job, and that access should require manual implementation after the requirement is verified by a supervisor.

Discretionary access control (DAC) and role-based access control (RBAC) are examples of systems based on a user's need to know. To ensure least privilege requires that the user's job be identified and each user be granted the lowest clearance required for their tasks. Another example is the implementation of views in a database. Need-to-know requires that the operator have the minimum knowledge of the system necessary to perform his task.

Separation of Duties

The concept of separation of duties prescribes that sensitive operations be divided among multiple users so that no one user has the rights and access to carry out the operation alone. Separation of duties is valuable in deterring fraud by ensuring that no single individual can compromise a system. It is considered a *preventive* administrative control. An example would be one person initiating a request for a payment and another authorizing that same payment. This is also sometimes referred to as *dual control*.

Job Rotation

From a security perspective, job rotation refers to the training of multiple users to perform the duties of a position to help prevent fraud by any individual employee. The idea is that by making multiple people familiar with the legitimate functions of the position, the higher the likelihood that unusual activities by any one person will be noticed. This is often used in conjunction with *mandatory vacations*, in which all users are required to take time off, allowing another to fill their position while gone, which enhances the opportunity to discover unusual activity. Beyond the security aspects of job rotation, additional benefits include:

- Trained backup in case of emergencies
- Protection against fraud
- Cross training of employees

Rotation of duties, separation of duties, and mandatory vacations are all administrative controls.

Sensitive Information Procedures

With an entire section of the CISSP exam blueprint (and a chapter of this book) devoted to access control and its use in preventing unauthorized access to sensitive data, it is obvious that the secure handling of sensitive information is critical. Although we tend to think in terms of the company's information, it is also critical that the company protect the private information of its customers and employees as well. A leak of users' and customers' personal information causes at a minimum embarrassment for the company and possibly fines and lawsuits.

Regardless of whether the aim is to protect company data or personal data, the key is to apply the access control principles described in Chapter 2, "Access Control," to both sets of data. When examining accessing access control procedures and policies, the following questions need to be answered:

- Is data available to the user that is not required for his job?
- Do too many users have access to sensitive data?

Record Retention

Proper access control is not possible without auditing. This allows us to track activities and discover problems before they are fully realized. Because this can sometimes lead to a mountain of data to analyze, only monitor the most sensitive of activities, and retain and review all records. Moreover, in many cases companies are required by law or regulation to maintain records of certain data.

Most auditing systems allow for the configuration of data retention options. In some cases the default operation is to start writing over the older records in the log when the maximum log size is full. Regular clearing and saving of the log can prevent this from happening and avoid the loss of important events. In cases of extremely sensitive data, having a server shut off access when a security log is full and cannot record any more events is even advisable.

Monitor Special Privileges

Inevitably some users, especially supervisors or those in the IT support department, will require special rights and privileges that other users do not possess. For example, it might be required that a set of users who work the Help Desk might need to be able to reset passwords or perhaps make changes to user accounts. These types of rights carry with them a responsibility to exercise the rights responsibly and ethically.

Although in a perfect world we would like to assume that we can expect this from all users, in the real world we know this is not always true. Therefore, one of the things to monitor is the use of these privileges. Although we should be concerned with the amount of monitoring performed and the amount of data produced by this monitoring, recording the exercise of special privileges should not be sacrificed, even if it means regularly saving the data as a log file and clearing the event gathering system.

Resource Protection

Enterprise resources include both assets we can see and touch (tangible), such as computers and printers, and assets we cannot see and touch (intangible), such as trade secrets and processes. Although typically we think of resource protection as preventing the corruption of digital resources and as the prevention of damage to physical resources, this concept also includes maintaining the availability of those resources. In this section, we discuss both aspects of resource protection.

Protecting Tangible and Intangible Assets

In some cases among the most valuable assets of a company are intangible ones such as secret recipes, formulas, and trade secrets. In other cases the value of the company is derived from its physical assets such as facilities, equipment, and the talents of its people. All are considered resources and should be included in a comprehensive resource protection plan. In this section, some specific concerns with these various types of resources are explored.

Facilities

Usually the largest tangible asset the organization has is the building in which it operates and the surrounding land. Physical security is covered extensively in Chapter 11, "Physical (Environmental) Security," but it bears emphasizing that vulnerability testing (discussed more fully later in this chapter) ought to include the security controls of the facility itself. Some examples of vulnerability testing as it relates to facilities include:

- Do doors close automatically, and does an alarm sound if they are held open too long?

- Are the protection mechanisms of sensitive areas, such as server rooms and wiring closets, sufficient and operational?

- Does the fire suppression system work?

- Are sensitive documents shredded as opposed to being thrown in the dumpster?

Beyond the access issues, the main systems that are needed to ensure operations are not disrupted include fire detection/suppression, HVAC (including temperature and humidity controls), water and sewage systems, power/backup power, communications equipment, and intrusion detection. For more detailed information on these issues, see Chapter 9, "Business Continuity and Disaster Recovery."

Hardware

Another of the more tangible assets that must be protected is all the hardware that makes the network operate. This includes not only the computers and printers with which the users directly come in contact, but also the infrastructure devices that they never see such as routers, switches, and firewall appliances. Maintaining access to these critical devices from an availability standpoint is covered later in the sections "Redundancy and Fault Tolerance" and "Backup and Recovery Systems."

From a management standpoint, these devices are typically managed remotely. Special care must be taken to safeguard access to these management features as well as protect the data and commands passing across the network to these devices. Some specific guidelines include:

- Change all default administrator passwords on the devices.
- Limit the number of users that have remote access to these devices.
- Rather than Telnet (which send commands in clear text) use an encrypted command-line tool such as Secure Shell (SSH).
- Manage critical systems locally.
- Limit physical access to these devices.

Software

Software assets include any propriety application, scripts, or batch files that have been developed in house that are critical to the operation of the organization. As discussed in Chapter 5, "Software Development Security," secure coding and development practices can help to prevent weaknesses in these systems. Attention must also be paid to preventing theft of these assets as well.

Moreover, closely monitoring the use of commercial applications and systems in the enterprise can prevent unintentional breach of licensing agreements. One of the benefits of only giving users the applications they require to do their job is that it limits the number of users that have an application, helping to prevent exhaustion of licenses for software.

Information Assets

Information assets are the last asset type that needs to be discussed but by no means are they the least important. The *primary* purpose of operations security is to safeguard information assets that are resident in the system. These assets include recipes, processes, trade secrets, product plans, and any other type of information that enables the enterprise to maintain competitiveness within its industry. The principles of data classification and access control discussed in Chapters 4 and 2, respectively, apply most critically to these assets. In some cases the dollar value of these assets might be difficult to determine although it might be clear to all involved that the asset is critical. For example, the secret formula for Coca-Cola has been closely guarded for many years due to its value to the company.

Asset Management

In the process of managing these assets, several issues must be addressed. Certainly access to the asset must be closely controlled to prevent its deletion, theft, or corruption (in the case of digital assets) and from physical damage (in the case of physical assets). Moreover, the asset must remain available when needed. This section covers methods of ensuring availability, authorization, and integrity.

Redundancy and Fault Tolerance

One of the ways to provide uninterrupted access to information assets is through redundancy and fault tolerance. Redundancy refers to providing multiple instances of either a physical or logical component such that a second component is available if the first fails. Fault tolerance is a broader concept that includes redundancy but refers to any process that allows a system to continue making information assets available in the case of a failure.

In some cases redundancy is applied at the physical layer, such as network redundancy provided by a dual backbone in a local network environment or by using multiple network cards in a critical server. In other cases redundancy is applied logically such as when a router knows multiple paths to a destination in case one fails.

Fault tolerance countermeasures are designed to combat threats to design reliability. Although fault tolerance can include redundancy, it also refers to systems such as Redundant Array of Independent Disks (RAID) in which data is written across multiple disks in such a way that a disk can fail and the data can be quickly made available from the remaining disks in the array without resorting to a backup tape. Be familiar with a number of RAID types because not all provide fault tolerance. RAID is covered in Chapter 9. Regardless of the technique employed for fault tolerance to operate, a system must be capable of detecting and correcting the fault.

Backup and Recovery Systems

Although a comprehensive coverage of backup and recovery systems is found in Chapter 9, it is important to emphasize here the role of operations in carrying out those activities. After the backup schedule has been designed, there will be daily tasks associated with carrying out the plan. One of the most important parts of this system is an ongoing testing process to ensure that all backups are usable in case a recovery is required. The time to discover that a backup did not succeed is during testing and not during a live recovery.

Identity and Access Management

Identity and access management are covered thoroughly in Chapter 2. From an operations perspective, it is important to realize that managing these things is an ongoing process that might require creating accounts, deleting accounts, creating and populating groups, and managing the permissions associated with all of these concepts. Ensuring that the rights to perform these actions are tightly controlled and that a formal process is established for removing permissions when they are no longer required and disabling accounts that are no longer needed is essential.

Another area to focus on is the control of the use of privileged accounts or accounts that have rights and permissions that exceed those of a regular user account. Although this obviously applies to built-in administrator or supervisor accounts (in some operating systems called root accounts) that have vast permissions, it also applies to accounts such as the Windows Power User account, which also confers some special privileges to the user.

Moreover, maintain the same tight control over the numerous built-in groups that exist in Windows to grant special rights to the group members. When using these groups, make note of any privileges held by the default groups that are not required for your purposes. You might want to remove some of the privileges from the default groups to support the concept of least privilege.

Media Management

Although media management was briefly discussed in Chapter 7, "Security Architecture and Design," a more detailed coverage is appropriate here. Be familiar with the following concepts and issues surrounding media management.

RAID

Redundant Array of Independent Disks (RAID) refers to a system whereby multiple hard drives are used to provide either a performance boost or fault tolerance for the data. When we speak of fault tolerance in RAID, we mean maintaining access to the data even in a drive failure without restoring the data from a backup media. The following are the types of RAID with which you should be familiar.

RAID 0, also called disk striping, writes the data across multiple drives. Although it improves performance, it does not provide fault tolerance. Figure 8-1 depicts RAID 0.

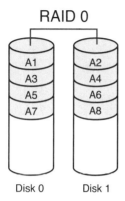

Figure 8-1 RAID 0

RAID 1, also called disk mirroring, uses two disks and writes a copy of the data to both disks, providing fault tolerance in the case of a single drive failure. Figure 8-2 depicts RAID 1.

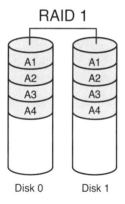

Figure 8-2 RAID 1

RAID 3, requiring at least three drives, also requires that the data is written across all drives like striping and then *parity information* is written to a single dedicated drive. The parity information is used to regenerate the data in the case of a single drive failure. The downfall is that the parity drive is a single point of failure if it goes bad. Figure 8-3 depicts RAID 3.

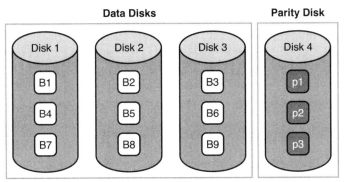

RAID 3 – Bytes Striped (and Dedicated Parity Disk)

Figure 8-3 RAID 3

RAID 5, requiring at least three drives, also requires that the data is written across all drives like striping and then parity information is written across all drives as well. The parity information is used in the same way as in RAID 3, but it is not stored on a single drive so there is no single point of failure for the parity data. With hardware RAID Level 5, the spare drives that replace the failed drives are usually hot swappable, meaning they can be replaced on the server while it is running. Figure 8-4 depicts RAID 5.

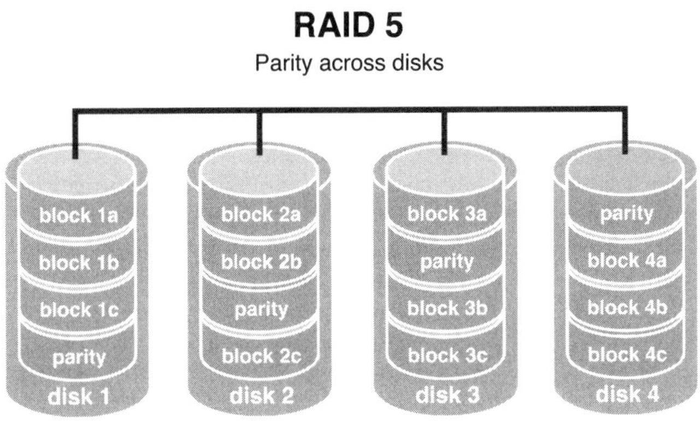

RAID 5
Parity across disks

Figure 8-4 RAID 5

RAID 7, though not a standard but a proprietary implementation, incorporates the same principles as RAID 5 but enables the drive array to continue to operate if any disk or any path to any disk fails. The multiple disks in the array operate as a single virtual disk.

Although RAID can be implemented with software or with hardware, certain types of RAID are faster when implemented with hardware. When software RAID is used, it is a function of the operating system. Both RAID 3 and 5 are examples of RAID types that are faster when implemented with hardware. Simple striping or mirroring (RAID 0 and 1), however, tend to perform well in software because they do not use the hardware-level parity drives. Table 8-1 summarizes the RAID types.

Table 8-1 RAID

RAID Level	Min. Number of Drives	Description	Strengths	Weaknesses
RAID 0	2	Data striping without redundancy	Highest performance	No data protection; one drive fails, all data is lost
RAID 1	2	Disk mirroring	Very high performance; very high data protection; very minimal penalty on write performance	High redundancy cost overhead; because all data is duplicated, twice the storage capacity is required
RAID 3	3	Byte-level data striping with dedicated parity drive	Excellent performance for large, sequential data requests	Not well-suited for transaction-oriented network applications; single parity drive does not support multiple, simultaneous read and write requests
RAID 5	3	Block-level data striping with distributed parity	Best cost/performance for transaction-oriented networks; very high performance, very high data protection; supports multiple simultaneous reads and writes; can also be optimized for large, sequential requests	Write performance is slower than RAID 0 or RAID 1

SAN

Storage area networks (SAN) are comprised of high-capacity storage devices that are connected by a high-speed private network (separate from the LAN) using storage-specific switches. This storage information architecture addresses the collection of data, management of data, and use of data.

NAS

Network-attached storage (NAS) serves the same function as SAN, but clients access the storage in a different way. In a NAS, almost any machine that can connect to the LAN (or is interconnected to the LAN through a WAN) can use protocols such as NFS, CIFS, or HTTP to connect to a NAS and share files. In a SAN, only devices that can use the Fibre channel SCSI network can access the data so it is typically done though a server with this capability. Figure 8-5 shows a comparison of the two systems.

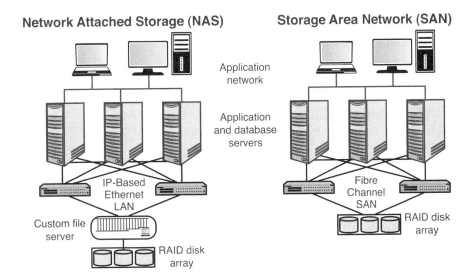

Figure 8-5 NAS and SAN

HSM

A Hierarchical Storage Management (HSM) system is a type of backup management system that provides a continuous online backup by using optical or tape "jukeboxes." It operates by automatically moving data between high-cost and low-cost storage media as the data ages. When continuous availability (24 hours-a-day processing) is required, HSM provides a good alternative to tape backups. It also strives to use the proper media for the scenario. For example, rewritable and erasable (CDR/W) optical disk is sometimes used for backups that require short time storage for changeable data, but require faster file access than tape.

Media History

Accurately maintain media library logs to keep track of the history of the media. This is important in that all media types have a maximum number of times they can safely be used. A log should be kept by a media librarian. This log should track all media (backup and other types such as OS installation discs). With respect to the backup media, use the following guidelines:

- Track all instances of access to the media.
- Track the number and location of backups.
- Track age of media to prevent loss of data through media degeneration.
- Inventory the media regularly.

Media Labeling and Storage

Plainly label all forms of storage media (tapes, optical, and so on) and store them safely. Some guidelines in the area of media control are to

- Accurately and promptly mark all data storage media.
- Ensure proper environmental storage of the media.
- Ensure the safe and clean handling of the media.
- Log data media to provide a physical inventory control.

The environment where the media will be stored is also important. For example, damage starts occurring to magnetic media above 100 degrees. The *Forest Green Book* is a Rainbow Series book that defines the secure handling of sensitive or classified automated information system memory and secondary storage media, such as degaussers, magnetic tapes, hard disks, floppy disks, and cards. The Rainbow Series is discussed in more detail in Chapter 4, "Information Security Governance and Risk Management."

Sanitizing and Disposing of Media

During media disposal, you must ensure no data remains on the media. The most reliable, secure means of removing data from magnetic storage media, such as a magnetic tape cassette, is through degaussing, which exposes the media to a powerful, alternating magnetic field. It removes any previously written data, leaving the media in a magnetically randomized (blank) state. Some other disposal terms and concepts with which you should be familiar are

- **Data purging:** Using a method such as degaussing to make the old data unavailable even with forensics. Purging renders information unrecoverable against laboratory attacks (forensics).

- **Data clearing:** Renders information unrecoverable by a keyboard. This attack extracts information from data storage media by executing software utilities, keystrokes, or other system resources executed from a keyboard.

- **Remanence:** Any data left after the media has been erased.

Network and Resource Management

Although security operations seems to focus its attention on providing confidentiality and integrity of data, availability of the data is also one of its goals. This means designing and maintaining processes and systems that maintain availability to resources despite hardware or software failures in the environment. Although this topic is covered more completely in Chapter 9, the following principles and concepts are available to assist in maintaining access to resources:

- **Redundant Hardware:** Failures of physical components, such as hard drives and network cards, can interrupt access to resources. Providing redundant instances of these components can help to ensure a faster return to access. In some cases changing out a component might require manual intervention, but in many cases these items are hot swappable (they can be changed with the device up and running) in which case a momentary reduction in performance might occur rather than a complete disruption of access.

- **Fault-Tolerant Technologies:** Taking the idea of redundancy to the next level are technologies that are based on multiple computing systems working together to provide uninterrupted access even in the event of a failure of one of the systems. Clustering of servers and grid computing are both great examples of this approach.

- **Service Level Agreements (SLAs):** SLAs are agreements about the ability of the support system to respond to problems within a certain timeframe while providing an agreed level of service. They can be internal between departments or external to a service provider. By agreeing on the quickness with which various problems are addressed, some predictability is introduced to the response to problems, which ultimately supports the maintenance of access to resources.

- **MTBF and MTTR:** Although SLAs are appropriate for services that are provided, a slightly different approach to introducing predictability can be used with regard to physical components that are purchased. Vendors typically publish values for a product's Mean Time Between Failure (MTBF), which describes how often a component fails on average. Another valuable metric typically provided is the Mean Time to Repair (MTTR), which describes the average amount of time it will take to get the device fixed and back online.

- **Single Point of Failure (SPOF):** Though not actually a strategy, it is worth mentioning that the ultimate goal of any of these approaches is to avoid an SPOF of failure in a system. All components and groups of components and devices should be examined to discover any single element that could interrupt access to resources if a failure occurs. Each SPOF should then be mitigated in some way.

Operations Processes

While technology can help us to prevent many problems and maintain access to critical resources, in many cases problems are created by the human beings managing the systems. Well-designed and tested policies and processes, exercised faithfully, can go a long way in preventing loss of data and loss of access to data. This section covers a number of critical procedures.

Incident Response Management

Inevitably security events will occur and the response to these events says much about how damaging the events will be to the organization. Incident response policies should be formally designed, well communicated, and followed. They should specifically address cyber-attacks against an organization's IT systems. Steps in the incident response system can include the following:

1. **Detect.** The first step is to detect the incident. All detective controls, such as auditing, discussed in Chapter 2, are designed to provide this capability. The worst sort of incident is the one that goes unnoticed.

2. **Respond.** The response to the incident should be appropriate for the type of incident. Denial of service (DoS) attacks against the web server would require a quicker and different response than a missing mouse in the server room. Establish standard responses and response times ahead of time.

3. **Report.** All incidents should be reported within a timeframe that reflects the seriousness of the incident. In many cases establishing a list of incident types and the person to contact when that type of incident occurs is helpful. Exercising attention to detail at this early stage while time-sensitive information is still available is critical.

4. **Recover.** Recovery involves a reaction designed to make the network or system that is affected functional again. Exactly what that means depend on the circumstances and the recovery measures that are available. For example, if fault-tolerance measures are in place, the recovery might consist of simply allowing one server in a cluster to fail over to another. In other cases it could mean restoring the server from a recent backup. The main goal of this step is to make all resources available again.

5. **Remediate.** This step involves eliminating any residual danger or damage to the network that still might exist. For example, in the case of a virus outbreak, it could mean scanning all systems to root out any additional effected machines. These measures are designed to make a more detailed mitigation when time allows.

6. **Review.** Finally, review each incident to discover what could be learned from it. Changes to procedures might be called for. Share lessons learned with all personnel who might encounter this type of incident again. Complete documentation and analysis is the goal of this step.

Change Management

All networks evolve, grow, and change over time. Companies and their processes also evolve and change, which is a good thing. But manage change in a structured way so as to maintain a common sense of purpose about the changes. By following recommended steps in a formal process, change can be prevented from becoming the tail that wags the dog. The following are guidelines to include as a part of any change control policy:

- All changes should be formally requested.
- Each request should be analyzed to ensure it supports all goals and polices.

- Prior to formal approval, all costs and effects of the methods of implementation should be reviewed.
- After they're approved, the change steps should be developed.
- During implementation, incremental testing should occur, relying on a predetermined fallback strategy if necessary.
- Complete documentation should be produced and submitted with a formal report to management.

One of the key benefits of following this method is the ability to make use of the documentation in future planning. Lessons learned can be applied and even the process itself can be improved through analysis.

Configuration Management

Although it's really a subset of change management, configuration management specifically focuses itself on bringing order out of the chaos that can occur when multiple engineers and technicians have administrative access to the computers and devices that make the network function. It follows the same basic process as that discussed under "Change Management," but perhaps takes on even greater importance considering the impact that conflicting changes can have (and in some immediately) on the network.

The functions of configuration management are:

- Report the status of change processing.
- Document the functional and physical characteristics of each configuration item.
- Perform information capture and version control.
- Control changes to the configuration items, and issue versions of configuration items from the software library.

NOTE In the context of configuration management, a *software library* is a controlled area accessible only to approved users who are restricted to the use of an approved procedure. A *configuration item* (CI) is a uniquely identifiable subset of the system that represents the smallest portion to be subject to an independent configuration control procedure. When an operation is broken into individual CIs, the process is called *configuration identification*.

Examples of these types of changes are:

- Operating system configuration
- Software configuration
- Hardware configuration

From a CISSP perspective, the biggest contribution of configuration management controls is ensuring that changes to the system do not unintentionally diminish security. Because of this, all changes must be documented, and all network diagrams, both logical and physical, *must* be updated constantly and consistently to accurately reflect the state of each configuration *now* and not as it was two years ago. Verifying that all configuration management policies are being followed should be an ongoing process.

In many cases it is beneficial to form a configuration control board. The tasks of the configuration control board can include

- Ensuring that changes made are approved, tested, documented, and implemented correctly.
- Meeting periodically to discuss configuration status accounting reports.
- Maintaining responsibility for ensuring that changes made do not jeopardize the soundness of the verification system.

In summary, the components of configuration management are:

- Configuration control
- Configuration status accounting
- Configuration audit

Patch Management

As configuration management is a subset of change management, patch management might be seen as a subset of configuration management. *Software patches* are updates released by vendors that either fix functional issues with or close security loopholes in operating systems, applications, and versions of firmware that run on the network devices.

To ensure that all devices have the latest patches installed, deploy a formal system to ensure that all systems receive the latest updates *after* thorough testing in a non-production environment. It is impossible for the vendor to anticipate every possible impact a change might have on business critical systems in the network. The enterprise is responsible for ensuring that patches do not adversely impact operations.

Audit and Review

Accountability is impossible without a record of activities and review of those activities. Capturing and monitoring audit logs provide the digital proof when someone who is performing certain activities needs to be identified. This goes for both the good guys and the bad guys. In many cases it is required to determine who misconfigured something rather than who stole something. Audit trails based upon access and identification codes establish individual accountability. The questions to address when reviewing audit logs include the following:

- Are users accessing information or performing tasks that are unnecessary for their jobs?
- Are repetitive mistakes (such as deletions) being made?
- Do too many users have special rights and privileges?

The level and amount of auditing should reflect the security policy of the company. Audits can be either self-audits or be performed by a third party. Self-audits always introduce the danger of subjectivity to the process. Logs can be generated on a wide variety of devices including intrusion detection systems (IDS), servers, routers, and switches. In fact, host-based IDS makes use of the operating system logs of the host machine.

When assessing controls over audit trails or logs, address the following questions:

- Does the audit trail provide a trace of user actions?
- Is access to online logs strictly controlled?
- Is there separation of duties between security personnel who administer the access control function and those who administer the audit trail?

Keep and store logs in accordance with the retention policy defined in the organization's security policy. They must be secured to prevent modification, deletion, and destruction. When auditing is functioning in a monitoring role, it supports the *detection* security function in the *technical* category. When formal review of the audit logs takes place, it is a form of *detective administrative* control. Reviewing audit data should be a function separate from the day-to-day administration of the system.

Operations Security Threats and Preventative Measures

As you have probably gathered by now, a wide variety of security threats face those charged with protecting the assets of an organization. Luckily, a wide variety of tools are available to use to accomplish this task. This section covers some common threats and mitigation approaches.

Clipping Levels

Clipping levels set a baseline for normal user errors, and violations exceeding that threshold will be recorded for analysis of why the violations occurred. When clipping levels are used, a certain number of occurrences of an activity might generate no information whereas recording of activities begins when a certain level is exceeded.

Clipping levels are used to

- Reduce the amount of data to be evaluated in audit logs
- Provide a baseline of user errors above which violations will be recorded

Deviations from Standards

One of the methods that you can use to identify performance problems that arise is by developing standards or baselines for the performance of certain systems. After these benchmarks have been established, deviations for the standards can be identified. This is especially helpful in identifying certain types of DoS attacks as they occur. Beyond the security benefit, it also aids in identifying systems that might need upgrading before the situation effects productivity.

Unusual or Unexplained Events

In some cases events occur that appear to have no logical cause. That should never be accepted as an answer when problems occur. Although the focus is typically on getting systems up and running again, the root causes of issues must be identified. Avoid the temptation to implement a quick workaround (often at the expense of security). When time permits, using a methodical approach to find exactly why the event happened is best, because inevitably the problem will come back if the root cause has not been addressed.

Unscheduled Reboots

When systems reboot on their own, it is typically a sign of hardware problems of some sort. Reboots should be recorded and addressed. Overheating is the cause of many reboots. Often reboots can also be the result of a DoS attack. Have a system monitoring in place to record all system reboots, and investigate any that are not initiated by a human or have occurred as a result of an automatic upgrade.

Trusted Recovery

When an application or operating system suffers a failure (crash, freeze, and so on), it is important that the system respond in a way that leaves the system in a secure state or that it makes a *trusted recovery*. A trusted recovery ensures that security is not breached when a system crash or other system failure occurs. You might recall that the *Orange Book* requires a system be capable of a trusted recovery for all systems rated B3 or A1.

Trusted Paths

A trusted path is a communication channel between the user or the program through which he is working and the trusted computer base (TCB). (Chapter 7 covers TCB.) The TCB provides the resources to protect the channel and prevent it from being compromised. Conversely, a communication path that is not protected by the system's normal security mechanisms is called a *covert channel*. Taking this a step further, if the interface offered to the user is secured in this way, it is referred to as a *trusted shell*.

Input/Output Controls

The main thrust of input/output control is to apply controls or checks to the input that is allowed to be submitted to the system. Performing input validation on all information accepted into the system can ensure that it is of the right data type and format and that it does not leave the system in an insecure state.

Also secure output of the system (printouts, reports, and so on). All sensitive output information should require a receipt before release and have proper access controls applied regardless of its format.

System Hardening

Another of the ongoing goals of operations security is to ensure that all systems have been hardened to the extent that is possible and still provide functionality. The hardening can be accomplished both on a physical and logical basis. Chapter 11 covers physical security of systems in detail. From a logical perspective

- Remove unnecessary applications.
- Disable unnecessary services.
- Block unrequired ports.
- Tightly control the connecting of external storage devices and media if it's allowed at all.

Vulnerability Management Systems

The importance of performing vulnerability and penetration testing has been emphasized throughout this book. A vulnerability management system is software that centralizes and to a certain extent automates the process of continually monitoring and testing the network for vulnerabilities. These systems can scan the network for vulnerabilities, report them, and in many cases remediate the problem without human intervention. Although they're a valuable tool in the toolbox, these systems, regardless of how sophisticated they might be, cannot take the place of vulnerability and penetration testing performed by trained professionals.

IDS/IPS

Setup, configuration, and monitoring of any intrusion detection and intrusion prevention systems (IDS/IPS) are also ongoing responsibilities of operations security. Many of these systems must be updated on a regular basis with the attack signatures that enable them to detect new attack types. The analysis engines that they use also sometimes have updates that need to be applied.

Moreover, the log files of systems that are set to log certain events rather than take specific actions when they occur need to have those logs archived and analyzed on a regular basis. Spending large sums of money on software that gathers information and then disregarding that information makes no sense whatsoever.

Chapter 2 discusses IDS and IPS in detail.

Monitoring and Reporting

Hopefully by now it is obvious that monitoring and reporting on the findings is another of the day-to-day responsibilities of operations security. Some key issues to keep in mind are:

- Reduce the data collected when monitoring as much as possible and still satisfy requirements.
- Ensure that report formats reflect the technical level and needs of the audience.

Antimalware/Antivirus

Finally, all updates of antivirus and antimalware software are the responsibility of operations security. For more detailed coverage of these procedures, see Chapter 5.

Exam Preparation Tasks

Review All Key Topics

Review the most important topics in this chapter, noted with the Key Topics icon in the outer margin of the page. Table 8-2 lists a reference of these key topics and the page numbers on which each is found.

Table 8-2 Key Topics

Key Topic Element	Description	Page Number
Section	Operations Security Concepts	343
List	RAID	349
List	Principles of managing resource access	355
List	Incident response steps	356

Complete the Tables and Lists from Memory

Print a copy of the CD Appendix A, "Memory Tables," or at least the section for this chapter, and complete the tables and lists from memory. The CD Appendix B, "Memory Tables Answer Key," includes completed tables and lists to check your work.

Define Key Terms

Define the following key terms from this chapter and check your answers in the glossary:

operations security, need-to-know/least privilege, separation of duties, job rotation, information assets, redundancy, fault tolerance, RAID 0, RAID 1, RAID 2, RAID 3, RAID 5, RAID 7, Storage Area Networks (SAN), Hierarchical Storage Management (HSM) system, data purging, data clearing, remanence, Mean Time Between Failure (MTBF), Mean Time to Repair (MTTR), NAS, software patches, trusted recovery, trusted path

Review Questions

1. Which of the following refers to allowing users access only to resources required to do their jobs?

    a. job rotation

    b. separation of duties

    c. need-to-know/least privilege

    d. mandatory vacation

2. Which of the following is an example of an intangible asset?

    a. disc drive

    b. recipes

    c. people

    d. server

3. Which of the following is *not* a guideline for securing hardware?

    a. Change all default administrator passwords on the devices

    b. Use Telnet rather than SSH

    c. Limit physical access to these devices

    d. Manage critical system locally

4. Which of the following is also called disk striping?

    a. RAID 0

    b. RAID 1

    c. RAID 2

    d. RAID 5

5. Which of the following is also called disk mirroring?

    a. RAID 0

    b. RAID 1

c. RAID 2

d. RAID 5

6. Which of the following is comprised of high-capacity storage devices that are connected by a high-speed private (separate from the LAN) network using storage specific switches?

   a. HSM

   b. SAN

   c. NAS

   d. RAID

7. Which of the following uses a method such as degaussing to make the old data unavailable even with forensics?

   a. data clearing

   b. data purging

   c. remanence

   d. data duplication

8. A backup power supply is an example of _____.

   a. SLAs

   b. MTBR

   c. redundancy

   d. cardinality

9. Which of the following describes the average amount of time it will take to get the device fixed and back online?

   a. MTBF

   b. MTTR

   c. HSM

   d. SLA

10. Which of the following is *not* a step in incident response management?

    a. detect

    b. respond

    c. monitor

    d. report

Answers and Explanations

1. **c.** When allowing access to resources and assigning rights to perform operations, the concept of least privilege (also called need-to-know) should always be applied. In the context of resource access, that means that the default level of access should be no access. Give users access only to resources required to do their jobs, and that access should require manual implementation after the requirement is verified by a supervisor.

2. **b.** In some cases among the most valuable assets of a company are intangible ones such as secret recipes, formulas, and trade secrets.

3. **b.** Rather than Telnet (which sends commands in clear text) use an encrypted command line tool such as Secure Shell (SSH).

4. **a.** RAID 0, also called disk striping, writes the data across multiple drives but although it improves performance, it does not provide fault tolerance.

5. **b.** RAID 1, also called disk mirroring, uses two disks and writes a copy of the data to both disks, providing fault tolerance in the case of a single drive failure.

6. **b.** Storage area networks (SAN) are comprised of high-capacity storage devices that are connected by a high-speed private (separate from the LAN) network using storage specific switches.

7. **b.** Purging renders information unrecoverable against laboratory attacks (forensics).

8. **c.** Failures of physical components such as hard drives and network cards can interrupt access to resources. Providing redundant instances of these components can help to ensure a faster return to access.

9. **b.** The Mean Time to Repair (MTTR) describes the average amount of time it will take to get the device fixed and back online.

10. **c.** The steps in incident response management are

    1. Detect
    2. Respond
    3. Report
    4. Recover
    5. Remediate
    6. Review

This chapter covers the following topics:

- **Business continuity and disaster recovery concepts:** This section explains disasters, disaster recovery and the disaster recovery plan, continuity planning and the business continuity plan, business impact analysis, contingency plan, availability, reliability, recoverability, and fault tolerance.

- **Business continuity scope and plan:** This includes a discussion of personnel components, project scope, and business continuity steps.

- **Business impact analysis development:** This section describes the process for performing a business impact analysis, including identifying the critical functions and systems, prioritizing functions and systems, identifying threats and vulnerabilities, and calculating risks.

- **Preventive controls:** This includes fault-tolerant technologies, insurance, data backup, and fire detection and suppression.

- **Recovery strategies:** This section covers categorizing asset recovery priorities, business process recovery, facility recovery, supply and technology recovery, user environment recovery, data recovery, and training personnel.

- **Critical teams and duties:** This includes the damage assessment team, legal team, media relations team, recovery team, relocation team, restoration team, salvage team, and security team.

- **Contingency plan:** This section discusses the development, usage, and maintenance of the contingency plan.

- **BCP testing:** This includes a checklist test, structured walk-through test, simulation test, parallel test, full-interruption test, and BCP maintenance.

CHAPTER 9

Business Continuity and Disaster Recovery

Organizations should never view business continuity and disaster recovery as a discretionary expense. Organizations must include business continuity and disaster recovery as part of any comprehensive security plan. No matter how diligent you are, your organization will be the victim of security breaches and disasters. If your organization appropriately plans for business continuity and disaster recovery, it will be able to recover from a breach or disaster in a timely and efficient manner. Without proper planning in this area, your organization could suffer irreparable damage.

This chapter explains the business continuity and disaster recovery concepts that you need to understand for the CISSP exam. The business continuity scope and plan and business impact analysis are vital parts of business continuity and disaster recovery. Preventive controls can be implemented but only provide a limited level of protection against disasters. An organization must develop recovery strategies to ensure that all assets can be recovered to the state they were in prior to the disaster. Organizations must also consider the teams involved in any disaster recovery and assign the appropriate duties to these teams. Contingency plans should also be developed to ensure that an organization's recovery occurs as planned. Finally, all aspects of the business continuity plan must be fully tested to ensure that the plan actually works. The plan should be maintained and kept current through a regular revision cycle.

Foundation Topics

Business Continuity and Disaster Recovery Concepts

Security professionals must be involved in the development of any business continuity and disaster recovery processes.

As a result, security professionals must understand the basic concepts involved in business continuity and disaster recovery planning, including the following:

- Disruptions

- Disasters
  - Technological
  - Manmade
  - Natural
- Disaster Recovery and the Disaster Recovery Plan (DRP)
- Continuity Planning and the Business Continuity Plan (BCP)
- Business Impact Analysis (BIA)
- Contingency Plan
- Availability
- Reliability
- Recoverability
- Fault Tolerance

Disruptions

A disruption is any unplanned event that results in the temporary interruption of any organizational asset, including processes, functions, and devices. Disruptions are grouped into three main categories: non-disaster, disaster, and catastrophe.

Non-disasters are temporary interruptions that occur due to malfunction or failure. Non-disasters might or might not require public notification and are much easier to recover from than disasters or catastrophes.

A *disaster* is a suddenly occurring event that has a long-term negative impact on life. Disasters require that the organization publicly acknowledge the event and provide the public with information on how the organization will recover. Disasters require more effort for recovery than non-disasters but less than catastrophes.

A *catastrophe* is a disaster that has a much wider and much longer impact. In most cases, a disaster is considered a catastrophe if facilities are destroyed, thereby resulting in the need for the rebuilding of the facilities and the use of a temporary offsite facility.

Disasters

A disaster is an emergency that goes beyond the normal response of resources. A disaster usually affects a wide geographical area and results in severe damage, injury, loss of life, and loss of property. Any disaster has negative financial and reputational effects on the organization. The severity of the financial and reputational damage is also affected by the amount of time the organization takes to recover from the disaster.

The causes of disasters are categorized into three main areas according to origin: technological disasters, man-made disasters, and natural disasters. A disaster is officially over when all business elements have returned to normal function at the original site. The primary concern during any disaster is personnel safety.

Technological Disasters

Technological disasters occur when a device fails. This failure can be the result of device defects, incorrect implementation, incorrect monitoring, or human error. Technological disasters are not usually intentional. If a technological disaster is not recovered from in a timely manner, an organization might suffer a financial collapse.

If a disaster occurs because of a deliberate attack against an organization's infrastructure, the disaster is considered a man-made disaster even if the attack is against a specific device or technology. In the past, all technological disasters were actually considered man-made disasters because technological disasters are usually due to human error or negligence. However, in recent years, experts have started categorizing technological disasters separately from man-made disasters, although the two are closely related.

Man-made Disasters

Man-made disasters occur through human intent or error. Man-made disasters include enemy attacks, bombings, sabotage, arson, terrorism, strikes or other job actions, infrastructure failures, personnel unavailability due to emergency evacuation, and mass hysteria. In most cases, man-made disasters are intentional.

Natural Disasters

Natural disasters occur because of a natural hazard. Natural disasters include flood, tsunami, earthquake, hurricane, tornado, and other such natural events. A fire that is not the result of arson is also considered a natural disaster.

Disaster Recovery and the Disaster Recovery Plan (DRP)

Disaster recovery minimizes the effect of a disaster and includes the steps necessary to resume normal operation. Disaster recovery must take into consideration all organizational resources, functions, and personnel. Efficient disaster recovery will sustain an organization during and after a disruption due to a disaster.

Each organizational function or system will have its own disaster recovery plan (DRP). The DRP for each function or system is created as a direct result of that function or system being identified as part of the business continuity plan (BCP). The DRP is implemented when the emergency occurs and includes the steps to restore functions and systems. The goal of DRP is to minimize or prevent property damage and prevent loss of life. More details on disaster recovery are given later in this chapter in the "Create Recovery Strategies" section.

Continuity Planning and the Business Continuity Plan (BCP)

Continuity planning deals with identifying the impact of any disaster and ensuring that a viable recovery plan for each function and system is implemented. Its primary focus is how to carry out the organizational functions when a disruption occurs.

The BCP considers all aspects that are affected by a disaster, including functions, systems, personnel, and facilities. It lists and prioritizes the services that are needed, particularly the telecommunications and IT functions. More details on continuity planning are given later in this chapter in the "Business Continuity Scope and Plan" section.

Business Impact Analysis (BIA)

A business impact analysis (BIA) is a functional analysis that occurs as part of business continuity and disaster recovery. Performing a thorough BIA will help business units understand the impact of a disaster. The resulting document that is produced from a BIA lists the critical and necessary business functions, their resource dependencies, and their level of criticality to the overall organization. More details on the BIA are given later in this chapter in the "Business Impact Analysis (BIA) Development" section.

Contingency Plan

The contingency plan is part of an organization's overall BCP. Although the BCP defines the organizational aspects that can be affected and the DRP defines how to recover functions and systems, the contingency plan provides instruction on what personnel should do until the functions and systems are restored to full functionality. Think of the contingency plan as a guideline for operation at a reduced state. It usually includes contact information for all personnel, vendor contract information, and equipment and system requirements.

Failure of the contingency plan is usually considered a management failure. A contingency plan, along with the BCP and DRP, should be reviewed at least once a year. As with all such plans, version control should be maintained. Copies should be provided to personnel for storage both onsite and offsite to ensure that personnel can access the plan in the event of the destruction of the organization's main facility.

Availability

As you already know, availability is one of the key principles of the confidentiality, integrity, and availability (CIA) triad and has been discussed in almost every defined CISSP domain. Availability is a main component of business continuity planning. The organization must determine the acceptable level of availability for each function or system. If the availability of a resource falls below this defined level, then specific actions must be followed to ensure that availability is restored.

In regard to availability, most of the unplanned downtime of functions and systems is attributed to hardware failure. Availability places emphasis on technology.

Reliability

Reliability is the ability of a function or system to consistently perform according to specifications. It is vital in business continuity to ensure that the organization's processes can continue to operate. Reliability places emphasis on processes.

Business Impact Analysis (BIA) Development

The BCP development depends most on the development of the BIA. The BIA helps the organization to understand what impact a disruptive event would have on the organization. It is a management-level analysis that identifies the impact of losing an organization's resources.

The four main steps of the BIA are as follow:

1. Identify critical processes and resources.
2. Identify outage impacts, and estimate downtime.
3. Identify resource requirements.
4. Identify recovery priorities.

The BIA relies heavily on any vulnerability analysis and risk assessment that is completed. The vulnerability analysis and risk assessment may be performed by the BCP committee or by a separately appointed risk assessment team. The risk assessment process is discussed in detail in the "Risk Assessment" section in Chapter 4, "Information Security Governance and Risk Management."

Identify Critical Processes and Resources

When identifying the critical processes and resources of an organization, the BCP committee must first identify all the business units or functional areas within the organization. After all units have been identified, the BCP team should select which individuals will be responsible for gathering all the needed data and select how to obtain the data.

These individuals will gather the data using a variety of techniques, including questionnaires, interviews, and surveys. They might also actually perform a vulnerability analysis and risk assessment or use the results of these tests as input for the BIA.

During the data gathering, the organization's business processes and functions and the resources upon which these processes and functions depend should be documented. This list should include all business assets, including physical and financial assets that are owned by the organization, and any assets that provide competitive advantage or credibility.

Identify Outage Impacts, and Estimate Downtime

After determining all the business processes, functions, and resources, the organization should then determine the criticality level of each resource.

As part of determining how critical an asset is, you need to understand the following terms:

- **Maximum tolerable downtime (MTD):** The maximum amount of time that an organization can tolerate a single resource or function being down. This is also referred to as maximum period time of disruption (MPTD).

- **Mean time to repair (MTTR):** The average time required to repair a single resource or function when a disaster or disruption occurs.

- **Mean time between failure (MTBF):** The estimated amount of time a device will operate before a failure occurs. This amount is calculated by the device vendor. System reliability is increased by a higher MTBF and lower MTTR.

- **Recovery time objective (RTO):** The shortest time period after a disaster or disruptive event within which a resource or function must be restored to avoid unacceptable consequences. RTO assumes that an acceptable period of downtime exists. RTO should be smaller than MTD.

- **Work recovery time (WRT):** The difference between RTO and MTD, which is the remaining time that is left over after the RTO before reaching the maximum tolerable.

- **Recovery point objective (RPO):** The point in time to which the disrupted resource or function must be returned.

Each organization must develop its own documented criticality levels. A good example of organizational resource and function criticality levels include critical, urgent, important, normal, and nonessential. Critical resources are those resources that are most vital to the organization's operation and should be restored within minutes or hours of the disaster or disruptive event. Urgent resources should be restored in 24 hours but are not considered as important as critical resources. Important resources should be restored in 72 hours but are not considered as important as critical or urgent resources. Normal resources should be restored in 7 days but are not considered as important as critical, urgent, or important resources. Nonessential resources should be restored within 30 days.

Each process, function, and resource must have its criticality level defined to act as an input into the DRP. If critical priority levels are not defined, a DRP might not be operational within the timeframe the organization needs to recover.

Identify Resource Requirements

After the criticality level of each function and resource is determined, you need to determine all the resource requirements for each function and resource. For example, an organization's accounting system might rely on a server that stores the accounting application, another server that holds the database, various client systems that perform the accounting tasks over the network, and the network devices and infrastructure that support the system. Resource requirements should also consider any human resources requirements. When human resources are unavailable, the organization can be just as negatively impacted as when technological resources are unavailable.

NOTE Keep in mind that the priority for any CISSP should be the safety of human life. Consider and protect all other organizational resources only after personnel are safe.

The organization must document the resource requirements for every resource that would need to be restored when the disruptive event occurs. This includes device name, operating system or platform version, hardware requirements, and device interrelationships.

Identify Recovery Priorities

After all the resource requirements have been identified, the organization must identify the recovery priorities. Establish recovery priorities by taking into consideration process criticality, outage impacts, tolerable downtime, and system resources. After all this information is compiled, the result is an information system recovery priority hierarchy.

Three main levels of recovery priorities should be used: high, medium, and low. The BIA stipulates the recovery priorities but does not provide the recovery solutions. Those are given in the DRP.

Recoverability

Recoverability is the ability of a function or system to be recovered in the event of a disaster or disruptive event. As part of recoverability, downtime must be minimized. Recoverability places emphasis on the personnel and resources used for recovery.

Fault Tolerance

Fault tolerance is provided when a backup component begins operation when the primary component fails. One of the key aspects of fault tolerance is the lack of service interruption.

Varying levels of fault tolerance can be achieved at most levels of the organization based on how much an organization is willing to spend. However, the backup component often does not provide the same level of service as the primary component. For example, an organization might implement a high-speed T1 connection to the Internet. However, the backup connection to the Internet that is used in the event of the failure of the T1 line might be much slower but at a much lower cost of implementation than the primary T1 connection.

Business Continuity Scope and Plan

As you already know, creating the BCP is vital to ensure that the organization can recover from a disaster or disruptive event. Several groups have established standards and best practices for business continuity. These standards and best practices include many common components and steps.

This section covers the personnel components, the project scope, and the business continuity steps that must be completed.

Personnel Components

The most important personnel in the development of the BCP is senior management. Senior management support of business continuity and disaster recovery drives the overall organizational view of the process. Without senior management support, this process will fail.

Senior management sets the overall goals of business continuity and disaster recovery. A business continuity coordinator should be named by senior management and leads the BCP committee. The committee develops, implements, and tests the BCP and DRP. The BCP committee should contain a representative from each business unit. At least one member of senior management should be part of this committee. In addition, the organization should ensure that the IT department, legal department, security department, and communications department are represented because of the vital role that these departments play during and after a disaster.

With management direction, the BCP committee must work with business units to ultimately determine the business continuity and disaster recovery priorities. Senior business unit managers are responsible for identifying and prioritizing time-critical systems. After all aspects of the plans have been determined, the BCP committee should be tasked with regularly reviewing the plans to ensure they remain current and viable. Senior management should closely monitor and control all business continuity efforts and publicly praise any successes.

After an organization gets into disaster recovery planning, other teams are involved. These teams are discussed in the "Critical Teams and Duties" section later in this chapter.

Project Scope

To ensure that the development of the BCP is successful, senior management must define the BCP scope. A business continuity project with an unlimited scope can often become too large for the BCP committee to handle correctly. For this reason, senior management might need to split the business continuity project into smaller, more manageable pieces.

When considering the splitting of the BCP into pieces, an organization might want to split the pieces based on geographic location or facility. However, an enterprise-wide BCP should be developed that ensures compatibility of the individual plans.

Business Continuity Steps

Many organizations have developed standards and guidelines for performing business continuity and disaster recovery planning. One of the most popular standards is

Special Publication (SP) 800-34 Revision 1 (R1) from the National Institute of Standards and Technology (NIST).

The following list summarizes the steps of SP 800-34 R1:

1. Develop contingency planning policy.
2. Conduct business impact analysis (BIA).
3. Identify preventive controls.
4. Create recovery strategies.
5. Develop business continuity plan (BCP).
6. Test, train, and exercise.
7. Maintain the plan.

Figure 9-1 shows a more detailed listing of the tasks included in SP 800-34 R1.

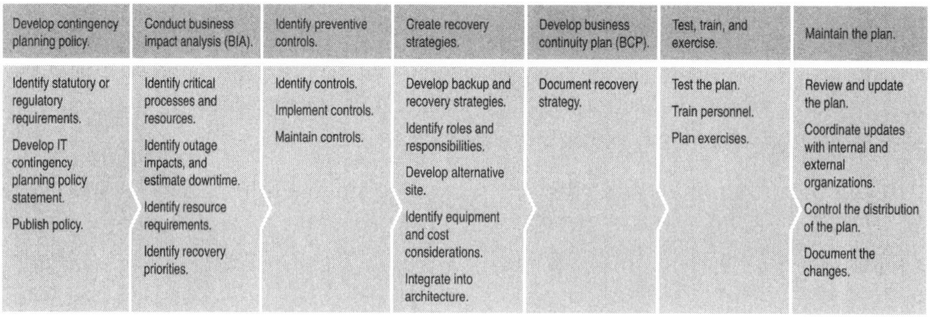

Figure 9-1 NIST Special Publication 800-34 Revision 1

Preventive Controls

Identifying the preventive controls is the third step of the business continuity steps as outlined in NIST SP 800-34 R1. If preventive controls are identified in the BIA, disasters or disruptive events might be mitigated or eliminated. These preventive measures deter, detect, and/or reduce impacts to the system. Preventive methods are preferable to actions that might be necessary to recover the system after a disruption if the preventive controls are feasible and cost effective.

The following sections discuss the primary preventive controls that organizations can implement as part of business continuity and disaster recovery, including redundant systems, facilities, and power; fault-tolerant technologies; insurance; data backup; and fire detection and suppression.

Redundant Systems, Facilities, and Power

In anticipation of disasters and disruptive events, organizations should implement redundancy for critical systems, facilities, and power and assess any systems that have been identified as critical to determine whether implementing redundant systems is cost effective. Implementing redundant systems at an alternate location often ensures that services are uninterrupted. Redundant systems include redundant servers, redundant routers, redundant internal hardware, and even redundant backbones. Redundancy occurs when an organization has a secondary component, system, or device that takes over when the primary unit fails.

Redundant facilities ensure that the organization maintains a facility at whatever level it chooses to ensure that the organizational services can continue when a disruptive event occurs. Redundant facilities are discussed in more depth later in this chapter.

Power redundancy is implemented using uninterruptible power supplies (UPSs) and power generators.

Fault-Tolerant Technologies

Fault tolerance enables a system to continue operation in the event of the failure of one or more components. Fault tolerance within a system can include fault-tolerant adapter cards and fault-tolerant storage drives. One of the most well-known fault tolerance systems is Redundant Array of Independent Disks (RAID). Chapter 8, "Operations Security," discusses RAID.

By implementing fault-tolerant technologies, an organization can ensure that normal operation occurs if a single fault-tolerant component fails.

Insurance

Although redundancy and fault tolerance can actually act as preventive measures against failures, insurance is not really a preventive measure. If an organization purchases insurance to provide protection in the event of a disruptive event, the insurance has no power to protect against the event itself. The purpose of the insurance is to ensure that the organization will have access to additional financial resources to help in the recovery.

Keep in mind that recovery efforts from a disruptive event can often incur large financial costs. Even some of the best estimates might still fall short when the actual recovery must take place. By purchasing insurance, the organization can ensure that key financial transactions, including payroll, accounts payable, and any recovery costs, are covered.

Insurance actual cost valuation (ACV) compensates property based on the value of the item on the date of loss plus 10 percent. However, keep in mind that insurance on any printed materials only covers inscribed, printed, or written documents, manuscripts, or records. It does not cover money and securities. A special type of insurance called *business interruption insurance* provides monetary protection for expenses and lost earnings.

Organizations should annually review insurance policies and update them as necessary.

Data Backup

Data backup provides prevention against data loss but not prevention against the disruptive event. All organizations should ensure that all systems that store important files are backed up in a timely manner. Users should also be encouraged to back up personal files that they might need. In addition, periodic testing of the restoration process should occur to ensure that the files can be restored.

Data recovery, including backup types and schemes and electronic backup, is covered in more detail later in this chapter.

Fire Detection and Suppression

Organizations should implement fire detection and suppression systems as part of any BCP. Fire detection and suppressions vary based on the method of detection/suppression used and are discussed in greater detail in the "Environmental Security" section of Chapter 11, "Physical (Environmental) Security."

Create Recovery Strategies

The next step in the business continuity process is to create recovery strategies. *Higher level* recovery strategies identify the order in which processes and functions are restored. *System-level* recovery strategies define how a particular system is to be restored. Keep in mind those individuals who best understand the system should define system recovery strategies. Although the BCP committee probably can develop the prioritized recovery lists and high-level recovery strategies, system administrators and other IT personnel need to be involved in the development of recovery strategies for IT assets.

Disaster recovery tasks include recovery procedures, personnel safety procedures, and restoration procedures. The overall business recovery plan should require a committee to be formed to decide the best course of action. This recovery plan committee receives its direction from the BCP committee and senior management.

All decisions regarding recovery should be made in advance and incorporated into the DRP. Any plans and procedures that are developed should refer to functions or processes, not specific individuals. As part of the disaster recovery planning, the recovery plan committee should contact critical vendors ahead of time to ensure that any equipment or supplies can be replaced in a timely manner.

When a disaster or disruptive event has occurred, the organization's spokesperson should report the bad news in an emergency press conference before the press learns of the news through another channel. The DRP should detail any guidelines for handling the press. The emergency press conference site should be planned ahead of time.

When resuming normal operations after a disruptive event, the organization should conduct a thorough investigation if the cause of the event is unknown. Personnel should account for all damage-related costs that occur as a result of the event. In addition, appropriate steps should be taken to prevent further damage to property.

The commonality between all recovery plans is that they all become obsolete. For this reason, they require testing and updating.

This section includes a discussion of categorizing asset recovery priorities, business process recovery, facility recovery, supply and technology recovery, user environment recovery, data recovery, and training personnel.

Categorize Asset Recovery Priorities

Discussed in the "Identify Outage Impacts, and Estimate Downtime" section earlier in this chapter, the RTO, WRT, and RPO values affect the recovery solutions that will be selected. An RTO stipulates the amount of time an organization will need to recover from a disaster, and an RPO stipulates the amount of data an organization can lose when a disaster occurs. The RTO, WRT, and RPO values are derived during the BIA process.

In developing the recovery strategy, the recovery plan committee takes the RTO, WRT, and RPO value and determines the recovery strategies that should be used to ensure that the organization meets these BIA goals.

Critical devices, systems, and applications need to be restored earlier than devices, systems, or applications that do not fall into this category. Keep in mind when classifying systems that most critical systems cannot be restored using manual methods. The recovery plan committee must understand the backup/restore solutions that are available and implement the system that will provide recovery within the BIA values and cost constraints. The window of time for recovery of data-processing capabilities is based on the criticality of the operations affected.

Business Process Recovery

As part of the DRP, the recovery plan committee must understand the interrelationships between the processes and systems. A business process is a collection of tasks that produce a specific service or product for a particular customer or customers.

For example, if the organization determines that an accounting system is a critical application and the accounting system relies on a database server farm, the DRP needs to include the database server as a critical asset. Although restoring the entire database server farm to restore the critical accounting system might not be necessary, at least one of the servers in the farm is necessary for proper operation.

Workflow documents should be provided to the recovery plan committee for each business process. As part of recovering the business processes, the recovery plan committee must also understand the process's required roles and resources, input and output tools, and interfaces with other business processes.

Facility Recovery

When dealing with an event that either partially or fully destroys the primary facility, the organization will need an alternate location from which to operate until the primary facility is restored. The DRP should define the alternate location and its recovery procedures.

The DRP should include not only how to bring the alternate location to full operation, but also how the organization will return from the alternate location to the primary facility after it is restored. Also, for security purposes, the DRP should include details on the security controls that were used at the primary facility and guidelines on how to implement these same controls at the alternate location.

The most important factor in locating an alternate location during the development of the DRP is to ensure that the alternate location is not affected by the same disaster. This might mean that the organization must select an alternate location that is in another city or geographic region. The main factors that affect the selection of an alternate location include the following:

- Geographic location
- Organizational needs
- Location's cost
- Location's restoration effort

Testing an alternate location is a vital part of any DRP. Some locations are easier to test than others. The DRP should include instructions on when and how to periodically test alternate facilities to ensure that the contingency facility is compatible with the primary facility.

The alternate locations that security professionals should understand for the CISSP exam include the following:

- Hot site
- Cold site
- Warm site
- Tertiary site
- Reciprocal agreements
- Redundant sites

Hot Site

A hot site is a leased facility that contains all the resources needed for full operation. This environment includes computers, raised flooring, full utilities, electrical and communications wiring, networking equipment, and UPSs. The only resource that must be restored at a hot site is the organization's data, often only partially. It should only take a few hours to bring a hot site to full operation.

Although a hot site provides the quickest recovery, it is the most expensive to maintain. In addition, it can be administratively hard to manage if the organization requires proprietary hardware or software. A hot site requires the same security controls as the primary facility and full redundancy, including hardware, software, and communication wiring.

Cold Site

A cold site is a leased facility that contains only electrical and communications wiring, air conditioning, plumbing, and raised flooring. No communications equipment, networking hardware, or computers are installed at a cold site until it is necessary to bring the site to full operation. For this reason, a cold site takes much longer to restore than a hot or warm site.

Although a cold site provides a slowest recovery, it is the least expensive to maintain. It is also the most difficult to test.

Warm Site

A warm site is a leased facility that contains electrical and communications wiring, full utilities, and networking equipment. In most cases, the only devices that are not included in a warm site are the computers. A warm site takes longer to restore than a hot site but less than a cold site.

A warm site is somewhere between the restoration time and cost of a hot site and cold site. It is the most widely implemented alternate leased location. Although testing a warm site is easier than testing a cold site, a warm site requires much more effort for testing than a hot site.

Figure 9-2 is a chart that compares the components deployed in these three sites.

	Hot Site	Warm Site	Cold Site
Electrical Connection	Yes	Yes	Yes
Peripherals	Yes	Some	None
Networking	Yes	None	None
Servers and Other Hardware	Yes	None	None
Applications	Yes	None	None

Figure 9-2 Hot Site, Warm Site, and Cold Site Comparison

Tertiary Site

A tertiary site is a secondary backup site that provides an alternate in case the hot site, warm site, or cold site is unavailable. Many large companies implement tertiary sites to protect against catastrophes that affect large geographic areas.

For example, if an organization requires a data center that is located on the coast, the organization might have its primary location in New Orleans, Louisiana and its hot site in Mobile, Alabama. This organization might consider locating a tertiary site in Miami, Florida, because a hurricane can affect both the Louisiana and Alabama Gulf coast.

Reciprocal Agreements

A reciprocal agreement is an agreement between two organizations that have similar technological needs and infrastructures. In the agreement, both organizations agree to act as an alternate location for the other if either of the organization's primary facilities are rendered unusable. Unfortunately in most cases, these agreements cannot be legally enforced.

A disadvantage of this site is that it might not be capable of handling the required workload and operations of the other organization.

> **NOTE** A mutual-aid agreement is a pre-arranged agreement between two organizations in which each organization agrees to provide assistance to the other in the event of a disaster.

Redundant Sites

A redundant or mirrored site is a site that is identically configured as the primary site. A redundant or mirrored site is not a leased site but is usually owned by the same organization as the primary site. The organization is responsible for maintaining the redundant site.

Although redundant sites are expensive to maintain, many organizations today see them as a necessary expense to ensure that uninterrupted service can be provided.

Supply and Technology Recovery

Although facility recovery is not often a concern with smaller disasters or disruptive events, almost all recovery efforts usually involve the recovery of supplies and technology. Organizations must ensure that any DRPs include guidelines and procedures for recovering supplies and technology. As part of supply and technology recovery, the DRP should include all pertinent vendor contact information in the event that new supplies and technological assets must be purchased.

The DRP must include recovery information on the following assets that must be restored:

- Hardware backup
- Software backup
- Human resources
- Heating, ventilation, and air conditioning (HVAC)
- Supplies
- Documentation

Hardware Backup

Hardware that must be included as part of the DRP includes client computers, server computers, routers, switches, firewalls, and any other hardware that is running on the organization's network. The DRP must include not only guidelines and procedures for restoring all the data on each of these devices, but also information regarding restoring these systems manually if the systems are damaged or completely destroyed. Legacy devices that are no longer unavailable in the retail market should also be identified.

> **NOTE** Data recovery is covered later in this chapter.

As part of preparing the DRP, the recovery plan team must determine the amount of time that it will take the hardware vendors to provide replacements for any damaged or destroyed hardware. Without this information documented, any recovery plans might be ineffective due to lack of resources. Organizations might need to explore other options, including purchasing redundant systems and storing them at an alternate location, if vendors are unable to provide replacement hardware in a timely manner. When replacement of legacy devices is possible, organizations should take measures to replace them before the disaster occurs.

Software Backup

Even if an organization has every device needed to restore its infrastructure, those devices are useless if the applications and software that run on the devices is not available. The applications and software includes any operating systems, databases, and utilities that need to be running on the device.

Many organizations might think that this requirement is fulfilled if they have a backup on either tape, DVD, or other media of all their software. But all software that is backed up usually requires at least an operating system to be running on the device on which it is restored. These data backups often also require that the backup management software is running on the backup device, whether that is a server or dedicated device.

All software installation media, service packs, and other necessary updates should be stored at an alternate location. In addition, all license information should be documented as part of the DRP. Finally, frequent backups of applications should be taken, whether this is through the application's internal backup system or through some other organizational backup. A backup is only useful if it can be restored so the DRP should fully document all the steps involved.

In many cases, applications are purchased from a software vendor, and only the software vendor understands the coding that occurs in the applications. Because there are no guarantees in today's market, some organizations might decide that they need to ensure that they are protected against a software vendor's demise. A software escrow is an agreement whereby a third party is given the source code of the software to ensure that the customer has access to the source code if certain conditions for the software vendor occur, including bankruptcy and disaster.

Human Resources

No organization is capable of operating without personnel. An occupant emergency plan specifically addresses procedures for minimizing loss of life or injury when a threat occurs. The human resources team is responsible for contacting all personnel in the event of a disaster. Contact information for all personnel should be stored onsite and offsite. Multiple members of the HR team should have access to the personnel contact information. Remember that personnel safety is always the primary concern. All other resources should be protected only after the personnel is safe.

After the initial event is over, the HR team should monitor personnel morale and guard against employee stress and burnout during the recovery period. If proper cross-training has occurred, multiple personnel can be rotated in during the recovery process. Any DRP should take into consideration the need to provide adequate periods of rest for any personnel involved in the disaster recovery process. It should also include guidelines on how to replace any personnel who is a victim of the disaster.

The organization must ensure that salaries and other funding to personnel continue during and after the disaster. Because funding can be critical both for personnel and for resource purchases, authorized, signed checks should be securely stored offsite. Lower-level management with the appropriate access controls should have the ability to disperse funds using these checks in the event that senior management is unavailable.

An executive succession plan should also be created to ensure that the organization follows the appropriate steps to protect itself and continue operation.

Supplies

Often disasters affect the ability to supply an organization with its needed resources, including paper, cabling, and even water. The organization should document any resources that are vital to its daily operations and the vendors from which these resources can be obtained. Because supply vendors can also be affected by the disaster, alternative suppliers should be identified.

Documentation

For disaster recovery to be a success, the personnel involved must be able to complete the appropriate recovery procedures. Although the documentation of all these procedures might be tedious, it is necessary to ensure that recovery occurs. In addition, each department within the organization should be asked to decide what departmental documentation is needed to carry out day-to-day operations. This documentation should be stored in a central location onsite, and a copy should be retained offsite as well. Specific personnel should be tasked with ensuring that this documentation is created, stored, and updated as appropriate.

User Environment Recovery

All aspects of the end user environment recovery must be included as part of the DRP to ensure that the end users can return to work as quickly as possible. As part of this user environment recovery, end user notification must occur. Users must be notified of where and when to report after a disaster occurs.

The actual user environment recovery should occur in stages, with the most critical functions being restored first. User requirements should be documented to ensure that all aspects of the user environment are restored. For example, users in a critical department might all need their own client computer. These same users might also need to access an application that is located on a server. If the server is not restored, the users will be unable to perform their job duties even if their client computers are available.

Finally, manual steps that can be used for any function should be documented. Because we are so dependent on technology today, we often overlook the manual methods of performing our job tasks. Documenting these manual methods might ensure that operations can still occur, even if they occur at a decreased rate.

Data Recovery

In most organizations, the data is one of the most critical assets when recovering from a disaster. The BCPs and DRPs must include guidelines and procedures for recovering data. However, the operations teams must determine which data is backed up, how often the data is backed up, and the method of backup used. So while this section discusses data backup, remember that the BCP teams do not actually make any data backup decisions. The BCP teams are primarily concerned with ensuring that the data that is backed up can be restored in a timely manner.

This section discusses the data backup types and schemes that are used as well as electronic backup methods that organizations can implement.

Data Backup Types and Schemes

To design an appropriate data recovery solution, security professionals must understand the different types of data backups that can occur and how these backups are used together to restore the live environments.

For the CISSP exam, security professionals must understand the following data backup types and schemes:

- Full backup
- Differential backup
- Incremental backup
- Copy backup
- Daily backup
- Transaction log backup
- First in, first out rotation scheme
- Grandfather/father/son rotation scheme

The three main data backups are full backups, differential backups, and incremental backups. To understand these three data backup types, you must understand the concept of archive bits. When a file is created or updated, the archive bit for the file is enabled. If the archive bit is cleared, the file will not be archived during the next backup. If the archive bit is enabled, the file will be archived during the next backup.

With a full backup, all data is backed up. During the full backup process, the archive bit for each file is cleared. A full backup takes the longest time and the most space to complete. However, if an organization only uses full backups, then only the latest full backup needs to be restored. Any backup that uses a differential or incremental backup will first start with a full backup as its baseline. A full backup is the most appropriate for offsite archiving.

In a differential backup, all files that have been changed since the last full backup will be backed up. During the differential backup process, the archive bit for each file is not cleared. A differential backup might vary from taking a short time and a small amount of space to growing in both the backup time and amount of space it needs over time. Each differential backup will back up all the files in the previous differential backup if a full backup has not occurred since that time. In an organization that uses a full/differential scheme, the full and the only the most recent differential backup must be restored, meaning only two backups are needed.

An incremental backup backs up all files that have been changed since the last full or incremental backup. During the incremental backup process, the archive bit for each file is cleared. An incremental backup usually takes the least amount of time and space to complete. In an organization that uses a full/incremental scheme, the full backup and each subsequent incremental backup must be restored. The incremental backups must be restored in order. If your organization completes a full backup on Sunday and an incremental backup daily Monday through Saturday, up to seven backups could be needed to restore the data.

Figure 9-3 shows a comparison of the three main backup types.

Backup Type	Data Backed Up	Backup Time	Restore Time	Storage Space
Full Backup	All Data	Slowest	Fast	High
Incremental Backup	Only New/Modified Files/Folders	Fast	Moderate	Lowest
Differential Backup	All Data Since Last Full	Moderate	Fast	Moderate

Figure 9-3 Backup Types Comparison

Copy and daily backups are two special backup types that are not considered part of any regularly scheduled backup scheme because they do not require any other backup type for restoration. Copy backups are similar to normal backups but do not reset the file's archive bit. Daily backups use a file's time stamp to determine whether it needs archiving. Daily backups are popular in mission-critical environments where multiple daily backups are required because files are updated constantly.

Transaction log backups are only used in environments where capturing all transactions that have occurred since the last backup is important. Transaction log backups help organizations to recover to a particular point in time and are most commonly used in database environments.

Although magnetic tape drives are still in use today and used to back up data, many organizations today back up their data to optical discs, including CD-ROMs, DVDs, and Blu-ray discs; high-capacity, high-speed magnetic drives; or other media. No matter the media used, retaining backups both onsite and offsite is important. Store onsite backup copies in a waterproof, heat-resistant, fire-resistant safe or vault.

As part of any backup plan, an organization should also consider the backup rotation scheme that it will use. Cost considerations and storage considerations often dictate that backup media is reused after a period of time. If this reuse is not planned in advance, media can become unreliable due to overuse. Two of the most popular backup rotation schemes are first in, first out and grandfather/father/son.

In the first in, first out (FIFO) scheme, the newest backup is saved to the oldest media. Although this is the simplest rotation scheme, it does not protect against data errors. If an error in data exists, the organization might not have a version of the data that does not contain the error.

In the grandfather/father/son scheme (GFS), three sets of backups are defined. Most often these three definitions are daily, weekly, and monthly. The daily backups are the sons, the weekly backups are the fathers, and the monthly backups are the grandfathers. Each week, one son advances to the father set. Each month, one father advances to the grandfather set.

Figure 9-4 displays a typical 5-day GFS rotation using 21 tapes. The daily tapes are usually differential or incremental backups. The weekly and monthly tapes must be a full backup.

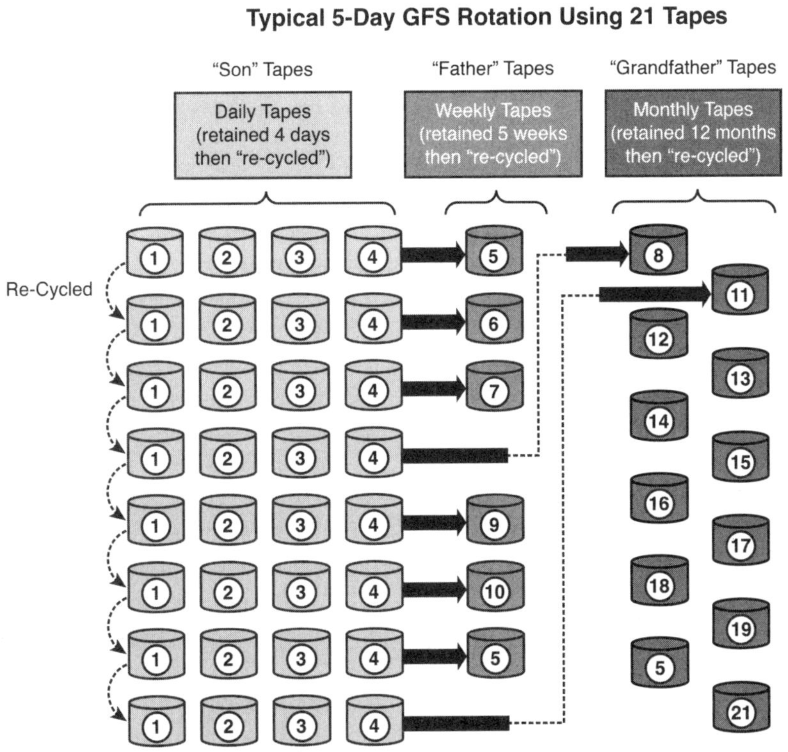

Figure 9-4 Grandfather/Father/Son Backup Rotation Scheme

Electronic Backup

Electronic backup solutions back up data quicker and more accurately than the normal data backups and are best implemented when information changes often.

For the CISSP exam, you should be familiar with the following electronic backup terms and solutions:

- **Electronic vaulting:** Copies files as modifications occur. This method occurs in real time.

- **Remote journaling:** Copies the journal or transaction log offsite on a regular schedule. This method occurs in batches.

- **Tape vaulting:** Creates backups over a direct communication line on a backup system at an offsite facility.

- **Hierarchical storage management (HSM):** Stores frequently accessed data on faster media and less frequently accessed data on slower media.

- **Optical jukebox:** Stores data on optical disks and uses robotics to load and unload the optical disks as needed. This method is ideal when 24/7 availability is required.

- **Replication:** Copies data from one storage location to another. Synchronous replication uses constant data updates to ensure that the locations are close to the same, whereas asynchronous replication delays updates to a predefined schedule.

High Availability

High availability in data recovery is a concept that ensures that data is always available using redundancy and fault tolerance. Most organizations implement high-availability solutions as part of any DRP.

High-availability terms and techniques that you must understand include the following:

- **Redundant Array of Independent Disks (RAID):** A hard-drive technology in which data is written across multiple disks in such a way that a disk can fail and the data can be quickly made available from remaking disks in the array without restoring a backup tape.

- **Storage-area network (SAN):** High-capacity storage devices that are connected by a high-speed private network using storage-specific switches.

- **Failover:** The capacity of a system to switch over to a backup system if a failure in the primary system occurs.

- **Failsoft:** The capability of a system to terminate non-critical processes when a failure occurs.

- **Clustering:** Refers to a software product that provides load-balancing services. With clustering, one instance of an application server acts as a master controller and distributes requests to multiple instances using round-robin, weighted round-robin, or least-connections algorithms.

- **Load balancing:** Refers to a hardware product that provides load-balancing services. Application delivery controllers (ADCs) support the same algorithms, but also use complex number-crunching processes, such as per-server CPU and memory utilization, fastest response times, and so on, to adjust the balance of the load. Load-balancing solutions are also referred to as farms or pools.

Training Personnel

Even if an organization takes the steps to develop the most thorough BCPs and DRPs, these plans are useless if the organization's personnel do not have the skills to completely recover the organization's assets when a disaster occurs. Personnel should be given the appropriate time and monetary resources to ensure that adequate training occurs. This includes allowing personnel to test any DRPs.

Training should be obtained from both internal and external sources. When job duties change or new personnel are hired, policies should be in place to ensure the appropriate transfer of knowledge occurs.

Critical Teams and Duties

Although the number one and number two priorities when a disaster occurs are personnel safety and health and damage mitigation, respectively, recovering from a disaster quickly becomes an organization's priority after these two are handled. However, no organization can recover from a disaster if the personnel are not properly trained and prepared. To ensure that personnel can perform their duties during disaster recovery, they must know and understand their job tasks.

During any disaster recovery, financial management is important. Financial management usually includes the chief financial officer and any other key accounting personnel. This group must track the recovery costs and assess the cash flow projections. They formally notify any insurers of claims that will be made. Finally, this group is responsible for establishing payroll continuance guidelines, procurement procedures, and emergency costs tracking procedures.

Organizations must decide which teams are needed during a disaster recovery and ensure that the appropriate personnel are placed on each of these teams. The disaster recovery manager directs the short-term recovery actions immediately following a disaster.

Organizations might need to implement the following teams to provide the appropriate support for the DRP:

- Damage assessment team
- Legal team
- Media relations team
- Recovery team
- Relocation team
- Restoration team
- Salvage team
- Security team

Damage Assessment Team

The damage assessment team is responsible for determining the disaster's cause and the amount of damage that has occurred to organizational assets. It identifies all affected assets and the critical assets' functionality after the disaster. The damage assessment team determines which assets will need to be restored and replaced and contacts the appropriate teams that need to be activated.

Legal Team

The legal team deals with all legal issues immediately following the disaster and during the disaster recovery. The legal team oversees any public relations events that are held to address the disaster, although the media relations team will actually deliver the message. The legal team should be consulted to ensure that all recovery operations adhere to federal and state laws and regulations.

Media Relations Team

The media relations team informs the public and media whenever emergencies extend beyond the organization's facilities according to the guidelines given in the DRP. The emergency press conference site should be planned ahead. When issuing public statements, the media relations team should be honest and accurate about what is known about the event and its effects. The organization's response to the media during and after the event should be unified.

A credible, informed spokesperson should deliver the organization's response. When dealing with the media after a disaster, the spokesperson should report bad news before the media discovers it through another channel. Anyone making disaster announcements to the public should understand that the audience for such announcements includes the media, unions, stakeholders, neighbors, employees, contractors, and even competitors.

Recovery Team

The recovery team's primary task is recovering the critical business functions at the alternate facility. This mostly involves ensuring that the physical assets are in place, including computers and other devices, wiring, and so on. The recovery team usually oversees the relocation and restoration teams.

Relocation Team

The relocation team oversees the actual transfer of assets between locations. This includes moving assets from the primary site to the alternate site and then returning those assets when the primary site is ready for operation.

Restoration Team

The restoration team actually ensures that the assets and data are restored to operations. The restoration team needs access to the backup media.

Salvage Team

The salvage team recovers all assets at the disaster location and ensures that the primary site returns to normal. The salvage team manages the cleaning of equipment, the rebuilding of the original facility, and identifies any experts to employ in the recovery process. In most cases, the salvage team declares when operations at the disaster site can resume.

Security Team

The security team is responsible for managing the security at both the disaster site and any alternate location that the organization uses during the recovery. Because the geographic area that the security team must manage after the disaster is often much larger, the security team might need to hire outside contractors to aid in this process. Using these outside contractors to guard the physical access to the sites and using internal resources to provide security inside the facilities is always better because the reduced state might make issuing the appropriate access credential to contractors difficult.

BCP Testing

After the BCP is fully documented, an organization must take measures to ensure that the plan is maintained and kept up to date. At a minimum, an organization must evaluate and modify the BCP and DRP on an annual basis. This evaluation usually involves some sort of test to ensure that the plans are accurate and thorough. Testing frequently is important because any plan is not viable unless testing has occurred. Through testing, inaccuracies, deficiencies, and omissions are detected.

Testing the BCP and DRP prepares and trains personnel to perform their duties. It also ensures that the alternate backup site can perform as needed. When testing occurs, the test is probably flawed if no issues with the plan are found.

The types of tests that are commonly used to assess the BCP and DRP include the following:

- Checklist test
- Table-top exercise
- Structured walk-through test
- Simulation test
- Parallel test
- Full-interruption test
- Functional drill
- Evacuation drill

Checklist Test

The checklist test occurs when managers of each department or functional area review the BCP. These managers make note of any modifications to the plan. The BCP committee then uses all the management notes to make changes to the BCP.

Table-top Exercise

A table-top exercise is the most cost-effective and efficient way to identify areas of overlap in the plan before conducting higher level testing. A table-top exercise is an informal brainstorming session that encourages participation from business leaders and other key employees. In a table-top exercise, the participants agree to a particular disaster scenario upon which they will focus.

Structured Walk-Through Test

The structured walk-through test involves representatives of each department or functional area thoroughly reviewing the BCP's accuracy. This type of test is the most important test to perform prior to a live disaster.

Simulation Test

In a simulation test, the operations and support personnel execute the DRP in a role-playing scenario. This test identifies omitted steps and threats.

Parallel Test

A parallel test validates the operation of a new system against its predecessor. The performance of the replacement system is compared to the primary system. If performance deficiencies are found, the BCP team researches ways to prevent these deficiencies from occurring.

Full-Interruption Test

A full-interruption test involves shutting down the primary facility and bringing the alternate facility up to full operation. This is a hard switch-over in which all processing occurs at the primary facility until the "switch" is thrown. This type of test requires full coordination between all the parties and includes notifying users in advance of the planned test. An organization should perform this type of test only when all other tests have been implemented and are successful.

Functional Drill

A functionality drill tests a single function or department to see whether the function's DRP is complete. This type of drill requires the participation of the personnel that perform the function.

Evacuation Drill

In an evacuation drill, personnel follow the evacuation or shelter-in-place guidelines for a particular disaster type. In this type of drill, personnel must understand the area to which they are to report when the evacuation occurs. All personnel should be accounted for at that time.

BCP Maintenance

After a test is complete, all test results should be documented, and the plans should be modified to reflect those results. The list of successful and unsuccessful activities from the tests will be the most useful to management when maintaining the BCP. All obsolete information in the plans should be deleted, and any new information should be added. In addition, modifying current information based on new regulations, laws, or protocols might be necessary.

Version control of the plans should be managed to ensure that the organization always uses the most recent version. In addition, the BCP should be stored in multiple locations to ensure that it is available if a location is destroyed by the disaster. Multiple personnel should have the latest version of the plans to ensure that the plans can be retrieved if primary personnel are unavailable when the plan is needed.

Exam Preparation Tasks

Review All Key Topics

Review the most important topics in this chapter, noted with the Key Topics icon in the outer margin of the page. Table 9-1 lists a reference of these key topics and the page numbers on which each is found.

Table 9-1 Key Topics for Chapter 9

Key Topic Element	Description	Page Number
Paragraph	Business continuity and disaster recovery concepts	369
Paragraph	Causes of disasters	371
List	BIA steps	373
Paragraph	Critical asset terms	374
List	SP 800-34 R1 steps	378
List	Alternate locations	383
List	Backup types and schemes	389
List	Electronic backup terms	392
List	High-availability terms	392
List	BCP teams	394
List	BCP tests	396

Complete the Tables and Lists from Memory

Print a copy of the CD Appendix A, "Memory Tables," or at least the section for this chapter, and complete the tables and lists from memory. The CD Appendix B, "Memory Tables Answer Key," includes completed tables and lists to check your work.

Define Key Terms

Define the following key terms from this chapter and check your answers in the glossary:

disruption, non-disaster disruption, disaster, catastrophe, technological disasters, man-made disasters, natural disasters, reliability, maximum tolerable downtime (MTD), mean time to repair (MTTR), mean time between failure (MTBF), recovery time objective (RTO), work recovery time (WRT), recovery point objective (RPO), hot site, cold site, warm site, tertiary site, reciprocal agreement, mutual aid agreement, redundant site, mirrored site, full backup, differential backup, incremental backup, copy backup, daily backups, transaction log backup, failover, failsoft.

Review Questions

1. What is a catastrophe?

    a. a temporary interruption that occurs due to malfunction or failure

    b. a suddenly occurring event that has a long-term negative impact on life

    c. a disaster that has a much wider and much longer impact than other disasters

    d. a disaster that occurs when a device fails

2. What is the first step in a business impact analysis (BIA)?

    a. Identify recovery priorities.

    b. Identify outage impacts, and estimate downtime.

    c. Identify resource requirements.

    d. Identify critical processes and resources.

3. What is recovery time objective (RTO)?

    a. the shortest time period after a disaster or disruptive event within which a resource or function must be restored to avoid unacceptable consequences

b. the point in time to which the disrupted resource or function must be returned

c. the maximum amount of time that an organization can tolerate a single resource or function being down

d. the average time required to repair a single resource or function when a disaster or disruption occurs

4. Which term is used for a leased facility that contains all the resources needed for full operation?

    a. cold site

    b. hot site

    c. warm site

    d. tertiary site

5. Which of the following is NOT a backup type?

    a. full

    b. incremental

    c. grandfather\father\son

    d. transaction log

6. Which electronic backup type stores data on optical disks and uses robotics to load and unload the optical disks as needed?

    a. optical jukebox

    b. hierarchical storage management

    c. tape vaulting

    d. replication

7. What is failsoft?

    a. the capacity of a system to switch over to a backup system if a failure in the primary system occurs

    b. the capability of a system to terminate non-critical processes when a failure occurs

    c. a software product that provides load-balancing services

    d. high capacity storage devices that are connected by a high-speed private network using storage-specific switches

8. Which team is NOT defined as part of the business continuity plan (BCP)?

    a. media relations team

    b. security team

    c. recovery team

    d. human resources team

9. Which test is the most cost-effective and efficient way to identify areas of overlap in the plan before conducting higher-level testing?

    a. table-top exercise

    b. checklist test

    c. parallel test

    d. simulation test

10. What is the first step in business continuity planning according to NIST SP 800-34 R1?

    a. Conduct Business Impact Analysis (BIA).

    b. Develop contingency planning policy.

    c. Identify preventive controls.

    d. Create recovery strategies.

Answers and Explanations

1. **c.** A catastrophe is a disaster that has a much wider and much longer impact than other disasters. A non-disaster disruption is a temporary interruption that occurs due to malfunction or failure. A disaster is a suddenly occurring event that has a long-term negative impact on life. A technological disaster is a disaster that occurs when a device fails.

2. **d.** The first step in a BIA is to identify critical processes and resources.

3. **a.** Recovery time objective (RTO) is the shortest time period after a disaster and disruptive event within which a resource or function must be restored to avoid unacceptable consequences.

4. **b.** A hot site is a leased facility that contains all the resources needed for full operation.

5. **c**. Grandfather\father\son is NOT a backup type. It is a backup rotation scheme.

6. **a**. An optical jukebox stores data on optical disks and uses robotics to load and unload the optical disks as needed.

7. **b**. Failsoft is the capability of a system to terminate non-critical processes when a failure occurs.

8. **d**. The human resources team is NOT defined as part of the BCP.

9. **a**. A table-top exercise is the most cost-effective and efficient way to identify areas of overlap in the plan before conducting higher level testing.

10. **b**. The first step in business continuity planning according to NIST SP 800-34 R1 is developing a contingency planning policy.

This chapter covers the following topics:

- **Computer crime concepts:** This section covers the different types of computer crimes, including computer-assisted crime, computer-targeted crime, incidental computer crime, and other computer crime concepts.

- **Major legal systems:** This includes civil code law, common law, criminal law, civil/tort law, administrative/regulatory law, customary law, religious law, and mixed law.

- **Intellectual property law:** This section describes intellectual property, including patents, trade secrets, trademarks, copyrights, software piracy and licensing issues, and internal protection.

- **Privacy:** This includes a discussion of personally identifiable information (PII), laws and regulations, and compliance.

- **Liability:** This section covers due care versus due diligence, negligence, and liability issues with personal information, hackers, third-party outsourcing, and contracts and procurement.

- **Incident response:** This section explains events versus incidents, incident response team and incident investigations, rules of engagement, and procedures.

- **Forensics and digital investigations:** This section explains how to identify, preserve, collect, examine, and analyze evidence and how to present findings. It also covers the IOCE/SWGDE, crime scene, MOM, chain of custody, and interviewing.

- **Evidence:** This section discusses the five rules of evidence, types of evidence, surveillance, search and seizure, media analysis, software analysis, network analysis, and hardware/embedded device analysis.

- **Security professional ethics:** This includes (ISC)^2 Code of Ethics, Computer Ethics Institute, Internet Architecture Board, and Organizational Ethics.

CHAPTER 10

Legal, Regulations, Investigations, and Compliance

Understanding applicable laws and regulations is a necessary part of any security professional's training. The security practices that an organization adopts are usually directly affected by the laws and regulations from local, state, and federal government. Tied in with this need to understand laws and regulations is the security professional's need to understand how to perform investigations. Even if the perpetrator of a security incident is discovered, the perpetrator cannot be held accountable for any crime if the individuals who performed the investigation did not adhere to appropriate investigatory laws and regulations. In the United States, the Secret Service and the Federal Bureau of Investigations (FBI) share the task of investigating computer crimes.

Computers have brought new opportunities for criminal acts to occur. Criminals are always looking for new ways to illegally break into networks and individual systems. But as we have discussed before, most security issues within an organization are perpetuated by its employees. Disgruntled employees in particular pose the greatest threat for an organization. The security professional's job is to ensure that all devices are updated in a timely manner and protected from attacks both from within and without. As we have mentioned before, there is no way to fully protect a network or system 100% of the time against 100% of the attacks, but security professionals must ensure that their organizations practice due care and due diligence as part of a comprehensive security plan.

Also keep in mind that the organization must provide a means for employees to report any computer incident or crime that they witnessed or are aware of while ensuring that employees feel safe doing so. In most cases, employees do not want to report incidents because they are afraid of being pulled into something with which they do not want to be involved. They are also often afraid of being accused of doing something that they did not do. Finally, employees might not report an incident or crime because they are not aware of the organization's security policies and procedures. Organizations should establish a culture that provides appropriate training and a means for reporting incidents.

This chapter covers all the topics regarding the legal, regulations, investigations, and compliance domain for the CISSP exam. It includes an explanation of computer crime concepts, major legal systems, intellectual property law, privacy, liability, incident response, evidence, and security professional ethics.

Foundation Topics

Computer Crime Concepts

Computer crimes today are usually made possible by a victim's carelessness. If a computer crime has occurred, proving criminal intent and causation is often difficult. Investigating and prosecuting computer crimes is made even more difficult because evidence is mostly intangible. Further affecting computer crime investigation is the fact that obtaining a trail of evidence of activities performed on a computer is hard.

Because of these computer crime issues, it is important that security professionals understand the following computer crime concepts:

- Computer-assisted crime
- Computer-targeted crime
- Incidental computer crime
- Computer prevalence crime
- Hackers versus crackers

Computer-Assisted Crime

A computer-assisted crime occurs when a computer is used as a tool to help commit a crime. This type of crime could be carried out without a computer but uses the computer to make committing the crime easier. Think of it this way: Criminals can steal confidential organizational data in many different manners. This crime is possible without a computer. But when criminals use computers to help them steal confidential organizational data, then a computer-assisted crime has occurred.

Computer-Targeted Crime

A computer-targeted crime occurs when a computer is the victim of an attack that's sole purpose is to harm the computer and its owner. This type of crime could not be carried out without a computer being used. Computer crimes that fit into this category include denial of service (DoS) and buffer overflow attacks.

Incidental Computer Crime

An incidental computer crime occurs when a computer is involved in a computer crime without being the victim of the attack or the attacker. A computer being used as a zombie in a botnet is part of an incidental computer crime.

Computer Prevalence Crime

A computer prevalence crime occurs due to the fact that computers are so widely used in today's world. This type of crime occurs only because computers exist. Software piracy is an example of this type of crime.

Hackers Versus Crackers

Hacker and *cracker* are two terms that are often used interchangeably in media but do not actually have the same meaning. Hackers are individuals who attempt to break into secure systems to obtain knowledge about the systems and possibly use that knowledge to carry out pranks or commit crimes. Crackers, on the other hand, are individuals who attempt to break into secure systems without using the knowledge gained for any nefarious purposes.

In the security world, the terms white hat, gray hat, and black hat are more easily understood and less often confused than the terms *hackers* and *crackers*. A white hat does not have any malicious intent. A black hat has malicious intent. A gray hat is considered somewhere in the middle of the two. A gray hat will break into a system, notify the administrator of the security hole, and offer to fix the security issues for a fee.

Major Legal Systems

Security professionals must understand the different legal systems that are used throughout the world and the components that make up the systems.

These systems include the following:

- Civil code law
- Common law
- Criminal law
- Civil/tort law
- Administrative/regulatory law
- Customary law
- Religious law
- Mixed law

Civil Code Law

Civil code law, developed in Europe, is based on written laws. It is a rule-based law and does not rely on precedence in any way. The most common legal system in the world, civil code law does not require lower courts to follow higher court decisions.

NOTE Do not confuse the civil code law of Europe with the United States civil/tort laws.

Common Law

Common law, developed in England, is based on customs and precedent because no written laws were available. Common law reflects on the morals of the people and relies heavily on precedence. In this system, the lower court must follow any precedents that exist due to higher court decisions. This type of law is still in use today in the United Kingdom, the United States, Australia, and Canada.

Today, common law uses a jury-based system, which can be waived so the case is decided by a judge. But the prosecution must provide guilt beyond a reasonable doubt. Common law is divided into three systems: criminal law, civil/tort law, and administrative/regulatory law.

Criminal Law

Criminal law covers any actions that are considered harmful to others. It deals with conduct that violates public protection laws. In criminal law, guilty parties might be imprisoned and/or fined. Criminal law is based on common law and statutory law. Statutory law is handed down by federal, state, or local legislating bodies.

Civil/Tort Law

In civil law, the liable party owes a legal duty to the victim. It deals with wrongs that have been committed against an individual or organization. Under civil law, the victim is entitled to compensatory, punitive, and statutory damages. Compensatory damages are those that compensate the victim for his losses. Punitive damages are those that are handed down by juries to punish the liable party. Statutory damages are those that are based on damages established by laws.

In civil law, the liable party has caused injury to the victim. Civil laws include economic damages, liability, negligence, intentional damage, property damage, personal damage, nuisance, and dignitary torts.

In the United States, civil law allows senior officials of an organization to be held liable for any civil wrongdoing by the organization. So if an organization is negligent, the senior officials can be pursued by any parties that were wronged.

Administrative/Regulatory Law

In administrative law, standards of performance or conduct are set by government agencies for organizations and industries to follow. Common areas that are covered by administrative law include public utilities, communications, banking, environment protection, and healthcare.

Customary Law

Customary law is based on the customs of a country or region. Customary law is not used in most systems in isolation, but rather incorporated into many mixed law systems, such as those used in many African countries, China, and Japan. Monetary fines or public service is the most common form of restitution in this legal system.

Religious Law

Religious law is based on religious beliefs. Although most religious law will be based on a particular religion and its primary written rules, cultural differences can vary from country to country and will affect the laws that are enforced.

Mixed Law

Mixed law combines two or more of the other law types. The most often mixed law uses civil law and common law.

Intellectual Property Law

Intellectual property law is a group of laws that recognizes exclusive rights for creations of the mind. Intellectual property is a tangible or intangible asset to which the owner has exclusive rights.

The intellectual property covered by this type of law includes the following:

- Patent
- Trade secret
- Trademark
- Copyright
- Software piracy and licensing issues

This section explains these types of intellectual properties and the internal protection of these properties.

Patent

A patent is granted to an individual or company to cover an invention that is described in the patent's application. When the patent is granted, only the patent owner can make, use, or sell the invention for a period of time, usually 20 years. Although it is considered one of the strongest intellectual property protections available, the invention becomes public domain after the patent expires, thereby allowing any entity to manufacture and sell the product.

Patent litigation is common in today's world. You commonly see technology companies, such as Apple, Hewlett-Packard, and Google, filing lawsuits regarding infringement on patents (often against each other). For this reason, many companies involve a legal team in patent research before developing new technologies. Being the first to be issued a patent is crucial in today's highly competitive market.

Any product that is produced that is currently undergoing the patent application process will usually be identified with the Patent Pending seal, shown in Figure 10-1.

Figure 10-1 Patent Pending Seal

Trade Secret

A trade secret ensures that proprietary technical or business information remains confidential. A trade secret gives an organization a competitive edge. Trade secrets include recipes, formulas, ingredient listings, and so on that must be protected against disclosure. After the trade secret is obtained by or disclosed to a competitor or the general public, it is no longer considered a trade secret.

Most organizations that have trade secrets attempt to protect these secrets using non-disclosure agreements (NDAs). These NDAs must be signed by any entity that has access to information that is part of the trade secret. Anyone who signs an NDA will suffer legal consequences if the organization is able to prove that the signer violated it.

Trademark

A trademark ensures that a symbol, sound, or expression that identifies a product or an organization is protected from being used by another organization. This trademark allows the product or organization to be recognized by the general public.

Most trademarks are marked with one of the designations shown in Figure 10-2.

If the trademark is not registered, an organization should use a capital TM. If the trademark is registered, an organization should use a capital R that is encircled.

Figure 10-2 Trademark Designations

Copyright

A copyright ensures that a work that is authored is protected for any form of reproduction or use without the consent of the copyright holder, usually the author or artist who created the original work. A copyright lasts longer than a patent. Although the U.S. Copyright Office has several guidelines to determine the amount of time a copyright lasts, the general rule for works created after January 1, 1978 is the life of the author plus 70 years.

In 1996, the World Intellectual Property Organization (WIPO) standardized the treatment of digital copyrights. Copyright management information (CMI) is licensing and ownership information that is added to any digital work. In this standardization, WIPO stipulated that CMI included in copyrighted material cannot be altered.

The symbol shown in Figure 10-3 denotes a work that is copyrighted.

Figure 10-3 Copyright Symbol

Software Piracy and Licensing Issues

To understand software piracy and licensing issues, professionals should understand the following terms that are used to differentiate between the types of software available:

- **Freeware:** Software available free of charge, including all rights to copy, distribute, and modify the software.
- **Shareware:** Software that is shared for a limited time. After a certain amount of time (the trial period), the software requires that the user purchase the software to access all the software's features. This is also referred to as trialware.
- **Commercial software:** Software that is licensed by a commercial entity for purchase in a wholesale or retail market.

Software piracy is the unauthorized reproduction or distribution of copyrighted software. Although software piracy is a worldwide issue, it is much more prevalent in Asia, Europe, Latin America, and Africa/Middle East. Part of the problem with software piracy stems from the cross-jurisdictional issues that arise. Obtaining the cooperation of foreign law enforcement agencies and government is often difficult or impossible. Combine this with the availability of the hardware needed to create pirated software and the speed with which it can be made, and you have a problem that will only increase over the coming years.

Security professionals and the organizations they work with must ensure that the organization takes measures to ensure that employees understand the implications of installing pirated software. In addition, large organizations might need to utilize an enterprise software inventory application that will provide administrators with a report on the software that is installed.

Internal Protection

As mentioned earlier in this chapter, employees are the greatest threat for any organization. For this reason, organizations should take measures to protect confidential resources from unauthorized internal access. Any information that is part of a patent, trade secret, trademark, or copyright should be marked and given the appropriate classification. Access controls should be customized for this information, and audit controls should be implemented that alert personnel should any access occur. Due care procedures and policies must be in place to ensure that any laws that protect these assets can be used to prosecute an offender.

Privacy

When considering technology and its use today, privacy is a major concern of users. This privacy concern usually covers three areas: which personal information can be shared with whom, whether messages can be exchanged confidentially, and whether and how one can send messages anonymously. Privacy is an integral part of any security measures that an organization takes.

As part of the security measures that organizations must take to protect privacy, personally identifiable information (PII) must be understood, identified, and protected. Organizations must also understand the privacy laws that governments have adopted. Finally, organizations must ensure that they comply with all laws and regulations regarding privacy.

Personally Identifiable Information (PII)

PII is any piece of data that can be used alone or with other information to identify a single person. Any PII that an organization collects must be protected in the strongest manner possible. PII includes full name, identification numbers (including driver's license number and Social Security number), date of birth, place of birth, biometric data, financial account numbers (both bank account and credit card numbers), and digital identities (including social media names and tags).

Keep in mind that different countries and levels of government can have different qualifiers for identifying PII. Security professionals must ensure that they understand international, national, state, and local regulations and laws regarding PII. As the theft of this data becomes even more prevalent, you can expect more laws to be enacted that will affect your job.

A complex listing of PII is shown in Figure 10-4.

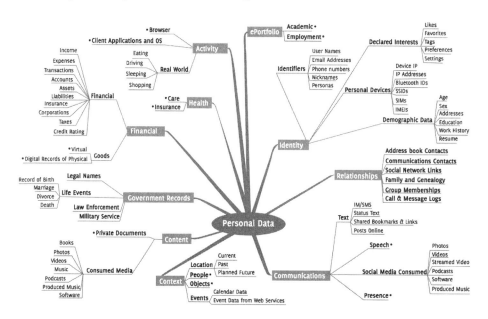

Figure 10-4 PII List

Laws and Regulations

Security professionals are usually not lawyers. As such, they are not expected to understand all the specifics of the laws that affect their organization. However, security professionals must be aware of the laws and at a minimum understand how those laws affect the operations of their organization. For example, a security professional at a healthcare facility would need to understand all security guidelines in the Health Insurance Portability and Accountability Act (HIPAA) as well as the Patient Protection and Affordable Care Act (PPACA) and Health Care and Education Reconciliation Act of 2010, commonly known as Obamacare.

NOTE At the time of publication of this book, Obamacare was not specifically part of the CISSP exam. The authors of this book are including Obamacare in anticipation of future revisions to the CISSP content.

This section discusses many of the laws that will affect a security professional. For testing purposes, you need not worry about all the details of the law. You simply need to understand the law's name(s), purpose, and the industry it affects (if applicable).

Sarbanes-Oxley (SOX) Act

The Public Company Accounting Reform and Investor Protection Act of 2002, more commonly known as the Sarbanes-Oxley (SOX) Act, affects any organization that is publicly traded in the United States. It controls the accounting methods and financial reporting for the organizations and stipulates penalties and even jail time for executive officers.

Health Insurance Portability and Accountability Act (HIPAA)

HIPAA, also known as the Kennedy-Kassebaum Act, affects all healthcare facilities, health insurance companies, and healthcare clearing houses. It is enforced by the Office of Civil Rights of the Department of Health and Human Services. It provides standards and procedures for storing, using, and transmitting medical information and healthcare data. HIPAA overrides state laws unless the state laws are stricter.

Gramm-Leach-Bliley Act (GLBA) of 1999

The Gramm-Leach-Bliley Act (GLBA) of 1999 affects all financial institutions, including banks, loan companies, insurance companies, investment companies, and credit card providers. It provides guidelines for securing all financial information and prohibits sharing financial information with third parties. This act directly affects the security of PII.

Computer Fraud and Abuse Act (CFAA)

The Computer Fraud and Abuse Act (CFAA) of 1986 affects any entities that might engage in hacking of "protected computers" as defined in the Act. It was amended in 1989, 1994, 1996; in 2001 by the Uniting and Strengthening America by Providing Appropriate Tools Required to Intercept and Obstruct Terrorism (USA PATRIOT) Act; in 2002 and in 2008 by the Identity Theft Enforcement and Restitution Act. A "protected computer" is a computer used exclusively by a financial institution or the U.S. government or used in or affecting interstate or foreign commerce or communication, including a computer located outside the United States that is used in a manner that affects interstate or foreign commerce or communication of the United States. Due to the inter-state nature of most Internet communication, any ordinary computer has come under the jurisdiction of the law, including cellphones. The law includes several definitions of hacking, including knowingly accessing a computer without authorization, intentionally accessing a computer to obtain financial records, U.S. government information, or protected computer information, and transmitting fraudulent commerce communication with the intent to extort.

Federal Privacy Act of 1974

The Federal Privacy Act of 1974 affects any computer that contains records used by a federal agency. It provides guidelines on collection, maintenance, use, and dissemination of PII about individuals that is maintained in systems of records by federal agencies on collecting, maintaining, using, and distributing PII.

Federal Intelligence Surveillance Act (FISA) of 1978

The Federal Intelligence Surveillance Act (FISA) of 1978 affects law enforcement and intelligence agencies. It was the first act to give procedures for the physical and electronic surveillance and collection of "foreign intelligence information" between "foreign powers" and "agents of foreign powers" and only applied to traffic within the United States. It was amended by the USA PATRIOT Act of 2001 and the FISA Amendments Act of 2008.

Electronic Communications Privacy Act (ECPA) of 1986

The Electronic Communications Privacy Act (ECPA) of 1986 affects law enforcement and intelligence agencies. It extended government restrictions on wiretaps from telephone calls to include transmissions of electronic data by computer and prohibited access to stored electronic communications. It was amended by the Communications Assistance to Law Enforcement Act (CALEA) of 1994, the USA PATRIOT Act of 2001, and the FISA Amendments Act of 2008.

Computer Security Act of 1987

The Computer Security Act of 1987 was superseded by the Federal Information Security Management Act (FISMA) of 2002. This Act was the first law written to require a formal computer security plan. It was written to protect and defend any of the sensitive information in the federal government systems and provide security for that information. It also placed requirements on government agencies to train employees and identify sensitive systems.

United States Federal Sentencing Guidelines of 1991

The United States Federal Sentencing Guidelines of 1991 affects individuals and organizations convicted of felonies and serious (Class A) misdemeanors. It provides guidelines to prevent sentencing disparities that existed across the United States.

Communications Assistance for Law Enforcement Act (CALEA) of 1994

The Communications Assistance for Law Enforcement Act (CALEA) of 1994 affects law enforcement and intelligence agencies. It requires telecommunications carriers and manufacturers of telecommunications equipment to modify and design their equipment, facilities, and services to ensure that they have built-in surveillance capabilities. This allows federal agencies to monitor all telephone, broadband Internet, and Voice over IP (VoIP) traffic in real time.

Personal Information Protection and Electronic Documents Act (PIPEDA)

The Personal Information Protection and Electronic Documents Act (PIPEDA) affects how private sector organizations collect, use, and disclose personal information in the course of commercial business in Canada. The Act was written to address European Union (EU) concerns over the security of PII in Canada. The law requires organizations to obtain consent when they collect, use, or disclose personal information and to have personal information policies that are clear, understandable, and readily available.

Basel II

Basel II affects financial institutions. It addresses minimum capital requirements, supervisory review, and market discipline. Its main purpose is to protect against risks the banks and other financial institutions face.

Payment Card Industry Data Security Standard (PCI DSS)

The Payment Card Industry Data Security Standard (PCI DSS) affects any organizations that handle cardholder information for the major credit card companies. The latest version is version 2.0. To prove compliance with the standard, an organization must be reviewed annually. Although it is not a law, this standard has affected the adoption of several state laws.

Federal Information Security Management Act (FISMA) of 2002

The Federal Information Security Management Act (FISMA) of 2002 affects every federal agency. It requires the federal agencies to develop, document, and implement an agency-wide information security program.

Economic Espionage Act of 1996

The Economic Espionage Act of 1996 covers a multitude of issues because of the way the Act was structured. But for the purposes of the CISSP exam, this Act affects companies that have trade secrets and any individuals who plan to use encryption technology for criminal activities. A trade secret does not need to be tangible to be protected by this Act. Per this law, theft of a trade secret is now a federal crime, and the United States Sentencing Commission must provide specific information in its reports regarding encryption or scrambling technology that is used illegally.

USA PATRIOT Act

The USA PATRIOT Act of 2001 affects law enforcement and intelligence agencies in the United States. Its purpose is to enhance the investigatory tools that law enforcement can use, including e-mail communications, telephone records, Internet communications, medical records, and financial records. When this law was enacted, it amended several other laws, including FISA and the ECPA of 1986.

Although the USA PATRIOT Act does not restrict private citizen use of investigatory tools, exceptions include if the private citizen is acting as a government agent (even if not formally employed), if the private citizen conducts a search that would require law enforcement to have a warrant, if the government is aware of the private citizen's search, or if the private citizen is performing a search to help the government.

Health Care and Education Reconciliation Act of 2010

The Health Care and Education Reconciliation Act of 2010 affects healthcare and educational organizations. For the CISSP exam, this Act increased some of the security measures that must be taken to protect healthcare information.

Employee Privacy Issues and Expectation of Privacy

Employee privacy issues must be addressed by all organizations to ensure that the organization is protected. However, organizations must give employees the proper notice of any monitoring that might be used. Organizations must also ensure that the monitoring of employees is applied in a consistent manner. Many organizations implement a no-expectation-of-privacy policy that the employee must sign after receiving the appropriate training. Keep in mind that this policy should specifically describe any unacceptable behavior. Companies should also keep in mind that some actions are protected by the Fourth Amendment. Security professionals and senior management should consult with legal counsel when designing and implementing any monitoring solution.

European Union

The EU has implemented several laws and regulations that affect security and privacy. The EU Principles on Privacy include strict laws to protect private data. The EU's Data Protection Directive provides direction on how to follow the laws set forth in the principles. The EU then created the Safe Harbor Privacy Principles to help guide U.S. organizations in compliance with the EU Principles on Privacy. Some of the guidelines include the following:

- Data should be collected in accordance with the law.
- Information collected about an individual cannot be shared with other organizations unless given explicit permission by the individual.
- Information transferred to other organizations can only be transferred if the sharing organization has adequate security in place.
- Data should be used only for the purpose for which it was collected.
- Data should be used only for a reasonable period of time.

NOTE Do not confuse the term *safe harbor* with *data haven*. According to the EU, a safe harbor is an entity that conforms to all the requirements of the EU Principles on Privacy. A data haven is a country that fails to legally protect personal data with the main aim being to attract companies engaged in the collection of the data.

The EU Electronic Security Directive defines electronic signature principles. In this directive, a signature must be uniquely linked to the signer and to the data to which it relates so that any subsequent data change is detectable. The signature must be capable of identifying the signer.

Export/Import Issues

Many organizations today develop trade relationships with organizations that are located in other countries. Organizations must be aware of the export and import laws of the countries of both the source and destination countries. Encryption technologies are some of the most restricted technologies in regard to import and export laws. Although the United States does limit the export of encryption technologies for national security reasons, other countries, such as China and Russia, limit the import of these same technologies because the countries do not want their citizens to have access to them.

Any organization that engages in export and import activities with entities based in other countries should ensure that legal counsel is involved in the process so that all laws and regulations are followed.

Compliance

Organizations must ensure that they are in compliance with all laws and regulations, including international regulations and laws. Senior management can no longer claim ignorance in regard to negligence of the organization. Because laws and regulations are constantly being enacted by government agencies, organizations must ensure that security professionals obtain the proper training to ensure compliance. As mentioned earlier in this section, the organization should obtain proper legal counsel to provide adequate protection against future prosecution, both for the organization and its senior management.

Liability

Liability is the status of being legally responsible to another entity because of your actions or negligence. With the advent of recent laws that hold senior management responsible for organizational liability, organizations and their senior management can no longer afford to turn a blind eye to security issues. Liability is one of the most important concepts in law so security professionals should be aware of its implications.

Security professionals must understand several liability concepts:

- Due diligence versus due care
- Negligence
- Liability issues, including personal information, hackers, third-party outsourcing, contracts, procurements, and vendors

Due Diligence Versus Due Care

Due diligence and *due care* are two related terms that affect liability. Due diligence means that an organization understands the security risks that it faces. Due care means that an organization takes all the actions it can reasonably take to prevent security issues or to mitigate damage if security breaches occur. Due care and due diligence often go hand-in-hand but must be understood separately before they can be considered together.

Due diligence is all about gathering information. Organizations must institute the appropriate procedures to determine any risks to organizational assets. Due diligence then provides the information necessary to ensure that the organization practices due care. Without adequate due diligence, due care cannot occur.

Due care is all about action. Organizations must institute the appropriate protections and procedures for all organizational assets, especially intellectual property. In due care, failure to meet minimum standards and practices is considered negligent. If an organization does not take actions that a prudent person would have taken under similar circumstances, the organization is negligent.

As you can see, due diligence and due care have a dependent relationship. When due diligence occurs, organizations will recognize areas of risk. Examples include an organization determining that regular personnel do not understand basic security issues, that printed documentation is not being discarded appropriately, and that employees are accessing files to which they should not have access. When due care occurs, organizations take the areas of identified risk and implement plans to protect against the risks. For the identified due diligence examples, due care examples to implement include providing personnel security awareness training, putting procedures into place for proper destruction of printed documentation, and implementing appropriate access controls for all files.

NOTE *Risk* is a term that is commonly associated with due diligence and due care. For more information on risk management, refer to Chapter 4, "Information Security Governance and Risk Management."

Negligence

Negligence means that an organization was careless and as a result of being careless, some person or organization was injured. Negligence serves as a basis for lawsuits. On any given day, examples exist of organizations who are being accused of negligence, and often these negligence suits involve legal action against senior management. Under the principle of culpable negligence, senior management can be held liable for losses that result from computer system breaches if senior management did not ensure that the organization exercised due care in protecting computer resources.

Penalties that an organization can accrue due to negligence can include both civil and criminal penalties. Civil penalties usually result in compensation being paid to the victim, and criminal penalties can result in fines and jail time. For this reason, organizations must ensure that unreasonable risks are prevented. *Proximate cause* is a term that is associated with negligence. Proximate cause proves that an injury to one party occurred due to the negligence of another party.

Liability Issues

As stated earlier, liability is the status of being legally responsible to another entity because of your actions or negligence. But often liability is not thoroughly understood because organizations do not fully analyze downstream liability.

Downstream liability refers to liability that an organization accrues due to partnerships with other organizations and customers. For example, consider an organization that does not have the appropriate procedures in place to ensure that its firewall has the security updates that it needs. If hackers later break into the network through this security hole and steal data used for identity theft, the customers can then sue the organization for negligence. This is an example of a downstream liability. Liability issues that an organization must consider include personal information, hackers, third-party outsourcing, and contracts and procurements.

As mentioned in the earlier section on PII, organizations have a legal obligation to protect any PII that it is collecting as well as the assets on which the PII resides. Organizations must also ensure that the appropriate procedures are in place to ensure that personnel do not inadvertently disclose PII by training personnel on proper handling procedures.

Hackers are most often interested in seeing how far their skills will take them. They often deviate from the accepted norms of security. Security professionals must ensure that they keep up with the latest techniques and tools used by hackers. Hackers often use tools such as Crack, John the Ripper, Nessus, Saint, Nmap, and L0phtCrack. Security professionals can then use these tools in an ethical manner to perform their own internal penetration testing.

Third-party outsourcing is also a liability that many organizations do not consider as part of their risk assessment. Any outsourcing agreement must ensure that the information that is entrusted to the other organization is protected by the proper security measures to fulfill all the regulatory and legal requirements.

Similar to third-party outsourcing, contract and procurement processes must be formalized. Organizations should establish procedures for managing all contracts and procurements to ensure that they include all the regulatory and legal requirements. Periodic reviews should occur to ensure that the contractual organization is complying with the guidelines of the contract.

Incident Response

Incident response is vital to every organization to ensure that any security incidents are detected, contained, and investigated. Incident response is the beginning of any investigation. After an incident has been discovered, incident response personnel perform specific tasks. During the entire incident response, the incident response team must ensure that they follow proper procedures to ensure that evidence is preserved.

As part of incident response, security professionals must understand the difference between events and incidents (see the following section). The incident response team must have the appropriate incident response procedures in place to ensure that the incident is handled, but the procedures must not hinder any forensic investigations that might be needed to ensure that parties are held responsible for any illegal actions. Security professionals must understand the rules of engagement and the authorization and scope of any incident investigation.

Event Versus Incident

In regard to incident response, a basic difference exists between events and incidents. An *event* is a change of state that occurs. Whereas events include both negative and positive events, incident response focuses more on negative events—events that have been deemed as negatively impacting the organization. An *incident* is a series of events that negatively impact an organization's operations and security.

Events can only be detected if an organization has established the proper auditing and security mechanisms to monitor activity. A single negative event might occur. For example, the auditing log might show that an invalid login attempt occurred. By itself, this login attempt is not a security concern. However, if many invalid login attempts occur over a period of a few hours, the organization might be undergoing an attack. The initial invalid login is considered an event, but the series of invalid login attempts over a few hours would be an incident, especially if it is discovered that the invalid login attempts all originated from the same IP address.

Incident Response Team and Incident Investigations

When establishing the incident response team, organizations must consider the technical knowledge of each individual. The members of the team must understand the organization's security policy and have strong communication skills. Members should also receive training in incident response and investigations.

When an incident has occurred, the primary goal of the team is to contain the attack and repair any damage caused by the incident. Security isolation of an incident scene should start immediately when the incident is discovered. Evidence must be preserved, and the appropriate authorities should be notified.

The incident response team should have access to the incident response plan. This plan should include the list of authorities to contact, team roles and responsibilities, an internal contact list, securing and preserving evidence procedures, and a list of investigations experts who can be contacted for help. A step-by-step manual should be created that the incident response team must follow to ensure that no steps are skipped. After the incident response process has been engaged, all incident response actions should be documented.

If the incident response team determines that a crime has been committed, senior management and the proper authorities should be contacted immediately.

Rules of Engagement, Authorization, and Scope

An organization ought to document the rules of engagement, authorization, and scope for the incident response team. The rules of engagement define which actions are acceptable and unacceptable if an incident has occurred. The authorization and scope provide the incident response team with the authority to perform an investigation and with the allowable scope of any investigation they must undertake.

The rules of engagement act as a guideline for the incident response team to ensure that they do not cross the line from enticement into entrapment. Enticement occurs when the opportunity for illegal actions is provided (luring) but the attacker makes his own decision to perform the action, and entrapment means to encourage someone to commit a crime that the individual might have had no intention of committing. Enticement is legal but does raise ethical arguments and might not be admissible in court. Conversely, entrapment is illegal.

Incident Response Procedures

When performing incident response, it is important that the incident response team follow incident response procedures. Depending on where you look, you might find different steps or phases included as part of the incident response process.

For the CISSP exam, you need to remember the following steps:

1. Detect the incident.
2. Respond to the incident.
3. Report the incident to the appropriate personnel.
4. Recover from the incident.
5. Remediate all components affected by the incident to ensure that all traces of the incident have been removed.
6. Review the incident, and document all findings.

The actual investigation of the incident occurs during the respond, report, and recover steps. Following appropriate forensic and digital investigation processes during the investigation can ensure that evidence is preserved.

The incident response process is shown in Figure 10-5.

Figure 10-5 Incident Response Process

NOTE To learn more about the incident response procedures, refer to the "Incident Response Management" section in Chapter 8.

Forensic and Digital Investigations

Computer investigations require different procedures than regular investigations because the timeframe for the investigator is compressed and an expert might be required to assist in the investigation. Also, computer information is intangible and often requires extra care to ensure that the data is retained in its original format. Finally, the evidence in a computer crime is much more difficult to gather.

After a decision has been made to investigate a computer crime, you should follow standardized procedures, including the following:

- Identify what type of system is to be seized.
- Identify the search and seizure team members.
- Determine the risk that the suspect will destroy evidence.

After law enforcement has been informed of a computer crime, the organization's investigator's constraints are increased. Turning the investigation over to law enforcement to ensure that evidence is preserved properly might be necessary.

When investigating a computer crime, evidentiary rules must be addressed. Computer evidence should prove a fact that is material to the case and must be reliable. The chain of custody must be maintained. Computer evidence is less likely to be admitted in court as evidence if the process for producing it must be documented.

Any forensic investigation involves the following steps:

1. Identification
2. Preservation
3. Collection
4. Examination
5. Analysis
6. Presentation
7. Decision

The forensic investigation process is shown in Figure 10-6.

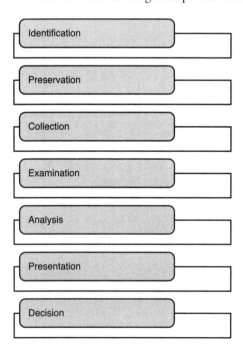

Figure 10-6 Forensic Investigation Process

The following sections cover these forensic investigation steps in detail as well as explain IOCE/SWGDE, the crime scene, MOM, the chain of custody, and interviewing.

Identify Evidence

The first step in any forensic investigation is to identify and secure the crime scene and identify the evidence. Identifying the evidence is done through reviewing audit logs, monitoring systems, analyzing user complaints, and analyzing detection mechanisms. Initially, the investigators might be unsure of which evidence is important. Preserving evidence that you might not need is always better than wishing you had evidence that you did not retain.

Identifying the crime scene is also part of this step. In digital investigations, the attacked system is considered the crime scene. In some cases, the system from which the attack originated can also be considered part of the crime scene. However, fully capturing the attacker's systems is not always possible. For this reason, you should ensure that you capture any data that can point to a specific system, such as capturing IP addresses, user names, and other identifiers.

Preserve and Collect Evidence

The next steps in forensic investigations include preserving and collecting evidence. This involves making system images, implementing chain of custody (which is discussed in detail in its own section later), documenting the evidence, and recording timestamps.

Before collecting any evidence, consider the order of volatility. This order ensures that investigators collect evidence from the components that are most volatile first.

The order of volatility is as follows:

1. Memory contents
2. Swap files
3. Network processes
4. System processes
5. File system information
6. Raw disk blocks

To make system images, you need to use a tool that creates a bit-level copy of the system. In most cases, you must isolate the system and remove it from production to create this bit-level copy. You should ensure that two copies of the image are retained. One copy of the image will be stored to ensure that an undamaged, accurate copy is available as evidence. The other copy will be used during the examination and analysis steps. Message digests should be used to ensure data integrity.

Although the system image is usually the most important piece of evidence, it is not the only piece of evidence you need. You might also need to capture data that is stored in cache, process tables, memory, and the registry. When documenting a computer attack, you should use a bound notebook to keep notes.

Remember that using experts in digital investigations to ensure that evidence is properly preserved and collected might be necessary. Investigators usually assemble a field kit to help in the investigation process. This kit might include tags and labels, disassembly tools, and tamper-evident packaging. Commercial field kits are available, or you could assemble your own based on organizational needs.

Examine and Analyze Evidence

After evidence has been preserved and collected, the investigator then needs to examine and analyze the evidence. While examining evidence, any characteristics, such as timestamps and identification properties, should be determined and documented. After the evidence has been fully analyzed using scientific methods, the full incident should be reconstructed and documented.

Present Findings

After an examination and analysis of the evidence, it must be presented as evidence in court. In most cases when presenting evidence in court, presenting the findings in a format the audience can understand is best. Although an expert should be used to testify as to the findings, it is important that the expert be able to articulate to a nontechnical audience the details of the evidence.

Decide

At the end of the court proceeding, a decision will be made as to the guilt or innocence of the accused party. At that time, evidence will no longer need to be retained. However, documenting any lessons learned from the incident is important. Any individuals involved in any part of the investigation should be a part of this lessons-learned session.

IOCE/SWGDE

The International Organization on Computer Evidence (IOCE) and Scientific Working Group on Digital Evidence (SWGDE) are two groups that study digital forensics and help to establish standards for digital investigations. Both groups release guidelines on many formats of digital information, including computer data, mobile device data, automobile computer systems data, and so on. Any investigators should ensure that they comply with the principles from these groups.

The main principles as documented by IOCE are as follows:

- The general rules of evidence should be applied to all digital evidence.
- Upon seizing digital evidence, actions taken should not change that evidence.
- When a person needs to access original digital evidence, that person should be suitably trained for the purpose.
- All activity relating to the seizure, access, storage, or transfer of digital evidence must be fully documented, preserved, and available for review.
- An individual is responsible for all actions taken with respect to digital evidence while the digital evidence is in his possession.

Crime Scene

A crime scene is the environment in which potential evidence exists. After the crime scene has been identified, steps should be taken to ensure that the environment is protected, including both the physical and virtual environment. To secure the physical crime scene, an investigator might need to isolate the systems involved by removing them from a network. However, the systems should NOT be powered down until the investigator is sure that all digital evidence has been captured. Remember: Live computer data is dynamic and is possibly stored in several volatile locations.

Access to the crime scene should be tightly controlled and limited only to individuals who are vital to the investigation. As part of the documentation process, make sure to note anyone who has access to the crime scene. After a crime scene is contaminated, no way exists to restore it to the original condition.

MOM

Documenting motive, opportunity, and means (MOM) is the most basic strategy for determining suspects. *Motive* is all about why the crime was committed and who committed the crime. *Opportunity* is all about where and when the crime occurred. *Means* is all about how the crime was carried out by the suspect. Any suspect that is considered must possess all three of these qualities. For example, a suspect might have a motive for a crime (being dismissed from the organization) and an opportunity for committing the crime (user accounts were not disabled properly) but might not possess the means to carry out the crime.

Understanding MOM can help any investigator narrow down the list of suspects.

Chain of Custody

At the beginning of any investigation, you should ask the questions who, what, when, where, and how. These questions can help get all the data needed for the chain of custody. The chain of custody shows who controlled the evidence, who secured the evidence, and who obtained the evidence. A proper chain of custody must be preserved to successfully prosecute a suspect. To preserve a proper chain of custody, the evidence must be collected following predefined procedures in accordance with all laws and regulations.

The primary purpose of the chain of custody is to ensure that evidence is admissible in court. Law enforcement officers emphasize chain of custody in any investigations that they conduct. Involving law enforcement early in the process during an investigation can help to ensure that the proper chain of custody is followed.

Interviewing

An investigation often involves interviewing suspects and witnesses. One person should be in charge of all interviews. Because evidence needs to be obtained, ensuring that the interviewer understands what information needs to be obtained and all the questions to cover is important. Reading a suspect his rights is ONLY necessary if law enforcement is performing the interview. Recording the interview might be a good idea to provide corroboration later when the interview is used as evidence.

If an employee is suspected of a computer crime, a representative of the human resources department should be involved in any interrogation of the suspect. The employee should only be interviewed by an individual who is senior to that employee.

Evidence

For evidence to be admissible, it must be relevant, legally permissible, reliable, properly identified, and properly preserved. *Relevant* means that it must prove a material fact related to the crime in that it shows a crime has been committed, can provide information describing the crime, can provide information regarding the perpetuator's motives, or can verify what occurred. *Reliability* means that it has not been tampered with or modified. *Preservation* means that the evidence is not subject to damage or destruction.

All evidence must be tagged. When creating evidence tags, be sure to document the mode and means of transportation, a complete description of evidence including quality, who received the evidence, and who had access to the evidence.

Any investigator must ensure that evidence adheres to the five rules of evidence (see the following section). In addition, the investigator must understand each type of evidence that can be obtained and how each type can be used in court. Investigators must follow surveillance, search, and seizure guidelines. Finally, investigators must understand the differences among media, software, network, and hardware/embedded device analysis.

Five Rules of Evidence

When gathering evidence, an investigator must ensure that the evidence meets the five rules that govern it:

- Be authentic.
- Be accurate.
- Be complete.
- Be convincing.
- Be admissible.

Because digital evidence is more volatile than other evidence, it still must meet these five rules.

Types of Evidence

An investigator must be aware of the types of evidence used in court to ensure that all evidence is admissible. Sometimes the type of evidence determines its admissibility.

The types of evidence that you should understand are as follows:

- Best evidence
- Secondary evidence
- Direct evidence
- Conclusive evidence
- Circumstantial evidence
- Corroborative evidence
- Opinion evidence
- Hearsay evidence

Best Evidence

The best evidence rule states that when evidence, such as a document or recording, is presented, only the original will be accepted unless a legitimate reason exists for why the original cannot be used. In most cases, digital evidence is not considered best evidence because investigators must capture *copies* of the original data and state.

However, courts can apply the best evidence rule to digital evidence in a case-by-case basis, depending on the evidence and the situation. In this situation, the copy must be proved by an expert witness who can testify as to the contents and confirm that it is an accurate copy of the original.

Secondary Evidence

Secondary evidence has been reproduced from an original or substituted for an original item. Copies of original documents and oral testimony are considered secondary evidence.

Direct Evidence

Direct evidence proves or disproves a fact through oral testimony based on information gathered through the witness's senses. A witness can testify on what he saw, smelled, heard, tasted, or felt. This is considered direct evidence. Only the witness can give direct evidence. No one else can report on what the witness told them because that is considered hearsay evidence.

Conclusive Evidence

Conclusive evidence does not require any other corroboration and cannot be contradicted by any other evidence.

Circumstantial Evidence

Circumstantial evidence provides inference of information from other intermediate relevant facts. This evidence makes a jury come to a conclusion by using a fact to imply that another fact is true or untrue. An example is implying that a former employee committed an act against an organization due to his dislike of the organization after his dismissal.

Corroborative Evidence

Corroborative evidence supports another piece of evidence. For example, if a suspect produces a receipt to prove he was at a particular restaurant at a certain time and then a waitress testifies that she waited on the suspect, then the waitress provides corroborating evidence through her testimony.

Opinion Evidence

Opinion evidence is based on what the witness thinks, feels, or infers regarding the facts. However, if an expert witness is used, that expert is able to testify on a fact based on his knowledge in a certain area. For example, a psychiatrist can testify as to conclusions on a suspect's state of mind. Expert testimony is not considered opinion evidence because of the expert's knowledge and experience.

Hearsay Evidence

Hearsay evidence, as mentioned earlier, is evidence that is secondhand where the witness does not have direct knowledge of the fact asserted but knows it only from being told by someone. In some cases, computer-based evidence is considered hearsay, especially if an expert cannot testify as to the accuracy and integrity of the evidence.

Surveillance, Search, and Seizure

Surveillance, search, and seizure are important facets of any investigation. Surveillance is the act of monitoring behavior, activities, or other changing information, usually of people. Search is the act of pursuing items or information. Seizure is the act of taking custody of physical or digital components.

Two types of surveillance are used by investigators: physical surveillance and computer surveillance. Physical surveillance occurs when a person's actions are reported or captured using cameras, direct observance, or closed-circuit TV (CCTV). Computer surveillance occurs when a person's actions are reported or captured using digital information, such as audit logs.

A search warrant is required in most cases to actively search a private site for evidence. For a search warrant to be issued, probable cause that a crime has been committed must be proven to a judge. The judge must also be given corroboration regarding the existence of evidence. The only time a search warrant does not need to be issued is during exigent circumstances, which are emergency circumstances that are necessary to prevent physical harm, the evidence destruction, the suspect's escape, or some other consequence improperly frustrating legitimate law enforcement efforts. Exigent circumstances will have to be proven when the evidence is presented in court.

Seizure of evidence can only occur if the evidence is specifically listed as part of the search warrant unless the evidence is in plain view. Evidence specifically listed in the search warrant can be seized, and the search can only occur in areas specifically listed in the warrant.

Search and seizure rules do not apply to private organizations and individuals. Most organizations warn their employees that any files stored on organizational resources are considered property of the organization. This is usually part of any no-expectation-of-privacy policy.

Media Analysis

Investigators can perform many types of media analysis, depending on the media type.

The following types of media analysis can be used:

- **Disk imaging:** Creates an exact image of the contents of the hard drive.
- **Slack space analysis:** Analyzes the slack (marked as empty or reusable) space on the drive to see whether any old (marked for deletion) data can be retrieved.
- **Content analysis:** Analyzes the contents of the drive and gives a report detailing the types of data by percentage.
- **Steganography analysis:** Analyzes the files on a drive to see whether the files have been altered or to discover the encryption used on the file.

Software Analysis

Software analysis is a little harder to perform because it often requires the input of an expert on software code.

Software analysis techniques include the following:

- **Content analysis:** Analyzes the content of software, particularly malware, to determine for which purpose the software was created.
- **Reverse engineering:** Retrieves the source code of a program to study how the program performs certain operations.
- **Author identification:** Attempts to determine the software's author.
- **Context analysis:** Analyzes the environment the software was found in to discover clues to determining risk.

Network Analysis

Network analysis involves the use of networking tools to provide logs and activity for evidence.

Network analysis techniques include the following:

- **Communications analysis:** Analyzes communication over a network by capturing all or part of the communication and searching for particular types of activity.
- **Log analysis:** Analyzes network traffic logs.
- **Path tracing:** Tracing the path of a particular traffic packet or traffic type to discover the route used by the attacker.

Hardware/Embedded Device Analysis

Hardware/embedded device analysis involves using the tools and firmware provided with devices to determine the actions that were performed on and by the device. The techniques used to analyze the hardware/embedded device vary based on the device. In most cases, the device vendor can provide advice on the best technique to use depending on what information you need. Log analysis, operating system analysis, and memory inspections are some of the general techniques used.

Security Professional Ethics

Ethics for any profession are the right and wrong actions that are the moral principle of that occupation. Security professionals, particularly those who hold the CISSP certification, should understand the ethics that are published by the International Information Systems Security Certification Consortium (ISC)^2, the Computer Ethics Institute, the Internet Architecture Board (IAB), and the organization they are employed by.

(ISC)^2 Code of Ethics

(ISC)^2 provides a strict Code of Ethics for its certificate holders. All certificate holders must follow the Code of Ethics. Any reported violations of the code are investigated. Certificate holders who are found to be guilty of violation will have their certification revoked.

The four mandatory canons for the Code of Ethics are as follows:

- Protect society, the common good, necessary public trust and confidence, and the infrastructure.
- Act honorably, honestly, justly, responsibly, and legally.
- Provide diligent and competent service to principals.
- Advance and protect the profession.

Any certificate holders are required to report any actions by other certificate holders that they feel are in violation of the Code. If a certificate holder is reported, a peer review committee will investigate the actions and make a decision as to the certificate holder's standing.

Certification is a privilege that must be earned and maintained. Certificate holders are expected to complete certain educational requirements to prove their continued competence in all aspects of security. They are also expected to promote the understanding and acceptance of prudent information security measures.

Computer Ethics Institute

The Computer Ethics Institute created the Ten Commandments of Computer Ethics. The following list summarizes these ten ethics:

- Do not use a computer for harm.
- Do not interfere with the computer work of other people.
- Do not snoop around in the computer files of other people.
- Do not use a computer to steal.
- Do not use a computer to lie.
- Do not install and use licensed software unless you have paid for it.
- Do not use another person's computer unless you have permission or have paid the appropriate compensation for said usage.
- Do not appropriate another person's intellectual output.
- Consider the consequences of the program you are writing or the system you are designing.
- Always use a computer in ways that ensure consideration and respect of other people and their property.

Internet Architecture Board

The IAB oversees the design, engineering, and management of the Internet. This board meets regularly to review Internet standardization recommendations. Internet ethics is just a small part of the area they cover. Ethics statements issued by the IAB usually detail any acts that they deem irresponsible. These actions include wasting resources, destroying data integrity, compromising privacy, and accessing resources that users are not authorized to access.

Request for Comments (RFC) 1087, called Ethics and the Internet, is the specific IAB document that outlines unethical Internet behavior. Refer to http://tools.ietf.org/html/rfc1087 for more information.

Organizational Ethics

Organizations should develop an internal ethics statement and ethics program. By adopting a formal statement and program, the organization is stressing to its employees that they are expected to act in an ethical manner in all business dealings.

Several laws in the United States can affect the development and adoption of an organizational ethics program. If an organization adopts an ethics program, the liability of the organization is often limited, even when the employees are guilty of wrongdoing, provided the organization ensures that personnel have been instructed on the organization's ethics.

Exam Preparation Tasks

Review All Key Topics

Review the most important topics in this chapter, noted with the Key Topics icon in the outer margin of the page. Table 10-1 lists a reference of these key topics and the page numbers on which each is found.

Table 10-1 Key Topics for Chapter 10

Key Topic Element	Description	Page Number
List	Computer crime concepts	406
List	Major legal systems	407
List	Intellectual property concepts	409
List	Software types	412

Key Topic Element	Description	Page Number
List	Liability concepts	420
List	Incident response procedures	425
List	Forensic investigation steps	426
List	Order of volatility	427
List	Five rules of evidence	431
List	Types of evidence	431
List	Media analysis types	434
List	Software analysis types	434
List	Network analysis types	435
List	(ISC)² Four Canons of Code of Ethics	436

Define Key Terms

Define the following key terms from this chapter and check your answers in the glossary:

computer-assisted crime, computer-targeted crime, incidental computer crime, computer prevalence crime, civil code law, common law, civil/tort law, compensatory damages, punitive damages, statutory damages, criminal law, administrative law, regulatory law, customary law, religious law, mixed law, patent, trade secret, trademark, copyright, software piracy, freeware, shareware, trialware, commercial software, personally identifiable information (PII), Public Company Accounting Reform and Investor Protection Act of 2002, Sarbanes-Oxley (SOX) Act, Health Insurance Portability and Accountability Act (HIPAA), Kennedy-Kassebaum Act, Gramm-Leach-Bliley Act (GLBA) of 1999, Computer Fraud and Abuse Act (CFAA) of 1986, protected computer, Federal Privacy Act of 1974, Federal Intelligence Surveillance Act (FISA) of 1978, Electronic Communications Privacy Act (ECPA) of 1986, Computer Security Act of 1987, United States Federal Sentencing Guidelines of 1991, Communications Assistance for Law Enforcement Act (CALEA) of 1994, Personal Information Protection and Electronic Documents Act (PIPEDA), Basel II, Payment Card Industry Data Security Standard (PCI DSS), Federal Information Security Management Act (FISMA) of 2002, Economic Espionage Act of 1996, Uniting and Strengthening America by Providing Appropriate Tools Required to Intercept and Obstruct Terrorism (USA PATRIOT) Act of 2001, Health Care and

Education Reconciliation Act of 2010, liability, due diligence, due care, negligence, downstream liability, crime scene, MOM, motive, opportunity, means, best evidence rule, secondary evidence, direct evidence, conclusive evidence, circumstantial evidence, corroborative evidence, opinion evidence, hearsay evidence, surveillance, search, seizure, physical surveillance, computer surveillance, disk imaging, slack space analysis, content analysis, and steganography analysis.

Review Questions

1. Which type of crime occurs when a computer is used as a tool to help commit a crime?

    a. computer-assisted crime

    b. incidental computer crime

    c. computer-targeted crime

    d. computer prevalence crime

2. Which type of law system is based on written laws and does not use precedence?

    a. common law

    b. civil code law

    c. criminal law

    d. customary law

3. Which of the following protects intellectual property such as a symbol, sound, or expression that identifies a product or an organization from being used by another organization?

    a. patent

    b. copyright

    c. trademark

    d. trade secret

4. What is another name for the Public Company Accounting Reform and Investor Protection Act of 2002?

    a. Kennedy-Kassebaum Act

    b. USA PATRIOT

    c. Obamacare

    d. Sarbanes-Oxley Act

5. Which term is the status of being legally responsible to another entity because of your actions or negligence?

   a. liability

   b. due care

   c. due diligence

   d. negligence

6. What is the first step of the incident response process?

   a. Respond to the incident.

   b. Detect the incident.

   c. Report the incident.

   d. Recover from the incident.

7. What is the second step of the forensic investigations process?

   a. Identification

   b. Collection

   c. Preservation

   d. Examination

8. Which of the following is NOT one of the five rules of evidence?

   a. Be accurate.

   b. Be complete.

   c. Be admissible.

   d. Be volatile.

9. Which type of evidence has been reproduced from an original or substituted for an original item?

   a. secondary evidence

   b. best evidence

   c. hearsay evidence

   d. direct evidence

10. Which of the following is NOT one of the four mandatory canons of the (ISC)² Code of Ethics?

    a. Provide diligent and competent service to principals.

    b. Always use a computer in ways that ensure consideration and respect of other people and their property.

    c. Advance and protect the profession.

    d. Act honorably, honestly, justly, responsibly, and legally.

Answers and Explanations

1. **a**. A computer-assisted crime occurs when a computer is used as a tool to help commit a crime. An incidental computer crime occurs when a computer is involved in a computer crime without being the victim of the attack or the attacker. A computer-targeted crime occurs when a computer is the victim of an attack in which the sole purpose is to harm the computer and its owner. A computer prevalence crime occurs due to the fact that computers are so widely used in today's world.

2. **b**. Civil code law is based on written laws and does not use precedence. Common law is the type of law based on customs and precedent because no written laws were available. Criminal law is the type of law that covers any actions that are considered harmful to others. Customary law is the type of law based on the customs of a country or region.

3. **c**. A trademark ensures that a symbol, sound, or expression that identifies a product or an organization is protected from being used by another organization. A patent is granted to an individual or company to cover an invention that is described in the patent's application. A copyright ensures that a work that is authored is protected from any form of reproduction or use without the consent of the copyright holder, usually the author or artist that created the original work. A trade secret gives an organization a competitive edge. Trade secrets include recipes, formulas, ingredient listings, and so on that must be protected against disclosure.

4. **d**. Another name for the Public Company Accounting Reform and Investor Protection Act of 2002 is the Sarbanes-Oxley Act. The Health Insurance Portability and Accountability Act is also known as the Kennedy-Kassebaum Act. The Uniting and Strengthening America by Providing Appropriate Tools Required to Intercept and Obstruct Terrorism Act is also known as the USA PATRIOT Act. The Health Care and Education Reconciliation Act of 2010 is also known as Obamacare.

5. **a.** Liability is the status of being legally responsible to another entity because of your actions or negligence. Due care means that an organization takes all the actions it can reasonably take to prevent security issues or to mitigate damage if security breaches occur. Due diligence means that an organization understands the security risks that it faces. Negligence means that an organization was careless and as a result of being careless, some person or organization was injured.

6. **b.** The steps of the incident response process are as follows:
    1. Detect the incident.
    2. Respond to the incident.
    3. Report the incident to the appropriate personnel.
    4. Recover from the incident.
    5. Remediate all components affected by the incident to ensure that all traces of the incident have been removed.
    6. Review the incident, and document all findings.

7. **c.** The steps of the forensic investigation process are as follows:
    1. Identification
    2. Preservation
    3. Collection
    4. Examination
    5. Analysis
    6. Presentation
    7. Decision

8. **d.** The five rules of evidence are as follows:
    - Be authentic.
    - Be accurate.
    - Be complete.
    - Be convincing.
    - Be admissible.

9. **a.** Secondary evidence has been reproduced from an original or substituted for an original item. Best evidence is an original item, such as an original document. Hearsay evidence is secondhand where the witness does not have direct knowledge of the fact asserted but knows it only from being told by someone. Direct evidence proves or disproves a fact through oral testimony based on information gathered through the witness's senses.

10. **b.** The four mandatory canons of the (ISC)² Code of Ethics are as follows:

    - Protect society, the common good, necessary public trust and confidence, and the infrastructure.
    - Act honorably, honestly, justly, responsibly, and legally.
    - Provide diligent and competent service to principals.
    - Advance and protect the profession.

This chapter covers the following topics:

- **Geographical threats:** Covers threats related to geography, including internal, external, natural, man-made, system, and politically motivated.

- **Site and facility design:** Describes defense models and concepts related to a secure site or facility such as Crime Prevention Through Environmental Design (CPTED), layered defense models, physical security plans, and facility selection issues.

- **Perimeter security:** Discusses the protection of the facility perimeter including gates, fences, perimeter intrusion protection, lighting, patrol forces, and perimeter access control.

- **Building and internal security:** Surveys important issues inside the facility such as doors, locks, biometrics, glass entries, visitor control, equipment room, and work area protection.

- **Environmental security:** Topics include fire protection, power supply, HVAC, water leakage and flooding, and the proper use of environmental alarms.

- **Equipment security:** Discusses proper corporate procedures designed to protect equipment; includes discussion on safes and vaults.

- **Personnel privacy and safety:** Covers guidelines for maintaining personnel privacy and safety alongside security.

CHAPTER 11

Physical (Environmental) Security

Many of the threats we have discussed are logical in nature; that is, they are attacks that can take place over a network. However, throughout this book the importance of preventing physical access to assets has been emphasized. This chapter undertakes a final and complete treatment of preventing intentional and unintentional damage to facilities, equipment, and people.

Foundation Topics

Geographical Threats

Many threats are a function of the geographic location of the office or facility. This section discusses a wide variety of threats and issues, some of which only apply to certain areas. The security professional must be prepared to anticipate and mitigate those issues.

Internal Versus External Threats

When talking about threats to the physical security of assets, we can frame the conversation by threats that appear from outside the organization and those that come from within the organization. Many of the mitigation techniques discussed in the following sections are designed to address maintaining perimeter security or access to the building or room, whereas other techniques are designed to address threats from those who might have some access to the room or building.

For example, an electric fence surrounding the facility is designed to prevent access to the building by those who should not have *any* access (an external threat), whereas a door lock system on the server room that requires a swipe of the employee card is designed to prevent access by those who are already in the building (an internal threat). Keep this in mind as you read the following sections.

Natural Threats

Many of the physical threats that must be addressed and mitigated are caused by the forces of nature. Building all facilities to withstand the strongest hurricanes, tornadoes, and earthquakes is not economically feasible because in many areas these events happen infrequently if ever. What *can* be done is to make a realistic assessment of the historical weather conditions of an area and perform a prudent cost-benefit analysis to determine which threats should be addressed and which should be accepted. This section discusses some of the major natural threats.

Hurricane/Tropical Storm

In certain areas, hurricanes and tropical storms are so frequent and unpredictable that all buildings are required to be capable of withstanding the more moderate instances of these storms. In other areas, doing that makes no sense even though these storms do occur from time to time. The location of the facility should dictate how much is spent in mitigating possible damages from these events.

Tornadoes

Although events of the last few years might seem to contradict this, over the long haul certain areas are more prone to tornadoes than others. A study of the rate and severity of tornadoes in an area from a historical perspective can help to determine measures that make sense for a particular location.

NOTE In recent tornado outbreaks, many cellphone towers were knocked out completely. In rural areas especially, communication with loved ones was next to impossible. In the Alabama tornado outbreak in April 2001, it took many individuals up to 72 hours to locate loved ones because of lack of communications. You can see how this loss of communication would affect a company, school, or even a hospital.

Earthquakes

Earthquakes should be treated in the same way as hurricanes, tropical storms, and tornadoes; that is, the location of the specific facility dictates the amount of preparation and the measures to take to address this risk. For example, facilities in California might give this issue more attention than those in the southeastern United States where these events are extremely rare.

Floods

Always take flooding into consideration because it is an event that can occur with the right circumstances just about anywhere. If at all possible, keep computing systems and equipment off the floor, and build server rooms and wiring closets on raised floors to help prevent damage that could occur in even a small flood.

System Threats

Some of the threats that exist are not from the forces of nature but from failures in systems that provide basic services, such as electricity and utilities. Although these problems can sometimes arise from events of nature, in this section we discuss guidelines for preparing and dealing with these events, which can occur in any location and in any type of weather conditions.

Electrical

Electricity is the lifeline of the organization and especially in regard to computing systems, outages are not only an inconvenience, but they can also damage equipment and cause loss of data. Moreover, when the plug is pulled, to a large degree the enterprise grinds to a halt in today's world.

For this reason, all mission-critical systems should have Uninterruptable Power Supplies (UPS) that can provide power on a short-term basis until the system can be cleanly shut down. In cases where power must be maintained for longer than a matter of minutes, make onsite generators available to provide the power to keep systems running on a longer term basis until power is restored.

Noise, humidity, and brownouts are also issues that affect the electricity supply. The recommended optimal relative humidity range for computer operations is 40% to 60%. Critical systems must be protected from both power sags and surges. Neither is good for equipment. Line conditioners placed between the system and the power source can help to even out these fluctuations and prevent damage.

Finally, the most prevalent cause of computer center fires is electrical distribution systems. Checking these systems regularly can identify problems before they occur.

Communications

Protecting the physical security of communication, such as email, telephone, and fax systems, is a matter of preventing unauthorized access to the physical communication lines (cables and so on) and physical and logical access to equipment used to manage these systems.

For example, in the case of email, the email servers should be locked away and access to them over the network must be tightly controlled with usernames and complex passwords.

In the case of fax machines, implementing policies and procedures can prevent sensitive faxes from becoming available to unauthorized persons. In some cases, preventing certain types of information from being transmitted with faxes might be necessary.

Many phone systems now have been merged into the data network using Voice over IP (VoIP). With these systems, routers and switches might be involved in managing the phone system and should be physically locked away and logically protected from network access in the same fashion as email servers. Because email and VoIP both use the data network, ensure that cabling is not exposed to tampering and malicious destruction.

Some additional considerations that can impact disaster recovery are

- Maintain fault tolerant connections to the Internet, such as when the primary connection is T1 but there is a backup dial-up or satellite connection.

- Establish phone connections to employees besides primary organizational phone connections. Know cellphone and home numbers for employee notification.

- Establish radio communications over the entire campus with repeater antennas to provide communication during emergencies. Many primary forms of communication (such as phone lines and cellphones) can go down.

NOTE To learn more about disasters and disaster recovery, refer to Chapter 9, "Business Continuity and Disaster Recovery."

Utilities

Some utilities systems, such as gas and water, can be routed into the facility through ducts and tunnels that might provide an unauthorized entry point to the building. Such ducts and tunnels that offer this opportunity should be monitored with sensors and access control mechanisms.

Any critical parts of the systems where cut-off valves and emergency shutdown systems are located should be physically protected from malicious tampering. In some cases covering and protecting these valves and controls using locking cages might be beneficial.

Man-Made Threats

Although many of the physical threats we face are a function of natural occurrences and random events, some of them are purposeful. This section explores some of the physical threats faced from malicious and careless humans. These threats come from both external forces and internal forces.

Explosions

Explosions can be both intentional and accidental. Intentional explosions can occur as a result of political motivation (covered in more detail in the section "Politically Motivated Threats") or they can simply be vandalism. Accidental explosions can be the result of a failure to follow procedures and the failure of physical components.

With regard to intentional explosions, the best defense is to prevent access to areas where explosions could do significant damage to the enterprise's operational components, such as server rooms, wiring closets, and areas where power and utilities enter the building. When an intentional explosion occurs, typically thought has been given to locating the explosive where the most harm can be done, so those areas should get additional physical protection.

Fire

Fires can happen anywhere and thus are a consideration at all times. Later in this chapter, you learn about both fire suppression and fire detection techniques. Address the threat of fire in the contexts of both an accident and an intentional attack. An *auxiliary station alarm* might be beneficial in many cases. This mechanism automatically causes an alarm originating in a data center to be transmitted over the local municipal fire or police alarm circuits for relaying to both the local police/fire station and the appropriate headquarters.

Fires can be classified using a standard system as shown in the following list. Later in this chapter, we talk about the proper extinguisher or suppression system for each type.

Class A	Ordinary combustibles
Class B	Flammable liquids, flammable gases
Class C	Electrical equipment
Class D	Combustible metals
Class K	Cooking oil or fat

With respect to construction materials, according to (ISC)², all walls must have a two-hour minimum fire rating in an information processing facility. Knowing that the most prevalent cause of computer center fires is electrical distribution systems is also useful. Regardless of the fire source, the first action to take is evacuating all personnel.

Vandalism

Vandalism in most cases results in defacement of walls, bathrooms, and such, but when critical components are accessible, it can impact operations. Cut cables and smashed devices are reasons stressed in preventing physical access to these components.

Even when all measures have been taken, vandalism can still cause problems. For example, a purposefully plugged toilet can flood a floor and damage equipment if undetected.

Fraud

In the context of physical security, fraud involves gaining access to systems, equipment, or the facility through deception. For example, a person who enters the facility posing as a serviceman or a person who tailgates and follows an employee through the card system are both forms of fraudulent physical access. Physical access control systems become critical to preventing this type of fraud and the damage it can lead to.

Theft

Preventing physical theft of company assets depends on preventing physical access to the facility. Physical theft is the risk that will most likely affect confidentiality, integrity, and availability (CIA). For assets that leave the facility, such as laptops, give thought to protecting sensitive data that might exist on them through the use of encryption, preferably through encrypted drives.

Collusion

Collusion occurs when two employees work together to accomplish a theft of some sort that could not be accomplished without their combined knowledge or responsibilities. In several chapters, you have read about using proper separation of duties to prevent a single person from controlling enough of a process to hide their actions.

Limiting the specific accesses of operations personnel forces an operator into collusion with an operator of a different category to have access to unauthorized data. Collusion is much less likely to occur from a statistical standpoint than a single person operating alone. When you consider this fact, the tradeoff in exchanging one danger for another is justified.

Politically Motivated Threats

Although it might seem at times like many more politically motivated threats exist today, these threats have always existed. The enterprise is often unwillingly dragged into these confrontations if they are seen as contributing to whatever the issue of the day might be. These threats can be costly in terms of lost productivity, destruction of company assets, and even physical danger to employees and officers of the company. This section covers some of the major ways these threats can manifest themselves along with measures to take that can lessen or mitigate the risk they present.

Strikes

Although strikes might be the least dangerous of the threats in this list, they can still damage the enterprise. In countries like the United States, basic rules of order have been established that prevent the worst of the possible outcomes, but even then an orderly strike can cost productivity and can hurt the image of the company. In other countries, strikes can be much more dangerous, especially when other political issues become intertwined with monetary issues.

Riots

Riots often occur seemingly out of nowhere, although typically an underlying issue explodes at some single incident. These events can be very dangerous as large mobs will often participate in activities that none of the individuals would normally do on their own. Often times the enterprise is seen as a willing participant in some perceived slight or wrong suffered by the rioters. In that case the company and its assets become a large and somewhat easy target.

Civil Disobedience

Civil disobedience is the intentional refusal to obey certain laws, demands, and commands of a government and is commonly, though not always, defined as being nonviolent resistance. One of the typical by-products of this is a disruption of some process to bring attention to the perceived injustice of the law or rule being broken.

It might also manifest itself as an action against some practice by the enterprise that might not be illegal but might be seen by some groups as harmful in some way. When this is the case the physical security of the facility becomes important as in some cases action might be taken to harm the facility.

Terrorist Acts

Increasingly, the threats of terrorist activity have caused a new focus on not only the security of facilities both at home and abroad but also of the physical safety of workers and officers. In many cases certain industries have found it beneficial to include emergency planning designed to address terrorist acts. Reactions to common scenarios are rehearsed to ensure the best possible outcome in the case of an attack.

Bombing

Bombing of facilities or company assets, once a rare occurrence, is no longer so in many parts of the world today. Increasingly, the enterprise is driven to include such considerations as local disturbance levels and general political unrest in an area before company sites are chosen. In many cases the simple threat of a bomb is enough to engage evacuation plans that are both costly and disruptive. Despite this, evacuation plans that address terrorist threats and bombings have become an integral part of any security policy, especially in certain parts of the world.

NOTE To learn more about disasters and disaster recovery, refer to Chapter 9.

Site and Facility Design

For many forward-thinking organizations, physical security considerations begin during site selection and design. These companies have learned that building in security is easier than patching the security after the fact. In this section, site selection and site building practices that can lead to increased physical security are covered.

Layered Defense Model

All physical security should be based in a *layered defense model*. In such a model, reliance should not be based on any single physical security concept but on the use of multiple approaches that support one another. The theory is that if one tier of defense (say, for example, perimeter security) fails that another layer will serve as a backup (such as locks on the server room door). Layering the concepts discussed in this chapter can strengthen the overall physical security.

CPTED

Crime Prevention Through Environmental Design (CPTED) refers to designing the facility from the ground up to support security. It is actually a broad concept that can be applied to any project (housing developments, office buildings, and retail establishments). It addresses the building entrance, landscaping, and interior design. It aims to create behavioral effects that reduce crime. The three main strategies that guide CPTED are covered in this section.

Natural Access Control

The natural access control concept applies to the entrances of the facility. It encompasses the placement of the doors, lights, fences, and even landscaping. It aims to satisfy security goals in the least obtrusive and aesthetically appealing manner. A single object can be designed in many cases to fulfill multiple security objectives.

For example, many buildings have bollards or large posts in the front of the building with lights on them. These objects serve a number of purposes. They protect the building entrance from cars being driven into it. The lights also brighten the entrance and discourage crime, and finally they can guide people to the entrance.

Natural access control also encourages the idea of creating *security zones* in the building. These areas can be labeled, and then card systems can be used to prevent access to more sensitive areas. This concept also encourages a minimization of entry points and a tight control over those entry points. It also encourages a separate entrance in the back for suppliers that is not available or highly visible to the public.

Natural Surveillance

Natural surveillance is the use of physical environmental features to promote visibility of all areas and thus discourage crime in those areas. The idea is to encourage the flow of people such that the largest possible percentage of the building is always populated, because people in an area discourage crime. It also attempts to maximize the visibility of all areas.

Natural Territorials Reinforcement

The goal of natural territorials reinforcement is to create a feeling of community in the area. It attempts to extend the sense of ownership to the employees. It also attempts to make potential offenders feel that their activities are at risk of being discovered. This is often implemented in the form of walls, fences, landscaping, and light design.

Physical Security Plan

Another important aspect of site and facility design is the proper convergence between the physical layout and the physical security plan. Achieving all the goals of CPTED is not always possible, and in cases where gaps exist, the physical security plan should include policies and/or procedures designed to close any gaps. The plan should address the following issues.

Deter Criminal Activity

Both the layout and supporting policies should deter criminal activity. For example, as many areas as possible should be open and easily seen. There should be a minimum of isolated and darkened areas. Signage that indicates cameras or onsite monitoring and the presence of guards can also serve as deterrents.

Delay Intruders

Another beneficial characteristic of the physical security plan is to add impediments to entry, such as locks, fences, and barriers. Any procedures that slow and monitor the entry of people into the facility can also help. The more delay the intruder encounters, the less likely he is to choose the facility and the more likely he is to be caught.

Detect Intruders

Systems and procedures should be in place that allow for criminal activity to be detected. Motion sensors, cameras, and the like are all forms of intruder detection. Logging all visitors could also be a form of deterrence.

Assess Situation

The plan should identify specific personnel and actions to be taken when an event occurs. Compiling a list of incident types that indicate an acceptable response, response time, and contact names might be beneficial. Written plans developed ahead of time provide a much more effective and consistent response.

Respond to Intrusions and Disruptions

The plan should also attempt to anticipate and develop appropriate responses to intruders and to common disruptions (power outages, utility problems, and so on). Although anticipating every potential event is impossible, creating a list covering possible intrusions and disruptions should be doable. Scripted responses can then be developed to ensure a consistent and predictable response to these events from all personnel.

Facility Selection Issues

When an organization moves to a new facility or enlarges an existing one, it is a great opportunity to include physical security issues in the site selection process or in the expansion plan. In this section, we look at some critical items to consider if this opportunity presents itself.

Visibility

The amount of visibility desired depends on the organization and the processes being carried out at the facility. In some cases having high visibility of the location to help promote the brand or for convenience of customers is beneficial. In other cases a lower profile is desired when sensitive operations are taking place. When this is the case, the likelihood of eavesdropping from outside the facility through windows should be considered. Considering common areas is also important. If possible, these areas should not be isolated or darkened. Place them in visible areas with lighting to discourage crime. This includes hallways, parking lots, and other shared areas.

Surrounding Area and External Entities

Considering the environment in which the facility is located is also important. What type of neighborhood is it? Is it an area that has a high crime rate, or is it isolated? Isolation can be good, but it also invites crime that might go undetected for a longer period of time. Also consider the distance to police stations, medical facilities, and fire stations as well. Finally, consider the nature of the operations of the surrounding businesses. Do they pose any sort of threat to your operations?

Accessibility

The ease with which employees and officers can access the facility is a consideration. What are the traffic conditions that the employees will encounter? If this is a new facility replacing an old one, is it inconvenient for the bulk of the employees? Do you risk losing employees over the commute? Is this location convenient to transportation options, such as train stations and airports? If lots of travel is required by your employees, accessibility could be important. If you often host employees from other locations on a temporary basis or host business partners, are safe accommodations nearby?

Construction

The materials used to construct the facility are another critical issue. But the issues to consider here do not stop at simply the makeup of the walls and ceilings, although that is crucial. It should also take into consideration the support systems built into the building. A complete list of items to look at includes

- Walls
- Doors
- Ceilings
- Windows
- Flooring
- HVAC
- Power source
- Utilities

- Fire detection and suppression

Some special considerations include the following:

- According to (ISC)², all walls must have a two-hour minimum fire resistant rating.
- Doors must resist forcible entry.
- Location and type of fire suppression systems should be known.
- Flooring in server rooms and wiring closets should be raised to help mitigate flooding damage.
- Backup and alternate power sources should exist.
- Separate AC units must be dedicated and air quality/humidity should be controlled for data centers and computer rooms.

Internal Compartments

In many areas of a facility, partitions are used to separate work areas. These partitions although appearing to be walls are not full walls in that that they do not extend all the way to the ceiling. When this construction approach is combined with a drop ceiling, also common in many buildings, an opportunity exists for someone to gain access to an adjoining room through the drop ceiling. All rooms that need to be secured, such as server rooms and wiring closets, should not have these types of walls.

Computer and Equipment Rooms

While we are on the subject of rooms that contain equipment to which physical access should be controlled, such as those that contain sensitive servers and crucial network gear, computer and equipment rooms should be locked at all times and secured and fitted with the following safeguards:

- Locate computer and equipment room in the center of the building, when possible.
- Computer and equipment rooms should have a single access door or point of entry.
- Avoid the top floors of buildings for computer and equipment rooms.
- Install and frequently test fire detection and suppression systems.
- Install raised flooring.

- Install separate power supplies for computer and equipment rooms when possible.
- Use only solid doors.

Perimeter Security

When considering the perimeter security of a facility, taking a holistic approach, sometimes known as the *concentric circle* approach, is sometimes helpful (see Figure 11-1). This approach relies on creating layers of physical barriers to information.

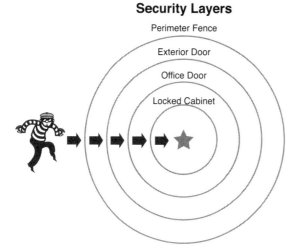

Figure 11-1 Concentric Circle Approach

In this section, we'll look at implementing this concept in detail.

Gates and Fences

The outermost ring in the concentric circle approach is comprised of the gates and fences that surround the facility. Within that are interior circles of physical barriers, each of which has its own set of concerns. In this section, considerations for barriers (bollards), fences, gates, and walls are covered.

Barriers (Bollards)

Barriers called *bollards* have become quite common around the perimeter of new office and government buildings. These are short vertical posts placed at the building's entrance way and lining sidewalks that help to provide protection from vehicles that might either intentionally or unintentionally crash into or enter the building or injure pedestrians. They can be made of many types of materials. The ones shown in Figure 11-2 are stainless steel.

Figure 11-2 Stainless Steel Bollards

Fences

Fencing is the first line of defense in the concentric circle paradigm. When selecting the type of fencing to install, consider the determination of the individual you are trying to discourage. Use the following guidelines with respect to height:

- Three to four feet tall fences deter only casual intruders.
- Six to seven feet tall fences are too tall to climb easily.
- Eight feet and taller fences deter more determined intruders, especially when augmented with razor wire.

Gates

Gates can be weak points in a fence if not handled correctly. Gates are rated by the Underwriters Laboratory in the following way. Each step up in class requires additional levels of protection.

Class 1: Residential use

Class 2: Commercial usage

Class 3: Industrial usage

Class 4: Restricted area

Walls

In some cases walls might be called for around a facility. When that is the case, and when perimeter security is critical, intrusion detection systems can be deployed to alert you of any breaching of the walls. These types of systems are covered in more detail in the next section.

Perimeter Intrusion Detection

Regardless of whether you use fences or walls, or even if you decide to deploy neither of these impediments, you can significantly reduce your exposure by deploying one of the following types of perimeter intrusion detection systems. All the systems described next are considered physical intrusion detection methods.

Infrared Sensors

Passive infrared systems (PIR) operate by identifying changes in heat waves in an area. Because the presence of an intruder would raise the temperature of the surrounding air particles, this system alerts or sounds an alarm when this occurs.

Electromechanical Systems

Electromechanical systems operate by detecting a break in an electrical circuit. For example, the circuit might cross a window or door and when the window or door is opened the circuit is broken, setting off an alarm of some sort. Another example might be a pressure pad placed under the carpet to detect the presence of individuals.

Photoelectric Systems

Photometric or photoelectric systems operate by detecting changes in the light and thus are used in windowless areas. They send a beam of light across the area and if the beam is interrupted (by a person, for example) the alarm is triggered.

Acoustical Detection Systems

Acoustical systems use strategically placed microphones to detect any sound made during a forced entry. These systems only work well in areas where there is not a lot of surrounding noise. They are typically very sensitive, which would cause many false alarms in a loud area, such as a door next to a busy street.

Wave Motion Detector

These devices generate a wave pattern in the area and detect any motion that disturbs the wave pattern. When the pattern is disturbed, an alarm sounds.

Capacitance Detector

These devices emit a magnetic field and monitor that field. If the field is disrupted, which will occur when a person enters the area, the alarm will sound.

CCTV

Closed-circuit television system (CCTV) uses sets of cameras that can either be monitored in real time or can record days of activity that can be viewed as needed at a later time. In very high security facilities, these are usually monitored. One of the main benefits of using CCTV is that it increases the guard's visual capabilities. Guards can monitor larger areas at once from a central location. CCTV is a category of physical surveillance, not computer/network surveillance.

Lighting

One of the best ways to deter crime and mischief is to shine a light on the areas of concern. In this section, we look at some types of lighting and some lighting systems that have proven to be effective. Lighting is considered a physical control for physical security.

Types of Systems

The security professional must be familiar with several types of lighting systems:

- **Continuous lighting:** An array of lights that provide an even amount of illumination across an area
- **Standby lighting:** A type of system that illuminates only at certain times or on a schedule
- **Movable lighting:** Lighting that can be repositioned as needed

- **Emergency lighting:** Lighting systems with their own power source to use when power is out

Types of Lighting

A number of options are available when choosing the illumination source or type of light. The following are the most common choices:

- **Fluorescent:** Very low pressure mercury-vapor gas-discharge lamp that uses fluorescence to produce visible light
- **Mercury vapor:** Gas-discharge lamp that uses an electric arc through vaporized mercury to produce light
- **Sodium vapor:** Gas-discharge lamp that uses sodium in an excited state to produce light
- **Quartz lamps:** A lamp consisting of an ultraviolet light source, such as mercury vapor, contained in a fused-silica bulb that transmits ultraviolet light with little absorption

Regardless of the light source, it will be rated by its *feet of illumination*. When positioning the lights, you must take this rating into consideration. For example, if a controlled light fixture mounted on a 5-meter pole can illuminate an area 30 meters in diameter, for security lighting purposes, the distance between the fixtures should be 30 feet. Moreover, there should be extensive exterior perimeter lighting of entrances or parking areas to discourage prowlers or casual intruders.

Patrol Force

An excellent augmentation to all other detection systems is the presence of a guard patrolling the facility. This option offers the most flexibility in reacting to whatever occurs. One of the keys to success is adequate training of the guards so they are prepared for any eventuality. There should be a prepared response for any possible occurrence. One of the main benefits of this approach is that guards can use discriminating judgment based on the situation, which automated systems cannot do.

Access Control

When granting physical access to the facility, a number of guidelines should be followed with respect to record keeping. Every successful and unsuccessful attempt to enter the facility, including those instances where admission was granted, should be recorded as follows:

- Date and time
- Specific entry point
- User ID employed during the attempt

Building and Internal Security

Although perimeter security is important, security within the building is also important as prescribed in the concentric circle model. This section covers issues affecting the interior of the facility.

Doors

A variety of door types and door materials can be used in buildings. They can either be hollow, which are used inside the building or solid, typically used at the edge of the building and in places where additional security is required. Some door types with which the security professional should be familiar and prepared to select for protection are

- **Vault doors:** Leading into walk-in safes or security rooms
- **Personnel doors:** Used by humans to enter the facility
- **Industrial doors:** Large doors that allow access to larger vehicles
- **Vehicle access doors:** Doors to parking building or lots
- **Bullet-resistant doors:** Doors designed to withstand firearms

Door Lock Types

Door locks can either be mechanical or electronic. *Electric locks* or *cipher locks* use a key pad that require the correct code to open the lock. These are programmable and organizations that use them should change the password frequently. Another type of door security system is a *proximity authentication device*, with which a programmable card is used to deliver an access code to the device either by swiping the card or in some cases just being in the vicinity of the reader. These devices typically contain the following *Electronic Access Control (EAC)* components:

- An electromagnetic lock
- A credential reader
- A closed door sensor

Turnstiles and Mantraps

Two special types of physical access control devices, mantraps and turnstiles, require mention as well. Although you might be familiar with a turnstile, which can be opened by scanning or swiping an access card, a mantrap is an unusual system with which you might not be familiar.

A *mantrap* is a series of two doors with a small room between them. The user is authenticated at the first door and then allowed into the room. At that point, additional verification occurs (such as a guard visually identifying the person) and then she is allowed through the second door. These doors are typically used only in very high security situations. Mantraps also typically require that the first door is closed, prior to enabling the second door to open. Figure 11-3 shows a mantrap design.

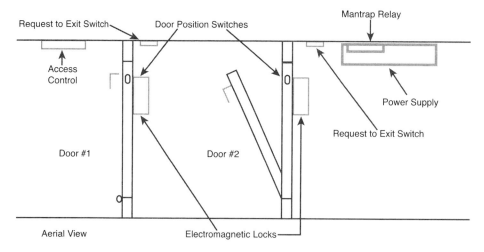

Figure 11-3 Mantrap

Locks

Locks are also used in places other than doors, such as protecting cabinets and securing devices. Types of mechanical locks with which you should be familiar are

- **Warded locks:** These have a spring-loaded bolt with a notch in it. The lock has wards or metal projection inside the lock with which the key will match and enable opening the lock. A warded lock design is shown in Figure 11-4.

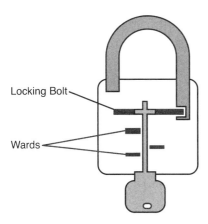

Figure 11-4 Warded Lock

- **Tumbler locks:** These have more moving parts than the warded lock, and the key raises the lock metal piece to the correct height. A tumbler lock design is shown in Figure 11-5.

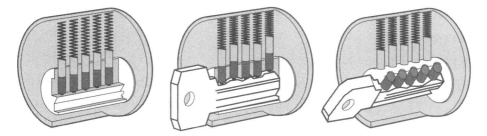

Figure 11-5 Tumbler Lock

- **Combination locks:** These require rotating the lock in a pattern that, if correct, lines the tumblers up, opening the lock. A combination lock design is shown in Figure 11-6.

In the case of device locks, laptops are the main item that must be protected because they are so easy to steal. Laptops should never be left in the open without being secured to something solid with a *cable lock*. These are vinyl-coated steel cables that connect to the laptop and then lock around an object.

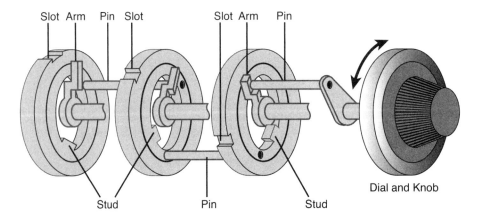

Figure 11-6 Combination Lock

Biometrics

The highest level of physical access control and the most expensive to deploy is a biometric device. Biometric devices are covered extensively in Chapter 2, "Access Control."

Glass Entries

Glass entryways include windows, glass doors, and glass walls, which have become common in many facilities. The proper glass must be selected for the situation. You should be familiar with the following types of glass:

- **Standard:** Used in residential area and is easily broken
- **Tempered:** Created by heating the glass, which gives it extra strength
- **Acrylic:** Made of polycarbonate acrylic; is much stronger than regular glass but produces toxic fumes when burned
- **Laminated:** Two sheets of glass with a plastic film between, which makes breaking it more difficult

In areas where regular glass must be used but security is a concern, glass can be used that is embedded with wire to reduce the likelihood of breaking and entering. An even stronger option is to supplement the windows with steel bars.

Visitor Control

Some system of identifying visitors and controlling their access to the facility must be in place. The best system is to have a human present to require all visitors to sign in before entering. If that is unfeasible, another option is to provide an entry point at which visitors are presented with a locked door and a phone that can be used to call and request access. Either of these methods helps to prevent unauthorized persons from simply entering the building and going where they please.

Another best practice with regard to visitors is to always accompany a contractor or visitor to their destination to help ensure they are not going where they shouldn't. In low security situations, this practice might not be necessary but is recommended in high security areas. Finally, log all visits as discussed in the "Access Control" section earlier in this chapter.

Equipment Rooms

Lock any areas where equipment is stored, and control access to them. Having a strict inventory of all equipment so theft can be discovered is also important. For data centers and server rooms, the bar is raised even higher. There will be more on this topic later in this section.

Work Areas

Some system should be in place to separate areas by security. Some specific places where additional security measures might be required are discussed in this section. Most of these measures apply to both visitors and employees. Prohibiting some employees from certain areas might be beneficial.

Secure Data Center

Data centers must be physically secured with lock systems and should *not* have drop ceilings. Some additional considerations for rooms that contain lots of expensive equipment are

- They should *not* be located on top floors or in basements.
- An off switch should be located near the door for easy access.
- Separate HVAC for these rooms is recommended.
- Environmental monitoring should be deployed to alert of temperature or humidity problems.
- Floors should be raised to help prevent water damage.
- All systems should have a UPS with the entire room connected to a generator.

Restricted Work Area

The facility might have areas that must be restricted to only the workers involved, even from other employees. In these cases physical access systems must be deployed using smart cards, proximity readers, keypads, or any of the other physical access mechanisms described in this book.

Environmental Security

Although most considerations concerning security revolve around preventing mischief, preventing damage to data and equipment from environmental conditions is also the responsibility of the security team because it addresses the *availability* part of the CIA triad. In this section, some of the most important considerations are covered.

Fire Protection

Fire protection has a longer history than many of the topics discussed in this book, and while the traditional considerations concerning preventing fires and fire damage still hold true, the presence of sensitive computing equipment requires different approaches to detection and prevention, which is the topic of this section.

Fire Detection

Several options are available for fire detection. You should be familiar with the following basic types of fire detection systems:

- **Smoke-activated:** Operates using a photoelectric device to detect variations in light caused by smoke particles.

- **Heat-activated (also called heat-sensing):** Operates by detecting temperature changes. These can either alert when a predefined temperature is met or alert when the rate of rise is a certain value.

- **Flame-actuated:** Optical devices that "look at" the protected area. They generally react faster to a fire than non-optical devices do.

Fire Suppression

Although certainly fire extinguishers (covered earlier in this chapter) are a manual form of fire suppression, other more automated systems also exist. You should be familiar with the following sprinkler system types:

- **Wet pipe:** Use water contained in pipes to extinguish the fire. In some areas, the water might freeze and burst the pipes, causing damage. These are also not recommended for rooms where equipment will be damaged by the water.
- **Dry pipe:** In this system, the water is not held in the pipes but in a holding tank. The pipes hold pressurized air, which is reduced when fire is detected allowing the water to enter the pipe and the sprinklers. This minimizes the chance of an accidental discharge. Figure 11-7 shows a comparison of wet and dry systems.

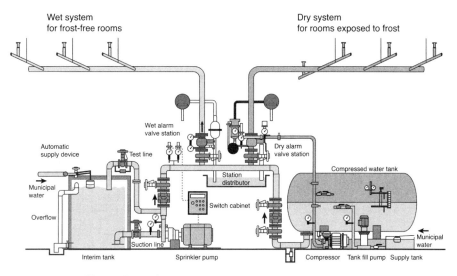

Figure 11-7 Wet and dry pipe systems

- **Preaction:** Operates like a dry pipe system except that the sprinkler head holds a thermal-fusible link that must be melted before the water is released. This is currently the recommended system for a computer room.
- **Deluge:** Allows large amounts of water to be released into the room, which obviously makes this not a good choice where computing equipment will be located.

At one time, fire suppression systems used Halon gas, which works well by suppressing combustion through a chemical reaction. However, these systems are no longer used because they have been found to damage the ozone layer.

EPA-approved replacements for Halon include:

- Water
- Argon
- NAF-S-III

Another fire suppression system that can be used in computer rooms that will not damage computers and is safe for humans is FM-200.

Power Supply

The power supply is the lifeblood of the enterprise and all of its equipment. In this section, we look common power issues and some of the prevention mechanisms and mitigation techniques that will allow the company to continue to operate when power problems arise.

Types of Outages

When discussing power issues, you should be familiar with the following terms:

- **Surge:** A prolonged high voltage
- **Brownout:** A prolonged drop in power that is below normal voltage
- **Fault:** A momentary power outage
- **Blackout:** A prolonged power outage
- **Sags:** A momentary reduction in the level of power

However, possible power problems go beyond partial or total loss of power. Power lines can introduce noise and interfere with communications in the network. In any case where large electric motors or source of certain types of light, such as florescent lighting, are present, shielded cabling should be used to help prevent Radio Frequency Interference (RFI) and Electromagnetic Interference (EMI).

Preventative Measures

Procedures to prevent static electricity from damaging components should also be observed. Some precautions to take are

- Use anti-static sprays.
- Maintain proper humidity levels.
- Use anti-static mats and wrist bands.

To protect against dirty power (sags and surges) and both partial and total power outages, the following devices can be deployed:

- **Power conditioners:** Go between the wall outlet and the device and smooth out the fluctuations of power delivered to the device, protecting against sags and surges.
- **Uninterruptible power supplies (UPS):** Go between the wall outlet and the device and use a battery to provide power if the source from the wall is lost.

HVAC

The heating and air conditioning systems are not just there for the comfort of the employees. The massive amounts of computing equipment deployed by most enterprises are even more dependent on these systems than humans. They won't complain; they'll just stop working. Computing equipment and infrastructure devices like routers and switches do not like the following conditions:

- **Heat:** Excessive heat causes reboots and crashes
- **Humidity:** Causes corrosion problems with connections
- **Low humidity:** Dry conditions encourage static electricity, which can damage equipment

With respect to temperature, some important facts to know are:

- At 100 degrees, damage starts occurring to magnetic media; in fact, floppy diskettes are the most susceptible to this.
- At 175 degrees, damage starts occurring to computers and peripherals.
- At 350 degrees, damage starts occurring to paper products.

In summary, the conditions need to be perfect for these devices. It is for this reason that AC units should be dedicated to the information processing facilities and on a separate power source than the other HVAC systems.

Water Leakage and Flooding

As much as computing systems dislike heat, they dislike water even more. It also can cause extensive damage to flooring, walls, and the facility foundation. Water detectors should be placed under raised floors and over dropped ceilings so that leaks in the ceiling and water under the floors are detected before they cause a problem.

Speaking of raised floors, in areas such as wiring closets, data centers, and server rooms, *all* floors should be raised to provide additional margin for error in the case of rising water.

Environmental Alarms

An error that causes a system to be vulnerable because of the environment in which it is installed is called an *environmental error*. Considering the various challenges presented by the environmental demands placed on the facility by the computing equipment and the costs of failing to address these needs, it behooves the enterprise to have some system that alerts when environmental conditions are less than desirable. An alert system such as a *hygrometer*, which monitors humidity, should be in place in areas where sensitive equipment resides. The system should also monitor temperature as well. These types of controls are considered physical controls.

Equipment Security

The physical security of the equipment has been stressed throughout this book. This section discusses corporate procedures concerning equipment and media and the use of safes and vaults for protecting other valuable physical assets.

Corporate Procedures

Physical security of equipment and media should be designed into the security policies and procedures of the company. These procedures should address the following issues.

Tamper Protection

It should *not* be possible for unauthorized persons to access and change the configuration of any devices. This means additional measures, such as the ones in the remainder of this section, should be followed to prevent this. Tampering includes defacing, damaging, or changing the configuration of a device. Integrity verification programs should be used by applications to look for evidence of data tampering, errors, and omissions.

Encryption

Encrypting sensitive data stored on devices can help to prevent the exposure of data in the event of a theft or in the event of inappropriate access of the device. Cryptography and encryption concepts are covered extensively in Chapter 6, "Cryptography."

Inventory

   Recognizing when items are stolen is impossible if no item count or inventory system exists. All equipment should be inventoried, and all relevant information about each device should be maintained and kept up to date. Maintain this information both electronically and in hard copy.

Physical Protection of Security Devices

   Security devices, such as firewalls, NAT devices, and intrusion detection and prevention systems, should receive the most attention because they relate to physical and logical security.

   Beyond this, devices that can be easily stolen, such as laptops, tablets, and smartphones, should be locked away. If that is not practical, then lock these types of devices to a stationary object. A good example of this is the cable locks used with laptops.

Tracking Devices

   When the technology is available, tracking of small devices can be used to help mitigate loss of both devices and their data. Many smartphones now include tracking software that allows you to locate the device after it has been stolen or lost by using either cell tower tracking or GPS. Deploy this technology when available.

   Another useful feature available on these same types of devices is a remote wipe feature. This allows sending a signal to a stolen device instructing it to wipe out the data contained on the device. Finally, these devices typically also come with the ability to remotely lock the device when misplaced.

Portable Media Procedures

   Strict control of the use of portable media devices can help prevent sensitive information from leaving the network. This includes floppy disks, CDs, DVDs, flash drives, thumb drives, and external hard drives. Although written rules should be in effect about the use of these devices, using security policies to prevent the copying of data to these media types is also possible. Allowing the copying of data to these drive types as long as the data is encrypted is also possible. If these functions are provided by the network operating system, you should deploy them.

Safes, Vaults, and Locking

   With respect to protecting physical assets such as laptops, smartphones, tablets, and so on, nothing beats locking the devices away. In cases where it is possible to do so, lockable cabinets are a good solution for storing these devices. In addition to selecting the proper lock (locks are discussed earlier in this chapter), all equipment should be inventoried, and a system devised for maintaining these counts as the devices come and go.

Some items require even more protection than a locked cabinet. Keep important legal documents and any other items of extreme value in a safe or a vault for the added protection these items require. Fire-proof safes and vaults can provide protection for contents even during a fire.

Personnel Privacy and Safety

The human resources are the most important assets the organization possesses. You might recall that in the event of a fire, the first action to always take is to evacuate all personnel. Their safety comes before all other considerations. Although equipment and in most cases the data can be recovered, human beings can neither be backed up nor replaced.

An Occupant Emergency Plan (OEP) provides coordinated procedures for minimizing loss of life or injury and protecting property damage in response to a physical threat. In a disaster of any type, personnel safety is the first concern.

NOTE More information on occupant safety can be found in Chapter 9.

The organization is responsible for protecting the privacy of each individual's information, especially as it relates to personnel and medical records. Although this expectation of privacy does not necessarily and usually does not extend to their activities on the network, both federal and state laws hold organizations responsible for the release of this type of information with violations resulting in heavy fines and potential lawsuits that result if the company is found liable.

NOTE More information on legal considerations regarding privacy appears in Chapter 10, "Legal, Regulations, Investigations, and Compliance."

Exam Preparation Tasks

As mentioned in the section "How to Use This Book" in the Introduction, you have a couple of choices for exam preparation: the exercises in this chapter and the exam simulation questions on the CD-ROM.

Review All Key Topics

Review the most important topics in this chapter, noted with the Key Topics icon in the outer margin of the page. Table 11-1 lists a reference of these key topics and the page numbers on which each is found.

Table 11-1 Key Topics

Key Topic Element	Description	Page Number
List	Fire extinguishers	450
Section	CPTED strategies	453
Bullet list	Fence types	459
List	Gates	460

Define Key Terms

Define the following key terms from this chapter and check your answers in the glossary:

system threats, natural threats, external threats, internal threats, man-made threats, auxiliary station alarm, Class A extinguisher, Class B extinguisher, Class C extinguisher, Class D extinguisher, Class K extinguisher, collusion, civil disobedience, layered defense model, Crime Prevention Through Environmental Design (CPTED), Natural Access Control, Natural Surveillance, Natural Territorials Reinforcement, concentric circle, bollards, Class 1 gate, Class 2 gate, Class 3 gate, passive infrared systems (PIR), electromechanical systems, photometric system, acoustical systems, wave motion detector, capacitance detector, closed circuit television system (CCTV), continuous lighting, standby lighting, movable lighting, emergency lighting, fluorescent lighting, mercury vapor lighting, sodium vapor lighting, quartz lamp lighting, feet of illumination, cipher locks, proximity authentication device, mantrap, warded locks, tumbler locks, combination lock, cable lock, standard glass, tempered glass, acrylic glass, laminated glass, smoke-activated sensor, heat-activated sensor, flame-actuated sensor, wet pipe extinguisher, dry pipe extinguisher, preaction extinguisher, deluge extinguisher, surge, brownout, fault, blackout, power conditioners, uninterruptible power supplies (UPS), environmental error, hygrometer

Review Questions

1. Which of the following is an example of preventing an internal threat?

    a. a door lock system on the server room

    b. an electric fence surrounding the facility

    c. armed guards outside the facility

    d. parking lot cameras

2. Which of the following is not an example of a natural threat?

    a. flood

    b. bombing

    c. earthquake

    d. tornado

3. Which of the following is a system threat?

    a. loss of utilities

    b. bombing

    c. earthquake

    d. tornado

4. What is the recommended optimal relative humidity range for computer operations?

    a. 10%–30 %

    b. 20%–40 %

    c. 30%–50 %

    d. 40%–60 %

5. What is the most prevalent cause of computer center fires?

    a. human error

    b. electrical distribution systems

    c. lighting systems

    d. arson

6. Which of the following is *not* an example of a man-made threat?

    a. bombing

    b. arson

    c. flood

    d. collusion

7. Which of the following extinguishers is designed to address electrical equipment fires?

    a. Class A

    b. Class B

    c. Class C

    d. Class D

8. Class K extinguishers are designed to address what type of fire?

    a. cooking oil or fat

    b. flammable liquids

    c. combustible metals

    d. ordinary combustibles

9. Which of the following is not a politically motivated threat?

    a. power outage

    b. bombing

    c. strike

    d. civil disobedience

10. Which of the following is *not* one of the three main strategies that guide CPTED?

    a. Natural Access Control

    b. Natural Surveillance Reinforcement

    c. Natural Territorials Reinforcement

    d. Natural Surveillance

Answers and Explanations

1. **a**. An electric fence surrounding the facility is designed to prevent access to the building by those who should not have *any* access (an external threat), whereas a door lock system on the server room that requires a swipe of the employee card is designed to prevent access by those who are already in the building (an internal threat).

2. **b**. A bombing is an example of a man-made threat.

3. **a**. Some of the threats that exist are not from the forces of nature but from failures in systems that provide basic services such as electricity and utilities.

4. **d**. The recommended optimal relative humidity range for computer operations is 40% to 60%.

5. **b**. The most prevalent cause of computer center fires is electrical distribution systems. These systems should be checked regularly to identify problems before they occur.

6. **c**. Floods are a natural threat.

7. **c**. Class C extinguishers are designed to address electrical equipment fires.

8. **a**. Class K extinguishers are designed to address cooking oil or fat fires.

9. **a**. Power outage is a system threat.

10. **b**. The three strategies are Natural Access Control, Natural Territorials Reinforcement, and Natural Surveillance.

Glossary

3DES *See* triple DES.

802.11a Operates in the 5GHz frequency with a maximum speed of 54 Mbps.

802.11b Operates in the 2.4GHz frequency with a maximum speed of 11 Mbps.

802.11f Standard for communication between access points.

802.11g Operates in the 2.4 GHz frequency with a maximum speed of 54 Mbps.

802.11n Operates in both the 2.4GHz and 5.0GHz frequencies with a maximum theoretical speed of 600 Mbps.

A

absolute addressing Addresses the entire primary memory space.

access control The means by which a subject's ability to communicate with or access an object is allowed or denied based on an organization's security requirements.

access control list A table that consists of the access rights that subjects have to a particular object. An ACL is about the object.

access control matrix A table that consists of a list of subjects, a list of objects, and a list of the actions that a subject can take upon each object.

access control policy A security policy that defines the method for identifying and authenticating users and the level of access that is granted to users.

access point A wireless transmitter and receiver that hooks into the wired portion of the network and provides an access point to this network for wireless devices.

accountability An organization's ability to hold users responsible for the actions they perform.

accreditation The formal acceptance of the adequacy of a system's overall security by the management.

ACL *See* access control list.

acoustical systems Detection systems that use strategically placed microphones to detect any sound made during a forced entry.

acrylic glass Made of polycarbonate acrylic, is much stronger than regular glass but produces toxic fumes when burned.

ActiveX A Microsoft technology that uses object-oriented programming (OOP) and is based on the COM and DCOM.

AD *See* architectural description.

ad hoc mode A wireless implementation in which there is no AP and stations communicate directly with one another.

Address Resolution Protocol (ARP) Resolves the IP address placed in the packet to a physical or layer 2 address (called a MAC address in Ethernet).

administrative control A security control that is implemented to administer the organization's assets and personnel and includes security policies, procedures, standards, and guidelines that are established by management.

administrative law A type of law where standards of performance or conduct are set by government agencies for organizations and industries to follow. Common areas that are covered include public utilities, communications, banking, environmental protection, and healthcare.

ADSL *See* asymmetric DSL.

advisory security policy A security policy that provides instruction on acceptable and unacceptable activities.

adware Tracks your Internet usage in an attempt to tailor ads and junk e-mails to your interests.

aggregation Assembling or compiling units of information at one sensitivity level and having the resultant totality of data being of a higher sensitivity level than the individual components.

agile This is a development model that puts more emphasis on continuous feedback and cross-functional teamwork.

AH *See* authentication header.

ALE *See* annualized rate of occurrence.

algorithm A mathematical function that encrypts and decrypts data. Also referred to as a cipher.

analog Represents the data as sound and is what is used in analog telephony.

annualized loss expectancy   The expected risk factor of an annual threat event. The acronym stands for annualized loss expectancy. The equation used is ALE = SLE × ARO.

annualized rate of occurrence   The estimate of how often a given threat might occur annually. This acronym stands for annualized rate of occurrence.

insert AP   *See* access point.

application layer (layer 7)   Where the encapsulation process begins. This layer receives the raw data from the application in use and provides services such as file transfer and message exchange to the application (and thus the user).

application level proxies   Perform deep packet inspection. This type of firewall understands the details of the communication process at layer 7 for the application of interest.

architectural description (AD)   Comprises the set of documents that convey the architecture in a formal manner.

architecture   Describes the organization of the system, including its components and their interrelationships along with the principles that guided its design and evolution.

ARO   *See* ARO.

ARP   *See* Address Resolution Protocol.

assembly languages   Languages that use symbols or mnemonics to represent sections of complicated binary code. Consequently, these languages use an assembler to convert the code to machine level.

asset value   *See* AV.

associative memory   Searches for a specific data value in memory rather than using a specific memory address.

asymmetric DSL (ADSL)   Usually provides uploads from 128Kbps to 384 Kbps and downloads up to 768 Kbps.

asymmetric encryption   An encryption method whereby a key pair, one private key and one public key, performs encryption and decryption. One key performs the encryption, whereas the other key performs the decryption. Also referred to as public key encryption.

asymmetric mode   In this mode, a processor is dedicated to a specific process or application and when work is done for that process, it always is done by the same processor.

asynchronous encryption   When encryption or decryption requests are processed from a queue.

asynchronous token   A token that generates the password based on a challenge/response technique with the authentication server, with the token device providing the correct answer to the authentication server's challenge.

Asynchronous Transfer Mode (ATM)   A cell-switching technology. It transfers fixed size (53 bytes) cells rather than packets and after a path is established, it will use the same path for the entire communication.

asynchronous transmission   Uses start and stop bits to communicate when each byte is starting and stopping.

atomicity   Either all operations are complete or the database changes are rolled back.

attenuation   The weakening of the signal as it travels down the cable and meets resistance. Occurs when the signal meets resistance as it travels through the cable. This weakens the signal and at some point (different in each cable type) the signal is no longer strong enough to be read properly at the destination.

ATM   *See* Asynchronous Transfer Mode.

authenticating server   The RADIUS server and the authenticator (AP, switch, remote access server) is the RADIUS client.

authentication   The act of validating a user with a unique identifier by providing the appropriate credentials.

authentication header (AH)   Part of IPsec that provides data integrity, data origin authentication, and protection from replay attacks.

authenticator   The component in a RADIUS environment to which an applicant is attempting to connect (AP, switch, remote access server).

authorization   The point after identification and authentication at which a user is granted the rights and permissions to resources.

auxiliary station alarm   A mechanism that automatically causes an alarm originating in a data center to be transmitted over the local municipal fire or police alarm circuits for relaying to both the local police/fire station and the appropriate headquarters.

AV   This acronym stands for asset value.

availability   A value that describes what percentage of the time the resource or the data is available. The tenet of the CIA triad that ensures that data is accessible when and where it is needed.

avalanche effect   The condition where any change in the key or plaintext, no matter how minor, will significantly change the ciphertext.

B

backdoor   A mechanism implemented in many devices or applications that gives the user who uses the backdoor unlimited access to the device or application. A piece of software installed by a hacker that allows him to return later and connect to the computer without going through the normal authentication process.

base relation   In SQL, a relation that is actually existent in the database.

baseband   Transmissions where the entire medium is used for a single transmission and then multiple transmission types are assigned time slots to use this single circuit.

Basel II   Recommendations from a banking association that affect financial institutions. They address minimum capital requirements, supervisory review, and market discipline with the purpose of protecting against risks the banks and other financial institutions face.

baseline   An information security governance component that acts as a reference point that is defined and captured to be used as a future reference. Both security and performance baselines are used.

basic rate (BRI) ISDN   Solution that provides three channels, two B channels that provide 64 Kbps each and a D channel that is 16 kbps for a total of 144 Kbps.

Bastion host   Device exposed directly to the Internet or to any untrusted network.

behavioral characteristics   Any measurable actions that are performed by a user.

Bell-LaPadula Model   First mathematical model of a multilevel system that used both the concepts of a state machine and those of controlling information flow.

best evidence rule   States that when evidence, such as a document or recording, is presented, only the original will be accepted unless a legitimate reason exists for why the original cannot be used.

BGP   *See* border gateway protocol.

Biba model   Concerns itself more with the integrity of information rather than the confidentiality of that information.

biometric acceptability   The likelihood that users will accept and follow the system.

biometric accuracy   How correct the overall biometric readings will be.

biometric throughput   The rate at which the biometric system will be able to scan characteristics and complete the analysis to permit or deny access.

blackout   A prolonged power outage.

block cipher   A cipher that performs encryption by breaking the message into fixed-length units.

Blowfish   A block cipher that uses 64-bit data blocks using anywhere from 32- to 448-bit encryption keys. Blowfish performs 16 rounds of transformation.

bluejacking   When an unsolicited message is sent to a Bluetooth-enabled device.

bluesnarfing   The unauthorized access to a device using the Bluetooth connection.

bluetooth   A wireless technology that is used to create Personal Area Networks (PANs).

bollards   Short vertical posts placed at the entrance way to building and lining sidewalks that help to provide protection from vehicles that might either intentionally or unintentionally crash into or enter the building or injure pedestrians.

boot sector virus   These infect the boot sector of a computer and either overwrite files or install code into the sector so the virus initiates at startup.

Border Gateway Protocol (BGP)   An exterior routing protocol considered to be a path vector protocol.

botnet   A collection of computers that act together in an attack; the individual computers are called zombies.

Brewer-Nash (Chinese Wall) model   Model that introduced the concept of allowing access controls to change dynamically based on a user's previous actions.

bridge federated identity model   *See* trusted third-party federated identity model.

BRI   *See* basic rate (BRI) ISDN.

broadband   Divides the medium into different frequencies.

broadcast   This is a transmission sent by a single system to all systems in the network. It is considered one to all.

brownout   A prolonged drop in power that is below normal voltage.

BSI   *See* build security in.

buffer overflow   Occurs when too much data is accepted as input to a specific process. Hackers can take advantage of this phenomenon by submitting too much data, which can cause an error, or in some cases execute commands on the machine if he can locate an area where commands can be executed.

build and fix   A development method that while certainly used in the past has been largely discredited and is now used as a template for how *not* to manage a development project. Simply put, using this method, the software is developed as quickly as possible and released.

build security in (BSI) An initiative that promotes a process-agnostic approach that makes security recommendations with regard to architectures, testing methods, code reviews, and management processes.

bus topology The earliest Ethernet topology used. In this topology, all devices are connected to a single line that has two definitive endpoints.

C

CA *See* certification authority.

cable lock Vinyl-coated steel cables that connect to the laptop and then lock around an object.

cable modems Internet access solution that can provide up to 50 Mbps over the coaxial cabling used for cable TV.

cache A relatively small amount (when compared to primary memory) of very high speed RAM, which holds the instructions and data from primary memory, that has a high probability of being accessed during the currently executing portion of a program.

CALEA *See* Communications Assistance for Law Enforcement Act (CALEA) of 1994.

candidate key An attribute in one relation that has values matching the primary key in another relation.

Capability Maturity Model Integration (CMMI) This comprehensive set of guidelines addresses all phases of the software development life cycle. It describes a series of stages or maturity levels that a development process can advance as it goes from the ad hoc (build and fix) model to one that incorporates a budgeted plan for continuous improvement

capability table A table that lists the access rights that a particular subject has to objects. A capability table is about the subject.

capacitance detector These devices emit a magnetic field and monitor that field. If the field is disrupted, which occurs when a person enters the area, the alarm will sound.

cardinality The number of rows in a relation.

Carrier Sense Multiple Access Collision Avoidance (CSMA/CA) Contention method used in an 802.11 wireless network.

Carrier Sense Multiple Access Collision Detection (CSMA/CD) Contention method used in 802.3 networks.

CAST-128 A block cipher that uses a 40- to 128-bit key that will perform 12 or 16 rounds of transformation on 64-bit blocks.

CAST-256 A block cipher that uses 128-, 160-, 192-, 224-, or 256-bit key that will perform 48 rounds of transformation on 128-bit blocks.

catastrophe A disaster that has a wide and long impact.

CBC *See* cipher block chaining.

CBC-MAC *See* cipher block chaining MAC.

CCTV *See* closed circuit television system.

CDMA *See* Code Division Multiple Access.

centralized access control An access control type in which a central department or personnel oversees the access for all organizational resources.

CER *See* crossover error rate.

certificate revocation list A list of digital certificates that a CA has revoked.

certification The technical evaluation of a system. The process of evaluating the software for its security effectiveness with regard to the customer's needs.

certification authority The entity that creates and signs digital certificates, maintains the certificates, and revokes them when necessary.

CFAA *See* Computer Fraud and Abuse Act of 1986.

CFB *See* cipher feedback.

Challenge Handshake Authentication Protocol (CHAP) Method for validating a password without sending the password across an untrusted network, where the server sends the client a set of random text called a challenge. The client encrypts the text with the password and sends it back. The server then decrypts it with the same password and compares the result with what was sent originally. If the results match, then the server can be assured that the user or system possesses the correct password without ever needing to send it across the untrusted network.

Channel Service Unit/Data Service Unit (CSU/DSU) Used to connect a LAN to a WAN.

CHAP *See* Challenge Handshake Authentication Protocol.

characteristic factors Factors that are something a person is, such as a fingerprint or facial geometry.

chosen ciphertext attack An attack that occurs when an attacker chooses the ciphertext to be decrypted to obtain the plaintext.

chosen plaintext attack An attack that occurs when an attacker chooses the plaintext to get encrypted to obtain the ciphertext.

cipher *See* algorithm.

cipher block chaining A DES mode in which each 64-bit block is chained together because each resultant 64-bit ciphertext block is applied to the next block. So plaintext message block one is processed by the algorithm using an initialization vector (IV). The resultant ciphertext message block one is XORed with plaintext message block two, resulting in ciphertext message two. This process continues until the message is complete.

cipher block chaining MAC A block-cipher MAC that operates in CBC mode.

cipher feedback A DES mode that works with 8-bit (or smaller) blocks and uses a combination of stream ciphering and block ciphering. Like CBC, the first 8-bit block of the plaintext message is XORed by the algorithm using a keystream, which is the result of an IV and the key. The resultant ciphertext message is applied to the next plaintext message block.

cipher locks Use a key pad that requires the correct code to open the lock.

ciphertext An altered form of a message that is unreadable without knowing the key and the encryption system used. Also referred to as a cryptogram.

ciphertext-only attack An attack that occurs when an attacker uses several encrypted messages (ciphertext) to figure out the key used in the encryption process.

circuit level proxies Firewall that operates at the session layer (layer 5) of the OSI model.

circuit-switching networks Establish a set path to the destination and only use that path for the entire communication.

circumstantial evidence Evidence that provides inference of information from other intermediate relevant facts.

civil code law A type of law based on written laws. It is a rule-based law and does not rely on precedence in any way.

civil disobedience The intentional refusal to obey certain laws, demands, and commands of a government and is commonly, though not always, defined as being nonviolent resistance.

civil/tort law A type of law where the liable party owes a legal duty to the victim. It deals with wrongs that have been committed against an individual or organization.

Clark-Wilson Integrity model Developed after the Biba model, this model also concerns itself with data integrity.

Class 1 gate A gate suitable for residential use.

Class 2 gate A gate suitable for commercial usage.

Class 3 gate A gate suitable for industrial usage.

Class A extinguisher Used for ordinary combustibles.

Class B extinguisher Used for flammable liquids and flammable gases.

Class C extinguisher Used for electrical equipment.

Class D extinguisher Used for combustible metals.

Class K extinguisher Used for cooking oil or fat.

cleanroom A development model that strictly adheres to formal steps and a more structured method. It attempts to prevent errors and mistakes through extensive testing.

cleartext *See* plaintext.

closed circuit television system (CCTV) Uses sets of cameras that can either be monitored in real time or can record days of activity that can be viewed as needed at a later time.

cloud computing The centralization of data in a web environment that can be accessed from anywhere anytime. Approach that makes resources available in a web-based data center so the resources can be accessed from anywhere.

CMMI *See* Capability Maturity Model Integration.

coaxial One of the earliest cable types to be used for networking was coaxial, the same basic type of cable that brought cable TV to millions of homes.

CobiT Framework that deals with IT governance.

Code Division Multiple Access (CDMA) A modulation technique used in mobile wireless.

cohesion A term used to describe how many different tasks a module can carry out. If it is limited to a small number or a single function, it is said to have high cohesion.

cold site A leased facility that contains only electrical and communications wiring, air conditioning, plumbing, and raised flooring.

collision An event that occurs when a hash function produces the same hash value on different messages. Occurs when two employees work together to accomplish a theft of some sort that could not be accomplished without their combined knowledge or responsibilities.

column or attribute A column in a table.

COM *See* Component Object Model.

combination lock Lock requires rotating the lock in a pattern, which if correct, lines up the tumblers, opening the lock.

commercial software Software that is licensed by a commercial entity for purchase in a wholesale or retail market.

common criteria System that uses Evaluation Assurance Levels (EALs) to rate systems with each representing a successively higher level of security testing and design in a system.

common law A type of law based on customs and precedent because no written laws were available. Common law reflects on the morals of the people and relies heavily on precedence.

Common Object Request Broker Architecture (CORBA) An open object-oriented standard developed by the Object Management Group (OMG).

Communications Assistance for Law Enforcement Act (CALEA) of 1994 A U.S. law that affects law enforcement and intelligence agencies. It requires telecommunications carriers and manufacturers of telecommunications equipment to modify and design their equipment, facilities, and services to ensure that they have built-in surveillance capabilities.

compensative control A security control that substitutes for a primary access control and mainly acts as a mitigation to risks.

compensatory damages Damages that compensate the victim for his losses.

Component Object Model (COM) A model for communication between processes on the same computer.

Computer Fraud and Abuse Act (CFAA) of 1986 A U.S. act that affects any entities that might engage in hacking of "protected computers" as defined in the Act.

computer prevalence crime A crime that occurs due to the fact that computers are so widely used in today's world. This type of crime occurs only because computers exist.

Computer Security Act of 1987 A U.S. act that was the first law written to require a formal computer security plan. It was written to protect and defend any of the sensitive information in the federal government systems and provide security for that information.

computer surveillance When a person's actions are reported or captured using digital information, such as audit logs.

computer-assisted crime A crime that occurs when a computer is used as a tool to help commit a crime.

computer-targeted crime A crime that occurs when a computer is the victim of an attack whose sole purpose is to harm the computer and its owner.

concealment cipher   A cipher that interspersed plaintext somewhere within other written material. Also referred to as a null cipher.

concentric circle   Approach that relies on creating layers of physical barriers to information.

conclusive evidence   Evidence that does not require any other corroboration.

confidentiality   The tenet of the CIA triad that ensures that data is protected from unauthorized disclosure.

confidentially   A characteristic provided if the data cannot be read.

confusion   The process of changing a key value during each round of encryption. Confusion is often carried out by substitution.

consistency   The transaction follows an integrity process that ensures that data is consistent in all places where it exists.

contamination   The intermingling or mixing of data of one sensitivity or need-to-know level with that of another.

content analysis   Analyzes the contents of a drive or software. If drive content analysis, it gives a report detailing the types of data by percentage. If software content analysis, it determines the purpose of the software.

context-dependent access control   A type of access that is based on subject or object attributes or environmental characteristics. Bases the access to data on multiple factors to help prevent inference.

Control Objectives for Information and Related Technology   *See* CobiT.

copy backup   A backup that backs up all the files, similar to full backups, but does not reset the file's archive bit.

copyright   An intellectual property type that ensures that a work that is authored is protected for any form of reproduction or use without the consent of the copyright holder, usually the author or artist that created the original work.

CORBA   *See* Common Object Request Broker Architecture.

corrective control   A security control that reduces the effect of an attack or other undesirable event.

corroborative evidence   Evidence that supports another piece of evidence.

counter mode (CTR)   A DES mode similar to OFB mode that uses an incrementing IV counter to ensure that each block is encrypted with a unique keystream. Also, the ciphertext is not chaining into the encryption process. Because this chaining does not occur, CTR performance is much better than the other modes.

countermeasure A control that is implemented to reduce potential risk.

coupling Describes how much interaction one module requires from another module to do its job. Low or loose coupling indicates a module does not need much help from other modules whereas high coupling indicates the opposite.

CPTED *See* Crime Prevention Through Environmental Design.

Crime Prevention Through Environmental Design (CPTED) Refers to designing the facility from the ground up to support security.

crime scene The environment in which potential evidence exists.

criminal law A type of law that covers any actions that are considered harmful to others. It deals with conduct that violates public protection laws.

CRL *See* Certificate Revocation List.

cross-certification federated identity model A federated identity model in which each organization certifies that every other organization is trusted.

crossover error rate The point in a biometric system at which FRR equals FAR.

crosstalk Occurs when the signals from the two wires (or more) interfere with one another and distort the transmission.

cryptanalysis The science of decrypting ciphertext without prior knowledge of the key or cryptosystem used. The purpose of cryptanalysis is to forge coded signals or messages that will be accepted as authentic.

cryptogram *See* ciphertext.

cryptography A science that either hides data or makes data unreadable by transforming it.

cryptology The science that studies encrypted communication and data.

cryptosystem The entire cryptographic process, including the algorithm, key, and key management functions. The security of a cryptosystem is measured by the size of the keyspace and available computational power.

cryptovariable *See* key.

CSMA/CA *See* Carrier Sense Multiple Access Collision Avoidance.

CSMA/CD *See* Carrier Sense Multiple Access Collision Detection.

CSU/DSU *See* Channel Service Unit/Data Service Unit.

CTR *See* counter mode.

customary law A type of law based on the customs of a country or region.

cybersquatting When domain names are registered with no intent to use them but with intent to hold them hostage.

D

DAC *See* discretionary access control.

daily backup A backup in which a file's time stamp is used to determine whether it needs archiving.

data clearing Renders information unrecoverable by a keyboard. This attack extracts information from data storage media by executing software utilities, keystrokes, or other system resources executed from a keyboard.

data link layer (layer 2) Responsible for determining what MAC addresses should be at each hop and adding them to part of the packet.

data mining A process of using special tools to organize the data into an even more useable format. It analyzes large data sets in a data warehouse to find non-obvious patterns.

data purging Uses a method such as degaussing to make the old data unavailable even with forensics. Purging renders information unrecoverable against laboratory attacks (forensics).

data structure Refers to the logical relationship between elements of data. It describes the extent to which elements, methods of access, and processing alternatives are associated and the organization of data elements.

data warehouse A repository of information from heterogeneous databases.

data warehousing A process of combining data from multiple databases or data sources in a central location called a warehouse. The warehouse is used to carry out analysis. The data is not simply combined but is processed and presented in a more useful and understandable way.

database locks Used when one user is accessing a record that prevents another user from accessing the record at the same time to prevent edits until the first user is finished.

database views Refers to the given set of data that a user or group of users can see when they access the database.

data-over-cable service interface specifications (DOCSIS) Standard for cable modem communications.

DCOM *See* Distributed Component Object Model.

DDoS *See* Distributed Denial of Service.

decentralized access control An access control type in which personnel closest to the resources, such as department managers and data owners, oversee the access control for individual resources.

decoding The process of changing an encoded message back into its original format.

decryption The process of converting data from ciphertext to plaintext. Also referred to as deciphering.

default stance The default security stance that is used by an organization. An allow-by-default stance permits access to any data unless a need exists to restrict access. A deny-by-default stance is much stricter because it denies any access that is not explicitly permitted.

defense in depth A security approach refers to deploying layers of protection.

degree The number of columns in a table.

deluge extinguisher Allows large amounts of water to be released into the room, which obviously makes it not a good choice for where computing equipment will be located.

demilitarized zone Network where systems are placed that will be accessed regularly from the untrusted network.

demultiplexer Takes a single input signal that carries many channels and separates those over multiple output.

DES *See* digital encryption standard.

DES-X A variant of DES that uses multiple 64-bit keys in addition to the 56-bit DES key. The first 64-bit key is XORed to the plaintext, which is then encrypted with DES. The second 64-bit key is XORed to the resulting cipher.

detective control A security control that detects an attack while it is occurring to alert appropriate personnel.

deterrent control A security control that deters potential attacks.

DHCP *See* Dynamic Host Configuration Protocol.

dial-up connection One that uses the PSTN. If it is initiated over an analog phone line, it requires a modem that converts the digital data to analog on the sending end with a modem on the receiving end converting it back to digital.

differential backup A backup in which all files that have been changed since the last full backup will be backed up and the archive bit for each file is not cleared.

diffusion The process of changing the location of the plaintext within the ciphertext. Diffusion is often carried out using transposition.

digital Signaling that is the type used in most computer transmissions has not an infinite number of possible values but only two, on and off.

digital certificate An electronic document that identifies the certificate holder.

digital encryption standard (DES) A symmetric algorithm that uses a 64-bit key, 8 bits of which are used for parity. The effective key length for DES is 56 bits. DES divides the message into 64-bit blocks. Sixteen rounds of transposition and substitution are performed on each block, resulting in a 64-bit block of ciphertext.

digital signature A method of providing sender authentication and message integrity. The message acts as an input to a hash function, and the sender's private key encrypts the hash value. The receiver can perform a hash computation on the received message to determine the validity of the message.

digital signature standard A federal digital security standard that governs the Digital Security Algorithm (DSA).

Digital Subscribers Line (DSL) A very popular option that provides a high-speed connection from a home or small office to the ISP. While it uses the existing phone lines, it is an always-on connection.

direct evidence Evidence that proves or disproves a fact through oral testimony based on information gathered through the witness's senses.

Direct Sequence Spread Spectrum (DSSS) One of two modulation technologies (along with FSSS) that were a part of the original 802.11 standard.

directive control A security control that specifies an acceptable practice within an organization.

disaster A suddenly occurring event that has a long-term negative impact on life.

discretionary access control An access control model in which the owner of the object specifies which subjects can access the resource.

disk imaging Creates an exact image of the contents of the hard drive.

disruption Any unplanned event that results in the temporary interruption of any organizational asset, including processes, functions, and devices.

distance vector Routing protocols that share their entire routing table with their neighboring routers on a schedule, thereby creating the most traffic of the three categories. They also use a metric called hop count. Hop count is simply the number of routers traversed to get to a network.

Distributed Component Object Model (DCOM) A model for communication between processes in different parts of the network.

Distributed Denial of Service (DDoS)   Attack where the perpetuator enlists the aid of other machines.

distributed object-oriented systems   When an application operates in a client-server framework as many do, the solution is performing distributed computing. This means that components on different systems must be able to both locate each other and communicate on a network.

DMZ   *See* demilitarized zone.

DNS   *See* Domain Name System.

DNS cache poisoning attack   The attacker attempts to refresh or update that record when it expires with a different address than the correct address.

DNSSEC   One of the newer approaches to preventing DNS attacks. Many current implementations of DNS software contain this functionality. It uses digital signatures to validate the source of all messages to ensure they are not spoofed.

DOCSIS   *See* data-over-cable service interface specifications.

domain   The set of allowable values that an attribute can take.

domain grabbing   Occurs when individuals register a domain name of a well-known company before the company has the chance to do so.

Domain Name System (DNS)   Resolves a computer name (or in the case of the web a domain name) to an IP address.

double-DES   A DES version that uses a 112-bit key length.

downstream liability   A type of liability that an organization accrues due to partnerships with other organizations and customers.

dry pipe extinguisher   In this system, the water is not held in the pipes but in a holding tank. The pipes hold pressurized air, which is reduced when fire is detected, allowing the water to enter the pipe and the sprinklers. This minimizes the chance of an accidental discharge.

DSL   *See* Digital Subscribers Line.

DSS   *See* Digital Signature Standard.

DSSS   *See* Direct Sequence Spread Spectrum.

dual control   A security measure that requires that two employees must be available to complete a specific task to complete the job. This security measure is part of separation of duties.

dual-homed firewall   One that has two network interfaces, one pointing to the internal network and another connected to the untrusted network.

due care   A legal term that is used when an organization took all reasonable measures to prevent security breaches and also took steps to mitigate damages caused by successful breaches.

due diligence   A legal term that is used when an organization investigated all vulnerabilities.

dumpster diving   A social engineering attack that occurs when attackers examine garbage contents to obtain confidential information.

durability   After it's verified, the transaction is committed and cannot be rolled back.

Dynamic Host Configuration Protocol (DHCP)   A service that can be used to automate the process of assigning an IP configuration to the devices in the network.

dynamic packet filtering firewall   Keeps track of that source port and dynamically adds a rule to the list to allow return traffic to that port.

E

E carriers   In Europe, a similar technology to T-carrier lines.

EAP   *See* Extensible Authentication Protocol.

ECB   *See* electronic code book.

Economic Espionage Act of 1996   A U.S. act that affects companies that have trade secrets and any individuals who plan to use encryption technology for criminal activities.

ECPA   *See* Electronic Communications Privacy Act (ECPA) of 1986.

EF   *See* exposure factor.

EIGRP   *See* Enhanced IGRP.

electromagnetic interference   Interference from power lines and other power sources.

electromechanical systems   Detection systems that operate by detecting a break in an electrical circuit. For example, the circuit might cross a window or door, and when the window or door is opened the circuit is broken, setting off an alarm of some sort.

electronic code book   A version of DES in which 64-bit blocks of data are processed by the algorithm using the key. The ciphertext produced can be padded to ensure that the result is a 64-bit block.

Electronic Communications Privacy Act (ECPA) of 1986   A U.S. act that affects law enforcement and intelligence agencies. It extended government restrictions on wiretaps from telephone calls to include transmissions of electronic data by computer and prohibited access to stored electronic communications.

e-mail spoofing   The process of sending an e-mail that appears to come from one source when it really comes from another.

embedded system   A piece of software built into a larger piece of software that is in charge of performing some specific function on behalf of the larger system.

emergency lighting   Lighting systems with their own power source to use when power is out.

EMI   *See* electromagnetic interference.

Encapsulating Security Payload (ESP)   Part of IPsec that provides data integrity, data origin authentication, protection from replay, and encryption.

encapsulation   Process where information is added to the header at each layer and then a trailer is placed on the packet before transmission.

encoding   The process of changing data into another form using code.

encryption   The process of converting data from plaintext to ciphertext. Also referred to as enciphering.

Enhanced IGRP (EIGRP)   A classless Cisco proprietary routing protocol that is considered a hybrid or advanced distance vector protocol.

enrollment time   The process of obtaining the sample that is used by a biometric system.

environmental error   An error called that causes a system to be vulnerable because of the environment in which it is installed.

ESP   *See* Encapsulating Security Payload.

Ethernet   A widely used layer 2 protocol, described in the 802.3 standard.

ethical hacking   *See* penetration testing.

exposure   A condition that occurs when an organizational asset is exposed to losses.

exposure factor   The percent value or functionality of an asset that will be lost when a threat event occurs.

Extensible Authentication Protocol (EAP)   Not a single protocol but a framework for port-based access control that uses the same three components that are used in RADIUS.

Extensible Markup Language (XML)   The most widely used web language.

external threats   Threats from perimeter security or access to the building or room.

extranet   A network logically separate from the intranet. It is an area where resources that will be accessed from the outside world are made available.

F

facial scan   A biometric scan that records facial characteristics, including bone structure, eye width, and forehead size.

fail safe state   Leaving system processes and components in a secure state when a failure occurs or is detected in the system.

fail soft   The termination of selected, non-critical processing when a hardware or software failure occurs.

failover   The capacity of a system to switch over to a backup system if a failure in the primary system occurs.

false acceptance rate   A measurement of the percentage of invalid users that will be falsely accepted by the system. This is called a Type II error.

false rejection rate   A measurement of valid users that will be falsely rejected by a biometric system. This is called a Type I error.

FAR   *See* false acceptance rate.

fault   A momentary power outage.

fault tolerance   A concept that includes redundancy but refers to any process that allows a system to continue making information assets available in the case of a failure.

feature extraction   The approach to obtaining biometric information from a collected sample of a user's physiological or behavioral characteristics.

FDDI   *See* Fiber Distributed Data Interface.

FDM   *See* Frequency Division Multiplexing.

FDMA   *See* Frequency Division Multiple Access.

Federal Information Security Management Act (FISMA) of 2002   A U.S. act that affects every federal agency. It requires the federal agencies to develop, document, and implement an agency-wide information security program.

Federal Intelligence Surveillance Act (FISA) of 1978   A U.S. act that affects law enforcement and intelligence agencies. It gives procedures for the physical and electronic surveillance and collection of "foreign intelligence information" between "foreign powers" and "agents of foreign powers" and only applies to traffic within the United States.

Federal Privacy Act of 1974   A U.S. act that affects any computer that contains records used by a federal agency. It provides guidelines collection, maintenance, use, and dissemination of personally identifiable information (PII) about individuals that is maintained in systems of records by federal agencies on collecting, maintaining, using, and distributing PII that is maintained in systems of records by federal agencies.

federated identity   A portable identity that can be used across businesses and domains.

feet of illumination   A measurement of lighting.

fetching   When a CPU gets instructions from memory.

FHSS   *See* Frequency Hopping Spread Spectrum.

Fiber Distributed Data Interface (FDDI)   Another layer 2 protocol that uses a ring topology and a fiber infrastructure.

fiberoptic   Cabling that uses a source of light that shoots down an inner glass or plastic core of the cable.

field-programmable gate array   A type of programmable logic device (PLD) that is programmed by blowing fuse connections on the chip or using an antifuse that makes a connection when a high voltage is applied to the junction.

File Transfer Protocol (FTP)   Used to transfer files from one system to another.

finger scan   A biometric scan that extracts only certain features from a fingerprint.

fingerprint scan   A biometric scan that scans the ridges of a finger for matching.

firewall   Device that inspects and controls the type of traffic allowed.

firmware   Type of ROM where a program is stored.

FISA   *See* Federal Intelligence Surveillance Act of 1978.

FISMA   *See* Federal Information Security Management Act of 2002.

flame actuated sensor   Optical devices that "look at" the protected area. They generally react faster to a fire than nonoptical devices do.

flash memory   A type of electrically programmable ROM.

fluorescent   Lighting system that uses very low pressure mercury-vapor, gas-discharge lamp that uses fluorescence to produce visible light.

foreign key   An attribute in one relation that has values matching the primary key in another relation. Matches between the foreign key to primary key are important because they represent references from one relation to another and establish the connection among these relations.

FPA *See* Federal Privacy Act of 1974.

FPGA *See* field-programmable gate array.

fractional T1 A part of a T1.

frame relay A layer 2 protocol used for WAN connections. The frame relay network is shared by customers of the provider.

freeware Software available free of charge, including all rights to copy, distribute, and modify the software.

Frequency Division Multiple Access (FDMA) One of the modulation techniques used in cellular wireless networks.

Frequency Division Multiplexing (FDM) A process used in multiplexing that divides the medium into a series of non-overlapping frequency sub-bands, each of which is used to carry a separate signal.

Frequency Hopping Spread Spectrum (FHSS) One of two technologies (along with DSSS) that were a part of the original 802.11 standard. It is unique in that it changes frequencies or channels every few seconds in a set pattern that both transmitter and receiver know.

FRR *See* false rejection rate.

FTP *See* File Transfer Protocol.

FTPS FTP that adds support for the Transport Layer Security (TLS) and the Secure Sockets Layer (SSL) cryptographic protocols.

full backup A backup in which all data is backed up and the archive bit for each file is cleared.

G

gateway Any device that performs some sort of translation or acts as a control point to entry and exit.

GLBA *See* Gramm-Leach-Bliley Act of 1999.

Global System Mobile (GSM) A type of cellphone that contains a Subscriber Identity Module (SIM) chip.

Graham-Denning model Deals with the delegation and transfer of rights.

Gramm-Leach-Bliley Act (GLBA) of 1999   A U.S. act that affects all financial institutions, including banks, loan companies, insurance companies, investment companies, and credit card providers. It provides guidelines for securing all financial information and prohibits sharing financial information with third parties.

grid computing   The process of harnessing the CPU power of multiple physical machines to perform a job.

GSM   *See* Global System Mobile.

guideline   An information security governance component that gives recommended actions that are much more flexible than standards, thereby providing allowance for circumstances that can occur.

H

hand geometry scan   A biometric scan that obtains size, shape, or other layout attributes of a user's hand but can also measure bone length or finger length.

hand topography scan   A biometric scan that records the peaks and valleys of the hand and its shape.

Harrison-Ruzzo-Ullman Model   Model that deals with access rights and restricts the set of operations that can be performed on an object to a finite set to ensure integrity.

hash   A one-way function that reduces a message to a hash value. If the sender's hash value is compared to the receiver's hash value, message integrity is determined. If the resultant hash values are different, then the message has been altered in some way, provided that both the sender and receiver used the same hash function.

hash MAC   A keyed-hash MAC that involves a hash function with symmetric key.

HAVAL   A one-way function that produces variable-length hash values, including 128 bits, 160 bits, 192 bits, 224 bits, and 256 bits, and uses 1,024-bit blocks.

HDSL   *See* High-Bit-Data-Rate DSL.

Health Care and Education Reconciliation Act of 2010   A U.S. law that affects healthcare and educational organizations. It increased some of the security measures that must be taken to protect healthcare information.

Health Insurance Portability and Accountability Act (HIPAA)   A U.S. act that affects all healthcare facilities, health insurance companies, and healthcare clearing houses. It provides standards and procedures for storing, using, and transmitting medical information and healthcare data.

hearsay evidence   Evidence that is secondhand where the witness does not have direct knowledge of the fact asserted but knows it only from being told by someone.

heat-activated sensor   Also called heat-sensing. Operates by detecting temperature changes. These can either alert when a predefined temperature is met or alert when the rate of rise is a certain value.

hierarchical database   In this model, data is organized into a hierarchy. An object can have one child (an object that is a subset of the parent object), multiple children, or no children.

hierarchical storage management (HSM) system   A type of backup management system that provides a continuous online backup by using optical or tape "jukeboxes."

High-Bit-Data-Rate DSL (HDSL)   Form of DSL that provides T1 speeds.

high-level languages   These instructions use abstract statements (for example, IF-THEN-ELSE) and are processor independent. They are easier to work with and their syntax is more similar to human language.

HIPAA   *See* Health Insurance Portability and Accountability Act (HIPAA).

HMAC   *See* Hash MAC.

honeynets   Networks that are configured to be attractive to hackers.

honeypots   Systems that are configured to be attractive to hackers and lure them into spending time attacking them while information is gathered about the attack.

host-based IDS   An IDS that monitors traffic on a single system.

hot site   A leased facility that contains all the resources needed for full operation.

HSM   *See* hierarchical storage management system.

HSSI interface   Found on both routers and multiplexers and provides a connection to services like frame relay and ATM. It operates at speeds up to 52 Mbps.

HTTP   This protocol is used to view and transfer web pages or web content.

HTTP-S   *See* HTTP-Secure.

HTTP-Secure   The implementation of HTTP running over the SSL/TLS protocol, which establishes a secure session using the server's digital certificate.

hub   A physical device (layer 1) that functions as a junction point for devices in a star topology. It is considered physical in that it has no intelligence.

hybrid   A combination of network topologies, including bus, star, and ring.

hybrid or advanced distance vector protocols   Exhibit characteristics of both distance vector and link state routing protocols.

hygrometer   An alert system that monitors humidity.

I

IaaS *See* infrastructure as a service.

ICMP *See* Internet Message Control Protocol.

ICMP redirect By crafting ICMP redirect packets, the attacker alters the route table of the host that receives the redirect message. This will change the way packets are routed in the network to his advantage.

IDEA *See* International Data Encryption Algorithm.

identification The act of a user professing an identity to an access control system.

IDS *See* intrusion detection system.

IGMP *See* Internet Group Management Protocol.

IKE *See* Internet Key Exchange.

IMAP *See* Internet Message Access Protocol.

implied addressing Refers to registers usually contained inside the CPU.

incidental computer crime A crime that occurs when a computer is involved in a computer crime without being the victim of the attack or the attacker.

incremental A refinement to the basic waterfall model that states that software should be developed in increments of functional capability.

incremental backup A backup in which all files that have been changed since the last full or incremental backup will be backed up and the archive bit for each file is cleared.

indirect addressing The type of memory addressing where the address location that is specified in the program instruction contains the address of the final desired location.

inference Occurs when someone has access to information at one level that allows them to infer information about another level.

information assets Recipes, processes, trade secrets, product plans, and any other type of information that enables the enterprise to maintain competitiveness within its industry.

information flow model Model that focuses on controlling flows that relate two versions of the same object.

Information Technology Security Evaluation Criteria (ITSEC) Addresses integrity and availability as well as confidentiality.

informative security policy A security policy that provides information on certain topics and acts as an educational tool.

infrared   Short distance wireless process that uses light rather than radio waves, in this case, infrared light.

infrastructure as a service (IaaS)   Involves the vendor providing the hardware platform or data center and the company installs and manages their own operating systems and application systems. The vendor simply provides access to the data center and maintains that access.

infrastructure mode   In this mode, all transmissions between stations go through the AP and no direct communication between stations occurs.

intangible assets   Include intellectual property, data, and organizational reputation.

Integrated Services Digital Network (ISDN)   Sometimes referred to as digital dial-up. The really big difference between ISDN and analog dial-up is the performance.

integrity   A characteristic provided if you can be assured that the data has not changed in any way. The tenet of the CIA triad that ensures that data is accurate and reliable.

Interior Gateway Protocol   An obsolete classful Cisco proprietary routing protocol.

intermediate system to intermediate system (IS-IS)   A complex interior routing protocol that is based on OSI protocols rather than IP.

internal threats   Threats from those who might have some access to the room or building.

International Organization for Standardization (ISO) and the International Electro technical Commission (IEC)   *See* ISO/IEC 27000.

International Data Encryption Algorithm   A block cipher that uses 64-bit blocks, which are divided into 16 smaller blocks. It uses a 128-bit key and performs eight rounds of transformations on each of the 16 smaller blocks.

Internet Group Management Protocol (IGMP)   Used when multicasting, which is a form of communication whereby one host sends to a group of destination hosts rather than a single host (called a unicast transmission) or to all hosts (called a broadcast transmission).

Internet Key Exchange (IKE)   Also sometimes referred to as IPsec Key Exchange, provides the authenticated material used to create the keys exchanged by ISAKMP used to perform peer authentication.

Internet Message Access Protocol (IMAP)   An application layer protocol for e-mail retrieval.

Internet Message Control Protocol (ICMP)   Used by the network devices to send a message regarding the success or failure of communications and used by humans for troubleshooting. When you use the programs PING or TRACEROUTE, you are using ICMP.

internet protocol (IP) Responsible for putting the source and destination IP addresses in the packet and for routing the packet to its destination.

Internet Security Association and Key Management Protocol (ISAKMP) Handles the creation of a security association for the session and the exchange of keys.

interrupt A signal used by an in/out device when it requires the CPU to perform some action.

intranet The internal network of the enterprise.

intrusion detection system (IDS) A system responsible for detecting unauthorized access or attacks against systems and networks.

intrusion prevention system (IPS) A system responsible for preventing unauthorized access or attacks against systems and networks.

IP *See* internet protocol.

IP address spoofing One of the techniques used by hackers to hide their trail or to masquerade as another computer. The hacker alters the IP address as it appears in the packet.

IPS *See* intrusion prevention system.

IPsec Can provide encryption, data integrity, and system-based authentication, which makes it a flexible option for protecting transmissions.

iris scan A biometric scan that scans the colored portion of the eye, including all rifts, coronas, and furrows.

ISAKMP *See* Internet Security Association and Key Management Protocol.

ISDN *See* Integrated Services Digital Network.

ISO/IEC 27000 These standards provide guidance to organizations in integrating security into the development and maintenance of software applications. Series establishes information security standards published jointly by the International Organization for Standardization (ISO) and the International Electrotechnical Commission (IEC).

isolation Transactions do not interact with other transactions until completion.

issue-specific security policy A security policy that addresses specific security issues.

ITSEC *See* Information Technology Security Evaluation Criteria.

J

Java applet   A small component created using Java that runs in a web browser. It is platform independent and creates intermediate code called byte code that is not processor-specific.

Java Database Connectivity (JDBC)   Makes it possible for Java applications to communicate with a database.

Java Platform, Enterprise Edition (J2EE)   A distributed component model that relies on the Java programming language. It is a framework used to develop software that provides APIs for networking services and uses an interprocess communication process that is based on CORBA.

JDBC   *See* Java Database Connectivity.

job rotation   A security measure that ensures that more than one person fulfills the job tasks of a single position within an organization. Refers to training of multiple users to perform the duties of a position to help prevent fraud by any individual employee.

joint analyses development model   Also called the Joint Application Development (JAD), this is a development model that uses a team approach. It uses workshops to both agree on requirements and to resolve differences. The theory is that by bringing all parties together at all stages that a more satisfying product will emerge at the end of the process.

K

Kennedy-Kassebaum Act   *See* Health Insurance Portability and Accountability Act (HIPAA).

Kerberos   An authentication protocol that uses a client-server model developed by MIT's Project Athena. It is the default authentication model in the recent editions of Windows Server and is also used in Apple, Sun, and Linux operating systems.

kernel proxy firewall   An example of a fifth-generation firewall. It inspects the packet at every layer of the OSI model but does not introduce the performance hit that an application layer firewall will because it does this at the kernel layer.

key   A parameter that controls the transformation of plaintext into ciphertext or vice versa. Determining the original plaintext data without the key is impossible. Also referred to as a cryptovariable.

key clustering   Occurs when different encryption keys generate the same ciphertext from the same plaintext message.

keyspace   All the possible key values when using a particular algorithm or other security measure. A 40-bit key would have 240 possible values, whereas a 128-bit key would have 2,128 possible values.

keystroke dynamics   A biometric system that measures the typing pattern that a user uses when inputting a password or other pre-determined phrase.

knowledge factors   Factors that are something a person knows.

knowledge-based systems   Also called expect systems, they use artificial intelligence to emulate human logic when solving problems. Rules-based programming instructs the system how to react through if-then statements.

known plaintext attack   An attack that occurs when an attacker uses the plaintext and ciphertext versions of a message to discover the key used.

L

L2TP   *See* layer 2 tunneling protocol.

laminated glass   Two sheets of glass with a plastic film between that it makes it more difficult to break.

LAN   Stands for local area network. A group of systems that are connected with a fast network connection. For purposes of this discussion, that is any connection over 10 Mbps and usually in a single location.

layer 2 tunneling protocol   A newer protocol that operates at layer 2 of the OSI model. It can use various authentication mechanisms like PPTP can, but does not provide any encryption. It is typically used with IPsec, a very strong encryption mechanism.

layer 3 switch   A switch with the routing function also built in.

layer 4 switches   Provide additional routing above layer 3 by using the port numbers found in the Transport layer header to make routing decisions.

layered defense model   In such a model, reliance should not be based on any single physical security concept but on the use of multiple approaches that support one another.

least privilege   A security principle that requires that a user or process is given only the minimum access privilege needed to perform a particular task.

liability   The status of being legally responsible to another entity because of your actions or negligence.

link state   Routing protocols that only share network changes (link outages and recoveries) with neighbors, thereby greatly reducing the amount of traffic generated. They also use a much more sophisticated metric that is based on many factors such as the bandwidth of each link on the path and the congestion on each link.

Lipner model   Shares characteristics with the Clark-Wilson model in that it separates objects into data and programs.

local area network   *See* LAN.

logic bomb   A type of malware that executes when an event takes place.

logical control   Software or hardware components used to restrict access.

M

MAC   *See* mandatory access control.

machine languages   Languages that deliver instructions directly to the processor.

macro viruses   These infect programs written in Word Basic, Visual Basic, or VB-Script that are used to automate functions. These viruses infect Microsoft Office files. They are easy to create because the underlying language is simple and intuitive to apply. These are especially dangerous in that they infect the operating system itself. They also can be transported between different operating systems as the languages are platform independent.

maintenance hook   A set of instructions built into the code that allows for one who knows about the so-called "back door" to use the instructions to connect to view and edit the code without using the normal access controls.

malware   A term that describes any software that harms a computer, deletes data, or takes actions the user did not authorize.

MAN   *See* Metropolitan Area Network.

management control   *See* administrative control.

mandatory access control   An access control model in which subject authorization is based on security labels.

man-made disasters   Disasters that occur through human intent or error.

man-made threats   Physical threats faced from malicious and careless humans.

mantrap   A series of two doors with a small room between them.

matrix-based model   Organizes tables of subjects and objects indicating what actions individual subjects can take upon individual objects.

maximum tolerable downtime   The maximum amount of time that an organization can tolerate a single resource or function being down.

MD2   A message digest algorithm that produces a 128-bit hash value and performs 18 rounds of computations.

MD4   A message digest algorithm that produces a 128-bit hash value and performs only 3 rounds of computations.

MD5   A message digest algorithm that produces a 128-bit hash value and performs 4 rounds of computations.

MD6   A message digest algorithm that produces a variable hash value, performing a variable number of computations.

mean time between failure (MTBF)   The estimated amount of time a device will operate before a failure occurs. Describes how often a component fails on average.

mean time to repair (MTTR)   The average time required to repair a single resource or function when a disaster or disruption occurs. Describes the average amount of time it will take to get a device fixed and back online.

means   How the crime was carried out by the suspect.

Media Access Control (MAC) addresses   In Ethernet, these are called physical addresses because these 48-bit addresses expressed in hexadecimal are permanently assigned to the network interfaces of devices.

memory card   A swipe card that contains user authentication information and is issued to valid users.

mercury vapor   Lighting system that uses an electric arc through vaporized mercury to produce light.

mesh topology   The most fault tolerant and the most expensive to deploy. In this topology, all devices are connected to all other devices.

Metro Ethernet   The use of Ethernet technology over a wide area.

Metropolitan Area Network (MAN)   A type of LAN that encompasses a large area such as the downtown of a city.

middleware   Software in a distributed environment that ties the client and server software together.

MIMO   *See* Multiple Input Multiple Output.

mirrored site   *See* redundant site.

mixed law   A type of law that combines two or more of the other law types. The most often mixed law uses civil law and common law.

mobile code   Instructions passed across the network and executed on a remote system. A code type that can be transferred across a network and then executed on a remote system or device.

mono-alphabetic substation cipher   A cipher that uses only one alphabet.

motive   Why the crime was committed and who committed the crime. MOM stands for motive, opportunity, and means.

movable lighting   Lighting that can be repositioned as needed.

MTBF   *See* mean time between failure.

MTD   *See* maximum tolerable downtime.

MTTR   *See* mean time to repair.

multicast   This is a signal received by all others in a group called a multicast group. It is considered one-to-many.

multilevel lattice models   Developed mainly to deal with confidentiality issues and focuses itself mainly on information flow.

multi-mode   Fiberoptic that uses several beams of light at the same time and uses LEDs as a light source.

multipartite virus   Virus that can infect both program files and boot sectors.

Multiple Input Multiple Output (MIMO)   Using multiple antennas, which allow for up to four spatial streams at a time.

multiplexer   A physical (layer 1) device that combines several input information signals into one output signal, which carries several communication channels, by means of some multiplex technique.

multitasking   The process of carrying out more than one task at a time.

mutual aid agreement   A pre-arranged agreement between two organizations in which each organization agrees to provide assistance to the other in the event of a disaster.

N

NAS   *See* network attached storage or network access server.

NAT   *See* network address translation.

natural access control   This concept applies to the entrances of the facility. It encompasses the placement of the doors, lights, fences, and even landscaping. It aims to satisfy security goals in the least obtrusive and asthetically appealing manner.

natural disasters Disasters that occur because of a natural hazard.

natural languages Languages whose goal is to create software that can solve problems on its own rather than require a programmer to create code to deal with the problem. Although it's not fully realized, it is a goal worth pursuing using knowledge-based processing and artificial intelligence.

natural surveillance The use of physical environmental features to promote visibility of all areas and thus discourage crime in those areas. The idea is to encourage the flow of people such that the largest possible percentage of the building is always populated, because people in an area discourage crime.

natural territorials reinforcement Goal is to create a feeling of community in the area. It attempts to extend the sense of ownership to the employees.

natural threats Physical threats that must be addressed and mitigated that are caused by the forces of nature.

need to know A security principle that defines what the minimums for each job or business function are.

need-to-know/least privilege Concept that users should only be given access to resources required to do their job.

negligence A term that means that an organization was careless, resulting in some person or organization being injured.

network access server (NAS) Device that controls access to a network.

network address translation A service that changes the private IP address to a public address that is routable on the Internet. When the response is returned from the Web, the NAT service receives it and translates the address back to the original private IP address and sends it back to the originator.

network attached storage (NAS) A form of network storage that uses the existing LAN network for access using file access protocols such as NFS or SMB.

network database Like the hierarchical model, data is organized into a hierarchy but unlike the hierarchical model, objects can have multiple parents.

network layer (layer 3) Information required to route the packet is added. This will be in the form of a source and destination logical address.

network-based IDS An IDS that monitors network traffic on a local network segment.

noise A term used to cover several types of interference than can be introduced to the cable that causes problems.

non-disaster disruptions   Temporary interruptions that occur due to malfunction or failure.

noninterference models   Model less concerned with the flow of information and more concerned with a subject's knowledge of the state of the system at a point in time; it concentrates on preventing the actions that take place at one level from altering the state presented to another level.

non-repudiation   Provides proof of the origin of data, thereby preventing the sender from denying that he sent the message and supporting data integrity.

O

object linking and embedding (OLE)   A method for sharing objects on a local computer that uses COM as its foundation.

object linking and embedding database (OLE DB)   A replacement for ODBC, extending its functionality to non-relational databases.

object-oriented database (OODB)   This model has the ability to handle a variety of data types and is more dynamic than a relational database. OODB systems are useful in storing and manipulating complex data, such as images and graphics.

object-oriented programming (OOP)   In OOP, objects are organized in a hierarchy in classes with characteristics called attributes attached to each. OOP emphasizes the employment of objects and methods rather than types or transformations as in other software approaches.

object-relational database   This model is the marriage of object-oriented and relational technologies combining the attributes of both.

OCSP   *See* online certificate status protocol.

ODBC   *See* open database connectivity.

OFB   *See* output feedback.

OFDM   *See* Orthogonal Frequency Division Multiplexing.

OLE   *See* object linking and embedding.

OLE DB   *See* object linking and embedding database.

OLTP ACID test   An Online Transaction Processing system is used to monitor for problems such as processes that stop functioning. Its main goal is to prevent transactions that don't happen properly or are not complete from taking effect. An ACID test ensures that each transaction has certain properties before it is committed.

one-time pad   The most secure encryption scheme that can be used. It works likes a running cipher in that the key value is added to the value of the letters. However, it uses a key that is the same length as the plaintext message.

one-way function   A mathematical function that can be more easily performed in one direction than in the other.

online certificate status protocol   An Internet protocol that obtains the revocation status of an X.509 digital certificate.

Online Transaction Processing system   *See* OLTP ACID test.

OODB   *See* object-oriented database.

OOP   *See* object-oriented programming.

open database connectivity (ODBC)   An API that allows communication with databases either locally or remotely.

open shortest path first (OSPF)   A standards-based link state protocol.

open systems interconnect (OSI) model   Created in the 1980s by the International Standards Organization (ISO) as a part of its mission to create a protocol set to be used as a standard for all vendors.

Open Web Application Security Project (OWASP)   An open-source application security project. This group creates guidelines, testing procedures, and tools to assist with web security. A group that monitors attacks, specifically web attacks. OWASP maintains a list of top 10 attacks on an ongoing basis.

operations security   Comprises the activities that support continual maintenance of the security of the system on a daily basis.

opinion evidence   Evidence that is based on what the witness thinks, feels, or infers regarding the facts.

opportunity   Where and when the crime occurred.

Orange Book   A collection of criteria based on the Bell-LaPadula model that is used to grade or rate the security offered by a computer system product.

organizational security policy   The highest level security policy adopted by an organization that outlines security goals.

Orthogonal Frequency Division Multiplexing (OFDM)   A more advanced technique of modulation where a large number of closely spaced orthogonal sub-carrier signals are used to carry the data on several parallel data streams. It is used in 802.11a and 802.11g. It makes speed up to 54 Mbps possible.

OSI   *See* open systems interconnect model.

OSPF *See* open shortest path first.

output feedback (OFB) A DES mode that works with 8-bit (or smaller) blocks that uses a combination of stream ciphering and block ciphering. However, OFB uses the previous keystream with the key to create the next keystream.

OWASP *See* Open Web Application Security Project.

ownership factors Factors that are something a person possesses, such as a password.

P

PaaS *See* platform as a service.

packet filtering firewalls Only inspect the header of the packet for allowed IP addresses or port numbers.

packet switching networks (such as the Internet or a LAN) Networks that group all transmitted data blocks, called packets. Each packet is treated individually with respect to routing.

palm scan A biometric scan that records fingerprint information from every finger as well as hand geometry information. Also referred to as a hand scan.

PAP *See* Password Authentication Protocol.

parasitic virus This is a virus that attaches itself to a file, usually an executable file, and then delivers the payload when the program is used.

passive infrared systems (PIR) Detection systems that operate by identifying changes in heat waves in an area.

Password Authentication Protocol (PAP) Provides authentication but the credentials are sent in cleartext and can be read with a sniffer.

PAT *See* Port Address Translation.

patch panels Operate at the physical layer of the OSI model and simply function as a central termination point for all the cables running through the walls from wall outlets, which in turn are connected to computers with cables.

patent An intellectual property type that covers an invention described in a patent application and is granted to an individual or company.

Payment Card Industry Data Security Standard (PCI DSS) A standard that affects any organizations that handle cardholder information for the major credit card companies. The latest version is version 2.0.

PBX *See* private branch exchange.

PCI DSS *See* Payment Card Industry Data Security Standard.

peer-to-peer computing Any client/server solution in which any platform may act as a client or server or both.

penetration testing A test that simulates an attack to identify any risks that can stem from the vulnerabilities of a system or device.

permutation *See* transposition.

Personal Information Protection and Electronic Documents Act (PIPEDA) An act from Canada that affects how private sector organizations collect, use, and disclose personal information in the course of commercial business. The Act was written to address European Union concerns over the security of PII.

personally identifiable information (PII) Any piece of data that can be used alone or with other information to identify a single person.

pharming A social engineering attack, similar to phishing, that actually pollutes the contents of a computer's DNS cache so that requests to a legitimate site are actually routed to an alternate site.

phishing A social engineering attack in which attackers try to learn personal information, including credit card information and financial data. A social engineering attack where a recipient is convinced to click on a link in an e-mail that appears to go to a trusted site but in fact goes to the hacker's site.

phone cloning A process where copies of the SIM chip are made allowing another user to make calls as the original user.

photometric system Operates by detecting changes in light and thus is used in windowless areas. It sends a beam of light across the area and if the beam is interrupted (by a person, for example), the alarm is triggered.

physical control A security control that protects an organization's facilities and personnel.

physical layer (layer 1) Responsible for turning the information into bits (ones and zeros) and sending it out on the medium.

physical surveillance When a person's actions are reported or captured using cameras, direct observance, or CCTV.

physiological characteristics Any unique physical attribute of the user, including iris, retina, and fingerprints.

PII *See* personally identifiable information.

ping of death attack Sends several oversized packets, which can cause the victim's system to be unstable at the least and possibly freeze up.

ping scanning   Basically pings every IP address and keeps track of which IP addresses respond to the ping.

PIPEDA   *See* Personal Information Protection and Electronic Documents Act.

pipelined processor   Overlaps the steps of different instructions whereas a scalar processor executes one instruction at a time.

plaintext   A message in its original format. Also referred to as cleartext.

platform as a service (PaaS)   Involves the vendor providing the hardware platform or data center and the software running on the platform. The company is still involved in managing the system.

Point-to-Point Protocol (PPP)   A layer 2 protocol that performs framing and encapsulation of data across point-to-point connections.

point-to-point tunneling protocol (PPTP)   A Microsoft protocol based on PPP. It uses built-in Microsoft Point-to-Point encryption and can use a number of authentication methods, including CHAP, MS-CHAP, and EAP-TLS.

policy   An information security governance component that outlines goals but does not give any specific ways to accomplish the stated goals.

polling   Contention method where a primary device polls each other device to see whether it needs to transmit.

polyalphabetic substation cipher   A cipher that uses multiple alphabets.

polyinstantiation   A process used to prevent data inference violations. It does this by enabling a relation to contain multiple tuples with the same primary keys with each instance distinguished by a security level. It prevents low-level database users from inferring the existence of higher level data. The development of a detailed version of an object from another object using different values in the new object.

polymorphic virus   This virus makes copies of itself, and then makes changes to those copies. It does this in hopes of avoiding detection of antivirus software.

polymorphism   The ability of different objects with a common name to react to the same message or input with different output.

POP   *See* Post Office Protocol.

Port Address Translation (PAT)   A specific version of NAT that uses a single public IP address to represent multiple private IP addresses.

port scan   This attack basically pings every address and port number combination and keeps track of which ports are open on each device as the pings are answered by open ports with listening services and not answered by closed ports.

Post Office Protocol (POP)   An application layer e-mail retrieval protocol.

POTS (Plain Old Telephone Service)   *See* public switched telephone network.

power conditioners   Go between the wall outlet and the device and smooth out the fluctuations of power delivered to the device protecting against sags and surges.

PPP   *See* Point-to-Point Protocol.

PPTP   *See* point-to-point tunneling protocol.

preaction extinguisher   Operates like a dry pipe system except that the sprinkler head holds a thermal-fusible link that must be melted before the water is released. This is currently the recommended system for a computer room.

presentation layer (layer 6)   Responsible for the manner in which the data from the application layer is represented (or presented) to the application layer on the destination device. If any translation between formats is required, it will take care of it.

preventive control   A security control that prevents an attack from occurring.

PRI ISDN   *See* Primary Rate ISDN (PRI).

primary key   Columns that make each row unique.

Primary Rate ISDN (PRI)   Solution that provides up to 23 B channels and a D channel for a total of 1.544 Mbps.

private branch exchange (PBX)   A private telephone switch that resides on the customer's premises. It has a direct connection to the telecommunication provider's switch. It performs call routing within the internal phone system.

private IP addresses   Three ranges of IPv4 addresses set aside to be used *only* within private networks and are *not* routable on the Internet.

private key encryption   *See* symmetric encryption.

privilege escalation   The process of exploiting a bug or weakness in an operating system to allow a user to receive privileges to which they are not entitled.

procedure   An information security governance component that includes all the detailed actions that personnel are required to follow.

process   A set of threads that are part of the same larger piece of work done for a specific application.

protected computer   A computer used exclusively by a financial institution or the U.S. government or used in or affecting interstate or foreign commerce or communication, including a computer located outside the United States that is used in a manner that affects interstate or foreign commerce or communication of the United States.

prototyping   The use of a sample of code to explore a specific approach to solving a problem before extensive time and cost have been invested in the approach.

proximity authentication device   A programmable card used to deliver an access code to the device either by swiping the card or in some cases just being in the vicinity of the reader.

proxy firewall   Creates the web connection between systems on their behalf but they can typically allow and disallow traffic on a more granular basis. Proxy firewalls actually stand between each connection from the outside to the inside and make the connection on behalf of the endpoints.

PSTN   *See* public switched telephone network.

Public Company Accounting Reform and Investor Protection Act of 2002   *See* Sarbanes-Oxley (SOX) Act.

public key encryption   *See* asymmetric encryption.

public switched telephone network (PSTN)   Also referred to as the Plain Old Telephone Service (POTS), this is the circuit-switched network that has been used for analog phone service for years and is now mostly a digital operation.

punitive damages   Damages that are handed down by juries to punish the liable party.

Q

qualitative risk analysis   A method of analyzing risk whereby intuition, experience, and best practice techniques are used to determine risk.

quartz lamp   A lamp consisting of an ultraviolet light source, such as mercury vapor, contained in a fused-silica bulb that transmits ultraviolet light with little absorption.

R

RA   *See* registration authority.

RAD   *See* Rapid Application Development.

radio frequency interference (RFI)   Interference from radio sources in the area.

RADIUS   *See* Remote Access Dial In User Service.

RAID 0 Also called disk striping, this method writes the data across multiple drives but while it improves performance, it does not provide fault tolerance.

RAID 1 Also called disk mirroring, it uses two disks and writes a copy of the data to both disks, providing fault tolerance in the case of a single drive failure.

RAID 2 In this system, the data is striped across all drives at the bit level and uses a hamming code for error detection. Hamming codes can detect up to two-bit errors or correct one-bit errors without detection of uncorrected errors.

RAID 3 Requires at least three drives. The data is written across all drives like striping and then parity information is written to a single dedicated drive; the parity information is used to regenerate the data in the case of a single drive failure.

RAID 5 Requires at least three drives. The data is written across all drives like striping and then parity information is spread across all drives as well. The parity information is used to regenerate the data in the case of a single drive failure.

RAID 7 While not a standard but a proprietary implementation, this system incorporates the same principles as RAID 5 but enables the drive array to continue to operate if any disk or any path to any disk fails. The multiple disks in the array operate as a single virtual disk.

Rapid Application Development (RAD) A development model in which less time is spent upfront on design while emphasis is placed on rapidly producing prototypes with the assumption that crucial knowledge can only be gained through trial and error.

RBAC *See* role-based access control.

RC4 A stream cipher that uses a variable key size of 40 to 2,048 bits and up to 256 rounds of transformation.

RC5 A block cipher that uses a key size of up to 2,048 bits and up to 255 rounds of transformation. Block sizes supported are 32, 64, or 128 bits.

RC6 A block cipher based on RC5 that uses the same key size, rounds, and block size.

reciprocal agreement An agreement between two organizations that have similar technological needs and infrastructures.

record Collection of related data items.

recovery control A security control that recovers a system or device after an attack has occurred.

recovery point objective The point in time to which the disrupted resource or function must be returned.

recovery time objective   The shortest time period after a disaster or disruptive event within which a resource or function must be restored to avoid unacceptable consequences.

Red Book   A collection of criteria based on the Bell-LaPadula model that addresses network security.

redundancy   Refers to providing multiple instances of either a physical or logical component such that a second component is available if the first fails.

redundant site   A site that is identically configured as the primary site.

reference monitor   A system component that enforces access controls on an object.

referential integrity   Requires that for any foreign key attribute, the referenced relation must have a tuple with the same value for its primary key.

registration authority   The entity in a PKI that verifies the requestor's identity and registers the requestor.

regulatory law   *See* administrative law.

regulatory security policy   A security policy that addresses specific industry regulations, including mandatory standards.

relation   Fundamental entity in a relational database in the form of a table.

relational database   Uses attributes (columns) and tuples (rows) to organize the data in two-dimensional tables.

reliability   The ability of a function or system to consistently perform according to specifications.

religious law   A type of law based on religious beliefs.

remanence   Any data left after the media has been erased.

Remote Access Dial In User Service (RADIUS)   An remote authentication standard defined in RFC 2138. RADIUS is designed to provide a framework that includes three components: supplicant, authenticator, and authenticating server.

residual risk   Risk that is left over after safeguards have been implemented.

retinal scan   A biometric scan that scans the retina's blood vessel pattern.

RFI   *See* radio frequency interference.

Rijndael algorithm   Uses three block sizes of 128, 192, and 256 bits. A 128-bit key with a 128-bit block size undergoes 10 transformation rounds. A 192-bit key with a 192-bit block size undergoes 12 transformation rounds. Finally, a 256-bit key with a 256-bit block size undergoes 14 transformation rounds.

ring   A physical ring topology is one in which the devices are daisy-chained one to another in a circle or ring.

RIP   *See* Routing Information Protocol.

RIPEMD-160   A message digest algorithm that produces a 160-bit hash value after performing 160 rounds of computations on 512-bit blocks.

risk   The probability that a threat agent will exploit a vulnerability and the impact of the probability.

risk acceptance   A method of handling risk that involves understanding and accepting the level of risk as well as the cost of damages that can occur.

risk avoidance   A method of handling risk that involves terminating the activity that causes a risk or choosing an alternative that is not as risky.

risk management   The process that occurs when organizations identify, measure, and control organizational risks.

risk mitigation   A method of handling risk that involves defining the acceptable risk level the organization can tolerate and reducing the risk to that level.

risk transfer   A method of handling risk that involves passing the risk on to a third party.

role-based access control   An access control model in which each subject is assigned to one or more roles.

rootkit   A set of tools that a hacker can use on a computer after he has managed to gain access and elevate his privileges to administrator.

routers   Use a routing table that tells the router in which direction to send traffic destined for a particular network.

Routing Information Protocol (RIP)   Standards-based distance vector protocol that has two versions, RIPv1 and RIPv2. Both use hop count as a metric.

row   A row in a table.

RPO   *See* recovery point objective.

RTO   *See* recovery time objective.

rule-based access control   An access control model in which a security policy is based on global rules imposed for all users.

running key cipher   A cipher that uses a physical component, usually a book, to provide the polyalphabetic characters.

S

SaaS *See* software as a service.

SABSA *See* Sherwood Applied Business Security Architecture.

safeguard *See* countermeasure.

SAML *See* Security Assertion Markup Language.

SAN *See* storage area networks.

Sarbanes-Oxley (SOX) Act A U.S. act that controls the accounting methods and financial reporting for the organizations and stipulates penalties and even jail time for executive officers and affects any organization that is publicly traded in the United States.

schema Description of a relational database.

screened host A firewall that is between the final router and the internal network.

screened subnet In this case, two firewalls are used and traffic must be inspected at both firewalls to enter the internal network.

search The act of pursuing items or information.

secondary evidence Evidence that has been reproduced from an original or substituted for an original item.

secret key encryption *See* symmetric encryption.

secure electronic transaction A protocol that secures credit card transaction information over the Internet.

Secure European System for Applications in a Multi-vendor Environment (SESAME) A project that extended Kerberos functionality to fix Kerberos weaknesses. It uses both symmetric and asymmetric cryptography to protect interchanged data and a trusted authentication server at each host.

Secure File Transfer Protocol (SFTP) This is an extension of the SSH. There have been a number of different versions with version 6 being the latest. Because it uses SSH for the file transfer, its uses TCP port 22.

secure shell (SSH) An application and protocol that is used to remotely log in to another computer using a secure tunnel.

secure sockets layer (SSL) A protocol developed by Netscape to transmit private documents over the Internet that implements either 40-bit (SSL 2.0) or 128-bit encryption (SSL 3.0).

Security Assertion Markup Language (SAML)   An XML-based open standard data format for exchanging authentication and authorization data between parties, in particular, between an identity provider and a service provider.

security domain   A set of resources that follow the same security policies and are available to a subject.

security kernel   The hardware, firmware, and software elements of a trusted computing base that implements the reference monitor concept.

security perimeter   The dividing line between the trusted parts of the system and those that are untrusted.

seizure   The act of taking custody of physical or digital components.

separation of duties   The concept that prescribes that sensitive operations be divided among multiple users so that no one user has the rights and access to carry out the operation alone. A security measure that ensures that one person is not capable of compromising organizational security. It prevents fraud by distributing tasks and their associated rights and privileges between more than one user.

Serial Line Interface Protocol (SLIP)   *See* SLIP.

Service Oriented Architecture (SOA)   An approach that operates on the theory of providing web-based communication functionality without requiring redundant code to be written per application. It uses standardized interfaces and components called service brokers to facilitate communication among web-based applications.

service set identifier (SSID)   A name or value assigned to identify the WLAN from other WLANs.

SESAME   *See* Secure European System for Applications in a Multi-vendor Environment.

session hijacking attack   The hacker attempts to place himself in the middle of an active conversation between two computers for the purpose of taking over the session of one of the two computers, thus receiving all data sent to that computer.

Session Initiation Protocol (SIP)   To control call sessions and multimedia over VoIP networks.

session layer (layer 5)   Responsible for adding information to the packet that makes a communication session between a service or application on the source device possible with the same service or application on the destination device.

SET   *See* secure electronic transaction.

SFTP   *See* Secure File Transfer Protocol.

shareware   Software that is shared for a limited time. After a certain amount of time (the trial period), the software requires that the user purchase the software to access all the software's features. This is also referred to as trialware.

Sherwood Applied Business Security Architecture (SABSA)   A model for guiding the creation and design of a security architecture. It attempts to enhance the communication process between stakeholders.

shoulder surfing   A social engineering attack that occurs when an attacker watches when a user enters login or other confidential data.

S-HTTP   Encrypts only the served page data and submitted data like POST fields, leaving the initiation of the protocol unchanged.

signaling system 7 (SS7)   Protocol to set up, control the signaling, and tear down a PSTN phone call.

signature dynamics   A biometric system that measures stroke speed, pen pressure, and acceleration and deceleration while the user writes his signature.

Simple Mail Transfer Protocol (SMTP)   A standard application layer protocol used between e-mail servers. This is also the protocol used by clients to send e-mail.

Simple Network Management Protocol (SNMP)   An application layer protocol that is used to retrieve information from network devices and to send configuration changes to those devices.

single loss expectancy   *See* SLE.

single mode   Fiberoptic that uses a single beam of light provided by a laser as a light source.

single sign-on   A system in which a user enters his login credentials once and can access all resources in the network.

SIP   *See* Session Initiation Protocol.

skipjack   A block-cipher, symmetric algorithm developed by the U.S. NSA that uses an 80-bit key to encrypt 64-bit blocks. It is used in the Clipper chip.

slack space analysis   Analyzes the slack (marked as empty or reusable) space on the drive to see whether any old (marked for deletion) data can be retrieved.

SLE   The monetary impact of each threat occurrence. This acronym stands for single loss expectancy. The equation used is SLE = AV × EF.

SLIP   An older remote access protocol that had been made obsolete by PPP.

smart card   An ICC that contains memory like a memory card but also contains an embedded chip like bank or credit cards.

SMDS   *See* Switched Multimegabit Data Service.

smoke activated sensor   Operates using a photoelectric device to detect variations in light caused by smoke particles.

SMTP   *See* Simple Mail Transfer Protocol.

smurf   This attack is also a DoS attack that uses a type of ping packet called an ICMP ECHO REQUEST.

smurf attack   In this attack, an attacker sends a large amount of UDP echo traffic to an IP broadcast address, all of it having a fake source address, which will, of course, be the target system.

SNMP   *See* Simple Network Management Protocol.

SOA   *See* Service Oriented Architecture.

SOCKS firewall   An example of a circuit-level firewall.

sodium vapor   Lighting system that uses sodium in an excited state to produce light.

software as a service (SaaS)   Involves the vendor providing the entire solution. They might provide you with an e-mail system, for example, whereby they host and manage everything for you.

Software Development Life Cycle   The goal of the software development life cycle is to provide a predictable framework of procedures designed to identify all requirements with regard to functionality, cost, reliability, and delivery schedule and ensure that each are met in the final solution.

software patches   Updates released by vendors that either fix functional issues with or close security loopholes in operating systems, applications, and versions of firmware that run on the network devices.

software piracy   The unauthorized reproduction or distribution of copyrighted software.

SONET   *See* synchronous optical networks.

SOX Act   *See* Sarbanes-Oxley Act.

spam   When e-mail is sent out on a mass basis that is not requested.

spear phishing   A phishing attack carried out against a specific target by learning about the target's habits and likes. The process of foisting a phishing attack on a specific person rather than a random set of people.

spiral   A development model that is an iterative approach but places more emphasis on risk analysis at each stage.

split knowledge   A security measure that ensures no single employee knows all the details to perform a task. This security measure is part of separation of duties.

spyware   Tracks your activities and can also gather personal information that could lead to identity theft.

SSH   *See* secure shell.

SSID   *See* service set identifier.

SSL   *See* secure sockets layer.

SSO   *See* single sign-on.

stakeholder   Individuals, teams, and departments, including groups outside the organization, with interests or concerns that should be considered.

standard   An information security governance component that describes how policies will be implemented within an organization.

standard glass   Used in residential areas and is easily broken.

standby lighting   A type of system that illuminates only at certain times or on a schedule.

star topology   The most common in use today. In this topology, all devices are connected to a central device (either a hub or a switch).

state machine models   By examining every possible state the system could be in and ensuring that the system maintains the proper security relationship between objects and subjects in each state, the system is said to be secure.

stateful firewalls   Aware of the proper functioning of the TCP handshake, keeps track of the state of all connections with respect to this process and can recognize when packets are trying to enter the network that don't make sense in the context of the TCP handshake.

statutory damages   Damages established by laws.

stealth virus   This is a virus that hides the modifications that it is making to the system to help avoid detection.

steganography   When a message is hidden inside another object, such as a picture or document.

steganography analysis   Analyzes the files on a drive to see whether the files have been altered or to discover the encryption used on the file.

storage area networks (SAN)   Comprised of high-capacity storage devices that are connected by a high-speed private (separate from the LAN) network using storage-specific switches.

strategic plans (or goals) Plans that guide the long-term security activities (3 to 5 years or more).

stream-based cipher A cipher that performs encryption on a bit-by-bit basis and uses keystream generators.

substitution The process of exchanging one byte in a message for another.

substitution cipher A cipher that uses a key to substitute characters of character blocks with different characters or character blocks.

superscalar A computer architecture characterized by a processor that enables concurrent execution of multiple instructions in the same pipeline stage.

supervisor mode Mode used when a computer system processes input/output instructions.

supplicant The component in a RADIUS environment seeking authentication.

surge A prolonged high voltage.

surveillance The act of monitoring behavior, activities, or other changing information, usually of people.

Switched Multimegabit Data Service (SMDS) A connectionless packet switched technology that communicates across an established public network.

switches Intelligent and operate at layer 2 of the OSI model. We say they map to this layer because they make switching decisions based on MAC addresses, which reside at layer 2.

symmetric encryption An encryption method whereby a single private key both encrypts and decrypts the data. Also referred to as a private or secret key encryption.

symmetric mode In this mode, the processors or cores are handed work on a round-robin basis, thread by thread.

SYN ACK attack In this attack, the hacker sends a large number of packets with the SYN flag set, which causes the receiving computer to set aside memory for each ACK packet it expects to receive in return. These packets never come and at some point the resources of the receiving computer are exhausted, making this a form of DoS attack.

synchronous encryption When encryption or decryption occurs immediately.

synchronous optical networks (SONET) Use fiber-based links that operate over lines measured in optical carrier (OC) transmission rates.

synchronous token A token generates a unique password at fixed time intervals with the authentication server.

synchronous transmission   Uses a clocking mechanism to synch up the sender and receiver.

system development life cycle   Process that provides clear and logical steps that should be followed to ensure the system that emerges at the end of the development process provides the intended functionality with an acceptable level of security.

system threats   Threats that exist not from the forces of nature but from failures in systems that provide basic services such as electricity and utilities.

system-specific security policy   A security policy that addresses security for a specific computer, network, technology, or application.

T

T carriers   Dedicated lines to which the subscriber has private access and does not share with another customer.

TACACS+   A Cisco proprietary authentication service that operates on Cisco devices, providing a centralized authentication solution.

tactical plans (or goals)   Plans that achieve the goals of the strategic plan and are shorter in length (6 to 18 months).

tangible assets   Include computers, facilities, supplies, and personnel.

TCB   *See* Trusted Computer Base.

TCP three-way handshake   Process of creating a state of connection between the two hosts before any data is transferred.

TCP/IP   Model has only four layers and is useful to study because it focuses its attention on TCP/IP.

TCSEC   *See* Trusted Computer System Evaluation Criteria.

TDM   *See* Time Division Multiplexing.

teardrop   The hacker sends malformed fragments of packets that when reassembled by the receiver cause the receiver to crash or become unstable.

technological disasters   Disasters that occur when a device fails.

Telnet   A remote access protocol used to connect to a device for the purpose of executing commands on the device.

tempered glass   Created by heating the glass which gives it extra strength.

tertiary site   A secondary backup site that provides an alternate in case the hot site, warm site, or cold site is unavailable.

The Open Group Architecture Framework   *See* TOGAF.

Thicknet   Type of coaxial with an official name of 10Base5.

Thinnet   Coaxial also called 10Base2; operates at 10 Mbps and although when it was named it was anticipated to be capable of running 200 feet, this was later reduced to 185 feet.

thread   An individual piece of work done for a specific process.

threat   A condition that occurs when a vulnerability is identified or exploited.

threat agent   The entity that carries out a threat.

three-legged firewall   Uses three interfaces, one connected to the untrusted network, one to the internal network, and another to a part of the network called a DMZ.

tiger   A hash function that produces 128-, 160-, or 192-bit hash values after performing 24 rounds of computations on 512-bit blocks.

Time Division Multiplexing (TDM)   Multiplexing where the transmissions take turns rather than send at the same time.

time-of-check/time-of-use attacks   An attack that attempts to take advantage of the sequence of events that take place as the system completes common tasks.

TLS/SSL   *See* transport layer security/secure sockets layer.

TOGAF   The Open Group Architecture Framework; has its origins in the U.S. Department of Defense and calls for an Architectural Development Method (ADM) that employs an iterative process that calls for individual requirements to be continuously monitored and updated as needed.

token passing   Contention method used is called in both FDDI and token ring. In this process, a special packet called a token is passed around the network. A station cannot send until the token comes around and is empty.

token ring   A proprietary layer 2 protocol that enjoyed some small success and is no longer widely used.

tort law   *See* civil/tort law.

total risk   The risk that an organization could encounter if it decides not to implement any safeguards.

TPM   *See* trusted platform module.

trade secret   An intellectual property type that ensures that proprietary technical or business information remains confidential. Trade secrets include recipes, formulas, ingredient listings, and so on that must be protected against disclosure.

trademark   An intellectual property type that ensures that the symbol, sound, or expression that identifies a product or an organization is protected from being used by another organization.

transaction log backup   A backup that captures all transactions that have occurred since the last backup.

transport layer (layer 4)   Receives all the information from layers 7, 6, and 5 and adds information that identifies the transport protocol in use and the specific port number that identifies the required layer 7 protocol.

transport layer security/secure sockets layer (TLS/SSL)   This is another option for creating secure connections to servers. It works at the application layer of the OSI model. It is used mainly to protect HTTP traffic or web servers.

transposition   The process of shuffling or reordering the plaintext to hide the original message. Also referred to as permutation.

transposition cipher   A cipher that scrambles the letters of the original message in a different order.

trapdoor   *See* backdoor.

trapdoor (encryption)   A secret mechanism that allows the implementation of the reverse function in a one-way function.

trialware   *See* shareware.

triple DES   A version of DES that increases security by using three 56-bit keys.

Trojan horse   A program or rogue application that appears to or is purported to do one thing but it does another when executed.

Trusted Computer Base (TCB)   Comprises the components (hardware, firmware, and/or software) that are trusted to enforce the security policy of the system and that, if compromised, jeopardize the security properties of the entire system.

Trusted Computer System Evaluation Criteria (TCSEC)   Developed by the National Computer Security Center (NCSC) for the U.S. Department of Defense to evaluate products.

trusted path   A communication channel between the user or the program through which he is working and the trusted computer base.

trusted platform module   A security chip installed on a computer motherboard that is responsible for managing symmetric and asymmetric keys, hashes, and digital certificates.

trusted recovery   The response of a system to a failure (such as a crash or freeze) that leaves the system in a secure state.

trusted shell   A secure interface to a system.

trusted third-party federated identity model   A federated identity model in which each organization subscribes to the standards of a third party.

tumbler locks   Lock with more moving parts than the warded lock with the key raising the lock metal piece to the correct height.

twisted pair   The most common type of network cabling found today is called twisted-pair cabling. It is called this because inside the cable are four pairs of smaller wires that are braided or twisted.

Twofish   A version of Blowfish that uses 128-bit data blocks using 128-, 192-, and 256-bit keys and performs 16 rounds of transformation.

U

unicast   This is a transmission from a single system to another single system. It is considered one-to-one.

uninterruptible power supplies (UPS)   Goes between the wall outlet and the device and uses a battery to provide power if the source from the wall is lost.

United States Federal Sentencing Guidelines of 1991   A U.S. act that affects individuals and organizations convicted of felonies and serious (Class A) misdemeanors.

Uniting and Strengthening America by Providing Appropriate Tools Required to Intercept and Obstruct Terrorism (USA PATRIOT) Act of 2001   A U.S. law that affects law enforcement and intelligence agencies in the United States. Its purpose is to enhance the investigatory tools that law enforcement can use, including e-mail communications, telephone records, Internet communications, medical records, and financial records.

UPS   *See* uninterruptible power supplies.

URL hiding   This attack takes advantage of the ability to embed URLs in web pages and e-mail.

USA PATRIOT Act   *See* Uniting and Strengthening America by Providing Appropriate Tools Required to Intercept and Obstruct Terrorism Act of 2001.

V

vascular scan   A biometric scan that scans the pattern of veins in the user's hand or face.

VDSL   *See* Very-High–Bit-Data-Rate DSL.

very long instruction word processor   A processor in which a single instruction specifies more than one *concurrent* operation.

Very-High–Bit-Data-Rate DSL (VDSL)   Form of DSL capable of supporting HDTV and VoIP.

very-high-level languages   A fourth generation of languages that focuses on abstract algorithms that hide some of the complexity from the programmer. This frees the programmer to focus on the real-world problems she is trying to solve rather than the details that go on behind the scenes.

view   The representation of the system from the perspective of a stakeholder or a set of stakeholders. Security is enforced through the use of views, which is the set of data available to a given user.

viewpoint   A template used to develop individual views that establish the audience, techniques, and assumptions made.

virtual firewalls   Software that has been specifically written to operate in the virtual environment.

virtual LAN   *See* VLAN.

Virtual Private Network (VPN)   Connections are those that use an untrusted carrier network but provide protection of the information through strong authentication protocols and encryption mechanisms.

Virtual Router Redundancy Protocol (VRRP)   Used to provide multiple gateways to clients for fault tolerance in the case of a router going down.

virus   A self-replicating program that infects software. It uses a host application to reproduce and deliver its payload and typically attaches itself to a file.

VLANs   These are logical subdivisions of a switch that segregate ports from one another as if they were in different LANs. These VLANs can also span multiple switches, meaning that devices connected to switches in different parts of a network can be placed in the same VLAN regardless of physical location.

voice pattern or print   A biometric system that measures the sound pattern of a user stating a certain words.

VoIP   When voice is encapsulated in packets and sent across packet switching networks.

VPN   *See* Virtual Private Network.

VRRP   *See* Virtual Router Redundancy Protocol.

V-shaped   A development model that differs primarily from the waterfall method in that verification and validation are performed at each step.

vulnerability   An absence or weakness of a countermeasure that is in place.

vulnerability assessment   An assessment method whereby an organization's network is tested for countermeasure absences or other security weaknesses.

W

war chalking   A practice that is typically used to accompany war driving. After the war driver has located a WLAN, he would indicate in chalk on the sidewalk the SSID and the types of security used on the network.

war driving   Driving around and locating WLANs with a laptop and a high-power antenna.

warded lock   Lock with a spring-loaded bolt with a notch in it. The lock has wards or metal projection inside the lock with which the key will match and enable opening the lock.

warm site   A leased facility that contains electrical and communications wiring, full utilities, and networking equipment.

WANs   *See* wide area networks.

WASC   *See* Web Application Security Consortium.

waterfall   A development model that breaks the process up into distinct phases. While somewhat of a rigid approach, it sees the process as a sequential series of steps that are followed without going back to earlier steps. This approach is called incremental development.

wave motion detector   These devices generate a wave pattern in the area and detect any motion that disturbs the accepted wave pattern. When the pattern is disturbed, an alarm sounds.

Web Application Security Consortium (WASC)   An organization that provides best practices for web-based applications along with a variety of resources, tools, and information that organizations can make use of in developing web applications.

WEP   *See* wired equivalent privacy.

wet pipe extinguisher   Uses water contained in pipes to extinguish the fire. In some areas, the water might freeze and burst the pipes causing damage. These are also not recommended for rooms where equipment will be damaged by the water.

whaling   Targets a single person who is someone of significance or importance. It might be a CEO, a COO, or CTO, for example.

wide area networks (WANs)   Used to connect LANs together (including MANs).

Wi-Fi protected access (WPA) Created to address the widespread concern with the inadequacy of WEP.

wired equivalent privacy (WEP) The first security measure used with 802.11. It was specified as the algorithm in the original specification. It can be used to both authenticate a device and encrypt the information between the AP and the device.

work factor (encryption) The amount of time and resources that would be needed to break the encryption.

work recovery time The difference between RTO and MTD, which is the remaining time that is left over after the RTO before reaching the maximum tolerable.

worm A type of malware that can spread without the assistance of the user.

WPA *See* Wi-Fi protected access.

WPA2 An improvement over WPA. WPA2 uses CCMP, based on Advanced Encryption Standard (AES) rather than TKIP.

WRT *See* work recovery time.

X-Z

X.25 Somewhat like frame relay in that traffic moves through a packet switching network. Uses mechanisms for reliability that are no longer required in today's phone lines and that create overhead.

XML *See* Extensible Markup Language.

XML: DB API Allows XML applications to interact with more traditional databases, such as relational databases.

Zachman framework A two-dimensional model that intersects communication interrogatives (such as what, why, and where) with various viewpoints (such as planner, owner, and designer).

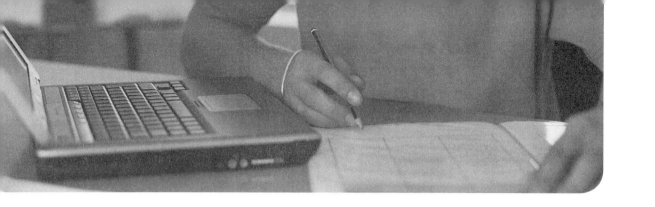

Index

Numbers

3DES (Triple DES)
  modes, 262-263, 495, 514
  overview, 262
10Base2 cabling, 88
10BaseT cabling, 89
10GBaseT cabling, 89
100BaseT cabling, 89
802.11 wireless standard
  amendments, 138
    802.11a, 138
    802.11b, 138
    802.11g, 138
  modulation techniques, 136
1000BaseT cabling, 89

A

A - Verified protection, 325
A1 - Verified Design, 325-326
absolute addressing, 306
acceptability (biometrics), 503
access control, 5-6
  accountability, 36
    auditing/reporting, 36-37
    penetration testing, 38-39
    vulnerability assessments, 37-38
  administration, 49-50
    centralized, 49
    decentralized, 49
    provisioning life cycle, 50
  authentication
    factors, 17
    identity/account management, 18-19
    knowledge factors, 17
    passwords, 19-22
  authorization, 28
    access control policies, 29
    default to no access, setting, 30
    directory services, 30-31
    federated identities, 35
    Kerberos, 32-34
    least privilege, 29-30, 343
    need to know principles, 29-30
    security domains, 35
    separation of duties, 29
    SESAME, 34
    SSO, 31-32
  Brewer-Nash model, 320
  categories, 39
    compensative, 40
    corrective, 40
    detective, 40
    deterrent, 40
    directive, 40
    preventive, 41
    recovery, 41

CIA triad, 12-14
default stance, 14
defense-in-depth strategy, 15, 298
facilities, 462-463
- *biometrics, 466*
- *door locks, 463*
- *doors, 463*
- *glass entries, 466*
- *locks, 464-465*
- *mantraps, 464*
- *perimeters.* See *perimeters*
- *turnstiles, 464*
- *visitors, 466-467*

Harrison-Ruzzo-Ullmen model, 321
identifying
- *relationships between resources and users, 16*
- *resources, 15*
- *users, 16*

least privilege, 343
lists (ACLs), 49
managing, 349
matrix, 48
models, 46
- *access control matrix, 48*
- *ACLs, 49*
- *capabilities tables, 48*
- *content-dependent, 48*
- *context-dependent, 48*
- *discretionary (DAC), 46*
- *mandatory (MAC), 47*
- *RBAC, 47*
- *rule-based, 48*

monitoring, 50
- *IDS.* See *IDS*
- *IPS, 52, 363*

natural, 453-454
policies, 29
resources, maintaining, 355-356
services, 302
threats, 52-53
- *backdoor/trapdoor, 57*
- *brute-force, 53*
- *buffer overflow, 55*
- *dictionary attacks, 53*
- *DOS/DDOS, 55*
- *dumpster diving, 55*
- *emanating, 57*
- *identity theft, 54*
- *malware, 56*
- *mobile code, 56*
- *passwords, 53*
- *phishing/pharming, 54*
- *shoulder surfing, 54*
- *sniffing, 57*
- *social engineering, 53*
- *spoofing, 56*

types, 41
- *administrative, 41-42*
- *logical/technical, 43-44*
- *physical, 43-45*

access points (APs), 137
accessibility (facilities), 456
accountability, 36
auditing/reporting, 36-37
- *audit trails, 37*
- *guidelines, 36*
- *scrubbing, 36*

penetration testing, 38-39
- *categories, 39*
- *performing, 38*
- *strategies, 38-39*

vulnerability assessments, 37-38

accreditation, 236-237, 329-330
accuracy (biometrics), 503
ACLs (access control lists), 49
acoustical detection systems, 461
Acquire/Develop phase (system development life cycle), 204-205
acrylic glass, 466
active cryptography attacks, 286
ActiveX, 224
AD (architectural description), 299
Ad Hoc mode (WLANs), 137
Adams, Carlisle, 265
addresses
   absolute, 306
   implied, 306
   indirect, 306
   IP
      classes, 80-81
      IPv4, 77-80, 82
      IPv6, 82
      NAT, 81-89
      public versus private, 81
      spoofing, 150
   logical, 306
   MAC, 82-83
   relative, 306
   Resolution Protocol (ARP), 75, 101-102
Adleman, Leonard, 267
administration
   access control, 49-50
      centralized, 49
      decentralized, 49
      provisioning life cycle, 50
   controls, 41-42, 484, 504
   security responsibilities, 190
administrative law, 409
ADSL (Asymmetric DSL), 128
advisory security policies, 185
adware, 232
AES (Advanced Encryption Standard), 263
aggregation, 334
Agile software development method, 216-217
AH (Authentication Header), 130
ALE (annual threat event), 178
algebraic attacks, 288
algorithms, 513. *See also* ciphers
   asymmetric, 255-256
      confidentiality, 256
      defined, 265
      Diffie-Hellman, 266
      ECC, 267-268
      El Gamal, 267
      Knapsack, 268
      private/public keys, 255
      RSA, 267
      strengths/weaknesses, 256, 495, 514
      zero-knowledge proof, 268
   defined, 245
   MD, 271
   SHA (Secure Hash Algorithm), 271-272
   symmetric, 253-254, 258
      3DES. See 3DES
      AES, 263
      block ciphers, 255
      Blowfish, 264
      CAST, 265
      DES. See DES
      IDEA, 263
      Initialization Vectors (IVs), 255
      key facts, 496, 514
      RC, 264

Skipjack, 264
stream-based ciphers, 254
strengths/weaknesses, 254, 495, 514
Twofish, 264
alternate facility locations, 382-385
   cold sites, 383
   hot sites, 383
   reciprocal agreements, 384
   redundant sites, 385
   selecting, 382
   tertiary sites, 384
   testing, 383
   warm sites, 384
ALU (arithmetic logic unit), 304
analog transmissions, 83
analytic attacks, 289
annual threat event, 178
anomaly-based IDS, 51, 507
antimalware software, 236
antivirus software, 236
application-based IDS, 52
application layer
   OSI, 67
   TCP/IP, 72
application-level proxies, 114
application owner security responsibilities, 191
APs (access points), 137
architectural description (AD), 299
architectures, 8
   defined, 299
   frameworks, 312-313
      ITIL, 172, 313
      SABSA, 168, 490, 509
      TOGAF, 166-167, 312, 489, 508
      Zachman, 312

maintenance, 330
system security, 310
   documentation, 314
   models. See *security, models*
   modes. See *security, modes*
   policies, 310
   requirements, 310-311
   zones, 311
systems, 298
   computing platforms, 300-301
   CPUs, 303-304
   design phase, 299
   development phase, 299
   input/output devices, 307
   ISO-IEC 42010:2011, 299
   maintenance phase, 299
   memory, 304-306
   multitasking, 308-309
   operating systems, 307-308
   security services, 302-303
threats, 330
   data flow control, 333
   database, 333-334
   maintenance hooks, 331
   OWASP, 333
   SAML, 332
   server-based attacks, 333
   time-of-check/time-of-use attacks, 331-332
   web-based attacks, 332
   XML, 332
arithmetic logic unit (ALU), 304
ARP (Address Resolution Protocol), 75, 101-102
assembly languages, 219
assessing risks. See *risks, assessment*

attacks 543

assets. *See also* resources
  critical, identifying, 374
  criticality, 374-375, 495-498, 517
  equipment security, 472-473
  managing, 348-349
    backup/recovery, 349
    fault tolerance, 348
    redundancy, 348
  protecting, 346
    corporate procedures, 472-473
    facilities, 346
    hardware, 347
    information assets, 347
    security device protection, 473-474
    software, 347
    threats, mitigating, 362-364
  qualitative risk analysis, 179
  quantitative risk analysis, 178-179
  tangible/intangible, 177
  technological, recovering
    hardware, 386
    software, 386-387
  threats
    clipping levels, 361
    deviations from standards, 361
    unexplained events, 361
  value, determining, 177
  vulnerabilities/threats, 177-178
associative memory, 306
assurance
  accreditation and certification, 329-330
  evaluation systems, 322
    Common Criteria, 328-329
    ITSEC, 326-327
    Rainbow Series. See *Rainbow Series*
    TCSEC, 323

asymmetric algorithms, 255-256
  confidentiality, 256
  defined, 265
  Diffie-Hellman, 266
  ECC, 267-268
  El Gamal, 267
  Knapsack, 268
  private/public keys, 255
  RSA, 267
  strengths/weaknesses, 256, 495, 514
  zero-knowledge proof, 268
Asymmetric DSL (ADSL), 128
asymmetric multitasking, 308
asynchronous encryption/decryption, 244, 493, 512
asynchronous transmissions, 84
ATM (Asynchronous Transfer Mode), 123
attacks. *See also* **threats**
  cryptography
    algebraic, 288
    analytic, 289
    birthday, 289
    brute-force, 288
    chosen ciphertext, 287
    chosen plaintext, 287
    ciphertext-only, 287
    dictionary, 289
    differential, 288
    factoring, 289
    frequency analysis, 288
    known plaintext, 287
    linear cryptanalysis, 288
    meet-in-the middle, 290
    passive versus active, 286
    replay, 289
    reverse engineering, 289

    social engineering, 287
    statistical, 289
  database, 333-334
    aggregation, 334
    contamination, 334
    inference, 334
  DNS, 145
    cache poisoning, 145
    cybersquatting, 147
    DDoS, 146
    DNSSEC, 146
    domain grabbing, 147
    DoS, 146
    URL hiding, 146
  email
    spam, 148
    spear phishing, 148
    spoofing, 147
    whaling, 148
  ICMP
    Fraggle, 144
    Ping of Death, 144
    ping scanning, 145
    redirect, 144
    Smurf, 144
  port scanning, 150
  server-based, 333
  session hijacking, 150
  SYN ACK, 149
  teardrop, 150
  time-of-check/time-of-use, 331-332
  web-based, 332
  wireless, 149
attenuation, 142-143
attributes, 225, 510

auditing
  accountability, 36-37
  committee security responsibilities, 189
  guidelines, 36
  policies, 360
  record retention, 345
  scrubbing, 36
  services, 303
  software security, 237
  trails, 37
auditor security responsibilities, 191
authentication
  categories, 481, 501
  characteristic factors, 23
    behavioral, 25
    biometric considerations, 26-28
    biometric methods ranked by effectiveness, 26-27
    biometric user acceptance rankings, 27
    physiological, 24-25
  cryptosystems, 250
  factors, 17
  knowledge factors, 17
    identity/account management, 18-19
    passwords, 19-22
  ownership factors, 22
    memory cards, 22-23
    smart cards, 23
    token devices, 22
  remote access protocols, 133
Authentication Header (AH), 130
author identification, 434
authorization, 28
  access control policies, 29
  cryptosystems, 251
  default to no access, setting, 30
  directory services, 30-31

federated identities, 35
incident response, 424
Kerberos, 32-34
    advantages, 33
    disadvantages, 33
    ticket-issuing process, 33
least privilege, 29-30, 343
need to know principles, 29-30
security domains, 35
separation of duties, 29
SESAME, 34
SSO, 31-32
    advantages, 31
    disadvantages, 32
    objectives, 31
    Open Group Single Sign-On Standard Web site, 31

availability, 298
business continuity planning, 373
high, 392-393, 498-499, 518
    clustering, 518
    failover, 518
    failsoft, 518
    load balancing, 518
    RAID, 518
    SAN, 518
resources, maintaining, 355-356

avalanche effect, 245, 513
awareness training (security), 193-194

B

B - Mandatory protection, 324
B1 - Labeled Security Protection, 324-325
B2 - Structured Protection, 325
B3 - Security Domains, 325

backdoor, 57, 235
backups
asset management, 349
business continuity, 380
copy, 390
daily, 390
differential, 390
electronic, 392
electronic vaulting, 498, 517
full, 389
hardware, 386
HSM, 498, 517
incremental, 390
optical jukeboxes, 517
remote journaling, 498, 517
replication, 498, 518
rotation schemes, 391
schemes, 391
software, 386-387
tape vaulting, 517
transaction log, 390
types, 389-390

barriers (perimeters), 459
base relations, 225, 510
baseband transmissions, 84-85
Basel II, 417
baselines (information security governance), 185-186
basic rate (BRI) ISDN, 127
bastion hosts, 115
BCP (business continuity plan), 372
contingency plans, 372-373
maintenance, 398
personnel
    components, 377
    training, 393

scope, 377
SP 800-34 Revision 1 standard, 378
tests, 396-397
   checklist, 396
   evacuation drills, 397
   full-interruption, 397
   functional drills, 397
   parallel, 397
   simulation, 397
   structured walk-through, 397
   table-top exercises, 397
behavioral characteristics (authentication), 25
Bell-LaPadula model, 317-318
   confidentiality, 318
   flow of information rules, 317
   limitations, 318
best evidence, 432
BGP (Border Gateway Protocol), 108
BIA (business impact analysis), 372-373
   critical processes/resources, identifying, 374
   criticality levels, 374-375
   fault tolerance, 376
   recoverability, 376
   recovery priorities, 376
   resource requirements, 375
   steps, 495, 516-517
Biba model, 319
biometric authentication, 25, 466
   considerations, 26-28
   effectiveness rankings, 26-27
   keystroke dynamics, 25
   signature dynamics, 25
   terms, 483

   user acceptance rankings, 27
   voice patterns, 25
birthday attacks, 289
black hats, 407
blackouts, 470
block ciphers, 255
Blowfish, 264
Bluejacking, 139
Bluesnarfing, 139
Bluetooth, 139
board of directors security responsibilities, 188
bollards, 459
bombings, 452
boot sector viruses, 231, 511
Border Gateway Protocol (BGP), 108
botnets, 232
boundary control services, 302
Brewer-Nash model, 320
BRI (basic rate) ISDN, 127
British Ministry of Defence Architecture Framework (MODAF), 168
broadband transmissions, 84-85
broadcast transmissions, 86
brownouts, 470
brute-force attacks, 288
BSI (Build Security In), 210
budgets (security), 194-195
buffer overflow, 55, 233-235
Build and Fix software development method, 211-212
Build Security In (BSI), 210
bullet-resistant doors, 463
bus topology, 92
business continuity, 8
   asset criticality, 495-498, 517
   availability, 373

backups
  electronic vaulting, 498, 517
  HSM, 498, 517
  optical jukeboxes, 517
  remote journaling, 498, 517
  replication, 498, 518
  tape vaulting, 517
BCP. *See* BCP
BIA, 372-373
  critical processes/resources, identifying, 374
  criticality levels, 374-375
  fault tolerance, 376
  recoverability, 376
  recovery priorities, 376
  resource requirements, 375
  steps, 495, 516-517
contingency plans, 372-373
continuity planning, 372
disaster recovery. *See* disaster recovery
disruptions, 370
high-availability, 498-499, 518
personnel training, 393
plan, 372
  personnel components, 377
  scope, 377
  SP 800-34 R1 standard, 378
preventive controls, 378
  data backups, 380
  fault tolerance, 379
  fire detection and suppression systems, 380
  insurance, 379-380
  redundancy, 379
recovery priorities, 376

recovery strategies, 380-381
  business processes, 382
  data. See *data, recovery*
  documentation, 388
  facilities, 382-385
  hardware, 386
  human resources, 387
  recovery priorities, categorizing, 381
  software, 386-387
  supplies, 387
  user environment, 388
reliability, 373
business impact analysis. *See* **BIA**
business process recovery, 382
business unit manager security responsibilities, 189

C

C - Discretionary protection, 324
C1 - Discretionary Security Protection, 324
C2 - Controlled Access Protection, 324
cable modems, 128
cabling, 87
  coaxial, 87-88
  fiberoptic, 89-91
  selecting, 87
  twisted pair, 88-90
    categories, 89-90
    shielded versus unshielded, 89
    types, 89
  WLAN security, 142
caches, 306
CALEA (Communications Assistance to Law Enforcement Act) of 1994, 417

candidate keys, 225, 511
capabilities tables, 48
Capability Maturity Model Integration (CMMI), 174, 218
capacitance detectors, 461
cardinality, 225, 511
cards
   memory, 22-23
   smart, 23
carrier lines
   E, 121
   OC, 122
   T, 121
Carrier Sense Multiple Access Collision Avoidance (CSMA/CA), 100
Carrier Sense Multiple Access Collision Detection (CSMA/CD), 99
CAs (certification authorities), 275-276
CAST (Carlisle, Adams, Stafford, Tavares) algorithm, 265
categories
   access control, 39
      compensative, 40
      corrective, 40
      detective, 40
      deterrent, 40
      directive, 40
      preventive, 41
      recovery, 41
   authentication, 481, 501
   IDS, 487-488, 503-507
   penetration testing, 39
   programming languages, 219
      assembly, 219
      high-level, 219
      machine, 219
      natural, 220
      very-high-level, 219
   routing protocols, 107
   security policies, 185
   twisted pair cabling, 89-90
CBC (Cipher Block Chaining), 260
CBC-MAC (cipher block chaining MAC), 274
CC (Common Criteria), 328-329
CCTV (closed-circuit television system), 461
CDMA (Code Division Multiple Access), 136
CDP (Cisco Discovery Protocol), 106
central processing units (CPUs), 303-304
centralized access control, 49
CEO (chief executive officer), 189
CER (crossover error rate), 503
certificate revocation lists (CRLs), 277
certificates. *See* digital certificates
certification, 329-330
   authorities (CAs), 275-276
   software, 236-237
Certified Information Systems Security Professional. *See* CISSP
CFAA (Computer Fraud and Abuse Act), 416
CFB (Cipher Feedback), 261
CFO (chief financial officer), 189
chain of custody, 430
change control policies, 356-357
change management (software development), 209
Channel Service Unit/Data Service Unit (CSU/DSU), 122

CHAP (Challenge Handshake Authentication Protocol), 133
characteristic factor authentication, 23
  behavioral characteristics, 25
  biometrics
    considerations, 26-28
    effectiveness rankings, 26-27
    user acceptance rankings, 27
  physiological characteristics, 24-25
checklist tests, 396
chief executive officer (CEO), 189
chief financial officer (CFO), 189
chief information officer (CIO), 189
chief privacy officer (CPO), 189
chief security officer (CSO), 189
Chinese Wall model, 320
chosen ciphertext attacks, 287
chosen plaintext attacks, 287
CIA (confidentiality, integrity, and availability) triad, 12-14, 160
CIDR (Classless Inter-Domain Routing), 80
CIO (chief information officer), 189
cipher-based MAC (CMAC), 274
Cipher Block Chaining (CBC), 260
cipher block chaining MAC (CBC-MAC), 274
Cipher Feedback (CFB), 261
ciphers. See also **algorithms**
  block, 255
  Caesar, 247
  concealment, 252
  hybrid, 256-257
  running key, 252
  scytale, 246
  stream-based, 254
  substitution, 252, 257
    defined, 252
    modulo 26, 252
    one-time pads, 257-258
    steganography, 258
  transposition, 253
  Vigenere, 248-249
ciphertext, 244, 512
ciphertext-only attacks, 287
circuit-level proxies, 114
circuit-switching networks, 123
circumstantial evidence, 432
Cisco Discovery Protocol (CDP), 106
CISSP (Certified Information Systems Security Professional), 2
  additional versions, 4
  exam specifications, 10
  goals, 4
  qualifications needed, 10
  signing up, 10
  sponsoring bodies, 2-4
  value, 5
civil code law, 408
civil disobedience, 452
civil law, 408-409
Clark-Wilson Integrity model, 319-320
classifications (data), 186
  commercial business, 186-187
  military and government, 187-188
Classless Inter-Domain Routing (CIDR), 80
Cleanroom software development method, 218
clearing data, 355
cleartext, 244, 493, 512
clipping levels, 21, 361

closed-circuit television system (CCTV), 461
cloud computing, 117-118, 335
clustering, 393, 518
CMAC (cipher-based MAC), 274
CMMI (Capability Maturity Model Integration), 174, 218
coaxial cabling, 87-88
COBIT (Control Objectives for Information and related Technology), 170, 314
Code Division Multiple Access (CDMA), 136
cognitive passwords, 20, 502
cohesion, 221
cold sites, 383
collaboration, 134-135
collisions, 98, 494, 513
   avoidance, 100
   cryptography, 245
   detection, 99
   domains, 98
collusion, 451
combination locks, 465
combination passwords, 19, 501
commercial business data classifications, 186-187
commercial software, 412
Committee of Sponsoring Organizations (COSO), 171
Common Body of Knowledge, 5
Common Criteria (CC), 328-329
common law, 408
Common Object Request Broker Architecture (CORBA), 222
communication. *See also* transmissions
   analysis, 435
   encryption levels
      end-to-end, 281
      link, 280
   threats, 447-448
   trusted entities, 277-278
Communications Assistance to Law Enforcement Act (CALEA) of 1994, 417
compartmented security mode, 321
compensative controls, 40
compiled code, 220
complex passwords, 19, 501
compliance (legal), 420
computer crimes
   computer-assisted, 406
   computer prevalence, 407
   computer-targeted, 406
   evidence, 430-431
      five rules, 431
      hardware/embedded device analysis, 435
      media analysis, 434
      network analysis, 435
      search warrants, 433
      seizure, 434
      software analysis, 434
      surveillance, 433
      types, 431-433
   hackers *versus* crackers, 407
   incident responses. *See* incident responses
   incidental, 406
   investigations, 9, 406
      chain of custody, 430
      crime scenes, 429
      decisions, 428
      examination and analysis, 428
      identification, 427

construction (facilities) 551

interviews, 430
IOCE/SWGDE, 428-429
law enforcement involvement, 426
MOM, 429
presentation, 428
preservation and collection, 427-428
process, 426
standardized procedures, 425
white/gray/black hat, 407
Computer Ethics Institute, Ten Commandments of Computer Ethics, 436
Computer Fraud and Abuse Act (CFAA), 416
Computer Security Act of 1987, 417
computers
equipment rooms (facilities), 457-458
prevalence crimes, 407
targeted crimes, 406
computing platforms, 300-301
distributed, 300
embedded, 301
mainframe/thin clients, 300
middleware, 301
mobile, 301
virtual, 301
concealment ciphers, 252
conclusive evidence, 432
confidentiality, 297
Bell-LaPadula model, 318
cryptosystems, 250
confidentiality, integrity, and availability (CIA) triad, 12-14, 160
configuration management
policies, 358-359
software development, 209

confusion, 245, 513
connections
LANs. *See* LANs
remote, 126
attacks, 149
authentication protocols, 133
cable, 128
dial-up, 126-127
DSL, 127-128
Internet security, 283
ISDN, 127
multimedia collaboration, 134-135
RADIUS, 132-133
SSL, 134, 283
TACACS, 132-133
Telnet, 134
TLS, 134, 284
VPNs, 129-132
satellite, 141
WANs
ATM, 123
circuit-switching, 123
CSU/DSU, 122
E lines, 121
frame relay, 123
HSSI, 124-125
OC lines, 122
packet-switching, 123
PPP, 124
PSTN, 125
SMDS, 124
T lines, 121
VoIP, 125-126
X.25, 124
wireless. *See* WLANs
construction (facilities), 456-457

contact/contactless cards, 23
contamination, 334
content analysis, 434
content-dependent access control, 48
contention methods, 97-101
   collisions, 98
   CSMA/CA, 100
   CSMA/CD, 99
   polling, 101
   token passing, 101
context analysis, 434
context-dependent access control, 48
contingency plans, 372-373
continuity planning, 372
continuous lighting systems, 461
Control Objectives for Information and related Technology (COBIT), 170, 314
controlled security mode, 322
controls
   administrative, 41-42, 484, 504
   compensative, 40
   corrective, 40
   detective, 40
   deterrent, 40
   directive, 40
   logical, 43-44, 485, 505
   NIST SP 800-53 families, 488, 507
   physical, 43-45, 486, 506
   preventive, 41
   recovery, 41
   technical, 43-44
cookies, 284-285
copy backups, 390
copyrights, 411-412
CORBA (Common Object Request Broker Architecture), 222

corrective controls, 40
corroborative evidence, 433
COSO (Committee of Sponsoring Organizations), 171
Counter Mode (CTR), 262
countermeasures, 161
coupling, 221
covert channels, 362
CPO (chief privacy officer), 189
CPTED (Crime Prevention through Environmental Design), 453
CPUs (central processing units), 303-304
crackers, 407
Crime Prevention through Environmental Design (CPTED), 453
crime scenes, 429
criminal activity, deterring, 454
criminal law, 408
critical processes/resources, identifying, 374
criticality (assets), 374-375, 495-498, 517
CRLs (certificate revocation lists), 277
cross-certification model, 35, 278
crossover error rate (CER), 503
crosstalk, 143
cryptanalysis, 245, 513
cryptography, 7
   3DES
      modes, 262-263, 495, 514
      overview, 262
   asymmetric, 255-256
      confidentiality, 256
      defined, 265
      Diffie-Hellman, 266
      ECC, 267-268

cryptography 553

 El Gamal, 267
 Knapsack, 268
 private/public keys, 255
 RSA, 267
 strengths/weaknesses, 256, 495, 514
 zero-knowledge proof, 268
asynchronous encryption/decryption, 512
attacks
 algebraic, 288
 analytic, 289
 birthday, 289
 brute-force, 288
 chosen ciphertext, 287
 chosen plaintext, 287
 ciphertext-only, 287
 dictionary, 289
 differential cryptanalysis, 288
 factoring, 289
 frequency analysis, 288
 known plaintext, 287
 linear cryptanalysis, 288
 meet-in-the-middle, 290
 passive versus active, 286
 replay, 289
 reverse engineering, 246
 social engineering, 287
 statistical, 289
avalanche effect, 245, 513
ciphertext, 244, 512
collisions, 245, 494, 513
confusion, 245, 513
cryptanalysis, 245, 513
cryptology, 245, 513
cryptosystems, 245, 250, 512
 authentication, 250
 authorization, 251
 confidentiality, 250
 integrity, 251
 non-repudiation, 251
decoding, 245, 513
decryption, 244, 493, 512
diffusion, 245, 513
digital certificates, 276, 493, 512
 CAs, 275-276
 classes, 277
 cross-certification, 278
 defined, 244
 requesting, 277
 revocation lists, 277
 trusted entity communication, 277-278
 X.509, 276-277
digital signatures, 244, 274-275, 493, 512
email, 281
 MIME, 282
 PGP, 281-282
 quantum cryptography, 282
 S/MIME, 282
encoding, 245, 513
encryption. *See* encryption
hash functions, 244, 512
 HAVAL, 272
 MD algorithms, 271
 one-way hash, 269-270
 RIPEMD-160, 272
 SHA, 271-272
 Tiger, 272
history, 246-247
 Caesar cipher, 247
 Kerckhoff principles, 249
 Lucifer project, 250

scytale ciphers, 246
World War II, 249-250
Internet, 283
cookies, 284-285
HTTP, 284
HTTPS, 284
IPsec, 285-286
remote access, 283
S-HTTP, 284
SET, 284
SSH, 285
SSL, 134, 283
TLS, 134, 284
keys
clustering, 245, 513
defined, 244, 512
management, 278-279
keyspace, 245, 513
life cycle, 246
MACs
CBC-MAC, 274
CMAC, 274
HMAC, 273
one-way functions, 246, 513
PKI, 275
CAs, 275-276
CRLs, 277
cross-certification, 278
digital certificates, 276-277
OCSP, 276
RAs, 275
trusted entity communication, 277-278
plaintext, 244, 493, 512
services, 303
substitution, 245, 494-495, 513

substitution ciphers, 257
defined, 252
modulo 26, 252
one-time pads, 257-258
steganography, 258
symmetric algorithms, 253-254, 258
3DES. See *3DES*
AES, 263
block ciphers, 255
Blowfish, 264
CAST, 265
DES. See *DES*
IDEA, 263
Initialization Vectors (IVs), 255
key facts, 496, 514
RC, 264
Skipjack, 264
stream-based ciphers, 254
strengths/weaknesses, 254, 495, 514
Twofish, 264
synchronous encryption/decryption, 244, 493, 512
TPM, 279-280
transposition, 245, 494, 513
trapdoors, 246, 514
Vigenere ciphers, 248-249
work factors, 246, 513
cryptology, 245, 513
cryptosystems, 245, 250, 512
authentication, 250
authorization, 251
confidentiality, 250
integrity, 251
non-repudiation, 251
CSMA/CA (Carrier Sense Multiple Access Collision Avoidance), 100

CSMA/CD (Carrier Sense Multiple Collision Detection), 99
CSO (chief security officer), 189
CSU/DSU (Channel Service Unit/Data Service Unit), 122
CTR (Counter Mode), 262
customary law, 409
cybersquatting, 147

D

D - Minimal protection, 324
DAC (discretionary access control), 46
daily backups, 390
damage assessment teams, 394
data
   availability, 298
   centers, 467
   classifications, 186
      commercial business, 186-187
      military and government, 187-188
   clearing, 355
   confidentiality, 297
   custodian security responsibilities, 190
   decoding, 245
   encoding, 245
   flow control, 333
   integrity. *See* integrity
   mining, 227, 334
   owner security responsibilities, 190
   purging, 355
   recovery, 388
      backup rotation schemes, 391
      backup types, 389-390
      electronic backups, 392
      high availability, 392-393
   remanence, 355
   structures, 222
   warehousing, 227
Data Link layer (OSI), 68-69
Data Terminal Equipment (DTE), 122
databases
   data
      mining, 227
      warehousing, 227
   locks, 228
   models, 224
      hierarchical, 226
      network, 226
      object-oriented, 226
      object-relational, 226
      relational, 225
   OLTP ACID tests, 229
   polyinstantiation, 228
   programming languages, 226-227
      JDBC, 227
      ODBC, 226
      OLE DB, 227
      XML, 227
   relational management systems. *See* relational databases
   threats, 228, 333-334
      aggregation, 334
      contamination, 334
      inference, 334
   views, 225, 228, 299, 511
DDoS (Distributed Denial of Service) attacks, 55, 146
DDR SDRAM (Double Data Rate Synchronous Dynamic Random Access Memory), 305
DDR2 SDRAM (Double Data Rate Two Synchronous Dynamic Random Access Memory), 305

DDR3-SDRAM (Double Data Rate Three Synchronous Dynamic Random Access Memory), 305
decentralized access control, 49
decoding, 245, 513
decryption, 493
   asynchronous, 244, 493, 512
   defined, 244, 512
   synchronous, 244, 493, 512
dedicated security mode, 321
de-encapsulation, 76, 129
defense-in-depth model, 15, 298
degaussing, 355
degrees, 225, 511
deluge sprinkler systems, 469
Demilitarized Zone (DMZ), 115
denial-of-service attacks, 144
Denial of Service (DoS) attacks, 55, 146
Department of Defense Architecture Framework (DoDAF), 168
DES (Digital Encryption Standard)
   defined, 259
   Double-DES, 259
   key length, 259
   modes, 259-262
      CBC, 260
      CFB, 261
      CTR, 262
      ECB, 259
      OFB, 261-262
DES-X, 259
design models, 8
design phase
   software development life cycle, 207
   system architecture, 299
detective controls, 40
deterrent controls, 40
Develop phase (software development life cycle), 207
development (software)
   knowledge-based systems, 229
   life cycle, 206
      change/configuration management, 209
      Design, 207
      Develop, 207
      Gather Requirements, 206-207
      Release/Maintain, 209
      Test/Validate, 208-209
   malware, 230
      botnets, 232
      logic bombs, 232
      protection, 235-236
      rootkits, 233
      spyware/adware, 232
      Trojan horses, 231
      viruses, 230-231
      worms, 231
   methods, 211
      Agile, 216-217
      Build and Fix, 211-212
      Cleanroom, 218
      CMMI, 218
      Incremental, 214
      JAD, 218
      Prototyping, 214
      RAD, 216
      Spiral, 215
      V-shaped, 213
      Waterfall, 212-213
   programming, 219
      ActiveX, 224
      assembly languages, 219

cohesion, 221
compiled versus interpreted code, 220
CORBA, 222
coupling, 221
data structures, 222
distributed object-oriented systems, 222
high-level languages, 219
Java, 223
machine languages, 219
mobile code, 223
natural languages, 220
object-oriented, 220-221
OLE, 223
polymorphism, 221
SOA, 223
very-high-level languages, 219
security, 210
 auditing, 237
 backdoors, 235
 BSI, 210
 buffer overflow, 233-235
 certification/accreditation, 236-237
 ISO/IEC 27000, 210
 malware protection, 235-236
 OWASP,
 privilege escalation, 235
 source code issues, 233
 WASC, 210
development (system life cycle), 202-204
 Acquire/Develop, 204-205
 Dispose, 205-206
 Implement, 205
 Initiate, 204
 Operate/Maintain, 205
development phase (system architecture), 299

deviations from standards, 361
devices
 embedded, analyzing, 435
 input/output, 307
 network, 109
  architecture, 115
  cloud computing, 117-118
  endpoint security, 119
  firewalls, 112-114
  gateways, 112
  honeypots, 117
  hubs, 109
  multiplexers, 109
  patch panels, 109
  PBXs, 116-117
  proxy servers, 116
  routers, 112
  switches, 110-111
  virtualization, 116
  VLANs, 111
 security, protecting, 473-474
  portable media, 473
  safes/vaults/locking, 474
  tracking devices, 473
DHCP (Dynamic Host Configuration Protocol), 102-103
dial-up connections, 126-127
dictionary attacks, 53, 289
differential backups, 390
differential cryptanalysis, 288
Diffie, Whitfield, 266
Diffie-Hellman algorithm, 266
diffusion, 245, 513
digital certificates, 276, 493, 512
 CAs, 275-276
 classes, 277
 cross-certification, 278

defined, 244
requesting, 277
revocation lists, 277
trusted entity communication, 277-278
X.509, 276-277
Digital Encryption Standard. *See* **DES**
Digital Signature Standard (DSS), 275
digital signatures, 244, 274-275, 493, 512
Digital Subscribers Line. *See* **DSL**
digital transmissions, 83
direct evidence, 432
Direct Memory Access (DMA), 306
Direct Sequence Spread Spectrum (DSSS), 136
directive controls, 40
directory services, 30-31
disaster recovery, 8, 371
  alternate facility locations, 383
  asset criticality, 374-375, 495-498, 517
  availability, 373
  backups
    electronic vaulting, 498, 517
    HSM, 498, 517
    optical jukeboxes, 517
    remote journaling, 498, 517
    replication, 498, 518
    tape vaulting, 517
  BIA, 372-373
    critical processes/resources, identifying, 374
    criticality levels, 374-375
    fault tolerance, 376
    recoverability, 376
    recovery priorities, 376
    resource requirements, 375
  business continuity plan, 372
    personnel components, 377
    scope, 377
    SP 800-34 Revision 1 standard, 378
  business processes, 382
  committee, 381
  contingency plans, 372-373
  continuity planning, 372
  data, 388
    backup rotation schemes, 391
    backup types, 389-390
    electronic backups, 392
    high availability, 392-393
  disasters, 371
    man-made, 371
    natural, 371
    technological, 371
  disruptions, 370
  documentation, 388
  DRP. *See* DRP
  facility alternate locations, 382-385
    cold sites, 383
    hot sites, 383
    reciprocal agreements, 384
    redundant sites, 385
    selecting, 382
    tertiary sites, 384
    testing, 383
    warm sites, 384
  financial management, 393
  hardware, 386
  high-availability, 498-499, 518
  human resources, 387
  personnel training, 393
  press, handling, 381

preventive controls, 378
  data backups, 380
  fault tolerance, 379
  fire detection and suppression systems, 380
  insurance, 379-380
  redundancy, 379
recovery priorities, 381
reliability, 373
software, 386-387
supplies, 387
teams
  damage assessment, 394
  legal, 394
  listing of, 394
  media relations, 395
  restoration, 395
  salvage, 395
  security, 395-396
user environment, 388
disasters, 371
  man-made, 371
  natural, 371
  technological, 371
discretionary access control (DAC), 46
disks
  imaging, 434
  mirroring, 350
  striping, 349
Dispose phase (system development life cycle), 205-206
disposing media, 355
disruptions, 370, 455
distance vector protocols, 107
Distributed Denial of Service (DDoS) attacks, 55, 146

distributed systems, 300
  cloud computing, 335
  grid computing, 335
  object-oriented, 222
  peer-to-peer computing, 335
DMA (Direct Memory Access), 306
DMZ (Demilitarized Zone), 49
DNS (Domain Name System) attacks, 103, 145-146
  cache poisoning, 145
  cybersquatting, 147
  DDoS, 146
  DNSSEC, 146
  domain grabbing, 147
  DoS, 146
  URL hiding, 146
DNSSEC (Domain Name System Security Extensions), 146
document exchanges/reviews, 192
documentation, 314
  COBIT, 314
  disaster recovery, 388
  ISO/IEC 27000 series, 314
DoDAF (Department of Defense Architecture Framework), 168
Domain Name System. *See* **DNS attacks**
Domain Name System Security Extensions (DNSSEC), 146
domains, 511
  authorization, 35
  collision, 98
  grabbing, 147
  relational databases, 225
door locks, 463
doors, 463
DoS (Denial of Service) attacks, 55, 146

Double Data Rate Synchronous Dynamic Random Access Memory (DDR SDRAM), 305
Double Data Rate Three Synchronous Dynamic Random Access Memory (DDR3-SDRAM), 305
Double Data Rate Two Synchronous Dynamic Random Access Memory (DDR2 SDRAM), 305
Double-DES, 259
downstream liability, 422
downtime, estimating, 374-375
DRP (disaster recovery plan), 372
   business processes, 382
   committee, 381
   data, 388
      backup rotation schemes, 391
      backup types, 389-390
      electronic backups, 392
      high availability, 392-393
   documentation, 388
   facility alternate locations, 382-385
      cold sites, 383
      hot sites, 383
      reciprocal agreements, 384
      redundant sites, 385
      selecting, 382
      tertiary sites, 384
      testing, 383
      warm sites, 384
   hardware, 386
   human resources, 387
   personnel training, 393
   press, handling, 381
   recovery priorities, categorizing, 381
   software, 386-387
   supplies, 387
   teams
      damage assessment, 394
      legal, 394
      listing of, 394
      media relations, 395
      restoration, 395
      salvage, 395
      security, 395-396
   tests, 396-397
      checklist, 396
      evacuation drills, 397
      full-interruption, 397
      functional drills, 397
      parallel, 397
      simulation, 397
      structured walk-through, 397
      table-top exercises, 397
   user environment, 388
dry pipe sprinkler systems, 469
DSL (Digital Subscribers Line), 127-128
   security, 128
   versions, 127-128
DSS (Digital Signature Standard), 275
DSSS (Direct Sequence Spread Spectrum), 136
DTE (Data Terminal Equipment), 122
dual-homed firewalls, 115
due care/diligence, 162, 421
dumpster diving, 55
Dynamic Host Configuration Protocol (DHCP), 102-103
dynamic packet filtering firewalls, 114
dynamic ports, 77
dynamic routing, 106

E

E carrier lines, 121
EAP (Extensible Authentication Protocol), 133
earthquakes, 446
eavesdropping, 57, 143
ECB (Electronic Code Book), 259
ECC (Elliptic Curve Cryptosystems), 267-268
Economic Espionage Act of 1996, 418
ECPA (Electronic Communications Privacy Act) of 1986, 416
EIGRP (Enhanced IGRP), 108
El Gamal, 267
electrical threats, 447
electromechanical systems, 460
electronic backups, 392
electronic vaulting, 392, 498, 517
Elliptic Curve Cryptosystems (ECC), 267-268
email
   attacks, 147-148
      spam, 148
      spear phishing, 148
      spoofing, 147
      whaling, 148
   cryptography, 281
      MIME, 282
      PGP, 281-282
      quantum cryptography, 282
      S/MIME, 282
emanating, 57
embedded device analysis, 435
embedded systems, 301
emergency lighting systems, 462
employee privacy issues, 419

Encapsulating Security Payload (ESP), 130
encapsulation, 129
encoding, 245, 513
encryption, 251, 493
   asymmetric algorithms, 255-256
      confidentiality, 256
      defined, 265
      Diffie-Hellman, 266
      ECC, 267-268
      El Gamal, 267
      Knapsack, 268
      private/public keys, 255
      RSA, 267
      strengths/weaknesses, 256, 495, 514
      zero-knowledge proof, 268
   asynchronous, 244, 493, 512
   ciphers
      block, 255
      concealment, 252
      hybrid, 256-257
      running key, 252
      stream-based, 254
      substitution, 252
      transposition, 253
   communication levels, 280-281
      end-to-end encryption, 281
      link, 280
   defined, 244, 512
   equipment protection, 472
   IVs, 255
   substitution ciphers, 257
      defined, 252
      modulo 26, 252
      one-time pads, 257-258
      steganography, 258

symmetric, 253-254, 258
    3DES. See 3DES
    AES, 263
    block ciphers, 255
    Blowfish, 264
    CAST, 265
    DES. See DES
    IDEA, 263
    Initialization Vectors (IVs), 255
    key facts, 496, 514
    RC, 264
    Skipjack, 264
    stream-based ciphers, 254
    strengths/weaknesses, 254, 495, 514
    Twofish, 264
synchronous, 244, 493, 512
TKIP, 140

end-to-end encryption, 281
endpoint security, 119
Enhanced IGRP (EIGRP), 108
Enigma machine, 249-250
enrollment time (biometrics), 503
enterprise resources. *See* **resource protection**
environmental security, 9
  alerts, 472
  fire protection, 468
    detection, 468
    suppression, 468-470
  HVAC, 471
  overview, 9
  power supplies, 470
    outages, 470
    preventative measures, 470-471
  water leakages/flooding, 471
equipment rooms, 467

equipment security, 472
  corporate procedures, 472-473
    encryption, 472
    inventory, 473
    tamper protection, 472
  security device protection, 473-474
    portable media, 473
    safes/vaults/locking, 474
    tracking devices, 473
ESP (Encapsulating Security Payload), 130
Ethernet 802.3, 94-96
ethical hacking. *See* **penetration testing**
ethics
  Computer Ethics Institute, Ten Commandments of Computer Ethics, 436
  Internet Architecture Board (IAB), 437
  (ISC)² Code of Ethics, 435-436
  organizational, 437
Ethics and the Internet (RFC 1087), 437
EU (European Union) privacy laws, 419
European E carrier lines, 121
evacuation drills, 397
evaluation systems
  Common Criteria, 328-329
  ITSEC, 326
    assurance requirements, 327
    functional requirements, 326-327
    TSEC, mapping, 327
  Rainbow Series. *See* Rainbow Series
  TCSEC, 323
events *versus* incidents, 423
evidence, 430-431
  analyzing, 428
  chain of custody, 430

collecting, 427-428
examining, 428
five rules, 431
hardware/embedded device analysis, 435
identifying, 427
IOCE/SWGDE, 428-429
media analysis, 434
network analysis, 435
presenting in court, 428
preserving, 427-428
search warrants, 433
seizure, 434
software analysis, 434
surveillance, 433
types
- *best, 432*
- *circumstantial, 432*
- *conclusive, 432*
- *corroborative, 433*
- *direct, 432*
- *hearsay, 433*
- *opinion, 433*
- *secondary, 432*

exam
prerequisites, 10
signing up, 10
specifications, 10

expert systems, 229
explosion threats, 449
export legal issues, 420
exposures, 161
Extensible Authentication Protocol (EAP), 133
exterior routing protocols, 106
external entities (facilities), 456
external geographical threats, 437
extranets, 120

F

facial scans, 25
facilities
access control, 463
- *biometrics, 466*
- *door locks, 463*
- *doors, 463*
- *glass entries, 466*
- *locks, 464-465*
- *mantraps, 464*
- *turnstiles, 464*
- *visitors, 466-467*

alternate locations, 382-385
- *cold sites, 383*
- *hot sites, 383*
- *reciprocal agreements, 384*
- *redundant sites, 385*
- *selecting, 382*
- *tertiary sites, 384*
- *testing, 383*
- *warm sites, 384*

design, 453
- *computer and equipment rooms, 457-458*
- *construction, 456-457*
- *CPTED, 453*
- *facility selection, 455*
- *internal compartments, 457*
- *layered defense model, 453*

environmental alerts, 472
fire protection, 468
- *detection, 468*
- *suppression, 468-470*

HVAC, 471

564   facilities

interior security
 data centers, 467
 equipment rooms, 467
 restricted work areas, 468
 work areas, 467
perimeters
 access control, 462-463
 acoustical detection systems, 461
 barriers, 459
 capacitance detectors, 461
 CCTV, 461
 electromechanical systems, 460
 fences, 459
 gates, 459-460
 infrared sensors, 460
 intrusion detection, 460
 lighting, 461-462
 natural access control, 453-454
 natural surveillance, 454
 natural territorials reinforcement, 454
 patrol force, 462
 photoelectric systems, 460
 walls, 460
 wave motion detectors, 461
physical security plan, 454-455
 criminal activity, deterring, 454
 delaying intruders, 455
 detecting intruders, 455
 intrusions/disruptions response, 455
 situation assessment, 455
power supplies, 470
 outages, 470
 preventative measures, 470-471
protection, 346
redundant, 379

selection
 accessibility, 456
 surrounding area/external entities, 456
 visibility, 456
water leakages/flooding, 471

factoring attacks, 289
failovers, 392, 518
failsoft, 393, 518
false rejection rate (FRR), 503
FAR (false acceptance rate), 503
Fast Ethernet, 89
fault tolerance
 asset management, 348
 BIA, 376
 business continuity, 379
 resource availability, 355
faults (power), 470
FDDI (Fiber Distributed Data Interface), 97, 120
FDMA (Frequency Division Multiple Access), 136
feature extraction (biometrics), 503
Federal Information Security Management Act (FISMA) of 2002, 418
Federal Intelligence Surveillance Act (FISA) of 1978, 416
Federal Privacy Act of 1974, 416
federated identities, 35
fences, 459
FHSS (Frequency Hopping Spread Spectrum), 136
Fiber Distributed Data Interface (FDDI), 97, 120
fiberoptic cabling, 89-91
Field Programmable Gate Array (FPGA), 305

FIFO (first in, first out) backup rotation scheme, 391
File Transfer Protocol (FTP), 104
File Transfer Protocol Secure (FTPS), 104
filters, 141
financial management (disaster recovery), 393
finger scans, 24
fingerprint scans, 24
fires, 449-450
    detection and suppression systems, 380
    protection, 468
        detection, 468
        suppression, 468-470
firewalls, 112-114
    application-level proxies, 114
    circuit-level proxies, 114
    deploying, 115
    dual-homed, 115
    dynamic packet filtering, 114
    kernel proxy, 114
    multihomed, 115
    packet filtering, 113
    proxy, 114
    screened hosts, 115
    screened subnet, 115
    SOCKS, 114
    stateful, 113
firmware, 305
first in, first out (FIFO) backup rotation scheme, 391
FISA (Federal Intelligence Surveillance Act) of 1978, 416
FISMA (Federal Information Security Management Act) of 2002, 418
five rules of evidence, 431
flame actuated fire detection, 468

flash memory, 305
floods
    facilities, 471
    natural, 447
fluorescent lighting, 462
foreign keys, 225, 511
forensic investigations. *See* investigations
FPGA (Field Programmable Gate Array), 305
Fraggle attacks, 144
frame relay, 123
frameworks, 312-313
    COBIT, 170, 314
    COSO, 171
    DoDAF, 168
    ITIL, 313
    listing of, 163-164
    MODAF, 168
    NIST SP 800-53, 170-171
    SABSA, 168, 312, 490, 509
    TOGAF, 168, 312
    Zachman, 166-167, 312, 489, 508
fraud, 450
freeware, 412
frequency analysis attacks, 288
Frequency Division Multiple Access (FDMA), 136
Frequency Hopping Spread Spectrum, 136
FRR (false rejection rate), 503
FTP (File Transfer Protocol), 104
FTPS (File Transfer Protocol Secure), 104
full backups, 389
full-interruption tests, 397
full-knowledge tests, 39

functional drills, 397
functions
  hash
    defined, 244, 512
    HAVAL, 272
    MD algorithms, 271
    one-way hash, 269-270
    RIPEMD-160, 272
    SHA, 271-272
    Tiger, 272
  one-way, 246
fuzzy expert systems, 229

G

gates, 459-460
gateways, 112
geographical threats, 445
  internal *versus* external, 437
  natural, 446-447
    earthquakes, 446
    floods, 447
    hurricanes/tropical storms, 446
    tornadoes, 446
GFS (grandfather/father/son) backup rotation scheme, 391
Gigabit Ethernet, 89
glass entryways, 466
GLBA (Gramm-Leach-Bliley Act), 415
government data classifications, 187-188
Graham-Denning model, 320
Gramm-Leach-Bliley Act (GLBA), 415
graphical passwords, 20, 502
gray hats, 407
grid computing, 335
GSM (Global System Mobile), 137

H

hackers, 407
Halon gas, 469
hand geometry scans, 24
handling
  risks, 180-181
  sensitive information, 344-345
hardware
  disaster recovery, 386
  evidence analysis, 435
  protection, 347
  redundant, 355
Harrison-Ruzzo-Ullmen model, 321
hash functions
  defined, 244, 512
  HAVAL, 272
  MD algorithms, 271
  one-way, 269-270
  RIPEMD-160, 272
  SHA, 271-272
  Tiger, 272
hash MAC (HMAC), 273
HAVAL hash function, 272
HDSL (High Bit-Rate DSL), 128
Health Care and Education Reconciliation Act of 2010, 418
Health Insurance Portability and Accountability Act (HIPAA), 415
hearsay evidence, 433
heat activated fire detection, 468
heating and air conditioning (HVAC), 471
Hellman, Martin, 266
hierarchical databases, 226
hierarchical storage management (HSM), 354, 392

high availability, 392-393, 498-499, 518
  clustering, 518
  failover, 518
  failsoft, 518
  load balancing, 518
  RAID, 518
  SAN, 518
High Bit-Rate DSL (HDSL), 128
high-level languages, 219
High-Speed Serial Interface (HSSI), 124-125
HIPAA (Health Insurance Portability and Accountability Act), 415
history
  cryptography, 246-247
    Caesar cipher, 247
    Kerckhoff principles, 249
    Lucifer project, 250
    scytale ciphers, 246
    Vigenere ciphers, 248-249
    World War II, 249-250
  media, 354
HMAC (hash MAC), 273
honeypots, 117
host-based IDS, 50-51
hot sites, 383
HSM (hierarchical storage management), 354, 392, 498, 517
HSSI (High-Speed Serial Interface), 124-125
HTTP (IIypertext Transfer Protocol), 104, 284
HTTPS (Hypertext Transfer Protocol Secure), 104, 284
hubs, 109
human resources recovery, 387
hurricanes, 446

HVAC (heating and air conditioning), 471
hybrid ciphers, 256-257
hybrid routing protocols, 107
hybrid topologies (networks), 94

I

IaaS (infrastructure as a service), 117
IAB (Internet Architecture Board), 437
IBM Lucifer project, 250
ICCs (integrated circuit cards), 23
ICMP (Internet Control Message Protocol), 74
  attacks, 143-144
    Fraggle, 144
    ICMP redirect, 144
    Ping of Death, 144
    ping scanning, 145
    Smurf, 144
  defined, 104
IDEA (International Data Encryption Algorithm), 263
identities
  federated, 35
  management, 18-19, 349
  theft, 54
IDS (Intrusion Detection System)
  acoustical, 461
  anomaly-based, 51, 507
  application-based, 52
  capacitance, 461
  categories, 487-488, 503-507
  CCTV, 461
  electromechanical systems, 460
  infrared sensors, 460
  operations security, 363

patrol force, 462
perimeters, 460
photoelectric systems, 460
responses, 455
rule-based, 52, 507
signature-based, 51, 503
wave motion, 461

IEC (International Electrotechnical Commission), 164

IGMP (Internet Group Management Protocol), 75

IGRP (Interior Gateway Routing Protocol), 108

IKE (Internet Key Exchange), 130

IMAP (Internet Message Access Protocol), 105

Implement phase (system development life cycle), 205

implied addressing, 306

import legal issues, 420

incident responses, 423
events *versus* incidents, 423
management, 356-357
procedures, 424-425
rules of engagement/authorization/ scope, 424
teams, 424
creating, 424
investigations, 424

incidental computer crimes, 406

incidents *versus* events, 423

incremental backups, 390

Incremental software development method, 214

indirect addressing, 306

industrial doors, 463

inference, 334

information
assets, protecting, 347
flow models, 316
life cycle, 188

information security governance, 6-7, 182-183
baselines, 185-186
components, 183
data classifications, 186
commercial businesses, 186-187
military and government, 187-188
guidelines, 186
information life cycle, 188
management approval, 182
Maturity Model, 330
organizational information security statements, 183
policies/procedures, 183-186
categories, 185
issue-specific, 185
organization security, 184
system-specific, 185
standards, 185

Information Technology Infrastructure Library (ITIL), 172, 313

Information Technology Security Evaluation Criteria. *See* **ITSEC**

informative security policies, 185

infrared sensors, 460

infrared wireless, 139

infrastructure as a service (IaaS), 117

Infrastructure mode (WLANs), 137

Initialization Vectors (IVs), 255

Initiate phase (system development life cycle), 204

input/output
    controls, 362
    devices, 307
insurance, 379-380
intangible asset protection, 177, 346
    facilities, 346
    hardware, 347
    information assets, 347
    software, 347
integrated circuit cards (ICCs), 23
Integrated Services Digital Network (ISDN), 127
integrity, 268-269, 297-298
    Biba model, 319
    Clark-Wilson model, 319-320
    cryptosystems, 251
    goals, 298
    hash functions
        HAVAL, 272
        MD algorithms, 271
        one-way hash, 269-270
        RIPEMD-160, 272
        SHA, 271-272
        Tiger, 272
    Lipner model, 320
    MACs
        CBC-MAC, 274
        CMAC, 274
        HMAC, 273
    services, 303
intellectual property laws, 409
    copyrights, 411-412
    internal protection, 413
    patents, 410
    software piracy and licensing issues, 412-413
    trademarks, 411
    trade secrets, 410-411
interior facility security, 463
    biometrics, 466
    data centers, 467
    door locks, 463
    doors, 463
    equipment rooms, 467
    glass entries, 466
    locks, 464-465
    mantraps, 464
    restricted work areas, 468
    turnstiles, 464
    visitors, 466-467
    work areas, 467
Interior Gateway Routing Protocol (IGRP), 108
interior routing protocols, 106
Intermediate system to Intermediate system (IS-IS) protocol, 108
internal compartments (facilities), 457
internal geographical threats, 437
International Data Encryption Algorithm (IDEA), 263
International Electrotechnical Commission (IEC), 164
International Information Systems Security Certification Consortium. *See* (ISC)^2
International Organization for Standardization (ISO), 164
International Organization on Computer Evidence (IOCE), 428-429
Internet Architecture Board (IAB), 437
Internet Control Message Protocol. *See* ICMP
Internet Group Management Protocol (IGMP), 75

Internet Key Exchange (IKE), 130
Internet layer (TCP/IP), 74-75
Internet Message Access Protocol (IMAP), 105
Internet Protocol (IP), 74
Internet security, 283
  cookies, 284-285
  HTTP, 284
  HTTPS, 284
  IPsec, 285-286
  remote access, 283
  S-HTTP, 284
  SET, 284
  SSH, 285
  SSL, 134, 283
  TLS, 134, 284
Internet Security Association and Key Management Protocol (ISAKMP), 130
interpreted code, 220
interviews (investigations), 430
intranets, 119-120
intruders
  delaying, 455
  detecting, 455
intrusion detection. *See* **IDS**
inventory, 473
investigations, 9, 425-426
  crime scenes, 429
  decisions, 428
  evidence, 430-431
    chain of custody, 430
    examining/analyzing, 428
    five rules, 431
    hardware/embedded device analysis, 435
    identifying, 427
    media analysis, 434
    network analysis, 435
    presenting in court, 428
    preserving and collecting, 427-428
    search warrants, 433
    seizure, 434
    software analysis, 434
    surveillance, 433
    types, 431-433
  incident responses
    incidents versus events, 423
    procedures, 424-425
    rules of engagement/authorization/scope, 424
    teams, 424
  interviews, 430
  IOCE/SWGDE, 428-429
  law enforcement involvement, 426
  MOM, 429
  process, 426
  standardized procedures, 425
IOCE (International Organization on Computer Evidence), 428-429
IP (Internet Protocol), 74
IP addresses
  classes, 80-81
  IPv4, 77-80, 82
  IPv6, 82
  NAT, 81-89
  public *versus* private, 81
  spoofing, 150
IPS (Intrusion Prevention System), 52, 363
IPsec, 285-286
  AH (Authentication Header), 130
  ESP, 130
  IKE, 130

ISAKMP, 130
VPNs, 130-132
IPv4
IPv6, compared, 82
overview, 77-80
IPv6, 82
iris scans, 25
IS-IS (Intermediate system to Intermediate system) protocol, 108
ISAKMP (Internet Security Association and Key Management Protocol), 130
(ISC)² International Information Systems Security Certification Consortium, 2-4
certifications offered, 4
Code of Ethics, 435-436
defined, 2
goals, 4
ISDN (Integrated Services Digital Network), 127
ISO (International Organization for Standardization), 164
ISO/IEC 27000 series
security architecture documentation, 314
software development security, 210
ISO-IEC 42010:2011, 166, 299
issue-specific security policies, 185
ITIL (Information Technology Infrastructure Library), 172, 313
ITSEC (Information Technology Security Evaluation Criteria), 326
assurance requirements, 327
functional requirements, 326-327
TSEC, mapping, 327
IVs (Initialization Vectors), 255

J

JAD (Joint Analyses Development) software development method, 218
Java
applets, 223
Database Connectivity (JDBC), 227
Enterprise Edition, 223
JDBC (Java Database Connectivity), 227
job rotation, 163, 344

K

KDC (Key Distribution Center), 33
Kerberos, 32-34
advantages, 33
disadvantages, 33
ticket-issuing process, 33
Kerckhoff principles, 249
kernel proxy firewalls, 114
kernels (security), 311
Key Distribution Center (KDC), 33
keys
clustering, 245, 513
defined, 244, 512
distribution center, 33
managing, 278-279
primary, 225, 511
keyspaces, 245, 513
keystroke dynamics scanning, 25
Knapsack, 268
knowledge-based systems, 229
knowledge factor authentication, 17
identity/account management, 18-19

passwords, 19-22
   changing, 21
   Linux, 21
   lockout policies, 21
   management, 20
   types, 19-20
   Windows, 22

known plaintext attacks, 287

L

L2TP (Layer 2 Tunneling Protocol), 130
labeling media, 354
laminated glass, 466
LANs (local area networks), 94
   contention methods, 97-101
      collisions, 98
      CSMA/CA, 100
      CSMA/CD, 99
      polling, 101
      token passing, 101
   Ethernet 802.3, 94-96
   FDDI, 97
   overview, 119
   Token Ring, 96
   wireless. *See* WLANs

laptop memory, 305
laws
   administrative, 409
   civil, 408-409
   civil code, 408
   common, 408
   compliance, 420
   criminal, 408
   customary, 409
   export/import issues, 420

   intellectual property, 409
      copyrights, 411-412
      internal protection, 413
      patents, 410
      software piracy and licensing issues, 412-413
      trade secrets, 410-411
      trademarks, 411
   liability, 420
      due diligence versus due care, 421
      issues, 422-423
      negligence, 421-422
   mixed, 409
   privacy, 415
      Basel II, 417
      CALEA of 1994, 417
      CFAA, 416
      Computer Security Act of 1987, 417
      Economic Espionage Act of 1996, 418
      ECPA of 1986, 416
      employee privacy issues, 419
      European Union, 419
      expectations of privacy, 419
      Federal Privacy Act of 1974, 416
      FISA of 1978, 416
      FISMA of 2002, 418
      GLBA, 415
      Health Care and Education Reconciliation Act of 2010, 418
      HIPAA, 415
      PCI DSS, 418
      PIPEDA, 417
      SOX Act, 415
      United States Federal Sentencing Guidelines of 1991, 417
      USA PATRIOT Act, 418
   religious, 409

Layer 2 Tunneling Protocol (L2TP), 130
layered defense model, 453
layers
   OSI
      Application, 67
      Data Link, 68-69
      Network, 68
      Physical, 69
      Presentation, 67
      Session, 67-68
      Transport, 68
   TCP/IP
      Application, 72
      Internet, 74-75
      Link, 76
      Transport, 72-74
LDAP (Lightweight Directory Access Protocol), 31
leaks (memory), 306
least privilege principles, 29-30, 343
legal systems, 9
   administrative, 409
   civil, 408-409
   civil code, 408
   common, 408
   criminal, 408
   customary, 409
   mixed, 409
   religious, 409
legal teams, 394
liability, 420
   due diligence *versus* due care, 421
   issues, 422-423
   negligence, 421-422

life cycles
   cryptography, 246
   information, 188
   software development, 206
      change/configuration management, 209
      design, 207
      develop, 207
      gather requirements, 206-207
      release/maintain, 209
      test/validate, 208-209
   system development, 203-204
      acquire/develop, 204-205
      dispose, 205-206
      implement, 205
      initiate, 204
      operate/maintain, 205
lighting, 461
   feet of illumination ratings, 462
   systems, 461-462
   types, 462
Lightweight Directory Access Protocol (LDAP), 31
linear cryptanalysis, 288
Link layer (TCP/IP), 76
links
   encryption, 280
   state protocols, 107
Linux password management, 21
Lipner model, 320
load balancing, 393, 518
local area networks. *See* **LANs**
locking
   databases, 228
   security devices, 474
lockout policies (passwords), 21
locks, 464-465

logic bombs, 232
logical addressing, 306
   IP classes, 80-81
   IPv4, 77-80, 82
   IPv6, 82
   NAT, 81-89
   public *versus* private, 81
logical controls, 43-44, 485, 505
logs
   analysis, 435
   audit, scrubbing, 36
   transaction log backups, 390
Lucifer project, 250

M

MAC (mandatory access control), 47
MAC (Media Access Control) addresses, 82-83, 141
machine languages, 219
macro viruses, 231, 511
MACs (Message Authentication Code), 273
   CBC-MAC, 274
   CMAC, 274
   HMAC, 273
mainframe platforms, 300
maintenance
   architecture, 330
   BCP, 398
   hooks, 331
   system architecture, 299
malware, 56, 230
   botnets, 232
   classes, 488, 507
   logic bombs, 232
   protection, 235-236
      antimalware software, 236
      antivirus software, 236
      security policies, 236
   rootkits, 233
   spyware/adware, 232
   Trojan horses, 231
   viruses, 230-231
   worms, 231
management
   accounts, 18-19
   controls, 41-42, 484, 504
   identity, 18-19
   security responsibilities, 189
managing
   access, 349
   assets, 348-349
      backup/recovery, 349
      fault tolerance, 348
      redundancy, 348
   configurations, 358-359
   finances during disaster recovery, 393
   identities, 349
   incident responses, 356-357
   keys, 278-279
   media
      disposal, 355
      HSM, 354
      labeling, 354
      media history, 354
      NAS, 353
      RAID, 349-352
      SAN, 353
   memory, 309
   passwords, 20, 482-483, 502-503
   patches, 359-360
   relational databases, 491-492, 510-511
   responsibilities. *See* responsibilities

risks, 181
  analysis teams, 182
  management teams, 181
  policies, 181
  vulnerabilities, 363
mandatory access control (MAC), 47
man-made disasters, 371
man-made threats, 449-451
  collusion, 451
  explosions, 449
  fires, 449-450
  fraud, 450
  theft, 450
  vandalism, 450
MANs (Metropolitan Area Networks), 120
mantraps, 464
matrix-based models, 315-316
maximum period time of disruption (MPTD), 374
maximum tolerable downtime (MTD), 374, 517
MD algorithms, 271
mean time between failure (MTBF), 356, 374, 517
mean time to repair (MTTR), 356, 374, 517
media
  analysis (evidence), 434
  disposal, 355
  history, 354
  labeling, 354
  managing
    HSM, 354
    NAS, 353
    RAID, 349-352
    SAN, 353
  multimedia collaboration, 134-135
  portable, 473
  relations teams, 395
Media Access Control (MAC) addresses, 82-83, 141
meet-in-the middle attacks, 290
memory, 304-306
  addressing
    absolute, 306
    implied, 306
    indirect, 306
    logical, 306
    relative, 306
  associative, 306
  caches, 306
  cards, authentication, 22-23
  DMA, 306
  leaks, 306
  managing, 309
  primary, 306
  RAM, 305
  ROM, 305
  TPM, 280
  virtual, 306
mercury vapor lighting, 462
mesh topology, 93-94
Message Authentication Code. *See* MACs
message integrity, 268-269
  hash functions
    HAVAL, 272
    MD algorithms, 271
    one-way hash, 269-270
    RIPEMD-160, 272
    SHA, 271-272
    Tiger, 272

576 message integrity

MACs
   CBC-MAC, 274
   CMAC, 274
   HMAC, 273
methodologies (security)
   CMMI, 174
   ISO/IEC 27000, 164-166
   ITIL, 172
   listing of, 163-164
   program life cycle, 174-175
   Six Sigma, 173
   top-down/bottom-up, 174
metrics (security), 194-195
Metro Ethernet, 120
Metropolitan Area Networks (MANs), 120
middleware, 301
military data classifications, 187-188
MIME (Multipurpose Internet Mail Extension), 282
mirrored sites, 385
mixed law, 409
mobile code, 56, 223
mobile computing platforms, 301
MODAF (British Ministry of Defence Architecture Framework), 168
models
   access control, 46
      ACLs, 49
      capabilities tables, 48
      content-dependent, 48
      context-dependent, 48
      discretionary, 46
      mandatory, 47
      matrix, 48
      RBAC, 47
      rule-based, 48

databases, 224
   hierarchical, 226
   network, 226
   object-oriented, 226
   object-relational, 226
   relational, 225
OSI, 66-67
   advantages, 66
   Application layer (layer 7), 67
   Data Link layer (layer 2), 68-69
   encapsulation/de-encapsulation, 76
   multi-layer protocols, 70
   Network layer (layer 3), 68
   Physical layer (layer 1), 69
   Presentation layer (layer 6), 67
   protocol mappings, 70
   Session layer, 67-68
   Transport layer (layer 4), 68
security
   Bell-LaPadula, 317-318
   Biba, 319
   Brewer-Nash, 320
   Clark-Wilson Integrity, 319-320
   Graham-Denning, 320
   Harrison-Ruzzo-Ullmen, 321
   Lipner, 320
   summary, 495, 514
   types, 315-316
software development, 211
   Agile, 216-217
   Build and Fix, 211-212
   Cleanroom, 218
   CMMI, 218
   Incremental, 214
   JAD, 218
   Prototyping, 214
   RAD, 216

Spiral, 215
V-shaped, 213
Waterfall, 212-213
TCP/IP, 71
Application layer, 72
ARP, 101-102
encapsulation/de-encapsulation, 76
Internet layer, 74-75
Link layer, 76
TCP/UDP ports, 77-78
Transport layer, 72-74
modes
3DES, 262-263, 495, 514
security, 321
compartmented, 321
dedicated, 321
multilevel, 322
system high, 321
modulation, 135
802.11 techniques, 136
cellular/mobile, 136-137
modulo 26 substitution cipher, 252
MOM (motive, opportunity, means), 429
monitoring
access control, 50
identity theft, 54
IDS, 50-52
IPS, 52
operations security, 363-364
reference, 311
services, 303
special privileges, 345
threats, 52-53
backdoor/trapdoor, 57
brute-force, 53
buffer overflow, 55

dictionary attacks, 53
DOS/DDOS, 55
dumpster diving, 55
emanating, 57
malware, 56
mobile code, 56
passwords, 53
phishing/pharming, 54
shoulder surfing, 54
sniffing, 57
social engineering, 53
spoofing, 56
motive, opportunity, means (MOM), 429
movable lighting systems, 461
MPTD (maximum period time of disruption), 374
MTBF (mean time between failure), 356, 374, 517
MTD (maximum tolerable downtime), 374, 517
MTTR (mean time to repair), 356, 374, 517
multicast transmissions, 85
multihomed firewalls, 115
multi-layer protocols, 70
multilevel
lattice models, 315
security mode, 322
multimedia collaboration, 134-135
multi-mode fiberoptic cabling, 89
multipartite viruses, 231, 511
multiplexers, 109
Multipurpose Internet Mail Extension (MIME), 282
multitasking, 308-309
mutual-aid agreements, 385

N

NAS (Network-Attached Storage), 353
NAT (Network Address Translation), 81-89, 105
National Information Assurance Certification and Accreditation Process (NIACAP), 329
National Institute of Standards and Technology Special Publication. *See* NIST SP
natural access control, 453-454
natural disasters, 371
natural languages, 220
natural surveillance, 454
natural territorials reinforcement, 454
natural threats, 446
    earthquakes, 446
    floods, 447
    hurricanes/tropical storms, 446
    tornadoes, 446
NDAs (non-disclosure agreements), 411
need-to-know principles, 29-30, 343
negligence, 421-422
Network Address Translation (NAT), 81-89, 105
Network-Attached Storage (NAS), 353
Network layer (OSI), 68
networks
    cabling, 87
        coaxial, 87-88
        fiberoptic, 89-91
        selecting, 87
        twisted pair, 88-90
    databases, 226
    devices, 109
        architecture, 115
        cloud computing, 117-118
        endpoint security, 119
        firewalls, 112-114
        gateways, 112
        honeypots, 117
        hubs, 109
        multiplexers, 109
        patch panels, 109
        PBXs, 116-117
        proxy servers, 116
        routers, 112
        switches, 110-111
        virtualization, 116
        VLANs, 111
    encapsulation/de-encapsulation, 76
    evidence analysis, 435
    IDS, 50
    IP addresses
        classes, 80-81
        IPv4, 77-80, 82
        IPv6, 82
        NAT, 81-89
        public versus private, 81
    LANs. *See* LANs
    MAC addresses, 82-83
    OSI model, 66-67
        advantages, 66
        Application layer (layer 7), 67
        Data Link layer (layer 2), 68-69
        multi-layer protocols, 70
        Network layer (layer 3), 68
        Physical layer (layer 1), 69
        Presentation layer (layer 6), 67
        protocol mappings, 70
        Session layer (layer 5), 67-68
        Transport layer (layer 4), 68

networks 579

protocols
    ARP, 101-102
    DHCP, 102-103
    FTP, 104
    FTPS, 104
    HTTP, 104
    HTTPS, 104
    ICMP, 104
    IMAP, 105
    POP, 105
    SFTP, 104
    SHTTP, 104
    SMTP, 105
    SNMP, 105-106
remote connections, 126
    authentication protocols, 133
    cable, 128
    dial-up, 126-127
    DSL, 127-128
    ISDN, 127
    multimedia collaboration, 134-135
    RADIUS, 132-133
    SSL, 134, 283
    TACACS, 132-133
    Telnet, 134
    TLS, 134, 284
    VPNs, 129-132
routing, 106
routing protocols
    BGP, 108
    categories, 107
    distance vector, 107
    EIGRP, 108
    hybrid, 107
    IGRP, 108
    IS-IS, 108
    link state, 107
    OSPF, 107
    RIP, 107
    security, 106
    static versus dynamic, 106
    types, 106
    VRRP, 108
security, 139-141
    attenuation, 142
    cabling, 142
    crosstalk, 143
    DNS attacks, 145-147
    eavesdropping, 143
    email attacks, 147-148
    ICMP attacks, 143-145
    IP address spoofing, 150
    MAC filters, 141
    noise, 142
    overview, 6-7
    port scanning, 150
    satellites, 141
    session hijacking, 150
    SYN ACK attacks, 149
    teardrop attacks, 150
    WEP, 140
    wireless, 149
    WPA, 140
    WPA2, 140
services
    DNS, 103
    NAT, 105
    PAT, 105
TCP/IP, 101-102
transmissions, 86
types
    extranets, 119-120
    intranets, 120

LANs, 119

MANs, 120

wireless. *See* WLANs

NIACAP (National Information Assurance Certification and Accreditation Process), 329

NIST (National Institute of Standards and Technology) SP (Special Publication)

800-30, 176

800-34 Revision 1, 378

800-53, 170-171, 488, 507

noise (WLANs), 142

non-disclosure agreements (NDAs), 411

noninterference models, 316

non-repudiation (cryptosystems), 251

normalization (databases), 225

null ciphers, 252

numeric passwords, 20, 502

O

Object Linking and Embedding (OLE), 223

Object Linking and Embedding Database (OLE DB), 227

object-oriented databases, 226

object-oriented programming (OOP), 220-221

object-relational databases, 226

Object Request Broker (ORB), 222

OC carrier lines, 122

OCSP (Online Certificate Status Protocol), 276

ODBC (Open Database Connectivity), 226

OEP (Occupant Emergency Plan), 474

OFB (Output Feedback), 261-262

OFDM (Orthogonal Frequency Division Multiplexing), 136

OFDMA (Orthogonal Frequency Division Multiple Access), 136

off-the-shelf software packages, 229

OLE (Object Linking and Embedding), 223

OLE DB (Object Linking and Embedding Database), 227

OLTP (Online Transaction Processing) ACID tests, 229

one-time pads, 257-258

one-time passwords, 20, 482, 502

one-way functions, 246, 514

one-way hash, 269-270

Online Certificate Status Protocol (OCSP), 276

Online Transaction Processing (OLTP) ACID tests, 229

onsite assessment security responsibilities, 192

OOP (object-oriented programming), 220-221

Open Database Connectivity (ODBC), 226

The Open Group Architecture Framework (TOGAF), 168, 312

Open Group Single Sign-On Standard website, 31

Open Shortest Path First (OSPF) protocol, 107

Open systems Interconnect model. *See* OSI model

Open Web Application Security Project (OWASP), 210, 333

Operate/Maintain phase (system development life cycle), 205

operating systems, 307-308

operations security, 8
  access management, 349
  job rotation, 344
  least privilege, 343
  preventative measures
    antivirus/antimalware, 364
    IDS/IPS, 363
    input/output controls, 362
    monitoring/reporting, 363-364
    system hardening, 362-363
    trusted paths, 362
    unscheduled reboots, 362
    vulnerability management, 363
  procedures, 356
    audits, 360
    change control, 357-358
    configuration management, 358-359
    incident response management, 356-357
    patches, 359-360
  RAID, 497, 514
  record retention, 345
  resource protection, 346
    access, maintaining, 355-356
    asset management, 348-349
    facilities, 346
    hardware, 347
    identity management, 349
    information assets, 347
    media management. See media, managing
    software, 347
    tangible/intangible assets, 346
  sensitive information procedures, 344-345
  separation of duties, 344
  special privileges, monitoring, 345
  threats
    clipping levels, 361
    deviations from standards, 361
    unexplained events, 361
opinion evidence, 433
optical jukeboxes, 392, 517
Orange Book, 323-326
  assurance requirements
    life cycle, 324
    operational, 323
  classification system, 324-326
    A - Verified protection, 325
    A1 - Verified Design, 325-326
    B - Mandatory protection, 324
    B1 - Labeled Security Protection, 324-325
    B2 - Structured Protection, 325
    B3 - Security Domains, 325
    C - Discretionary protection, 324
    C1 - Discretionary Security Protection, 324
    C2 - Controlled Access Protection, 324
    D - Minimal protection, 324
ORB (Object Request Broker), 222
order of volatility, 427
organizations
  ethics, 437
  information security governance. See information security governance
  security policies, 184
Orthogonal Frequency Division Multiple Access (OFDMA), 136
Orthogonal Frequency Division Multiplexing (OFDM), 136
OSI (Open Systems Interconnect) model, 66-67
  advantages, 66
  encapsulation/de-encapsulation, 76

layers
    Application (layer 7), 67
    Data Link (layer 2), 68-69
    Network (layer 3), 68
    Physical (layer 1), 69
    Presentation (layer 6), 67
    Session (layer 5), 67-68
    Transport (layer 4), 68
multi-layer protocols, 70
protocol mappings, 70
OSPF (Open Shortest Path First) protocol, 107
outages (power)
    impacts, identifying, 374-375
    types, 470
Output Feedback (OFB), 261-262
OWASP (Open Web Application Security Project), 210, 333
ownership factor authentication, 22
    memory cards, 22-23
    smart cards, 23
    token devices, 22

P

PaaS (platform as a service), 118
packets
    filtering firewalls, 113
    switching networks, 123
PACs (Privileged Attribute Certificates), 34
palm/hand scans, 24
PAP (Password Authentication Protocol), 133
parallel tests, 397
parasitic viruses, 231, 511
partial-knowledge tests, 39

passive cryptography attacks, 286
passive infrared systems (PIR), 460
passphrase passwords, 19, 502
passwords
    changing, 21
    Linux, 21
    lockout policies, 21
    managing, 20, 482-483, 502-503
    static, 481-482
    threats, monitoring, 53
    types, 481-482, 501-502
        cognitive, 20
        combination, 19
        complex, 19
        graphical, 20
        numeric, 20
        one-time, 20, 482
        passphrase, 19
        standard, 19
        static, 19
    Windows, 22
PAT (Port Address Translation), 105
patches
    management, 359-360
    panels, 109
patents, 410
paths
    tracing, 435
    trusted, 362
patrol force, 462
PBXs (private branch exchanges), 116-117
PCI DSS (Payment Card Industry Data Security Standard), 418
peer-to-peer computing, 335
penetration testing, 38-39
    categories, 39

performing, 38
strategies, 38-39
perimeters, 458
   access control, 462-463
   acoustical detection systems, 461
   barriers, 459
   capacitance detectors, 461
   CCTV, 461
   electromechanical systems, 460
   fences, 459
   gates, 459-460
   infrared sensors, 460
   intrusion detection, 460
   lighting
      feet of illumination ratings, 462
      systems, 461-462
      types, 462
   patrol force, 462
   photoelectric systems, 460
   walls, 460
   wave motion detectors, 461
Personal Information Protection and Electronic Documents Act (PIPEDA), 417
personally identifiable information (PII), 414
personnel
   components (BCP), 377
   doors, 463
   privacy, protecting, 474
   safety, 474
   security responsibilities, 192-193
PGP (Pretty Good Privacy), 281-282
pharming, 54
phishing, 54, 148
photoelectric systems, 460
physical addressing, 82-83

physical controls, 43-45, 472, 486, 506
Physical layer (OSI), 69
physical security, 9
   equipment, 472
      corporate procedures, 472-473
      security device protection, 473-474
   geographical threats, 445
      internal versus external, 445
      natural, 446-447
   interior building, 463
      biometrics, 466
      data centers, 467
      door locks, 463
      doors, 463
      equipment rooms, 467
      glass entries, 466
      locks, 464-465
      mantraps, 464
      restricted work areas, 468
      turnstiles, 464
      visitors, 466-467
      work areas, 467
   lighting, 461
      feet of illumination ratings, 462
      systems, 461-462
      types, 462
   man-made threats, 449
      collusion, 451
      explosions, 449
      fires, 449-450
      fraud, 450
      theft, 450
      vandalism, 450
   natural access control, 453-454
   perimeters, 458
      access control, 462-463

584   physical security

    acoustical detection systems, 461
    barriers, 459
    capacitance detectors, 461
    CCTV, 461
    electromechanical systems, 460
    fences, 459
    gates, 459-460
    infrared sensors, 460
    intrusion detection, 460
    patrol force, 462
    photoelectric systems, 460
    walls, 460
    wave motion detectors, 461
personnel
    privacy, 474
    safety, 474
politically motivated threats, 451-452
    bombings, 452
    civil disobedience, 452
    riots, 451
    strikes, 451
    terrorist acts, 452
site and facility design, 453
    computer and equipment rooms, 457-458
    construction, 456-457
    CPTED, 453
    facility selection, 455
    internal compartments, 457
    layered defense model, 453
    natural surveillance, 454
    natural territorials reinforcement, 454
    physical security plan, 454-455
system threats, 447
    communications, 447-448
    electrical, 447
    utilities, 448

physiological characteristics (authentication), 24-25
PII (personally identifiable information), 414
Ping of Death, 144
ping scanning, 145
PIPEDA (Personal Information Protection and Electronic Documents Act), 417
PIR (passive infrared systems), 460
PKI (Public Key Infrastructure), 275
    CAs, 275-276
    CRLs, 277
    cross-certification, 278
    digital certificates, 276
        classes, 277
        requesting, 277
        X.509, 276-277
    OCSP, 276
    RAs, 275
    trusted entity communication, 277-278
plaintext, 244, 493, 512
platform as a service (PaaS), 118
PLD (Programmable Logic Device), 305
Point-to-Point Protocol (PPP), 124, 126
Point-to-Point Tunneling Protocol (PPTP), 129-130
policies
    access control, 29
    corporate, 472-473
        encryption, 472
        inventory, 473
        tamper protection, 472
    equipment security, 472-473
        encryption, 472

    inventory, 473
    tamper protection, 472
  incident response, 424-425
  information security governance, 183-186
    categories, 185
    issue-specific, 185
    organizational security, 184
    system-specific, 185
  job rotation, 344
  least privilege, 29-30, 343
  lockout, 21
  malware protection, 236
  operations, 356
    audits, 360
    change control, 356-359
    configuration management, 358-359
    incident response management, 356-357
    patches, 359-360
  portable media, 473
  record retention, 345
  risk management, 181
  sensitive information, 344-345
  separation of duties, 344
  special privileges, monitoring, 345
politically motivated threats, 451-452
  bombings, 452
  civil disobedience, 452
  riots, 451
  strikes, 451
  terrorist acts, 452
polling, 101
polyinstantiation (databases), 228
polymorphic viruses, 231, 511
polymorphism, 221
POP (Post Office Protocol), 105

portable media procedures, 473
ports
  address translation (PAT), 105
  scanning attacks, 150
  TCP/UDP, 77-78
Post Office Protocol (POP), 105
power
  conditioners, 471
  outages
    impacts, 374-375
    types, 470
  preventative measures, 470-471
  redundancy, 379
  supplies, 470
PPP (Point-to-Point-Protocol), 124, 126
PPTP (Point-to-Point Tunneling Protocol), 129-130
preaction sprinkler systems, 469
preemptive multitasking, 309
prerequisites for exam, 10
Presentation layer (OSI), 67
Pretty Good Privacy (PGP), 281-282
preventive controls, 41
PRI (primary rate) ISDN, 127
primary keys, 228, 511
primary memory, 306
primary rate (PRI) ISDN, 127
privacy, 413
  expectations, 419
  laws, 415
    Basel II, 417
    CALEA of 1994, 417
    CFAA, 416
    Computer Security Act of 1987, 417
    Economic Espionage Act of 1996, 418
    ECPA of 1986, 416

employee privacy issues, 419
European Union, 419
expectations of privacy, 419
Federal Privacy Act of 1974, 416
FISA of 1978, 416
FISMA of 2002, 418
GLBA, 415
Health Care and Education Reconciliation Act of 2010, 418
HIPAA, 415
PCI DSS, 418
PIPEDA, 417
SOX Act, 415
United States Federal Sentencing Guidelines of 1991, 417
USA PATRIOT Act, 418
personnel, protecting, 474
PII (personally identifiable information), 414
private branch exchanges (PBXs), 116-117
private IP addresses, 81
private key encryption. *See* **symmetric algorithms**
Privileged Attribute Certificates (PACs), 34
privileges
escalation, 235
special, monitoring, 345
procedures. *See* **policies**
process/policy reviews, 192
professional ethics. *See* **ethics**
programmable logic device (PLD), 305
programming, 219
ActiveX, 224
cohesion, 221
compiled *versus* interpreted code, 220

CORBA, 222
coupling, 221
data structures, 222
distributed object-oriented systems, 222
Java
applets, 223
Enterprise Edition, 223
languages
assembly, 219
databases, 226-227
high-level, 219
machine, 219
natural, 220
very-high-level, 219
mobile code, 223
object-oriented, 220-221
OLE, 223
polymorphism, 221
SOA, 223
protocols
anomaly-based IDS, 51
ARP, 75, 101-102
CHAP, 133
DHCP, 102-103
EAP, 133
FDDI, 97
frame relay, 123
FTP, 104
FTPS, 104
HTTP, 104, 284
HTTPS, 104, 284
ICMP. *See* ICMP
IGMP, 75
IMAP, 105
IP, 74
IPsec, 285-286

ISAKMP, 130
L2TP, 130
OCSP, 276
OSI
   mapping, 70
   multi-layer, 70
PAP, 133
POP, 105
PPP, 124, 126
PPTP, 129-130
remote authentication, 133
routing
   BGP, 108
   categories, 107
   distance vector, 107
   EIGRP, 108
   hybrid, 107
   IGRP, 108
   IS-IS, 108
   link state, 107
   OSPF, 107
   RIP, 107
   security, 106
   static versus dynamic, 106
   types, 106
   VRRP, 108
SFTP, 104
SHTTP, 104, 284
SIP, 125
SLIP, 126
SMTP, 105
SNMP, 105-106
SSL, 134, 283
TCP
   functionality examples, 74
   ports, 77-78
   three-way handshake, 73
   UDP, compared, 73
TCP/IP. *See* TCP/IP
Telnet, 134
TKIP, 140
TLS, 134, 284
Token Ring, 96
UDP
   ports, 77-78
   TCP, compared, 73
Prototyping software development method, 214
provisioning life cycle, 50
proxy firewalls, 113-114
proxy servers, 116
PSTN (Public Switched Telephone Network), 125
public IP addresses, 81
public key encryption. *See* **asymmetric algorithms**
Public Key Infrastructure. *See* **PKI**
punitive damages, 408
purging data, 355

Q

qualitative risk analysis, 179
quantitative risk analysis, 178-179
quantum cryptography, 282
quartz lamps, 462

R

RAD (Rapid Application Development) software development method, 216
RADIUS (Remote Authentication Dial In User Service), 132-133

RAID (Redundant Array of Independent Disks), 349-352
  data recovery, 392
  defined, 518
  implementing, 352
  levels
    0 (disk striping), 349
    1 (disk mirroring), 350
    3, 350
    5, 351
    7, 351
    summary, 352
Rainbow Series, 323
  Orange Book, 323-326
    classification system, 324-326
    life cycle assurance requirements, 324
    operational assurance requirements, 323
  Red Book, 326
RAM (Random Access Memory), 305
Rapid Application Development (RAD) software development method, 216
RAs (Registration Authorities), 275
RBAC (role-based access control), 47
RC algorithms, 264
Read Only Memory (ROM), 305
reciprocal agreements, 384
records
  defined, 225
  retention, 345
recoverability, 376
recovery
  asset management, 349
  controls, 41
  disasters. *See* disaster recovery
  point objective (RPO), 375, 517
  priorities, 376, 381
  time objective (RTO), 374, 517
  trusted, 362
Red Book, 326
redundancy
  asset management, 348
  hardware, 355
  sites, 385
  systems, facilities, power, 379
  Virtual Router Redundancy Protocol (VRRP), 108
Redundant Array of Independent Disks. *See* **RAID**
reference monitors, 311
referential integrity, 225, 522
Registration Authorities (RAs), 275
regulations. *See* **laws**
regulatory law, 409
regulatory security policies, 185
relational databases, 225
  attributes, 225
  base relations, 225
  cardinality, 225
  degrees, 225
  domains, 225
  keys
    candidate, 225
    foreign, 225
    primary, 225
  managing, 510
  normalization, 225
  records, 225
  referential integrity, 225
  relations, 225
  schemas, 225
  tuples, 225
  views, 225
relations, 225

relative addresses, 306
Release/Maintenance phase (software development life cycle), 209
religious law, 409
remanence (media disposal), 355
Remote Authentication Dial In User Service (RADIUS), 132-133
remote connections, 126
   attacks, 149
   authentication protocols, 133
   cable, 128
   dial-up, 126-127
   DSL, 127-128
      security, 128
      versions, 127-128
   Internet security, 283
   ISDN, 127
   multimedia collaboration, 134-135
   RADIUS, 132-133
   SSL, 134, 283
   TACACS, 132-133
   Telnet, 134
   TLS, 134, 284
   VPNs, 129-132
      encapsulation/de-encapsulation, 76, 129
      IPsec, 130-132
      L2TP, 130
      PPTP, 129-130
remote journaling, 392, 498, 517
replay attacks, 289
replication, 392, 498, 518
reporting
   accountability, 36-37
   operations security, 363-364
Request for Comments (RFC) 1087, 437

requirements
   ITSEC, 326
      assurance, 327
      functional, 326-327
   Orange Book assurance, 323-326
      life cycle, 324
      operational, 323
   resources, 375
   system security, 310-311
residual risks, 180
resource protection, 346
   access
      maintaining, 355-356
      management, 349
   asset management, 348-349
      backup/recovery systems, 349
      fault tolerance, 348
      redundancy, 348
   identity management, 349
   media management
      HSM, 354
      labeling, 354
      media disposal, 355
      media history, 354
      NAS, 353
      RAID, 349-352
      SAN, 353
   preventative measures
      antivirus/antimalware, 364
      IDS/IPS, 363
      input/output controls, 362
      monitoring/reporting, 363-364
      system hardening, 362-363
      trusted paths, 362
      trusted recovery, 362
      vulnerability management, 363

tangible/intangible assets, 346
   facilities, 346
   hardware, 347
   information assets, 347
   software, 347
threats
   clipping levels, 361
   deviations from standards, 361
   unexplained events, 361
resources. *See also* **assets**
  critical, identifying, 374
  criticality levels, 374-375
  identifying, 15
  protection. *See* resource protection
  relationships with users, identifying, 16
  requirements, 375
    application owners, 183
    audit committee, 189
    auditors, 191
    board of directors, 188
    data custodians, 190
    data owners, 190
    document exchange/review, 192
    management, 189
    onsite assessment, 192
    personnel, 192-193
    process/policy reviews, 192
    security administrators, 190
    security analysts, 191
    supervisors, 191
    system administrators, 190
    system owners, 190
    third-party governance, 191
    users, 191
responsibilities, 188
restoration teams, 395

restricted work areas, 468
retina scans, 25
reverse engineering, 289, 434
RFC (Request for Comments) 1087, 437
ring topology, 91
riots, 451
RIP (Routing Information Protocol), 107
RIPEMD-160 hash function, 272
risks
  assessment, 175
    asset value, determining, 177
    handling risks, 180-181
    NIST SP 800-30, 176
    qualitative risk analysis, 179
    quantitative risk analysis, 178-179
    safeguards, selecting, 179-180
    total risk versus residual risk, 180
    vulnerabilities/threats, 177-178
  defined, 161
  handling, 180-181
  managing, 6-7, 181
    analysis teams, 182
    management teams, 181
    policies, 181
  residual, 180
  total, 180
Rivest, Shamri, Adleman (RSA) algorithm, 267
Rivest, Ron, 267
role-based access control (RBAC), 47
ROM (Read Only Memory), 305
rootkits, 233
routers, 112
routing
  networks, 106

protocols
  BGP, 108
  categories, 107
  distance vector, 107
  EIGRP, 108
  hybrid, 107
  IGRP, 108
  IS-IS, 108
  link state, 107
  OSPF, 107
  RIP, 107
  security, 106
  static versus dynamic, 106
  types, 106
  VRRP, 108
Routing Information Protocol (RIP), 107
RPO (recovery point objective), 375, 517
RSA (Rivest, Shamir, Adleman) algorithm, 267
RTO (recovery time objective), 374
rule-based
  access control, 48
  IDS, 52, 507
rules of engagement (incident response), 424
running key ciphers, 252

S

SaaS (software as a service), 118
SABSA (Sherwood Applied Business Security Architecture) framework, 168, 312, 490, 509
safeguards, selecting, 179-180
safes, 474
sags, 470

salvage teams, 395
SAML (Security Assertion Markup Language), 332
SAN (Storage Area Networks)
  data recovery, 392
  defined, 353
Sarbanes-Oxley (SOX) Act, 415
satellite connection security, 141
schemas, 225, 510
Scientific Working Group on Digital Evidence (SWGDE), 428-429
scope (incident responses), 424
screened host firewalls, 115
screened subnet firewall, 115
scrubbing, 36
scytale ciphers, 246
SDRAM (Synchronous Dynamic Random Access Memory), 305
SDSL (Symmetric DSL), 128
search warrants, 433
secondary evidence, 432
secret key encryption. *See* symmetric algorithms
Secure Electronic Transactions (SETs), 284
Secure European System for Applications in a Multi-vendor Environment (SESAME), 34
Secure Hash Algorithm (SHA), 271-272
Secure-HTTP (SHTTP), 104, 284
Secure MIME (S/MIME), 282
Secure Shell. *See* SSH
Secure Sockets Layer (SSL), 134, 283
security
  budgets, 194-195
  effectiveness, 194-195
  job rotation, 163

methodologies
    CMMI, 174
    ISO/IEC 27000 Series, 164-166
    ITIL, 172
    listing of, 163-164
    program life cycle, 174-175
    Six Sigma, 173
    top-down/bottom-up, 174
metrics, 194-195
models
    Bell-LaPadula, 317-318
    Biba, 319
    Brewer-Nash, 320
    Clark-Wilson Integrity, 319-320
    Graham-Denning, 320
    Harrison-Ruzzo-Ullmen, 321
    Lipner, 320
    summary, 495, 514
    types, 315-316
modes, 321
    compartmented, 321
    dedicated, 321
    multilevel, 322
    system high, 321
teams, 395-396

Security Assertion Markup Language (SAML), 332

security device protection, 473-474
    portable media, 473
    safes/vaults/locking, 474
    tracking devices, 473

seizure of evidence, 434

sensitive information procedures, 344-345

separation of duties, 29, 163, 344

Serial Line Internet Protocol (SLIP), 126

servers
    attacks, 333
    proxy, 116
Service Level Agreements (SLAs), 356
Service-Oriented Architecture (SOA), 223
service set identifiers (SSIDs), 137
services
    directory, 30-31
    DNS attacks, 103, 145-146
        cache poisoning, 145
        cybersquatting, 147
        DDoS, 146
        DNSSEC, 146
        domain grabbing, 147
        DoS, 146
        URL hiding, 146
    network
        DNS, 103
        NAT, 105
        PAT, 105
    public cloud computing, 117-118
    RADIUS, 132-133
    security, 302-303
        access control, 302
        auditing, 303
        boundary control, 302
        cryptography, 303
        integrity, 303
        monitoring, 303
    SMDS, 124
    TACACS/TACACS+, 132-133
SESAME (Secure European System for Applications in a Multi-vendor Environment), 34
Session Initiation Protocol (SIP), 125
Session layer (OSI), 67-68

SETs (Secure Electronic Transactions), 284
SFTP (SSH File Transfer Protocol), 104
SHA (Secure Hash Algorithm), 271-272
Shamir, Adi, 267
shareware, 412
Sherwood Applied Business Security Architecture (SABSA), 168, 312, 490, 509
shielded twisted pair (STP) cabling, 89
shoulder surfing, 54
SHTTP (Secure-HTTP), 104, 284
signature-based IDS, 51, 503
signature dynamics scanning, 25
signing up for the exam, 10
Simple Mail Transfer Protocol (SMTP), 105
Simple Network Management Protocol (SNMP), 105-106
simple passwords, 19
simulation tests, 397
single loss expectancy (SLE), 178
single mode fiberoptic cabling, 89
Single Point of Failure (SPOF), 356
single sign-on. *See* SSO
SIP (Session Initiation Protocol), 125
site design, 453
  computer and equipment rooms, 457-458
  construction, 456-457
  CPTED, 453
  facility selection, 455
    accessibility, 456
    surrounding area/external entities, 456
    visibility, 456
  internal compartments, 457
  layered defense model, 453
  lighting, 461
    feet of illumination ratings, 462
    systems, 461-462
    types, 462
  natural access control, 453-454
  natural surveillance, 454
  natural territorials reinforcement, 454
  perimeters, 458
    access control, 462-463
    acoustical detection systems, 461
    barriers, 459
    capacitance detectors, 461
    CCTV, 461
    electromechanical systems, 460
    fences, 459
    gates, 459-460
    infrared sensors, 460
    intrusion detection, 460
    patrol force, 462
    photoelectric systems, 460
    walls, 460
    wave motion detectors, 461
  physical security plan, 454-455
    criminal activity, deterring, 454
    delaying intruders, 455
    detecting intruders, 455
    intrusions/disruptions response, 455
    situation assessment, 455
Six Sigma, 173
Skipjack, 264
slack space analysis, 434
SLAs (Service Level Agreements), 356
SLE (single loss expectancy), 178
SLIP (Serial Line Internet Protocol), 126

Small Outline DIMM (SODIMM), 305
smart cards, 23
SMDS (Switched Multimegabit Data Service), 124
S/MIME (Secure MIME), 282
smoke activated fire detection, 468
SMTP (Simple Mail Transfer Protocol), 105
Smurf attacks, 144
sniffing, 57
SNMP (Simple Network Management Protocol), 105-106
SOA (Service-Oriented Architecture), 223
social engineering threats, 53, 287
SOCKS firewalls, 114
SODIMM (Small Online DIMM), 305
sodium vapor lighting, 462
software
    commercial, 412
    development. *See* software development
    disaster recovery, 386-387
    evidence analysis, 434
    freeware, 412
    piracy and licensing issues, 412-413
    protection, 347
    shareware, 412
software as a service (SaaS), 118
software development
    knowledge-based systems, 229
    life cycle, 206
        change/configuration management, 209
        design, 207
        Develop, 207
        Gather Requirements, 206-207
        Release/Maintain, 209
        Test/Validate, 208-209
    malware, 230
        botnets, 232
        logic bombs, 232
        protection, 235-236
        rootkits, 233
        spyware/adware, 232
        Trojan horses, 231
        viruses, 230-231
        worms, 231
    methods, 211
        Agile, 216-217
        Build and Fix, 211-212
        Cleanroom, 218
        CMMI, 218
        Incremental, 214
        JAD, 218
        Prototyping, 214
        RAD, 216
        Spiral, 215
        V-shaped, 213
        Waterfall, 212-213
    programming, 219
        ActiveX, 224
        assembly languages, 219
        cohesion, 221
        compiled versus interpreted code, 220
        CORBA, 222
        coupling, 221
        data structures, 222
        distributed object-oriented systems, 222
        high-level languages, 219
        Java, 223
        machine languages, 219
        mobile code, 223

natural languages, 220
object-oriented, 220-221
OLE, 223
polymorphism, 221
SOA, 223
very-high-level languages, 219
security, 210
auditing, 237
backdoors, 235
BSI, 210
buffer overflow, 233-235
certification/accreditation, 236-237
ISO/IEC 27000, 210
malware protection, 235-236
overview, 7
OWASP, 210
privilege escalation, 235
source code issues, 233
WASC, 210
SONET (Synchronous Optical Networks), 120, 122
source code issues (software), 233
SOX (Sarbanes-Oxley) Act, 415
SP (Special Publication) 800-34 Revision 1, 378
spam, 148
spear phishing, 148
special privileges, monitoring, 345
Special Publication (SP) 800-34 Revision 1, 378
Spiral software development method, 215
SPOF (Single Point of Failure), 356
sponsoring bodies, 2-4
spoofing, 56
email, 147
IP addresses, 150

sprinkler systems, 469
spyware, 56, 232
SSH (Secure Shell)
File Transfer Protocol (SFTP), 104
Internet security, 285
SSIDs (service set identifiers), 137
SSL (Secure Sockets Layer), 134, 283
SSO (single sign-on), 31-32
advantages, 31
authorization, 31
disadvantages, 32
Open Group Single Sign-On Standard website, 31
stakeholders, 299
standard glass, 466
standard passwords, 19, 501
standards
deviations, 361
information security governance, 185
ISO/IEC 27000, 164-166
wireless
802.11a, 138
802.11b, 138
802.11g, 138
standby lighting systems, 461
star topology, 92
state machine models, 315
stateful firewalls, 113
static passwords, 19, 481-482, 501
static routing, 106
statistical anomaly-based IDS, 51
statistical attacks, 289
statutory damages, 408
stealth viruses, 231, 511
steganography, 258, 434

storage. *See also* memory
   HSM, 354, 392, 498, 517
   NAS, 353
   SAN
      data recovery, 392
      defined, 353
Storage Area Networks. *See* **SAN**
STP (shielded twisted pair) cabling, 89
stream-based ciphers, 254
strikes, 451
structured walk-through tests, 397
substitution, 245, 494-495, 513
substitution ciphers, 257
   defined, 252
   modulo 26, 252
   one-time pads, 257-258
   steganography, 258
supervisor security responsibilities, 191
supplies, recovering, 387
surges (power), 470
surrounding areas (facilities), 456
surveillance, 433
SWGDE (Scientific Working Group on Digital Evidence), 428-429
Switched Multimegabit Data Service (SMDS), 124
switches, 110-111
   layer 3 *versus* layer 4, 111
   transparent bridging, 110
symmetric algorithms, 253-254, 258
   3DES
      modes, 262-263, 495, 514
      overview, 262
   AES, 263
   block ciphers, 255

Blowfish, 264
CAST, 265
DES
   defined, 259
   Double-DES, 259
   key length, 259
   modes, 259-262
IDEA, 263
Initialization Vectors (IVs), 255
key facts, 496, 514
RC, 264
Skipjack, 264
stream-based ciphers, 254
strengths/weaknesses, 254, 495, 514
Twofish, 264
Symmetric DSL (SDSL), 128
symmetric multitasking, 308
SYN ACK attacks, 149
Synchronous Dynamic Random Access Memory (SDRAM), 305
synchronous encryption/decryption, 244, 493, 512
Synchronous Optical Networks (SONET), 120, 122
synchronous transmissions, 84
systems
   administrator security responsibilities, 190
   architecture, 298
      computing platforms, 300-301
      CPUs, 303-304
      design phase, 299
      development phase, 299
      input/output devices, 307
      ISO-IEC 42010:2011, 299
      maintenance, 299

memory, 304-306

multitasking, 308-309

operating systems, 307-308

security services, 302-303

development life cycle, 203-204

Acquire/Develop, 204-205

Dispose, 205-206

Implement, 205

Initiate, 204

Operate/Maintain, 205

distributed, 300

cloud computing, 335

grid computing, 335

peer-to-peer computing, 335

embedded, 301

hardening, 362-363

high security mode, 321

owner security responsibilities, 190

ports, 77

redundant, 379

security architecture, 310

documentation, 314

frameworks. See *frameworks*

models. See *security, models*

modes. See *security, modes*

policies, 310

requirements, 310-311

zones, 311

specific security policies, 185

threats, 447

communications, 447-448

electrical, 447

utilities, 448

T

T carrier lines, 121

table-top exercises, 397

tables

capabilities, 48

routing, 106

TACACS+ (Terminal Access Controller Access-Control System Plus), 132-133

TACACS (Terminal Access Controller Access-Control System), 132-133

tamper protection, 472

tangible asset protection, 177, 346

facilities, 346

hardware, 347

information assets, 347

software, 347

tape vaulting, 392, 517

Tavares, Stafford, 265

TCB (Trusted Computer Base), 310

TCP (Transmission Control Protocol), 72

functionality examples, 74

ports, 77-78

three-way handshake, 73

UDP, compared, 73

TCP/IP, 71

ARP, 101-102

encapsulation/de-encapsulation, 76

IP, 74

layers

Application, 72

Link, 76

Internet, 74-75

Transport, 72-74

TCP
- *functionality examples*, 74
- *ports*, 77-78
- *three-way handshake*, 73
- *UDP, compared*, 73

TCP/UDP ports, 77-78

TCSEC (Trusted Computer System Evaluation Criteria)
- ITSEC, mapping, 327
- overview, 323

TDMA (Time Division Multiple Access), 136

teams
- disaster recovery
  - *damage assessment*, 394
  - *legal*, 394
  - *listing of*, 394
  - *media relations*, 395
  - *restoration*, 395
  - *salvage*, 395
  - *security*, 395-396
- incident response, 424
  - *creating*, 424
  - *investigations*, 424
  - *procedures*, 424-425
  - *rules of engagement/authorization/ scope*, 424

teardrop attacks, 150
technical controls, 43-44
technological disasters, 371

technologies, recovering
- hardware, 386
- software, 386-387

telecommunications, 6
Telnet, 134
tempered glass, 466

Ten Commandments of Computer Ethics, 436

Terminal Access Controller Access-Control System (TACACS), 132-133

Terminal Access Controller Access-Control System Plus (TACACS+), 132-133

Temporal Key Integrity Protocol (TKIP), 140

terrorist acts, 452
tertiary sites, 384

Test/Validate phase (Software Development Life Cycle), 208-209

testing
- alternate facility locations, 383
- BCP/DRP, 396-397
  - *checklist tests*, 396
  - *evacuation drills*, 397
  - *full-interruption tests*, 397
  - *functional drills*, 397
  - *parallel tests*, 397
  - *simulation tests*, 397
  - *structured walk-through tests*, 397
  - *table-top exercises*, 397
- OLTP ACID, 229
- penetration, 38-39
  - *categories*, 39
  - *performing*, 38
  - *strategies*, 38-39

theft, 450
Thicknet, 87
thin client platforms, 300
Thinnet, 88

third-party
- governance security responsibilities, 191
- outsourcing, 422

threats. *See also* **attacks**
- access control, 52-53
    - *backdoor/trapdoor, 57*
    - *brute-force, 53*
    - *buffer overflow, 55*
    - *dictionary attacks, 53*
    - *DoS/DDoS, 55*
    - *dumpster diving, 55*
    - *emanating, 57*
    - *identity theft, 54*
    - *malware, 56*
    - *mobile code, 56*
    - *passwords, 53*
    - *phishing/pharming, 54*
    - *shoulder surfing, 54*
    - *sniffing, 57*
    - *social engineering, 53*
    - *spoofing, 56*
- agents, 161
- architecture, 330
    - *data flow control, 333*
    - *maintenance hooks, 331*
    - *OWASP, 333*
    - *SAML, 332*
    - *server-based attacks, 333*
    - *time-of-check/time-of-use attacks, 331-332*
    - *web-based, 332*
    - *XML, 332*
- assets, 177-178
- data mining warehouses, 334
- database, 228, 333-334
    - *aggregation, 334*
    - *contamination, 334*
    - *inference, 334*
- defined, 161
- distributed systems
    - *cloud computing, 335*
    - *grid computing, 335*
    - *peer-to-peer computing, 335*
- geographical, 444
- networks, 142-150
    - *attenuation, 142-143*
    - *cabling, 142*
    - *crosstalk, 143*
    - *DNS attacks, 145-146*
    - *eavesdropping, 143*
    - *email attacks, 147-148*
    - *ICMP attacks, 143-144*
    - *noise, 142*
- operations
    - *antivirus/antimalware, 364*
    - *clipping levels, 361*
    - *deviations from standards, 361*
    - *IDS/IPS, 363*
    - *input/output controls, 362*
    - *monitoring/reporting, 363-364*
    - *system hardening, 362-363*
    - *trusted paths, 362*
    - *trusted recovery, 362*
    - *unexplained events, 361*
    - *vulnerability management, 363*
- physical
    - *internal versus external, 437*
    - *man-made, 449-451*
    - *natural, 446-447*
    - *politically motivated, 451-452*
    - *system, 447-449*
- software, 230
    - *backdoors, 235*
    - *botnets, 232*
    - *buffer overflow, 233-235*
    - *logic bombs, 232*

malware protection, 235-236
privilege escalation, 235
rootkits, 233
source code issues, 233
spyware/adware, 232
Trojan horses, 231
viruses, 230-231
worms, 231
throughput rate, 503
Tiger hash functions, 272
Time Division Multiple Access (TDMA), 136
time-of-check/time-of-use attacks, 331-332
TKIP (Temporal Key Integrity Protocol), 140
TLS (Transport Layer Security), 134, 284
TOGAF (The Open Group Architecture Framework), 168, 312
tokens
device authentication methods, 22
passing, 101
ring, 96
topologies (networks), 89
bus, 92
hybrid, 94
mesh, 93-94
ring, 91
star, 92
tornadoes, 446
tort law, 408-409
total risks, 180
TPM (Trusted Platform Module), 279-280
tracking devices, 473
trade secrets, 410-411
trademarks, 411

traffic anomaly-based IDS, 51
transaction log backups, 390
Transmission Control Protocol. *See* **TCP**
transmissions, 83
analog *versus* digital, 83
asynchronous *versus* synchronous, 84
broadband *versus* baseband, 84-85
broadcast, 86
multicast, 85
unicast, 85
wired *versus* wireless, 86
transparent bridging, 110
Transport layer
OSI, 68
TCP/IP, 72-74
TCP functionality, 74
TCP three-way handshake, 73
TCP/IP and UDP headers, 73
Transport Layer Security (TLS), 134, 284
transposition, 245, 253, 494, 513
trapdoors, 57, 246, 514
Triple DES. *See* **3DES**
Trojan horses, 56, 231
tropical storms, 446
trust
levels. *See also* Rainbow Series
accreditation and certification, 329-330
evaluation systems, 326-329
paths, 362
recovery, 362
Trusted Computer Base (TCB), 310
Trusted Computer System Evaluation Criteria (TCSEC), 323, 327
Trusted Platform Module (TPM), 279-280

trusted third-party model (federated identities), 35
tumbler locks, 465
tuples, 225, 510
turnstiles, 464
twisted pair cabling, 88-90
  categories, 89-90
  shielded *versus* unshielded, 89
  types, 89
Twofish, 264
Type I authentication, 17
  identity/account management, 18-19
  passwords, 19-22
    changing, 21
    Linux, 21
    lockout policies, 21
    management, 20
    types, 19-20
    Windows, 22
Type II authentication, 22
  memory cards, 22-23
  smart cards, 23
  token devices, 22
Type III authentication, 23
  behavioral characteristics, 25
  biometrics
    considerations, 26-28
    effectiveness rankings, 26-27
    user acceptance rankings, 27
  physiological characteristics, 24-25

U

UDP (User Datagram Protocol)
  ports, 77-78
  TCP, compared, 73
unexplained events, 361

unicast transmissions, 85
United States Federal Sentencing Guidelines of 1991, 417
unshielded twisted pair (UTP) cabling, 89
UPS (uninterruptible power supplies), 471
URL hiding, 146
USA PATRIOT (Uniting and Strengthening America by Providing Appropriate Tools Required to Intercept and Obstruct Terrorism) Act, 418
User Datagram Protocol. *See* UDP
users
  environment recovery, 388
  identifying, 16
  job rotation, 344
  least privilege, 29-30, 343
  ports, 77
  relationships with resources, identifying, 16
  security responsibilities, 191
  separation of duties, 344
  special privileges, monitoring, 345
utilities systems threats, 448
UTP (unshielded twisted pair) cabling, 89

V

V-shaped software development method, 213
value of CISSP certification
  enterprise, 5
  security professionals, 5
vandalism, 450
vascular scans, 25
vaults, 463, 474

VDSL (Very High Bit-Rate DSL), 128
vehicle access doors, 463
Very High Bit-Rate DSL (VDSL), 128
very-high-level languages, 219
viewpoints, 299
views, 225, 228, 299, 511
Vigenere ciphers, 248-249
virtual local area networks (VLANs), 111
virtual memory, 306
virtual platforms, 301
Virtual Private Networks. *See* **VPNs**
Virtual Router Redundancy Protocol (VRRP), 108
virtualization, 116
viruses
 antivirus software, 236
 boot sector, 231, 511
 defined, 56
 Trojan horses, 231
 macro, 231, 511
 multipartite, 231, 511
 parasitic, 231, 511
 polymorphic, 231, 511
 stealth, 231, 511
 types, 492, 511
 worms, 231
visibility (facility selection), 456
visitor control, 466-467
VLANs (virtual local area networks), 111
voice pattern scanning, 25
VoIP (Voice over IP), 125-126
VPNs (Virtual Private Networks), 129-132
 encapsulation/de-encapsulation, 129
 IPsec, 130-132
 L2TP, 130
 PPTP, 129-130
VRRP (Virtual Router Redundancy Protocol), 108
vulnerabilities. *See also* **threats**
 assessments, 37-38
 assets, 177-178
 defined, 160
 managing, 363

W

walls (perimeters), 460
WANs (wide area networks), 121
 ATM, 123
 carrier lines
  E, 121
  OC, 122
  T, 121
 circuit-switching, 123
 CSU/DSU, 122
 frame relay, 123
 HSSI, 124-125
 packet-switching, 123
 PPP, 124
 PSTN, 125
 SMDS, 124
 VoIP, 125-126
 X.25, 124
warchalking, 149
wardriving, 149
warm sites, 384
WASC (Web Application Security Consortium), 210
water leakages, 471
Waterfall software development method, 212-213

WLANs (wireless networks) 603

wave motion detectors, **461**
web-based attacks, **332**
websites
  CIDR, 80
  CISSP registration, 10
  ISO, 166
  Open Group Single Sign-On Standard, 31
  RFC 1087, 437
WEP (Wired Equivalent Privacy), 140
wet pipe sprinkler systems, 469
whaling, 148
white hats, 407
wide area networks. *See* **WANs**
Wi-Fi Protected Access. *See* **WPA**
Windows password management, 22
WIPO (World Intellectual Property Organization), 412
Wired Equivalent Privacy (WEP), 140
wired/wireless transmissions, 86
WLANs (wireless networks), 135
  802.11 techniques, 136
  access points, 137
  attacks, 149
  Bluetooth, 139
  cellular/mobile, 136-137
  CSMA/CA, 100
  infrared, 139
  Infrastructure mode *versus* Ad Hoc mode, 137
  modulation, 135
    802.11 techniques, 136
    cellular/mobile, 136-137
  security, 139-141
    MAC filters, 141
    WEP, 139-140
    WPA, 140
    WPA2, 140
  SSIDs, 137
  standards, 138
    802.11a, 138
    802.11b, 138
    802.11f, 138
  structure
    access points, 137
    SSIDs, 137
  TCP/IP model, 71
    ARP, 101-102
    Application layer, 72
    encapsulation/de-encapsulation, 76
    Internet layer, 74-75
    IP, 74
    Link layer, 76
    TCP. See TCP
    TCP/UDP ports, 77-78
    Transport layer, 72-74
  threats, 142-150
    attenuation, 142-143
    cabling, 142
    crosstalk, 143
    DNS attacks, 145-146
    eavesdropping, 143
    email attacks, 147-148
    ICMP attacks, 143-144
    noise, 142
  topologies, 89
    bus, 92
    hybrid, 94
    mesh, 93604+-94
    ring, 91
    star, 92

transmissions, 83
    analog versus digital, 83
    asynchronous versus synchronous, 84
    broadband versus baseband, 84-85
    multicast, 85
    unicast, 85
    wired versus wireless, 86
WANs
    ATM, 123
    circuit-switching, 123
    CSU/DSU, 122
    E carrier lines, 121
    frame relay, 123
    HSSI, 124-125
    OC carrier lines, 122
    overview, 121
    packet-switching, 123
    PPP, 124
    PSTN, 125
    SMDS, 124
    T carrier lines, 121
    VoIP, 125-126
    X.25, 124
work areas (facilities), 467
work factors, 246, 513
World Intellectual Property Organization (WIPO), 412
World War II cryptography, 249-250
worms, 56, 231
WPA (Wi-Fi Protected Access)
    overview, 140
    personal *versus* enterprise versions, 140
WPA2 (Wi-Fi Protected Access 2)
    overview, 140
    personal *versus* enterprise versions, 140
WRT (work recovery time), 374, 517

X

X.25, 124
X.400 directory service standard, 31
X.500 directory service standard, 30
X.509 certificates, 276-277
XML
    architecture threats, 332
    databases, 227

Z

Zachman framework, 166-167, 312, 489, 508
zero-knowledge
    proof, 268
    tests, 39
zones (security), 311

PEARSON

ALWAYS LEARNING

PEARSON IT CERTIFICATION

Pearson IT Certification
THE LEADER IN IT CERTIFICATION LEARNING TOOLS

Visit pearsonITcertification.com today to find:

- IT CERTIFICATION EXAM information and guidance for

  Pearson is the official publisher of Cisco Press, IBM Press, VMware Press and is a Platinum CompTIA Publishing Partner—CompTIA's highest partnership accreditation

- EXAM TIPS AND TRICKS from Pearson IT Certification's expert authors and industry experts, such as
  - *Mark Edward Soper* – CompTIA
  - *David Prowse* – CompTIA
  - *Wendell Odom* – Cisco
  - *Kevin Wallace* – Cisco and CompTIA
  - *Shon Harris* – Security
  - *Thomas Erl* – SOACP

- SPECIAL OFFERS – pearsonITcertification.com/promotions

- REGISTER your Pearson IT Certification products to access additional online material and receive a coupon to be used on your next purchase

CONNECT WITH PEARSON IT CERTIFICATION

Be sure to create an account on **pearsonITcertification.com** and receive members-only offers and benefits

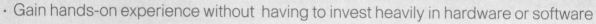

Try Safari Books Online FREE for 15 days
Get online access to Thousands of Books and Videos

  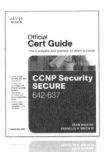  

FREE 15-DAY TRIAL + 15% OFF*
informit.com/safaritrial

> ### Feed your brain
> Gain unlimited access to thousands of books and videos about technology, digital media and professional development from O'Reilly Media, Addison-Wesley, Microsoft Press, Cisco Press, McGraw Hill, Wiley, WROX, Prentice Hall, Que, Sams, Apress, Adobe Press and other top publishers.

> ### See it, believe it
> Watch hundreds of expert-led instructional videos on today's hottest topics.

WAIT, THERE'S MORE!

> ### Gain a competitive edge
> Be first to learn about the newest technologies and subjects with Rough Cuts pre-published manuscripts and new technology overviews in Short Cuts.

> ### Accelerate your project
> Copy and paste code, create smart searches that let you know when new books about your favorite topics are available, and customize your library with favorites, highlights, tags, notes, mash-ups and more.

* Available to new subscribers only. Discount applies to the Safari Library and is valid for first 12 consecutive monthly billing cycles. Safari Library is not available in all countries.

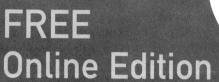

Your purchase of **CISSP Cert Guide** includes access to a free online edition for 45 days through the **Safari Books Online** subscription service. Nearly every Pearson IT Certification book is available online through **Safari Books Online**, along with thousands of books and videos from publishers such as Addison-Wesley Professional, Cisco Press, Exam Cram, IBM Press, O'Reilly Media, Prentice Hall, Que, Sams, and VMware Press.

Safari Books Online is a digital library providing searchable, on-demand access to thousands of technology, digital media, and professional development books and videos from leading publishers. With one monthly or yearly subscription price, you get unlimited access to learning tools and information on topics including mobile app and software development, tips and tricks on using your favorite gadgets, networking, project management, graphic design, and much more.

Activate your FREE Online Edition at
informit.com/safarifree

STEP 1: Enter the coupon code: RJGMNVH.

STEP 2: New Safari users, complete the brief registration form.
Safari subscribers, just log in.

If you have difficulty registering on Safari or accessing the online edition,
please e-mail customer-service@safaribooksonline.com